ANALYZE THIS

ACCT
Are you in?

WHAT IF...

...all students wanted to read their textbook?

70% The percentage of students who report that they read their textbooks and earn a 3.5 grade point average or higher in school.*

...coming to class was something every student desired?

34% The percentage of students who go to every class during a semester.*

...we could encourage a better teaching and learning experience in accounting classrooms?

88% The percentage of students who are interested in learning from a streamlined textbook.*

...we gave students a book with online homework for less than $100 retail?

84% The percentage of students surveyed who prefer ACCT over a traditional book.**

...we gave students engaging resources to help them study?

98% The percentage of students surveyed who want to use the ACCT reference cards.**

*According to a survey of 1,000 students via SurveyU.com. | **According to a survey of 238 accounting students at 2- and 4-year schools.

SOUTH-WESTERN
CENGAGE Learning™

Financial ACCT, 2010 Edition

Godwin, Alderman

Vice President of Editorial, Business:
Jack W. Calhoun

Editor-in-Chief: Rob Dewey

Publisher/Director, 4LTR Press:
Neil Marquardt

Senior Acquisitions Editor:
Matthew Filimonov

Supervising Developmental Editor:
Aaron Arnsparger

Senior Project Manager, 4LTR Press:
Michelle Lockard

Senior Marketing Manager: Kristen Hurd

Senior Marketing Communications
Manager: Libby Shipp

Marketing Coordinator: Heather McAuliffe

Senior Content Project Manager: Cliff
Kallemeyn

Media Editor: Chris Valentine

Senior Frontlist Buyer, Manufacturing:
Doug Wilke

Production Service: LEAP Publishing
Services, Inc.

Compositor: MPS Limited, A Macmillan
Company

Senior Art Director: Stacy Jenkins Shirley

Internal and Cover Designer: KeDesign,
Mason, OH

Cover Image: ®iStock Images

Senior Image Rights Acquisition Account
Manager: Deanna Ettinger

Photo Researcher: Terri Miller

Brief Contents Images: © Kristian Sekulic/
Shutterstock.com, © iStockphoto.com/
alvarez, © iStockphoto.com/quavondo,
and © Yuri Arcurs/Shutterstock.com

For product information and technology assistance, contact us at
Cengage Learning Customer & Sales Support, 1-800-354-9706

For permission to use material from this text or product, submit all requests online at **www.cengage.com/permissions** Further permissions questions can be emailed to **permissionrequest@cengage.com**

Library of Congress Control Number: 2010920950

ISBN 13: 978-0-538-79896-9
ISBN 10: 0-538-79896-3

South-Western Cengage Learning
5191 Natorp Boulevard
Mason, OH 45040
USA

Cengage Learning products are represented in Canada by Nelson Education, Ltd.

For your course and learning solutions, visit **www.cengage.com**
Purchase any of our products at your local college store or at our preferred online store **www.ichapters.com**

Printed in the United States of America
1 2 3 4 5 6 7 13 12 11 10

ACCT

Brief Contents

ACCT

© ISTOCKPHOTO.COM/SEAN LOCKE

Contents

© MONKEY BUSINESS IMAGES/SHUTTERSTOCK.COM

5 Internal Control and Cash 88

6 Receivables 106

© ISTOCKPHOTO.COM/ANDREW RICH

© YURI ARCURS/SHUTTERSTOCK.COM

© YURI ARCURS/SHUTTERSTOCK.COM

11 Statement of Cash Flows 224

© DMITRIV SHIRONOSOV/SHUTTERSTOCK.COM

12 Financial Statement Analysis 248

IT'S ALL ABOUT
THE HOMEWORK!

CengageNOW™ is an **easy-to-use online resource** that helps you **study in less time** to **get the grade you want** – NOW.

CengageNOW™ comes FREE with each new copy of ACCT and features:
- End-of-chapter homework from the textbook written by the authors
- eBook
- Quizzes, games, e-lectures, and more!

How to Register Your Access Code:
1. Launch a Web browser. Go to www.cengage.com/login and click on "Create My Account." Already have an account? Enter your email/password under "Sign In."
2. Enter your access code in the field provided, exactly how it appears on your card.
3. New users: Enter your account information and click "Continue."
4. Record your email address and password below and store it in a secure location for future visits.

[Email Address: _____]
[Password: _____]

Want Extra Problems?
CengageNOW comes automatically with this book and offers additional exercises and problems to give you a variety of assignment options. You can create static assignments or algorithmic assignments and you can also assign cases and longer problems.

Through the **4LTR+ Custom Program,** you can package these additional exercises with your students' textbooks for just $5. Students will see the additional exercises in CengageNOW if you assign them, but some may also prefer to use them in a printed format.

www.4ltrpress.cengage.com/4ltrplusbc.html

ACCT

REVIEW!

ACCT puts a multitude of study aids at your fingertips. After reading the chapters, check out these resources for further help:

• **Review Cards,** found in the back of your book, include all learning objectives, key concepts and definitions, and visual summaries for each chapter.

• **Online Printable Flash Cards** give you additional ways to check your comprehension of key accounting concepts.

• Other great tools to help you review include **interactive games, E-Lectures, online tutorials,** and **quizzes**.

Go to 4ltrpress.cengage.com/acct to find plenty of resources to help you *Review!*

MAKING
IT REAL!

ACCT will prepare you for the real world by showing you how accounting information is used to make business decisions.

Throughout the text, take a look at the Making It Real features that highlight everyday businesses.

Home Depot Analysis boxes found within each chapter give students experience with analyzing financial data found in Home Depot's 2008 Annual Report. The excerpted annual report is located in the back of the text.

Each chapter contains a wealth of recent financial statements from today's leading companies such as Wendy's, Bed, Bath and Beyond, American Eagle Outfitters, Domino's Pizza, and many, many more.

Each chapter's final learning objective usually includes a discussion of analysis that includes both vertical and horizontal presentation as well as coverage of important ratios that relate to the chapter topics.

ACCT

comprehensive chart of accounts

Assets

Cash
Petty cash
Accounts receivable
Allowance for bad debts
Fuel
Interest receivable
Inventories/Inventory
Supplies
Office supplies
Prepaid insurance
Prepaid rent
Notes receivable
Other current assets
Short-term investments
Long-term investments
Property, plant and equipment
Land
Buildings
Accumulated depreciation—buildings
Equipment
Accumulated depreciation—equipment
Studio equipment
Accumulated depreciation—studio equipment
Automobiles
Accumulated depreciation—automobiles
Truck
Accumulated depreciation—truck
Delivery Van
Accumulated depreciation—delivery van
Boat
Computers
Gas can
Lawn mower
Patents
Other assets

Liabilities

Accounts payable
Bond interest payable
Dividends payable
Dividends payable—common stock
Dividends payable—preferred stock
Federal income tax payable
FICA taxes payable
Interest payable
Income tax payable
Notes payable-short-term
Salaries payable
Sales tax payable
State income tax payable
Utilities Payable
Unearned revenue
Unearned service revenue
Bonds payable
Discount on bonds payable
Premium on bonds payable
Mortgage payable
Notes payable—long-term

Equity

Capital stock
Common stock
Common Stock to be Distributed
Additional paid in capital
Additional paid in capital—Treasury stock
Preferred stock
Retained earnings
Dividends
Treasury stock

Revenues

Sales
Sales discounts
Sales returns and allowances
Revenue
Service revenue
Interest revenue
Bowling revenue
Gain on disposal

Expenses

Cost of sales
Cost of goods sold
Administrative expenses
Advertising expense
Bad debt expense
Cash over and short
Commission expense
Depreciation expense
Depreciation expense—building
Depreciation expense—truck
Freight-in/transportation-in
Fuel expense
Gain on redemption of bonds
General and administrative expenses
Income tax expense
Insurance expense
Interest expense
Loss on disposal
Loss on redemption of bonds
Miscellaneous expense
Operating expenses
Operating permit expense
Payroll tax expense
Permit expense
Postage expense
Purchases
Rent expense
Salaries expense
Selling expenses
Service charge expense
Supplies expense
Utilities expense

*Note: Cost of sales and cost of goods sold are listed first since they are used to compute gross profit.

Financial Accounting

Introduction

Imagine for a moment that you are home for the summer and decide to mow lawns to make some money. With $100 of your own money and $200 borrowed from a relative, you purchase a $260 lawn mower, a $20 gas can, and $20 of gas. During June, you mow 40 lawns at $10 each, buy $175 of additional gasoline, and pay your relative $1 of interest. At the end of June, you have $194 in cash, $10 of gasoline, and $30 due from customers.

Given this information, can you tell what happened to your business in June? Were you profitable? What do you have to show for your efforts? How can you tell? Getting answers to such questions requires accounting.

Accounting is the process of identifying, measuring, and communicating economic information to permit informed judgments and decisions. Put more simply, accounting is the "language of business." When you want to know about the financial results of a business, you must understand and speak accounting. The purpose of this book is to teach you this language.

With this overall purpose in mind, the current chapter introduces the basic terms, principles and rules that comprise the grammar of the accounting language. It does so by creating the June financial statements of the lawn service scenario described above. At the end of the chapter, you should be familiar with the four main financial statements of accounting. You should also have a working accounting vocabulary that can be built upon in the following chapters.

Learning Objectives

After studying the material in this chapter, you should be able to:

LO1 Describe the four assumptions made when communicating accounting information.

LO2 Describe the purpose and structure of an income statement and the terms and principles used to create it.

LO3 Describe the purpose and structure of a balance sheet and the terms and principles used to create it.

LO4 Describe the purpose and structure of a statement of retained earnings and how it links the income statement and the balance sheet.

LO5 Describe the purpose and structure of a statement of cash flows and the terms and principles used to create it.

LO6 Describe the qualitative characteristics that make accounting information useful.

LO7 Describe the conceptual framework of accounting.

LO1 Beginning Assumptions

Accounting The process of identifying, measuring, and communicating economic information to permit informed judgments and decisions.

The purpose of accounting is to identify, measure, and communicate economic information about a particular entity to interested users. As a foundation for accomplishing this purpose, accountants make the following four assumptions: economic entity, time period, monetary unit, and going concern.

Accounting, the "language of business," would describe this picture as a guy using an asset (the lawn mower) to generate a revenue (the money he will be paid).

© eSTOCK PHOTO/ALAMY

Economic Entity Assumption

The **economic entity assumption** states that the financial activities of a business can be separated from the financial activities of the business's owner(s). This assumption allows a user to examine a company's accounting information without concern that the information includes the personal affairs of the owner(s). For the lawn service example in the introduction, this means that personal activities such as buying gasoline for your automobile should not be included with business activities such as buying

Economic entity assumption Accountants assume that the financial activities of a business can be separated from the financial activities of the business's owner(s).

MAKING IT REAL

After conducting its 2008 audit of General Motors Corporation, the public accounting firm Deloitte & Touche LLP wrote the following in its auditor's report:

"[General Motors'] recurring losses from operations, stockholders' deficit, and inability to generate sufficient cash flow to meet its obligations and sustain its operations raise substantial doubt about its ability to continue as a going concern."

This language is commonly known as a going concern opinion. The auditor uses it to inform the public of its opinion that the company's continued operations are in doubt. A going concern opinion does not always mean that the company will cease operations. But it does mean that there is significant doubt that the company will continue without significant changes. In the case of General Motors, those significant changes came on June 1, 2009, when the company filed for Chapter 11 bankruptcy protection.

Going concern opinions are designed to protect a company's stakeholders and allow them to make decisions with the most accurate information available. In General Motors' situation, the going concern opinion accurately predicted the future and gave external users an early warning of the likely bankruptcy.

gasoline for the lawn mower. These activities can and should be accounted for separately.

Time Period Assumption

Business owners and other interested parties usually do not want to wait long before they receive information about how a business is doing. They want periodic measurements of the business's success or failure. Accountants therefore assume that economic information can be meaningfully captured and communicated over short periods of time, even if those time periods are somewhat artificial, such as one month or one quarter. This is known as the **time period assumption**.

Most companies communicate to users on both a quarterly and annual basis. In fact, publicly traded companies such as Starbucks are required by law to file quarterly and annual financial statements with the Securities and Exchange Commission (SEC). For the lawn service example, the time period is the month of June.

Monetary Unit Assumption

The **monetary unit assumption** assumes that the dollar is the most effective means to communicate economic activity. If an economic activity cannot be expressed in dollars, then it is not recorded in the accounting system. It assumes further that the dollar is reasonably stable with respect to inflation and deflation. As a result, accountants do not adjust economic values based on inflation or deflation. A dollar earned in 1980 is the same as a dollar earned in 2010.

Going Concern Assumption

The **going concern assumption** states that a company will continue to operate into the foreseeable future. This assumption enables accountants to use certain techniques that will be described later in the chapter. Unless there is evidence to the contrary, most companies are

Time period assumption Accountants assume that economic information can be meaningfully captured and communicated over short periods of time.

Monetary unit assumption Accountants assume that the dollar is the most effective means to communicate economic activity.

Going concern assumption Accountants assume that a company will continue to operate into the foreseeable future.

On Home Depot's income statement, in Appendix C, you can find the following four descriptions: 1) The Home Depot, Inc, and Subsidiaries, 2) amounts in millions, 3) Fiscal Year Ended February 1, 2009. Which assumption does each description best relate?

1) economic entity, 2) monetary unit, 3) time period

assumed to be going concerns. Those that are not going concerns are often in the process of liquidation (that is, selling their resources and paying off their obligations). Because the lawn service will continue through the summer, it is a going concern at the end of June.

LO2 Reporting Profitability: The Income Statement

One of the first questions asked of any business is whether it makes money. Stated differently in "accounting" words, is the business profitable? Does it generate more resources than it uses? Accounting provides answers to these questions with a financial statement called an *income statement*. An income statement reports a company's *revenues* and *expenses*.

Revenues

A **revenue** is an increase in resources resulting from the sale of goods or the provision of services. Receiving $10 for mowing a lawn is an example of a revenue. You have $10 more than you did previously because you provided a service. Other revenue common to businesses is investment income.

Revenues are recorded according to the revenue recognition principle. The **revenue recognition principle** states that a revenue should be recorded when a resource has been earned. A resource is earned when either the sale of the good or the provision of the service is substantially complete and collection is reasonably assured.

Given these definitions, total June revenues for the lawn service are as follows. You have only one source of revenue—mowing lawns. Assuming that your customers will pay, your lawn service creates a revenue each time a lawn is mowed. So, if you mowed 40 lawns

at $10 each, revenues total $400 for the month. Of those revenues, you have received payment for all except $30.

Expenses

An **expense** is a decrease in resources resulting from the sale of goods or provision of services. The gasoline consumed while mowing lawns is an example of an expense. Other expenses common to businesses are wages, taxes, advertising, and utilities.

Expenses are recorded according to the matching principle. The **matching principle** states that expenses should be recorded in the period resources are used to generate revenues. For example, since fuel is used to mow lawns in June, June expenses should include the fuel used.

Given these definitions, total June expenses for the lawn service are as follows. Unlike the revenue side, the lawn service has three sources of expenses. The first is fairly clear—fuel. The amount of fuel used during June can be calculated as follows from the given information:

Amount on hand on June 1	$ 20
+ Amount purchased during June	175
− Amount on hand on June 30	(10)
Amount used during June	$185

Therefore, fuel expense is $185.

Revenue An increase in resources resulting from the sale of goods or the provision of services.

Revenue recognition principle The principle that a revenue should be recorded when a resource has been earned.

Expense A decrease in resources resulting from the sale of goods or provision of services.

Matching principle The principle that expenses should be recorded in the period resources are used to generate revenues.

The second expense relates to your borrowing. You paid your relative $1 at the end of June to compensate her for loaning you $200. Paying for the use of someone else's money is called interest. Therefore, interest expense is $1.

The third expense relates to your equipment—the lawn mower and the gas can. Because this equipment was used in June to generate revenues, the matching principle requires that some portion of the equipment's cost be expensed in June. This is called depreciation expense. Chapter 8 will discuss the various methods for calculating depreciation expense, but for now we will keep things simple. Assuming that the equipment will be used for four months, it is reasonable to expense one-fourth of the equipment's cost each month. This equals $65 for the lawn mower ($260 cost ÷ 4 months) and $5 for the gas can ($20 cost ÷ 4 months). Therefore, depreciation expense for June is $70.

The Income Statement

Once a company's revenues and expenses are calculated, they are reported on an income statement. An **income statement** is a financial statement that shows a company's revenues and expenses over a specific period of time. Its purpose is to demonstrate the financial success or failure of the company over that specific period of time. When revenues exceed expenses, a company generates net income. When expenses exceed revenues,

Income statement A financial statement that reports a company's revenues and expenses over a specific period of time.

> The income statement's purpose is to demonstrate the financial success or failure of the company over a specific period of time.

a company generates a net loss. The basic structure of the statement is as follows:

Revenues − Expenses = Net Income or Net Loss

Given the revenues and expenses determined previously, the lawn service's June income statement would appear as Exhibit 1-1. It contains the company name, the statement name, and the time reference, which for this example is the month of June. It also shows that the lawn service generated $144 of net income during June.

Exhibit 1-1 Income Statement for Lawn Service, Inc.

Lawn Service, Inc.
Income Statement
For the Month Ending June 30

Revenues		$400
Expenses:		
Fuel	$185	
Interest	1	
Depreciation	70	
Total expenses		256
Net income		$144

HOME DEPOT ANALYSIS

Look at Home Depot's income statement in Appendix C. The statement contains two revenues and five expenses. Can you identify them? What was the company's net income for the most current year?

Revenues: net sales; interest and investment income

Expenses: cost of sales; selling, general and administrative; depreciation and amortization; interest expense; provision for income taxes

Net income (called net earnings): $2,260 million

LO3 Reporting Financial Position: The Balance Sheet

Another important issue for any business is its current financial position. What does the business own? What does it owe? Accounting provides answers to these questions with a financial statement called a *balance sheet*. A balance sheet reports a company's *assets*, *liabilities*, and *equity*.

Assets

An asset is a resource of a business. More formally, an **asset** is an economic resource that is objectively measurable, that results from a prior transaction, and that will provide future economic benefit. Cash is a good example of an asset. It can be counted, it is received through a transaction with someone else, and it can be used to buy things in the future. Other common assets include merchandise inventory, equipment, supplies, and investments.

Assets are recorded and reported according to the historical cost principle, which is often shortened to the cost principle. The **cost principle** states that assets should be recorded and reported at the cost paid to acquire them.

Given these definitions, the lawn service has several assets at the end of June—$194 of cash, $10 of remaining fuel, and $30 of receivables from customers. It also has a lawn mower and a gas can, but the value of those assets are calculated a little differently because they will be used over several periods. The lawn mower originally cost $260, but the matching principle required the expensing of $65 of that cost in June. As a result, the lawn mower's remaining cost is $195 ($260 − $65). A similar calculation is performed for the gas can. Because $5 of the total $20 cost of the gas can was expensed during June, the remaining cost is $15 ($20 − $5). Again, Chapter 8 will discuss in much more detail the accounting for equipment.

Liabilities

A liability is an obligation of a business. More formally, a **liability** is an obligation of a business that results from a past transaction and will require the sacrifice of economic resources at some future date. Examples of liabilities common to businesses include notes payable to creditors, accounts payable to vendors, salaries

payable to employees, and taxes payable to governments. The only liability of the lawn service at the end of June is the $200 borrowed from your relative, who is considered a creditor. As will be explained below, the business does not have a liability for the $100 of your own money that was contributed to the company. You are an owner, not a creditor.

Equity

Equity is the difference between a company's assets and liabilities and represents the share of assets that are claimed by the company's owners. An example of equity with which you may be familiar is home equity. A homeowner's equity refers to the difference between the value of the home and the amount owed to the bank. Equity in accounting is the same principle except that it refers to the difference between the cost of the business's assets and its liabilities.

A company can generate equity in two ways. The first is through contributed capital. **Contributed capital** is defined as the resources that investors contribute to a business in exchange for an ownership interest. The $100 that you, the owner, put into the lawn service is contributed capital. Note here that contributed capital is not a revenue. The increase of $100 did not result from the lawn service providing a service or selling a product. It came by selling an ownership interest. The most common method that companies use to generate contributed capital is the sale of common stock to investors.

The second way a company generates equity is through profitable operations. When a company generates net income, it can either distribute those profits to owners or retain them in the business to grow the business further. Profits that are distributed to owners

Asset An economic resource that is objectively measurable, results from a prior transaction, and will provide future economic benefit.

Cost principle The principle that assets should be recorded and reported at the cost paid to acquire them.

Liability An obligation of a business that results from a past transaction and will require the sacrifice of economic resources at some future date.

Equity The difference between a company's assets and liabilities, representing the share of assets that is claimed by the company's owners.

Contributed capital The resources that investors contribute to a business in exchange for ownership interest.

Because a balance sheet is reported at a specific point in time, it is often referred to as a snapshot of a business.

are called **dividends**. Note here that dividends are not an expense of a company. They are simply a distribution of company assets to owners. Profits that are retained in the business are called **retained earnings.** A company's retained earnings therefore represent the equity generated and retained from profitable operations. Since the lawn service did not distribute any assets to you, the owner, it retained the entire $144 of June earnings.

The Balance Sheet

A company's assets, liabilities, and equity are reported on a balance sheet. A **balance sheet** is a financial statement that shows a company's assets, liabilities, and equity at a specific point in time. Its purpose is to show, at a given point in time, a company's resources and its claims against those resources. Because a balance sheet is reported at a specific point in time, it is often referred

Dividends Profits that are distributed to owners.

Retained earnings Profits that are retained in the business.

Balance sheet A financial statement that reports a company's assets, liabilities, and equity at a specific point in time.

to as a snapshot of a business. The basic structure of the statement is as follows:

Assets = Liabilities + Equity

Given the assets, liabilities, and equity determined previously, the lawn service's balance sheet would appear as Exhibit 1-2. It contains the company name, the statement name, and the time reference, which for this example is June 30.

Notice that total assets equal total liabilities plus total equity. This will always be the case for any business. An entity's assets are always claimed by someone. Either they are owed to someone (in this case, your relative) or claimed by an owner (in this case, you). No asset of any business is ever unclaimed. This relationship between assets, liabilities, and equity is represented by the following equation, known as the fundamental accounting equation: **Assets = Liabilities + Equity.** This fundamental accounting equation is what the balance sheet reports. That is why it is called a *balance* sheet.

Exhibit 1-2 Balance Sheet for Lawn Service, Inc.

Lawn Service, Inc.
Balance Sheet
June 30

Cash	$194	
Accounts receivable	30	
Supplies (fuel)	10	
Lawn mower	195	
Gas can	15	
Total assets		$444
Note payable to relative	$200	
Total liabilities		$200
Contributed capital	$100	
Retained earnings	144	
Total equity		244
Total liabilities and equity		$444

HOME DEPOT ANALYSIS

Look at Home Depot's balance sheet in Appendix C. Write out in numbers the company's accounting equation (A = L + E) for the most current year. How many different assets does the company disclose?

1) A = L + E: $41,164 = $23,387 + $17,777

2) **Fourteen different assets are listed on Home Depot's balance sheet.**

LO4 Reporting Equity: The Statement of Retained Earnings

Owners of a business are usually interested in how their equity is growing as a result of profitable operations. They are also interested in how that equity is distributed in the form of dividends. Such information is reported on the statement of retained earnings. A **statement of retained earnings** shows the change in a company's retained earnings over a specific period of time. The basic structure of the statement is as follows:

> Retained Earnings, Beginning Balance
> +/– Net Income/Loss
> – Dividends
> = Retained Earnings, Ending Balance

The lawn service's statement of retained earnings would appear as Exhibit 1-3. It contains the company name, the statement name, and the time reference, which for this example is the month of June.

Your business started with no retained earnings but generated net income of $144 in June. Since none of that income was distributed through dividends, the business retained all of those net assets. Therefore, retained earnings increased from $0 to $144.

Exhibit 1-3 Statement of Retained Earnings for Lawn Service, Inc.

Lawn Service, Inc. Statement of Retained Earnings For the Month Ending June 30	
Retained earnings, June 1	$ 0
+ Net income	144
– Dividends	0
Retained earnings, June 30	$144

Linking the Income Statement and the Balance Sheet

In addition to showing the change in retained earnings, the statement of retained earnings links the income statement and the balance sheet. A company cannot calculate its retained earnings balance at the end of the

When preparing financial statements, the income statement must be prepared first, followed by the statement of retained earnings and then the balance sheet.

period without factoring in the income earned during the period. The statement of retained earnings provides this link by including net income in the calculation of retained earnings, which is then reported on the balance sheet. This means that when preparing financial statements for any business, the income statement must be prepared first, followed by the statement of retained earnings and then the balance sheet. A graphical depiction of these links is included in Exhibit 1-4.

Exhibit 1-4 Relationship Among Financial Statements

Income Statement

Revenues	$400
– Expenses	256
Net income	$144

Statement of Retained Earnings

Retained earnings, June 1	$ 0
+ Net income	144
– Dividends	0
Retained earnings, June 30	$144

Balance Sheet

Total assets	$444
Liabilities	200
Contributed capital	100
Retained earnings	144
Total liabilities and equity	$444

Statement of retained earnings A financial statement that reports the change in a company's retained earnings over a specific period of time.

HOME DEPOT ANALYSIS

ook at Home Depot's statement of stockholders' equity in Appendix C. Which column of the statement contains the statement of retained earnings? For the most recent year presented, is the amount for net income the same as net income on the income statement? Is the balance in retained earnings the same as the balance on the balance sheet?

The statement of stockholders' equity has nine columns of numerical data. The fourth numerical column from the left (with "Retained Earnings" as the header) is Home Depot's statement of retained earnings. In the most recent year presented, the amount for net income is $2,260, which is the number shown on the income statement, and the balance in retained earnings is $12,093, which is the same balance shown on the balance sheet.

LO5 Reporting Cash Flows: The Statement of Cash Flows

Another important issue for any business is its management of cash. Where does a company get its cash? Where does its cash go? Will there be enough cash to pay bills? Accounting provides answers to these questions with a financial statement called a *statement of cash flows*. A statement of cash flows reports a company's cash inflows and outflows from its *operating*, *investing*, and *financing activities*.

Financing Activities

Most businesses must raise funds to begin. Borrowing money from creditors and receiving contributions from investors are both ways to finance a business's operations. Therefore, generating and repaying cash from creditors and investors are considered *financing activities*. In the lawn service example, you contributed $100 of your own money and borrowed $200 from a relative. Both of these inflows are from financing activities. Therefore, the cash inflow in June from financing activities is $300.

Investing Activities

Once a company has raised sufficient capital from creditors and investors, it usually acquires the revenue-

generating assets that it needs for operations. The buying and selling of such assets are considered *investing activities*. In the lawn service example, you paid $260 for the lawn mower and $20 for the gas can. Therefore, the cash flows from investing activities were –$280. In other words, the lawn service experienced a cash outflow of $280 in June from investing activities.

Operating Activities

After the proper equipment is acquired, a business can begin operations. Operating a business includes the purchase of supplies, the payment of employees, and the sale of products. These transactions are considered *operating activities*. In the lawn service example, cash flows from operations in the month of June included $370 received from customers for mowing their lawns, $195 ($20 + $175) paid for gasoline to operate the lawn mower, and $1 paid to your relative for the right to use her $200. As a result, the net cash inflow from operating activities for the month was $174 ($370 – $195 – $1).

The Statement of Cash Flows

The details of cash inflows and outflows for a business are reported on a *statement of cash flows*. The **statement of cash flows** is a financial statement that shows a company's sources and uses of cash over a specific period of time. Its purpose is to inform users about how and why a company's cash changed during the period. The basic structure of the statement is as follows:

Statement of cash flows A financial statement that reports a company's sources and uses of cash over a specific period of time.

An important issue for any business is its management of cash. Where does a company get its cash? Where does its cash go? Will there be enough cash to pay bills?

Cash Flows Provided (Used) by Operating Activities
+/− Cash Flows Provided (Used) by Investing Activities
+/− Cash Flows Provided (Used) by Financing Activities
= Net Increase (Decrease) in Cash

Exhibit 1-5 Statement of Cash Flows for Lawn Service, Inc.

Lawn Service, Inc.
Statement of Cash Flows
For the Month Ending June 30

Operating activities		
Cash received from customers	$ 370	
Cash paid for fuel	(195)	
Cash paid for interest	(1)	
Net cash provided by operating activities		$ 174
Investing activities		
Cash paid for lawn mower	$(260)	
Cash paid for gas can	(20)	
Net cash used by investing activities		(280)
Financing activities		
Cash received from borrowing	$ 200	
Cash received from contributions	100	
Net cash provided by financing activities		300
Net increase in cash		$ 194
Cash balance, June 1		0
Cash balance, June 30		$ 194

Given the cash inflows and outflows described previously, the lawn service's June statement of cash flows would appear as Exhibit 1-5. It contains the company name, the statement name, and the time reference, which for this example is the month of June. It also shows a net change in cash from June 1 to June 30 of $194.

Note that the ending cash balance on the statement agrees with the cash balance shown on the balance sheet in Exhibit 1-2. Since $280 of the $300 of cash generated from financing activities was invested into the lawn mower and the gas can, the majority of the $194 of cash on hand was generated through operations. This, of course, is a good sign and bodes well for your ability to generate enough cash in the future both to pay your relative and to keep for yourself.

LO6 Qualitative Characteristics of Accounting Information

Even though accounting is a very quantitative process and the financial statements introduced thus far are full of numbers, accounting information must possess certain qualitative characteristics to be considered useful. The following qualitative characteristics help ensure that accounting information is indeed useful.

Understandability

Accounting information should first and foremost be understandable. **Understandability** refers to the ability of accounting information to "be comprehensible to those who have a reasonable understanding of business. . . and are willing to study the information with reasonable

Understandability The ability of accounting information to "be comprehensible to those who have a reasonable understanding of business...and are willing to study the information with reasonable diligence."

HOME DEPOT ANALYSIS

Look at Home Depot's statement of cash flows in Appendix C. How much cash did Home Depot generate or use for operating, investing, and financing activities during the most recent year?

Operating Activities: Generated $5,528 million
Investing Activities: Used $1,729 million
Financing Activities: Used $3,680 million

diligence" (SFAC No. 2, par. 40). Notice that this definition puts much of the responsibility on the user of accounting information. Users must be willing to spend a "reasonable" amount of time studying the information. No specifics are given on what is a "reasonable" amount of time, but it is obvious that the more time you spend studying accounting information, the more you will understand.

Relevance

Relevance refers to the capacity of accounting information to make a difference in decisions. Accounting information has this capacity when it possesses feedback value or predictive value. *Feedback value* refers to the ability to assess past performance, while *predictive value* refers to the ability to form expectations of future performance. In the lawn service example, four financial statements were created to demonstrate the financial activities for June. The statements provided feedback on the success of the business, but they also provided the data to generate expectations about July. As a result, the financial statements are relevant to our decision making, which makes them useful.

In addition to having feedback or predictive value, accounting information must be *timely* to be relevant. Information that helps you forecast August revenues is relevant when it is received in July, not when it is received in September. Information is relevant only if it is generated on a timely basis.

Reliability

Reliability refers to the extent to which accounting information can be depended upon to represent what it purports to represent, both in description and in number. To be considered reliable, accounting information should be verifiable, should have representational faithfulness, and should be neutral.

Relevance The capacity of accounting information to make a difference in decisions.

Reliability The extent to which accounting information can be depended upon to represent what it purports to represent, both in description and in number.

Comparability The ability to use accounting information to compare or contrast the financial activities of different companies.

Consistency The ability to use accounting information to compare or contrast the financial activities of the same entity over time.

Information is *verifiable* if it can be proven to be free from error. One can often prove that accounting information is free from error by comparing the information to an original source document such as an invoice or a contract. For example, the original cost of the lawn mower in your lawn service is verifiable because you could check the cost against the amount included on the sales receipt. If the two agree, the information is free from error and you can depend on it.

Information has *representational faithfulness* when the description corresponds to the underlying phenomenon. For example, in your lawn service, you purchased a gas can to store your gas. In your balance sheet, the gas can was reported as an asset. This reporting was a faithful representation of what the item truly was—a resource.

Information is *neutral* if it is presented in a way that is unbiased toward or against the reporting entity. In other words, neutral information does not portray an entity in a more or less favorable light than the information requires. In the lawn service example, income was reported to be $144, not more or less. The $144 figure was a neutral measure of the activities of the service.

Comparability

Comparability refers to the ability to use accounting information to compare or contrast the financial activities of different companies. Being able to compare information across companies allows an entity to assess its market position within an industry, to gauge its success against a competitor, and/or to set future goals based on industry standards.

Comparability does not imply uniformity. Accounting rules allow for some discretion in the manner in which accounting is applied to economic phenomenon. As a result, two businesses with the same economic phenomenon could have different accounting information because they use different acceptable accounting methods. Because such differences in accounting methods are a challenge to comparability, accounting rules require that entities disclose the accounting methods that they use so that information can be more easily compared across entities. Usually, such methods are disclosed in the notes to the financial statements, which are discussed in Chapter 2.

Consistency

Consistency refers to the ability to use accounting information to compare or contrast the financial activities

Materiality thresholds vary across different companies and different settings.

of the same entity over time. Consistency is obviously highest when an entity uses the same accounting methods year after year. In such a case, year-to-year comparisons can be very useful because they can reveal trends that help in generating expectations about future performance. However, entities sometimes change the manner in which they account for a particular economic event. Because such changes hinder consistency, accounting rules require that changes be disclosed by the company so that interested parties can assess the effect of the change. Such disclosures are usually found in the notes to the financial statements.

Materiality

Materiality is a concept that is closely related to relevance in that it refers to the threshold at which an item begins to affect decision making. Items meeting or exceeding the threshold are said to be material—that is, they are large enough to possibly affect decision making. Items below the threshold are said to be immaterial—that is, they are small enough that they will not affect decision making. The threshold varies across different companies and across different settings. As a company gets larger, its materiality threshold usually gets larger as well. Often, the materiality threshold is set at some percentage of assets or sales.

To see how materiality is applied, consider the following example from the lawn service. When you purchased the gas can for $20, the matching principle required that its cost be spread out over its useful life of four months. Suppose that instead of spreading out the cost, you expensed it entirely in the month it was purchased. Doing so would violate the matching principle and would result in $20 of expense instead of $5, which would lower net income from $144 to $129. Would such a violation affect your decision making about the service? Probably not. In other words, violation of the

matching principle is immaterial because the $15 error is not large enough to affect your decision making.

While materiality is largely quantitative in nature, the materiality threshold is not always solely a function of dollar amounts. For example, an error of $1,000 in a routine transaction may be considered immaterial while a $1,000 error in a nonroutine transaction may be considered material. In addition, transactions that a company may consider immaterial may be considered material by users of the information. Materiality judgments are just that—judgments—and should be made with caution. Furthermore, just because something is immaterial does not mean that errors in accounting should be accepted and condoned. Accounting information must be reliable, so it should be free from error as much as possible.

Conservatism

Conservatism refers to the manner in which accountants deal with uncertainty regarding economic situations. When accountants are faced with uncertainty about how to account for or report a particular transaction or situation, conservatism dictates that they use the accounting that is least likely to overstate the company's assets and revenues or to understate the company's liabilities and expenses. A common example of conservatism in action is the lower-of-cost-or-market rule for inventory. According to this rule, inventory must be recorded and reported at the lower of its cost or its current market value. This ensures that the value of inventory is not overstated. Other applications of conservatism will be discussed in subsequent chapters.

> **Materiality** The threshold at which a financial item begins to affect decision making.
>
> **Conservatism** The manner in which accountants deal with uncertainty regarding economic situations.

LO7 The Conceptual Framework

This chapter introduced many of the terms, principles, assumptions, and qualitative characteristics that are necessary to communicate the financial activities and position of a business. While they were initially described as the grammar of the financial accounting language, they are more formally known as components of the conceptual framework of accounting. The **conceptual framework of accounting** is the collection of concepts that guide the manner in which accounting is practiced.

The following tables summarize the elements of this conceptual framework. They will provide a good reference for you as you proceed through the remaining

> **Conceptual framework of accounting** The collection of concepts that guide the manner in which accounting is practiced.

Terms Used to Identify and Describe Economic Information

Term	Definition	Reported on the
Asset	A resource of a business	Balance sheet
Liability	An obligation of a business	Balance sheet
Equity	The difference between assets and liabilities	Balance sheet
Contributed capital	Equity resulting from contributions from owners	Balance sheet
Retained earnings	Equity resulting from profitable operations	Balance sheet and statement of retained earnings
Revenue	An increase in assets resulting from selling a good or providing a service	Income statement
Expense	A decrease in assets resulting from selling a good or providing a service	Income statement
Dividend	A distribution of profits to owners	Statement of retained earnings

Principles Used to Measure Economic Information

Principle	Definition	Ramification
Revenue recognition	Revenues are recorded when they are earned.	The receipt of cash is not required to record a revenue.
Matching	Expenses are recorded in the time period when they are incurred to generate revenues.	For many assets, the cost of the asset must be spread over the periods that it is used.
Cost	Assets are recorded and maintained at their historical costs.	Except in a few cases, market values are not used for reporting asset values.

Assumptions Made When Communicating Economic Information

Assumption	Definition	Ramification
Economic entity	The financial activities of a business can be accounted for separately from the business's owners.	We do not have to worry that the financial information of the owner is mixed with the financial information of the business.
Monetary unit	The dollar, unadjusted for inflation, is the best means of communicating accounting information in the United States.	All transactions in foreign currencies are converted to dollars.
Time period	Accounting information can be communicated effectively over short periods of time.	Most businesses prepare quarterly and annual financial statements.
Going concern	The company for which we are accounting will continue its operations indefinitely.	If an entity is not selling its assets, then the cost principle is appropriate.

chapters. As you tackle more complex accounting methods and procedures, keep in mind that they are simply extensions of the basic grammar presented in the tables. So, with a good understanding of the conceptual framework, you have the grammar necessary to begin your study of accounting.

Qualitative Characteristics that Make Accounting Information Useful

Term	Definition	Ramification
Understandability	Accounting information should be comprehensible by those willing to spend a reasonable amount of time studying it.	Users must spend a reasonable amount of time studying accounting information for it to be understandable.
Relevance	Accounting information should have the capacity to affect decisions.	Information should have predictive or feedback value and should be timely.
Reliability	Accounting information should be dependable to represent what it purports to represent.	Information should be free from error, a faithful representation, and neutral.
Comparability	Accounting information should be comparable across different companies.	Entities must disclose the accounting methods that they use so that comparisons across companies can be made.
Consistency	Accounting information should be comparable across different time periods within a company.	An entity should use the same accounting methods year to year and disclose when they change methods.
Materiality	The threshold over which an item could begin to affect decisions.	When an amount is small enough, normal accounting procedures are not always followed.
Conservatism	When uncertainty exists, accounting information should present the least optimistic alternative.	An entity should choose accounting techniques that guard against overstating revenues or assets.

Financial Statements Used to Communicate Economic Information

Statement	Purpose	Structure	Links to Other Statements
Balance sheet	Shows a company's assets, liabilities, and equity at a specific point in time	Assets = Liabilities + Equity	The balance in retained earnings comes from the statement of retained earnings. The balance in cash should agree with the ending cash balance on the statement of cash flows.
Income statement	Shows a company's revenues and expenses over a specific period of time	Revenue − Expenses = Net Income/Loss	Net income goes to the statement of retained earnings to compute retained earnings.
Statement of retained earnings	Shows the changes in a company's retained earnings over a specific period of time	Beginning Retained Earnings +/− Net Income/Loss − Dividends = Ending Retained Earnings	Ending retained earnings goes to the balance sheet.
Statement of cash flows	Shows a company's inflows and outflows of cash over a specific period of time	Operating Cash Flows +/− Investing Cash Flows +/− Financing Cash Flows = Net change in cash	The ending cash balance on the statement of cash flows should agree with the balance in cash on the balance sheet.

STUDY TOOLS
CHAPTER 1

CHAPTER REVIEW CARD

❏ Learning Objective and Key Concept Reviews

❏ Key Definitions and Formulas

ONLINE (Located at 4ltrpress.cengage.com/acct)

❏ Flash Cards and Crossword Puzzles

❏ Conceptual and Computational Interactive Quizzes

❏ E-Lectures

❏ Static, Algorithmic, and Additional Homework Activities
(as directed by your instructor)

EXERCISES

1. Accounting Terms LO2, 3, 4, 5

Consider the following information:

a. Revenues during the period
b. Supplies on hand at the end of the year
c. Cash received from borrowings during the year
d. Total liabilities at the end of the period
e. Dividends paid during the year
f. Cash paid for a building
g. Cost of buildings owned at year end

Required

Indicate whether you would find each of the above items on the income statement (IS), the balance sheet (BS), the statement of retained earnings (SRE), or the statement of cash flows (SCF).

2. Accounting Terms LO3

Consider the following information:

a. Accounts receivable
b. Salaries payable
c. Office supplies
d. Land
e. Common stock
f. Notes payable

Required

Indicate whether each of the above items is an asset (A), a liability (L), or part of equity (E).

3. Accounting Terms LO2, 3, 4

Consider the following information:

Item	Appears On	Classified As
1. Salaries expense	_____	_____
2. Equipment	_____	_____
3. Cash	_____	_____

Item	Appears On	Classified As
4. Accounts payable	_____	_____
5. Buildings	_____	_____
6. Contributed capital	_____	_____
7. Retained earnings	_____	_____
8. Interest revenue	_____	_____
9. Advertising expense	_____	_____

Required

Classify each of the items above according to (1) whether it appears on the income statement or balance sheet and (2) whether it is classified as a revenue, expense, asset, liability, or equity.

4. Accounting Terms LO2, 3, 4

The following items were recently taken from an income statement and balance sheet for Tiger Inc.

a. Income tax expense
b. Interest expense
c. Sales
d. Receivables
e. Retained earnings
f. Inventories
g. Accounts payable
h. Common stock
i. Cost of sales

Required

Identify whether each item would appear on the balance sheet or the income statement.

5. Statement of Cash Flows LO5

The following information is for Pasture Corp.:

Cash received from customers	$65,000
Cash received from lenders	20,000
Cash paid to suppliers	20,000
Cash paid for new equipment	50,000
Cash paid for dividend	4,000

Required

Indicate on what section of the statement of cash flows each item would appear and calculate Pasture's net change in cash.

6. Links Between Financial Statements LO2, 3, 4

Below are incomplete financial statements for Sterling Inc.

Balance Sheet

Assets

Cash	$ 8,000
Inventory	22,000
Building	40,000
Total assets	$70,000

Liabilities and Stockholders' Equity

Liabilities	
Accounts payable	$ 7,000
Stockholders' equity	
Common stock	(a)
Retained earnings	(b)
Total liabilities & stockholders' equity	$70,000

Income Statement

Sales	$90,000
Cost of sales	(c)
Administrative expenses	20,000
Net income	$ (d)

Statement of Retained Earnings

Retained earnings, beginning balance	$20,000
Net income	(e)
Dividends	10,000
Retained earnings, ending balance	$60,000

Required

Calculate the missing amounts.

7. Principles and Assumptions LO1, 3

The following basic accounting principles and assumptions were discussed in the chapter:

- Economic entity
- Going concern
- Monetary unit
- Cost principle
- Time period

_____ 1. Lester Company has a division in Germany. Before preparing the financial statements for the company and the foreign division, Lester translates the financial statements of its Germany division from the euro to U.S. dollars.

_____ 2. Matt enters into a partnership to start a bike shop with a friend. Each partner makes an initial cash investment of $8,000. Matt opens a checking account in the name of the company and transfers $8,000 from his personal account into the new account.

_____ 3. Dreamland Inc. has always prepared financial statements with a year-end of May 31. However, the company is going to sell stock to the public for the first time and is required by the SEC to give quarterly financial reports.

_____ 4. Platt Corp. purchases a fifty acre plot of land to build the world's largest factory. The company recorded the property at the amount of cash given to acquire it.

_____ 5. Lockbox Corp. is in its ninetieth year of business. The owner of the company is going to retire in two months and turn the company over to his son.

Required
Fill in the blank with the appropriate principle or assumption.

8. Balance Sheet Equation LO3

Consider the following information:

Assets	Liabilities	Stockholders' Equity
50,000	25,000	?
30,000	?	17,000
?	45,000	15,000
68,000	?	13,000
?	14,000	6,000

Required
Use the accounting equation to fill in the missing amounts.

9. Balance Sheet Equation LO3

Consider the following information:
a. Jenkins Company starts the year with $50,000 in assets and $40,000 in liabilities. Net income for the year is $12,500, and no dividends are paid. How much is the owners' equity at the end of the year?

b. McCay Inc. doubles the amount of its assets from the beginning to the end of the year. Liabilities at the end of the year are $50,000, and owners' equity is $30,000. What is the amount of McCay's assets at the beginning of the year?

c. During the year the liabilities of Hudson Corp. triple. Assets at the beginning of the year were $40,000, and owners' equity is $20,000. What is the amount of liabilities at the end of the year?

Required
Use the accounting equation to answer each of the independent questions above.

10. Qualitative Characteristics LO6

The following qualitative characteristics of accounting were discussed in the chapter:

- Consistency
- Relevance
- Understandability
- Comparability
- Conservatism
- Materiality
- Reliability

_____ 1. The ability of accounting information to be comprehensible to those who have a reasonable understanding of business and are willing to study the information with reasonable diligence.

_____ 2. The capacity to affect business decisions.

_____ 3. The dependability of accounting information.

_____ 4. The ability to compare and contrast the financial activities of the same company over a period of time.

_____ 5. The threshold over which an item begins to affect decision making.

_____ 6. The way in which accountants deal with uncertainty.

_____ 7. The ability to compare and contrast the financial activities of different companies.

Required
Fill in the blank with the appropriate characteristic.

11. Assumptions and Principles LO1, 2, 3

Harbor Corp. had the following situations during the year:
a. Inventory with a cost of $186,400 is reported at its market value of $235,600.
b. Harbor added four additional weeks to its fiscal year so that it could make its income look stronger. Past years were 52 weeks.
c. Harbor's CEO purchased a yacht for personal use and charged it to the company.
d. Revenues of $25,000 earned in the prior year were recorded in the current year.

Required
In each situation, identify the assumption or principle that has been violated and discuss how Harbor should have handled the situation.

12. Financial Statements   LO2, 3, 4, 5

Listed below are questions posed by various users of a company's financial statements.

User	Questions	Financial Statement
Stockholder	How did this year's sales figures compare with last year's sales figures?	_____
Banker	How much in borrowings does the company have on its books?	_____
Supplier	How much does the company owe its suppliers in total?	_____
Stockholder	How much did the company pay in dividends last year?	_____
Advertising agent	How much money was used to advertise in order to generate sales?	_____
Banker	What was the company's total interest cost last year?	_____

Required
Fill in the blank with the financial statement (income statement, balance sheet, statement of retained earnings, or statement of cash flows) the user would most likely use to find this information.

PROBLEMS

13. Prepare Financial Statements   LO2, 4

This information relates to York Inc. for the year:

Advertising expense	$ 2,400
Dividends paid	7,000
Rent expense	10,400
Retained earnings, January 1	57,000
Salaries expense	28,000
Service revenue	61,000
Utilities expense	1,800

Required
Prepare an income statement and a statement of retained earnings for the year.

14. Prepare Financial Statements   LO2, 3, 4

The following items are available from the records of Honky Tonk Records Inc. at the end of the year.

Accounts payable	$27,000
Accounts receivable	21,000
Advertising expense	6,000
Buildings	76,000
Capital stock	30,000
Cash	6,320
Notes payable	70,000
Salaries expense	9,500
Sales revenue	16,820
Studio equipment	25,000

Required
Prepare a balance sheet from the above information. Hint: You must first calculate the balance in retained earnings.

15. Preparing Financial Statements   LO2, 3, 4

On June 1 you begin an ocean tour business for the summer by contributing $600 in exchange for capital stock and borrowing $1,000 from your parents. With your money, you purchase a used boat for $1,200; supplies consisting of snorkels, fins, masks, and life-jackets for $240; a June operating permit for $25; and gasoline for $135. You anticipate that the boat and the gear will last only three months. You decide to charge $25 per passenger. At the end of the month of June, you have serviced 240 customers and purchased and used an additional $200 in gasoline. Included in those 240 customers were two neighbors who promised future payment which you have not received (totaling $225). You also pay your parents $5 for monthly interest.

Required
Prepare an income statement and a statement of retained earnings for the month ending June 30 and a balance sheet at June 30.

- All exercises and problems from the text are available online in static and algorithmic versions.
- Additional multiple choice, exercises, problems, and cases are available online in CengageNOW or as an enrichment module that can be customized into this text.

Chapter 1: Financial Accounting   19

Corporate Financial
Statements

Introduction

Chapter 1 introduced the terms, assumptions, principles, and statements that accounting uses to capture and communicate a company's economic activities. This chapter takes a more detailed look at the accounting information provided by companies, particularly public corporations such as Bed Bath & Beyond. Specifically, the chapter introduces the classified balance sheet, the multi-step income statement, and the statement of stockholders' equity. Each of these three financial statements represents a more detailed version of the balance sheet, the income statement, and the statement of retained earnings covered in Chapter 1. The chapter also introduces two analysis techniques, horizontal and vertical analyses, that are simple but powerful tools for generating a more thorough understanding of a company's balance sheet and income statement. At the end of this chapter, you should be comfortable reading through and using the financial statements of most any company.

Learning Objectives

After studying the material in this chapter, you should be able to:

LO1 Describe the three major forms of business.

LO2 Define generally accepted accounting principles and their origins.

LO3 Describe the main classifications of assets, liabilities, and equity in a classified balance sheet.

LO4 Describe the main subtotals of income on a multi-step income statement.

LO5 Analyze the balance sheet and the income statement using horizontal and vertical analyses.

LO6 Describe the purpose of a statement of stockholders' equity.

LO7 Describe the types of information usually disclosed along with financial statements.

LO1 Business Forms

One of the first decisions that any new business faces is the form that it will take. Businesses have the following three basic options:

- Sole proprietorship
- Partnership
- Corporation

A **sole proprietorship** is a business owned by one person and is the most common type of business in the United States. In a sole proprietorship, the owner maintains complete control of the business, bears all the risk of failure, and reaps all the rewards of success. For

Sole proprietorship A business owned by one person.

Inventory is one of the biggest assets for retailers like Bed Bath & Beyond. Because of its importance, it is reported separately on the company's classified balance sheet.

© AP IMAGES/KEVORK DJANSEZIAN

accounting purposes, a sole proprietorship is accounted for separately from the proprietor's personal affairs. This is an application of the economic entity assumption. For tax purposes, though, a sole proprietor's business is not separated from the proprietor. The income from the business is reported on Schedule C of the owner's personal tax return.

A **partnership** is a business that is formed when two or more proprietors join together to own a business. Partnerships can be established by either a written or oral agreement and can include any number of partners. Partnerships are formed for various reasons, such as joining proprietors with different skills, combining

Partnership A business that is formed when two or more proprietors join together to own a business.

CHAPTER 2

ACCT

CHEERS MIX by Mikasa

Balloons (s/4) $39.99
Martini (s/4) $39.99
Shot glass (s/6) $39.99

Chapter 2: Corporate Financial Statements

21

One of the first decisions that any new business faces is the form that it will take.

resources, and spreading the financial risk of the business among several people. Like sole proprietorships, a partnership is considered a separate accounting entity from the individual partners. However, also like sole proprietorships, a partner's share of partnership income is reported on the partner's individual tax return.

A **corporation** is a separate legal entity that is established by filing articles of incorporation in a state, usually with the secretary of state's office. Once a corporation is formed, it sells stock to individuals who want to own part of the corporation. This is one of the main reasons that corporations are formed—the ability to raise capital through the sale of ownership interests. It is also why corporation owners are called stockholders. Like a sole proprietorship and a partnership, a corporation is accounted for separately from its owners. However, it is also taxed separately. Income generated by a corporation is taxed on a corporate tax return, not on the stockholders' individual tax returns.

Corporations can take several forms, one of which is a public corporation. A **public corporation** is one in which ownership is available to the public at large. The stock of a public corporation is usually bought and sold on an open exchange such as the New York Stock Exchange (NYSE) or the National Association of Securities Dealers Automated Quotes (NASDAQ). Such corporations are said to be *publicly traded*. Examples of publicly traded corporations are Microsoft, Kellogg, and Bed Bath & Beyond. From this point forward, this text will focus on the accounting for publicly traded corporations. This will allow you to see accounting issues in companies with which you may be familiar.

LO2 Generally Accepted Accounting Principles

When accounting for their economic activities, public corporations must follow *generally accepted accounting principles*. **Generally accepted accounting principles (GAAP)** are the accounting standards, rules, principles, and procedures that comprise authoritative practice for financial accounting. These principles have been developed over time by several regulatory bodies, the most significant of which are listed as follows.

- Securities and Exchange Commission
- Financial Accounting Standards Board
- American Institute of Certified Public Accountants

The **Securities and Exchange Commission (SEC)** is the federal agency charged to protect investors and

Corporation A separate legal entity that is established by filing articles of incorporation in a state.

Public corporation A separate legal entity in which ownership is available to the public at large.

Generally accepted accounting principles The accounting standards, rules, principles, and procedures that comprise authoritative practice for financial accounting.

Securities and Exchange Commission The federal agency charged to protect investors and maintain the integrity of securities markets.

HOME DEPOT ANALYSIS

Look at the full company name at the top of any of Home Depot's financial statements in Appendix C. Can you tell from the name what form of business Home Depot uses?

The full company name is "The Home Depot, Inc. and Subsidiaries." Inc. stands for incorporated. Thus, Home Depot is a corporation.

maintain the integrity of securities markets. Established by Congress after the 1929 stock market crash, the SEC was given the authority to determine the rules by which publicly traded companies would disclose information to their owners. However, instead of writing all of the rules itself, the SEC delegated much of its accounting rule-making authority to the accounting profession. Today, the accounting organization that sets major accounting standards is the Financial Accounting Standards Board.

The **Financial Accounting Standards Board (FASB)** is a standard setting body whose mission is "to establish and improve standards of financial accounting and reporting for the guidance and education of the public, including issuers, auditors, and users of financial information." The FASB usually tackles large issues, such as the accounting for pensions, leases, stock options, and derivatives. It also maintains the conceptual framework discussed in Chapter 1. The Board consists of seven full-time voting members who oversee a standard-setting process of research, deliberation, public input, and board approval. Once the FASB establishes a rule or standard, it is then enforced by the SEC.

While the FASB is accounting's main standard-setting body, the **American Institute of Certified Public Accountants (AICPA)** also plays a role in establishing accounting rules. The AICPA, which is the professional organization of certified public accountants, maintains a board that establishes rules that are often more technical and more specific to certain industries. For example, the AICPA has issued rules for determining profits in the film industry. The rules set by the AICPA are also enforced by the SEC.

Each of these organizations are based in the United States. However, accounting is practiced throughout the world, and there is a movement to develop one set of international accounting standards to be used by all

> The accounting organization that **sets major accounting standards** is the Financial Accounting Standards Board.

countries. The **International Accounting Standards Board (IASB)** is a board, similar to the FASB, whose mission is to develop a single set of high quality standards requiring transparent and comparable information. Those standards, which have both similarities to and differences from GAAP, are called **International Financial Reporting Standards (IFRS)**. Because adoption of IFRS is voluntary, the effectiveness of the IASB at accomplishing its mission has been somewhat limited. However, the IASB and the FASB have both agreed to a commitment

Financial Accounting Standards Board The standard setting body whose mission is "to establish and improve standards of financial accounting and reporting for the guidance and education of the public, including issuers, auditors, and users of financial information."

American Institute of Certified Public Accountants The professional organization of certified public accountants whose board establishes rules that are often more technical and more specific to certain industries.

International Accounting Standards Board A board, similar to the FASB, whose mission is to develop a single set of high quality standards requiring transparent and comparable information.

International Financial Reporting Standards Standards issued by the International Accounting Standards Board.

HOME DEPOT ANALYSIS

Look at the third paragraph in Home Depot's Independent Auditor's Report in Appendix C. According to the auditor, are Home Depot's financial statements prepared in accordance with GAAP?

Yes. As the Independent Auditor's Report states, the financial information is presented "in conformity with accounting principles generally accepted in the United States of America."

to the convergence of U.S. and international standards. At some time in the future, the world may very well use one set of global accounting standards set by a global board. But for now, public companies traded on U.S. exchanges must use Generally Accepted Accounting Principles.

LO3 The Classified Balance Sheet

Chapter 1 introduced the balance sheet. A balance sheet is a financial statement that summarizes a company's assets, liabilities, and equity at a given point in time. The balance sheet shown in Chapter 1 reported every account of the company. However, most public corporations are much too large to report every account, so they prepare a classified balance sheet instead. A **classified balance sheet** groups together accounts of similar nature and reports them in a few major classifications.

The following sections discuss the various asset, liability, and equity classifications commonly used on classified balance sheets. The February 28, 2009, classified balance sheet of Bed Bath & Beyond in Exhibit 2-1 will be used as an illustration. As you review the statement, note that all numbers except per share data are in thousands, meaning that each reported number has three 0's missing. Note also that two years of data are presented, with the most recent year listed first. This is the normal format for most corporate balance sheets. It is also why such statements are often called *comparative* balance sheets.

Classified balance sheet A type of balance sheet that groups together accounts of similar nature and reports them in a few major classifications.

Current asset Any asset that is reasonably expected to be converted to cash or consumed within one year of the balance sheet date.

Long-term investments The investments in the common stock or debt of another entity that will not be sold within a year.

Fixed assets The tangible resources that are used in a company's operations for more than one year and are not intended for resale.

Assets

An asset is a resource of a business. Assets are generally grouped into five main categories on a classified balance sheet:

- current assets
- long-term investments
- fixed assets
- intangible assets
- other assets

Current Assets A **current asset** is any asset that is reasonably expected to be converted to cash or consumed within one year of the balance sheet date. Common examples include cash, investments that will mature or be sold within a year, accounts receivable from customers, inventories, and other assets such as prepaid insurance. Current assets are listed in order of their liquidity, which refers to the speed with which a resource can be converted to cash. Cash is listed first, followed by short-term investments, receivables, inventories, and then finally other assets.

Bed Bath & Beyond reports four current assets totaling over $2.5 billion on its February 28, 2009, balance sheet. As you might expect from a retailer, the vast majority of those assets (over $1.6 billion) is in *Merchandise inventories*, with a substantial amount also in *Cash and cash equivalents*. The company also reports some *Short-term investment securities* and *Other current assets*.

Long-Term Investments **Long-term investments** are a company's investments in the common stock or debt of another entity that will not be sold within a year. Companies typically list any long-term investments as their first noncurrent asset. Bed Bath & Beyond reports $221 million in *Long-term investment securities*.

Fixed Assets **Fixed assets** are the tangible resources that are used in a company's operations for more than one year and are not intended for resale. Examples include land, buildings, equipment, furniture, and fixtures.

Bed Bath & Beyond reports over $1.1 billion of fixed assets on its February 28, 2009, balance sheet, making them the second largest asset, which makes sense for a retailer. Note, however, that the company uses the term *Property and equipment, net* rather than fixed assets. This is a common name for fixed assets. Note also the word "net" in the description. Most fixed assets are subject to depreciation, which is the process

Exhibit 2-1 Bed Bath & Beyond Classified Balance Sheet

BED BATH & BEYOND INC. AND SUBSIDIARIES
Consolidated Balance Sheets
(in thousands, except per share data)

	February 28, 2009	March 1, 2008
Assets		
Current assets:		
Cash and cash equivalents	$ 668,209	$ 224,084
Short-term investment securities	2,000	—
Merchandise inventories	1,642,339	1,616,981
Other current assets	250,251	238,646
Total current assets	2,562,799	2,079,711
Long-term investment securities	221,134	326,004
Property and equipment, net	1,148,435	1,121,906
Other assets	336,475	316,472
Total assets	$4,268,843	$3,844,093
Liabilities and Shareholders' Equity		
Current liabilities:		
Accounts payable	$ 514,734	$ 570,605
Accrued expenses and other current liabilities	247,508	258,989
Merchandise credit and gift card liabilities	165,621	171,252
Current income taxes payable	25,105	13,266
Total current liabilities	952,968	1,014,112
Deferred rent and other liabilities	227,209	192,778
Income taxes payable	88,212	75,375
Total liabilities	1,268,389	1,282,265
Shareholders' equity:		
Preferred stock—$0.01 par value; authorized - 1,000 shares;		
no shares issued or outstanding	—	—
Common stock—$0.01 par value; authorized - 900,000 shares;		
issued 314,678 and 312,229 shares, respectively;	3,147	3,122
Additional paid-in capital	878,568	813,568
Retained earnings	4,154,921	3,729,766
Treasury stock, at cost	(2,031,642)	(1,983,590)
Accumulated other comprehensive loss	(4,540)	(1,038)
Total shareholders' equity	3,000,454	2,561,828
Total liabilities and shareholders' equity	$ 4,268,843	$ 3,844,093

of expensing the cost of an asset over its useful life. Therefore, fixed assets are reported "net" of any depreciation to date. Chapter 8 will discuss depreciation in much more detail.

Intangible Assets An **intangible asset** is a resource that is used in operations for more than one year, is not intended for resale, and has no physical substance. Examples include trademarks, patents, franchise rights, copyrights, and goodwill. Like fixed assets, intangible assets are subject to depreciation (although it is actually called amortization instead of depreciation) and are reported net of amortization to date. Bed Bath & Beyond does not separately report any intangible assets.

Other Assets **Other assets** are those resources that do not fit well into one of the other classifications. The classification can also include those assets that are small enough that they do not warrant separate reporting. Bed Bath & Beyond reports approximately $336 million

> **Intangible asset** A resource that is used in operation for more than one year, is not intended for resale, and has no physical substance.
>
> **Other assets** Resources that do not fit well into one of the other asset classifications or are small enough that they do not warrant separate reporting.

in *Other assets*. According to additional information provided by the company, the $336 million balance includes the company's intangible assets.

Liabilities

A liability is an obligation of a business. Liabilities are generally classified into two main categories on a classified balance sheet:

- Current liabilities
- Long-term liabilities

Current Liabilities
A **current liability** is an obligation that is reasonably expected to be satisfied within one year. Examples include accounts payable to vendors, salaries payable to employees, and taxes payable to taxing authorities. Even long-term debt, if maturing within one year, is classified as a current liability.

Bed Bath & Beyond reports four current liabilities totaling almost $953 million on its February 28, 2009, balance sheet. The largest is almost $515 million in *Accounts payable*, which is the amount owed to suppliers. Over $247 million is listed in *Accrued expenses and other current liabilities*, which likely represents obligations relating to employees, advertising, or other operating matters. Also, over $165 million is reported in *Merchandise credit and gift card liabilities*. This represents the value of unredeemed gift cards and other credits. Finally, the company reports about $25 million of *Current income taxes payable*, which is the amount owed to taxing authorities based on the income earned previously.

Long-Term Liabilities
A **long-term liability** is an obligation that is not expected to be satisfied within one year. Examples include notes payable, mortgage payable, and bonds payable. Bed Bath & Beyond has very few long term liabilities at February 28, 2009. It reports $227 million in *Deferred rent and other liabilities* and $88 million in *Income taxes payable*.

Equity

Equity is the difference between a company's assets and its liabilities. It is generated from the following two sources:

- Retained earnings
- Contributed capital

Retained earnings is the amount of equity a company generates by being profitable and retaining those profits in the business. **Contributed capital** is the amount of equity a company generates through the sale of stock to investors. Such equity is often referred to as capital stock. Examples of capital stock include common stock and preferred stock.

Like most publicly traded companies, Bed Bath & Beyond reports its equity accounts in one general section called Shareholders' Equity. The largest balance in the section is the $4.1 billion of *Retained earnings*. This balance indicates a very strong record of profits in previous years. The second largest balance is *Treasury stock*, which has a $2 billion balance. Treasury stock is created when a company buys back its stock from investors. The account therefore represents the amount of contributed capital that has been returned to owners. That is why the number is a negative—because it is a reduction to equity. A more in-depth analysis of treasury stock and equity in general will be left for Chapter 10.

Current liability An obligation that is reasonably expected to be satisfied within one year.

Long-term liability An obligation that is not expected to be satisfied within one year.

Retained earnings The amount of equity a company generates by being profitable and retaining those profits in the business.

Contributed capital The amount of equity a company generates through the sale of stock to investors.

Single-step income statement Calculates total revenues and total expenses and then determines net income in one step by subtracting total expenses from total revenues.

LO4 The Multi-Step Income Statement

Chapter 1 also introduced the income statement. The income statement is a financial statement that summarizes a company's revenues and expenses over a period of time. Companies generally use one of two forms for their income statements—a single-step statement or a multi-step statement.

A **single-step income statement** calculates total revenues and total expenses and then determines net income in one step by subtracting total expenses from total revenues. The income statement prepared in Chapter 1 was a single-step income statement. The major advantage of a single-step statement is its simplicity. However, the disadvantage is that it does not present the information in a manner that is very useful. As a result, most companies prepare multi-step income statements.

A **multi-step income statement** calculates income by grouping certain revenues and expenses together and calculating several subtotals of income. These subtotals provide information on the profitability of various aspects of the company's operations. While most companies prepare multi-step statements, there is some slight variation in how they are prepared. However, most include either some or all of the following four subtotals of income.

- Gross profit
- Operating profit
- Income before taxes
- Net income

The following sections discuss these subtotals that are commonly used by companies. For illustration purposes, Exhibit 2-2 contains Bed Bath & Beyond's income statement for the fiscal year ended February 28, 2009. Note that the company uses the title, *Consolidated Statements of Earnings,* rather than income statement. Note also that like the balance sheet, the numbers are in thousands. However, unlike the balance sheet, the income statement reports three years of data. The presentation of multiple years of data therefore yields comparative income statements.

Gross Profit

In a multi-step statement, sales revenue is listed first. **Sales revenue,** which is often labeled net sales, is the resources that a company generates during a period from selling its inventory. Listed next is cost of sales. **Cost of sales,** which is sometimes called cost of goods sold, represents the cost of the inventory that was sold during a period. Subtracting cost of sales from net sales then yields the first subtotal of income, gross profit. **Gross profit,** which is sometimes called gross margin, represents the profit that a company generates when considering only the sales price and the cost of the product sold. It therefore represents the gross dollar markup that a company is able to achieve when selling its inventory.

For the fiscal period ended February 28, 2009, Bed Bath & Beyond generated over $7.2 billion in *Net sales.* With *Cost of sales* of over $4.3 billion, the company generated a *Gross profit* of approximately $2.9 billion for the year. Note that with a profit of $2.9 billion on inventory costing $4.3 billion, the average markup on inventory was around 67% of its cost ($2.9 ÷ $4.3). That is, on average, an inventory item costing the company $100 sold for $167.

> **Multi-step income statement** Calculates income by grouping certain revenues and expenses together and calculating several subtotals of income.
>
> **Sales revenue** The resources that a company generates during a period from selling its inventory.
>
> **Cost of sales** The cost of the inventory sold during a period.
>
> **Gross profit** The profit that a company generates when considering only the sales price and the cost of the product sold.

Exhibit 2-2 Bed Bath & Beyond Multi-step Income Statement

Consolidated Statements of Earnings
Bed Bath & Beyond Inc. and Subsidiaries

	FISCAL YEAR ENDED		
(in thousands)	February 28, 2009	March 1, 2008	March 3, 2007
Net sales	$7,208,340	$7,048,942	$6,617,429
Cost of sales	4,335,104	4,123,711	3,782,027
Gross profit	2,873,236	2,925,231	2,835,402
Selling, general and administrative expenses	2,199,340	2,087,209	1,946,001
Operating profit	673,896	838,022	889,401
Interest income	9,412	27,210	43,478
Earnings before provision for income taxes	683,308	865,232	932,879
Provision for income taxes	258,185	302,424	338,635
Net earnings	$ 425,123	$ 562,808	$ 594,244

© iSTOCKPHOTO.COM/ALBERT LOZANO

Just like individuals do, corporations must pay taxes on their incomes.

Operating Profit

After gross profit is reported, operating expenses are listed. **Operating expenses** are the expenses that a company incurs during normal operations. Such expenses are recurring, meaning that they are incurred year after year as the company runs its business. Examples include advertising, salaries, utilities, depreciation, and insurance.

In most multi-step statements, operating expenses are summed together and subtracted from gross profit

---

Operating expenses Recurring expenses that a company incurs during normal operations.

Operating profit The profit that a company generates when considering both the cost of the inventory and the normal expenses incurred to operate the business.

Other revenue and expenses Revenues and expenses generated outside of normal operations.

Income before taxes The profit that a company generates when considering all revenues and expenses except for income taxes.

---

to yield the second subtotal of income, operating profit. **Operating profit** represents the profit that a company generates when considering both the cost of the inventory and the normal expenses incurred to operate the business. Other names for operating profit include income from operations or operating income.

Bed Bath & Beyond reports almost $2.2 billion of operating expenses in one expense line labeled *Selling, general and administrative expenses*. This is a common description for general operating expenses. Subtracting these operating expenses from gross profit yields an *Operating profit* of about $673 million. So, after considering its two major expenses—cost of inventory and operating expenses—Bed Bath & Beyond's $7.2 billion in sales yielded about $673 million in profits.

Income Before Taxes

In addition to cost of sales and operating expenses, companies sometimes generate revenues and expenses that are outside of their normal operations. Common examples include interest revenue and interest expense. Such items are listed separately as **other revenues and expenses** and are netted against operating profit to yield the third subtotal of income, income before taxes. **Income before taxes,** also called earnings before income taxes and other similar titles, represents the profit that a company generates when considering all revenues and expenses except for income taxes.

After reporting its operating profit, Bed Bath & Beyond reports *Interest income* of approximately $9 million. This $9 million, which likely represents the revenues generated from the company's investment portfolios, is added to operating profit to yield *Earnings before provision for income taxes* of $683 million.

HOME DEPOT ANALYSIS

Look at Home Depot's Income Statement in Appendix C. What form of income statement does the company use?

Home Depot uses a multi-step income statement. It shows several subtotals of income, including Gross Profit, Operating Income, Earnings Before Provision for Income Taxes, and Net Earnings.

Net Income

Like individuals, corporations must pay taxes on their incomes. Usually, the amount of tax in a given period is listed separately on a multi-step statement as provision for income taxes. **Provision for income taxes** is the amount of income tax expense for a given period. When this provision is subtracted from income before taxes, the final income measure, **net income,** is determined. Bed Bath & Beyond reports a $258 million *Provision for income taxes*. Subtracting that from income before taxes yields *Net earnings* of approximately $425 million.

In summary, Bed Bath & Beyond's multi-step income statement provides a picture of how the company generated its profits in the last period. It generated $2.9 billion in profits due to its inventory markups. Once it subtracted its operating expenses, it had profits of $674 million remaining. After considering other revenues and taxes, $425 million of profits remained from the original sales of $7.2 billion.

LO5 **Horizontal and Vertical Analyses**

The previous sections demonstrate that financial statements communicate economic information about a company to interested parties. For example, investors and creditors learn from Bed Bath & Beyond's income statement that the company earned $425 million of income in the most recent year. This is useful information because it demonstrates that the company was profitable during the year. However, the information can be even more useful if it is compared to something else. For example, is $425 million better or worse than last year? Is it high enough given sales for the period? How does it compare to competitors? Such comparisons provide the necessary context for a more thorough understanding of a company's financial activities. Such context can be easily generated through two techniques called horizontal and vertical analyses.

Horizontal Analysis

Horizontal analysis is a method of analyzing a company's account balances over time. It is normally conducted on both the balance sheet and the income statement. The analysis calculates both the absolute and percentage change in each account balance on a financial statement. As a result, it is very useful in identifying promising or troubling trends in a company. The analysis is called "horizontal" because the calculation compares an account's balance across the columns of yearly data—that is, horizontally across the financial statement.

Horizontal analysis is calculated as follows. First, the dollar change in an account is determined. This is defined as the current year balance less the prior year balance. The dollar change is then divided by the prior year balance to yield a percentage change. These two calculations are shown below.

$$\text{Dollar change in account balance} = \text{Current year balance} - \text{Prior year balance}$$

$$\text{Percentage change in account balance} = \frac{\text{Dollar change}}{\text{Prior year balance}}$$

To illustrate, consider the *Merchandise inventories* balance from Bed Bath & Beyond's balance sheet in Exhibit 2-1:

	February 28, 2009	March 1, 2008
Merchandise inventories	$1,642,339	$1,616,981

The company's inventory increased $25,358 from March 1, 2008 to February 28, 2009. Dividing that increase by the March 1, 2008 balance yields a percentage change of 1.6%. These calculations are shown in the following table. Also shown are similar calculations

	Inventories	Net earnings
Current Year Balance	$1,642,339	$ 425,123
− Prior Year Balance	− $1,616,981	− $ 562,808
Dollar Change	$ 25,358	$(137,685)
Dollar change	$25,358	$(137,685)
Prior year balance	$1,616,981	$562,808
= Percentage change	= 1.6%	= −24.4%

> **Provision for income taxes** The amount of income tax expense for a given period.
>
> **Net income** The final income measure after the provision for income taxes is subtracted from income before taxes.
>
> **Horizontal analysis** A method of analyzing a company's account balances over time by calculating absolute and percentage changes in each account.

for a horizontal analysis of *Net earnings* from the company's income statement in Exhibit 2-2. Note that the *Net earnings* calculations result in a negative percentage change.

For a full horizontal analysis, both dollar and percentage changes are calculated for each account on both the balance sheet and the income statement. Exhibit 2-3 contains a horizontal analysis of Bed Bath

& Beyond's balance sheet and income statement. The column headings show the general calculations, with CY and PY representing current year and prior year, respectively.

An examination of the balance sheet shows overall growth. *Total assets* in the most recent year were $424,750, or 11%, higher than the prior year. All assets except *Long-term investment securities* increased from the

Exhibit 2-3 Horizontal Analysis of Bed Bath & Beyond's Balance Sheet and Income Statement

Balance Sheet				
	CY Feb 28, 2009	PY March 1, 2008	(CY – PY) $ Change	(CY – PY) PY % Change
Assets				
Current assets:				
Cash and cash equivalents	$ 668,209	$ 224,084	$ 444,125	198.2%
Short-term investment securities	2,000	0	2,000	N/A
Merchandise inventories	1,642,339	1,616,981	25,358	1.6%
Other current assets	250,251	238,646	11,605	4.9%
Total current assets	2,562,799	2,079,711	$ 483,088	23.2%
Long-term investment securities	221,134	326,004	$ (104,870)	−32.2%
Property and equipment, net	1,148,435	1,121,906	26,529	2.4%
Other assets	336,475	316,472	20,003	6.3%
Total assets	$4,268,843	$3,844,093	$ 424,750	11.0%
Liabilities and Shareholders' Equity				
Current liabilities:				
Accounts payable	$ 514,734	$ 570,605	$ (55,871)	−9.8%
Accrued expenses and other current liabilities	247,508	258,989	(11,481)	−4.4%
Merchandise credit and gift card liabilities	165,621	171,252	(5,631)	−3.3%
Current income taxes payable	25,105	13,266	11,839	89.2%
Total current liabilities	952,968	1,014,112	$ (61,144)	−6.0%
Deferred rent and other liabilities	227,209	192,778	$ 34,431	17.9%
Income taxes payable	88,212	75,375	12,837	17.0%
Total liabilities	1,268,389	1,282,265	$ (13,876)	−1.1%
Shareholders' equity:				
Common stock	3,147	3,122	$ 25	0.8%
Additional paid-in capital	878,568	813,568	65,000	8.0%
Retained earnings	4,154,921	3,729,766	425,155	11.4%
Treasury stock, at cost	(2,031,642)	(1,983,590)	(48,052)	2.4%
Accumulated other comprehensive loss	(4,540)	(1,038)	($3,502)	337.4%
Total shareholders' equity	3,000,454	2,561,828	$ 438,626	17.1%
Total liabilities and shareholders' equity	$4,268,843	$3,844,093	$ 424,750	11.0%

Income Statement				
FISCAL YEAR ENDED	Feb 28, 2009	March 1, 2008	$ Change	% Change
Net sales	$7,208,340	$7,048,942	$ 159,398	2.3%
Cost of sales	4,335,104	4,123,711	211,393	5.1%
Gross profit	2,873,236	2,925,231	$ (51,995)	−1.8%
Selling, general and administrative expenses	2,199,340	2,087,209	112,131	5.4%
Operating profit	673,896	838,022	$ (164,126)	−19.6%
Interest income	9,412	27,210	(17,798)	−65.4%
Earnings before provision for income taxes	683,308	865,232	$ (181,924)	−21.0%
Provision for income taxes	258,185	302,424	(44,239)	−14.6%
Net earnings	$ 425,123	$ 562,808	$ (137,685)	−24.5%

Common-size statements allow investors and creditors to compare companies of vastly different sizes.

prior year, with *Cash and cash equivalents* having the largest increase by far. Since *Total liabilities* decreased 1.1%, the company's asset growth was not generated by borrowing from creditors. Rather, the company grew by being profitable. *Total shareholders' equity* was up 17.1% from the prior year, with the majority of that increase caused by a substantial increase in *Retained earnings*.

An examination of the income statement also shows growth. *Net sales* were 2.3% higher than the prior year. However, *Cost of sales* were 5.1% higher and *Selling, general and administrative expenses* were 5.4% higher. When a company's expenses grow faster than its sales revenues, its profitability will decline. That decline can be seen in all of the company's profit subtotals. Current-year *Gross profit, Operating profit,* and *Net earnings* were all lower than the prior year.

In summary, horizontal analysis of the balance sheet and income statement shows that Bed Bath & Beyond is growing and is profitable overall. That is the good news. The bad news is that the company was not as profitable this year as it was in the prior year. Horizontal analysis has provided the context for a much more thorough understanding of the financial statements.

Vertical Analysis

Vertical analysis is a method of comparing a company's account balances within one year. It also is normally conducted on both the balance sheet and the income statement. The analysis is calculated by dividing each account balance by a base account, yielding a percentage. The base account is total assets for balance sheet accounts and net sales or revenues for income statement accounts. These two calculations are shown below.

	For the Balance Sheet	For the Income Statement
Percentage	$\dfrac{\text{Account balance}}{\text{Total Assets}}$	$\dfrac{\text{Account balance}}{\text{Net Sales or Revenue}}$

The product of a vertical analysis is sometimes called a common-size financial statement. A **common-size financial statement** is a statement in which all accounts have been standardized by the overall size of the

company. Common-size statements are very useful because they allow investors and creditors to determine the importance of each account to the overall company and to compare that importance to other companies, even those of vastly different sizes.

To illustrate, consider again the *Merchandise inventories* balance from Bed Bath & Beyond's balance sheet in Exhibit 2-1 (see page 25). Also shown are the company's *Total assets*.

	February 28, 2009	March 1, 2008
Merchandise inventories	$1,642,339	$1,616,981
Total assets	4,268,843	3,844,093

A vertical analysis divides each inventory balance by total assets for that year. These calculations are shown in the following table. Also shown are similar calculations that would be made for a vertical analysis of *Net earnings* from the company's income statement in Exhibit 2-2. The only difference is that *Net earnings* is divided by *Net sales*, not *Total assets*.

	Current Year	Prior Year
Inventory Balance	$1,642,339	$1,616,981
Total Assets	$4,268,843	$3,844,093
= Percentage of Total Assets	= 38.5%	= 42.1%
Net Earnings	$425,123	$562,808
Net Sales	$7,208,340	$7,048,942
= Percentage of Net Sales	= 5.9%	= 8.0%

For a full vertical analysis, percentages are calculated for every account on each financial statement. Exhibit 2-4 contains a vertical analysis of Bed Bath & Beyond's balance sheet and income statement. The column headings show the general calculations, with CY and PY representing current year and prior year, respectively.

An examination of the balance sheet shows that the bulk of Bed Bath & Beyond's assets are held in *Merchandise inventories* and *Property and equipment*. Note, however, that both percentages decreased slightly from the prior year. Note also that the percentage in *Cash*

> **Vertical analysis** A method of comparing a company's account balances within one year by dividing each account balance by a base amount to yield a percentage.
>
> **Common-size financial statement** A statement in which all accounts have been standardized by the overall size of the company.

Exhibit 2-4 Vertical Analysis of Bed Bath & Beyond's Balance Sheet and Income Statement

Balance Sheet

	CY Feb. 28, 2009	CY CY Total assets	PY March 1, 2008	PY PY Total assets
Assets				
Current assets:				
Cash and cash equivalents	$ 668,209	15.7%	$ 224,084	5.8%
Short-term investment securities	2,000	0.0%	0	0.0%
Merchandise inventories	1,642,339	38.5%	1,616,981	42.1%
Other current assets	250,251	5.9%	238,646	6.2%
Total current assets	2,562,799	60.0%	2,079,711	54.1%
Long-term investment securities	221,134	5.2%	326,004	8.5%
Property and equipment, net	1,148,435	26.9%	1,121,906	29.2%
Other assets	336,475	7.9%	316,472	8.2%
Total assets	$4,268,843	100.0%	$3,844,093	100.0%
Liabilities and Shareholders' Equity				
Current liabilities:				
Accounts payable	$ 514,734	12.1%	$ 570,605	14.8%
Accrued expenses and other current liabilities	247,508	5.8%	258,989	6.7%
Merchandise credit and gift card liabilities	165,621	3.9%	171,252	4.5%
Current income taxes payable	25,105	0.6%	13,266	0.3%
Total current liabilities	952,968	22.3%	1,014,112	26.4%
Deferred rent and other liabilities	227,209	5.3%	192,778	5.0%
Income taxes payable	88,212	2.1%	75,375	2.0%
Total liabilities	1,268,389	29.7%	1,282,265	33.4%
Shareholders' equity:				
Common stock	3,147	0.1%	3,122	0.1%
Additional paid-in capital	878,568	20.6%	813,568	21.2%
Retained earnings	4,154,921	97.3%	3,729,766	97.0%
Treasury stock, at cost	(2,031,642)	−47.6%	(1,983,590)	−51.6%
Accumulated other comprehensive loss	(4,540)	−0.1%	(1,038)	0.0%
Total shareholders' equity	3,000,454	70.3%	2,561,828	66.6%
Total liabilities and shareholders' equity	$4,268,843	100.0%	$3,844,093	100.0%

Income Statement

FISCAL YEAR ENDED	CY Feb. 28, 2009	CY CY Net Sales	PY March 1, 2008	PY PY Net Sales
Net sales	$7,208,340	100.0%	$7,048,942	100.0%
Cost of sales	4,335,104	60.1%	4,123,711	58.5%
Gross profit	2,873,236	39.9%	2,925,231	41.5%
Selling, general and administrative expenses	2,199,340	30.5%	2,087,209	29.6%
Operating profit	673,896	9.3%	838,022	11.9%
Interest income	9,412	0.1%	27,210	0.4%
Earnings before provision for income taxes	683,308	9.5%	865,232	12.3%
Provision for income taxes	258,185	3.6%	302,424	4.3%
Net earnings	$ 425,123	5.9%	$ 562,808	8.0%

and cash equivalents increased significantly to 15.7% of assets. This shows that as Bed Bath & Beyond grew its assets during the year, it chose to keep more in the form of cash. More cash provides for more flexibility.

Regarding liabilities and equity, the largest liability is *Accounts payable*, while the largest equity account is *Retained earnings*. These make sense for a successful retailer. The analysis also reveals Bed Bath & Beyond's capital structure. Capital structure refers to the degree to which a company's assets are generated from liabilities versus equity. In general, a capital structure more heavily weighted towards liabilities is riskier. According to the vertical analysis, Bed Bath & Beyond generated 29.7% of assets from *Total liabilities* and 70.3% from *Total shareholders' equity* in the most recent year. This is a relatively low-risk capital structure.

MAKING IT REAL

A company's balance sheet often reflects its business model, and a vertical analysis can help you identify one model from another. For example, take the following vertical analyses of selected assets from the 2008 balance sheets of two well-known retailers—Amazon and Wal-Mart. Can you tell which company is which?

	Company A	Company B
Cash and cash equivalents	33.3%	4.4%
Accounts receivable	9.9%	2.4%
Inventories	16.8%	21.1%
Fixed assets, net	10.3%	58.5%

Both Amazon and Wal-Mart are in the business of selling inventory, but their models are different. Wal-Mart is a traditional "bricks and mortar" company that sells its inventory in stores, while Amazon is a dot com company that sells its inventory online. Therefore, Wal-Mart should have a greater percentage of its total assets in fixed assets. Company B has 58.5% of its assets in fixed assets. Therefore, Company B is Wal-Mart.

An examination of the income statement shows that *Cost of sales* was 60.1% of *Net sales* and *Selling, general and administrative expenses* were 30.5%. Taken together, these two major expense categories consumed over 90% of the company's sales revenues. The result was that *Net earnings* were 5.9% of *Net sales*. This means that the company earned almost 6 cents of profit for every dollar of sales. Note that this percentage is much lower than the 8.0% achieved in the prior year.

HOME DEPOT ANALYSIS

Conduct and interpret horizontal and vertical analyses of Home Depot's inventory and cost of sales found in Appendix C.

Inventory
H/A: ($10,673 − $11,731) / $11,731 = −9.0%
V/A: $10,673 / $41,164 = 25.9%
Cost of Sales
H/A: ($47,298 − $51,352) / $51,352 = −7.9%
V/A: $47,298 / $71,288 = 66.3%

The horizontal analyses indicate that both inventory and cost of sales decreased during the year. This reveals that the company is both keeping less inventory on its shelves and selling less. However, the vertical analyses indicate that inventory is still a significant part of Home Depot's business. Inventory makes up over one-fourth of Home Depot's assets. Moreover, for every dollar of sales, Home Depot spends about 66 cents on the merchandise sold. This leaves only 34 cents to cover all other expenses and generate a profit.

The statement of retained earnings links a company's income statement and balance sheet.

© YURI ARCURS / SHUTTERSTOCK.COM

As seen in the horizontal analysis, Bed Bath & Beyond is profitable, but its profits are declining.

LO6 **The Statement of Stockholders' Equity**

Chapter 1 introduced the statement of retained earnings. The statement of retained earnings links a company's income statement and balance sheet by showing how net income and dividends change the company's retained earnings balance. All corporations prepare a statement of retained earnings, but most show it as a component of a more comprehensive statement of stockholders' equity.

A **statement of stockholders' equity** is a financial statement that shows how and why each equity account in the company's balance sheet changed from one year to the next. It therefore focuses not only on retained earnings, but also on other equity accounts relating to a company's contributed capital.

For illustration purposes, Exhibit 2-5 contains Bed Bath & Beyond's statement of shareholders' equity for the fiscal year ended February 28, 2009. Like the income statement, this statement reports three years of data. However, unlike the income statement, each column reflects the activity in a specific equity account rather than a period of time. The five columns of the statement

refer to the five equity accounts from the classified balance sheet. That is, the balances at the bottom of the statement are the same balances from the most recent balance sheet. Note that the numbers are in thousands. Note also that Bed Bath & Beyond uses the word *shareholders'* in the title rather than stockholders'.

The first two accounts, *Common Stock* and *Additional Paid-In Capital,* represent the capital that has been contributed to the company through the issuance of stock. Chapter 10 will discuss in more detail why contributed capital is divided into two accounts. For now, you simply need to add the balances together to yield the total amount received to date. The activity in these accounts for the fiscal year ending February 28, 2009, is located on the bottom third of the statement. The columns of information indicate that the company generated contributed capital during the year primarily through transactions with employees.

The third account, *Retained Earnings,* represents the equity that has been generated through profitable operations and retained in the business. The retained earnings column is in fact Bed Bath & Beyond's statement of retained earnings. In each year presented, net income is added to the beginning retained earnings balance, but no dividends are subtracted. This is because Bed Bath & Beyond elects not to pay dividends.

The fourth account is *Treasury Stock.* Treasury stock is common stock that the company has purchased back from stockholders. Since the purchase of treasury stock is effectively a return of capital to owners, the balance in treasury stock is subtracted from stockholders' equity. The company has been very active in repurchasing its stock over the three years. Treasury stock will be covered in more detail in Chapter 10.

The last account, *Accumulated Other Comprehensive Income (Loss),* is beyond the scope of this chapter.

> **Statement of stockholders' equity** A financial statement that shows how and why each equity account in the company's balance sheet changed from one year to the next.

Exhibit 2-5 Bed Bath & Beyond's Statement of Shareholders' Equity

Consolidated Statements of Shareholders' Equity
Bed Bath & Beyond Inc. and Subsidiaries

(in thousands)	Common Stock Shares	Common Stock Amount	Additional Paid-in Capital	Retained Earnings	Treasury Stock Shares	Treasury Stock Amount	Accumulated Other Comprehensive Income (Loss)	Total
Balance at February 25, 2006	306,156	$3,062	$ 575,559	$2,632,224	(25,166)	$(948,395)	$ —	$2,262,450
Net earnings				594,244				594,244
Shares sold under employee stock option plans, including tax benefit	2,603	26	61,628					61,654
Issuance of restricted shares,	991	10	(10)					—
Stock-based compensation expense, net			61,744					61,744
Repurchase of common stock, including fees					(7,510)	(301,002)		(301,002)
Adoption of SAB 108			38,288	(72,612)				(34,324)
Adoption of SFAS No. 158							4,385	4,385
Balance at March 3, 2007	**309,750**	**3,098**	**737,209**	**3,153,856**	**(32,676)**	**(1,249,397)**	**4,385**	**2,649,151**
Adoption of FIN 48				13,102				13,102
Comprehensive Income (Loss):								
Net earnings				562,808				562,808
Temporary impairment of auction rate securities, net							(4,516)	(4,516)
Pension adjustment, net of							(736)	(736)
Currency translation							(171)	(171)
Comprehensive Income								557,385
Shares sold under employee stock option plans, including tax benefit	1,463	14	31,367					31,381
Issuance of restricted shares,	1,016	10	(10)					—
Stock-based compensation expense, net			45,002					45,002
Repurchase of common stock, including fees					(20,633)	(734,193)		(734,193)
Balance at March 1, 2008	**312,229**	**3,122**	**813,568**	**3,729,766**	**(53,309)**	**(1,983,590)**	**(1,038)**	**2,561,828**
Comprehensive Income (Loss):								
Net earnings				425,123				425,123
Change in temporary impairment of auction rate securities, net of taxes							(615)	(615)
Unrealized loss included in net earnings, net of taxes							3,528	3,528
Pension adjustment, net of							(4,593)	(4,593)
Currency translation							(1,822)	(1,822)
Comprehensive Income								421,621
Shares sold under employee stock option plans, including tax benefit	1,218	12	19,910					19,922
Issuance of restricted shares,	1,224	13	(13)					—
Stock-based compensation expense, net			44,906					44,906
Director fees paid in stock	7		197					197
Repurchase of common stock, including fees					(1,668)	(48,052)		(48,052)
SFAS No. 158 change in measurement date effect				32				32
Balance at February 28, 2009	**314,678**	**$ 3,147**	**$ 878,568**	**$4,154,921**	**(54,977)**	**$(2,031,642)**	**$ (4,540)**	**$3,000,454**

LO7 Information Beyond the Financial Statements

A company's financial statements contain a significant amount of information about the financial activities and position of the company. However, they are not exhaustive, and much information that is useful to creditors and investors is not included on the statements. As a result, companies like Bed Bath & Beyond prepare and report additional information beyond the financial statements. These items are normally included in a company's annual report that is distributed to all shareholders annually. Three items of significance are the following:

- Notes to the financial statements
- Auditor's report
- Management's Discussion and Analysis

Notes to the Financial Statements

At the bottom of each of Bed Bath & Beyond's financial statements is the following quote: *See accompanying Notes to the Consolidated Financial Statements.* A company's financial statements cannot communicate or disclose to users all the information necessary to adequately understand the financial activities and condition of an entity. Additional information, both quantitative and qualitative, is necessary and can be found in the notes to the financial statements.

The **notes to the financial statements** are the textual and numerical information immediately following the financial statements that (1) disclose the accounting methods used to prepare the financial statements, (2) disclose additional detail and explanation of account balances, and (3) provide information not recognized in the financial statements. Financial statements should not be examined without considering the notes to the financial statements.

The content of the notes to the financial statements varies by company, but there are some similarities across companies. First, the first note of practically all companies summarizes the significant accounting policies used

to prepare the financial statements. For example, you can find how a company accounted for its inventory, how the company uses estimates, and how the company recognizes its revenue. This note is especially useful in maintaining the comparability of financial statements across companies. Second, most companies include a note for each of their significant accounts. These notes can vary depending on the type of business, but most companies have notes for significant items such as property and equipment, income taxes, and employee benefit plans, among other things. Exhibit 2-6 contains the titles of the notes to Bed Bath & Beyond's most recent financial statements.

Auditor's Report

How do you know if Bed Bath & Beyond's financial statements and notes can be depended upon to be a fair depiction of its financial condition? Since you don't have the ability to determine whether the reported numbers are reliable, you must rely on a third party to provide assurance that the information is reliable. This is why all annual reports contain an *independent auditor's report.*

Exhibit 2-6 Bed Bath & Beyond's Notes to the Financial Statements

Bed Bath & Beyond Notes:

1. Summary of Significant Accounting Policies and Related Matters
2. Acquisition
3. Staff Accounting Bulletin No. 108, Considering the Effects of Prior Year Misstatements When Quantifying Misstatements in Current Year Financial Statements
4. Property and Equipment
5. Lines of Credit
6. Fair Value Measurements
7. Investment Securities
8. Provision for Income Taxes
9. Transactions and Balances with Related Parties
10. Leases
11. Employee Benefit Plans
12. Commitments and Contingencies
13. Supplemental Cash Flow Information
14. Stock-Based Compensation
15. Summary of Quarterly Results (Unaudited)

Notes to the financial statements The additional textual and numerical information immediately following the financial statements.

An **independent auditor's report** is a report, prepared by a certified public accountant for the public shareholder, stating an opinion on whether the financial statements present fairly, in conformity with GAAP, the company's financial condition and results of operations and cash flows. Exhibit 2-7 contains Bed Bath & Beyond's most recent auditor's report.

As you can see in the above report, KPMG, one of the largest public accounting firms in the world, performed the audit. KPMG's opinion is stated in the first sentence of the third paragraph—"the consolidated financial statements . . . present fairly, in all material respects, the financial position of Bed Bath & Beyond Inc. . . . and the results of their operations and their cash flows. . . ." This type of opinion, which is known as an unqualified opinion, is what all companies hope

Since you don't have the ability to determine whether a company's reported numbers are reliable, you must rely on a third party to provide assurance that the information is reliable.

Independent auditor's report A report, prepared by a certified public accountant for the public shareholder, stating an opinion on whether the financial statements present fairly, in conformity with GAAP, the company's financial condition and results of operations and cash flows.

Exhibit 2-7 Bed Bath & Beyond's Auditor's Report

REPORT OF INDEPENDENT REGISTERED PUBLIC ACCOUNTING FIRM

The Board of Directors and Shareholders
Bed Bath & Beyond Inc.:

We have audited the accompanying consolidated balance sheets of Bed Bath & Beyond Inc. and subsidiaries (the Company) as of February 28, 2009 and March 1, 2008, and the related consolidated statements of earnings, shareholders' equity, and cash flows for each of the fiscal years in the three-year period ended February 28, 2009. In connection with our audits of the consolidated financial statements, we have also audited the financial statement schedule. These consolidated financial statements and financial statement schedule are the responsibility of the Company's management. Our responsibility is to express an opinion on these consolidated financial statements and financial statement schedule based on our audits.

We conducted our audits in accordance with the standards of the Public Company Accounting Oversight Board (United States). Those standards require that we plan and perform the audit to obtain reasonable assurance about whether the financial statements are free of material misstatement. An audit includes examining, on a test basis, evidence supporting the amounts and disclosures in the financial statements. An audit also includes assessing the accounting principles used and significant estimates made by management, as well as evaluating the overall financial statement presentation. We believe that our audits provide a reasonable basis for our opinion.

In our opinion, the consolidated financial statements referred to above present fairly, in all material respects, the financial position of Bed Bath & Beyond Inc. and subsidiaries as of February 28, 2009 and March 1, 2008, and the results of their operations and their cash flows for each of the fiscal years in the three-year period ended February 28, 2009, in conformity with U.S. generally accepted accounting principles. Also in our opinion, the related financial statement schedule, when considered in relation to the basic consolidated financial statements taken as a whole, presents fairly, in all material respects, the information set forth therein.

As discussed in the Notes to the consolidated financial statements, the Company changed its methods of accounting for the fair value option for certain financial assets and financial liabilities and for fair value measurements in the fiscal year ended February 28, 2009 due to the adoption of Statement of Financial Accounting Standards ("SFAS") No. 159, "The Fair Value Option for Financial Assets and Financial Liabilities—Including an amendment of FASB Statement No. 115" and SFAS No. 157, "Fair Value Measurements". Further, as discussed in the Notes to the consolidated financial statements, the Company changed its method of accounting for uncertain tax positions in the fiscal year ended March 1, 2008 due to the adoption of the provisions of FASB Interpretation No. 48, "Accounting for Uncertainty in Income Taxes—an Interpretation of FASB Statement No. 109".

We also have audited, in accordance with the standards of the Public Company Accounting Oversight Board (United States), the Company's internal control over financial reporting as of February 28, 2009, based on criteria established in Internal Control—Integrated Framework issued by the Committee of Sponsoring Organizations of the Treadway Commission (COSO), and our report dated April 28, 2009 expressed an unqualified opinion on the effectiveness of the Company's internal control over financial reporting.

KPMG LLP

Short Hills, New Jersey
April 28, 2009

to receive. With this assurance from KPMG, users can consider the financial statements reliable.

Management's Discussion and Analysis

In addition to financial statements, notes, and the auditor's report, all annual reports contain a section called Management's Discussion and Analysis. **Management's Discussion and Analysis (MD&A)** is a discussion and analysis of the financial activities of the company by the company's management. The MD&A normally precedes the financial statements in the annual report and contains, among other things, comments on the company's results of operations, its ability to satisfy its current obligations, and its expansion plans.

In some areas, the MD&A is useful in understanding past performance. For example, management usually compares the current year's operating results to the prior year's and explains the reasons for any differences. In other areas, the MD&A is useful in generating expectations for the future. For example, management often discloses how many stores it plans to open or how much in new property and equipment it plans to purchase in the coming year.

Given that the MD&A provides feedback value and predictive value, it is therefore relevant information and should be read along with the financial statements. Exhibit 2-8 contains two excerpts from Bed Bath & Beyond's most recent MD&A.

Management's Discussion and Analysis A discussion and analysis of the financial activities of the company by the company's management.

Exhibit 2-8 Excerpts from Bed Bath & Beyond's Management's Discussion and Analysis

Net Sales
Net sales in fiscal 2008 (fifty-two weeks) increased $159.4 million to $7.208 billion, representing an increase of 2.3% over $7.049 billion of net sales in fiscal 2007 (fifty-two weeks), which increased $431.5 million or 6.5% over the $6.617 billion of net sales in fiscal 2006 (fifty-three weeks). For fiscal 2008, the increase in net sales was generated by the Company's new store sales increase of 4.6% partially offset by the decrease in comparable store sales. For fiscal 2007, approximately 82% of the increase in net sales was attributable to an increase in the Company's new store sales, 26% of the increase was attributable to the acquisition of buybuy BABY, 15% of the increase was attributable to the increase in comparable store sales, all partially offset by 23% as a result of an additional week of sales in fiscal 2006.

Expansion Program
The Company is engaged in an ongoing expansion program involving the opening of new stores in both new and existing markets, the expansion or relocation of existing stores and the continuous review of strategic acquisitions. In the 17 year period from the beginning of fiscal 1992 to the end of fiscal 2008, the chain has grown from 34 to 1,037 stores. Total square footage grew from 0.9 million square feet at the beginning of fiscal 1992 to 32.1 million square feet at the end of fiscal 2008. During fiscal 2008, the Company opened a total of 67 new stores, including 49 BBB stores throughout the United States and Canada, 11 CTS stores, one Harmon store and six buybuy BABY stores, and closed one Harmon store, all of which resulted in the aggregate addition of approximately 1.9 million square feet of store space. The Company opened its first international BBB store in Ontario, Canada in December 2007 and opened three additional stores in Canada during fiscal 2008. Since May 2008, the Company, through a joint venture, operates two stores in Mexico under the name "Home & More."

STUDY TOOLS
CHAPTER 2

CHAPTER REVIEW CARD

❏ Learning Objective and Key Concept Reviews

❏ Key Definitions and Formulas

ONLINE (Located at 4ltrpress.cengage.com/acct)

❏ Flash Cards and Crossword Puzzles

❏ Conceptual and Computational Interactive Quizzes

❏ E-Lectures

❏ Static, Algorithmic, and Additional Homework Activities
(as directed by your instructor)

EXERCISES

1. Classified Balance Sheet LO3

The following is a list of accounts:
- Supplies
- Accounts Receivable
- Retained Earnings
- Mortgage Payable
- Short-Term Investment
- Inventories
- Cash
- Patents
- Common Stock
- Accounts Payable
- Property, Plant, and Equipment
- Income Taxes Payable

Required
Indicate the appropriate classification of each as a Current Asset, Long-Term Investment, Fixed Asset, Intangible Asset, Other Asset, Current Liability, Long-Term Liability, Contributed Capital, or Retained Earnings.

2. Classified Balance Sheet LO3

The following are independent cases:

	Sally's Fish & Chips	Brina's Bar & Grill	Ely's Tanning Salon
ASSETS			
Current assets	3,000	2,500	4,500
Long-term investments	45,500	_____	60,000
Fixed assets	125,750	100,000	150,000
Intangible assets	32,250	55,250	15,000
Other assets	_____	35,500	6,500
Total assets	**220,000**	**225,750**	_____
LIABILITIES			
Current liabilities	15,500	7,000	_____
Long-term liabilities	45,000	_____	65,500
Total liabilities	_____	**75,000**	**69,000**
STOCKHOLDERS' EQUITY			
Capital stock	55,000	_____	67,500
Retained earnings	_____	105,000	_____
Total liabilities and stockholders' equity	**220,000**	_____	_____

Required
Fill in each blank with the appropriate dollar amount.

3. Miscellaneous Terms LO1, 7

Consider the following definitions:
1. A form of business in which multiple entities join together
2. Information following the financial statements that provides additional information and disclosures.
3. A form of business that is established by filing proper forms in a state.
4. A report that attests to the fair presentation of a company's financial statements.
5. The most common form of business.
6. Analysis of a company's financial activities that focuses on results of operations, ability to pay debts, and expansion plans.

Required
Match the definition with the following terms: Sole proprietorship; Management's Discussion and Analysis; Notes to the financial statements; Partnership; Auditor's Report; Corporation.

4. Generally Accepted Accounting Principles LO2

Consider the following definitions:
1. The accounting rules followed by U.S. corporations.
2. The governmental entity whose mission is to protect investors.
3. The accounting organization that contributes rules for more technical issues.
4. The major accounting rule-making body in the United States.
5. The international accounting rule-making body.

Required
Match each definition with one of the following terms: FASB; AICPA; SEC; IASB; GAAP.

5. Classified Balance Sheet LO3

These items were taken from the financial statements of Auburn Bowling Lanes at December 31:

Building	$60,200
Accounts receivable	14,520
Prepaid insurance	4,680
Cash	20,840
Equipment	63,680
Land	61,200
Insurance expense	780
Depreciation expense	5,360
Interest expense	2,600
Mortgage payable	103,040
Common stock	66,000
Retained earnings	40,000
Interest payable	3,600
Bowling revenues	18,180
Accounts payable	12,480

Required

Prepare a classified balance sheet, assuming that $13,600 of the mortgage payable will be paid next year.

6. Multi-Step Income Statement LO4

The following are all independent cases:

	The Bike Shop	The Rental Center	The Uniform Center
Sales revenue	$ _____	$ 78,000	$ 35,000
Cost of sales	45,000	_____	_____
Gross profit	18,000	_____	7,000
Selling expenses	_____	9,000	3,000
General and administrative expenses	2,800	_____	1,500
Total operating expenses	8,800	13,600	_____
Net income	9,200	25,400	2,500

Required

Fill in each blank with the appropriate dollar amount.

7. Multi-Step Income Statement LO4

These items were taken from the financial statement of Brown's Used Cars at December 31:

Utilities expense	$ 17,650
Interest expense	50
Selling expenses	14,600
Administrative expense	15,230
Interest revenue	500
Cost of sales	75,620
Net sales	154,900

Required

Prepare a multi-step income statement assuming Brown's falls into the 30% tax bracket.

8. Financial Statement Accounts LO3, 4, 6

The following is a list of accounts:

Treasury Stock	Interest Payable
Interest Revenue	Common Stock
Buildings	Cost of Sales
Dividends	Administrative Expense
Accounts Payable	Additional Paid-In Capital
Retained Earnings	Cash

Required

Identify if each account would appear on the balance sheet, income statement, and/or statement of stockholders' equity.

9. Horizontal and Vertical Analyses LO4, 5

Comparative income statements are available for Johanna's Fine Furs:

	2010	2009
Sales	$850,000	$800,000
Cost of sales	325,000	275,000
Gross profit	525,000	525,000
Operating expenses	175,000	120,000
Operating profit	350,000	405,000
Income tax expense	105,000	121,500
Net income	$245,000	$283,500

Required

Perform horizontal and vertical analyses on each of the items in the above comparative income statements. Round percentages to one decimal point (i.e., 10.1%).

10. Horizontal and Vertical Analyses LO3, 5

Comparative balance sheet data is available for Ellis Enterprises.

	2010	2009
Total Assets	$850,000	$700,000
Total Liabilities	$240,000	$280,000
Total Equity	$610,000	$420,000

Required

Perform horizontal and vertical analyses on each of the items above. Round percentages to one decimal point (i.e., 10.1%). If generating company assets through debt is considered more risky than generating company assets through equity, is Ellis more or less risky in 2010?

11. Horizontal Analysis LO4, 5

A horizontal analysis of company's sales revenue resulted in a $1.5 million change from 2009 to 2010, which equaled a percentage change of 22.8%.

Required

1. Interpret the dollar change and percentage change.
2. Of the list below, which item(s) would potentially explain the results of the analysis?
   a. A sales promotion was highly successful.
   b. A manufacturing plant was offline for much of the year due to maintenance.
   c. The company opened several new stores.
   d. The company lost market share to a new competitor.
   e. The company issued $1.5 million of stock during the year.

PROBLEMS

12. Prepare a Classified Balance Sheet LO3

Bay Company thinks there may be a problem with its balance sheet.

Bay Company
Classified Balance Sheet
For the Year Ending December 31

Assets			Liabilities and Stockholders' Equity		
Current assets			Current liabilities		
Buildings	$70,000		Accounts payable	$16,000	
Interest revenue	11,000		Interest expense	39,000	
Equipment	41,000		Total current liabilities		$ 55,000
Cash	8,000		Stockholders' equity		
Other current assets	4,000		Retained earnings	$50,000	
Total current assets		$ 134,000	Common stock	35,000	
Accounts receivable	$12,000		Bonds payable	40,000	
Land	20,000		Total stockholders' equity		125,000
Interest payable	14,000				
Total noncurrent assets		46,000	Total liabilities and		
Total assets		$180,000	stockholders' equity		$180,000

Required
Prepare a corrected classified balance sheet.

13. Prepare a Multi-Step Income Statement   LO4

The auditor for Foshee Corporation noticed that its income statement was incorrect.

Foshee Corporation
Income Statement
December 31

Sales revenue		$130,000
Cost of sales		80,000
Accounts receivable		19,500
Gross profit		30,500
Interest expense	15,000	
Selling expense	13,000	
Total operating expenses		(28,000)
Operating profit		2,500
Interest revenue	16,500	
Interest payable	4,000	8,500
Income before taxes		11,000
Income tax expense		(12,850)
Net income (loss)		$ (1,850)

Required
Prepare a corrected multi-step income statement.

14. Prepare and Analyze the Classified Balance Sheet   LO3, 5

The following balance sheet items are available from Carnell Inc. as of December 31, 2010:

	2010	2009
Accounts payable	$ 75,500	$ 35,035
Accounts receivable	50,000	85,065
Automobiles	24,000	24,000
Bonds payable, due 12/31/2014	125,000	25,000
Buildings	240,000	300,000
Capital stock, $5 par	100,000	80,000
Cash	15,000	25,635
Income taxes payable	12,250	16,465
Interest payable	13,755	7,550
Inventory	25,650	27,270
Land	300,000	200,000
Long-term investments	125,000	100,000
Notes payable, due 6/30/2011	100,000	100,000
Office supplies	12,500	13,500
Additional paid-in capital	200,000	190,000
Patents	6,000	6,000
Prepaid rent	10,150	12,275
Retained earnings	146,295	306,135
Salaries and wages payable	35,500	33,560

Required
a. Prepare a comparative, classified balance sheet for Carnell, Inc.
b. Perform horizontal and vertical analyses and interpret the results. Round percentages to one decimal point (i.e., 10.1%).
c. Assume the same information above except that in 2010, Bonds payable is $0 while Retained earnings is $271,295. Does this new information change any interpretations previously made?

15. Prepare and Analyze the Multi-Step Income Statement   LO4, 5

The following income statement items are available from Dansby Inc. for the years ending December 31, 2009, and 2010:

	2010	2009
Cost of sales	$48,596	$ 58,896
Depreciation expense	5,565	6,589
Income tax expense	2,217	2,684
Insurance expense	4,897	5,236
Interest expense	2,584	2,695
Interest revenue	4,287	4,189
Sales revenue	95,950	106,569
Supplies expense	1,654	2,106
Salaries expense	19,320	21,012
Commissions expense	4,879	6,010
Advertising expense	2,200	3,200
Rent expense	7,634	7,856

Required

a. Prepare a comparative, multi-step income statement for Dansby, Inc.
b. Perform horizontal and vertical analyses and interpret the results. Round percentages to one decimal point (i.e., 10.1%).
c. Assume the following change in information: Cost of sales in 2009, $45,670, and Cost of sales in 2010, $62,470. Does this new information change any interpretations previously made?

REMEMBER

- All exercises and problems from the text are available online in static and algorithmic versions.
- Additional multiple choice, exercises, problems, and cases are available online in CengageNOW or as an enrichment module that can be customized into this text.

Recording
Accounting Transactions

Introduction

After studying the material in this chapter, you should be able to:

LO1 Describe the purpose of an accounting information system.

LO2 Analyze the effect of accounting transactions on the accounting equation.

LO3 Understand how T-accounts and debits and credits are used in a double-entry accounting system.

LO4 Describe the purpose of the journal, ledger, and trial balance.

LO5 Record and post accounting transactions and prepare a trial balance and financial statements.

The first two chapters of this book focused on how economic information is communicated to users through financial statements: the balance sheet, the income statement, the statement of stockholders' equity, and the statement of cash flows. This chapter and Chapter 4 focus on how the activities of a business are captured by the accounting system so that these financial statements can be prepared. More specifically, Chapters 3 and 4 describe the accounting cycle. Because financial statements must be prepared periodically, the process of capturing and reporting information is a repetitive process, or cycle. This chapter explores the first three steps in the accounting cycle. The next chapter explores the remaining steps.

LO1 The Accounting Information System

A company's **accounting information system** is the system that identifies, records, summarizes, and communicates the various transactions of a company. Accounting information systems vary widely, ranging from manual, pencil-and-paper systems in some organizations to highly complex electronic systems in other organizations. However different their forms, though, all accounting systems are built to capture and report the effects of a company's *accounting transactions*.

An **accounting transaction** is any economic event that affects a company's assets, liabilities, or equity at the time of the event. Examples include the purchase of equipment, the consumption of supplies in operations, and the issuance of debt or stock. In each example, the event increases or decreases a specific asset, liability, or equity account of the company. Accounting transactions between a company and an external party (for example, an equipment purchase or the issuance of stock) are *external* transactions, while transactions within a company (the consumption of supplies) are *internal* transactions.

Accounting information system The system that identifies, records, summarizes, and communicates the various transactions of a company.

Accounting transaction Any economic event that affects a company's assets, liabilities or equity at the time of the event.

Much like a video camera, an accounting information system captures business activity so that others can view it.

© JEFF GREENBERG/ALAMY

To record accounting transactions and summarize the resulting information, companies use accounts. An **account** is an accounting record that accumulates the activity of a specific item and yields the item's balance. For example, a company's cash account is increased and decreased as cash is received and paid, and it shows the amount of cash held at any point in time. The various accounts that a company uses to capture its business activities are often listed in a **chart of accounts**. An example, complete with numerical references for each account, is found in Exhibit 3-1.

Charts of accounts will vary across companies. For example, a bank will have accounts relating to customer deposits while a biotech company will have accounts relating to research and development.

> **Account** An accounting record that accumulates the activity of a specific item and yields the item's balance.
>
> **Chart of accounts** The list of accounts that a company uses to capture its business activities.

Accounting information systems are built to capture and report the effects of a company's accounting transactions.

Exhibit 3-1 Chart of Accounts

100–199	ASSETS
100	Cash
101	Accounts Receivable
110	Supplies
120	Equipment
200–299	LIABILITIES
210	Accounts Payable
211	Unearned Revenues
230	Notes Payable
300–399	EQUITY
300	Common Stock
350	Retained Earnings
400–499	REVENUES
400	Service Revenue
500–599	EXPENSES
501	Administrative Expense
502	Advertising Expense
600–699	DIVIDENDS

Of course, there certainly will be many commonalities across charts of accounts—for example, practically every company will have an account for cash—but there

Dual nature of accounting Every accounting transaction must affect at least two accounts.

will be differences depending on the company's activities. As a result, you can tell a lot about what a company does if you have its chart of accounts.

LO2 Accounting Transactions and the Accounting Equation

All accounting transactions must be recorded in the accounting information system. To understand the nature of recording transactions, it is best to start with the fundamental accounting equation:

$$\text{Assets} = \text{Liabilities} + \text{Equity}$$

The equation states that a company's assets must always equal the sum of its liabilities and equity. This means that any change to one part of the equation must be accompanied by a second change to another part. For example, suppose that a transaction increases an asset account. For the equation to stay in balance, the transaction must also either decrease another asset account or increase a liability or equity account. This means that every accounting transaction must affect at least two accounts. This is known as the **dual nature of accounting**.

Transaction Analysis

To illustrate how accounting transactions affect the accounting equation, consider the following ten transactions in the first month of operations of Circle Films, a company that documents weddings, birthdays, and other significant life events. Although the example is a small hypothetical company, the transactions would be treated in the same way by all companies, large or small.

HOME DEPOT ANALYSIS

Look at Home Depot's Balance Sheet in Appendix C and determine how many accounts it uses to report its assets, liabilities, and equity. Also, consider the scenario when one stockholder of Home Depot sells his or her stock to another stockholder. Is this an economic event relating to Home Depot? Is it an accounting transaction?

Home Depot's Balance Sheet reports 31 different accounts, comprised of 15 asset accounts, 11 liability accounts, and 5 equity accounts.

When Home Depot's stock is sold on the New York Stock Exchange, the sale is an economic event of interest to Home Depot. However, because Home Depot is not involved in the transaction, it is not an accounting transaction.

Transaction Analysis

TRANSACTION #1:   After incorporating, Circle Films issues 3,000 shares of common stock to investors for $15,000 cash. Because Circle Films receives cash of $15,000, assets increase. Its equity also increases because investors have contributed cash for an ownership interest in the company. More specifically, Circle Films' common stock increases.

	Assets	=	Liabilities	+	Equity
	Cash	=		+	Common Stock
Prior Bal.	$ 0				$ 0
#1	+$15,000				+$15,000
New Bal.	$15,000				$15,000
	$15,000	=	$0	+	$15,000

TRANSACTION #2:   Circle Films purchases a video camera for $9,000 and memory cards for $1,000. In this transaction, the company is exchanging one asset (cash) for other assets (equipment and supplies). Therefore, assets both increase and decrease by $10,000. The net effect is no change in total assets.

	Assets			=	Liabilities	+	Equity
	Cash	Supplies	Equipment	=		+	Common Stock
Prior Bal.	$15,000	$ 0	$ 0				$15,000
#2	−$10,000	+$1,000	+$9,000				
New Bal.	$ 5,000	$1,000	$9,000				$15,000
	$15,000			=	$0	+	$15,000

TRANSACTION #3:   Circle Films receives a $1,500 payment immediately after filming a customer's wedding. Since Circle Films is receiving cash, assets increase. But unlike the previous transaction in which assets were exchanged, the increase in assets in this transaction results from filming the wedding. Recall from Chapter 1 that an inflow of assets from providing a service is a revenue. Revenues increase net income and therefore retained earnings. As a result, Circle Films' equity increases.

	Assets			=	Liabilities	+	Equity	
	Cash	Supplies	Equipment	=		+	Common Stock	Retained Earnings
Prior Bal.	$5,000	$1,000	$9,000				$15,000	$ 0
#3	+$1,500							+$1,500
New Bal.	$6,500	$1,000	$9,000				$15,000	$1,500
	$16,500			=	$0	+	$16,500	

TRANSACTION #4: Circle Films receives a $2,000 deposit from a customer to film her parents' fiftieth wedding anniversary. In this transaction, Circle Films again receives cash from a customer, so assets increase. However, it has not yet provided the service, so it has an obligation to the customer. As a result, Circle Films' liabilities increase for the amount of cash received.

	Assets			=	Liabilities	+	Equity	
	Cash	Supplies	Equipment	=	Unearned Revenue	+	Common Stock	Retained Earnings
Prior Bal.	$6,500	$1,000	$9,000		$ 0		$15,000	$1,500
#4	+$2,000				+$2,000			
New Bal.	$8,500	$1,000	$9,000		$2,000		$15,000	$1,500
	$18,500			=	$2,000	+	$16,500	

TRANSACTION #5: Circle Films paid $250 cash to run an ad in the local paper. Because Circle Films paid cash, assets decrease. The decrease in assets results from advertising its business. Recall from Chapter 1 that a decrease in assets from operating a business is an expense. Expenses decrease net income and therefore retained earnings. As a result, Circle Films' equity decreases.

	Assets			=	Liabilities	+	Equity	
	Cash	Supplies	Equipment	=	Unearned Revenue	+	Common Stock	Retained Earnings
Prior Bal.	$8,500	$1,000	$9,000		$2,000		$15,000	$1,500
#5	−$ 250							−$ 250
New Bal.	$8,250	$1,000	$9,000		$2,000		$15,000	$1,250
	$18,250			=	$2,000	+	$16,250	

TRANSACTION #6: Circle Films films a dance competition, leaving a $3,500 invoice with the customer. Because Circle Films receives no cash at the time of the competition, it is tempting to conclude that there is no accounting transaction and therefore no effect on the accounting equation. However, not all accounting transactions affect cash. By completing the job and leaving an invoice with the customer, Circle Films now has a receivable from the customer. Therefore, assets increase. And because the receivable is generated by providing a service, the firm has additional revenues and therefore more equity. So, equity increases as well. Note that this transaction is very similar to transaction #3, with the only difference being the type of asset that increases.

	Assets				=	Liabilities	+	Equity	
	Cash	Accounts Receivable	Supplies	Equipment	=	Unearned Revenue	+	Common Stock	Retained Earnings
Prior Bal.	$8,250	$ 0	$1,000	$9,000		$2,000		$15,000	$1,250
#6		+$3,500							+$3,500
New Bal.	$8,250	$3,500	$1,000	$9,000		$2,000		$15,000	$4,750
	$21,750				=	$2,000	+	$19,750	

TRANSACTION #7: Circle Films purchases another $9,000 video camera by signing a nine-month promissory note requiring the payment of principal and interest at maturity. Interest is charged at a 6% annual rate. Like transaction #2, Circle Films receives equipment, so assets increase. Unlike transaction #2, though, Circle Films promises to pay cash and interest in nine months instead of paying cash. Therefore, its liabilities increase.

		Assets			=	Liabilities		+	Equity	
	Cash	Accounts Receivable	Supplies	Equipment	=	Unearned Revenue	Notes Payable	+	Common Stock	Retained Earnings
Prior Bal.	$8,250	$3,500	$1,000	$ 9,000		$2,000	$ 0		$15,000	$4,750
#7				+$ 9,000			+$9,000			
New Bal.	$8,250	$3,500	$1,000	$18,000		$2,000	$9,000		$15,000	$4,750
			$30,750		=		$11,000	+		$19,750

TRANSACTION #8: Circle Films receives $3,500 from the customer in payment of the open invoice from transaction #6. In this transaction, Circle Films exchanges one asset for another. It receives cash in satisfaction of the receivable that was created when the service was performed. As a result, cash increases while receivables decrease. There is no change in total assets.

		Assets			=	Liabilities		+	Equity	
	Cash	Accounts Receivable	Supplies	Equipment	=	Unearned Revenue	Notes Payable	+	Common Stock	Retained Earnings
Prior Bal.	$ 8,250	$3,500	$1,000	$18,000		$2,000	$9,000		$15,000	$4,750
#8	+$ 3,500	−$3,500								
New Bal.	$11,750	$ 0	$1,000	$18,000		$2,000	$9,000		$15,000	$4,750
			$30,750		=		$11,000	+		$19,750

TRANSACTION #9: Circle Films pays wages of $2,000 to its employees. In this case, its cash decreases by $2,000, so its assets decrease. Since the payments are an outflow of assets from operating the business, the payments are an expense, which is a reduction to equity. Therefore, equity decreases.

		Assets			=	Liabilities		+	Equity	
	Cash	Accounts Receivable	Supplies	Equipment	=	Unearned Revenue	Notes Payable	+	Common Stock	Retained Earnings
Prior Bal.	$11,750	$0	$1,000	$18,000		$2,000	$9,000		$15,000	$4,750
#9	−$ 2,000									−$2,000
New Bal.	$ 9,750	$0	$1,000	$18,000		$2,000	$9,000		$15,000	$2,750
			$28,750		=		$11,000	+		$17,750

TRANSACTION #10: At the end of the month, Circle Films pays its owners a $1,500 cash dividend. In this transaction, cash and therefore assets decrease. Payments to a company's owners are dividends. Recall from Chapter 1 that dividends decrease retained earnings, so equity decreases as well.

	Assets				=	Liabilities		+	Equity	
	Cash	Accounts Receivable	Supplies	Equipment	=	Unearned Revenue	Notes Payable	+	Common Stock	Retained Earnings
Prior Bal.	$9,750	$0	$1,000	$18,000		$2,000	$9,000		$15,000	$2,750
#10	−$1,500									−$1,500
New Bal.	$8,250	$0	$1,000	$18,000		$2,000	$9,000		$15,000	$1,250
		$27,250			=	$11,000		+	$16,250	

Summary of Transactions

The ten transactions of Circle Films are summarized in Exhibit 3-2. Circle Films started the month with nothing but an idea and ended the month with $27,250 in assets, $11,000 in liabilities, and $16,250 in equity. As you review the exhibit, note that changes to the left side of the equation equaled changes to the right side of the equation for all transactions. As a result, the accounting equation was always in balance. Note also that every transaction affected at least two specific accounts. Sometimes the transaction affected two asset accounts (#2 and #8), sometimes an asset and a liability account (#4 and #7), and sometimes an asset and an equity account (#1, #3, #5, #6, #9, and #10). Any combination affecting assets, liabilities, and equity can occur, as long as the equation stays in balance.

Exhibit 3-2 Transaction Summary for Circle Films

	Assets				=	Liabilities		+	Equity	
	Cash	Accounts Receivable	Supplies	Equipment	=	Unearned Revenue	Notes Payable	+	Common Stock	Retained Earnings
#1	+15,000				=			+	+15,000	
#2	−10,000		+1,000	+9,000	=			+		
#3	+1,500				=			+		+1,500
#4	+2,000				=	+2,000		+		
#5	−250				=			+		−250
#6		+3,500			=			+		+3,500
#7				+9,000	=		+9,000	+		
#8	+3,500	−3,500			=			+		
#9	−2,000				=			+		−2,000
#10	−1,500				=			+		−1,500
	$8,250	$0	$1,000	$18,000	=	$2,000	$9,000	+	$15,000	$1,250
		$27,250			=	$11,000		+	$16,250	

LO3 The Double-Entry Accounting System

While the preceding analysis is an excellent way to understand and visualize the effect of accounting transactions, accounting information systems do not record transactions using plusses and minuses in a tabular format since such an approach, while accurate, would be very cumbersome. Rather, they use a *double-entry system* that traces its origins back to a mathematical treatise written in the fifteenth century by a Franciscan monk, Luca Pacioli. The double-entry system is based on the dual nature of accounting demonstrated in the preceding transaction analyses. That is, every accounting transaction affects at least two accounts, so accounting systems record those transactions with a "double" or "two-fold" entry. The following sections explain the mechanics of this double-entry system, starting with the T-account.

The T-Account

All accounts can be characterized or represented in the following form known as a T-account due to its resemblance to a capital T.

Account Name

Debit Side	Credit Side

The name of the account is listed at the top with two columns appearing below. The left column is the *debit* side while the right column is the *credit* side. The term **debit** simply means left side of an account while the term **credit** simply means right side of an account.

T-accounts work as follows. When a transaction affects an account balance, the amount of the transaction is entered on the account's debit side or credit side, depending on the transaction. You will see how transactions are recorded shortly. An entry on the debit side is called a "debit," while an entry on the credit side is called a "credit." Once all entries are made, the balance in an account is determined by separately adding up all debits and all credits and subtracting the smaller total from the larger, leaving the difference as the account balance. The following three examples illustrate this process.

You can tell a lot about what a company does if you have its chart of accounts.

Examples of T-Account Mechanics

Asset		Liability		Equity	
1,000	5,000	2,000	6,000	7,000	2,000
4,000	3,000	1,000	4,000		3,000
8,000		3,000			3,000
5,000			4,000		1,000

The areas between the horizontal lines contain the activity in each account, with the account balance below. The asset account has three debit entries totaling $13,000 and two credit entries totaling $8,000, leaving a debit balance of $5,000. The liability account has debit entries totaling $6,000 and credit entries totaling $10,000, resulting in a $4,000 credit balance. The equity account has a $1,000 credit balance after having $7,000 of debit entries and $8,000 of credit entries.

It is no coincidence that in this example the asset account has a debit balance while the liability and equity accounts have credit balances. In a double-entry system, asset accounts should normally have debit balances while liability and equity accounts should normally have credit balances. Such "normal" balances mirror the accounting equation, where assets are on the left side of the equal sign and liabilities and equity are on the right side.

Normal Account Balances

Asset Accounts		Liability Accounts		Equity Accounts	
Normal Balance			Normal Balance		Normal Balance

Accounting Equation

Assets	=	Liabilities	+	Equity

Debit The left side of an account.

Credit The right side of an account.

Any change to the accounting equation must be accompanied by a second change.

This arrangement of normal balances is the key to how a double-entry system works. To keep the accounting equation balanced, a double-entry system must keep debit balances equal to credit balances. This means that every accounting transaction must be recorded with equal changes to debit and credit balances. That, again, is why the system is "double-entry." How debits and credits are used to change account balances is discussed next.

Debit and Credit Rules

In a double-entry system, changes in account balances are recorded according to the following basic rules.

To *increase* an account balance	Record transaction on the same side as the normal balance.
To *decrease* an account balance	Record transaction on the opposite side as the normal balance.

These two rules seem simple enough, but their application can be confusing at first because different accounts have different normal balances. The following sections demonstrate how these rules are applied to asset, liability, and equity accounts. Also demonstrated is how these rules are applied to the three types of accounts that affect equity: revenues, expenses, and dividends. Once you have mastered the mechanics of these six types of accounts, you should be able to record most any accounting transaction correctly.

Asset Accounts   Asset accounts have normal debit balances. Therefore, increases to assets are recorded on the debit side while decreases are recorded on the credit side.

Asset Accounts	
Record increases on debit side	Record decreases on credit side
Balance	

To illustrate, suppose that a company starts the day with $5,000 in cash, receives $300 from a customer, and pays $250 to a vendor. The beginning balance of $5,000 is recorded on the debit side of the cash T-account. The increase of $300 is also recorded on the debit side, but the $250 decrease in cash is recorded on the side opposite of the normal balance—the credit side. Netting the debit and credit sides yields a debit balance of $5,050.

Cash	
5,000	250
300	
5,050	

Liability and Equity Accounts   Liability and equity accounts have normal credit balances. Therefore, increases are recorded on the credit side, while decreases are recorded on the debit side.

Liability and Equity Accounts	
Record decreases on debit side	Record increases on credit side
	Balance

To illustrate a liability account, suppose that a company owing $2,500 to a vendor buys an additional $150 of product on account and then pays $850 of its obligation. The beginning balance of $2,500 is recorded on the credit side of the Accounts Payable T-account. The additional payable of $150 is also recorded on the credit side. In contrast, the $850 payment, which is a reduction to the payable, is recorded on the debit side. Netting the debit and credit sides yields a credit balance of $1,800.

Accounts Payable	
850	2,500
	150
	1,800

To illustrate an equity account, suppose that a company has $34,000 of common stock outstanding. The company then issues additional common stock for $10,000 and later buys back and retires $6,000 of stock. The original $34,000 balance appears on the credit side of the Common Stock T-account. Since the Common Stock account has a normal credit balance, the $10,000 increase is recorded on the credit side while the $6,000 decrease is recorded on the opposite or debit side of the account. Netting the debit and credit sides yields a credit balance of $38,000.

```
            Common Stock
        6,000 | 34,000
              | 10,000
              |_____
              | 38,000
```

Revenue Accounts

Revenue Accounts When a company generates a revenue, it is increasing its equity. As demonstrated previously, increasing an equity account requires a credit entry. Therefore, revenue accounts are set up so that they also are increased with a credit entry. That is, revenue accounts have normal credit balances and are increased with credit entries and decreased with debit entries.

Revenue Accounts	
Record decreases on debit side	Record increases on credit side
	Balance

To illustrate, suppose that a company has $115,000 in existing service revenue. The company then earns an additional $13,000 in revenue. Since the Service Revenue account has a normal credit balance, both the existing $115,000 balance and the $13,000 increase are shown on the credit side, resulting in a balance of $128,000.

```
            Service Revenue
              | 115,000
              |  13,000
              |_____
              | 128,000
```

Expense and Dividend Accounts When a company incurs expenses or pays dividends, it is decreasing its equity. As demonstrated previously, decreasing equity requires a debit entry. Therefore, for expense and dividend accounts to effectively reduce equity, they have normal debit balances. Expense and dividend accounts are therefore increased with debit entries and decreased with credit entries.

Expense and Dividend Accounts	
Record increases on debit side	Record decreases on credit side
Balance	

> Any combination affecting assets, liabilities and equity can occur in a transaction, as long as the accounting equation stays in balance.

To illustrate an expense, suppose that a company has $66,000 in salaries expense when it incurs an additional $6,000 in salaries expense. Since the Salaries Expense account has a normal debit balance, both the $66,000 in existing expense and the $6,000 increase should be recorded on the debit side of the account, yielding a balance of $72,000.

```
          Salaries Expense
        66,000 |
         6,000 |
        _____|
        72,000 |
```

Summary of Debit and Credit Rules

You have now seen each major type of account and how the debit and credit columns are used to increase or decrease those accounts. For asset, expense, and dividend accounts, increases are recorded in the debit column and decreases are recorded in the credit column. For liability, equity, and revenue accounts, increases are recorded in the credit column and decreases are recorded in the debit column. A summary of these rules is presented in Exhibit 3-3.

Exhibit 3-3 Summary of Debit and Credit Rules

Type of Account	Normal Balance	Increase with a	Decrease with a
Asset	Debit	Debit	Credit
Liability	Credit	Credit	Debit
Equity	Credit	Credit	Debit
Revenue	Credit	Credit	Debit
Expense	Debit	Debit	Credit
Dividend	Debit	Debit	Credit

In a double-entry system, asset accounts have debit balances while liability and equity accounts have credit balances.

LO4 Recording Transactions in the Accounting System

This section examines the actual process of recording accounting transactions in a double-entry system. Accounting transactions are not recorded directly in T-accounts. Instead, accounting transactions are first recorded in a journal. Once recorded, the information is transferred or posted to a ledger. Information in the ledger is then summarized in a worksheet known as a trial balance. Financial statements are then prepared from the information in the trial balance.

The Journal

A **journal** is a chronological record of transactions. Because the journal is where transactions are first recorded into the accounting system, it is often called the book of original entry. Entries recorded in the journal are called *journal entries*. Companies can have various types of journals in which they record transactions, but since the mechanics of all journals are the same, we will focus on the most basic of journals, the general journal.

Journal A chronological record of transactions.

The general journal and an example journal entry take the form shown in Exhibit 3-4.

Exhibit 3-4 General Journal Form

General Journal			
Date	Account and Explanation	Debit	Credit
Date of transaction	Account(s) Debited	Amount	
	Account(s) Credited		Amount
	(Explanation of transaction)		

At the far left of the journal is a column for the transaction date. To the right of the date is a column to record the names of the accounts affected by the transaction and an explanation. The account(s) receiving debit entries are listed first followed by the account(s) receiving credit entries, which are slightly indented. To the right of the account names are debit and credit columns to record the monetary amounts of the transaction. As explained previously, the totals in the debit and credit columns should be the same for each transaction. When an accounting transaction is recorded in the general journal, we often say that the transaction has been *journalized*.

The general journal is useful in that it contains in one place a chronological record of all the accounting transactions of a company. Thus, a company can examine its journal if it has a question about whether a transaction was recorded or whether it was recorded correctly. However, the general journal is not very useful if a company is trying to determine the balance in a particular account. To get an account balance, one would have to find all journal entries affecting that account and then compute a balance. To avoid such a time-consuming task, the information recorded in the general journal is transferred to a *ledger*.

HOME DEPOT ANALYSIS

Look at Home Depot's Income Statement in Appendix C. Which of the accounts would be increased with a credit entry? Would the remaining accounts be increased with a debit entry?

Home Depot's income statement lists eight different accounts. Of those accounts, Net Sales and Interest and Investment Income would be increased with a credit entry. Both of these accounts are revenue accounts. The other six accounts are expense accounts and are increased with a debit entry.

When an accounting transaction is recorded in the general journal, we often say that the transaction has been *journalized*.

© KRISTIAN SEKULIC/SHUTTERSTOCK.COM

The Ledger

A **ledger** is a collection of accounts and their balances. While most companies have various types of ledgers containing different accounts, we will focus on the most basic type of ledger, the general ledger. The general ledger is nothing more than a collection of T-accounts for a company, which means that the general ledger contains both the activity and balances of all company accounts.

Account balances in the general ledger are updated as follows. When an accounting transaction is recorded in the general journal, the amounts recorded in the debit and credit columns are transferred to the debit and credit columns of the respective T-accounts in the ledger. This process of copying or transferring the information from the journal to the ledger is called *posting* and results in up-to-date account balances. Thus, companies look to the ledger for balances in their accounts.

The Trial Balance

After accounting transactions are recorded in the journal and posted to the ledger, companies prepare a trial balance. A **trial balance** is a listing of accounts and their balances at a specific point in time. In a trial balance, all accounts in a company's ledger are listed in a column on the left. Asset accounts are listed first, followed by liability accounts, equity accounts, and then revenue, expense, and dividend accounts. Each account's balance from the ledger is listed in the appropriate debit or credit column. At the bottom of each column, a total is calculated. The form of the trial balance is shown in Exhibit 3-5.

Ledger A collection of accounts and their balances.

Trial balance A listing of accounts and their balances at a specific point in time.

MAKING IT REAL

Although the text primarily discusses a manual accounting system, there are several popular computerized accounting information systems utilized by small businesses. Two of the most popular are QuickBooks® and Peachtree®.

QuickBooks is favored largely for its simplicity and ease of use for individuals with little to no accounting experience. Peachtree is a more sophisticated accounting system designed for a user with more accounting knowledge than the average person.

Both systems provide banking, general ledger, accounts payable, accounts receivable, payroll, and inventory

features and can keep track of income and expenses by customer, job, and department. Many reports can be created by both systems to analyze business performance. Both systems also provide security features to ensure only authorized users are accessing the businesses' accounting information.

Overall, such computerized systems are a great tool for businesses because they help ensure that a company's accounting information is captured and communicated effectively and efficiently.

© DAVID YOUNG-WOLFF/PHOTOEDIT

Exhibit 3-5 Trial Balance Form

	Debit	Credit
Asset Account(s)	Amount	
Liability Account(s)		Amount
Equity Account(s)		Amount
Revenue Account(s)		Amount
Expense Account(s)	Amount	
Dividends	Amount	
Totals	Total Debits	Total Credits

A trial balance serves several functions. First and foremost, a trial balance proves that total debit balances equal total credit balances. If they are unequal, then the accounting equation is out of balance and a correction is warranted. Second, a trial balance summarizes in one place all accounts of an entity and their respective balances. Financial statements are then prepared from those balances. Finally, a trial balance is helpful in making any necessary adjustments to account balances at the end of an accounting period. We will see this function in Chapter 4.

LO5 Comprehensive Example: Journal Entries to Financial Statements

The following section uses the Circle Films transactions to demonstrate the recording of transactions in the journal, the posting of information to the ledger, the preparation of a trial balance, and the preparation of financial statements.

Recording Transactions in the Journal and Posting to the Ledger

Circle Films entered into ten transactions. A four-step process will be used to demonstrate how to properly record each transaction and post it to the ledger. First, the accounts affected by the transaction will be identified. Second, the relevant debit/credit rules for those accounts will be identified. Third, the transaction will be recorded

in the journal. Fourth, the transaction will be posted to the ledger. This four-step process can be followed when recording and posting any accounting transaction.

Transaction #1   Circle Films issued 3,000 shares of common stock for $15,000.

Step 1—What accounts are affected and how?
Circle Films receives cash, so cash increases. Circle Films issues common stock, so common stock increases.

Step 2—What debit and credit entries are required?
Cash is an asset, so debit the Cash account to increase it. Common Stock is an equity account, so credit the Common Stock account to increase it.

Step 3—Record the journal entry.

#1	Cash	15,000	
	Common Stock		15,000
	(Owners invest cash in business)		

Assets	=	Liabilities	+	Equity
+15,000				+15,000

Step 4—Post the information to the ledger.

Cash			Common Stock	
15,000				15,000
15,000				15,000

Transaction #2   Circle Films buys a $9,000 video camera and $1,000 of memory cards for $10,000 cash.

Step 1—What accounts are affected and how?
Circle Films receives a camera and some tapes, so both equipment and supplies increase. Circle Films pays with cash, so cash decreases.

Step 2—What debit and credit entries are required?
Equipment and supplies are assets, so debit the Equipment and Supplies accounts to increase them. Cash is also an asset, so credit the Cash account to decrease it.

Step 3—Record the journal entry.

#2	Equipment	9,000	
	Supplies	1,000	
	Cash		10,000
	(Purchase video camera and tapes)		

Assets	=	Liabilities	+	Equity
+9,000				
+1,000				
−10,000				

Step 4—Post the information to the ledger.

Cash		Supplies		Equipment	
15,000	10,000	1,000		9,000	
5,000		1,000		9,000	

Transaction #3   Circle Films films a wedding for $1,500 cash.

Step 1—What accounts are affected and how?
Circle Films receives cash, so cash increases. The increase in cash results from Circle Films providing its service, so service revenue increases.

Step 2—What debit and credit entries are required?
Cash is an asset, so debit the Cash account to increase it. Revenues increase equity, so credit the Service Revenue account to increase it.

Step 3—Record the journal entry.

#3	Cash	1,500	
	Service Revenue		1,500
	(Provide service to customer)		
	Assets	=	Liabilities	+	Equity
	+1,500				+1,500

Step 4—Post the information to the ledger.

Cash		Service Revenue	
15,000	10,000		1,500
1,500			
6,500			1,500

Transaction #4   Circle Films receives $2,000 to film a future reception.

Step 1—What accounts are affected and how?
Circle Films receives cash, so cash increases. Because Circle Films has not yet performed the required service, it has a new liability to the customer called unearned revenue.

Step 2—What debit and credit entries are required?
Cash is an asset, so debit the Cash account to increase it. Unearned Revenue is a liability, so credit the Unearned Revenue account to increase it.

Step 3—Record the journal entry.

#4	Cash	2,000	
	Unearned Revenue		2,000
	(Cash received in advance of		
	providing service to customer)		
	Assets	=	Liabilities	+	Equity
	+2,000		+2,000		

Step 4—Post the information to the ledger.

Cash		Unearned Revenue	
15,000	10,000		2,000
1,500			2,000
2,000			
8,500			

Transaction #5   Circle Films pays $250 cash for advertising.

Step 1—What accounts are affected and how?
Circle Films pays cash, so cash decreases. The decrease in cash results from Circle Films' advertising its service, so advertising expense increases.

Step 2—What debit and credit entries are required?
Cash is an asset, so credit the Cash account to decrease it. Expenses decrease equity, so debit the Advertising Expense account to increase it.

Step 3—Record the journal entry.

#5	Advertising Expense	250	
	Cash		250
	(Pay for advertising)		
	Assets	=	Liabilities	+	Equity
	−250				−250

Step 4—Post the information to the ledger.

Cash		Advertising Expense	
15,000	10,000	250	
1,500	250	250	
2,000			
8,250			

Transaction #6   Circle Films films an event for $3,500 and leaves an invoice with the customer.

Step 1—What accounts are affected and how?
Circle Films performed a service for a customer, so its service revenue increases. Circle Films has not

yet received any payment from the customer, so its accounts receivable also increases.

Step 2—What debit and credit entries are required? Accounts Receivable is an asset, so debit the Accounts Receivable account to increase it. Revenues increase equity, so credit the Service Revenue account to increase it.

Step 3—Record the journal entry.

#6	Accounts Receivable	3,500	
	Service Revenue		3,500
	(Provide service to customer on account)		

Assets	=	Liabilities	+	Equity
+3,500				+3,500

Step 4—Post the information to the ledger.

Accounts Receivable		Service Revenue	
3,500			1,500
			3,500
3,500			5,000

Transaction #7 Circle Films buys another camera by signing a $9,000 note payable.

Step 1—What accounts are affected and how? Circle Films receives a camera, so equipment increases. It signs a note for payment, so notes payable increases.

Step 2—What debit and credit entries are required? Equipment is an asset, so debit the Equipment account to increase it. Notes Payable is a liability, so credit the Notes Payable account to increase it.

Step 3—Record the journal entry.

#7	Equipment	9,000	
	Notes Payable		9,000
	(Purchase of a video camera with a promissory note)		

Assets	=	Liabilities	+	Equity
+9,000		+9,000		

Step 4—Post the information to the ledger.

Equipment		Notes Payable	
9,000			9,000
9,000			9,000
18,000			

Transaction #8 Circle Films receives $3,500 from a customer in payment of services provided.

Step 1—What accounts are affected and how? Circle Films receives cash, so cash increases. Circle Films collects a receivable from a customer, so its accounts receivable decreases.

Step 2—What debit and credit entries are required? Cash is an asset, so debit the Cash account to increase it. Accounts Receivable is also an asset account, so credit the Accounts Receivable account to decrease it.

Step 3—Record the journal entry.

#8	Cash	3,500	
	Accounts Receivable		3,500
	(Receive payment from customer)		

Assets	=	Liabilities	+	Equity
+3,500				
−3,500				

Step 4—Post the information to the ledger.

Cash		Accounts Receivable	
15,000	10,000	3,500	3,500
1,500	250	0	
2,000			
3,500			
11,750			

Transaction #9 Circle Films pays $2,000 in salaries to employees.

Step 1—What accounts are affected and how? Circle Films pays cash, so cash decreases. This reduction in cash results from salaries paid to employees, so salaries expense increases.

Step 2—What debit and credit entries are required? Cash is an asset, so credit the Cash account to decrease it. Expenses decrease equity, so debit the Salaries Expense account to increase it.

Step 3—Record the journal entry.

#9	Salaries Expense	2,000	
	Cash		2,000
	(Pay salaries to employees)		

Assets	=	Liabilities	+	Equity
−2,000				−2,000

Step 4—Post the information to the ledger.

Cash		Salaries Expense	
15,000	10,000	2,000	
1,500	250	2,000	
2,000	2,000		
3,500			
9,750			

Transaction #10 Circle Films pays $1,500 in dividends to the owners.

Step 1—What accounts are affected and how?
Circle Films pays cash, so cash decreases. The cash payment is a distribution of company assets to the owners, so dividends increase.

Step 2—What debit and credit entries are required?
Cash is an asset, so credit the Cash account to decrease it. Dividends decrease equity, so debit the Dividends account to increase it.

Step 3—Record the journal entry.

#10	Dividends	1,500	
	Cash		1,500
	(Pay dividends to owners)		

Assets	=	Liabilities	+	Equity
−1,500				−1,500

Step 4—Post the information to the ledger.

Cash		Dividends	
15,000	10,000	1,500	
1,500	250	1,500	
2,000	2,000		
3,500	1,500		
8,250			

Summary After recording and posting the ten transactions, Circle Films' complete Journal and Ledger would appear as follows:

General Journal

Transaction	Account	Debit	Credit
#1	Cash	15,000	
	Common Stock		15,000
#2	Equipment	9,000	
	Supplies	1,000	
	Cash		10,000
#3	Cash	1,500	
	Service Revenue		1,500
#4	Cash	2,000	
	Unearned Revenue		2,000
#5	Advertising Expense	250	
	Cash		250
#6	Accounts Receivable	3,500	
	Service Revenue		3,500
#7	Equipment	9,000	
	Notes Payable		9,000
#8	Cash	3,500	
	Accounts Receivable		3,500
#9	Salaries Expense	2,000	
	Cash		2,000
#10	Dividends	1,500	
	Cash		1,500

General Ledger

Cash		Accounts Receivable		Supplies	
15,000	10,000	3,500	3,500	1,000	
1,500	250			1,000	
2,000	2,000	0			
3,500	1,500				
8,250					

Equipment		Unearned Revenue		Notes Payable	
9,000			2,000		9,000
9,000					
18,000			2,000		9,000

Common Stock		Service Revenue		Advertising Expense	
	15,000		1,500	250	
			3,500		
	15,000		5,000	250	

Salaries Expense		Dividends	
2,000		1,500	
2,000		1,500	

Preparing a Trial Balance

Once all transactions are recorded in the journal and posted to the ledger, a trial balance can be prepared.

Circle Films Trial Balance May 31		
	Debit	Credit
Cash	$ 8,250	
Supplies	1,000	
Equipment	18,000	
Unearned Revenue		$ 2,000
Notes Payable		9,000
Common Stock		15,000
Service Revenue		5,000
Advertising Expense	250	
Salaries Expense	2,000	
Dividends	15,000	
Total	$31,000	$31,000

Recall that a trial balance is a listing of all accounts and their balances at a specific point in time, starting with assets and followed by liabilities, equity, revenues, expenses, and dividends. Therefore, it is a summary of the balances in the ledger. You can confirm that the trial balance includes only the balances from the general ledger by reviewing again Circle Films' ledger on the previous page. As expected, total debit balances of $31,000 equal total credit balances of $31,000 in the trial balance.

Preparation of Financial Statements

Once the trial balance is finished, the final product of the accounting system can be prepared—the financial statements. As demonstrated in Chapter 1, the income statement must be prepared first, followed by the statement of retained earnings, and then the balance sheet.

The income statement shows a company's revenues and expenses. Circle Films' May 31 trial balance contains only one revenue account and two expense accounts. Therefore, its income statement for the month of May would appear as follows.

Circle Films Income Statement For the Month Ending May 31		
Service revenue		$5,000
Advertising expense	$ 250	
Salaries expense	2,000	
Total expenses		2,250
Net income		$2,750

With net income calculated, Circle Films' statement of retained earnings can be prepared. Recall from Chapter 1 that the statement of retained earnings takes the beginning balance in retained earnings, adds net income, and subtracts dividends to yield the current balance in retained earnings. Its May 31 trial balance shows no balance in beginning retained earnings because it just started its business. It also shows a $1,500 balance in dividends. Combining these two balances with net income yields the following statement of retained earnings for the month of May:

Circle Films Statement of Retained Earnings For the Month Ending May 31	
Retained earnings, May 1	$ 0
+ Net income	2,750
− Dividends	1,500
Retained earnings, May 31	$1,250

© ISTOCKPHOTO.COM/SCOTT KOCHSIEK

With retained earnings calculated, the company's balance sheet can be prepared. A balance sheet shows a company's assets, liabilities, and equity at a point in time. Circle Films' May 31 trial balance shows four asset accounts, two liability accounts, and one equity account (Common Stock). These seven accounts, along with the amount of retained earnings from the May statement of retained earnings, should be included on the balance sheet. Therefore, its May 31 balance sheet would appear as follows:

Circle Films Balance Sheet May 31	
Cash	$ 8,250
Supplies	1,000
Equipment	18,000
Total assets	$27,250
Unearned revenue	$ 2,000
Notes payable	9,000
Common stock	15,000
Retained earnings	1,250
Total liabilities and stockholders' equity	$27,250

STUDY TOOLS
CHAPTER 3

CHAPTER REVIEW CARD
- ❏ Learning Objective and Key Concept Reviews
- ❏ Key Definitions and Formulas

ONLINE (Located at 4ltrpress.cengage.com/acct)
- ❏ Flash Cards and Crossword Puzzles
- ❏ Conceptual and Computational Interactive Quizzes
- ❏ E-Lectures
- ❏ Static, Algorithmic, and Additional Homework Activities (as directed by your instructor)

EXERCISES

1. Transaction Analysis LO2

The following is a list of independent economic events:

1. Purchased inventory on account.
2. Paid dividends at the end of the year.
3. Received cash in payment for services.
4. Issued common stock for $10,000.
5. Paid rent in cash.
6. Received a bill for expenses incurred.
7. Bought stock in another company.
8. Billed customers for services.

Required

Indicate whether each transaction increases, decreases, or has no effect on assets, liabilities, and stockholders' equity.

2. Transaction Analysis LO2

The following are a few possible ways in which the accounting equation can be affected by a transaction:

Assets	=	Liabilities	+	Stockholders' Equity
1. Increase		Increase		
2. Decrease				Decrease
3. Increase				Increase
4. Increase/ Decrease				
5. Decrease		Decrease		

Required

Describe at least two situations that could result in each of the outcomes listed.

3. Normal Balances LO3

The following is a list of possible accounts found in a trial balance:

1. Accounts Receivable
2. Common Stock
3. Cash
4. Retained Earnings
5. Accounts Payable
6. Salaries Expense
7. Investments
8. Service Revenue
9. Dividends

Required

Indicate each account's normal balance and the effect of a debit and a credit to the account.

4. Transaction Analysis LO2, 3

Tsunami, Inc., entered into the following transactions in one month of operations:

1. Purchased $3,000 of computers on account.
2. Issued $7,500 of common stock to investors in exchange for cash.

3. Purchased supplies for $300 in cash.
4. Billed customers $25,000 for services rendered.
5. Paid salaries of $3,500 to employees.
6. Paid dividends to stockholders in the amount of $1,000.
7. Received $5,000 cash in payment of services billed in the previous month.
8. Paid the computer company in cash for purchase in (1).
9. Borrowed $50,000 from the bank.

Required

a. Indicate the specific accounts affected by each transaction.
b. Indicate whether those accounts were increased or decreased.
c. Designate the normal balances for each of the specific accounts.

5. Recording Transactions LO3, 4, 5

Prepare journal entries for the transactions listed in the preceding exercise (omitting explanations).

6. Recording Transactions LO3, 4, 5

The following information pertains to York Rafting Company:

Jan. 2   Issued common stock to investors for $25,000.
     3   Bought $3,500 of supplies on account.
     4   Paid rent for January in the amount of $1,200.
     9   Billed a customer $7,000 for services provided.
   16   Paid $1,500 cash to vendor for the previous purchase of supplies.
   24   Borrowed $10,000 from local bank.
   26   Received payment for billing made on January 9.

Required

Prepare journal entries for each transaction (omitting explanations).

7. Posting Transactions LO4, 5

Post the journal entries prepared in the preceding exercise to their appropriate T-accounts and prepare a trial balance at January 31.

8. Transaction Analysis LO2, 4, 5

The following is a tabular analysis of transactions in the month of September for the Fresh Company:

	Cash	+ Accounts Receivable	+ Supplies	+ Equipment	=	Accounts Payable	+	Stockholders' Equity	Additional Information
1.	+2,000	+7,000						+9,000	Sales Revenue
2.			+1,000			+1,000			
3.	−500					−500			
4.	−1,500							−1,500	Dividends Paid
5.	−750							−750	Advertising Expense
6.	+10,000							+10,000	Issued Common Stock
7.	+5,000	−5,000							
8.	−2,000							−2,000	Rent Expense
9.						+2,500		−2,500	Utilities Expense
10.				+5,000		+5,000			

Required

a. Provide a probable explanation for each individual event.
b. Recreate the appropriate journal entries.
c. Prepare an income statement for the month of September.
d. Prepare a statement of retained earnings for the month of September. Assume beginning Retained Earnings is $1,000.

9. Posting Information   LO4, 5

The following is the general journal of Dee's Fur Company for the month of November:

Date	Account Titles	Debit	Credit
Nov. 1	Cash	15,000	
	Common Stock		15,000
8	Equipment	5,000	
	Accounts Payable		3,000
	Cash		2,000
11	Accounts Receivable	7,500	
	Sales Revenue		7,500
18	Accounts Payable	1,700	
	Cash		1,700
21	Cash	5,000	
	Notes Payable		5,000
24	Dividends	1,500	
	Cash		1,500
25	Cash	3,500	
	Accounts Receivable		3,500

Required

a. Post the journal entries to the appropriate T-accounts assuming Dee's Fur starts its business in November.
b. Prepare a trial balance for the month ending November 30.

10. Trial Balance   LO4, 5

During the audit of Hines Brewery, the auditor discovered the following errors:

1. A purchase of equipment in the amount of $3,500 was recorded as a debit to Equipment for $350 and a credit to Accounts Payable for $350.
2. A credit of $5,600 to Sales Revenue in the general journal was posted to the general ledger at $6,500.
3. $1,000 cash paid for salaries incurred in previous months was recorded as a debit to Salaries Expense and a credit to Cash.
4. A journal entry recording a purchase of supplies on account was recorded for the correct amounts twice in the general ledger.
5. A credit posting to Service Revenue of $4,000 was omitted.

Required

Indicate whether or not the trial balance will still balance after the error and then indicate the manner in which the trial balance will be incorrect (for example, Revenue will be overstated by $500).

PROBLEMS

11. Transaction Analysis   LO2

On January 1, Gels and Shells, Inc., was established and entered into the following transactions during its first month of business:

1. Issued common stock of $50,000 in exchange for cash.
2. Purchased equipment worth $24,000 (paid in cash).
3. Purchased supplies of $6,000 on account.
4. Received bill for advertising in the newspaper for $235.
5. Billed customers $14,680 for services.
6. Paid salaries of $2,015.
7. Received payment of $6,023 from customers for bills in (5).
8. Received $5,000 cash for services to be performed at a later date.
9. Paid $4,500 to suppliers for purchase in (3).
10. Received bill for utilities in the amount of $175.

11. Paid dividends of $300 to stockholders.
12. Borrowed $10,000 from bank on a long-term basis.
13. Paid interest on loan from bank, $100.

Required

a. Show the effects of each transaction on the accounting equation by preparing a tabular analysis using the following column headings: Cash, Accounts Receivable, Supplies, Property and Equipment, Accounts Payable, Unearned Revenue, Notes Payable, Common Stock, Retained Earnings.
b. Prepare an income statement for the month of January.
c. Prepare a statement of retained earnings for the month of January.
d. Prepare a balance sheet at January 31.

12. Recording Transactions LO3, 4, 5

Darby Consulting, Inc., was established on March 1, and during March, Darby recorded the following transactions:

Mar. 1 Issued $10,000 common stock in exchange for cash.
    3 Purchased office supplies on account, $300.
    7 Paid rent for the next three months, $1,500.
    8 Paid cash towards the March 3 purchase of supplies, $175.
  11 Billed customers for services rendered, $5,780.
  12 Paid cash for advertising, $700.
  25 Received payment from customers previously billed, $4,500.
  28 Paid dividends to stockholders, $200.
  29 Paid salaries, $1,200.
  29 Paid utilities, $760.

Required

a. Prepare journal entries for each transaction (omitting explanations).
b. Post journal entries to appropriate T-accounts.
c. Prepare a trial balance at March 31.
d. Prepare an income statement and a statement of retained earnings for the month of March. Prepare a balance sheet at the end of March.

13. Recording Transactions LO3, 4, 5

The trial balance for ShirtCraft, Inc., at January 31 is shown as follows:

ShirtCraft, Inc. Trial Balance January 31		
	Debit	**Credit**
Cash	$ 5,600	
Accounts Receivable	12,890	
Supplies	9,235	
Prepaid Rent	1,500	
Property, Plant, & Equipment	30,500	
Accounts Payable		$ 7,625
Unearned Revenue		6,400
Notes Payable		15,000
Common Stock		25,000
Sales Revenue		9,650
Salaries Expense	2,300	
Utilities Expense	650	
Dividends	1,000	
Totals	$63,675	$63,675

During February the following transactions occurred:

Feb. 1 Billed customers for orders shipped, $2,500.
    1 Paid $150 interest on note from bank.
    4 Received payment from customers billed in January, $4,500.
    8 Bought office supplies on account, $560.
  12 Completed an order for which payment had previously been received in January, $3,500.
  18 Paid creditors for purchase of supplies in January, $1,895.
  26 Paid dividends to stockholders, $1,000.
  27 Paid salaries of $2,100; paid utilities of $775.

Required

a. Prepare opening T-accounts for the month of February.
b. Prepare journal entries for transactions in the month of February.
c. Post journal entries to appropriate T-accounts.
d. Prepare trial balance at February 28.

REMEMBER

- All exercises and problems from the text are available online in static and algorithmic versions.
- Additional multiple choice, exercises, problems, and cases are available online in CengageNOW or as an enrichment module that can be customized into this text.

Accrual Accounting
and Adjusting Entries

Introduction

Chapter 3 introduced the first three steps in the accounting cycle—recording transactions, posting information to the ledger, and preparing a trial balance from which financial statements are prepared. This chapter explores the remaining steps in the cycle. This includes the adjusting process that leads to accrual-based financial statements and the closing process that prepares the accounting system for the next period. Both the adjusting and closing processes occur at the end of each accounting period.

Learning Objectives

After studying the material in this chapter, you should be able to:

LO1 Describe how income is measured and reported under the accrual and cash bases of accounting.

LO2 Identify the four major circumstances in which adjusting journal entries are necessary.

LO3 Record and post adjusting journal entries, and prepare an adjusted trial balance and financial statements.

LO4 Describe the purpose of the closing process and prepare closing entries.

LO5 Describe the steps of the accounting cycle.

LO1 Accrual and Cash Bases of Accounting

One of the main functions of the accounting information system is to record the revenues and expenses that a business generates. In accounting, there are two possible bases for recording revenues and expenses—the cash basis and the accrual basis. The main difference between the two is the timing of when revenues and expenses are recorded.

The **cash basis of accounting** records revenues when cash is received and records expenses when cash is paid. The best example of a cash basis accounting system is your personal checking account. Revenues such as job wages are recorded only when you are paid. Expenses such as utilities are recorded only when you write the check.

In contrast, the **accrual basis of accounting** records revenues when they are earned and records expenses when they are incurred. This is an application of the revenue recognition and matching principles, respectively, discussed in Chapter 1. In an accrual accounting system, revenues such as job wages are recorded when earned, regardless of when payment is received. Likewise, expenses such as utilities are recorded when used, regardless of when payment is made. A summary of each basis is as follows.

Cash basis of accounting Records revenues when cash is received and records expenses when cash is paid.

Accrual basis of accounting Records revenues when they are earned and records expenses when they are incurred.

When a retailer like American Eagle Outfitters sells a gift card, it records a liability. It records a revenue when the customer redeems the card.

© BRENDAN MCDERMID/REUTERS/LANDOV

	Cash Basis	**Accrual Basis**
Record revenues when:	Cash is received	Revenue is earned
Record expenses when:	Cash is paid	Expense is incurred

To illustrate the difference between the cash and accrual bases, suppose that a neighbor leaves town for the months of June and July and asks you to collect his mail and newspapers. Before he leaves, he pays you $100. Suppose further that you agree to pay a friend $40 to do the work, but you pay him at the end of July after the work is completed. Income for June and July under each basis would be calculated as follows.

The best example of a cash basis accounting system is your personal checking account.

Under the cash basis, June revenues are $100 because you received $100 during the month. Likewise, June expenses are $0 because you paid nothing during the month. As a result, June income is $100. For July, you received no money but paid your friend $40, so revenues are $0 and expenses are $40. Therefore, July income is –$40.

	Cash Basis			Accrual Basis		
	June	July	Total	June	July	Total
Revenues	$100	$ 0	$100	$50	$50	$100
– Expense	0	40	40	20	20	40
Net Income	$100	$(40)	$ 60	$30	$30	$ 60

Under the accrual basis, revenues for June are $50 because you earned half of the $100 during June. And, even though you don't pay your friend until July, he provided half of the agreed labor in June, so June expenses are $20. As a result, June income is $30. Because the exact same circumstances occur in July, income for July is also $30.

The comparative income statements show that although each basis results in the same $60 of cumulative income, monthly income varies considerably. The cash-based statement reports that you generated a $100 profit one month and a $40 loss the next, while the accrual-based statement reports that you generated $30 in profits each month. Given that your activities were exactly the same each month, accrual-based income of $30 each month makes more sense than a $100 profit and a $40 loss. Even though both bases result in the same $60 income over the long term, the accrual basis provides a better representation of income over the two shorter periods of time. As a result, the accrual basis is required by Generally Accepted Accounting Principles.

Reporting Accrual- and Cash-Based Income

Because Generally Accepted Accounting Principles require the accrual basis, income statements report accrual-based income. However, cash basis information is also useful in understanding the financial condition of a company. A company that generates accrual income but never generates cash is a company that will soon fail. As a result, cash-based income is reported on the statement of cash flows. Recall from Chapter 1 that the operating activities section of a company's statement of cash flows calculates and reports the cash generated from operating the business. Cash generated from operations is the same as cash-based income.

To illustrate, consider the following condensed version of the operating activities section of American Eagle Outfitters' statement of cash flows shown in Exhibit 4-1.

American Eagle Outfitters uses the indirect method of reporting operating cash flows, which means that it calculates cash-based income by adjusting accrual-based income. The top line shows income on an accrual basis. For the current year, American Eagle Outfitters generated over $179 million of income under the accrual basis. This number would also be found on American Eagle Outfitters' income statement. After $123 million of adjustments, cash basis income is determined to be over $302 million. Cash basis income is much greater than accrual basis income. In all three years presented, income on a cash basis is greater than income on an accrual basis.

Exhibit 4-1 American Eagle Outfitters' Condensed Statement of Cash Flows—Operating Activities

(in thousands) For the Years Ended	01/31/09	02/02/08	02/03/07
Operating activities:			
Net income	$179,061	$400,019	$387,359
Adjustments to reconcile net income to cash provided:			
Depreciation and amortization	133,141	110,753	89,698
⋮	⋮	⋮	⋮
Accrued liabilities	(19,188)	(2,598)	33,047
Total adjustments	123,132	64,251	361,909
Net cash provided by operating activities	$302,193	$464,270	$749,268

In Appendix C, look at the Revenues paragraph in Home Depot's Note 1: Summary of Significant Accounting Policies. How can you tell from that paragraph that Home Depot uses the accrual basis of accounting?

Also, look at Home Depot's statement of cash flows in Appendix C. Over the three years presented, what was the total net income on a cash basis and how does that compare to total net income on an accrual basis?

The Revenues paragraph states that the company recognizes revenues when the customer takes possession of the merchandise or receives the service (that is, when the revenue is earned). It further states that when a customer pays in advance, the company records a "Deferred Revenue" because it has not yet earned the revenue, even though cash has been received.

The company's statement of cash flows shows that cash basis income was greater than accrual basis income in all years presented.

	2009	2008	2007	Total
Net income (cash basis):	$5,528	$5,727	$7,661	$18,916
Net income (accrual basis):	$2,260	$4,395	$5,761	$12,416

LO2 Adjusting Journal Entries

To ensure that revenues and expenses are properly recorded under an accrual basis, accounting information systems use adjusting journal entries. **Adjusting journal entries** are entries made in the general journal to record revenues that have been earned but not recorded and expenses that have been incurred but not recorded. The process of recording and posting adjusting entries is the fourth step in the accounting cycle and occurs at the end of each accounting period after the trial balance is prepared. After adjusting entries are journalized and posted, an "adjusted" trial balance is then prepared, from which financial statements are generated.

While adjusting entries can vary significantly across companies, they all arise because the exchange of cash does not always coincide with the earning of a revenue or incurrence of an expense. For example, sometimes cash is received *before* a revenue is earned while at other times cash is received *after* a revenue is earned. Likewise, sometimes cash is paid *before* an expense is incurred while at other times cash is paid *after* an expense is incurred. These four basic scenarios are the reasons that adjusting journal entries are necessary. Each scenario is listed in the following table and is discussed in the following sections.

Scenario	Classification of Adjusting Entry
1. Cash is received before revenue is earned	Deferred Revenue
2. Cash is received after revenue is earned	Accrued Revenue
3. Cash is paid before expense is incurred	Deferred Expense
4. Cash is paid after expense is incurred	Accrued Expense

Scenario 1: Deferred Revenue

Companies sometimes receive cash before they earn the revenue. For example, airlines get your money before you fly. When a company receives cash before it provides the service, it has a *deferred revenue*. The term *deferred* is used because at the time of cash receipt, the company has not yet provided the promised service and therefore cannot record a revenue in its accounting system. Instead, it must record a liability. Recording of the revenue must be *deferred* until the revenue is earned.

Adjusting journal entries Entries made in the general journal to record revenues that have been earned but not recorded and expenses that have been incurred but not recorded.

HOME DEPOT ANALYSIS

Look at the Revenues, Prepaid Advertising, and Self Insurance paragraphs in Home Depot's Note 1: Summary of Significant Accounting Policies, found in Appendix C. Do these paragraphs represent examples of deferred revenues, accrued revenues, deferred expenses, or accrued expenses?

The Revenue paragraph explains the example of receiving payment before providing the good or service (deferred revenue). The Prepaid Advertising paragraph explains the example of making payment before consuming the advertising (deferred expense). The Self Insurance paragraph explains the recording of a liability before payment of claims against the company (accrued expense).

Subscription Revenue To illustrate a deferred revenue adjustment, suppose that a company sells 12-month subscriptions to its monthly magazine. On October 1, the company receives a total of $1,200 for 20 subscriptions. To record this transaction, the company would record the following entry in its general journal:

Oct. 1	Cash	1,200	
	Unearned Subscription Revenue		1,200
	(To record cash received for future magazines)		

Assets	=	Liabilities	+	Equity
+1,200		+1,200		

This entry first increases the Cash account by the amount received. And, because the company now has an obligation to its customers to deliver the magazines, the entry also increases a liability account called Unearned Subscription Revenue. As a result, both assets and liabilities are increasing. The entry would then be posted to the relevant T-accounts as follows:

Cash		Unearned Subscription Revenue		Subscription Revenue	
1,200			1,200		0
1,200			1,200		0

Suppose further that the company prepares financial statements at the end of each month. As of October 31, the company has provided one month of magazines and has therefore earned one month of revenue, or $100 ($1,200 ÷ 12 months). Because the accounting system does not yet reflect this earned revenue, the following adjusting journal entry should be made on October 31:

Oct. 31	Unearned Subscription Revenue	100	
	Subscription Revenue		100
	(To record revenue earned during October)		

Assets	=	Liabilities	+	Equity
		−100		+100

This entry increases the Subscription Revenue account by the amount earned during the month and decreases the liability account Unearned Subscription Revenue by the same amount. As a result, liabilities are decreasing and equity is increasing. The entry would be posted to the relevant T-accounts as follows:

Cash		Unearned Subscription Revenue		Subscription Revenue	
1,200			1,200		0
		100			100
1,200			1,100		100

After posting, the Subscription Revenue T-account reflects the $100 earned in the current period while the Unearned Subscription Revenue T-account reflects the remaining $1,100 to be earned over the next 11 months. These two accounts have been *adjusted* so that they properly reflect revenues earned during October and liabilities owed on October 31. The Cash account is not affected by the adjusting journal entry. Cash was exchanged and recorded on October 1.

General Rule When a company receives cash before it provides a service, the company should always increase a liability account for the amount received. As the company provides the service, the liability account is adjusted down (decreased) and the related revenue account is adjusted up (increased). So, the adjusting journal entry for this scenario will always be a reduction to a liability account and an increase to a revenue account, as shown in Exhibit 4-2.

Scenario 2: Accrued Revenue

Companies often provide a service and then collect the cash. When a company earns a revenue before it receives cash, it has an *accrued revenue*. The term *accrue* means to accumulate or increase. An accrued revenue is another name for a receivable.

The **process of recording and posting adjusting entries** is the fourth step in the accounting cycle and occurs at the end of each accounting period after the trial balance is prepared.

Service Revenue To illustrate an accrued revenue adjustment, suppose that an accounting firm agrees to provide a service to a client for a $1,000 fee. The firm completes its work on September 23, bills the client

Exhibit 4-2 Entries in a Deferred Revenue Scenario

	Receipt of Cash		Provide Service		End of Period	
Cash	$$			Liability	$$	
Liability	$$			Revenue	$$	

MAKING IT REAL

Although gift cards have existed for many years, their ever-growing popularity in recent times is causing some accounting issues for retailers.

Many people would assume that retailers record revenue with each gift card purchased. However, the transfer of merchandise is required for revenue to be recognized. Therefore, gift card sales represent a deferred revenue, which is a liability. Revenue is not generated until the gift card is redeemed. For companies like American Eagle Outfitters, this liability is significant and, as a result, is a separate line item on the balance sheet. American Eagle Outfitters reports over $42 million in unredeemed gift cards at January 31, 2009.

Gift cards create another accounting challenge because of "breakage"—gift cards that are never redeemed. When a retailer determines that a card will not be redeemed, it can reduce its liability and increase its revenue for the breakage estimate. American Eagle Outfitters follows this practice. In the notes to its financial statements, the company states that it "determines an estimated gift card breakage rate by continuously evaluating historical redemption data and the time when there is a remote likelihood that a gift card will be redeemed. The Company recorded $12.2 million of revenue related to gift card breakage during Fiscal 2008."

on October 10, and receives payment on October 21. Suppose further that the accounting firm prepares its own financial statements at the end of each month, which in this case is September 30.

Because the accrual basis requires that revenues be recorded in the period in which they are earned, the accounting firm must record the $1,000 of revenue on September 30 with the following adjusting journal entry:

Sept. 30	Accounts Receivable	1,000	
	Service Revenue		1,000
	(To record revenue earned during September)		

Assets	=	Liabilities	+	Equity
+1,000				+1,000

The entry increases the Accounts Receivable account for the amount that the client owes the firm and increases the Service Revenue account for the amount that the firm has earned. As a result, both assets and equity are increasing. The preceding entry would be posted to the relevant T-accounts as follows:

Cash		Accounts Receivable		Service Revenue	
0		**1,000**		**1,000**	
0		1,000		1,000	

After posting, the Service Revenue T-account reflects the $1,000 earned in the current period while the Accounts Receivable T-account reflects the $1,000 of expected cash receipts from the client. These two accounts have been *adjusted* so that they properly reflect revenues earned during September and receivables held on September 30.

When the customer pays cash on October 21, the following entry is made:

Oct. 21	Cash	1,000	
	Accounts Receivable		1,000
	(To record receipt of cash)		

Assets	=	Liabilities	+	Equity
+1,000				
−1,000				

This entry increases the Cash account and decreases the Accounts Receivable account for the amount collected. As a result, although specific asset accounts are changing, total assets remain unchanged. No revenue is recorded because it was recorded in the prior period when it was earned. The entry would be posted to the relevant T-accounts as follows:

Cash		Accounts Receivable	
0		1,000	
1,000			**1,000**
1,000		0	

General Rule When a company earns a revenue before it receives cash, the company should always increase a receivable account and a revenue account for the amount earned. In other words, the receivable account should be adjusted up (increased) and the revenue account should also be adjusted up (increased). When the company collects the receivable, the receivable account is decreased and the cash account is increased. So, the adjusting journal entry for this scenario will always be an increase to an asset account and an increase to a revenue account, as shown in Exhibit 4-3.

Exhibit 4-3 Entries in an Accrued Revenue Scenario

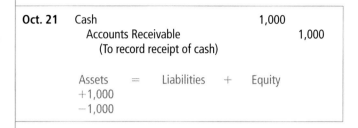

End of Period

Receipt of Cash

Provide Service

Receivable $$
Revenue $$

Cash $$
Receivable $$

Scenario 3: Deferred Expense

Companies often pay cash before they incur an expense. You need look no further than your own personal expenses to find numerous examples of payments made before you use the service. One example is insurance. You pay for insurance for several months in advance and are then covered.

When a company pays for a resource before it uses or consumes it, the company has a *deferred expense*. We use the term *deferred* because at the time of cash payment for the resource, the company has yet to use or consume the resource it is acquiring and therefore cannot record an expense in the accounting system. Instead, it records an asset. Recording of the expense must be *deferred* until the expense is incurred. You should note that a *deferred expense* is nothing more than an asset—a resource to be used.

Insurance Expense   To illustrate a deferred expense adjustment, suppose that on March 1, a company purchases a 12-month general liability insurance policy for $36,000. To record this transaction, the company would record the following entry in its general journal:

Mar. 1	Prepaid Insurance	36,000	
	Cash		36,000
	(To record purchase of insurance)		

Assets	=	Liabilities	+	Equity
−36,000				
+36,000				

This entry increases the asset account Prepaid Insurance to reflect the amount of insurance bought and decreases the Cash account for the same. Since both of these accounts are assets, this entry does not change total assets. The entry would then be posted to the relevant T-accounts as follows. For illustration purposes, assume that the cash account has a $100,000 balance prior to the entry.

Cash		Prepaid Insurance		Insurance Expense	
100,000	36,000	36,000		0	
64,000		36,000		0	

Suppose further that the company prepares financial statements at the end of March. As of March 31, the company has been covered for one month and has therefore consumed one month of insurance, or $3,000 ($36,000 ÷ 12 months). Because the accounting system does not yet reflect this expense, the following adjusting journal entry should be made on March 31:

Mar. 31	Insurance Expense	3,000	
	Prepaid Insurance		3,000
	(To record expense incurred during March)		

Assets	=	Liabilities	+	Equity
−3,000				−3,000

This entry increases the Insurance Expense account by the amount consumed during the month and decreases the asset account Prepaid Insurance by the same amount. As a result, both assets and equity are decreasing. The entry would be posted to the relevant T-accounts as follows:

Cash		Prepaid Insurance		Insurance Expense	
100,000	36,000	36,000		0	
			3,000	3,000	
64,000		33,000		3,000	

After posting, the Insurance Expense T-account reflects the $3,000 of insurance that was consumed in the current period while the Prepaid Insurance T-account reflects the remaining $33,000 of insurance to be consumed over the next eleven months. These two accounts have been *adjusted* so that they properly reflect expenses incurred during March and unexpired assets on March 31. The Cash account is not affected by the adjusting journal entry. Cash was exchanged and recorded on March 1.

Depreciation Expense   Another example of an expense where cash is paid before the expense is incurred is depreciation. Depreciation is the process of spreading out over their useful lives the cost of non-current assets such as equipment and buildings. For example, suppose that on August 1, a company purchases a delivery truck for $40,000. This transaction would be recorded into the accounting system as follows:

Aug. 1	Equipment	40,000	
	Cash		40,000
	(To record purchase of truck)		

Assets	=	Liabilities	+	Equity
−40,000				
+40,000				

This entry increases the asset account Equipment to reflect the cost of the truck and decreases the Cash account for the same. Since both of these accounts are assets, this entry does not change total assets. The entry would then be posted to the relevant T-accounts as follows. We will assume that the cash account has a $70,000 balance prior to the entry.

Cash		Equipment		Depreciation Expense	
70,000	40,000	40,000		0	
30,000		40,000		0	

Suppose further that the company prepares financial statements at the end of August. As of August 30, the company has used the truck for one month and should therefore record some amount of expense associated with the use of the truck. If we assume for simplicity that the amount of expense to be recognized in the current month is $1,000, the following adjusting journal entry should be made on August 31:

Aug. 31	Depreciation Expense	1,000	
	Accumulated Depreciation		1,000
	(To record expense incurred during August)		

Assets	=	Liabilities	+	Equity
−1,000				−1,000

This entry increases the Depreciation Expense account by the amount of expense allocated to the current month. However, instead of decreasing the Equipment account directly, the entry increases Accumulated Depreciation. We discuss accumulated depreciation in detail in Chapter 8, but for now you should know that the account is a contra-asset account that accumulates depreciation expense to date and is subtracted from the Equipment account to yield the net balance of the asset. As a result of the entry, both assets and equity are decreasing. Equity is decreasing because the company recorded an expense. Assets are decreasing because the net balance of Equipment and Accumulated Depreciation at the end of August is now $39,000 ($40,000 – $1,000). The entry would be posted to the relevant T-accounts as follows:

Equipment		Accumulated Depreciation		Depreciation Expense	
40,000			0	0	
			1,000	1,000	
40,000			1,000	1,000	

The Depreciation Expense and Accumulated Depreciation accounts have been *adjusted* so that they properly reflect the $1,000 of expenses incurred during August and the $39,000 of net unexpired balance of Equipment on August 31.

General Rule When a company pays cash before it incurs an expense, the company should always increase an asset account for the amount paid. As the company consumes the asset, the asset account is adjusted down (decreased) and the related expense account is adjusted up (increased). Depending on the type of asset, either the actual asset account will be decreased or a related contra-asset account will be increased. So, the adjusting journal entry for this scenario will always be a reduction to an asset account and an increase to an expense account, as shown in Exhibit 4-4.

Exhibit 4-4 Entries for a Deferred Expense Scenario

Scenario 4: Accrued Expense

Companies often incur expenses and pay for them later. A good example is employee salaries. Practically all companies pay their employees after the employees have provided labor for the company. When this occurs, the company has an *accrued expense*. An accrued expense is another name for a liability.

Salaries Expense To illustrate an accrued expense adjustment, suppose that a company's daily payroll is $1,000. The company pays its employees via direct deposit every Saturday for the work the employees have provided through Friday. Suppose further that the company prepares its financial statements on April 30, which is a Friday.

Because the accrual basis requires that expenses be recorded in the period in which they are incurred, the company must record the $5,000 of expense on April 30 with the following adjusting journal entry:

Apr. 30	Salaries Expense	5,000	
	Salaries Payable		5,000
	(To record salaries incurred during April)		

Assets	=	Liabilities	+	Equity
		+5,000		−5,000

The preceding entry increases the Salaries Expense account for the $5,000 of salaries incurred for the week and increases the Salaries Payable account for the same since it owes the employees those salaries. As a result, liabilities are increasing and equity is decreasing. The preceding entry would be posted to the relevant T-accounts as follows:

Cash		Salaries Payable		Salaries Expense	
8,000			5,000	5,000	
8,000			5,000	5,000	

After posting, the Salaries Expense T-account reflects the $5,000 incurred in the current period while the Salaries Payable T-account reflects the $5,000 owed to employees on April 30. These two accounts have been *adjusted* so that they properly reflect expenses incurred during April and the payable owed on April 30.

The Cash account is not affected by the adjusting journal entry. Cash, which has an $8,000 balance for illustrative purposes, will be paid on Saturday, May 1.

When the company pays its employees, the following entry would be made:

May 1	Salaries Payable	5,000	
	Cash		5,000
	(To record payment of cash)		

Assets	=	Liabilities	+	Equity
−5,000		−5,000		

The entry decreases the Cash account for the $5,000 paid to employees and decreases the Salaries Payable account by the same $5,000. No expense is recorded because it was recorded in the prior period when the expense was incurred. As a result, both assets and liabilities are decreasing. The entry would be posted to the relevant T-accounts as follows:

Cash		Salaries Payable	
8,000			5,000
	5,000	5,000	
3,000			0

Interest Expense Interest is another example of incurring an expense before cash is paid. For example, suppose that a company borrows $10,000 on November 1. The annual interest rate on the loan is 6%, and interest is payable on the first day of each month. Suppose further that the company prepares its financial statements on November 30.

As of November 30, the company has used the borrowed money for one month, so it has incurred one month's worth of interest. To calculate the amount of interest, we simply multiply the principal amount ($10,000) by the annual interest rate (6%) and by the relevant number of periods (1 month out of 12, or 1/12). So, interest for the month of November is:

$$\text{Principal} \times \text{annual rate} \times \text{time} = \$10{,}000 \times 0.06 \times 1/12$$
$$= \$50$$

Therefore, the following adjusting journal entry should be made on November 30:

Nov. 30	Interest Expense	50	
	Interest Payable		50
	(To record interest incurred during November)		

Assets	=	Liabilities	+	Equity
		+50		−50

The preceding entry increases the Interest Expense account for the $50 of interest for November and increases the Interest Payable account for the same. As a result, liabilities are increasing and equity is decreasing. The preceding entry would be posted to the relevant T-accounts as follows:

Cash	Interest Payable	Interest Expense
1,000	50	50
1,000	50	50

After posting, the Interest Expense T-account reflects the $50 incurred in the current period and the Interest Payable T-account reflects the $50 owed to the bank on November 30. These two accounts have been *adjusted* so that they properly reflect expenses incurred during November and the payable owed on November 30.

The Cash account is not affected by the adjusting journal entry. Cash, which has a $1,000 balance for illustrative purposes, will be paid on December 1. On that date, the following entry would be made:

Dec. 1	Interest Payable	50	
	Cash		50
	(To record payment of cash)		

Assets	=	Liabilities	+	Equity
−50		−50		

The preceding entry decreases the Cash account for the $50 paid to the bank and decreases the Interest Payable account by the same $50. As a result, both assets and liabilities are decreasing. The entry would be posted to the relevant T-accounts as follows:

Cash	Interest Payable
1,000	50
50	50
950	0

General Rule   When a company incurs an expense before it pays cash, the company should always increase a payable account and an expense account for the amount incurred. In other words, the payable account should be adjusted up (increased) and the expense account should also be adjusted up (increased). When the company pays the liability, the liability account is reduced and the cash account is decreased. So, the adjusting journal entry for this scenario will always be an increase to a liability account and an increase to an expense account, as shown in Exhibit 4-5.

Summary of Adjusting Journal Entries

Exhibit 4-6 summarizes the four scenarios that give rise to adjusting journal entries and the characteristics of the relevant entries.

As you review this exhibit, consider the following generalizations of all adjusting entries:

1. The purpose of adjusting entries is to record revenues that have been earned but not recorded and expenses that have been incurred but not recorded.

Exhibit 4-5 Entries in an Accrued Expense Scenario

Exhibit 4-6 Summary of Adjusting Journal Entry Scenarios

Scenario	Classification	Entry Before End of Period	Adjusting Entry at End of Period	Entry After End of Period

Cash is received *before* revenue is earned	Deferred Revenue	Cash $$
		  Liability $$
			Liability $$
			  Revenue $$	

Cash is received *after* revenue is earned	Accrued Revenue		Receivable $$
			  Revenue $$
				Cash $$
				  Receivable $$

Cash is paid *before* expense is incurred	Deferred Expense	Prepaid Asset $$
		  Cash $$
			Expense $$
			  Prepaid Asset $$	

Cash is paid *after* expense is incurred	Accrued Expense		Expense $$
			  Payable $$
				Payable $$
				  Cash $$

2. Every adjusting journal entry will affect at least one revenue or one expense account. In addition, every adjusting journal entry will affect at least one asset or liability account. This means that every adjusting entry will affect at least one account from the income statement and one account from the balance sheet.

3. Adjusting journal entries arise because the timing of revenue and expense recognition differs from the exchange of cash. Therefore, cash will never be increased or decreased in an adjusting entry.

LO3 Comprehensive Example: Adjusting Journal Entries

To illustrate the process of making adjusting journal entries from a trial balance and then preparing an adjusted trial balance, the Circle Films example from Chapter 3 will be continued. As a result of the transactions entered into by Circle Films during its first month of operations, the following unadjusted trial balance was prepared at May 31. Notice that it is an unadjusted trial balance because adjusting entries have not yet been made.

Circle Films
Unadjusted Trial Balance
May 31

	Debit	Credit
Cash	$ 8,250	
Supplies	1,000	
Equipment	18,000	
Unearned Revenue		$ 2000
Notes Payable		9,000
Common Stock		15,000
Service Revenue		5,000
Advertising Expense	250	
Salaries Expense	2,000	
Dividends	1,500	
Totals	$31,000	$31,000

In addition to these accounts and balances, the following information was available on May 31:

1. On May 31, Circle Films filmed the retirement reception for the customer who paid $2,000 on May 10 (see transaction #4 in Chapter 3 on page 48).

2. On May 31, Circle Films filmed the first night of a two-night local play. The second night will be filmed on June 1, at which time Circle Films will bill the customer. The customer has agreed to pay Circle Films $1,500 for each night.

3. After a physical count, Circle Films determined that it had $650 of supplies remaining.

4. The interest rate for the promissory note is 6%.

5. Circle Films estimates that depreciation for May on its two cameras totals $600.

Given this information, the following adjusting entries can be prepared.

Journalizing and Posting Adjusting Entries

Adjustment #1 (Deferred Revenue) Circle Films has now filmed the retirement reception, so it no longer has a liability to the customer. It has a revenue instead. However, the trial balance still shows the $2,000 liability. Thus, the adjusting entry to adjust the liability down and the revenue up is as follows:

May 31	Unearned Revenue	2,000	
	Service Revenue		2,000
	(To record revenue earned)		

$$\begin{array}{ccccc} \text{Assets} & = & \text{Liabilities} & + & \text{Equity} \\ & & -2,000 & & +2,000 \end{array}$$

The entry would be posted to the relevant T-accounts as follows:

Unearned Revenue		Service Revenue	
	2,000		5,000
2,000			2,000
	0		7,000

Adjustment #2 (Accrued Revenue) Circle Films filmed one night of a local play. Therefore, it has earned revenue for one night, or $1,500. The trial balance does not reflect this because Circle Films has not issued a bill, so the adjusting journal entry to adjust receivables and revenues up is as follows:

May 31	Accounts Receivable	1,500	
	Service Revenue		1,500
	(To record revenue earned)		

$$\begin{array}{ccccc} \text{Assets} & = & \text{Liabilities} & + & \text{Equity} \\ +1,500 & & & & +1,500 \end{array}$$

The entry would be posted to the relevant T-accounts as follows:

Accounts Receivable		Service Revenue	
0			5,000
1,500			2,000
			1,500
1,500			8,500

Adjustment #3 (Deferred Expense) Circle Films has $650 in supplies on hand. However, the trial balance shows $1,000 in the Supplies account, which is the amount that Circle Films originally purchased. Therefore, Circle Films must have used $350 of supplies ($1,000 − $650). To adjust the Supplies account down from $1,000 to $650 and to record the $350 in expense, the following adjusting journal is required.

May 31	Supplies Expense	350	
	Supplies		350
	(To record expense incurred)		

$$\begin{array}{ccccc} \text{Assets} & = & \text{Liabilities} & + & \text{Equity} \\ -350 & & & & -350 \end{array}$$

The entry would be posted to the relevant T-accounts as follows:

Supplies		Supplies Expense	
1,000		0	
	350	350	
650		350	

Adjustment #4 (Accrued Expense) Circle Films must pay interest on the promissory note at a 6% annual rate. Therefore, after one month, Circle Films has incurred $45 of interest expense ($9,000 × 6% × 1/12). This expense and the related obligation are not reflected in the trial balance because they have not yet been recorded. To record them, the following adjusting entry is required:

May 31	Interest Expense	45	
	Interest Payable		45
	(To record expense incurred)		

$$\begin{array}{ccccc} \text{Assets} & = & \text{Liabilities} & + & \text{Equity} \\ & & +45 & & -45 \end{array}$$

Once an adjusted trial balance is prepared, financial statements can be generated.

The entry would be posted to the relevant T-accounts as follows:

Interest Payable		Interest Expense	
	0	0	
	45	45	
	45	45	

Adjustment #5 (Deferred Expense) Circle determines that depreciation on its cameras should be $600 for the month of May. To record this depreciation, the following adjusting entry is required.

May 31	Depreciation Expense	600	
	Accumulated Depreciation		600
	(To record expense incurred)		

Assets	=	Liabilities	+	Equity
−600				−600

The entry would be posted to the relevant T-accounts as follows:

Equipment		Depreciation Expense		Accumulated Depreciation	
18,000		0			0
		600			600
18,000		600			600

Preparing an Adjusted Trial Balance

Once all of the preceding adjusting entries are journalized and posted to the ledger, an adjusted trial balance can be prepared. Like the previous trial balance, the adjusted trial balance simply lists all balances from the ledger. Since the ledger now reflects several adjustments, so does the adjusted trial balance.

The following is Circle Films' May 31 adjusted trial balance. The accounts that were either created or adjusted by the adjusting entries are highlighted.

© ISTOCKPHOTO.COM/ZEFFSS1

Circle Films
Adjusted Trial Balance
May 31

	Debit	Credit
Cash	$ 8,250	
Accounts Receivable	1,500	
Supplies	650	
Equipment	18,000	
Accumulated Depreciation		$ 600
Unearned Revenue		0
Interest Payable		45
Notes Payable		9,000
Common Stock		15,000
Service Revenue		8,500
Supplies Expense	350	
Interest Expense	45	
Depreciation Expense	600	
Advertising Expense	250	
Salaries Expense	2,000	
Dividends	1,500	
Totals	$33,145	$33,145

Preparing Financial Statements

Once all revenues and expenses are recorded and an adjusted trial balance is prepared, financial statements can be generated. Recall from Chapter 1 that the income statement should be prepared first. Using the adjusted revenue and expense account balances from the adjusted trial balance, Circle Films' income statement for the month of May would appear as follows:

Circle Films
Income Statement
For the Month Ending May 31

Revenues		$ 8,500
Expenses		
Supplies expense	$ 350	
Interest expense	45	
Depreciation expense	600	
Advertising expense	250	
Salaries expense	2,000	
Total expenses		3,245
Net income		$ 5,255

© YURI ARCURS/SHUTTERSTOCK.COM

After a period ends and financial statements are prepared, all temporary accounts must be reset to zero for the start of the next period.

With net income calculated, Circle Films' statement of retained earnings can be prepared. Recall that the statement of retained earnings takes the beginning balance in Retained Earnings, adds net income, and subtracts dividends to yield the current balance in Retained Earnings. Circle Films' May 31 adjusted trial balance shows no balance in beginning Retained Earnings and a $1,500 balance in dividends. Therefore, Circle Films' statement of retained earnings for the month of May would appear as follows.

Circle Films Statement of Retained Earnings For the Month Ending May 31	
Retained earnings, May 1	$ 0
Add: Net income	5,255
Less: Dividends	(1,500)
Retained earnings, May 31	$ 3,755

With Retained Earnings calculated, Circle Films' balance sheet can be prepared. Circle Films' May 31 adjusted trial balance shows several balance sheet accounts, starting with Cash and continuing through Common Stock. These accounts, along with the amount of Retained Earnings from the May statement of retained earnings, should be included on the balance

sheet. Therefore, Circle Films' May 31 balance sheet would appear as follows.

Circle Films Balance Sheet May 31			
Cash			$ 8,250
Accounts receivable			1,500
Supplies			650
Equipment		$18,000	
Less: Accumulated depreciation		600	17,400
Total assets			$27,800
Interest payable		$ 45	
Notes payable		9,000	
Total liabilities			$ 9,045
Common stock		$15,000	
Retained earnings		3,755	
Total stockholders' equity			18,755
Total liabilities and stockholders' equity			$27,800

LO4 Closing Process

After financial statements are prepared, companies conduct the closing process. The **closing process** is the process of transferring all revenue, expense, and dividend account balances to the Retained Earnings account. This transfer is necessary for two reasons.

First, revenue, expense, and dividend accounts are **temporary accounts**, meaning that they accumulate balances only for the current period. After the period ends and financial statements are prepared, all temporary

Closing process The process of transferring all revenue, expense, and dividend account balances to the Retained Earnings account.

Temporary accounts Accounts that accumulate balances only for the current period.

accounts must be reset to zero for the start of the next period.

Second, the transfer updates the Retained Earnings account to its proper end-of-period balance. In the preceding example, the balance in Retained Earnings is generated from the statement of retained earnings, not the adjusted trial balance. The closing process is the mechanism that updates the actual Retained Earnings account balance in the ledger.

The closing process is accomplished with several entries. **Closing entries**, which are made in the journal and posted to the ledger, eliminate the balances in all temporary accounts and transfer those balances to the Retained Earnings account. Usually, one entry is made for revenues, one for expenses, and a final entry for dividends. To illustrate, the temporary accounts from Circle Films' adjusted trial balance are shown in the following partial adjusted trial balance:

Circle Films
Partial Adjusted Trial Balance
May 31

	Debit	Credit
Service Revenue		$8,500
Supplies Expense	$ 350	
Interest Expense	45	
Depreciation Expense	600	
Advertising Expense	250	
Salaries Expense	2,000	
Dividends	1,500	

Circle Films has one revenue account with an $8,500 credit balance. To eliminate that balance and transfer it to the Retained Earnings account, the following closing entry is required.

May 31	Service Revenue	8,500	
	Retained Earnings		8,500
	(To close revenue account)		

In this entry, the revenue balance is eliminated while the Retained Earnings account is increased.

Expense and dividend accounts are closed in a similar fashion. To eliminate those balances and transfer them to Retained Earnings, the following closing entries are required.

May 31	Retained Earnings	3,245	
	Supplies Expense		350
	Interest Expense		45
	Depreciation Expense		600
	Advertising Expense		250
	Salaries Expense		2,000
	(To close expense accounts)		

May 31	Retained Earnings	1,500	
	Dividends		1,500
	(To close dividend account)		

In the first entry, all expense accounts are eliminated, and the Retained Earnings account is decreased for the same. In the second entry, the dividend account is eliminated, and the Retained Earnings account is decreased for the same.

All three closing entries would be posted to the appropriate T-accounts as follows.

Retained Earnings		Supplies Expense		Interest Expense	
	8,500	350		45	
3,245			350		45
1,500					
	3,755	0		0	

Depreciation Exp.		Advertising Expense		Salaries Expense	
600		250		2,000	
	600		250		2,000
0		0		0	

Service Revenue		Dividends	
	8,500	1,500	
8,500			1,500
	0	0	

Notice that after the closing entries are posted, all revenue, expense, and dividend accounts have zero balances as desired. They are now ready to begin the next reporting period. Also, Retained Earnings has a $3,755

Closing entries Entries made in the journal and posted to the ledger that eliminate the balances in all temporary accounts and transfer those balances to the Retained Earnings account.

credit balance. This is the balance reported on Circle Films' statement of retained earnings and balance sheet. In other words, the Retained Earnings account now has the proper balance at the end of the period.

As a final check that all accounts have been properly closed, a new trial balance is prepared. Appropriately called a post-closing trial balance, it contains all account balances for the beginning of the next accounting period. Circle Films' post-closing trial balance is as follows.

Circle Films Post-Closing Trial Balance May 31		
	Debit	Credit
Cash	$ 8,250	
Accounts Receivable	1,500	
Supplies	650	
Equipment	18,000	
Accumulated Depreciation		$ 600
Interest Payable		45
Notes Payable		9,000
Common Stock		15,000
Retained Earnings		3,755
Totals	$28,400	$28,400

Accounting cycle The sequence of steps in which an accounting information system captures, processes, and reports a company's accounting transactions during a period.

LO5 The Accounting Cycle— A Summary

This and the previous chapter covered the accounting cycle. The **accounting cycle** is the sequence of steps in which an accounting information system captures, processes, and reports a company's accounting transactions during a period. Chapter 3 demonstrated the first three steps—how to record journal entries in the journal, post the information to the ledger, and prepare a trial balance. This chapter demonstrated the two major processes that occur at the end of the period—adjusting and closing. The adjusting process includes the recording and posting of adjusting entries and the preparation of an adjusted trial balance, from which financial statements are prepared. The closing process includes the recording and posting of closing entries and the preparation of a post-closing trial balance. Once closing is completed, the accounting information system is prepared to begin the next period. Exhibit 4-7 summarizes these steps.

Exhibit 4-7 The Accounting Cycle

1. Journalize and post accounting transactions.
2. Prepare a trial balance.
3. Journalize and post adjusting entries.
4. Prepare an adjusted trial balance.
5. Prepare financial statements.
6. Journalize and post closing entries.
7. Prepare a post-closing trial balance.

STUDY TOOLS CHAPTER 4

CHAPTER REVIEW CARD

❑ Learning Objective and Key Concept Reviews

❑ Key Definitions and Formulas

ONLINE (Located at 4ltrpress.cengage.com/acct)

❑ Flash Cards and Crossword Puzzles

❑ Conceptual and Computational Interactive Quizzes

❑ E-Lectures

❑ Static, Algorithmic, and Additional Homework Activities (as directed by your instructor)

EXERCISES

1. Cash and Accrual Income   LO1

During 2010, Stacker Enterprises earned $55,000 from services provided and incurred $15,500 of expenses. At the end of the year, Stacker had received cash for $35,750 of the revenues and had paid $11,600 of the expenses. Also during 2010, Stacker received $3,500 cash for services to be performed in 2011 and paid $4,500 for rent for the first six months of 2011.

Required
Determine 2010 net income under (a) the cash basis and (b) the accrual basis of accounting.

2. Adjusting Journal Entries   LO2, 3

Following are several independent accounting situations:
1. Interest of $1,500 on a loan outstanding during 2010 is due on January 1, 2011.
2. Received $100,000 in 2010 for a service project that is 45% complete at year-end.
3. Received a $450 utility bill for the month of December on January 3, 2011.
4. $750 of prepaid rent for the month of December has expired.
5. $5,000 of revenue for services performed on December 14, 2010, is uncollected.
6. Prepay $6,500 of insurance on December 31, 2010, for the entire year of 2011.
7. Intend to buy a warehouse on January 1, 2011, for $125,000.
8. Property, Plant, and Equipment depreciation is $5,000 for the year.

Required
For each independent situation, determine the basic type of adjustment, if any, that is needed on December 31, 2010 (deferred revenue, deferred expense, accrued revenue, accrued expense). What would be the cumulative effect on 2010 net income of all adjustments made in situations 1–8?

3. Adjusting Journal Entries   LO2, 3

The following selected accounts were taken from the general ledger of the Cone Corporation on September 30 before adjusting entries have been made. Cone makes adjusting entries *quarterly*.

	Debit	Credit
Supplies	4,000	
Prepaid Rent	5,400	
Building	100,000	
Notes Receivable	25,000	
Accumulated Depreciation		20,000
Unearned Revenue		8,500

Additional Information:
1. Rent expires at a rate of $900 per month.
2. Supplies on hand total $2,000.
3. Utilities incurred in September but not yet recorded or paid are $500.
4. The building depreciates at a rate of $2,700 per quarter.
5. $5,000 of the $8,500 unearned revenue has been earned during the quarter.
6. Interest of $250 on the note receivable has been earned but not yet recorded.

Required
Prepare the necessary adjusting journal entries at September 30.

4. Adjusting Journal Entries   LO2, 3

For each of the transactions for Cone Corporation in Exercise 3, indicate the amount of the increase or decrease on the appropriate element of the balance sheet or income statement. The first transaction has been completed as an example.

	Balance Sheet			Income Statement		
Transaction	Assets	Liability	Equity	Revenues	Expenses	Net Income
1.	−2,700	NE	−2,700	NE	+2,700	−2,700
2.						
3.						
4.						
5.						
6.						

5. Adjusting Journal Entries   LO2, 3

In its first year of operations, Lien Corporation entered into the following transactions, among others:
1. January 1: Bought equipment with a 7-year useful life, $105,000.
2. March 31: Prepaid one year's rent, $24,000.
3. July 1: Took out a loan from the bank at an annual interest rate of 8%, $20,000.
4. August 1: Received payment for services not yet rendered, $12,000.

On December 31, Lien has earned $8,000 of the $12,000 in transaction 4 and has incurred $450 of utilities. Lien prepares adjusting entries on an annual basis.

Required
Prepare journal entries for transactions 1–4. Prepare any adjusting journal entries needed at December 31. Assume that the equipment depreciates evenly over its useful life.

6. Adjusting Journal Entries   LO2, 3

Coy Williams, a first-year accountant at Protein Plus, has asked you to review the following items for potential errors. Protein Plus has a December 31 year-end.

1. Did not adjust the Prepaid Insurance account for the $6,600 of insurance that expired during the year.
2. Recorded a full year of accrued interest on a $20,000, 10% note payable that was entered into on July 1. Interest is payable each July 1.
3. Did not record $8,500 of depreciation on an office building.
4. Recorded revenues of $12,000 when payment was received for a job that will be completed next year.
5. Recorded $600 of utilities expense for December even though Protein Plus will not pay the bill until January of next year.

Required
Determine if Coy made any errors in the five items. For those in which an error was made, prepare the entry that Coy should have made. What was the net effect of Coy's errors on the net income of Protein Plus?

7. Closing Process   LO4
A partial adjusted trial balance is shown as follows for Sparks Electricity:

Sparks Electricity Partial Adjusted Trial Balance June 30		
	Debit	Credit
Retained Earnings		$17,150
Service Revenue		30,500
Advertising Expense	$ 1,200	
Depreciation Expense	10,750	
Interest Expense	560	
Salaries Expense	5,000	
Supplies Expense	2,500	
Utilities Expense	2,080	
Dividends	1,000	

Required
a. Prepare Sparks' income statement and statement of retained earnings for the month of June.
b. Prepare the appropriate closing entries at June 30.
c. What is the purpose of "closing the books" at the end of an accounting period?

8. Closing Process   LO4
The following T-accounts contain the December postings to the general ledger of Swoops, Inc. The December 1 postings are beginning balances, while the December 31 postings are closing entries.

Service Revenue

12/31	75,000	12/1	64,000
		12/8	4,000
		12/24	3,000
		12/30	4,000

Salaries Expense

12/1	15,000	12/31	17,000
12/15	1,000		
12/30	1,000		

Supplies Expense

12/1	1,800	12/31	2,500
12/30	700		

Depreciation Expense

12/1	4,400	12/31	4,800
12/30	400		

Interest Expense

12/1	1,500	12/31	1,800
12/24	300		

Retained Earnings

12/31	2,500	12/1	51,550
12/31	26,100	12/31	75,000

Dividends

12/1	2,000	12/31	2,500
12/15	500		

Required
Recreate the closing journal entries made by Swoops on December 31.

PROBLEMS

9. Cash and Accrual Income   LO1, 2

Olga Industries keeps records under the cash basis of accounting rather than the accrual basis. Olga's 2010 income statement and additional data from 2009 and 2010 are as follows:

Olga Industries	
Cash-Basis Income Statement	
For the Year Ending December 31, 2010	
Revenues	$54,000
Expenses	35,000
Net income	$19,000

Additional Information:

	12/31/09	12/31/10
Accrued Revenues	6,000	8,000
Unearned Revenues	13,000	4,500
Accrued Expenses	5,000	4,000
Prepaid Expenses	10,000	9,500

All accrued revenues and expenses as of 12/31/09 were collected and paid, respectively, in 2010. All unearned revenues as of 12/31/09 were earned in 2010, and all prepaid expenses as of 12/31/09 were used in 2010 or have expired.

Required

Convert revenues and expenses from the cash basis to the accrual basis and recalculate income. Briefly explain why each adjustment is made.

10. Adjusting Entries and Trial Balance   LO2, 3

The unadjusted trial balance of Sweet Cheeks Facial Spa is shown as follows:

Sweet Cheeks Facial Spa		
Unadjusted Trial Balance		
September 30		
	Debit	Credit
Cash	$ 3,500	
Supplies	2,250	
Equipment	18,000	
Unearned Revenue		$ 1,500
Notes Payable		10,000
Common Stock		10,000
Service Revenue		4,000
Advertising Expense	650	
Salaries Expense	600	
Dividends	500	
Totals	$25,500	$25,500

Additional Information:
1. On September 30, Sweet Cheeks completed a women's retreat for which it had received payment in August, $1,500.
2. On September 30, Sweet Cheeks rendered service on credit, $500.
3. Monthly depreciation on Sweet Cheeks' equipment is $150.
4. The interest rate on the promissory note is 6%.
5. A count of the supplies revealed $500 of supplies remaining.
6. Assume the trial balance was last adjusted on August 31.

Required

Prepare all necessary adjusting entries for the month of September and prepare an adjusted trial balance as of September 30.

11. Adjusting Entries and Financial Statements   LO2, 3

The June 30 unadjusted trial balance of Prime Realty appears as follows.

Prime Realty		
Unadjusted Trial Balance		
June 30		
	Debit	Credit
Cash	$ 6,900	
Accounts Receivable	4,500	
Supplies	2,250	
Prepaid Rent	6,300	
Equipment	18,000	
Accumulated Depreciation		$ 900
Unearned Revenue		1,500
Notes Payable		10,000
Common Stock		20,200
Service Revenue		11,200
Advertising Expense	650	
Depreciation Expense	900	
Interest Expense	150	
Rent Expense	2,100	
Salaries Expense	1,700	
Dividends	350	
Totals	$43,800	$43,800

Additional Information:
1. Rent expires at a rate of $700 per month.
2. Monthly depreciation on equipment is $300.
3. Interest on the 6% promissory note is paid quarterly on April 1, July 1, October 1, and January 1.
4. Performed services for which payment was received in April, $800.
5. Received utility bill to be paid next month, $500.
6. Services to customers earned during June but unrecorded at June 30, $2,500.
7. Supplies on hand totaled $1,500 at June 30.
8. Owed employees for salaries for the last week of June to be paid in July, $800.
9. Prime Realty prepares adjusting entries each quarter. Adjustments were last made on March 31.

Required

a. Prepare all adjusting journal entries for the second quarter of operations.

b. Post journal entries to T-accounts using totals on the unadjusted trial balance as the opening balances.

c. Prepare an adjusted trial balance as of June 30.

d. Prepare an income statement and a statement of retained earnings for the six months ending June 30.

e. Prepare a classified balance sheet as of June 30.

12. Adjusting Entries and Closing Entries   LO2, 3, 4

The unadjusted and adjusted trial balances of Wang, Inc., are shown as follows:

	Wang, Inc.			
	Trial Balance			
	December 31			
	Unadjusted Trial Balance		**Adjusted Trial Balance**	
	Debit	**Credit**	**Debit**	**Credit**
Cash	$ 8,000		$ 8,000	
Accounts Receivable	12,250		16,250	
Supplies	2,400		1,200	
Prepaid Insurance	6,400		5,600	
Buildings	250,000		250,000	
Land	75,000		75,000	
Accumulated Depreciation		$ 25,000		$ 50,000
Salaries Payable		0		2,000
Utilities Payable		15,450		20,950
Unearned Revenue		9,500		7,000
Note Payable		75,000		75,000
Capital Stock		150,000		150,000
Retained Earnings		22,100		22,100
Service Revenue		75,500		82,000
Advertising Expense	8,500		8,500	
Depreciation Expense	0		25,000	
Insurance Expense	0		800	
Salaries Expense	8,000		10,000	
Supplies Expense	0		1,200	
Utilities Expense	0		5,500	
Dividends	2,000		2,000	
Totals	$372,550	$372,550	$409,050	$409,050

Required

a. Compare the unadjusted trial balance and the adjusted trial balance and recreate all adjusting journal entries that were made at December 31.

b. Prepare the income statement and a statement of retained earnings for the year. Also prepare a classified balance sheet at December 31.

c. Prepare necessary closing entries.

13. The Accounting Cycle   LO2, 3, 4, 5

Ruberstein, Inc., was founded on April 1 and entered into the following transactions:

Apr. 1 Issued common stock to shareholders in exchange for cash, $20,000.

1 Purchased a delivery van, $13,000.

1 Purchased a one-year insurance policy to be consumed evenly over the next 12 months, $4,800.

1 Took out a loan from First Bank, $20,000.

6 Hired two new employees on salary of $1,000 a month each.

6 Received prepayment for a contracted job to be performed in May, $4,500.

7 Purchased office supplies on credit, $1,200.

8 Billed customers for services provided, $7,500.

12 Paid to have an ad placed on a billboard, $1,300.

18 Billed customers for services provided, $8,600.

24 Paid dividends to stockholders, $1,000.

30 Received utility bills for the month of April to be paid next month, $740.

30 Prepaid the next six months of rent starting with May, $3,600.

Additional Information:

1. April depreciation for the delivery van is $217.

2. Interest on the loan from the bank is paid annually at a rate of 6%.

3. An inventory count of office supplies at April 30 showed $500 of supplies on hand.

4. Prepaid insurance has expired.

5. Employees' salaries earned but to be paid next month, $2,000.

Required

a. Journalize the transactions for the month of April.

b. Post the journal entries to the general ledger using T-accounts.

c. Prepare a trial balance as of April 30.

d. Prepare all necessary adjusting journal entries and post the entries to the appropriate T-accounts.

e. Prepare an adjusted trial balance as of April 30.

f. Prepare an income statement and a statement of retained earnings for the month of April. Also prepare a classified balance sheet as of April 30.

g. Prepare all closing entries for the temporary accounts and post the entries to the appropriate T-accounts.

h. Prepare a post-closing trial balance as of April 30.

> **REMEMBER**

- All exercises and problems from the text are available online in static and algorithmic versions.
- Additional multiple choice, exercises, problems, and cases are available online in CengageNOW or as an enrichment module that can be customized into this text.

IT'S ALL ABOUT
THE HOMEWORK!

CengageNOW™ is an **easy-to-use online resource** that helps you **study in less time** to **get the grade you want** – NOW.

CengageNOW™ comes FREE with each new copy of ACCT and features:
- End-of-chapter homework from the textbook written by the authors
- eBook
- Videos, quizzes, games, e-lectures, and more!

How to Register Your Access Code:
1. Launch a Web browser. Go to www.cengage.com/login and click on "Create My Account." Already have an account? Enter your email/password under "Sign In."
2. Enter your access code in the field provided, exactly how it appears on your card.
3. New users: Enter your account information and click "Continue."
4. Record your email address and password below and store it in a secure location for future visits.

[Email Address: _____]
[Password: _____]

Want Extra Problems?
CengageNOW comes automatically with this book and offers 250 additional exercises to give you a variety of assignment options. You can create static assignments or algorithmic assignments and you can also assign cases and longer problems.

Through the **4LTR+ Custom Program,** you can package these additional exercises with your students' textbooks for just $5. Students will see the additional exercises in CengageNOW if you assign them, but some may also prefer to use them in a printed format.

www.4ltrpress.cengage.com/4ltrplusbc.html

ACCT

Internal Control
and Cash

Introduction

This chapter examines the concepts of internal control and how those concepts affect the accounting for cash. Internal control is a company-wide process that seeks to improve a company's operations and its financial reporting. Among other things, internal control helps a company protect its assets. There are few assets that are more prone to theft than cash, so internal control is quite relevant and important to the accounting for cash.

This chapter begins with the role and overall concepts of internal control and then examines two control activities relating to cash—bank reconciliations and petty cash funds. The chapter concludes with how cash is reported and how a company's cash position can be analyzed.

Learning Objectives

After studying the material in this chapter, you should be able to:

LO1 Describe the role of internal control in a business.

LO2 Describe the five components of internal control.

LO3 Understand two methods of internal control over cash—bank reconciliations and petty cash funds.

LO4 Describe the reporting of cash.

LO5 Evaluate cash through the calculation and interpretation of horizontal, vertical, and ratio analyses.

LO1 Internal Control

In recent years, there have been numerous widely publicized accounting frauds. Major corporations such as Enron, WorldCom, and HealthSouth failed as a result of fraudulent activity. Many began to question the reliability and integrity of financial reporting of publicly traded companies.

Faced with this crisis, the United States Congress passed the Sarbanes-Oxley Act (SOX) in July 2002. The act sought to restore public confidence in financial reporting by enacting major changes in the manner in which accounting is practiced in the United States. Several of those changes focused on *internal control*.

In its broadest sense, internal control is the process that a company's management uses to help the company meet its operational and financial reporting objectives. More specifically, **internal control** is the system of policies and procedures that a company puts in place to provide reasonable assurances that:

- the company's operations are effective and efficient,

Internal control The system of policies and procedures used in a company to promote efficient and effective operations, reliable financial reporting, and compliance with laws and regulations.

CHAPTER 5

Making pizza is probably the most prominent process at a Domino's location, but equally important are internal control processes, especially in the collection of customer payments.

© AP IMAGES/PAUL SANCYA

- the company's financial reporting is reliable, and
- the company is complying with applicable laws and regulations.

All companies have systems of internal control. The only question is how strong or weak those systems are.

Recognizing that internal control affects a company's success or failure, Section 404 of SOX contained several new requirements for publicly traded companies regarding internal control. One of the most important requirements is that corporations include in their annual reports

Internal control report Annual report in which management states its responsibility for internal control and provides an assessment of its internal control.

to shareholders an **internal control report** containing the following two items:

- A statement that it is management's responsibility to establish and maintain an adequate internal control structure and procedures for financial reporting.

- An assessment of the effectiveness of the internal control structure and procedures for financial reporting for the most recent year.

These requirements publicly place the burden of internal controls squarely on management. Management must take responsibility for, as well as provide an assessment of, internal control. This forces management to be engaged with respect to its internal control.

In addition to requiring an internal control report, SOX also requires management to obtain an annual audit of its internal control structure and its assessment. In other words, SOX requires an independent, third-party evaluation of management's assessment. This evaluation is performed by the public accounting firm performing the company's financial audit.

To illustrate these requirements, Exhibit 5-1 contains Domino's Pizza's most recent internal control report as well as excerpts from the audit report of Domino's auditor, PricewaterhouseCoopers. The highlighted sections of the internal control report show that Domino's management (1) takes responsibility for its internal control, (2) states that it has conducted an evaluation of the effectiveness of its internal control, and (3) concludes that its internal control is effective. The highlighted portion of the audit report shows that the audit firm agrees. Based on its audit of Domino's internal controls, PricewaterhouseCoopers' opinion is that Domino's maintained effective internal control over financial reporting during the most recent period. This is the opinion that management wants to receive.

> All companies have systems of **internal control**. The only question is how strong or weak those systems are.

Exhibit 5-1 Internal Control Reporting by Domino's Pizza

Management Report on Internal Controls

The management of Domino's Pizza, Inc. is responsible for establishing and maintaining adequate internal control over financial reporting. Internal control over financial reporting is defined in Rule 13A-15(f) promulgated under the Exchange Act, as a process designed by, or under the supervision of the Company's principal executive and principal financial officers and effected by the Company's board of directors, management and other personnel, to provide reasonable assurance regarding the reliability of financial reporting and the preparation of financial statements for external purposes in accordance with generally accepted accounting principles.

Because of its inherent limitations, internal control over financial reporting may not prevent or detect misstatements. Also, projections of any evaluation of effectiveness to future periods are subject to the risk that controls may become inadequate because of changes in conditions, or that the degree of compliance with the policies or procedures may deteriorate.

Under the supervision and with the participation of the Company's management, including its Chief Executive Officer and Chief Financial Officer, the Company conducted an evaluation of the effectiveness of its internal control over financial reporting as of December 28, 2008 based on the framework in *Internal Control—Integrated Framework* issued by the Committee of Sponsoring Organizations of the Treadway Commission. Based on that evaluation, management concluded that its internal control over financial reporting was effective as of December 28, 2008.

The effectiveness of the Company's internal control over financial reporting as of December 28, 2008, has been audited by PricewaterhouseCoopers LLP, an independent registered public accounting firm, as stated in their report which appears herein.

Excerpt from Report of Independent Registered Public Accounting Firm

To the Stockholders and Board of Directors of Domino's Pizza, Inc.:

In our opinion, the consolidated financial statements … present fairly, in all material respects, the financial position of Domino's Pizza, Inc. and its subsidiaries at December 28, 2008 and December 30, 2007, and the results of their operations and their cash flows for each of the three years in the period ended December 28, 2008 in conformity with accounting principles generally accepted in the United States of America. … Also in our opinion, the Company maintained, in all material respects, effective internal control over financial reporting as of December 28, 2008, based on criteria established in *Internal Control—Integrated Framework* issued by the Committee of Sponsoring Organizations of the Treadway Commission (COSO).

PricewaterhouseCoopers LLP
Detroit, Michigan
February 24, 2009

The *COSO Framework* is the standard for understanding what good internal control looks like in an organization.

Before leaving Exhibit 5-1, note that both reports contain an italicized reference to *Internal Control—Integrated Framework*. This title refers to an influential report released in 1992 by the Committee of Sponsoring Organizations (COSO) of the Treadway Commission. The report was the culmination of the committee's exhaustive research and deliberation on the elements of sound internal control. The committee's objective was to provide a common understanding of internal control—a framework for implementing good internal control practices. Its success is clear. The *Framework* has become the standard for understanding what good internal control looks like in an organization, and it is the basis for the discussion in this chapter.

LO2 Components of Internal Control

The broad purpose of internal control is to help management achieve effective and efficient operations, reliable financial reporting, and compliance with laws and regulations. *Internal Control—Integrated Framework* states that good internal control consists of the following five interrelated components:

- Control Environment
- Risk Assessment
- Control Activities
- Information and Communication
- Monitoring

Control Environment

The **control environment** is the foundation for all other components of internal control. It is the atmosphere in which the members of an organization conduct their activities and carry out their responsibilities. The control environment is often called the "tone at the top" because it reflects the overall control consciousness of an organization.

Many factors affect an organization's control environment. One of the most important is the overall integrity and ethical values of personnel. These attributes translate into standards of behavior that can permeate throughout an organization's operations. Other factors include management's philosophy and operating style, the assignment of authority and responsibility, and the general structure of an organization. Each of these factors contributes to the overall corporate culture within which internal control operates. Without a sound control environment, the remaining elements of internal control suffer.

> **Control environment** The atmosphere in which the members of an organization conduct their activities and carry out their responsibilities.

HOME DEPOT ANALYSIS

Look at the Report of Independent Registered Public Accounting Firm accompanying Home Depot's financial statements in Appendix C. What was the auditor's opinion regarding the effectiveness of Home Depot's internal control?

In the auditor's opinion, The Home Depot, Inc. maintained, in all material respects, effective internal control over financial reporting as of February 1, 2009, based on criteria established in *Internal Control—Integrated Framework* issued by the Committee of Sponsoring Organizations of the Treadway Commission.

The control environment is often called the "tone at the top" because it reflects the overall control consciousness of an organization.

Risk Assessment

All organizations face a variety of risks that threaten the achievement of organizational objectives. **Risk assessment** refers to the identification and analysis of these risks, with the goal of effectively managing them. Because business conditions change throughout time, risk assessment is an ongoing organizational activity.

Organizational risks can arise from both external and internal sources. External sources might include new competitors, changing customer expectations, or even natural catastrophes. Internal sources might include inadequate workforce training, errors in financial reporting of activities, or theft of assets by employees.

Once an organization identifies its risks, the risks can be analyzed with the following general process:

- Estimate the significance of a risk

- Assess the likelihood of the risk occurring

- Consider what actions should be taken to manage the risk

Risks of minor significance or those with a lower likelihood of occurrence generally do not warrant serious concern. For example, the risk of a meteorite destroying a company's warehouse can likely be ignored. In contrast, significant risks with higher likelihood demand considerable attention. For example, the risk of an employee stealing cash from customer collections likely requires some attention. That attention comes in the form of control activities.

Control Activities

Control activities are the policies and procedures management establishes to address the risks that might

Risk assessment The identification and analysis of the risks that threaten the achievement of organizational objectives.

Control activities The policies and procedures established to address the risks that threaten the achievement of organizational objectives.

prevent the organization from achieving its objectives. Although specific control activities vary widely across organizations, they generally fall into one of several categories.

Establishing Responsibility A critical factor in good internal control is establishing responsibility for the performance of a given task. When responsibility is clear, two benefits arise. First, the employee knows that he or she will be held accountable for completion of the task. Second, management knows who to consult if the task is not completed satisfactorily.

A good example is a retailer's cashiers. Each cashier is assigned sole responsibility over a specific cash drawer. No other cashier has access to or responsibility for that drawer. If a drawer is returned to the company short of cash, management knows exactly who to speak to. As a result, cashiers are motivated to perform their tasks well, and the risk of theft or error is reduced.

Maintaining Adequate Documentation Accounting information is useful only when it is reliable, which means that it must be free from error. Control activities are necessary in all organizations to promote error-free accounting records. Consider the sale of a company's inventory as an example. Good control practices would require that the sale be documented on a sales invoice, preferably a sequentially numbered one so that the sale will neither be lost nor recorded twice. The invoice might also require the employee's initials to establish responsibility for the sale, and it will have multiple copies to be sent throughout the organization for proper fulfillment and recording of the sale. Such invoices and processes are increasingly computerized, which brings additional controls that further reduce the introduction of errors into the accounting system.

Segregation of Duties Segregation of duties is a technique that limits one person's control over a particular task or area of a company. Often called separation of duties, it is accomplished by spreading responsibility among multiple employees so that one employee's work can serve as a check against another's work. For example, consider the process of ordering, receiving, and paying for merchandise. If one employee handles all three tasks, there is greater risk of error and possibly theft of assets. However, if these three tasks are handled by different employees, errors by one employee can be caught by another employee. Moreover, unless the employees work unethically together, company assets are more protected against theft.

Physical Security Good internal control includes an effort to safeguard company assets and records. Most of these safeguarding controls are meant to prevent the loss of assets. Examples include secured facilities, fire and alarm systems, computer passwords and encryption, video monitors, and door sensors that signal when product is inappropriately taken from a store. Other controls are meant to detect the loss of assets. An example is the periodic counting of inventory for comparison to accounting records. Significant discrepancies can then be investigated.

Independent Verification Independent verification is the process of reviewing and reconciling information within an organization. This is particularly useful when reconciling an asset balance with the accounting records for that asset. An example would be a bank reconciliation, where the bank's balance and the company's balance are reconciled. Often, the most effective verifications are conducted on a surprise basis and are conducted by individuals who have no connection to the process or the employee being verified. Internal audit divisions of organizations commonly perform such verifications.

Information and Communication

Information and communication is another element of sound internal control. **Information and communication** refers to the need for the open flow of relevant information throughout an organization. Information must be captured and communicated in a form and a timeframe that enables employees to complete their responsibilities. This requires information systems that produce relevant and reliable reports. It also requires both upward and downward lines of communication. Management must communicate with employees, and employees must communicate with management.

Monitoring

Monitoring refers to the assessment of the quality of an organization's internal control. Monitoring can be accomplished in two ways. The first is through ongoing activities. For example, in his recurring daily responsibilities, a supervisor can check for evidence that a control activity is functioning properly. He or she can also ask employees if they understand the controls in place

> **Control activities** are necessary in all organizations to promote error-free accounting records.

and if those controls are being completed. The second is through a separate evaluation. The audit of internal controls required by SOX is an example of a separate evaluation. In both ways, the purpose of monitoring is to continuously improve internal control.

Limitations of Internal Control

Regardless of how well internal control is designed within an organization, it can provide only reasonable assurances that a company is meeting its objectives. Internal control systems are limited in their effectiveness because of (1) the human element and (2) cost-benefit analysis.

The *human element* refers to the fact that internal controls are often based on human judgment and action. Despite our best efforts, we all make mistakes at times, and internal control cannot eliminate them all. Furthermore, employees can purposefully circumvent controls for personal gain. Sometimes this will be a manager who overrides the control activities in place. Other times this will be multiple employees working together to circumvent existing controls. Such collusion among employees can be very effective at defeating a company's internal controls.

Cost-benefit analysis refers to the cost of implementing a control activity versus the benefit that the control provides. For example, a company could install retina-scanning security systems for its warehouses to decrease the risk of theft. However, the cost of the installation may far outweigh the marginal advantage that retina-scanning security provides over normal lock-and-key security. In such a case, security would be limited to lock-and-key because the cost of the extra security would far outweigh its benefit.

> **Information and communication**
> Required for the open flow of relevant information throughout an organization.
>
> **Monitoring** The assessment of the quality of an organization's internal control.

> Collusion among employees can be very effective at defeating a company's internal controls.

LO₃ Cash Controls

© MONKEY BUSINESS IMAGES/SHUTTERSTOCK.COM

The best asset to use in demonstrating internal control is cash. Cash is a highly desired asset. It is easily concealed, taken, and converted into other assets with only a small chance of detection. As a result, companies normally institute many controls to safeguard their cash and to report it properly. Two of these controls are bank reconciliations and petty cash funds. Each is discussed in the following sections.

Bank Reconciliations

Most companies keep the majority of their cash in a bank. This in itself is a good control procedure because it limits opportunities for theft. It is difficult to steal cash when it is locked up in the bank. The use of a bank also provides two sources of independent record keeping. That is, both the company and the bank keep a record of all cash transactions between them. As a result, a company can compare these records to verify its cash balance. This comparison is called a bank reconciliation.

A **bank reconciliation** is the process of reconciling the differences between the cash balance on a bank statement and the cash balance in a company's records. The purpose of a bank reconciliation is twofold. First, it confirms the accuracy of both the bank's and the company's cash records. Second, it determines the actual cash balance to be reported on the company's balance sheet. A bank reconciliation is prepared as follows:

- Reconcile the bank balance to the actual cash balance

- Reconcile the company's book balance to the actual cash balance

- Adjust the company's book balance to the actual cash balance

Reconciling the Bank Balance The first step in a bank reconciliation is to adjust the cash balance reported on the bank statement to the company's actual cash balance. The bank balance will differ from the actual cash balance and will therefore need adjustment for two main reasons.

The first reason relates to deposits and payments made by the company that are not reflected on the bank statement. For example, a **deposit in transit** is a deposit that has been made by the company but does not appear on the bank statement because it had not cleared the bank as of the statement date. Because the cash is now in the bank, deposits in transit should be added to the bank's cash balance. An **outstanding check** is a check that has been distributed by the company but does not appear on the bank statement because it had not cleared the bank as of the statement date. Because the cash is no longer in the bank, outstanding checks should be subtracted from the bank cash balance.

The second reason relates to errors made by the bank. Although bank errors are rare, they do occur and must also be reconciled. An error can result in the need to add to or subtract from the bank balance. For example, suppose that the bank erroneously records a $1,450 deposit as $1,540. The bank balance is overstated by $90 and should therefore be reduced by $90. In contrast, suppose that the bank records a $10 check as $100. In that case, the bank balance is understated by $90 and should be increased $90.

Once all adjustments to the bank balance are made, the adjusted bank balance should equal the actual cash balance to be reported on the balance sheet.

Bank reconciliation The process of reconciling the differences between the cash balance on a bank statement and the cash balance in a company's records.

Deposit in transit A deposit that has been made by the company but has not cleared the bank as of the statement date.

Outstanding check A check that has been distributed by the company but has not cleared the bank as of the statement date.

> A bank reconciliation confirms the accuracy of a company's cash records and determines the actual balance to be reported on the balance sheet.

Reconciling the Company Book Balance The second step in a bank reconciliation is to adjust the cash balance reported on the company's books to the actual cash balance. The company book balance may differ from the actual cash balance, and therefore need adjustment, for two main reasons.

The first reason relates to bank activities that change a company's cash balance but have not been recorded by the company. Usually, companies are notified of these changes through bank memoranda. More specifically, a **credit memorandum** is notification of an addition to the cash balance on the bank statement. Credit memoranda arise when the bank collects cash on behalf of the company—often through the collection of a company receivable or interest on a note. Credit memoranda should be added to the company's book balance. A **debit memorandum** is notification of a subtraction from the cash balance on the bank statement. Common examples are fees charged for banking services and customer checks returned for insufficient funds. Both of these examples reflect cash that the company no longer has, so they should be subtracted from the company's book balance.

The second reason relates to errors made in the company's cash records. For example, suppose that during the reconciliation a company discovers that it erroneously recorded for $100 a check written as $1,000. The company's balance is overstated by $900 and should be reduced by $900.

Adjusting the Cash Balance Once the bank balance and the company's book balance are reconciled, the company's cash balance must be adjusted to the actual cash balance determined by the reconciliations. Therefore, the third step in a bank reconciliation is to record the journal entries necessary to adjust the company's book balance to the actual cash balance. The journal entries are based on the credit and debit memoranda and errors identified during the reconciliation of the company's balance.

Bank Reconciliation Example

To illustrate a bank reconciliation, suppose that Chapman Enterprises maintains an account with Great Plains Bank. At the end of March, Chapman shows a cash balance of $54,567 while Great Plains shows a balance of $49,880. The differences result from the following:

1. Deposits of $6,450 on March 30 and $1,236 on March 31 do not appear on the March 31 bank statement since they had not cleared the bank as of March 31.

   Resolution: These are deposits in transit. Add them to the bank balance.

2. Checks written in late March for $589 (#1987), $900 (#1990), and $1,180 (#1991) do not appear on the March 31 bank statement since they had not cleared the bank as of March 31.

   Resolution: These are outstanding checks. Subtract them from the bank balance.

3. The March 31 bank statement shows the collection of a $550 receivable from one of Chapman's customers and a $50 monthly service fee. Chapman had not recorded either of these two items.

   Resolution: The collection is a credit memorandum. Add it to Chapman's cash balance. The fee is a debit memorandum. Subtract it from Chapman's cash balance.

4. The March 31 bank statement shows that a $220 customer check was returned to the bank for nonsufficient funds (NSF). Chapman had not recorded this item.

   Resolution: The NSF check is a debit memorandum because no cash was received from the customer's check that Chapman deposited earlier. Subtract it from Chapman's cash balance.

5. A check clearing the bank for $400 was erroneously recorded in Chapman's records at $450. The check was written to pay off an open account payable.

   Resolution: Chapman recorded $50 too much for the check. Therefore, Chapman's cash is understated by $50. Add the $50 to Chapman's cash balance.

Credit memorandum An addition to the cash balance on the bank statement for items such as the collection of interest.

Debit memorandum A subtraction from the cash balance on the bank statement for items such as service charges.

Chapman's resulting bank reconciliation is shown as follows. The top half shows the reconciliation of the bank balance while the bottom half shows the reconciliation of the company's book balance.

Chapman Bank Reconciliation March 31		
Balance per bank statement		$49,880
Add deposits in transit:		
March 30	$6,450	
March 31	1,236	7,686
Deduct outstanding checks:		
No. 1987	$ 589	
No. 1990	900	
No. 1991	1,180	2,669
Actual cash balance		$54,897
Balance per company records		$54,567
Add:		
Collection of receivable	$ 550	
Error by Chapman	50	600
Deduct:		
Monthly service charge	$ 50	
NSF check	220	270
Actual cash balance		$54,897

Both reconciliations correctly show an actual cash balance of $54,897. To adjust the company's cash balance to that actual balance, the following entries must be made. Note that each of the four entries comes from the four adjustments made in the reconciliation of the book balance to the actual balance.

Entry 1—Collection of the Receivable
Chapman updates its cash balance to reflect the bank's collection of the receivable.

Mar. 31	Cash	550	
	Accounts Receivable		550
	(To record the collection of a receivable by the bank)		

Assets	=	Liabilities	+	Equity
+550				
−550				

Entry 2—Correction of Error
Chapman corrects the error made when the $400 check was recorded for $450. This requires Chapman to add back to both cash and accounts payable.

Mar. 31	Cash	50	
	Accounts Payable		50
	(To correct error)		

Assets	=	Liabilities	+	Equity
+50		+50		

Entry 3—Monthly Service Charge
Chapman records the monthly service charge as an expense. As a result, both assets and equity decrease.

Mar. 31	Service Charge Expense	50	
	Cash		50
	(To record monthly expense for bank account)		

Assets	=	Liabilities	+	Equity
−50				−50

Entry 4—NSF Check
Chapman records the effect of a check returned for non-sufficient funds by reinstating the receivable and reducing its cash balance. Since the check was no good, the receivable has not yet been collected. Chapman must now try to collect again.

Mar. 31	Accounts Receivable	220	
	Cash		220
	(To reinstate customer receivable)		

Assets	=	Liabilities	+	Equity
+220				
−220				

After these four entries are recorded, the company's cash balance is updated to the actual cash balance.

Petty Cash Funds

Most companies require that all disbursements of cash be made with a check. This is a basic control activity that allows a company to better monitor its cash outflows. However, there are many instances when only a minor amount of cash is needed and the process of writing a check is burdensome. Examples would include postage

for small mailings and the purchase of miscellaneous office supplies. To handle such cases, companies often establish a petty cash fund.

A **petty cash fund** is an amount of cash kept on hand to pay for minor expenditures. While the size and scope of a petty cash fund will vary across companies, its operation will involve the following three activities:

- Establishing the fund
- Making payments from the fund
- Replenishing the fund

Establishing the Fund A petty cash fund is established by writing a check for the amount of the fund, cashing the check, and placing the cash under the care of an employee designated as custodian. A journal entry is then made to record the establishment of the fund.

To illustrate, suppose that on May 1, Barnett Design Group cashes a $100 check to establish a petty cash fund and gives the cash to John Stephens, the custodian. On this date, Barnett would record the following entry.

May 1	Petty Cash		100	
	Cash			100
	(To establish $100 petty cash fund)			
	Assets	= Liabilities	+	Equity
	+100			
	−100			

The entry increases Petty Cash and decreases Cash. Notice that there is no change in total assets. Barnett has simply designated $100 to be used in a petty cash fund. Barnett still has its cash. It has not yet disbursed any cash outside of the company.

Making Payments from the Fund After the fund is established, the cash is used to pay for qualifying expenditures. Payments are usually made in one of two ways. Cash can be taken from the fund to make payment, or employees can seek reimbursement from the fund for payments they have personally made. In either case, the custodian should collect receipts for the use of any cash. As payments are made from petty cash, no journal entries are made. Journal entries are recorded only when the fund is replenished.

Replenishing the Fund As the cash in the fund decreases, the fund must be replenished. To do so, the remaining cash in the fund is counted, and the company cashes a check for the amount that brings the total cash in the fund back to the original balance. The receipts in the fund are then used as documentation for recording expenses.

To illustrate, suppose that on May 31, Stephens examines the petty cash fund and prepares the following report.

Petty Cash Fund Replenishment Report	
Petty cash fund	$100
Less: cash remaining in the fund	15
Cash requested to replenish fund	$ 85
Receipts in the fund:	
Postage	$ 25
Office supplies	47
Miscellaneous	13
Total receipts	$ 85

The report shows that the fund needs $85 to be fully replenished. It also shows that there are receipts totaling $85. As a result, Barnett would cash a check for $85 to replenish the fund and record expenses as follows.

May 31	Postage Expense		25	
	Supplies Expense		47	
	Miscellaneous Expense		13	
	Cash			85
	(To replenish petty cash fund and record various expenses)			
	Assets	= Liabilities	+	Equity
	−85			−25
				−47
				−13

The entry increases the three expense accounts related to the expenditures and decreases the Cash account for the amount of the check. Because Barnett is recording the expenses resulting from fund use, the entry reduces both assets and equity. This same type of entry would be repeated each time the fund is replenished.

Cash Over and Short When a petty cash fund is replenished, the amount of cash needed for replenishment should equal the total amount of receipts. However, this will not always be the case. Sometimes, the custodian will not obtain all receipts or will give incorrect change, resulting in a discrepancy between the cash needed for replenishment and the amount of receipts. In such cases, the discrepancy is charged to an account called Cash Over and Short. Cash Over and Short is a temporary account that can have either a debit or credit balance, depending on the situation. A debit

Petty cash fund An amount of cash kept on hand to pay for minor expenditures.

balance increases expenses while a credit balance decreases expenses.

To illustrate, assume the same facts as previously except that Stephens counts only $13 of cash in the fund before replenishment.

Petty Cash Fund Replenishment Report	
Petty cash fund	$100
Less: Cash remaining in the fund	13
Cash requested to replenish fund	$ 87
Receipts in the fund:	
Postage	$ 25
Office supplies	47
Miscellaneous	13
Total receipts	$ 85

In this case, a check must be written for $87 to fully replenish the fund. However, there is only $85 of receipts. The $2 difference is charged to the Cash Over and Short account as follows.

May 31	Postage Expense	25	
	Supplies Expense	47	
	Miscellaneous Expense	13	
	Cash Over and Short	2	
	Cash		87
	(To replenish petty cash fund and record various expenses)		

Assets	=	Liabilities	+	Equity
−87				−25
				−47
				−13
				− 2

In this entry, the Cash Over and Short account is debited, which indicates an increase to expenses. Most likely, the balance would be reported as a miscellaneous expense.

Cash A medium of exchange.

Cash equivalent Any investment that is readily convertible into cash and has an original maturity of three months or less.

Restricted cash Cash a company has restricted for a specific purpose.

> Cash takes many forms—the coins and dollar bills in your pocket, your checking and savings accounts, even a check from a friend that has not yet been deposited.

LO4 Reporting Cash and Cash Equivalents

At its most basic level, **cash** is a medium of exchange. A general rule is that something is cash if you can deposit it into a bank and readily use it to pay someone. Cash takes many forms—the coins and dollar bills in your pocket, your checking and savings accounts, even a check from a friend that has not yet been deposited. Money orders and travelers checks are other examples of cash.

In addition to these forms of cash, companies often hold investments that are so much like cash that they are deemed to be *equivalent to cash*. A **cash equivalent** is any investment that (1) is readily convertible into a known amount of cash and (2) has an original maturity of three months or less. Examples of cash equivalents can include Treasury bills, certificates of deposit, money market accounts, and commercial paper, as long as they mature in three months or less. Cash equivalents are so much like cash that they are combined with cash for reporting purposes.

Cash and cash equivalents are reported on the balance sheet as a current asset. Most companies report their balances in the first line of the balance sheet. In some cases, though, a company will restrict some of its cash for a specific purpose. For example, a company may designate a certain amount of cash for the payment of interest. To inform investors and creditors of such restrictions, companies will report such **restricted cash** separately from cash and cash equivalents.

An example of such a company is Domino's Pizza. Exhibit 5-2 contains the first two accounts of Domino's 2008 balance sheet as well as the notes to the financial statements addressing the company's cash balances.

As you can see, Domino's has over $45 million in cash and cash equivalents at the end of 2008. It reports even more in restricted cash—almost $79 million. Domino's

Exhibit 5-2 Cash Information from Domino's 2008 Annual Report

Balance Sheet

(in thousands)	2008	2007
Cash and cash equivalents	$45,372	$11,344
Restricted cash	78,871	80,951

Notes to the financial statements

Cash and Cash Equivalents

Cash equivalents consist of highly liquid investments with original maturities of three months or less at the date of purchase. These investments are carried at cost, which approximates fair value.

Restricted Cash

Restricted cash includes $42.0 million of cash held for future interest payments, $26.4 million cash held in interest reserves, $10.0 million cash held for capitalization of entities and $0.5 million of other restricted cash.

notes disclose the purpose of this restriction. The majority of restricted cash is intended for interest payments.

LO5 Analyzing Cash

A company's management of cash is critical to its success. If a company can't keep enough cash, it can quickly run into major problems. The following sections examine the cash position of Papa John's International. The examination will require the cash balance from the company's balance sheet and various items from its statement of cash flows. The required information is found in Exhibit 5-3, excerpted from Papa John's 2008 Annual Report.

Exhibit 5-3 Account Balances from Papa John's 2008 Annual Report

Source	Accounts	2008	2007	2006
Balance Sheet	Cash and cash equivalents	$ 10,987	$ 8,877	
	Total assets	$386,468	$401,817	
Statement of Cash Flows	Net cash provided by operating activities	$ 73,063	$ 61,591	$ 85,601
	Net cash used in investing activities	(26,232)	(55,323)	(53,562)
	Net cash used in financing activities	(44,129)	(10,617)	(41,327)
	Additional investing activity detail:			
	Purchase of property and equipment	(29,271)	(31,148)	(39,352)
	Acquisitions	(183)	(24,983)	(31,943)
	Additional financing activity detail:			
	Proceeds (repayments) from line of credit	(10,500)	37,500	47,500
	Acquisition of Company common stock	(37,697)	(72,871)	(106,292)

HOME DEPOT ANALYSIS

Home Depot's balance sheet in Appendix C reports Cash and Cash Equivalents of $519 million. Looking at the Cash Equivalents paragraph in Home Depot's first note, what types of investments does the company include in cash equivalents?

Home Depot's Cash Equivalents note states that its cash equivalents include high-grade commercial paper, money market funds, and U.S. government agency securities.

Horizontal and Vertical Analyses

A good place to start the analysis of any asset account is horizontal and vertical analyses. Recall from Chapter 2 that horizontal analysis calculates the dollar change in an account balance, defined as the current year balance less the prior year balance, and divides that change by the prior year balance to yield the percentage change. Vertical analysis divides each account balance by a base account, yielding a percentage. The base account for an analysis of cash is total assets. These calculations are summarized as follows:

Horizontal Analysis

$$\text{Dollar change in account balance} = \text{Current year balance} - \text{Prior year balance}$$

$$\text{Percentage change in account balance} = \frac{\text{Dollar change}}{\text{Prior year balance}}$$

Vertical Analysis

$$\text{Percentage} = \frac{\text{Cash}}{\text{Total Assets}}$$

Given Papa John's information in Exhibit 5-3, horizontal and vertical analyses of cash result in the following:

Horizontal Analysis

	Change	Percentage Change
Cash and cash equivalents	$\begin{aligned} 10,987 \\ -8,877 \\ \hline 2,110 \end{aligned}$	$\dfrac{2,110}{8,877} = 23.8\%$

Vertical Analysis

	2008	2007
Cash and cash equivalents	$\dfrac{10,987}{386,468} = 2.8\%$	$\dfrac{8,877}{401,817} = 2.2\%$

The horizontal analysis shows that Papa John's cash balance increased a little over $2 million in 2008, which equals a 23.8% increase over the prior year. The vertical analysis shows that cash made up about 2.8% of total assets in 2008. This was also an increase

MAKING IT REAL

Cash on hand is critical to any successful business. Without available cash, a company cannot pay its bills and obligations.

Recently, companies have begun holding onto their cash as long as possible due to stricter limits related to bank loans. These companies need their cash to finance their day-to-day operations and many are less focused on paying their obligations in a timely manner.

Large companies are in the prime position to take advantage of smaller companies in order to maximize their cash on hand. Large corporations often represent a large percentage of sales for smaller businesses. Therefore, these small businesses are forced to accept delayed payment in order to maintain a supplier relationship with their large customers. At the same time, these large corporations require payment from their customers in a timely manner or the customers will quickly be faced with collection litigation. This double standard is possible because of the wide-reaching power and resources many large corporations possess.

Until credit requirements are again loosened, companies will continue to hoard their available cash for daily operations and will push the limits of making good on their obligations.

© STEPHEN COBURN/SHUTTERSTOCK.COM

Operating activities include those transactions necessary to run the business. This would include selling a product, paying employees, and advertising. According to Exhibit 5-3, Papa John's generated over $73 million in cash from operations during 2008, which is an improvement over 2007.

Investing activities include the buying and selling of revenue-generating assets such as buildings and equipment. Papa John's reports a net cash outflow of over $26 million from investing activities in 2008. The majority of that outflow was due to the purchase of property and equipment.

Financing activities include the raising and repayment of capital through debt and equity. During 2008, Papa John's reports over $44 million in cash outflows from financing activities. This outflow was due mostly to the acquisition of its own common stock and the repayment of a credit facility, which is a form of debt.

With this information, you can conclude that Papa John's cash increased only $2 million during 2008 because it used most of the cash generated through operations to purchase operational assets and to repay investors and creditors. This seems to be a good use of its cash.

Free Cash Flow

A company needs to generate enough cash to pay its bills. It also needs to generate enough to maintain its operational assets and to reward its shareholders with

from the prior year, when cash made up only 2.2% of total assets.

While the preceding analysis shows that Papa John's cash increased during 2008, it does not indicate why cash increased. To find out why, investors and creditors can look at the information on company's statement of cash flows. Recall from Chapter 1 that the statement of cash flows classifies a company's cash inflows and outflows into three main categories—operating activities, investing activities, and financing activities.

HOME DEPOT ANALYSIS

Using Home Depot's financial statements in Appendix C, calculate and interpret (1) horizontal and vertical analyses of cash and (2) free cash flow.

Horizontal Analysis

($519 – $445) / $445 = 16.6%

Vertical Analysis

$519 / $41,164 = 1.3%

The 16.6% horizontal analysis indicates that cash increased during the year by more than 16%. The 1.3% vertical analysis indicates that a very small portion of Home Depot's assets are in the form of cash.

Free Cash Flow

Cash Flows from Operating Activities	$5,528
Less: Capital Expenditures	(1,847)
Less: Dividends	(1,521)
Free Cash Flow	$2,160

Home Depot generated enough cash from operations to fund its capital expenditures and its dividends and to have over $2.2 billion of free cash flow. This amount shows that Home Depot is able to generate cash for other company purposes.

dividends. If a company can generate more cash than it needs for these commitments, it is generating free cash flow.

Free cash flow is the excess cash a company generates beyond what it needs to invest in productive capacity and pay dividends to stockholders. That is, free cash flow is a measure of a company's ability to generate cash for expansion, for other forms of improved operations, or for increased returns to stockholders. While free cash flow can be defined in many ways, the most straightforward definition is as follows:

Free Cash Flow

Cash Flows from Operating Activities
Less: Capital Expenditures
Less: Dividends
Free Cash Flow

The ratio starts with cash flows from operating activities, which is a measure of a company's ability to generate cash from its current operations. Capital expenditures refers to the amount a company spends on fixed assets during the year. Dividends are payments

to stockholders during the year. Each of these items is found on the statement of cash flows.

From the information in Exhibit 5-3, Papa John's free cash flow for the most recent two years is calculated as follows:

Free Cash Flow

	2008	2007
Cash Flows from Operating Activities	$73,063	$61,591
Less: Capital Expenditures	(29,271)	(31,148)
Less: Dividends	0	0
Free Cash Flow	$43,792	$30,443

In each year, Papa John's produces positive free cash flow. And, from the statement of cash flow information in Exhibit 5-3, you can get an idea of how it has used that free cash flow. Notice the large cash outflows in the additional financing activity detail. In the three years reported, the company paid out $37,697, $72,871, and $106,292 for "Acquisition of Company common stock." Papa John's has been buying back its common stock from its shareholders.

Free cash flow The excess cash a company generates beyond what it needs to invest in productive capacity and pay dividends to stockholders.

STUDY TOOLS CHAPTER 5

CHAPTER REVIEW CARD

❏ Learning Objective and Key Concept Reviews

❏ Key Definitions and Formulas

ONLINE (Located at 4ltrpress.cengage.com/acct)

❏ Flash Cards and Crossword Puzzles

❏ Conceptual and Computational Interactive Quizzes

❏ E-Lectures

❏ Static, Algorithmic, and Additional Homework Activities (as directed by your instructor)

EXERCISES

1. Internal Control   LO1, 2

The following items relate to internal control:
1. Sarbanes-Oxley Act of 2002
2. Management's Report on Internal Control
3. *Internal Control—Integrated Framework*
4. Five elements of internal control

Required
Provide a brief explanation of each of these items.

2. Internal Control Activities   LO1, 2

Douglas Company has the following internal control procedures:
1. A pre-numbered shipping document is used for each shipment to customers.
2. The employee who writes checks cannot make entries in the general ledger.
3. An internal auditor reconciles the bank statement each month.
4. The company stores inventory in a room that is monitored by cameras.
5. The manager is required to authorize purchases before they are made by employees.

Required
For each item, identify the internal control principle that is being followed.

3. Internal Control Activities   LO1, 2

Percy Printers uses the following control procedures.
1. Checks are not pre-numbered because the purchasing manager must approve payments before checks are signed.
2. The company's accountant records the receipt of cash and checks and makes deposits at the bank.
3. The employee who works the register reconciles cash to receipts at the end of the day.
4. Employees know that the internal auditor will do a bank reconciliation at the end of each month.
5. Petty cash is kept in a back room but is not monitored during the day.
6. A cashier lets another employee work his assigned register while he helps a customer.

Required
Identify the problem with each internal control procedure.

4. Bank Reconciliation Items   LO3

Luther's Grille is preparing a bank reconciliation for the month of March and needs help with the following items:
1. A customer's $125 check was deposited on March 31 but does not appear on the bank statement.
2. A check clearing for $35 was recorded by Luther's Grille for $53.
3. The bank statement shows a $45 NSF check.
4. A service charge of $50 was reported on the bank statement.
5. The bank statement shows that the bank collected $80 of interest on Luther's Grille's behalf.
6. A charge of $30 for internet banking was reported on the bank statement.
7. A $100 check written on March 31 does not appear on the bank statement.

Required
Identify whether each item is (1) an addition to the book balance, (2) a deduction from the book balance, (3) an addition to the bank balance, or (4) a deduction from the bank balance.

5. Bank Reconciliation Items   LO3

Consider the following two independent situations:
1. A company's January 31 bank reconciliation shows deposits in transit of $1,500. The company's books indicate deposits of $23,000 for the month of February, but the bank statement indicates deposits of $21,750 for February.
2. A company's January 31 bank reconciliation indicates outstanding checks of $2,500. The company's books indicate disbursements of $17,950 for the month of February, but the bank statement shows $18,900 of disbursements for February.

Required
For situation 1, determine deposits in transit at February 28. For situation 2, determine outstanding checks at February 28.

6. Prepare Bank Reconciliation   LO3

McKnight Company's June 30 bank statement shows a balance of $14,750. McKnight's books show a June 30 cash balance of $13,600. McKnight also has the following information:
1. Deposits in transit as of June 30, $1,000
2. Outstanding checks as of June 30, $2,500
3. $100 service charge reported on the bank statement
4. NSF check returned with bank statement, $1,500
5. Interest on note receivable collected by the bank, $1,250

Required
Prepare McKnight's bank reconciliation as of June 30 and prepare any necessary journal entries resulting from the reconciliation. What is the actual cash balance that should be reported on the June 30 balance sheet?

7. Prepare Bank Reconciliation LO3

The following bank statement for the month of May is for El Guapo Industries:

Bank Statement

	Checks	Deposits	Balance
Balance, May 1			12,000
Deposits recorded during May		46,000	
Checks cleared during May	34,000		
NSF checks—Hugo Company	2,500		
Interest collected on note receivable		5,600	
Bank service charge	35		
Service charge for new checks	65		
Balance, May 31			27,000

The following information was taken from the books at El Guapo:

Balance, May 1	$12,000
Deposits during May	48,500
Checks written during May	36,500

Required
Prepare El Guapo's May bank reconciliation and prepare any necessary journal entries resulting from the reconciliation.

8. Petty Cash LO3

On June 1, CWA Enterprises established a petty cash fund for $250. On June 30, the fund's custodian prepares a report showing $76.25 in cash remaining and receipts of $36.50 for postage, $76.45 for office supplies, and $60.80 for miscellaneous items. The custodian presents the report to the company accountant, who replenishes the fund.

Required
Prepare all necessary journal entries for the month of June.

9. Petty Cash LO3

On January 1, Martin Co. establishes a petty cash fund in the amount of $500. On January 31, the fund is replenished. Before replenishment, there was $128.75 remaining in the petty cash drawer and the following receipts: freight-in costs, $103.50; postage, $50; office supplies, $198; and miscellaneous expenses, $22.

Required
Prepare all journal entries necessary to record the establishment of the fund and the end-of-the-month entry to record the replenishment.

10. Reporting Cash and Cash Equivalents LO4

The following is a list of items that may or may not be included in the cash and cash equivalents total on the balance sheet:

1. Cash in checking account
2. Petty cash on hand
3. Shares of Coca-Cola common stock
4. Certificate of deposit maturing in 45 days
5. Certificate of deposit that matures in 120 days
6. One-month Treasury bills
7. Undeposited check from a customer
8. A customer's check returned by the bank and marked NSF

Required
For each of the stated items, indicate whether the item should be included or excluded from the Cash and Cash Equivalents total.

11. Reporting Cash and Cash Equivalents LO4

The CPA Company invested in the following items during November and December of 2010:

November	
60-day Treasury bills	$15,000
Preferred stock	25,500
CD, due date 1/31/2012	34,000
CD, due date 2/1/2011	50,000
December	
Common stock	$60,000
Commercial paper, maturity date of 1/15/2011	90,000

Required
Determine the total of cash and cash equivalents that should be reported on the December 31, 2010, balance sheet, assuming that cash on hand totaled $5,500.

12. Evaluate Cash LO5

In its annual report, Kraft Foods reports the following account balances:

Cash and cash equivalents, 12/31/08	$ 1,244
Cash and cash equivalents, 12/31/07	567
Total assets	63,078
Cash flows from operating activities	4,141
Capital expenditures	1,367
Dividends	1,663

Required
a. Prepare horizontal and vertical analyses of Kraft's cash balance.
b. Calculate free cash flow.

PROBLEMS

13. Prepare Bank Reconciliation LO3

The bank statement for the month of September and the general ledger cash account for September of the Helms Foundation are as follows.

Bank Statement			
Date	**Disbursements**	**Deposits**	**Balance**
Sept. 1			33,450
3	560		32,890
4		4,000	36,890
6	910		35,980
9	150		35,830
13		13,500	49,330
15	900		48,430
16	875		47,555
18	8,000		39,555
19	775		38,780
22	450		38,330
25		6,000	44,330
26	5,000		39,330
27	650		38,680
30		1,000	39,680
30	75		39,605
30	65		39,540

Cash			
Sept. 1	35,980	Sept. 5	150
12	13,500	8	875
24	6,000	9	900
30	9,000	10	8,000
		11	775
		17	5,000
		19	450
		22	650
		23	850
		25	900
		28	1,200

Two checks were outstanding at the end of August: one for $560 and one for $910. There was one deposit in transit at the end of August for $4,000. The last two disbursements on the bank statement were service charges by the bank, and the $1,000 deposit of September 30 represents a note receivable collected by the bank for Helms.

Required
Prepare a bank reconciliation for the month of September, and prepare any journal entries required by Helms at September 30.

14. Evaluate Cash LO5

In their annual reports, Walgreens and CVS report the following account balances:

	Walgreens	CVS
Cash and cash equivalents, 12/31/08	$ 443	$1,352.4
Cash and cash equivalents, 12/31/07	255	1,056.6
Total assets	22,410	60,959.9
Cash flows from operating activities	3,039	3,947.1
Capital expenditures	2,225	2,179.9
Dividends	376	383.0

Required
Calculate and interpret (a) horizontal and vertical analyses of cash balance and (b) free cash flow for both companies. How do the cash positions compare?

CASE

15. Research and Analysis LO1, 4, 5

Access the 2009 annual report for WD-40 Company by clicking on the *Investors* and *Financial Reports* links at www.wd40company.com.

Required
1. Conduct horizontal and vertical analyses of WD-40 Company's cash balance.
2. Examine the company's statement of cash flows and determine the major ways in which the company has been using its cash in the past three years.
3. Examine the Report of Independent Registered Public Accounting Firm and locate PricewaterhouseCoopers' opinion of WD-40 Company's internal control over financial reporting.
4. Based on your answers above, write a paragraph explaining your opinion of WD-40 Company's cash position. Use your answers as supporting facts.

REMEMBER

- All exercises and problems from the text are available online in static and algorithmic versions.
- Additional multiple choice, exercises, problems, and cases are available online in CengageNOW or as an enrichment module that can be customized into this text.

Receivables

Introduction

This chapter examines the accounting for receivables. Specifically, the chapter focuses on how companies account for the recording, the collection, and the noncollection of accounts receivable. After a discussion of how to analyze a company's receivable position, the chapter concludes with the accounting for a second type of receivable, a note receivable.

LO1 Recording and Reporting Accounts Receivable

A receivable represents a company's claim on the assets of another entity. The most common type of receivable is an account receivable. An **account receivable** is an amount owed by a customer who has purchased the company's product or service. Sometimes these receivables are referred to as trade receivables because they arise from the trade of the company.

Recording Accounts Receivable

Receivables are recorded at the time of the sale. To illustrate, suppose that on June 4 Furio Company sells $1,000 of product to a customer on account. Furio would record the revenue and receivable arising from the sale with the following entry. Note that this example ignores the effects on Furio's inventory and cost of goods sold. These will be covered in Chapter 7.

June 4	Accounts Receivable	1,000	
	Sales		1,000
	(To record sale on account)		

Assets	=	Liabilities	+	Equity
+1,000				+1,000

Account receivable An amount owed by a customer who has purchased the company's product or service.

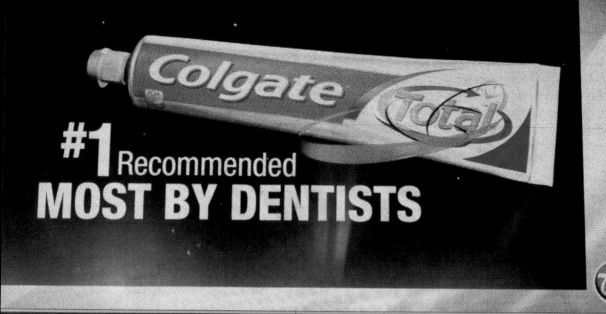

Companies like Colgate-Palmolive commonly sell their products on account. Unfortunately, the receivables that are created are not always collected.

© RICHARD LEVINE/ALAMY

Both assets and equity increase as a result of this sale. When Furio collects the receivable, it will increase its cash and eliminate the receivable.

In some cases, a customer will return a product instead of paying for it, and this affects the accounts receivable balance. To illustrate, suppose that on June 10, the customer returns a $150 product because it is not needed. Furio would record the return with the following entry. Again, the example focuses only on the effect on receivables and ignores the effects on inventory and cost of goods sold.

June 10	Sales Returns and Allowances	150	
	Accounts Receivable		150
	(To record sales return)		

Assets	=	Liabilities	+	Equity
−150				−150

The entry decreases Accounts Receivable for the sales price of the product. However, instead of decreasing the Sales account directly, the entry increases Sales Returns and Allowances. Sales Returns and Allowances is a contra-revenue account, meaning that its balance is subtracted from sales when calculating a company's net sales. Companies use this account to maintain a record of returns each period. Like the Sales account, Sales Returns and Allowances is a temporary account whose balance is zeroed-out at the end of each period.

In addition to returns, companies sometimes provide discounts to customers if they pay within a certain time period. For example, sales are commonly made with terms 2/10, n/30, meaning that customers can receive a 2% discount if they pay within 10 days of the invoice. To illustrate, suppose that Furio grants terms of 2/10, n/30. On June 12 the customer pays the remaining $850 bill. By qualifying for a 2% discount, the customer saves $17 ($850 × 2%) and pays only $833. Furio would record the receipt of payment as follows:

June 12	Cash	833	
	Sales Discounts	17	
	Accounts Receivable		850
	(To record payment)		

Assets	=	Liabilities	+	Equity
+833				−17
−850				

The entry increases Cash for the $833 payment and decreases Accounts Receivable for the full $850 balance. The difference, which equals the discount of $17 for timely payment, goes into the Sales Discounts account. Like Sales Returns and Allowances, the Sales Discounts account is a contra-revenue account that is subtracted from sales when calculating net sales. Companies use this account to maintain a record of discounts each period. It is a temporary account whose balance is zeroed-out at the end of each period.

Reporting Accounts Receivable

Because accounts receivable are expected to be collected quickly, they are classified and reported as current assets. However, companies do not normally collect all of their receivables because customers do not

Net realizable value The amount of cash that a company expects to collect from its total accounts receivable.

> Companies must follow the principle of conservatism and report their accounts receivable at net realizable value.

always pay their bills. Among other reasons, customers have financial hardships, relocate without paying, or simply refuse to pay. As a result, companies must follow the principle of conservatism and report their accounts receivable at net realizable value.

Net realizable value is the amount of cash that a company expects to collect from its total or gross accounts receivable balance. It is calculated by subtracting from gross receivables the amount that a company does not expect to collect. For example, a company that has $1,000 of gross receivables but does not expect to collect $50 of them has receivables with a net realizable value of $950. The amount that a company does not expect to collect is usually called an allowance. How companies estimate and record the allowance will be examined later in the chapter.

To illustrate the reporting of receivables, consider the following receivables balances from Colgate-Palmolive's 2008 balance sheet.

Receivables Balances from Colgate-Palmolive's 2008 Balance Sheet		
(in millions)	2008	2007
Receivables, net of allowances of $47.4 and $50.6	1,591.9	1,680.7

Colgate-Palmolive reports a net realizable value of receivables of approximately $1.7 billion in 2007 and $1.6 billion in 2008. It also states textually that its receivables are *net of allowances of $47.4 and $50.6*. Again, the term *allowances* refers to the amount of receivables that Colgate-Palmolive expects to be uncollectible. At the end of 2007, the company was allowing for $50.6 million of uncollectible receivables. At the end of 2008, the allowance had fallen to $47.4 million.

To demonstrate the relation among gross receivables, the allowance, and net realizable value of receivables, Colgate-Palmolive's numbers are recast as follows. Note that gross accounts receivable is the one value that is not reported by the company.

	2008	2007
Gross accounts receivable	$1,639.3	1,731.3
Less: Allowance	47.4	50.6
Net realizable value	$1,591.9	$1,680.7

	2008	2007
Gross accounts receivable	$512	$465
Less: Allowance	7	5
Net realizable value	$505	$460

While Colgate-Palmolive provides the allowance balance on the face of the balance sheet, many companies do not. They simply report their receivables at "net" and disclose the allowance for uncollectible accounts in their notes to the financial statements. An example is The Clorox Company. The following shows both the company's receivables balances from its 2008 balance sheet and its Revenue Recognition note.

Receivables Balances and Revenue Recognition Note from The Clorox Company's 2008 Balance Sheet and Notes

(amounts in millions)	2008	2007
Receivables, net	$505	$460

Revenue Recognition
The Company provides for an allowance for doubtful accounts based on its historical experience and a periodic review of its accounts receivable. Receivables were presented net of an allowance for doubtful accounts of $7 and $5 at June 30, 2008 and 2007, respectively.

As you can see, The Clorox Company provides the same information as Colgate-Palmolive. You just have to look in a different place to find it. As in the previous example, these numbers are recast to demonstrate how they were calculated.

LO₂ Uncollectible Receivables

As stated in the previous section, most companies are unable to collect all of their accounts receivable. Losses from the inability to collect accounts receivable are recorded in the accounting system as **bad debt expense**.

Because uncollectible accounts are a normal part of any business, bad debt expense is considered an operating expense. It is included in the calculation of net income but is usually combined with other operating expenses on the income statement. Thus, you will rarely find a company's bad debt expense listed separately on its income statement. If you do, it is likely bad news because the amount was large enough to warrant individual reporting.

There are two methods to account for bad debt expense:

- direct write-off method
- allowance method

Each method is discussed in the following sections.

Bad debt expense The expense resulting from the inability to collect accounts receivable.

HOME DEPOT ANALYSIS

Look at Home Depot's Balance Sheet in Appendix C. How can you tell whether the company's receivables are reported at net realizable value?

Home Depot reports the following for receivables: "Receivables, net." The "net" indicates that the reported balance is gross receivables less the allowance balance. The Accounts Receivable paragraph in Note 1 discloses that the allowance balance (Home Depot refers to it as the "valuation reserve") is not material. That is, the balance is small enough that it will not affect the evaluation of Home Depot's reported receivables. Therefore, the actual allowance value is not reported.

Direct Write-off Method

Under the **direct write-off method**, bad debt expense is recorded when a company determines that a receivable is uncollectible and removes it from its records. The receivable is eliminated or "written off" the company's accounting records, and bad debt expense is recorded for the amount of the receivable.

To illustrate, suppose that Thompson Inc. makes a $4,000 credit sale to Brandon LLC during October 2010. In April 2011, Thompson determines that it will be unable to collect from Brandon. Thompson would make the following entries to reflect this activity:

Oct. 2010	Accounts Receivable	4,000	
	Sales		4,000
	(To record sale on account)		

Assets	=	Liabilities	+	Equity
+4,000				+4,000

April 2011	Bad Debt Expense	4,000	
	Accounts Receivable		4,000
	(To record bad debt expense and write off receivable)		

Assets	=	Liabilities	+	Equity
−4,000				−4,000

The first entry records the account receivable created from the sale. Both assets and equity increase as a result.

The second entry increases Bad Debt Expense to reflect the loss incurred from the inability to collect from Brandon. It also decreases Accounts Receivable to remove the receivable from Thompson's records. As a result of this write-off, both assets and equity decrease. All write-offs under the direct method will result in the same basic entry. The only difference will be the dollar amount.

The major advantage of the direct write-off method is its simplicity. When an account is deemed uncollectible,

Direct write-off method Method in which bad debt expense is recorded when a company determines that a receivable is uncollectible and removes it from its records.

Allowance method Method in which companies use two entries to account for bad debt expense—one to estimate the expense and a second to write off receivables.

Because uncollectible accounts are a normal part of any business, **bad debt expense** is considered an operating expense.

it is written off and an expense is recorded. The major disadvantage is that it can violate the matching principle. The matching principle requires that expenses be matched as closely as possible to the period in which the related revenues are recognized. In the preceding example, the revenue is recorded in 2010, but the expense is recorded in 2011. Assuming that Thompson prepares financial statements at the end of December, the expense is not matched to the year of the sale.

Because the direct method violates the matching principle, generally accepted accounting principles prohibit its use. The only exception to this prohibition is when bad debt expense is immaterial to the company. An expense is immaterial if it is small enough that failure to report it properly does not alter decision making. For example, if a company's bad debt expense totals $100 when it has $1 million in sales, failure to follow the matching principle will not likely affect decisions about the company. For most companies, though, bad debt expense is material, so they must use the allowance method.

Allowance Method

While the direct write-off method accounts for uncollectible receivables with one entry, the **allowance method** splits the accounting into two entries—one to record an estimate of bad debt expense and another to write off receivables when they become uncollectible. Both of these entries are described in the following sections.

Recording Bad Debt Expense The purpose of the allowance method is to match the expense from uncollectible receivables to the period in which those receivables were created. To achieve this purpose, a company must record bad debt expense *at the end of each accounting period*. However, at the end of the period, the company does not yet know which receivables will be uncollectible.

Because of this inability to know which specific receivables will turn out to be uncollectible, the allowance

Because the direct method violates the matching principle, generally accepted accounting principles prohibit its use.

method requires a company to set up an "allowance" for uncollectible receivables when recording bad debt expense. That is, instead of writing off specific receivables at year end, a company increases a contra-asset account called Allowance for Bad Debts. **Allowance for bad debts** represents the dollar amount of receivables that a company believes will ultimately be uncollectible. As described earlier, its balance is subtracted from gross receivables to yield the receivables' net realizable value.

To illustrate, suppose that Duncan Sports makes credit sales of $800,000 during 2009. Based on past experience, Duncan estimates that $8,000 of these sales will not be collected. Duncan would therefore make the following entries to record this activity:

During 2009	Accounts Receivable	800,000	
	Sales		800,000
	(To record sales on account)		

Assets	=	Liabilities	+	Equity
+800,000				+800,000

End of 2009	Bad Debt Expense	8,000	
	Allowance for Bad Debts		8,000
	(To record bad debt expense)		

Assets	=	Liabilities	+	Equity
−8,000				−8,000

The first entry increases Accounts Receivable and Sales for the credit sales during the year. This increases both assets and equity. The second entry increases both Bad Debt Expense and Allowance for Bad Debts by $8,000. This effectively matches the expense of future uncollectible receivables to 2009 sales. It also reduces Duncan's net realizable value of receivables by $8,000 because it is now allowing for $8,000 of those receivables to be uncollectible. As a result, both assets and equity decrease.

The same basic entry will be recorded each time bad debt expense is estimated under the allowance method. The only difference will be the amount of the estimate, which will depend on circumstances and the estimation method a company uses. Methods of estimating bad debt expense are covered later in the chapter.

Recording a Write-Off Regardless of the method used to account for uncollectible receivables, a company must write off a receivable when it is deemed to be uncollectible. Under the direct write-off method, the company records bad debt expense at the time of the write-off. However, under the allowance method, bad debt expense has already been estimated and recorded and an allowance balance created for uncollectible receivables. Therefore, instead of increasing bad debt expense at the time of the write-off, the company reduces the balance in the allowance account.

To illustrate, suppose that Duncan Sports determines in 2010 that a $2,500 receivable from William Johnson is uncollectible and decides to write it off the books. Duncan would make the following entry:

2010	Allowance for Bad Debts	2,500	
	Accounts Receivable		2,500
	(To record write-off)		

Assets	=	Liabilities	+	Equity
−2,500				
+2,500				

The entry decreases Accounts Receivable and decreases an equal amount of Allowance for Bad Debts. Note that the entry has no effect on total assets or net income. More specifically, the entry has no effect on Duncan's net realizable value of receivables. This is because both the asset account and the contra-asset account are decreasing by the same amount, thereby offsetting one another. Duncan now knows that Johnson will not pay, but Duncan had already allowed for that possibility. Therefore, Duncan's expected cash receipts are unchanged. This will be the case for all write-offs under the allowance method.

Recording the Recovery of a Write-Off Occasionally, a company will collect a receivable that it had previously written off. For example, suppose that Johnson pays his bill in full later during 2010. When this payment occurs, the following two entries are made:

> **Allowance for bad debts** The dollar amount of receivables that a company believes will ultimately be uncollectible.

The allowance method requires a company to estimate its bad debt expense and to set up an "allowance" for uncollectible receivables.

2010	Accounts Receivable	2,500	
	Allowance for Bad Debts		2,500
	(To reverse the original write-off)		
	Cash	2,500	
	Accounts Receivable		2,500
	(To collect the receivable)		

Assets	=	Liabilities	+	Equity
+2,500				
−2,500				

The first entry simply reverses the original entry writing off the receivable. The second entry records the collection of cash and the reduction of the receivable.

Percentage-of-sales approach Method that estimates bad debt expense as a percentage of sales.

Notice that once again there is no effect on total assets by either of these two entries.

LO3 Estimating Bad Debt Expense

The previous section demonstrated how to record bad debt expense under the allowance method. This section demonstrates how to estimate the amount of bad debt expense to be recorded.

When estimating bad debt expense companies may use one of two different approaches.

- percentage-of-sales approach
- percentage-of-receivables approach

Both approaches use information such as past experience, industry norms or trends, and current customer credit ratings to make the estimate as accurate as possible. Each approach is discussed in the following sections.

Percentage-of-Sales Approach

Under the **percentage-of-sales approach**, bad debt expense is a function of a company's sales. It is calculated by multiplying sales for the period by some percentage

MAKING IT REAL

Most companies have a good idea of how long it takes them to collect their receivables. However, sometimes shocks to the economy can cause significant delays in collections. Take the recent recession and economic downturn. Customer payments have slowed significantly. The reduced cash flow is especially damaging to small businesses that might not have sufficient cash on hand to pay their own suppliers. This turns into a never-ending cycle where buyers and sellers are both past due on their bills and reduces the cash flow to the entire economy.

To combat this, companies are being forced to alter their collections policies. Traditionally, buyers with delinquent accounts would have their credit slashed or cancelled. Now, companies are considering alternative approaches which do not place undue pressure on the customer in the hopes of maintaining an agreeable relationship. The CEO of The UnitedCompanies Inc., a Houston-based company, began making personal calls to buyers with accounts more than 60 days past due. Some companies stop shipping to buyers until their accounts are made current. Others are implementing technology into the collections process to facilitate faster and easier payment.

The bottom line is that delayed collection of accounts receivable affects both the business and the customer. Longer collection cycles mean that businesses have a diminished cash flow and have to struggle to make do with less cash on hand. Without timely collections, many businesses are put in a situation where they might face delinquency with their own vendors or even bankruptcy from lack of liquidity.

© SEAN PRIOR/SHUTTERSTOCK.COM

set by the company. For example, suppose a company with $250,000 of sales in 2010 estimates that it will not collect 4% of those sales. The estimate for bad debt expense at the end of 2010 would be $10,000 ($250,000 × 4%). The entry to record the estimate is shown below.

End of 2010	Bad Debt Expense	10,000	
	Allowance for Bad Debts		10,000
	(To record bad debt expense)		

Assets	=	Liabilities	+	Equity
−10,000				−10,000

The advantages of this approach are its simplicity and the fact that it results in very good matching. Bad debt expense for a period is primarily a function of sales for that period. The main disadvantage is that no consideration is given to the resulting balance in the Allowance for Bad Debts account. It is simply the existing balance plus the current estimate. Since the allowance account is used to compute net realizable value, the percentage-of-sales approach results in a less meaningful net realizable value of receivables.

Percentage-of-Receivables Approach

Under the **percentage-of-receivables approach**, bad debt expense is a function of a company's receivables balance. It is calculated in two steps. The first step is to calculate what the balance in the Allowance for Bad Debts account should be. This is accomplished by multiplying accounts receivable by a percentage set by the company. The second step is to adjust the allowance account to that calculated balance. The amount of the adjustment is bad debt expense for the period.

To illustrate, suppose that a company has a receivables balance of $24,000 at the end of 2010. Based on past experience, the company expects that 2% of its receivables balance will be uncollectible. As a result, the balance in the allowance account at year end should be 2% of receivables, or a $480 credit balance ($24,000 × 2%). The next step is to make the adjustment.

Since the allowance method for bad debts relies on estimates, a company's allowance balance prior to adjustment can have either a debit or credit balance. A debit balance means that the company has experienced greater write-offs during the year than expected. A credit balance indicates that write-offs have been less than expected. Whether the balance is a debit or credit does not require a company to correct its bad debt expense from the prior year. However, it does affect the adjustment for the current year.

To illustrate, assume that the allowance account has a $100 credit balance prior to adjustment. To get the balance to a $480 credit requires a $380 credit entry. Therefore, bad debt expense for the period is $380. This is illustrated as follows.

Allowance for Bad Debts

	100	Existing balance
	380	Adjustment required = Bad Debt Expense
	480	Desired balance ($24,000 × 2%)

End of 2010	Bad Debt Expense	380	
	Allowance for Bad Debts		380
	(To record bad debt expense)		

Assets	=	Liabilities	+	Equity
−380				−380

In contrast, assume that the allowance account has a $50 debit balance prior to adjustment. In that case, the necessary adjustment is a $530 credit entry. Therefore, bad debt expense for the period is $530. This is illustrated as follows.

Allowance for Bad Debts

50		Existing balance
	530	Adjustment required = Bad Debt Expense
	480	Desired balance ($24,000 × 2%)

End of 2010	Bad Debt Expense	530	
	Allowance for Bad Debts		530
	(To record bad debt expense)		

Assets	=	Liabilities	+	Equity
−530				−530

The major advantage of the percentage-of-receivables approach is that it results in a very meaningful net realizable value. This is because the allowance account is determined as a set percentage of receivables. The disadvantage is that it does not match expenses as well as the percentage-of-sales approach. This is because the adjustment necessary is a function of both the set percentage and a company's prior experience with write-offs. As a result, current expenses are affected by prior year experiences.

Aging of Accounts Receivable Many companies use a more refined version of the percentage-of-receivables approach. Recognizing that receivables

> **Percentage-of-receivables approach**
> Method that estimates bad debt expense as a percentage of receivables.

become less collectible as they get older, companies often prepare aging schedules for their receivables. An **aging schedule** is a listing and summation of accounts receivable by their ages. Normally, receivables that are outstanding for 30 days or less are considered current and are grouped together. Receivables outstanding longer than 30 days are considered past due and are grouped together in 30-day increments. Companies then apply increasing uncollectible percentages to older receivables.

To illustrate, suppose that SC Works prepares an aging schedule at the end of 2010 as shown in Exhibit 6-1. SC Works reports $66,600 of receivables and breaks them into Current and several categories of Past Due. Each category is assigned an expected percentage of uncollectable receivables that rises as the age of the receivables increases. The necessary allowance balance is then calculated by summing the totals from each category.

> Recognizing that receivables become less collectible as they get older, companies often prepare **aging schedules** for their receivables.

an aging schedule provides a more accurate estimate of the allowance for bad debts and therefore a better estimate of bad debt expense. But an aging schedule has another benefit. It is a good internal control activity.

Recall from Chapter 5 that control activities are one of the five elements of a good internal control system. They are procedures put in place to assist companies in operating and reporting efficiently and effectively. Keeping track

Exhibit 6-1 Aging Schedule of Accounts Receivable—SC Works

| Customer | Current | Number of Days Past Due | | | | Total |
		1–30	31–60	61–90	Over 90	
Ellis Manufacturing			$4,100			$ 4,100
Clayburn Company					$2,400	$ 2,400
MAG, Incorporated				$2,750		$ 2,750
Others	$44,450	$10,400	$1,000	$1,200	$ 300	$57,350
Totals	$44,450	$10,400	$5,100	$3,950	$2,700	$66,600
* % Uncollectible	1%	3%	15%	30%	50%	
Allowance Balance	$ 4,450	$ 312	$ 765	$1,185	$1,350	$ 8,062

Assuming that SC Works has a credit balance of $870 in the allowance account prior to recording bad debt expense, the company would make the following entry to record bad debt expense.

Allowance for Bad Debts

	870	Existing balance
	7,192	Adjustment required = Bad Debt Expense
	8,062	Desired balance

End of 2010	Bad Debt Expense	7,192	
	Allowance for Bad Debts		7,192
	(To record bad debt expense)		

Assets	=	Liabilities	+	Equity
−7,192				−7,192

As you can see, the entry to record bad debt expense is the same as previously described. The difference is that

Aging schedule A listing of accounts receivable by their ages.

of receivables and their ages helps meet these objectives. For example, an aging schedule provides the information a company needs to pursue its receivables effectively. It also provides information for future credit decisions. A company may hesitate to provide credit to customers who have past due receivables.

LO4 Analyzing Accounts Receivable

Any investor, creditor, or manager of a company should be interested in how well a company manages its accounts receivable. Because a receivable is an uncollected sale, the main question that should be asked of a company is how well it collects its receivables. In general, better collection means better management of receivables.

The following sections examine how well Colgate-Palmolive collects its receivables. The examination

An aging schedule provides a more accurate estimate of the allowance for bad debts and therefore a better estimate of bad debt expense.

will require information from the company's balance sheet and its income statement. The required information is found in Exhibit 6-2, excerpted from Colgate-Palmolive's 2008 Annual Report.

Exhibit 6-2 Account Balances from Colgate-Palmolive's 2008 Annual Report

Source	Accounts	2008	2007
Income Statement	Net Sales	$15,329.9	$13,789.7
Balance Sheet	Net Accounts Receivable	$ 1,591.9	$ 1,680.7
	Allowance for Bad Debts	47.4	50.6
	Total assets	9,979.3	10,112.0

Horizontal and Vertical Analyses

A good place to start the analysis of accounts receivable is with horizontal and vertical analyses. Recall from Chapter 2 that horizontal analysis calculates the dollar change in an account balance, defined as the current year balance less the prior year balance, and divides that change by the prior year balance to yield the percentage change. Vertical analysis divides each account balance by a base account, yielding a percentage. The base account is total assets for balance sheet accounts and net sales or total revenues for income statement accounts. These calculations are summarized as follows:

Horizontal Analysis

$$\text{Dollar change in account balance} = \text{Current year balance} - \text{Prior year balance}$$

$$\text{Percentage change in account balance} = \frac{\text{Dollar change}}{\text{Prior year balance}}$$

Vertical Analysis

	For the Balance Sheet	For the Income Statement
Percentage =	$\dfrac{\text{Account Balance}}{\text{Total Assets}}$	$\dfrac{\text{Account Balance}}{\text{Net Sales or Revenue}}$

Given Colgate-Palmolive's financial information in Exhibit 6-2, horizontal and vertical analyses of accounts receivable and sales result in the calculations shown below. Note that the net realizable value of receivables, as reported on the balance sheet, is used in the calculations.

The calculations show slight improvement in Colgate-Palmolive's receivables position. Horizontal analysis shows that the company's receivables balance decreased $88.8 million, or 5.3%, in 2008. Horizontal analysis of sales shows growth in sales of $1,540 million, or 11.2%, during the year, so it does not appear that receivables are lower because sales have fallen. Vertical analysis shows that receivables as a percentage of assets were down slightly, from 16.6% in 2007 to 16.0% in 2008.

For comparison purposes, the 2008 horizontal and vertical analyses of The Clorox Company are listed on the next page. The calculations show that The Clorox

Horizontal Analysis

	Change	Percentage Change
Accounts receivable	$\begin{array}{r} 1,591.9 \\ -1,680.7 \\ \hline (88.8) \end{array}$	$\dfrac{(88.8)}{1,680.7} = -5.3\%$
Net sales	$\begin{array}{r} 15,329.9 \\ -13,789.7 \\ \hline 1,540.2 \end{array}$	$\dfrac{1540.2}{13,789.7} = 11.2\%$

Vertical Analysis

	2008		2007	
Accounts receivable	$\dfrac{1,591.9}{9,979.3}$	= 16.0%	$\dfrac{1,680.7}{10,112.0}$	= 16.6%
Net sales	$\dfrac{15,329.9}{15,329.9}$	= 100%	$\dfrac{13,789.7}{13,789.7}$	= 100%

Because a receivable is an uncollected sale, the main question that should be asked of a company is how well it collects its receivables.

		Horizontal Analysis	Vertical Analysis
Accounts receivable	Colgate	(5.3%)	16.0%
	Clorox	9.8%	10.7%
Net sales	Colgate	11.2%	100%
	Clorox	8.8%	100%

Company maintains less receivables as a percentage of assets, but also that its change in receivables more closely mirrors the change in sales.

Receivables Turnover Ratio

The preceding analysis indicates that Colgate-Palmolive appears to be managing its receivables well. Another means to assess the management of receivables is to calculate a company's receivables turnover ratio. The **receivables turnover ratio** compares a company's credit sales during a period to its average receivables balance during that period. It is calculated as follows:

$$\text{Receivables Turnover Ratio} = \frac{\text{Credit Sales}}{\text{Average Receivables}}$$

Where average receivables is:

$$\frac{\text{Beginning Receivables} + \text{Ending Receivables}}{2}$$

Because the ratio divides credit sales during a period by the average receivables balance during the period, it indicates how many times during a period a company generates and collects receivables. In general, companies want this ratio to be higher rather than lower because a higher ratio indicates that the company collects, or turns over, its receivables faster.

Colgate-Palmolive's 2008 receivables turnover ratio is calculated as follows from the information in Exhibit 6-2. Note that net sales is used instead of net credit sales. While net credit sales would be preferable, it is infrequently reported by companies, so net sales is used as a substitute.

$$\frac{15,329.9}{(1,591.9 + 1,680.7)/2} = 9.4$$

The 9.4 ratio indicates that Colgate-Palmolive's 2008 sales were 9.4 times its average receivables balance. In other words, the company was able to generate and collect its receivables balance over nine times in 2008.

Because the receivables turnover ratio is sometimes difficult to interpret, it is often converted into the days-in-receivables ratio. The **days-in-receivables ratio** divides the receivables turnover ratio into 365 days to express, in days, how long it takes a company to generate and collect its receivables. Thus, the days-in-receivables ratio is calculated as follows:

$$\text{Days-in-Receivables Ratio} = \frac{365}{\text{Receivables Turnover Ratio}}$$

$$\frac{365}{9.4} = 38.8$$

A ratio of 38.8 indicates that it takes Colgate-Palmolive about 39 days to generate and collect the average receivable. Whether this is good or bad requires some comparison. In the prior year, Colgate-Palmolive's ratio was 42.4. The Clorox Company's 2008 ratio was 33.5 days. So, you can conclude that Colgate-Palmolive is getting better at collecting its receivables, but it is not quite as efficient as The Clorox Company.

Allowance Ratio

One additional ratio that is useful in analyzing a company's management of receivables is the allowance ratio. The **allowance ratio** compares the allowance account to gross accounts receivable to determine the percentage of receivables that are expected to be uncollectible in the future. It is calculated as follows:

$$\text{Allowance Ratio} = \frac{\text{Allowance for Bad Debts}}{\text{Gross Accounts Receivable}}$$

Where gross accounts receivable is:

Net Accounts Receivable + Allowance for Bad Debts

Receivables turnover ratio A comparison of credit sales to receivables that measures a company's ability to generate and collect receivables.

Days-in-receivables ratio A conversion of the receivables turnover ratio that expresses a company's ability to generate and collect receivables in days.

Allowance ratio A comparison of the allowance account to receivables that measures the percentage of receivables that are expected to be uncollectible in the future.

Using Home Depot's financial statements in Appendix C, calculate and interpret (1) horizontal and vertical analyses of accounts receivable and sales, (2) receivables turnover and days-in-receivables ratios, and (3) the allowance ratio.

(1) Horizontal Analysis

Accounts Receivable: $($972 − $1,259)/$1,259 = -22.8\%$

Sales: $($71,288 − $77,349)/$77,349 = -7.8\%$

Vertical Analysis

Accounts Receivable: $972/$41,164 = 2.4\%$

Sales: $71,288/$71,288 = 100\%$

The −22.8% horizontal analysis indicates that receivables decreased during the year by almost 23%. With the company's decrease in sales of 7.8%, a decrease in receivables is not alarming. The 2.4% vertical analysis indicates that a very small portion of Home Depot's assets are in the form of receivables.

(2) Receivables Turnover Ratio:

$$71,288/[($972 + $1,259)/2] = 63.9$$

Days-in-Receivables: $365/63.9 = 5.7$ days

The 63.9 receivables turnover ratio indicates that Home Depot generates and collects its receivables very quickly—about 64 times each year. The days-in-receivables ratio of 5.7 also indicates that receivables are collected rapidly. We should note here that Home Depot sells very little merchandise on credit. Rather, it accepts third-party credit cards, which pay Home Depot each day for the charges made by cardholders. This helps the company to keep receivables balances extremely low given its large sales volume.

(3) Allowance Ratio: Not applicable

In its first note, Home Depot discloses that its "valuation reserve related to accounts receivable was not material..." This means that Home Depot's allowance balance is effectively zero, which yields an allowance ratio of 0%. Home Depot expects to collect virtually all of its outstanding accounts receivable.

A higher ratio indicates that a company expects more receivables to be uncollectible. In general, a company would want this ratio to be as low as possible. Colgate-Palmolive's allowance ratio for 2008 and 2007 is calculated as follows from the information in Exhibit 6-2.

2008		2007	
$\dfrac{47.4}{1,591.9 + 47.4}$ =	2.9%	$\dfrac{50.6}{1,680.7 + 50.6}$ =	2.9%

For 2007 and 2008, Colgate-Palmolive expected that it would not collect 2.9% of its receivables, or about 3 cents per dollar of receivables. For comparison purposes, The Clorox Company's 2008 ratio was 1.4%. Again, like the receivables turnover ratio, this shows that Colgate-Palmolive collects its receivables at a high rate, but not as high as The Clorox Company.

LO5 Notes Receivable

An account receivable is an amount owed by a customer who has purchased the company's product or service. Sometimes, because of a customer's poor credit rating or because of the size of the transaction, a company will enter into a more formal agreement with the customer beyond a normal account receivable. This is often accomplished through a promissory note.

A **promissory note** is a written promise to pay a specific sum of money on demand or at some specific date in the future. Promissory notes can be used to formalize

> **Promissory note** A written promise to pay a specific sum of money on demand or at some specific date in the future.

© YURI ARCURS/SHUTTERSTOCK.COM

Promissory notes can be used to formalize a receivable or to loan money to another entity.

a receivable or to loan money to another entity. In most cases, promissory notes require the payment of both principal and interest. The company that will receive the principal and interest is called the *payee*. The customer or borrower who will pay the interest and principal is called the *maker* of the note. This chapter focuses on the accounting of the payee.

When a company accepts a promissory note, it has a **note receivable**. Like other assets, a note receivable is reported on the balance sheet. However, its classification depends on its terms. If the note is due within a year, it is classified as a current asset. Otherwise, it is a non-current asset.

Accounting for a note receivable usually requires entries to record the following:

- Issuance of the note

- Interest earned on the note

- Collection of the note

To illustrate, suppose that on October 1, 2009, Bentonville Machine Works sells a lathe to Tilbury Designs for $12,000. Bentonville accepts a six-month, 8% promissory note from Tilbury for payment. The note stipulates that Bentonville will receive both principal and interest from Tilbury on March 31, 2010.

Recording the Note

A note receivable is recorded at its face value, which is $12,000 in this example. Therefore, Bentonville would record the sale of the lathe and the resulting note receivable as follows:

Oct. 1 2009	Note Receivable	12,000	
	Sales		12,000
	(To record sale in exchange for a promissory note)		

Assets	=	Liabilities	+	Equity
+12,000				+12,000

Note receivable An asset created when a company accepts a promissory note.

In this entry, Bentonville increases Note Receivable to reflect the receipt of the promissory note and increases Sales to reflect the inflow of assets resulting from the sale. As a result, both assets and equity increase. As in previous examples in this chapter, the effects on inventory and cost of goods sold are ignored.

Recording Interest

Most promissory notes require that the maker pay interest to the payee. The amount of interest is a function of (1) the principal or face value of the note, (2) the annual interest rate, and (3) the length of time the note is outstanding. The calculation is as follows:

> Interest = Principal × Annual Rate of Interest × Time Outstanding

In this example, Bentonville's note receivable is outstanding for only six months. As a result, interest of 8% will be charged for six of the twelve months of the year. Therefore, interest over the life of the note is $480, calculated as follows.

$$\text{Interest} = \text{Principal} \times \text{Annual Rate of Interest} \times \text{Time Outstanding}$$
$$= \$12,000 \times .08 \times 6/12 \text{ months}$$
$$= \$480$$

According to the calculation, Bentonville will receive $480 of interest at the maturity of the note. However, the revenue recognition principle requires companies to record interest revenue when it is earned, even if cash will not be received until later. Assuming that Bentonville has a fiscal year-end prior to the maturity of the note, it must make an adjusting journal entry to record interest earned during the year. Recall from Chapter 4 that such an entry is an accrual adjusting entry.

To illustrate, suppose that Bentonville prepares financial statements on December 31. Bentonville has not yet received any interest payment from Tilbury because payment is not required until March 31, 2010. However, Bentonville has earned three months of interest, calculated as follows.

$$\begin{aligned} \text{Interest earned} &= \text{Principal} \times \text{Annual Rate of} \\ &\quad\text{Interest} \times \text{Time Outstanding} \\ &= \$12{,}000 \times .08 \times 3/12 \text{ months} \\ &= \$240 \end{aligned}$$

On December 31, Bentonville would record this interest revenue as follows.

Dec. 31 2009	Interest Receivable	240	
	Interest Revenue		240
	(To record interest earned on note)		
	Assets = Liabilities + Equity		
	+240 +240		

This entry increases Interest Receivable to reflect the additional receivable Bentonville now has from Tilbury. Bentonville will report this receivable on its balance sheet until the interest is paid in March 2010. The entry also increases Interest Revenue to reflect the inflow of assets attributable to the year 2009. As a result, both assets and equity increase.

Collecting the Note

The collection of a note receivable is much like the collection of an account receivable. When a note is collected, the note receivable is decreased and cash is increased. However, when a note receivable requires interest to be paid, the collection of the note often includes the collection of interest as well. This is the case for Bentonville.

On March 31, 2010, Bentonville collects cash and interest from Tilbury. The total interest over the six months Bentonville held the note is $480. The principal is $12,000. Therefore, Bentonville receives $12,480 in cash, recorded as follows:

Mar. 31 2010	Cash	12,480	
	Interest Receivable		240
	Note Receivable		12,000
	Interest Revenue		240
	(To record collection of note)		
	Assets = Liabilities + Equity		
	+12,480 +240		
	−12,000		
	−240		

This entry has four parts. First, the entry increases Cash for the amount of cash collected by Bentonville. Second, it decreases Interest Receivable to eliminate the asset that was created by the December 31 adjusting entry. Third, the entry decreases Note Receivable by its principal value because the note has been collected and is no longer outstanding. Finally, the entry increases Interest Revenue for the three months of interest (January, February, and March) earned in the current period ($12,000 × 8% × 3/12). This interest revenue will be reported on Bentonville's 2010 income statement. The result of the entry is a net increase to assets of $240 and an increase to equity of $240. If this seems low to you, remember that equity was increased substantially when the sale was made and the note created. When Bentonville collects the note, it is simply exchanging one asset for another. The net $240 increase to assets and equity results from the interest earned during the three months of the current year.

STUDY TOOLS
CHAPTER 6

CHAPTER REVIEW CARD
- ❑ Learning Objective and Key Concept Reviews
- ❑ Key Definitions and Formulas

ONLINE (Located at 4ltrpress.cengage.com/acct)
- ❑ Flash Cards and Crossword Puzzles
- ❑ Conceptual and Computational Interactive Quizzes
- ❑ E-Lectures
- ❑ Static, Algorithmic, and Additional Homework Activities (as directed by your instructor)

EXERCISES

1. Recording Accounts Receivable LO1

On February 4, Campbell Company sells inventory to a customer for $6,000. Terms of the sale are 1/15, net 30. On February 10, the customer returns $500 of merchandise. The customer pays on February 15.

Required
Prepare all journal entries to record the merchandise sale, its return, and the collection of the receivable. Ignore any effects on inventory or cost of goods sold.

2. Reporting Accounts Receivable LO1

A company reports the following for accounts receivable:

	2010	2009
Accounts receivable, net of allowance of $234 and $267	$5,432	$4,905

Required
For each year, determine the company's total or gross accounts receivable, net realizable value of accounts receivable, and allowance for bad debts balance. What does net realizable value represent?

3. Uncollectible Receivables LO2

Carnes Inc. reported the following information in its latest annual report:

Allowance for bad debts, beginning balance	$1,775
Bad debt expense for the year	325
Accounts receivable written off during the year	256

Required
Determine which method of accounting for bad debts Carnes uses, record all journal entries associated with the allowance account for the year, and determine the ending balance in the allowance account.

4. Accounting for Uncollectible Receivables LO2

The following information pertains to Godwin Motors, who uses the allowance method for receivables:

	2010	2009
Gross receivables	$ 648,750	$ 580,498
Allowance for bad debts	33,560	24,650
Net revenues	7,555,000	6,325,000

Required
a. Assuming that Godwin Motors recorded bad debt expense of $25,600 in 2010, what amount of accounts receivable were written off in 2010?
b. Prepare the journal entries to record the 2010 bad debt expense and the 2010 write-offs of uncollectible accounts.
c. Assuming that Godwin made all sales on credit, what amount of cash was collected in 2010?

5. Uncollectible Receivables LO2, 3

At December 31, Vicki's Designers had gross accounts receivable of $346,000. Historically, Vicki's Designers has estimated bad debt expense as 5% of gross receivables.

Required
a. Calculate bad debt expense for the year, assuming that the allowance account currently has (1) a credit balance of $5,000 and (2) a debit balance of $1,200.
b. Assume that on December 30, an account receivable of $2,000 was deemed uncollectible and written off. Prepare the journal entry to record this event. What effect does this have on (1) 2010 net income and (2) the net realizable value of receivables?

6. Estimating Bad Debt Expense LO3

Buster's Furniture provides the following information for the year:

Net credit sales for the year	$985,750
Accounts receivable at year-end	450,000
Allowance for bad debts at year-end	18,000 credit

Required
Estimate bad debt expense for 2010 as (a) 5% of accounts receivable and (b) 2% of net credit sales, and discuss why Buster's Furniture might choose one method over the other.

7. Aging Schedule for Accounts Receivable LO3

Outdoor Living has the following accounts receivable at year end, broken down by age:

Age	Amount
Current	$150,000
One month overdue	40,000
Two months overdue	18,000
Three months overdue	8,000

Prior experience has shown that the company will probably collect 95% of its current receivables and that the collection percentage will fall by 15% for each additional month an account receivable remains outstanding past its due date.

Required
Develop an estimate of Outdoor Living's allowance account balance and prepare the journal entry for bad debt expense, assuming that the allowance has an existing (a) $4,000 credit balance and (b) $1,000 debit balance.

8. Analyzing Receivables LO4

The following information was taken from the annual report of SC Enterprises:

	2010	2009
Sales	$240,000	$250,000
Total assets	840,000	825,000
Accounts receivable	125,000	78,000

Required
Prepare and interpret horizontal and vertical analyses of all three accounts. Should the owners of the business be concerned?

9. Analyzing Receivables   LO4
The following information pertains to Skelton Resorts:

Credit sales	$450,000
Net accounts receivable, beginning	63,000
Net accounts receivable, ending	54,000
Allowance for bad debts, ending	5,000

Required
Compute Skelton's receivables turnover ratio, days-in-receivables ratio, and allowance ratio.

10. Recording Notes Receivable   LO5
On April 1, 2010, Fly Corporation accepted cash of $15,000 and a six-month, 6%, $75,000 interest-bearing note from Gonzo, Inc., as settlement of an account receivable. Fly has a fiscal year-end of June 30, and Gonzo paid the principal and the interest on time.

Required
Identify the note's maker and payee and prepare all appropriate journal entries from the acceptance of the note to the maturity date.

11. Interest on Notes Receivable   LO5
Consider the following independent scenarios.

On 9/1, a company accepts a $10,000, 5%, 8-month note receivable.
On 3/1, a company accepts a $20,000, 8%, 6-month note receivable.
On 6/15, a company accepts a $15,000, 10%, 4-month note receivable.

Required
Assuming a December 31 year-end, calculate current-year interest revenue for each scenario.

PROBLEMS

12. Accounts Receivable Entries   LO1, 2, 3
During 2011, CE Electronics entered into the following transactions:

Sales on account	$1,400,000
Collections of credit sales	1,225,000
Wrote off accounts deemed uncollectible	20,000
Received payments on accounts previously written off	7,500

On its 2010 balance sheet, CE reported gross accounts receivable of $707,000 and an allowance account of $43,000.

Required
Prepare all journal entries to record each of the transactions that occurred in 2011 and the journal entry to record bad debt expense at the end of 2011, assuming that 7% of accounts receivable at the end of 2011 are uncollectible.

13. Comparing Methods for Uncollectible Receivables   LO2, 3
The following data pertains to the operations of Knight Corporation for 2010:

Net credit sales	$725,000
Net income (before bad debt expense)	135,000
Write-offs of uncollectible accounts	17,500
Estimated uncollectible percentage of net credit sales	3%

The controller is trying to decide which method of accounting for bad debts to use. The company is attempting to maximize its net income to meet projected figures. The bad debt expense is material to the company's financial statements.

Required
a. Calculate bad debt expense for 2010 under the direct write-off method and the allowance method.
b. Compute net income under both methods (assume a tax bracket of 30%).
c. Does Knight have the option of which method to use under GAAP?

14. Analyzing Receivables   LO4
The following information was taken from the annual reports of two high-end jewelry retailers:

	Company A	Company B
Net accounts receivable, 2010	$ 584,000	$ 460,000
Net accounts receivable, 2009	505,000	398,000
Net revenues, 2010	2,425,000	2,195,000
Net revenues, 2009	2,200,000	1,500,000

Required
a. Calculate the 2010 receivables turnover ratio for both companies.
b. Compare the two companies. Which one is more efficient with their receivables?
c. What other methods and factors would one consider when evaluating receivables? What one other comparison demonstrates one company's efficiency over the other?

CASE

15. Research and Analysis   LO1, 4
Access the 2008 annual report for Under Armour, Inc. by clicking on the *Investor Relations, Financials,* and *Annual Report & Proxy* links at www .underarmour.com.

Required

1. Examine the company's income statement and balance sheet and conduct horizontal and vertical analyses of net revenues and accounts receivable.
2. Examine the company's Accounts Receivable note. What is the company's 2008 balance in its allowance for bad debts account? What factors are considered when estimating the balance? How often is the balance reviewed? What likelihood does the company require before it writes off a receivable?
3. With the gathered information, calculate the company's receivables turnover and days-in-receivables ratios for 2008 and the company's allowance ratio for 2008 and 2007.
4. Based on your answers above, write a paragraph explaining your opinion of Under Armour's accounts receivable position. Use your answers as supporting facts.

Inventory

Introduction

This chapter examines the accounting for inventory. In particular, it examines how companies record their inventory and how they determine the cost of the inventory that is sold. It also examines how errors in inventory can affect income for multiple periods, how inventory can be estimated if needed, and how inventory must be adjusted if its market value falls below its cost. The chapter concludes with how to analyze a company's inventory position. The appendix covers inventory accounting under a periodic system.

LO1 Recording, Expensing, and Reporting Inventory

Inventory is a tangible resource that is held for resale in the normal course of operations. For a retailer, inventory is the merchandise on the shelves or in the warehouse. For a manufacturer, inventory also includes the raw materials and work in process related to producing a finished product. This chapter focuses exclusively on the merchandise inventory of a retailer. You will study the issues concerning raw materials, work in process, and finished goods when you take a managerial accounting course.

As you consider the definition of inventory, note that the phrase "intended for resale" differentiates inventory from other operational assets. A tractor that Caterpillar Corp. intends to sell is inventory, while an identical tractor used in Caterpillar's operations is a fixed asset. Furthermore, the phrase "in the normal course of operations" means that some assets for sale are not classified as inventory. For example, Wal-Mart may vacate a store to relocate within a community. Although the vacated building is put up for sale, it is not classified as inventory because Wal-Mart is not in the business of selling buildings.

Inventory A tangible resource that is held for resale in the normal course of operations.

Learning Objectives

After studying the material in this chapter, you should be able to:

LO1 Describe inventory and how it is recorded, expensed, and reported.

LO2 Calculate the cost of goods sold using different inventory costing methods.

LO3 Understand the income and tax effects of inventory cost flow assumptions.

LO4 Analyze the effects of inventory errors.

LO5 Demonstrate how inventory is estimated.

LO6 Apply the lower-of-cost-or-market rule to inventory.

LO7 Evaluate inventory through the calculation of horizontal, vertical, and ratio analyses.

LO8 Appendix: Record purchases and calculate the cost of goods sold under a periodic system.

For a retailer, inventory is an important asset, and accounting for it properly affects both the balance sheet and the income statement.

© CARSTEN REISINGER/ALAMY

Recording Inventory

Following the cost principle, inventory is recorded at its acquisition cost. This includes all costs incurred to get the inventory delivered and, if necessary, prepared for resale. It also includes any reductions granted by the vendor or supplier after purchase. Examples of items affecting the cost of inventory would include, but not be limited to, the following.

- purchase price
- taxes paid
- costs for shipping the product
- insurance during transit

- labor required to assemble the product
- returns to and allowances from the vendor
- purchase discounts from the vendor

For a retailer, inventory is the merchandise on the shelves or in the warehouse. For a manufacturer, inventory also includes the raw materials and work in process related to producing a finished product.

While inventory is recorded at cost, how it is recorded into the accounting system depends on the inventory system that a company uses. A **perpetual inventory system** updates the inventory account each time inventory is bought or sold—that is, perpetually. Therefore, purchases of inventory are recorded directly into the Inventory account. In contrast, a **periodic inventory system** updates the inventory account only at the end of an accounting period—that is, periodically. Instead of recording purchases into the inventory account, they are recorded in an account called Purchases, which is a temporary account that is closed into Inventory at the end of the period. This chapter will demonstrate inventory accounting under a perpetual system. The periodic system is demonstrated in the appendix to the chapter.

To illustrate the recording of inventory, suppose that Devon Gifts purchases $20,000 of inventory on account on October 10. The purchase would be recorded as follows:

Oct. 10	Inventory	20,000	
	Accounts Payable		20,000
	(To record purchase of inventory)		

| Assets | = | Liabilities | + | Equity |
| +20,000 | | +20,000 | | |

Both assets and liabilities increase as a result of this transaction.

In some cases, a company must pay for the transportation necessary to obtain the inventory. Such additional costs are called *transportation-in* and are added to the overall cost of the inventory. To illustrate, suppose that Devon pays a third-party carrier $300 to transport the inventory to its warehouse. Devon would record the payment with the following entry:

Oct. 10	Inventory	300	
	Cash		300
	(To record transportation-in)		

| Assets | = | Liabilities | + | Equity |
| +300 | | +300 | | |

Sometimes, a company will return inventory to the vendor or seek some reduction in the cost of the inventory due to defective merchandise. The former is called a *purchase return*, while the latter is a *purchase allowance*. Both reduce the cost of the inventory purchased.

To illustrate, suppose that on October 12 Devon is granted a $1,000 reduction in the cost of the merchandise due to blemishes on the inventory. Even though Devon keeps the inventory, its cost has decreased due to the purchase allowance. Therefore, Devon would reduce the cost of the inventory and its payable to the vendor with the following entry:

Oct. 12	Accounts Payable	1,000	
	Inventory		1,000
	(To record purchase allowance granted by vendor)		

| Assets | = | Liabilities | + | Equity |
| −1,000 | | −1,000 | | |

In addition to returns and allowances, companies sometimes receive discounts from vendors if payment is made within a certain time period. Such *purchase discounts* reduce the cost of the inventory. To illustrate, suppose that Devon pays its remaining $19,000 bill to the vendor on October 15, which qualifies Devon for a 1% discount. As a result, Devon would save $190 ($19,000 × 1%) and pay only $18,810. The entry to record payment would be as follows:

Oct. 15	Accounts Payable	19,000	
	Inventory		190
	Cash		18,810
	(To record payment)		

Assets	=	Liabilities	+	Equity
−190		−19,000		
−18,810				

The entry decreases Accounts Payable for the full $19,000 (since the debt is paid in full) and decreases Cash for the $18,810 payment. The difference is a reduction to Inventory because the purchase discount of $190 has reduced the cost of the inventory. Both assets and liabilities decrease.

Given the preceding activity, Devon's *net purchases* of inventory can be calculated as follows:

Gross purchases	$20,000
Add: Transportation-in	300
Less: Purchase returns and allowances	(1,000)
Purchase discounts	(190)
Net purchases	$19,110

Expensing Inventory

Inventory becomes an expense when it is sold. The account Cost of Goods Sold or Cost of Sales is used to capture the amount of inventory expensed during a period. Like the recording of inventory purchases, the recording of cost of goods sold depends on a company's inventory system. Under a perpetual system, cost of goods sold is updated each time inventory is sold—that is, perpetually. Under a periodic system, cost of goods sold is calculated and recorded only at the end of the period—that is, periodically. Again, this chapter will demonstrate inventory accounting under a perpetual system, with the periodic system demonstrated in the appendix to the chapter.

To illustrate the recording of cost of goods sold, suppose that on November 2 Devon sells inventory costing $400 for $600 cash. Devon would record the sale with the following two entries:

Nov. 2	Cash	600	
	Sales		600
	(To record sale of inventory)		

Assets	=	Liabilities	+	Equity
+600				+600

Nov. 2	Cost of Goods Sold	400	
	Inventory		400
	(To record sale of inventory)		

Assets	=	Liabilities	+	Equity
−400				−400

The first entry records the effect of the sale on Devon's cash and revenues. Both Cash and Sales increase for the amount of the sale. As a result, both assets and equity increase by $600.

The second entry records the effect of the sale on Devon's inventory and expenses. Cost of Goods Sold increases for the cost of the inventory sold. Inventory decreases for the same amount. As a result, both assets and equity decrease by $400.

The net effect of both entries on assets and equity is a $200 increase, which is equal to the profit that Devon earned on the sale.

Reporting Inventory and Cost of Goods Sold

Inventory is expected to be sold within a year. Therefore, it is reported on the balance sheet as a current asset. Because cost of goods sold is usually a large and important expense for a retailer, it is normally reported as a separate line item on the income statement just below sales.

To illustrate, consider the following excerpts from Wal-Mart's 2008 balance sheet and income statement, with relevant lines highlighted.

As you might expect from the world's largest retailer, inventory is an important asset. Wal-Mart reported Inventories of over $34 billion at the end of 2008—by far its largest current asset. It also reported over $306 billion in Cost of Sales for 2008, by far its largest expense. The same importance is seen in the 2008 financial statements of Wal-Mart's smaller but fierce rival, Target. Target reported $6.7 billion in inventory, and cost of sales of $44.1 billion is easily its largest expense.

Because cost of goods sold is usually a large expense for a retailer, it is normally reported separately on the income statement.

© ISTOCKPHOTO.COM/QUAVONDO

Excerpts from Wal-Mart's 2008 Financial Statements

amounts in millions

Current Assets	
Cash and Cash Equivalents	$ 7,275
Receivables	3,905
Inventories	34,511
Prepaid Expenses and Other	3,063
Current Assets of Discontinued Operations	195
Total Current Assets	$ 48,949
Income Statement	
Revenues:	
Net Sales	$401,244
Membership and Other Income	4,363
Total Revenues	$405,607
Cost and expenses:	
Cost of Sales	$306,158
Operating, Selling, General and Admin. Expenses	76,651
Operating income	$ 22,798

LO₂ Inventory Costing Methods

The previous section demonstrated the manner in which inventory and cost of goods sold are recorded under a perpetual system. When a sale is made, Inventory is decreased and Cost of Goods Sold is increased for the cost of the inventory that is sold. This section demonstrates how companies determine the cost of the inventory sold.

To determine the cost of inventory sold, companies can use one of the following four inventory costing methods.

- specific identification
- first-in, first-out (FIFO)
- last-in, first-out (LIFO)
- moving average

To illustrate each method, the following example will be used. Suppose that Nell Farms sells a specialty maple syrup that it purchases from Waverly Manufacturing. During the month of September, Nell experiences the following inventory activity:

		Units	Unit Cost	Total
Sept. 1	Beginning Inventory	40	$12	$480
Sept. 4	Purchase	60	$13	$780
Sept. 10	Sale	(65)		
Sept. 15	Purchase	30	$14	$420
Sept. 23	Purchase	45	$15	$675
Sept. 30	Sale	(50)		

HOME DEPOT ANALYSIS

Look at Home Depot's balance sheet and income statement in Appendix C. What name does the company use for its inventory and cost of goods sold? Is inventory the company's largest current asset? What is its cost? Is cost of goods sold the company's largest expense?

Home Depot uses the names Merchandise Inventories and Cost of Sales. Merchandise Inventories is the company's largest current asset and second largest asset only to Buildings. Its cost is $10,673 million. Cost of Sales of $47,298 million is by far the largest expense of the company.

Exhibit 7-1 Calculations for Specific Identification Method

	Transaction	Inventory Purchased			Inventory Sold			Inventory on Hand		
Sept. 1	Beginning Inventory							40	$12	$ 480
Sept. 4	Purchase #1	60	$13	$780				40	$12	$ 480
								60	$13	780
								100		$1,260
Sept. 10	Sell 65 units				30	$12	$360	10	$12	$ 120
					35	$13	455	25	$13	325
					65		$815	35		$ 445
Sept. 15	Purchase #2	30	$14	$420				10	$12	$ 120
								25	$13	325
								30	$14	420
								65		$ 865
Sept. 23	Purchase #3	45	$15	$675				10	$12	$ 120
								25	$13	325
								30	$14	420
								45	$15	675
								110		$1,540
Sept. 30	Sell 50 units				10	$12	$120	0	$12	$ 0
					20	$13	260	5	$13	65
					10	$14	140	20	$14	280
					10	$15	150	35	$15	525
					50		$670	60		$ 870

Specific Identification

The **specific identification method** determines cost of goods sold based on the actual cost of each inventory item sold. To use this method, a retailer must know which inventory item is sold and the exact cost of that particular item. As a result, the method is most likely to be used by companies whose inventory is unique. Examples might include an antiques store or a fine jeweler.

For illustration purposes, suppose that Nell specifically identifies each of its inventory items and provides the detailed inventory activity as shown in Exhibit 7-1.

Exhibit 7-1 shows that the September 10 sale consisted of thirty $12 units and thirty-five $13 units for a total cost of $815. The September 30 sale consisted of ten $12 units, twenty $13 units, ten $14 units, and ten $15 units, for a total cost of $670. Together, cost of goods sold for September is $1,485 ($815 + $670). The 60 units remaining in ending inventory, as shown in the bottom right corner of Exhibit 7-1, have a cost of $870.

Because most companies cannot track the actual cost of every inventory item that is sold, they cannot use the specific identification method. Instead, they must make an *assumption* about the cost of inventory sold. They can assume that the cost of the inventory sold is the cost of the first unit purchased, the last unit purchased, or an average of all purchases. Each of these three assumptions is described as follows.

First-In, First-Out (FIFO)

The **first-in, first-out (FIFO) method** calculates cost of goods sold based on the assumption that the first unit

> **Specific identification method** Determines cost of goods sold based on the actual cost of each inventory item sold.
>
> **First-in, first-out method** Calculates cost of goods sold based on the assumption that the first unit of inventory available for sale is the first unit sold.

Exhibit 7-2 Calculations for FIFO Method

	Transaction	Inventory Purchased			Inventory Sold			Inventory on Hand		
Sept. 1	Beginning Inventory							40	$12	$ 480
Sept. 4	Purchase #1	60	$13	$780				40	$12	$ 480
								60	$13	780
								100		$1,260
Sept. 10	Sell 65 units				40	$12	$480	0	$12	$ 0
					25	$13	325	35	$13	455
					65		$805	35		$ 455
Sept. 15	Purchase #2	30	$14	$420				35	$13	$ 455
								30	$14	420
								65		$ 875
Sept. 23	Purchase #3	45	$15	$675				35	$13	$ 455
								30	$14	420
								45	$15	675
								110		$1,550
Sept. 30	Sell 50 units				35	$13	$455	0	$13	$ 0
					15	$14	210	15	$14	210
					50		$665	45	$15	675
								60		$ 885

of inventory available for sale is the first unit sold. That is, inventory is assumed to be sold in the order that it is purchased. For most companies, the FIFO assumption matches the actual physical flow of their inventory. However, companies are not required to choose the assumption that matches their physical flow.

Exhibit 7-2 illustrates the calculation of cost of goods sold under the FIFO method.

At each sale, the FIFO method requires Nell to assign the costs of the first units purchased to cost of goods sold. On September 10, Nell sold 65 units. It therefore assumes that it sold all 40 units of beginning inventory and 25 of the units in Purchase #1. The total cost of those 65 units was $805.

For the September 30 sale, Nell assumes that it sold the 35 units remaining from Purchase #1 and 15 units of Purchase #2. The total cost of those 50 units was $665.

As a result of these two calculations, cost of goods sold for September is $1,470 ($805 + $665). The 60 units remaining in ending inventory, as shown in the bottom right corner of Exhibit 7-2, have a cost of $885.

Last-In, First-Out (LIFO)

The **last-in, first-out (LIFO) method** calculates cost of goods sold based on the assumption that the last unit of inventory available for sale is the first unit sold. That is, inventory is assumed to be sold in the opposite order of its purchase. Exhibit 7-3 illustrates the calculations under the LIFO method.

At each sale, the LIFO method requires Nell to assign the costs of the last or most recent units purchased to cost of goods sold. On September 10, Nell sold 65 units. It therefore assumes that it sold all 60 units of Purchase #1 and 5 of the units from beginning inventory. The total cost of those 65 units was $840.

For the September 30 sale, Nell assumes that it sold all 45 units of Purchase #3 and 5 units of Purchase #2. The total cost of those 50 units was $745.

Last-in, first-out method Calculates cost of goods sold based on the assumption that the last unit of inventory available for sale is the first unit sold.

Exhibit 7-3 Calculations for LIFO Method

	Transaction	Inventory Purchased			Inventory Sold			Inventory on Hand		
Sept. 1	Beginning Inventory							40	$12	$ 480
Sept. 4	Purchase #1	60	$13	$780				40	$12	$ 480
								60	$13	780
								100		$1,260
Sept. 10	Sell 65 units				5	$12	$ 60	35	$12	$ 420
					60	$13	780	0	$13	0
					65		$840	35		$ 420
Sept. 15	Purchase #2	30	$14	$420				35	$12	$ 420
								30	$14	420
								65		$ 840
Sept. 23	Purchase #3	45	$15	$675				35	$12	$ 420
								30	$14	420
								45	$15	675
								110		$1,515
Sept. 30	Sell 50 units				5	$14	$ 70	35	$12	$ 420
								25	$14	350
					45	$15	675	0	$15	0
					50		$745	60		$ 770

As a result, cost of goods sold for September is $1,585 ($840 + $745). Ending inventory, as shown in the bottom right corner of Exhibit 7-3, has a cost of $770.

Moving Average

The **moving average method** calculates cost of goods sold based on the average unit cost of all inventory available for sale. That is, the cost of each inventory item sold is assumed to be the average cost of all inventory available for sale at that time.

To calculate cost of goods sold at each sale date, a retailer must calculate the average unit cost of the inventory available for sale on that date. This calculation is conducted as follows:

$$\text{Average Unit Cost} = \frac{\text{Cost of Goods Available for Sale}}{\text{Units Available for Sale}}$$

Once the average unit cost is known, it is multiplied by the units sold to determine cost of goods sold.

Exhibit 7-4 contains Nell's calculations under the moving average method. Note that the average unit cost is rounded to the nearest penny, while inventory sold and inventory on hand is rounded to the nearest dollar.

At the September 10 sale, Nell has 100 units available for sale at a total cost of $1,260. Therefore, the average unit cost is $12.60 ($1,260 ÷ 100). Nell uses that unit cost to determine the costs of the inventory sold and the inventory that remains. Having sold 65 units, Nell's cost of goods sold on September 10 is $819 (65 × $12.60). The cost of the 35 units on hand after the sale is therefore $441 (35 × $12.60).

For the September 30 sale, Nell must recalculate the average unit cost because it has purchased additional units of inventory. This is why the term "moving average" is used—because the average cost per unit can change during the period as new purchases are made.

Moving average method Calculates cost of goods sold based on the average unit cost of all inventory available for sale.

Exhibit 7-4 Calculations for Moving Average Method

	Transaction	Inventory Purchased			Inventory Sold			Inventory on Hand		
Sept. 1	Beginning Inventory							40	$12.00	$ 480
Sept. 4	Purchase #1	60	$13	$780				40	$12.00	$ 480
								60	$13.00	780
								100		$1,260
Sept. 10	Sell 65 units				65	$12.60	$819	35	$12.60	$ 441
Sept. 15	Purchase #2	30	$14	$420				35	$12.60	$ 441
								30	$14.00	420
								65		$ 861
Sept. 23	Purchase #3	45	$15	$675				35	$12.60	$ 441
								30	$14.00	420
								45	$15.00	675
								110		$1,536
Sept. 30	Sell 50 units				50	$13.96	$698	60	$13.96	$ 838

At September 30, Nell has 110 units available for sale at a total cost of $1,536. Therefore, the new average unit cost, rounded to the nearest cent, is $13.96 ($1,536 ÷ 110). Having sold 50 units, Nell's cost of goods sold on September 30 is $698 (50 × $13.96).

As a result of these two calculations, cost of goods sold for September is $1,517 ($819 + $698). Ending inventory, as shown in the bottom right corner of Exhibit 7-4, has an average unit cost of $13.96, for a total cost of $838 (60 × $13.96).

LO3 Comparing Inventory Costing Methods

The previous sections show that a company's choice of inventory costing methods affects both its cost of goods sold and its ending inventory. To summarize these effects, Exhibit 7-5 puts Nell's inventory data in a form known as the cost of goods sold model and compares the results of each of the three cost flow assumptions. The specific identification method is omitted from the comparison because of its infrequent use.

HOME DEPOT ANALYSIS

Look at the Merchandise Inventories paragraph of Home Depot's first note in Appendix C. What cost flow assumption does the company use? As a result, which inventory units are represented by the $10,673 million balance on the company's balance sheet, and which units are represented by the $47,298 million cost of sales on the company's income statement?

The note indicates that the company uses the FIFO method. Therefore, the $10,673 million balance in inventory represents the last inventory units that the company purchased. The $47,298 million balance in cost of sales represents the cost of the first inventory units purchased.

Exhibit 7-5 Comparison of Inventory Costing Methods

	Units	FIFO	Moving Average	LIFO
Beginning Inventory	40	$ 480	$ 480	$ 480
Add: Net Purchases	135	1,875	1,875	1,875
Cost of Goods Available for Sale	175	$2,355	$2,355	$2,355
Less: Ending Inventory	60	885	838	770
Cost of Goods Sold	115	$1,470	$1,517	$1,585

Because inventory costing methods affect both income statement and balance sheet accounts, a company must disclose the method that it uses. It must also use the same method consistently.

The cost of goods sold model summarizes a company's inventory activity during a period by adding purchases to beginning inventory to yield cost of goods available for sale. This represents the total cost of the inventory that could have been sold during the period. That cost is then allocated to either what was sold (cost of goods sold) or what was not sold (ending inventory).

In Nell's case, it began the month of September with 40 units costing $480 and bought an additional 135 units costing $1,875 during the month. So, it could have sold up to 175 units with a total cost of $2,355. This is the case regardless of the inventory costing system chosen. However, the cost of the 115 units sold and the 60 units unsold depends on the cost flow assumption.

The FIFO method assigns the costs of the first and, in this case, less expensive units purchased to cost of goods sold, thereby yielding the lowest cost of goods sold. It also assigns the costs of the last and more expensive units to ending inventory, thereby yielding the highest ending inventory.

In contrast, the LIFO method assigns the costs of the last and, in this case, more expensive units to cost of goods sold, resulting in the highest cost of goods sold. The costs of the first and less expensive units are assigned to ending inventory, resulting in the lowest ending inventory.

The moving average assigns the average costs of all units purchased to cost of goods sold. Therefore, it yields cost of goods sold and ending inventory that fall in between the FIFO and LIFO extremes.

When a company experiences rising prices for its inventory, these relative differences will continue. These relationships are summarized as follows:

	Ending Inventory	Cost of Goods Sold
FIFO yields:	Highest	Lowest
Moving average yields:	Middle	Middle
LIFO yields:	Lowest	Highest

Because of these differences in both income statement accounts and balance sheet accounts, a company must disclose the inventory costing method that it uses. It must also use the same method consistently. These requirements allow for meaningful comparisons of inventory activity across different companies and across different periods within the same company.

While companies can use any of the four costing methods, some choose the LIFO method because of the resulting tax deferral. A **tax deferral** is a temporary delay in the payment of income taxes. Tax deferrals are beneficial because a company can keep and use its cash for a longer period of time.

To illustrate, suppose that Nell generated revenues of $5,240 from its sale of inventory during September. Suppose further that Nell incurred $1,850 in operating expenses during the month and that it is subject to a tax rate of 40%. Exhibit 7-6 contains comparative multi-step income statements prepared under each inventory costing method.

Exhibit 7-6 Comparative Income Statements

	FIFO	Moving Average	LIFO
Sales	$5,240	$ 5,240	$5,240
Cost of goods sold	(1,470)	(1,517)	(1,585)
Gross margin	$3,770	$ 3,723	$3,655
Operating expenses	(1,850)	(1,850)	(1,850)
Income before taxes	$1,920	$1,873	$1,805
Income taxes (40%)	(768)	(749)	(722)
Net income	$1,152	$1,124	$1,083

Tax deferral A temporary delay in the payment of income taxes.

Comparing the income tax obligations under the LIFO and FIFO assumptions (which are the two extremes), you can see that Nell can defer $46 in taxes ($768 − $722) if it uses the LIFO method rather than the FIFO method. In other words, it can write a $722 check to the taxing authority instead of a $768 check. Keep in mind, though, that this deferral is only temporary. If Nell sold its entire inventory in the next period, the deferral would be eliminated.

The general amount of tax deferral a company generates from using LIFO can be determined from information found in the notes to the financial statements. Companies that use the LIFO method must disclose the LIFO reserve. The **LIFO reserve** is the difference between the inventory reported on the balance sheet and what inventory would be if reported on a FIFO basis. The reserve is cumulative, meaning that it represents the cumulative difference between LIFO and FIFO over the years. Thus, the amount of taxes deferred can be calculated by multiplying the reserve by the company's tax rate.

To illustrate, consider the following excerpt from Safeway's 2008 inventory note.

Excerpts from Safeway's 2008 Inventory Note

Merchandise inventory of $1,740 million at year-end 2008 and $1,886 million at year-end 2007 is valued . . . on a last-in, first-out ("LIFO") basis. . . . Such LIFO inventory had a ("FIFO") . . . cost of $1,838 million at year-end 2008 and $1,949 million at year-end 2007.

Given this information, Safeway's 2008 LIFO reserve in millions is calculated as follows:

	2008
Inventories valued at FIFO	$1,838
Inventories valued at LIFO	1,740
LIFO reserve	$ 98

Assuming a tax rate of 30%, the taxes that Safeway has deferred as of the end of 2008 are $29.4 million ($98 × 30%).

LIFO reserve The difference between the LIFO inventory reported on the balance sheet and what inventory would be if reported on a FIFO basis.

LO4 Inventory Errors

Under a perpetual inventory system, the inventory account is updated each time inventory is bought or sold. However, most companies take a physical count of inventory at least once a year to confirm that the inventory balance from the accounting system matches the actual inventory on hand. Taking a physical inventory is an example of an internal control procedure discussed in Chapter 5. By counting inventory, a company can determine if it has lost inventory due to theft, damage, or errors in accounting.

Errors in the counting of inventory affect both the balance sheet (through inventory) and the income statement (through cost of goods sold). Moreover, because ending inventory in one period becomes beginning inventory in the next period, an error can affect not only the current period, but also the next period. To understand the effect of errors, consider the following scenario.

Suppose that Baggett Company has 3,000 units of inventory on January 1, 2010, and purchases an additional 34,000 units during the year. Included in those purchases are 1,000 units that ship on December 30. According to the shipping terms, Baggett owns the units while in transit, so they are properly included in its purchases. However, when Baggett counts its inventory on December 31, 2010, the 1,000 units are erroneously omitted from the count.

To demonstrate the effect of this error, the information is put into the cost of goods sold model. For simplicity purposes, each unit of inventory is assumed to cost Baggett $1.

In the year of the error (2010)

	Correct	As Counted	Effect
Beginning inventory	$ 3,000	$ 3,000	Not affected
Add: Net purchases	34,000	34,000	Not affected
Cost of goods available for sale	$37,000	$37,000	Not affected
Less: Ending inventory	5,000	4,000	Understated
Cost of goods sold	$32,000	$33,000	Overstated

The model shows that the counting error does not affect beginning inventory or purchases during 2010. These were recorded correctly. Because inventory was omitted from the count, ending inventory is understated by 1,000 units, or $1,000. This, in turn, results in cost

By counting inventory, a company can determine if it has lost inventory due to theft, damage, or errors in accounting.

of goods sold being overstated by $1,000. In the period of the error, assets are understated by $1,000 and cost of goods sold is overstated by $1,000. As a result, net income, and therefore equity, are also understated by $1,000.

The effect of the counting error is not limited to the year of the error. Because Baggett's ending inventory becomes beginning inventory in the next period, the effects of the 2010 counting error spill into 2011. To demonstrate, suppose that in 2011 Baggett purchases an additional 41,000 units of inventory and properly counts ending inventory at 6,000 units. The following cost of goods sold model shows how the error in 2010 affects 2011, even though no error is made in 2011.

In the period after the error (2011)

	Correct	As Counted	Effect
Beginning inventory	$ 5,000	$ 4,000	Understated
Add: Net purchases	41,000	41,000	Not affected
Cost of goods available for sale	$46,000	$45,000	Understated
Less: Ending inventory	6,000	6,000	Unaffected
Cost of goods sold	$40,000	$39,000	Understated

Beginning inventory for 2011 is now understated by 1,000 units. As a result, the inventory available for sale is also understated by 1,000 units. If ending inventory for 2011 is properly counted, then the inventory sold is understated by the same 1,000 units. If it is assumed that all units were purchased for $1 each, then the cost of goods sold model shows that the ending inventory account has the correct balance of $6,000, while the cost of goods sold balance is understated by $1,000 ($39,000 versus the correct $40,000 balance). Thus, while the balance sheet in 2011 is not affected by the 2010 counting error (since inventory is now correctly counted), the 2011 income statement is affected since the beginning inventory value in the cost of goods sold model is understated.

The preceding scenario is an example of a counterbalancing inventory error. A counterbalancing error is an error whose effect on net income is corrected in the period after the error. Note that there was only one error in this scenario—the failure to include 1,000 units of inventory in the final inventory count of 2010. However, the error affected cost of goods sold in two years.

In 2010, cost of goods sold was overstated by $1,000 because *ending* inventory was incorrect. Cost of goods sold was reported as $33,000 when it should have been $32,000. In 2011, cost of goods sold was understated by $1,000 because *beginning* inventory was incorrect. Cost of goods sold was reported as $39,000 when it should have been $40,000. The overstatement in cost of goods sold in 2010 was followed by an equal understatement in 2011. In this way, the inventory error is counterbalancing.

The effects of such errors on inventory, cost of goods sold, and related financial measures are listed in in Exhibit 7-7.

Not all inventory errors are counterbalancing. For example, if a particular warehouse of inventory is not counted year after year, the error will not work itself out. However, a discussion of noncounterbalancing errors will be left to more advanced accounting courses.

Exhibit 7-7 Effect of Inventory Errors

	If inventory is understated		If inventory is overstated	
	Current period	Next period	Current period	Next period
Inventory	Understated	Correct	Overstated	Correct
Cost of goods sold	Overstated	Understated	Understated	Overstated
Net income	Understated	Overstated	Overstated	Understated
Total assets	Understated	Correct	Overstated	Correct

Estimating Ending Inventory

company must sometimes estimate its inventory bal-ance. One example is when inventory is destroyed by a natural catastrophe. Another example is when a company prepares interim financial statements. In such cases, a company can estimate its ending inventory with the gross profit method.

The **gross profit method** of estimating inventory uses a company's gross profit percentage to estimate cost of goods sold and then ending inventory. To apply the method, a company first subtracts its normal gross profit from its sales to yield an estimate of its cost of goods sold. That estimate is then put into the cost of goods sold model to estimate ending inventory.

To illustrate, assume that Alsup Hardware is pre-paring interim financial statements at the end of its first quarter and needs to estimate cost of goods sold and ending inventory. Alsup has generated quarterly sales of $400,000. In past quarters, Alsup's gross profit percent-age has averaged 45%. Assuming that this quarter is similar to prior quarters, Alsup can estimate that gross profit on current-quarter sales is $180,000.

Current quarter sales (actual)	$400,000
Historical gross profit percentage	× 45%
Gross profit (estimated)	$180,000

Gross profit method A method of estimating inventory using a company's gross profit percentage to estimate cost of goods sold and then ending inventory.

> A company must sometimes estimate its inventory balance. One example is when inventory is destroyed by a natural catastrophe. Another example is when a company prepares interim financial statements.

Alsup can then estimate cost of goods sold for the period as $220,000.

Current quarter sales (actual)	$400,000
Gross profit (estimated)	(180,000)
Cost of goods sold (estimated)	$220,000

Now that Alsup has estimated cost of goods sold, it can calculate its ending inventory by plugging the cost of goods sold estimate into the cost of goods sold model. Based on past financial reports and purchase records, Alsup knows that it started the quarter with $200,000 in inventory and bought $90,000 of inventory during the quarter. This means that Alsup had $290,000 in inven-tory available for sale during the period. With $220,000 in estimated cost of goods sold, the cost of goods sold model yields a $70,000 estimate for ending inventory.

Beginning inventory (actual)	$200,000
Add: Net purchases (actual)	90,000
Cost of goods available for sale (actual)	$290,000
Less: Cost of goods sold (estimated)	(220,000)
Ending inventory (estimated)	$ 70,000

MAKING IT REAL

Inventory errors can originate from many different sources. Consider what happened at Winnebago Indus-tries in its second quarter of 2005. During a review of its physical inventory counts, it was determined that a formula in an electronic worksheet was incorrect. The error in the formula resulted in an overstatement of quarter-ending inven-tory of approximately $2.8 million, which led to an equal understatement of cost of goods sold for the quarter. The error in cost of goods sold resulted in a $1.8 million after-tax overstatement of quarterly earnings. Since actual earnings were $12.6 million and reported earn-ings were $14.4 million, the mistake was a 14% overstatement of actual earnings. After finding the problem, the company corrected its financial statements and released them to the public with a state-ment that the previously released financial statements could not be relied upon due to the inventory counting error.

© AP IMAGES/CHARLIE NEIBERGALL

LO6 Lower-of-Cost-or-Market

The cost principle requires that inventory be recorded at its cost. However, because of the principle of conservatism, accounting rules require that inventory be reported on the balance sheet at its market value if the market value is lower than the inventory's cost. This is known as the **lower-of-cost-or-market (LCM) rule**.

The lower-of-cost-or-market rule is applied at the end of each accounting period by comparing inventory costs to market values. For purposes of our comparison, an inventory's market value is equal to the cost to replace the inventory. Companies have some discretion in how LCM is applied. For example, they can compare costs and market values of (1) inventories in total, (2) major groups of inventories, or (3) individual inventory items. When the cost is lower than the market value, nothing further is done. However, when the market value is lower than the cost, the company must adjust its inventory down to the lower market value.

To illustrate, suppose that Dryden Company provides the December 31 inventory information shown in Exhibit 7-8.

Because of the principle of conservatism, accounting rules require that inventory be reported on the balance sheet at its market value if the market value is lower than the inventory's cost.

Dryden uses one of these two approaches, no adjustment to inventory is needed. However, if Dryden applies LCM to individual inventory items, it will need to adjust its inventory. The individual comparison yields a value of $1,300. Since this is lower than the inventory's cost of $1,420, the inventory must be adjusted down to $1,300. This is accomplished with the following entry:

Dec. 31	Cost of Goods Sold	120	
	Inventory		120
	(To adjust inventory to market)		

	Assets	=	Liabilities	+	Equity
	−120				−120

Exhibit 7-8 LCM Calculation for Dryden Company as of December 31

Item	Units	Unit Cost	Unit Market	Total Cost	Total Market	Total	Two Groups	Individual Items
A	5	$ 40	$ 80	$ 200	$ 400			$ 200
B	8	$ 65	$ 50	520	400			400
Group 1				$ 720	$ 800		$ 720	
C	4	$100	$160	$ 400	$ 640			400
D	10	$ 30	$ 50	300	500			300
Group 2				$ 700	$1,140		700	
Total				$1,420	$1,940	$1,420	$1,420	$1,300

Dryden has four types of inventory (A, B, C, and D) separated into two groups (1 and 2). Cost and market values are computed for each inventory type, each inventory group, and total inventory. The three right columns show the value that should be reported for inventory when applying LCM to total inventories, to the two groups of inventory, and to each individual inventory item.

When applied to total inventories and to the two groups of inventory, the lower-of-cost-or-market value is equal to the inventory's cost of $1,420. Therefore, if

The journal entry increases Cost of Goods Sold to reflect the loss in value of the inventory and decreases Inventory to adjust the account down to the $1,300 market value. As a result, both assets and equity decrease. Dryden's inventory is now ready to be reported on the balance sheet at its more conservative market value.

Lower-of-cost-or-market rule Requires inventory to be reported on the balance sheet at its market value if the market value is lower than the inventory's cost.

Any investor, creditor, or manager of a company should be interested in how well a company manages its inventory. A company manages its inventory by buying and selling efficiently and effectively.

LO7 Evaluating a Company's Management of Inventory

Any investor, creditor, or manager of a company should be interested in how well a company manages its inventory. A company manages its inventory by buying and selling efficiently and effectively.

The following sections examine the effectiveness of Target Corporation in managing its inventory. The examination will require information from the company's balance sheet and income statement. The required information is found in Exhibit 7-9, excerpted from Target's 2008 annual report.

Exhibit 7-9 Account Balances from Target's 2008 Annual Report

Source	Accounts	2008	2007
Income Statement	Net sales	$62,884	$61,471
	Cost of sales	$44,157	$42,929
Balance Sheet	Inventory	$ 6,705	$ 6,780
	Total assets	$44,106	$44,560

Horizontal and Vertical Analyses

An easy and useful place to start an examination of inventory is with horizontal and vertical analyses. Recall from Chapter 2 that horizontal analysis calculates the dollar change in an account balance, defined as the current-year balance less the prior-year balance, and divides that change by the prior-year balance to yield the percentage change. Vertical analysis divides each account balance by a base account, yielding a percentage. The base account is total assets for balance sheet accounts and net sales or total revenues for income statement accounts. These calculations are summarized as follows:

Horizontal Analysis

$$\text{Dollar change in account balance} = \text{Current-year balance} - \text{Prior-year balance}$$

$$\text{Percentage change in account balance} = \frac{\text{Dollar change}}{\text{Prior-year balance}}$$

Vertical Analysis

$$\text{Percentage} = \frac{\text{Balance Sheet}}{\frac{\text{Account Balance}}{\text{Total Assets}}} \text{ or } \frac{\text{Income Statement}}{\frac{\text{Account Balance}}{\text{Net Sales or Revenue}}}$$

Given Target's financial information in Exhibit 7-9, horizontal and vertical analyses of inventory and cost of sales result in the following.

Horizontal Analysis

	Change	Percentage Change
Inventory	$\begin{array}{r}6,705 \\ -6,780 \\ \hline (75)\end{array}$	$\dfrac{(75)}{6,780} = -1.1\%$
Cost of sales	$\begin{array}{r}44,157 \\ -42,929 \\ \hline 1,228\end{array}$	$\dfrac{1,228}{42,929} = 2.9\%$

Vertical Analysis

	2008	2007
Inventory	$\dfrac{6,705}{44,106} = 15.2\%$	$\dfrac{6,780}{44,560} = 15.2\%$
Cost of sales	$\dfrac{44,157}{62,884} = 70.2\%$	$\dfrac{42,929}{61,471} = 69.8\%$

HOME DEPOT ANALYSIS

Look at Home Depot's inventory note in Appendix C. Does it follow the lower-of-cost-or-market rule?

Home Depot discloses that its inventory is reported at the lower-of-cost-or-market value. Cost is determined on a FIFO basis.

Inventory Turnover Ratio

While horizontal and vertical analyses are useful for generating information about inventory, a more direct way to assess a company's ability to sell its inventory is to calculate the inventory turnover ratio. The **inventory turnover ratio** compares the cost of goods sold during a period to the average inventory balance during that period. It is calculated as follows:

$$\text{Inventory Turnover Ratio} = \frac{\text{Cost of Goods Sold}}{\text{Average Inventory}}$$

Where average inventory is:

$$\frac{\text{Beginning Inventory} + \text{Ending Inventory}}{2}$$

Because this ratio compares the cost of all inventory sold to the average cost of inventory on hand, it indicates how many times a company is able to sell its inventory balance in a period. All other things being equal, a higher ratio indicates that the company sold more inventory while maintaining less inventory on hand. This means that the company generated more sales revenue while reducing the costs of stocking inventory on the shelves.

Target's 2008 inventory turnover ratio is calculated as follows.

$$\frac{44,157}{(6,705 + 6,780) \div 2} = 6.5$$

The 6.5 ratio indicates that Target's cost of goods sold for 2008 was 6.5 times its average inventory balance. For every dollar of inventory on its shelves, on average, Target was able to sell over $6.00 of inventory during the period.

Because the turnover ratio is sometimes difficult to interpret, it is often converted into the days-in-inventory ratio. The **days-in-inventory ratio** converts the inventory turnover ratio into a measure of days by dividing the

The calculations show a fairly stable inventory position. Horizontal analysis of inventory shows a $75 million decrease, which equals a 1.1% reduction. Vertical analysis indicates that inventories made up 15.2% of Target's total assets in both 2007 and 2008. So, although inventory stocks were down slightly, the decrease mirrored an overall decrease in Target's total assets.

The analysis of cost of goods sold shows an increase of $1,228 million, which equals a 2.9% increase. Furthermore, vertical analysis indicates that cost of goods sold was 69.8% of sales in 2007 and 70.2% of sales in 2008. The reason for this increase is that cost of goods sold increased faster than sales. This is a trend that should warrant observation in the future.

For comparison purposes, the 2008 horizontal and vertical analyses of Wal-Mart are listed in Exhibit 7-10. Notice that Wal-Mart also experienced a decline in inventory and an increase in cost of goods sold. Further, Wal-Mart's cost of goods sold is a higher percentage of sales (76.3% versus 70.2%).

Exhibit 7-10 Target versus Wal-Mart Comparison

	Account	Horizontal Analysis	Vertical Analysis
Target	Inventory	−1.1%	15.2%
	Cost of goods sold	2.9%	70.2%
Wal-Mart	Inventory	−1.8%	21.1%
	Cost of goods sold	6.9%	76.3%

Inventory turnover ratio Compares cost of goods sold during a period to the average inventory balance during that period and measures the ability to sell inventory.

Days-in-inventory ratio Converts the inventory turnover ratio into a measure of days by dividing the turnover ratio into 365 days.

Using Home Depot's information in Appendix C, calculate and interpret (1) horizontal and vertical analyses of inventory and cost of goods sold, (2) inventory turnover ratio, and (3) days-in-inventory ratio.

(1) Horizontal Analysis

Inventory: ($10,673 − $11,731)/11,731 = −9.0%

Cost of Goods Sold: ($47,298 − $51,352)/51,352 = −7.9%

Vertical Analysis

Inventory: $10,673/$41,164 = 25.9%

Cost of Goods Sold: $47,298/$71,288 = 66.3%

The −9.0% and −7.9% horizontal analysis of inventory and cost of goods sold shows that Home Depot sold and stocked less inventory during the year. The 25.9% vertical analysis of inventory shows that over a quarter of the company's assets are tied up in inventory. This seems reasonable, given that Home Depot is a "big box" retailer. The 66.3% vertical analysis of cost of goods sold indicates that inventory cost is a very large expense for the company. For the average dollar of sales, the cost of the inventory sold was about 66 cents.

(2) Inventory Turnover Ratio

$47,298/($10,673 + $11,731) ÷ 2 = 4.2

(3) Days-in-Inventory

365/4.2 = 86.9 days

The 4.2 inventory turnover ratio indicates that Home Depot buys and sells its inventory about 4 times each year. The days in inventory ratio of 86.9 indicates that it takes the company almost three months to sell through its inventory.

---

turnover ratio into 365 days. Thus, the days-in-inventory ratio is calculated as follows:

$$\frac{365}{6.5} = 56.2$$

A ratio of 56.2 indicates that it takes Target about 56 days to sell as much inventory as it keeps on hand. Naturally, Target wants this ratio to be as low as possible. Its rival Wal-Mart generated a 41.5 ratio in 2008. This means it takes Target about 14 days longer than Wal-Mart to sell as much inventory as it has on hand.

Purchases An account used to accumulate the cost of all purchases.

Transportation-in An account that accumulates the transportation costs of obtaining the inventory.

Purchase Returns and Allowances An account that accumulates the cost of all inventory returned to vendors as well as the cost reductions from vendor allowances.

LO8 Appendix—Periodic Inventory System

A periodic inventory system does not update the inventory and cost of goods sold accounts during the period. When purchases are made, they are recorded in a temporary account called Purchases. When sales are made, the resulting revenue is recorded, but not the cost of goods sold. As a result, companies that use a periodic system must calculate and update the inventory and the cost of goods sold accounts at the end of the period. The following sections demonstrate the recording of purchases and the determination of ending inventory and cost of goods sold under a periodic system.

Recording Inventory

A periodic system uses the following four temporary accounts to capture the cost of inventory purchases during a period. The **Purchases** account accumulates the cost of all purchases. The **Transportation-in** account accumulates the transportation costs of obtaining the inventory. Both of these increase the cost of inventory. The **Purchases Returns and Allowances** account accumulates

When purchases are made in a periodic inventory system, they are recorded in a temporary account called Purchases. When sales are made, the resulting revenue is recorded, but not the cost of goods sold.

the cost of all inventory returned to vendors as well as the cost reductions from vendor allowances. The **Purchase Discounts** account accumulates the cost reductions generated from vendor discounts granted for prompt payment. Both of these reduce the cost of inventory. Each of the four accounts is closed at the end of the period when the inventory and the cost of goods sold accounts are updated.

To illustrate the recording of inventory with these accounts, the example used in the chapter is repeated. Suppose that Devon Gifts purchases $20,000 of inventory on account on October 10. The purchase would be recorded as follows:

Oct. 10	Purchases	20,000	
	Accounts Payable		20,000
	(To record purchase of inventory)		

Assets	=	Liabilities	+	Equity
+20,000		+20,000		

Suppose further that Devon pays a third-party carrier $300 cash to transport the inventory to its warehouse. Devon would record the payment with the following entry:

Oct. 10	Transportation-in	300	
	Cash		300
	(To record transportation-in)		

Assets	=	Liabilities	+	Equity
+300		+300		

Suppose further that on October 12 Devon is granted a $1,000 reduction in the cost of the merchandise due to blemishes on the inventory. Devon would reduce its payable to the vendor and record the allowance as follows.

Oct. 12	Accounts Payable	1,000	
	Purchase Returns and Allowances		1,000
	(To record purchase allowance granted by vendor)		

Assets	=	Liabilities	+	Equity
−1,000		−1,000		

Finally, suppose that Devon pays its remaining $19,000 bill to the vendor on October 15, which qualifies Devon for a 1% discount. As a result, Devon would save $190 ($19,000 × 1%) and pay only $18,810. The entry to record payment would be as follows:

Oct. 15	Accounts Payable	19,000	
	Purchase Discounts		190
	Cash		18,810
	(To record payment)		

Assets	=	Liabilities	+	Equity
−190		−19,000		
−18,810				

The entry decreases Accounts Payable for the full $19,000 and decreases Cash for the $18,810 payment. The difference is an addition to Purchase Discounts.

Given the preceding activity, Devon's **net purchases** of inventory can be calculated as follows:

Purchases	$20,000
Add: Transportation-in	300
Less: Purchase returns and allowances	(1,000)
Purchase discounts	(190)
Net purchases	$19,110

This is the same cost of net purchases as calculated under the perpetual system discussed in the chapter. Whether using a periodic or perpetual system, the cost of net purchases is the same. It is just captured in different accounts.

Inventory Costing Methods

A periodic system does not update the Inventory and the Cost of Goods Sold accounts during the period.

Purchase Discounts An account that accumulates the cost reductions generated from vendor discounts granted for prompt payments.

Net purchases The value of inventory purchased and transportation-in less purchase returns and allowances and purchase discounts.

Thus, the balances in these accounts must be calculated at the end of the period. This is accomplished in the following three steps:

1. Count the inventory on hand at the end of the period.

2. Use an inventory costing method to assign a cost to the ending inventory.

3. Calculate cost of goods sold using the cost of goods sold model.

To illustrate this process, the example used in the chapter is repeated. Suppose that during the month of September, Nell Farms experiences the following inventory purchases:

		Units	Unit Cost	Total
Sept. 1	Beginning inventory	40	$12	$480
Sept. 4	Purchase	60	$13	$780
Sept. 15	Purchase	30	$14	$420
Sept. 23	Purchase	45	$15	$675

At the end of the month, Nell counts 60 units on hand. Nell's cost of goods sold model for September is therefore as follows:

	Units	Cost
Beginning inventory	40	$ 480
Add: Net purchases	135	1,875
Cost of goods available for sale	175	$2,355
Less: Ending inventory	60	???
Cost of goods sold	115	???

To calculate the cost of the 60 units in ending inventory and therefore the cost of the 115 units sold, Nell must use one of the four inventory costing methods.

Specific Identification

Under the specific identification method, Nell determines the cost of ending inventory based on the actual cost of the units on hand. Suppose that Nell knows that the costs of the 60 units are five $13 units, twenty $14 units, and thirty-five $15 units. It can therefore calculate the cost of ending inventory as follows:

	Units	Unit Cost	Total Cost
Sept. 4 purchase	5	$13	$ 65
Sept. 15 purchase	20	$14	$280
Sept. 23 purchase	35	$15	$525
Ending inventory	60		$870

Plugging this cost of ending inventory into the cost of goods sold model yields Nell's cost of goods sold of $1,485.

	Units	Cost
Cost of goods available for sale	175	$2,355
− Ending inventory	60	870
= Cost of goods sold	115	$1,485

First-In, First-Out (FIFO)

Under the FIFO method, Nell assumes that the first units of inventory purchased are the first units sold. As a result, the costs of the last (most recent) purchases are assigned to ending inventory. It can therefore calculate the cost of ending inventory as follows:

	Units	Unit Cost	Total Cost
Sept. 23 purchase	45	$15	$675
Sept. 15 purchase	15	$14	210
Ending inventory	60		$885

The cost of all 45 units purchased on September 23 and 15 of the units purchased on September 15 are assigned to ending inventory, yielding a cost of $885. Plugging this into the cost of goods sold model yields Nell's cost of goods sold of $1,470.

	Units	Cost
Cost of goods available for sale	175	$2,355
− Ending inventory	60	885
= Cost of goods sold	115	$1,470

Last-In, First-Out (LIFO)

Under the LIFO method, Nell assumes that the last units of inventory purchased are the first units sold. As a result, the costs of the first purchases are assigned to ending inventory. Nell can therefore calculate the cost of ending inventory as follows:

	Units	Unit Cost	Total Cost
Beginning inventory	40	$12	$480
Sept. 4 purchase	20	$13	260
Ending inventory	60		$740

The cost of all 40 units of beginning inventory and 20 of the units purchased on September 4 are assigned to ending inventory, yielding a cost of $740. Plugging this into the cost of goods sold model yields Nell's cost of goods sold of $1,615.

	Units	Cost
Cost of goods available for sale	175	$2,355
− Ending inventory	60	740
= Cost of goods sold	115	$1,615

Weighted Average

Under the weighted average method, Nell assumes that the cost of each unit in ending inventory is the average cost of all units available for sale during the period. The weighted average cost per unit is calculated as follows:

$$\frac{\text{Weighted Average}}{\text{Unit Cost}} = \frac{\text{Cost of Goods Available for Sale}}{\text{Units Available for Sale}}$$

Note here that under a periodic system, the average unit cost is based on all the inventory available to be sold during the period. As a result, the average unit cost does not change during the period. Therefore, it is called a weighted average instead of a moving average (as under the perpetual system).

Nell's weighted average cost per unit, rounded to the nearest cent, is calculated as follows:

$$\frac{\$2,355}{175} = \$13.46$$

Nell can therefore calculate the cost of ending inventory as follows, rounded to the nearest dollar:

	Units	Unit Cost	Total Cost
Ending inventory	60	$13.46	$808

Plugging this into the cost of goods sold model yields Nell's cost of goods sold of $1,547.

	Units	Cost
Cost of goods available for sale	175	$2,355
− Ending inventory	60	808
= Cost of goods sold	115	$1,547

STUDY TOOLS
CHAPTER 7

CHAPTER REVIEW CARD

❑ Learning Objective and Key Concept Reviews

❑ Key Definitions and Formulas

ONLINE (Located at 4ltrpress.cengage.com/acct)

❑ Flash Cards and Crossword Puzzles

❑ Conceptual and Computational Interactive Quizzes

❑ E-Lectures

❑ Static, Algorithmic, and Additional Homework Activities (as directed by your instructor)

EXERCISES

1. Determine Inventory Costs LO1

Mary Cosmetics sells specialty lipstick for a retail price of $12.25 each. Mary purchases each tube for $5.00 and pays the following additional amounts: $1.50 per tube in freight charges, $0.40 per tube in taxes, and $2 per tube in commissions to employees for sales.

Required

Compute the cost of each tube of lipstick.

2. Record Inventory Purchases LO1

Heston Company purchases inventory with a list price of $7,000 for $6,300 on account. Heston pays a transportation company $200 to deliver the inventory. Upon receipt, Heston notices some defects, contacts the vendor, and receives a $500 allowance. Heston pays the vendor three days later, which qualifies Heston for a 2% discount.

Required

Prepare all journal entries Heston would make to record the preceding activity and calculate Heston's net purchases.

3. Inventory Purchases LO1, 2

Consider the following separate situations.

	William's Widgets	Sarah's Sofas	Clay's Cars
Beginning inventory	$4,000	$2,350	$ (e)
Purchases (gross)	4,230	(c)	7,340
Purchase returns	470	800	550
Purchase discounts	(a)	458	310
Transportation-in	150	500	420
Cost of goods available for sale	(b)	7,320	8,790
Ending inventory	1,890	1,750	(f)
Cost of goods sold	5,220	(d)	7,590

Required

Compute the missing amounts.

4. Inventory Costing Methods LO2

Avant Corporation's November inventory activity is as follows. Avant uses a perpetual inventory system.

Date	Transaction	Units	Unit Cost	Total Cost
11/1	Beginning inventory	32	$55	$1,760
11/7	Purchase	45	60	2,700
11/9	Sale	50		
11/14	Purchase	52	65	3,380
11/30	Sale	61		

Required

Compute the ending inventory and cost of goods sold under the FIFO, LIFO, and moving average costing methods.

5. Inventory Costing Methods LO2

Hahn Hardware provides the following information relating to its June inventory activity. Hahn uses a perpetual inventory system.

Date	Transaction	Units	Unit Cost	Total Cost
June 1	Inventory	13	$8.00	$104.00
June 7	Purchase	22	9.50	209.00
June 12	Sale	20		
June 18	Purchase	10	10.25	102.50
June 20	Sale	14		
June 26	Purchase	16	11.00	176.00
June 30	Sale	15		

Required

1. Put Hahn's given information into a cost of goods sold model. What is unknown?
2. Compute the ending inventory and cost of goods sold using the FIFO, LIFO, and moving average costing methods. Round dollar amounts to the nearest penny.
3. Calculate the sum of the ending inventory and cost of goods sold for each method. What do you notice about the answer for each method?

6. Inventory Errors LO4

Goodwin Grocery reported the following financial facts for 2009 and 2010.

	2009	2010
Beginning inventory	$ 20,000	$ 30,000
Cost of goods purchased	150,000	175,000
Cost of goods available for sale	$170,000	$205,000
Ending inventory	30,000	35,000
Cost of goods sold	$140,000	$170,000

Goodwin made two accounting errors during the years:

1. 2009 ending inventory was understated by $3,000.
2. 2010 ending inventory was overstated by $4,000.

Required

Compute Goodwin's correct cost of goods sold for each year.

7. Inventory Errors LO4

FMA Company reported the following income statement data.

	2009	2010
Sales	$210,000	$250,000
Beginning inventory	32,000	40,000
Cost of goods available for sale	205,000	242,000
Ending inventory	40,000	52,000
Cost of goods sold	165,000	190,000
Gross profit	45,000	60,000

Inventory balances at January 1, 2009, and December 31, 2010, are correct. However, the ending inventory at December 31, 2009, is overstated by $5,000.

Required

Prepare corrected data for 2009 and 2010, identify all accounts that were affected by the error and whether they were overstated or understated, and calculate the cumulative two-year effect of the inventory error on gross profit.

8. Estimating Inventory LO5

Clayburn Enterprises reported the following information for the current year:

Sales	$800,000
Beginning inventory	25,000
Purchases	502,000
Gross profit percentage	40%

Required

Using the gross profit method, estimate Clayburn's cost of goods sold for the year and the ending inventory at year end. Explain why a company might need to estimate its ending inventory.

9. Applying Lower-of-Cost-or-Market LO6

Kay Mart Company is preparing financial statements and provides the following information about several of its major inventory items.

Ending Inventory as of December 31

Item	Quantity on Hand	Unit Cost When Acquired	Replacement Cost (Market Value) as of December 31
R	25	$15	$19
S	60	22	20
T	34	30	33
U	50	10	11
V	13	50	55

Required

If Kay Mart uses the lower-of-cost-or-market rule (LCM), what should it report as the balance of inventory if (1) one market value is computed for all inventories or (2) a market value is computed for each inventory type?

10. Analyzing Inventory LO7

The following information is provided for three different companies: A, B, and C.

in millions	A	B	C
Beginning inventory	$ 569	$ 774	$ 989
Ending inventory	423	214	356
Cost of goods sold	1,376	1,232	1,771
Sales	2,232	1,836	3,025

Required

Calculate the inventory turnover ratio and days in inventory ratio for each company. How do the companies compare?

11. Analyzing Inventory LO7

Comparative income statements for Berg Company are given as follows.

Berg Company
Comparative Income Statements
For the Years Ended December 31, 2010 and 2009

	2010	2009
Net sales	$812,000	$812,000
Cost of goods sold	649,600	664,364
Gross profit	$162,400	$147,636
Operating expenses	84,448	79,724
Net income	$ 77,952	$ 67,912

Required

Prepare horizontal and vertical analyses of Berg's income statement data and comment on the current status of the company.

12. Appendix—Inventory Costing Methods (Periodic System) LO8

Hahn Hardware provides the following information relating to its June inventory. Hahn uses a periodic inventory system and sold 49 units during the month.

Date	Transaction	Units	Unit Cost	Total Cost
June 1	Inventory	13	8.00	$104.00
June 7	Purchase	22	9.50	209.00
June 18	Purchase	10	10.25	102.50
June 26	Purchase	16	11.00	176.00
	Totals	61		$591.50

Required

1. Put Hahn's given information into a cost of goods sold model. What is unknown?
2. Compute the ending inventory and cost of goods sold using the FIFO, LIFO, and weighted average costing methods.
3. Calculate the sum of the ending inventory and cost of goods sold for each method. What do you notice about the answer for each method?

13. Appendix—Inventory Costing Methods LO8

Avant Corporation's November inventory activity follows. Avant uses a periodic inventory system.

Date	Transaction	Units	Unit Cost	Total Cost
11/1	Beginning inventory	32	$55	$1,760
11/7	Purchase	45	60	2,700
11/14	Purchase	52	65	3,380
11/30	Ending inventory	18		

Required

1. Compute the ending inventory and cost of goods sold under the FIFO, LIFO, and weighted average costing assumptions.
2. Which costing assumption gives the highest ending inventory? Highest cost of goods sold? Why?
3. Explain why the average item cost is not $60 under the weighted average costing assumption.

PROBLEMS

14. Effects of Inventory Costing Methods on Income LO2

Martin Merchandising has hired you to examine whether the company should use the LIFO or FIFO inventory costing assumption. The company uses a perpetual inventory system and has supplied the following information for the month:

Beginning inventory, 2,000 units at $40	$ 80,000
Purchases on June 4, 12,000 units at $45	540,000
Sales on June 18, 10,500 units at $77	808,500
Operating expenses (excluding taxes)	148,000
Company tax rate	35%

Required

Prepare multi-step income statements under the LIFO and FIFO costing assumptions. Explain to Martin the advantages and disadvantages of using each inventory costing method. Use the income statements to support your explanation.

15. Recording Inventory Activity   LO1, 2, 6

Campbell Candy Company starts the month of January with 40 boxes of Tiger Bars costing $20 each. The following transactions occurred during the month.

Jan. 2   Purchased 15 additional boxes for $22 each. Paid with cash.

Jan. 4   Paid freight costs of $30 on January 2 purchase.

Jan. 10 Sold 45 boxes for $40 each.

Jan. 27 Purchased 10 additional boxes on account for $23 each.

Required

Assuming that Campbell uses a perpetual inventory system and the FIFO costing method, prepare all necessary journal entries related to Campbell's inventory activity.

Suppose that the inventory has a replacement value of $375 at the end of the month. What entry, if any, is required?

16. Analyzing Inventory   LO7

The following is comparative financial data for JK Martin Company and Stratton Company. All balance sheet data are as of December 31, 2009, and December 31, 2010.

Required

1. Prepare a vertical analysis of the 2010 income data for JK Martin Company and Stratton Company. Is one company more profitable than the other?
2. Prepare a horizontal analysis of the 2010 financial data for JK Martin Company and Stratton Company using 2009 as the base year. What does this analysis show?

3. Compute the inventory turnover and days in inventory ratios for 2010 for JK Martin Company and Stratton Company. Do these ratios change your conclusions about these companies?

17. Appendix—Recording Inventory Activity   LO8

Campbell Candy Company starts the month of January with 40 boxes of Tiger Bars costing $20 each. The following transactions occurred during the month.

Jan. 2   Purchased 15 additional boxes for $22 each. Paid with cash.

Jan. 4   Paid freight costs of $30 on January 2 purchase.

Jan. 10 Sold 45 boxes for $40 each.

Jan. 27 Purchased 10 additional boxes on account for $23 each.

Required

Assuming that Campbell uses a periodic inventory system, prepare all necessary journal entries related to Campbell's inventory activity. Calculate the cost of goods sold and the ending inventory under the FIFO, LIFO, and weighted average costing methods.

CASE

18. Research and Analysis   LO1, 3, 6, 7

Access the 2008 annual report for Safeway, Inc. by clicking on the *Investors* and *Annual Reports* links at www.safeway.com.

Required

1. Examine the company's income statement and balance sheet and conduct horizontal and vertical analyses of the company's cost of goods sold and inventory balances.
2. Examine the company's merchandise inventories note to its financial statements. What inventory

	JK Martin Company		Stratton Company	
	2010	2009	2010	2009
Net sales	$2,000,000		$550,000	
Cost of goods sold	1,100,000		240,000	
Operating expenses	305,000		75,000	
Income tax expense	52,000		6,500	
Cash	85,070	$ 82,508	16,100	$ 15,777
Inventory	250,000	225,000	70,000	65,600
Property & equipment	525,000	500,000	140,000	125,000
Current liabilities	65,000	75,000	35,000	30,000
Long-term liabilities	109,000	88,000	29,000	24,800
Common stock, $10 par	490,000	490,000	115,000	115,000
Retained earnings	173,000	147,520	40,756	30,289

costing method(s) does the company use to account for its inventory? How often does the company take a physical count of its inventory? Does the company follow the lower-of-cost-or-market rule?

3. Using the LIFO reserve disclosed on the balance sheet and assuming a 35% marginal income tax rate, determine how much in taxes the company has deferred at the end of 2008.

4. Calculate the inventory turnover and days-in-inventory ratios for 2008.

5. Based on your answers above, write a paragraph explaining your opinion of Safeway's inventory position. Use your answers as supporting facts.

Fixed Assets
and Intangible Assets

Introduction

This chapter examines the accounting for property and equipment, or as it is sometimes called, "fixed assets." For most companies, the objectives associated with fixed assets are fairly simple. They want to acquire fixed assets, use them productively for some period of time, and then dispose of them. Thus, the chapter examines these three activities—the acquisition of fixed assets, the depreciation of fixed assets over their useful lives, and the disposal of fixed assets. It also examines a few issues that arise during the life of a fixed asset, such as additional expenditures and revisions of original estimates. The chapter then focuses on how to analyze a company's fixed asset position. It concludes with the accounting for intangible assets.

LO1 Recording, Expensing, and Reporting Fixed Assets

A **fixed asset** is any tangible resource that is expected to be used in the normal course of operations for more than one year and is not intended for resale. Examples include land, buildings, equipment, furniture, fixtures, etc. Fixed assets are reported on the balance sheet and are classified as noncurrent assets because they are used for more than one year.

As you consider the definition of a fixed asset, note that the phrase "not intended for resale" differentiates a fixed asset from inventory. A computer that Dell Corporation makes for sale is inventory, while an identical computer used by an employee in business operations is a fixed asset. Also, note that the phrase "used in the normal course of operations" differentiates a fixed asset from an investment. Land on which a company builds a manufacturing plant is a fixed asset, while land bought to be sold to a developer is an investment. The company's intended use of the asset dictates how the asset is classified.

Fixed asset A tangible resource that is expected to be used in operations for more than one year and is not intended for resale.

Acct

Learning Objectives

After studying the material in this chapter, you should be able to:

LO1 Describe fixed assets and how they are recorded, expensed, and reported.

LO2 Calculate and compare depreciation expense using straight-line, double-declining-balance, and units-of-activity methods.

LO3 Understand the effects of adjustments that may be made during a fixed asset's useful life.

LO4 Record the disposal of fixed assets.

LO5 Evaluate fixed assets through the calculation and interpretation of horizontal, vertical, and ratio analyses.

LO6 Describe the cash flow effect of acquiring fixed assets.

LO7 Describe intangible assets and how they are recorded, expensed, and reported.

Accounting for fixed assets like this truck involves recording the purchase, depreciating the asset over its life, and then disposing of it.

© ISTOCKPHOTO.COM/ELENA ELISSEEVA

Recording Fixed Assets

Following the cost principle, fixed assets should be recorded at the cost of acquiring them. This includes all costs incurred to get the asset delivered, installed, and ready to use. Examples of expenditures to include in the cost of a fixed asset would therefore include, but not be limited to, the following:

- purchase price
- taxes paid on the purchase
- fees such as closing costs paid to attorneys
- delivery costs
- insurance costs during transit
- installation costs

To illustrate, suppose that Dozier Building Supply buys a delivery truck with a purchase price of $60,000, additional state sales taxes of $3,600, and a county fee of $400. Prior to receiving the truck, Dozier has the dealer paint the company's logo on the doors and install a specialized GPS. The dealer charges an additional $1,000 for this. Finally, Dozier pays an insurance company an additional $1,400 in premiums to add the truck to its coverage for the coming year. Given the preceding items, the cost of Dozier's truck is determined as follows:

Purchase price	$60,000
Sales taxes	3,600
County fee	400
Installation of logo and GPS	1,000
Total cost	$65,000

All of the costs except for the insurance are necessary to get the asset into its condition and location for intended use and are therefore included in the cost of the truck. The insurance covers the truck during its operations and is therefore an operating expense during the year. Assuming that Dozier paid cash to the dealer, the entry to record the purchase of the truck would be as follows:

Delivery Truck	65,000	
Cash		65,000
(To record the purchase of truck)		

Assets	=	Liabilities	+	Equity
+65,000				
−65,000				

Consider another example. Suppose a company purchases a tract of land for a new building site. The purchase price is $500,000 plus $25,400 in taxes and fees paid to the realtor, the bank, and the attorneys. Included on the land are four small buildings that must be removed at a total cost of $12,000. Also, the land requires $100,000 in logging, grading, and filling before it can be used. The timber harvested from the logging is sold for $20,000. The total cost of the land is as follows:

Purchase price	$500,000
Taxes and fees	25,400
Removal of buildings	12,000
Logging, grading, and filling	100,000
Less: Sales of timber	(20,000)
Total cost	$617,400

In this case, each cost is included in the asset because the land is not in the condition for use until each of the activities is completed. Notice also that the proceeds from the sale of the timber reduce the cost of the land.

Expensing Fixed Assets

A fixed asset converts to an expense as it is used or consumed. The expensing of fixed assets is accomplished through *depreciation*. **Depreciation** is the process of allocating the cost of a fixed asset over its useful life. Depreciation is an application of the matching principle—because a fixed asset is used to generate revenues period after period, some of its cost should be expensed in, or matched to, those same periods. The amount of expense recognized each period is known as **depreciation expense**. The cumulative amount of depreciation expense recognized to date is known as **accumulated depreciation**.

Some students experience some confusion with depreciation because of its everyday use in our language. For example, it is often said that a new car "depreciates" in value once it is driven off the dealer's lot. When utilized in this way, the term depreciation implies a decline or loss in value because the car is used. For our purposes, depreciation is a process of allocating an asset's cost, not a method of determining an asset's market value.

While depreciation applies to fixed assets, not all fixed assets are depreciated. Depreciation applies only to those assets with limited useful lives. An asset has a

Depreciation The process of systematically and rationally allocating the cost of a fixed asset over its useful life.

Depreciation expense The portion of a fixed asset's cost that is recognized as an expense in the current period.

Accumulated depreciation The cumulative amount of depreciation expense recognized to date on a fixed asset.

For accounting purposes, depreciation is a process of allocating an asset's cost, not a method of determining an asset's market value.

limited useful life when its revenue generating potential is limited by wear and tear and/or obsolescence. Most fixed assets such as equipment and buildings have limited useful lives and are therefore subject to depreciation. The major exception to this is land, which has an unlimited useful life. As a result, land is not subject to depreciation.

Depreciation expense is normally calculated at the end of an accounting period and recorded with an adjusting journal entry. Regardless of the fixed asset being depreciated or the facts of the calculation, the general form of the entry is the same: Depreciation Expense and Accumulated Depreciation are increased.

To illustrate, suppose that Dozier calculates its truck's depreciation as $10,000 for the first year. At year-end, Dozier would make the following entry:

Year-end	Depreciation Expense	10,000	
	Accumulated Depreciation		10,000

Assets	=	Liabilities	+	Equity
−10,000				−10,000

This entry increases Depreciation Expense for the $10,000 of cost allocated to the current period. However, instead of decreasing Delivery Truck, the entry increases Accumulated Depreciation, which is a contra-asset account that accumulates all depreciation recorded to date. Its balance is subtracted from the fixed asset account to yield the net book value of the fixed asset. We will see an example of this later in the chapter. The result of this entry is a decrease to both equity and assets.

Like other expenses, depreciation expense is reported on the income statement. Some companies, such as the Wendy's/Arby's Group, report it as a separate line item. A condensed version of Wendy's/Arby's Group's 2008 operating expenses follows:

Wendy's/Arby's Group 2008 Condensed Operating Expenses

in thousands	
Costs and expenses	
Cost of sales	$1,415,534
General and administrative	248,718
Depreciation and amortization	88,315
Goodwill impairment	460,075
Other	23,769
Total	$2,236,411

Other companies, such as McDonald's Corporation and Burger King Holdings, do not separately disclose depreciation expense. Rather, they include it in a larger expense category, usually in Administrative Expenses. The operating expense portion of McDonald's 2008 income statement is shown as follows:

McDonald's 2008 Condensed Operating Expenses

in millions	
OPERATING COSTS AND EXPENSES	
Company-operated restaurant expenses:	
Food & paper	$ 5,586.1
Payroll & employee benefits	4,300.1
Occupancy & other operating expenses	3,766.7
Franchised restaurants—occupancy expenses	1,230.3
Selling, general & administrative expenses	2,355.5
Impairment and other charges, net	6.0
Other operating (income) expense, net	(165.2)
Total operating costs and expenses	$17,079.5

No reference is made to depreciation expense on the statement, but this does not mean that McDonald's had no depreciation expense. To find it, we must consult the notes to the financial statements. The following is an excerpt from McDonald's Property and Equipment note:

Excerpt from McDonald's 2008 Property and Equipment Note

Depreciation and amortization expense related to continuing operations was (in millions): 2008—$1,161.6; 2007—$1,145.0; 2006—$1,146.3.

L ook at Home Depot's Balance Sheet in Appendix C. What general name does the company use for its fixed assets and what specific fixed asset accounts does it list? What is the historical cost of its fixed assets, how much depreciation expense has been accumulated to date, and what is the net book value of those fixed assets? What does the company report for depreciation expense for the current year?

Home Depot uses the name Property and Equipment for fixed assets. It lists the following six specific accounts: Land; Buildings; Furniture, Fixtures and Equipment; Leasehold Improvements; Construction in Progress; and Capital Leases. It reports a cost of $36,477 for its Property and Equipment. It also reports Accumulated Depreciation and Amortization to date of $10,243 million. Together, these result in a net book value of $26,234 million. Depreciation and Amortization for the current year is reported as $1,785 million on the income statement.

This note shows that over $1 billion in depreciation expense is included in one of the six operating expense subtotals in McDonald's 2008 income statement. Even though you don't see it on the income statement, it is there as a component of the reported expenses.

Reporting Fixed Assets

Fixed assets are reported on the balance sheet, usually as a separate line item just below current assets. A condensed version of Wendy's/Arby's 2008 balance sheet follows:

Wendy's/Arby's Group 2008 Condensed Balance Sheet	
in thousands	
Total current assets	$ 380,838
Property and equipment, net	1,770,372
Other assets	2,494,410
Total assets	$4,645,620

Notice first that Wendy's/Arby's uses "Property and Equipment" instead of "Fixed Assets." Because

the bulk of fixed assets for most companies is property, buildings, and equipment, most companies use some variation of the term "property, plant and equipment" to describe their fixed assets. Notice also that Wendy's/Arby's description includes the word "net." The term "net" is an abbreviation for the phrase *net book value*. **Net book value** represents the cost of a fixed asset that has not yet been depreciated. It is calculated by subtracting the accumulated depreciation to date from the cost of the fixed asset. For example, an asset costing $5,000 with $1,000 of accumulated depreciation would have a net book value of $4,000.

Because Wendy's/Arby's only reports the net number on the balance sheet, those interested in how the net book value was calculated would need to consult the notes to the financial statements. Wendy's/Arby's discloses the following condensed data in its property and equipment note:

Wendy's/Arby's 2008 Property and Equipment Note	
in thousands	
Property and equipment, at cost	$1,977,253
Accumulated depreciation and amortization	(206,881)
Net property and equipment	$1,770,372

At the end of 2008, Wendy's/Arby's held fixed assets with a total cost of almost $1.98 billion and accumulated depreciation of approximately $207 million. Netting those together yields the $1.77 billion net book value reported on the balance sheet.

Net book value The unexpired cost of a fixed asset, calculated by subtracting accumulated depreciation from the cost of the fixed asset.

While Wendy's/Arby's reports the cost and accumulated depreciation amounts in its notes, other companies, such as McDonald's, report both amounts directly on their balance sheets.

McDonald's 2008 Fixed Assets Section of Balance Sheet	
in millions	
Property and equipment, at cost	$31,152.4
Accumulated depreciation and amortization	(10,897.9)
Net property and equipment	$20,254.5

McDonald's lists over $31 billion in cost of fixed assets and almost $11 billion in accumulated depreciation of those assets. Thus, the net book value of its fixed assets is over $20 billion.

LO2 Calculating Depreciation Expense

When a company owns depreciable assets, it must calculate depreciation expense each period. Doing so requires the following information about the asset:

- Cost
- Salvage Value
- Useful Life
- Depreciation Method

Cost refers to the historical cost of the asset being depreciated. This is the amount that was recorded when the asset was purchased. **Salvage value** refers to the market value of the asset at the end of its useful life. It is the amount the company expects to receive when the asset is sold, traded-in, or scrapped. The difference between an asset's cost and its salvage value is the asset's net cost to the company, or its **depreciable cost**. The depreciable cost is the total amount that should be depreciated over time. **Useful life** refers to the length of time the asset will be used in operations.

Depreciation method refers to the method used to calculate depreciation expense. Generally accepted accounting principles allow the use of several different methods for calculating depreciation expense. This chapter focuses on the following three methods:

- Straight-line
- Double-declining-balance
- Units-of-activity

To illustrate how depreciation expense is calculated under each method, the Dozier Building Supply example will be continued. The following information about Dozier's delivery truck is available:

- Purchase Date: January 1, 2010
- Cost: $65,000
- Estimated Salvage Value: $15,000
- Estimated Useful Life: 5 years or 100,000 miles

Straight-Line Method

The **straight-line method** of depreciation spreads depreciation expense evenly over each year of the asset's useful life. It is a very simple calculation. The depreciable cost of the asset is divided by the useful life of the asset (in years) to yield the amount of depreciation expense per period. This calculation is shown below:

$$\text{Depreciation Expense} = \frac{\text{Cost} - \text{Salvage Value}}{\text{Useful Life}}$$

For Dozier's delivery truck, annual depreciation expense under the straight-line method would therefore be:

$$\text{Depreciation Expense} = \frac{\$65,000 - \$15,000}{5} = \$10,000$$

Cost The historical cost of a fixed asset being depreciated.

Salvage value An estimate of the value of a fixed asset at the end of its useful life.

Depreciable cost The difference between an asset's cost and its salvage value.

Useful life The length of time a fixed asset is expected to be used in operations.

Depreciation method The method used to calculate depreciation expense, such as the straight-line method, the double-declining-balance method, and the units-of-activity method.

Straight-line method A depreciation method that results in the same amount of depreciation expense each year of the asset's useful life.

Dozier would record the depreciation expense with the following adjusting journal entry at the end of the first year:

Dec. 31 2010	Depreciation Expense	10,000	
	Accumulated Depreciation		10,000

Assets	=	Liabilities	+	Equity
−10,000				−10,000

The same entry would be made at the end of each year through 2014. Exhibit 8-1 illustrates depreciation for the entire useful life of the asset.

Double-Declining-Balance Method

The **double-declining-balance method** of depreciation is an accelerated method that results in more depreciation expense in the early years of an asset's life and less depreciation expense in the later years of an asset's life. As a result, the double-declining-balance method often matches expenses to revenues better than the straight-line method. More depreciation expense is recorded when the asset is more useful.

To calculate depreciation expense under the double-declining-balance method, the rate of depreciation is determined first by taking the straight-line rate

Exhibit 8-1 Depreciation Schedule—Straight-Line Method

Year	Calculation	Depreciation Expense	Accumulated Depreciation	Net Book Value
			$ 0	$65,000
2010	($65,000 − $15,000) / 5	$10,000	10,000	55,000
2011	($65,000 − $15,000) / 5	10,000	20,000	45,000
2012	($65,000 − $15,000) / 5	10,000	30,000	35,000
2013	($65,000 − $15,000) / 5	10,000	40,000	25,000
2014	($65,000 − $15,000) / 5	10,000	50,000	15,000

The depreciation schedule highlights several items. First, depreciation expense is the same each period. This will always be true under the straight-line method.

Second, the accumulated depreciation account grows each year by $10,000 until the balance equals the depreciable cost of the asset. This is no coincidence. The final balance in accumulated depreciation is the total of all depreciation expense recorded during the asset's life. Therefore, the balance should equal the asset's depreciable cost. This will be true regardless of the depreciation method used.

Finally, the net book value decreases each year by $10,000 until it equals the salvage value estimated for the asset. This is no coincidence either. Net book value represents the remaining unexpired cost of the asset. Therefore, an asset's final net book value should always equal the estimated salvage value at the end of the asset's useful life. This will be true regardless of the depreciation method used.

of depreciation and doubling it (hence, the word *double* in the name). For example, if an asset has a four-year life, it has a straight-line rate of 25% (calculated by dividing 100% by four years). The straight-line rate is then doubled to 50%. An asset with a five-year life would have a 20% straight-line rate, which would be doubled to 40%. The doubled rate is then multiplied by the net book value of the asset to yield the amount of depreciation expense for the period. This calculation is shown as follows:

$$\text{Depreciation Expense} = \text{Depreciation Rate} \times \text{Net Book Value}$$
$$= (\text{Straight-Line Rate} \times 2)$$
$$\times (\text{Cost} - \text{Accumulated Depreciation})$$

Before depreciation expense for Dozier is calculated, note again that the depreciation rate is applied to the net book value of the asset, not its depreciable cost. Because an asset's net book value declines as the asset is depreciated, the amount of depreciation expense will therefore differ each period. In fact, depreciation expense will become smaller and smaller each period as the depreciation rate is applied to a smaller net book

Double-declining-balance method A depreciation method that accelerates depreciation expense into the early years of an asset's life.

value. This stands in contrast to the straight-line method and is why the name of this method contains the words *declining balance*.

Under the double-declining-balance method, Dozier's depreciation expense for the first year of the asset's life is calculated as follows:

$$\text{Depreciation Expense for 2010} = (20\% \times 2) \times (\$65,000 - \$0) = \$26,000$$

You can now see how the double-declining-balance method *accelerates* the depreciation. Instead of $10,000 of expense as under the straight-line method, depreciation expense in the first year is $26,000. In other words, $16,000 of depreciation expense is accelerated to the first year by using the double-declining-balance method instead of the straight-line method.

In the second year of the asset's life, the same formula is used. However, the resulting depreciation expense is lower because the depreciation rate is applied to a lower net book value. With $26,000 in depreciation to date, the accumulated depreciation balance is $26,000, yielding a net book value of $39,000 ($65,000 − $26,000). Therefore, depreciation expense in the second year would be:

$$\text{Depreciation Expense for 2011} = (20\% \times 2) \times (\$65,000 - \$26,000) = \$15,600$$

tion of $41,600). Therefore, the calculation of depreciation expense for the third year is as follows:

$$\text{Depreciation Expense for 2012} = (20\% \times 2) \times (\$65,000 - \$41,600) = \$9,360$$

Now, at this point we need to be careful. Over an asset's life, an entity cannot record more total depreciation than the asset's depreciable cost. Regardless of how much depreciation expense is calculated to be, an asset's accumulated depreciation balance should never exceed the asset's depreciable cost. In our example, Dozier's depreciable cost is $50,000. Accumulated depreciation after 2011 is $41,600. Therefore, depreciation expense in 2012 is limited to $8,400. This calculation is as follows:

Depreciable cost of asset ($65,000 − $15,000)	$50,000
Less: Accumulated depreciation at the end of 2011	41,600
Remaining depreciation to be taken	$ 8,400

Even though the calculation yields $9,360, depreciation expense for 2012 is limited to $8,400. And, because Dozier's truck is fully depreciated after 2012, there is no depreciation expense for the remaining two years of the truck's life.

A schedule of depreciation for all five years is shown in Exhibit 8-2. The calculated amounts in 2012 are struck through and are replaced with the necessary amounts.

Exhibit 8-2 Depreciation Schedule—Double-Declining-Balance Method

Year	Calculation	Depreciation Expense	Accumulated Depreciation	Net Book Value
			$ 0	$65,000
2010	(20% × 2) × ($65,000 − $0)	$26,000	26,000	39,000
2011	(20% × 2) × ($65,000 − $26,000)	15,600	41,600	23,400
2012	(20% × 2) × ($65,000 − $41,600)	~~9,360~~	~~50,960~~	~~14,040~~
		8,400	50,000	15,000
2013		0	50,000	15,000
2014		0	50,000	15,000

As you can see, depreciation expense for the second year is lower than the first year, but it is still more than would be calculated under the straight-line method. In other words, depreciation expense is still being accelerated to the early years of the asset's life.

In the third year of the asset's life, the same formula is used again, but this time the net book value is $23,400 (cost of $65,000 less accumulated deprecia-

Note that, as expected, depreciation expense is accelerated to the early years of the asset's life. Note also that, like the straight-line method, the double-declining-balance method results in a total of $50,000 of depreciation expense and a resulting net book value that is equal to the estimated salvage value of $15,000. The only difference between the methods is when depreciation expense is recognized.

Units-of-Activity Method

Both the straight-line and double-declining-balance methods are a function of the passage of time rather than the actual use of the asset. Each method assumes that the calculated depreciation is a reasonable representation of the actual usage of the asset. In contrast, the **units-of-activity method** of depreciation calculates depreciation based on actual asset activity. Because it relies on an estimate of an asset's lifetime activity, the method is limited to those assets whose units of activity can be determined with some degree of accuracy.

Calculating depreciation expense under the units-of-activity method starts by calculating depreciation per unit of expected activity. Depreciation per unit of expected activity is the depreciable cost of the asset divided by the estimated units of activity over the life of the asset.

$$\text{Depreciation Expense per Unit} = \frac{\text{Cost} - \text{Salvage Value}}{\text{Useful Life in Units}}$$

For Dozier's truck, depreciation expense per unit will be a function of miles driven. Since Dozier estimates that the truck will be driven 100,000 miles, its estimated depreciation per mile would be $0.50 per mile.

$$\text{Depreciation Expense per Unit} = \frac{\$65,000 - \$15,000}{100,000 \text{ miles}}$$
$$= \$0.50 \text{ per mile}$$

With a $0.50 per mile rate, the actual miles driven in a given year is needed to calculate depreciation expense. Assume that Dozier drives the truck 24,000 miles in 2010. Its depreciation expense for 2010 would therefore be $12,000.

$$\text{Depreciation Expense} = \$0.50 \times 24,000 = \$12,000$$

Similar calculations would be made for the next four years of the asset's life. A depreciation schedule, complete with the actual miles driven in each of the five years, is shown in Exhibit 8-3.

Exhibit 8-3 Depreciation Schedule—Units-of-Activity Method

Year	Calculation	Depreciation Expense	Accumulated Depreciation	Net Book Value
			$ 0	$65,000
2010	$0.50 × 24,000 miles	$12,000	12,000	53,000
2011	$0.50 × 22,000 miles	11,000	23,000	42,000
2012	$0.50 × 27,000 miles	13,500	36,500	28,500
2013	$0.50 × 17,000 miles	8,500	45,000	20,000
2014	$0.50 × 10,000 miles	5,000	50,000	15,000

Note that this calculation is very similar to the straight-line calculation. Depreciable cost is divided by estimated life. But, instead of calculating depreciation expense per year, depreciation expense per unit is calculated. Once depreciation expense per unit is known, depreciation expense is determined by multiplying the per unit rate by the actual units of activity during the period. The calculation is as follows:

$$\text{Depreciation Expense} = \text{Depreciation Expense per Unit} \times \text{Actual Units of Activity}$$

As you review the schedule, note that depreciation expense fluctuates as the asset's activity fluctuates. As a result, depreciation expense is a function of usage. Second, note that the total number of miles driven over the five years equals 100,000 miles. This assumption is made for simplicity. However, had Dozier driven the truck more than 100,000 miles, total depreciation expense over the life of the asset would still be limited to $50,000, the asset's depreciable cost.

Comparing Depreciation Methods

The calculations in the previous sections demonstrate that a company's depreciation expense in a given year will depend on the depreciation method chosen. For comparative purposes, Exhibit 8-4 summarizes the annual depreciation for Dozier's truck as well as the resulting net book values under the three methods.

Units-of-activity method A depreciation method in which depreciation expense is a function of the actual usage of the asset.

One of the most common reasons that companies choose one depreciation method over another is the effect on taxes.

Exhibit 8-4 Comparison of Three Depreciation Methods

Straight-Line			Double-Declining-Balance			Units-of-Activity		
Year	Depr. Exp.	NBV	Year	Depr. Exp.	NBV	Year	Depr. Exp.	NBV
2010	$10,000	$55,000	2010	$26,000	$39,000	2010	$12,000	$53,000
2011	10,000	45,000	2011	15,600	23,400	2011	11,000	42,000
2012	10,000	35,000	2012	8,400	15,000	2012	13,500	28,500
2013	10,000	25,000	2013	0	15,000	2013	8,500	20,000
2014	10,000	15,000	2014	0	15,000	2014	5,000	15,000
	$50,000			$50,000			$50,000	

The summary demonstrates that total depreciation expense over the life of the asset is $50,000 regardless of the method chosen. However, each method arrives at $50,000 differently. The straight-line method depreciates the same amount each year. The double-declining-balance method accelerates depreciation into the early years of the asset's life. The units-of-activity method depreciates different amounts each year depending on the asset's usage. No depreciation method is right. They are just different, and companies choose to use one over another for different reasons. One of the most common reasons is the effect on taxes.

Like all expenses, depreciation expense reduces net income, which in turn reduces income taxes. Assuming a 40% tax rate in the example above, the $50,000 of depreciation on the truck will lower taxes by $20,000. The advantage of the double-declining-balance method is that all of the tax savings are realized in three years rather than five. This is beneficial to a company because the company can temporarily use the cash that would otherwise be paid to the government.

Many companies take advantage of this tax effect by using one method of depreciation for tax purposes and another for financial reporting purposes. The Internal Revenue Service (IRS) allows companies to use a depreciation method known as the Modified Accelerated Cost Recovery System (MACRS). As its name implies, MACRS is an accelerated method much like the double-declining-balance method. However, the IRS does not require that a company use the same method on its tax return that it does for its financial statements. As a result, many companies that use MACRS for taxes use the straight-line method for financial reports.

Regardless of the method chosen, companies must disclose their choices in the notes to their financial statements so that comparisons can be made among different companies. This is an application of the qualitative characteristic of comparability. The disclosure is sometimes found in a note dedicated solely to fixed assets. However, most companies like McDonald's put it in the first note summarizing the significant accounting policies used to prepare financial statements.

McDonald's 2008 Disclosure of Depreciation Method

Property and equipment are stated at cost, with depreciation and amortization provided using the straight-line method over the following estimated useful lives: buildings—up to 40 years; leasehold improvements—the lesser of useful lives of assets or lease terms, which generally include option periods; and equipment—three to 12 years.

LO₃ Adjustments Made During a Fixed Asset's Useful Life

Since fixed assets are used for multiple years, companies sometimes must make adjustments as new information is available or as new activity occurs. These adjustments can arise from the following:

- Changes in estimates
- Additional expenditures to improve the fixed asset
- Significant declines in the asset's market value

Changes in Depreciation Estimates

Calculating depreciation expense requires that a company estimate the asset's useful life and its salvage value. These estimates are normally based on previous company experience with similar assets as well as factors such as the manufacturer's recommendations. As a result, they are usually fair and reasonable. However, estimates can differ from actual experience. When such errors are small and will not affect decision making, they are usually ignored. When the estimates are materially wrong, though, revisions can be made. We call this a change in estimate.

When an estimate is changed, the change is made prospectively, meaning that the change affects only the calculation of current and future depreciation expense. Depreciation expense for prior years is not retroactively corrected. Once an estimate is revised, current and future depreciation expense is calculated with the new estimate. This is done by (1) determining the remaining depreciable cost of the asset at the time of the revision and (2) depreciating that cost over the remaining useful life using the same depreciation method.

To illustrate, suppose that Thomas Supply purchases a machine for $90,000 on January 1, 2010. Thomas estimates that the machine will have a 10-year useful life and a $10,000 salvage value. Thomas uses the straight-line method of depreciation and records $8,000 of depreciation expense [($90,000 − $10,000) ÷ 10] each year as follows:

Dec. 31	Depreciation Expense	8,000	
	Accumulated Depreciation		8,000
	(To record depreciation expense)		

Assets	=	Liabilities	+	Equity
−8,000				−8,000

When actual experience shows that a past estimate was incorrect, accountants **change the estimate going forward** instead of correcting the past.

Now suppose that on January 1, 2014, Thomas decides that the machine will last only eight years rather than the ten years originally estimated and will have a salvage value of only $6,000 rather than $10,000. When these revisions are made, Thomas does not correct the four previous depreciation expense entries of $8,000 because they were based on reasonable estimates at the time. Instead, Thomas calculates the remaining depreciable cost of the asset and spreads it out over the remaining useful life.

To do this, Thomas must first calculate the net book value of the asset on the date of revision. This represents the unexpired cost of the asset.

Net book value at the time of estimate revision:

Cost of the asset, January 1, 2010	$90,000
Less: Accumulated depreciation for four years	32,000
Net book value on January 1, 2014	$58,000

Next, Thomas subtracts from the net book value the asset's salvage value, which will result in the asset's remaining depreciable cost. Keep in mind that Thomas uses the revised salvage value. This is shown as follows:

Depreciable cost for future depreciation:

Net book value on January 1, 2014	$58,000
Less: Estimated salvage value	6,000
Remaining depreciable cost	$52,000

Finally, under the straight-line method Thomas calculates depreciation expense by dividing the remaining depreciable cost by the remaining useful life. In this case, the total useful life is now estimated to be eight years instead of ten, which means that there are only four years remaining instead of six.

Depreciation expense under revised estimates:	
Remaining depreciable cost	$52,000
Divided by remaining useful life	÷ 4
Annual depreciation expense	$13,000

Because classifying expenditures as **capital or revenue** is subjective, two accountants may classify the same expenditure differently.

With this new depreciation expense calculated, Thomas would make the following journal entry at the end of Years 5 through 8.

Dec. 31	Depreciation Expense	13,000	
	Accumulated Depreciation		13,000
	(To record depreciation expense)		

Assets	=	Liabilities	+	Equity
−13,000				−13,000

So, Thomas depreciates $8,000 per year in Years 1 through 4 and $13,000 per year in Years 5 through 8. This results in $84,000 of total depreciation over the life of the asset, which is equal to the original cost of the asset less its revised salvage value ($90,000 − $6,000 = $84,000).

When a company has a material change in a fixed asset estimate, it will disclose the change in the notes to its financial statements. Exhibit 8-5 is an example from IBM, which in 1999 reduced income $404 million due to a change in useful life estimates on computers.

Exhibit 8-5 Change in Estimate—IBM

Change in Estimate
As a result of a change in the estimated useful life of personal computers from five years to three years, the company recognized a charge in the second quarter of 1999 of $404 million ($241 million after tax, $0.13 per diluted common share). In the second quarter of 1999, the company wrote off the net book value of personal computers that were three years old or older and, therefore, had no remaining useful life. The remaining book value of the assets will be depreciated over the remaining new useful life.

Expenditures After Acquisition

Most fixed assets require expenditures throughout their useful lives. You have to think no further than your personal automobile to see this. The purchasing price is only the first cost. Expenditures for oil changes, tune ups, minor repairs, and even major repairs come later. So, how are these additional expenditures treated from an accounting standpoint?

The accounting treatment for expenditures made during the useful life of a fixed asset depends on whether they are classified as *capital* or *revenue* expenditures. A **capital expenditure** increases the expected useful life or productivity of the asset. An example would be a new engine for an automobile. Capital expenditures are added to the cost of the asset and depreciated over the asset's remaining useful life. A **revenue expenditure** maintains the expected useful life or productivity of the asset. An example would be an oil change. Revenue expenditures are expensed in the period in which they are incurred. They are not added to the cost of the asset.

To illustrate, suppose that a company purchases a fixed asset for $50,000 on January 1, 2010. The company estimates the asset's useful life and salvage value at five years and $0, respectively. Using the straight-line depreciation method, the company records $10,000 of depreciation expense each year. Now suppose that on January 1, 2014, during the fifth year of the asset's life, the company incurs $1,000 in ordinary maintenance and $8,000 for upgrades. The upgrades allow the machine to be used productively in 2015 and 2016.

Given this information, the $1,000 is a revenue expenditure and should be expensed as follows:

Capital expenditure An expenditure that increases the expected useful life or productivity of a fixed asset.

Revenue expenditure An expenditure that maintains the expected useful life or productivity of a fixed asset.

Jan. 1	Maintenance Expense	1,000	
2014	Cash		1,000
	(To record normal maintenance)		

Assets	=	Liabilities	+	Equity
−1,000				−1,000

In contrast, the $8,000 for upgrades is a capital expenditure since the asset's useful life is extended two years. It should therefore be capitalized with the following entry:

Jan. 1	Fixed Asset	8,000	
2014	Cash		8,000
	(To record upgrade to asset)		

Assets	=	Liabilities	+	Equity
+8,000				
−8,000				

Notice that this entry results in an increase and decrease to assets rather than a change in equity. This is because the company is capitalizing the expenditure rather than expensing it.

With this addition to the cost of the asset, depreciation expense for 2014 must be recalculated. To do so, the company follows the same general procedures used in the change of estimate scenario. It first calculates the net book value of the asset and then adds the capital expenditure to obtain the updated net book value. This is shown as follows:

Net book value after the capital expenditure:

Cost of the asset, January 1, 2010	$50,000
Less: Accumulated depreciation for four years	40,000
Net book value on January 1, 2014	$10,000
Add: Upgrades made in 2014	8,000
Updated net book value on January 1, 2014	$18,000

Next, the company subtracts the asset's salvage value to get the remaining depreciable cost. Under the straight-line method of depreciation, the depreciable cost is then divided by the remaining useful life to obtain depreciation expense. In 2014, 2015, and 2016, the company will record $6,000 of depreciation expense each year.

> The classification of expenditures as capital expenditures rather than revenue expenditures was the source of one of the largest frauds in recent history.

Depreciation expense after capital expenditure:

Updated net book value on January 1, 2014	$18,000
Less: Estimated salvage value	0
Remaining depreciable cost on January 1, 2014	$18,000
Divided by remaining useful life	÷ 3
Annual depreciation expense	$ 6,000

While the classification of post-acquisition expenditures may seem rather unimportant, it is actually an area of great interest because of the potential for fraudulent behavior by companies. One of the largest corporate frauds in recent history centered on the treatment and reporting of revenue expenditures. In 2002, it was discovered that WorldCom was treating operating expenses associated with telecommunication lines as capital expenditures. Instead of appearing on the income statement as expenses, these costs were recorded as assets on the balance sheet. This resulted in a gross understatement of current expenses and overstatement of net income. Over the seven quarters that it committed this fraud, the company overstated its results by several billion dollars. After several years of investigation and prosecution, the chief executive officer of the company was found guilty of nine counts of securities fraud, conspiracy, and filing false documents.

Asset Impairment

Sometimes, a fixed asset's market value will fall substantially due to changing market conditions, technological improvements, or other factors. When a fixed asset's market value falls materially below its net book value and the decline in value is deemed to be *permanent*, the asset is considered *impaired*. Accounting rules require companies to write impaired assets down from their book values to their market values. This, like the lower-of-cost-or-market rule with inventory, is an application of the concept of conservatism.

L ook at Home Depot's first note to its financial statements in Appendix C. There is one paragraph describing expenditures for a certain type of activity where the treatment of the expenditures is very similar to the capital and revenue expenditures described in this text. What is this activity?

The activity is software costs. Home Depot describes in the Capitalized Software Costs paragraph that certain expenditures associated with the development of software are capitalized into Furniture, Fixtures, and Equipment and then amortized over the software's useful life, which is three to six years. All expenditures not meeting the requirements for capitalization are expensed in the period incurred.

To illustrate, suppose a company has equipment that makes a unique toy that becomes extremely popular. The equipment has a net book value of $140,000 and a higher market value. Suppose further that the toy suddenly loses its popularity, and the company is unable to alter the machine to produce anything else. As a result, the market value of the machine plummets to $40,000. The company deems this decline in market value to be permanent and declares that the asset is impaired. The asset impairment would be recorded as follows:

Loss on Impairment	100,000	
Fixed Asset		100,000
(To record permanent impairment of asset)		

Assets	=	Liabilities	+	Equity
−100,000				−100,000

In the above entry, a Loss on Impairment is increased to reflect the decline in value of the asset. This reduces equity. Because this loss is not a result of normal operations, the loss would be included among Other Revenues and Expenses on the income statement. In addition, the Fixed Asset account is decreased to reflect the reduced value. This reduces assets. After the impairment entry, depreciation expense would be calculated based on the revised depreciable cost and remaining useful life.

Asset impairments are not uncommon. In fact, current accounting rules require companies to periodically assess whether any of their fixed assets are impaired. Consider the note to Eli Lilly's financial statements as shown in Exhibit 8-6.

While the note speaks of issues that are beyond the scope of this book, you can at least see that asset impairments can be material to a company's financial results. Eli Lilly recorded over $154 million in impairments in one year.

LO4 Disposing of Fixed Assets

When a company decides that it no longer needs a fixed asset, it usually disposes of the asset in one of three ways. When the asset has no value, it will simply be discarded. When the asset still has value, it will either be sold or traded in for another asset, often a

Exhibit 8-6 Asset Impairment—Eli Lilly

Note 4: Asset Impairment and Other Site Charges
In December 2005, management approved, as part of our ongoing efforts to increase productivity and reduce our cost structure, decisions that resulted in non-cash charges of $154.6 million for the write-down of certain impaired assets, and other charges of $17.3 million, primarily related to contract termination payments. The impaired assets, which have no future use, include manufacturing buildings and equipment no longer needed to supply projected capacity requirements, as well as obsolete research and development equipment. The impairment charges are necessary to adjust the carrying value of the assets to fair value.

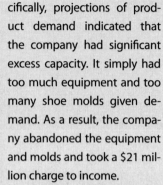

© AP IMAGES/AP PHOTO/FRANK AUGSTEIN

The value of a company's equipment can be impaired or reduced for many reasons. One of those is a decrease in demand for the product that the equipment makes. Take Crocs, Inc., as an example.

Crocs, Inc., is well known for its lightweight and colorful ventilated clogs. The company burst onto the scene in 2002 with the launch of its Beach™ model, and demand grew quickly. The company responded by rapidly diversifying into different styles and increasing production capacity and warehouse space. By 2007, the company was generating record profits of $168 million.

But things quickly changed. Demand for Crocs' products fell in 2008, resulting in a $185 million overall loss. Approximately 11% of that loss, or $21 million, was attributable to impairment charges on its manufacturing equipment. Specifically, projections of product demand indicated that the company had significant excess capacity. It simply had too much equipment and too many shoe molds given demand. As a result, the company abandoned the equipment and molds and took a $21 million charge to income.

And unfortunately for the company, the impairments continued into 2009. For the first six months of 2009, Crocs has recognized $17 million in asset impairment charges related to shoe molds and distribution facilities.

---

newer model. Since the accounting for trading an asset is beyond the scope of this book, we will focus on the first two cases—discarding or selling the asset.

The accounting for the disposal of a fixed asset consists of the following three steps:

1. Update depreciation on the asset.
2. Calculate gain or loss on the disposal.
3. Record the disposal.

The first step is to record any necessary depreciation expense to update the accumulated depreciation account. Usually, this means that depreciation expense must be recorded for a partial period. For example, a company that records annual depreciation expense on December 31 and sells equipment on the following February 15 must record depreciation expense for one and one-half months at the time of disposal.

The second step is to calculate any gain or loss on the disposal by comparing the asset's net book value to the proceeds from the asset's sale, if any. When the proceeds exceed the net book value, a gain on disposal is recognized. When the net book value exceeds the proceeds, a loss on disposal is recognized. This is summarized below:

Gain on Disposal =
    Proceeds from Sale > Net Book Value

Loss on Disposal =
    Proceeds from Sale < Net Book Value

The third and final step is to prepare a journal entry that decreases the asset account and its related accumulated depreciation account. If the asset is sold and cash is received, the entry must also record the increase in cash. Finally, any gain or loss on the disposal must be recorded.

To illustrate, suppose that a company purchases a machine on January 1, 2010, for $30,000. The company estimates the useful life and salvage value to be four years and $2,000, respectively. The company uses the straight-line method of depreciation and records depreciation expense annually on December 31. Given these facts, annual depreciation expense for the machine is $7,000 [($30,000 − $2,000) / 4].

Loss Example

Suppose further that the company sells the machine on June 30, 2012, for $12,000. To account for this sale, the company must first update the accumulated depreciation account. The asset has been used for six months since the last time depreciation was recorded (December 31), so the company must record six months of depreciation expense. Since annual depreciation expense is $7,000, six months of depreciation would be half of that, or $3,500. Therefore, the following entry would be made on June 30, 2012:

June 30 2012	Depreciation Expense	3,500	
	Accumulated Depreciation		3,500

Assets	=	Liabilities	+	Equity
−3,500				−3,500

As a result of this entry, the accumulated depreciation account is updated to a balance of $17,500 ($7,000 in 2010, $7,000 in 2011, and $3,500 in 2012). With this balance, the gain/loss on disposal can be calculated as follows:

Proceeds from sale		$12,000
Cost of machine	$30,000	
Less: accumulated depreciation	17,500	
Net book value at June 30, 2012		12,500
Loss on sale		$ (500)

Because the asset's net book value of $12,500 exceeds the sale proceeds of $12,000, the company generates a $500 loss. With this information, the company can prepare the following journal entry to record the disposal:

June 30 2012	Cash	12,000	
	Accumulated Depreciation	17,500	
	Loss on Disposal	500	
	Machine		30,000

Assets	=	Liabilities	+	Equity
+12,000				−500
+17,500				
−30,000				

The entry first decreases the Machine account by $30,000 to eliminate the account. A common mistake is to think that the Machine account should be decreased by its net book value of $12,500. But remember that

fixed assets are recorded and maintained at their costs, so the balance in the Machine account is $30,000 prior to disposal. Second, the entry decreases Accumulated Depreciation by $17,500. Because the company no longer has the asset, it should no longer maintain accumulated depreciation for the asset. Third, the entry increases the Cash account to reflect the asset received from selling the machine. Finally, the entry increases a Loss on Disposal account to reflect the loss on sale. This account is reported on the income statement among Other Revenues and Expenses. As a result of the entry, assets and equity decrease by $500, the amount of the loss.

Gain Example

To illustrate a gain example, suppose that the company sells the machine on March 31, 2013, for $8,000. After updating depreciation, the Accumulated Depreciation account would have a balance of $22,750:

Three full years (2010, 2011, 2012)	$21,000
One-fourth of 2013 ($7,000 × ¼)	1,750
Accumulated depreciation at March 31, 2013	$22,750

Therefore, the machine's net book value and the gain/loss on disposal at March 31, 2013, can be calculated as follows:

Proceeds from sale		$8,000
Cost of machine	$30,000	
Less: accumulated depreciation	22,750	
Net book value at March 31, 2013		7,250
Gain on sale		$ 750

Because the sale proceeds of $8,000 exceed the asset's net book value of $7,250, the company generates a

> **A loss on the sale of a fixed asset** is reported in other expenses so that operating expenses include only those expenses related to normal operations.

$750 gain. With this information, the following journal entry can be prepared to record the disposal:

Mar. 31 2013	Cash	8,000	
	Accumulated Depreciation	22,750	
	Gain on Disposal		750
	Machine	30,000	
	Assets = Liabilities + Equity		
	+ 8,000 +750		
	+22,750		
	−30,000		

Like the loss example, the entry decreases the Machine account by $30,000. It also decreases the machine's Accumulated Depreciation account by $22,750 to eliminate the account and increases the Cash account by $8,000 to reflect the asset received from selling the machine. Finally, the entry increases a Gain on Disposal account to reflect the gain on sale. Like the loss example, the net effect on the accounting equation is an equal change in assets and equity, with this example resulting in a $750 increase to both.

LO5 Evaluating a Company's Management of Fixed Assets

Because fixed assets comprise the largest category of assets for most companies, it is usually a good idea to evaluate a company's management of its fixed assets. A company manages fixed assets by acquiring them, using them productively, and then replacing them. Therefore, two issues of importance for any company with fixed assets would be as follows:

1. How productive are the company's fixed assets in generating revenues?

2. What is the condition of the company's fixed assets?

The following sections examine these issues for the fixed assets of McDonald's. The examination will require information from the company's balance sheet, income statement, and notes to the financial statements. The required information is found in Exhibit 8-7, excerpted from McDonald's 2008 Annual Report.

Horizontal and Vertical Analyses

A good place to start an analysis of fixed assets is with horizontal and vertical analyses. Recall from Chapter 2 that horizontal analysis calculates the dollar change in an account balance, defined as the current year balance less the prior year balance, and divides that change by the prior year balance to yield the percentage change. Vertical analysis divides each account balance by a base account, yielding a percentage. The base account is total assets for balance sheet accounts and net sales or total revenues for income statement accounts. These calculations are summarized as follows:

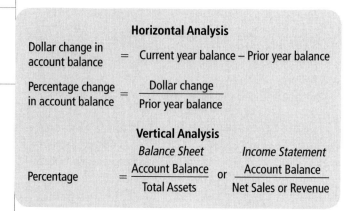

Exhibit 8-7 Account Balances from McDonald's 2008 Annual Report

Source	Accounts	2008	2007
Income Statement	Total revenues	$ 23,522.4	$ 22,786.6
Balance Sheet	Property and equipment, at cost	$ 31,152.4	$ 32,203.7
	Less: Accumulated depreciation	(10,897.9)	(11,219.0)
	Net property and equipment	$ 20,254.5	$ 20,984.7
	Total assets	$ 28,461.5	$ 29,391.7
Notes to Financial Statements	Depreciation expense	$ 1,161.6	$ 1,145.0

Given McDonald's financial information in Exhibit 8-7, horizontal and vertical analyses of fixed assets and depreciation expense result in the following. Note that the net book value of property and equipment is used in the calculations. Note also that vertical analysis is conducted on both years of data.

Horizontal Analysis

	Dollar Change	Percentage Change
Property and equipment	$\dfrac{20{,}254.5 - 20{,}984.7}{(730.2)}$	$\dfrac{(730.2)}{20{,}984.7} = -3.5\%$
Depreciation expense	$\dfrac{1{,}161.6 - 1{,}145.0}{16.6}$	$\dfrac{16.6}{1{,}145.0} = 1.5\%$

Vertical Analysis

	2008	2007
Property and equipment	$\dfrac{20{,}254.5}{28{,}461.5} = 71.2\%$	$\dfrac{20{,}984.7}{29{,}391.7} = 71.4\%$
Depreciation expense	$\dfrac{1{,}161.6}{23{,}522.4} = 4.9\%$	$\dfrac{1{,}145.0}{22{,}786.6} = 5.0\%$

The calculations show a fairly stable fixed asset position. Horizontal analysis shows a slight decrease of 3.5% in fixed assets and a slight increase of 1.5% in depreciation expense from 2007 to 2008. Vertical analysis shows that fixed assets make up a large part of McDonald's asset base. In each year, slightly over 71% of the assets are fixed assets. Furthermore, depreciation expense is shown to be about 5% in each year. This tells us that for every dollar in sales revenue, the company incurs about a nickel in depreciation expense. Overall, both of these analyses indicate fairly stable fixed assets over the two-year period.

For comparison purposes, the following table lists the 2008 horizontal and vertical analyses of Burger

		Horizontal Analysis	Vertical Analysis
Fixed Assets	McDonald's	−3.5%	71.2%
	Burger King	9.3%	35.8%
Depreciation Expense	McDonald's	1.5%	4.9%
	Burger King	5.4%	4.8%

King Holdings. While McDonald's has a larger percentage of its total assets in fixed assets, Burger King is increasing its fixed assets and depreciation at a greater rate.

Fixed Asset Turnover Ratio

The preceeding analyses indicate that McDonald's fixed assets were stable. But they do not indicate whether the company is using those fixed assets productively to generate revenues. One means to find out is to calculate the fixed asset turnover ratio. The **fixed asset turnover ratio** compares total revenues during a period to the average net book value of fixed assets during that period. It is calculated as follows:

$$\text{Fixed Asset Turnover Ratio} = \frac{\text{Total Revenues}}{\text{Average Net Book Value of Fixed Assets}}$$

where average net book value is:

$$\frac{\text{Beginning Net Book Value} + \text{Ending Net Book Value}}{2}$$

Because this ratio compares total revenues to fixed assets, it indicates the productivity of every dollar invested in fixed assets. In general, companies want this ratio to be higher rather than lower. All other things equal, a higher ratio indicates that the company is using its fixed assets more effectively to produce more revenue.

McDonald's 2008 fixed asset turnover ratio is calculated as follows.

$$\frac{23{,}522.4}{(20{,}254.5 + 20{,}984.7) \div 2} = 1.14$$

The 1.14 ratio shows that McDonald's total revenues for 2008 were 1.14 times the average net book value of its fixed assets. In other words, for every dollar of fixed assets, on average, McDonald's was able to generate $1.14 in revenue during the period. Whether this is good or bad requires some comparison. Wendy's/Arby's 2008 fixed asset turnover ratio was 1.60, while Burger King's was 2.67. McDonald's trails its two rivals in generating revenues from its fixed assets.

Fixed asset turnover ratio A comparison of total revenues to the average net book value of fixed assets that measures the productivity of fixed assets.

Using Home Depot's information in Appendix C, calculate and interpret (1) horizontal and vertical analyses of fixed assets and depreciation expense, (2) fixed asset turnover ratio, and (3) average life and average age of fixed assets.

(1) Horizontal Analysis

Fixed assets: ($26,234 − $27,476) / $27,476 = (4.5%)
Depreciation Expense: ($1,785 − $1,702) / $1,702 = 4.9%

Vertical Analysis

Fixed assets: $26,234 / $41,164 = 63.7%
Depreciation Expense: $1,785 / $71,288 = 2.5%

The horizontal analysis shows that while depreciation expense was up slightly, overall fixed assets actually decreased during the year. The 63.7% vertical analysis of fixed assets shows how important fixed assets are to the company. Almost two-thirds of its assets are in fixed assets. The 2.5% vertical analysis of depreciation expense indicates that although the company has large fixed assets, depreciation expense consumes less than three cents per dollar of sales in the most recent year.

(2) Fixed Asset Turnover Ratio:

$$\$71,288 / (\$26,234 + \$27,476)/2 = 2.66$$

The 2.66 fixed asset turnover ratio indicates that Home Depot generates $2.66 in sales for every $1 of fixed assets that it owns. This could provide Home Depot with a benchmark expectation for stores. For example, a store with $10 million of fixed assets could be expected to generate about $27 million in sales.

(3) Average Life Ratio: $26,234 / $1,785 = 14.7 years
Average Age Ratio: $10,243 / $1,785 = 5.7 years

The 14.7 average life ratio shows that Home Depot's average fixed asset has about a 15-year life. The 5.7 average age ratio indicates that the company's fixed assets are relatively young, having been used for only 5 or so years. Taken together, these two ratios indicate that Home Depot will not need significant fixed asset replacement in the near term.

Average Life and Age of Fixed Assets

In addition to understanding the productivity of fixed assets, it is a good idea to understand the condition of a company's fixed assets. Fixed assets in poor condition are usually less productive and normally require significant expenditures either to repair or replace. While a user of McDonald's financial statements cannot physically examine the company's fixed assets, one way to get a rough idea of the general condition of a company's fixed assets is to look at the age of the assets in comparison to their useful lives. This can be accomplished by calculating the average useful life and average age of the assets.

The **average useful life of fixed assets** represents the number of years, on average, that a company expects to use its fixed assets. It is calculated as follows:

$$\text{Average Useful Life} = \frac{\text{Cost of Fixed Assets}}{\text{Depreciation Expense}}$$

The ratio divides the total cost of fixed assets by the amount of annual depreciation expense to approximate the number of years that it will take to fully depreciate the assets. A higher number represents a longer useful life. You may notice that this ratio is basically a rearrangement of the calculation of straight-line depreciation. Therefore, the ratio works best when the company uses the straight-line method.

The **average age of fixed assets** represents the number of years, on average, that the company has used its fixed assets. It is calculated as follows:

Average useful life of fixed assets A comparison of the cost of fixed assets to depreciation expense that estimates the number of years, on average, that a company expects to use its fixed assets.

Average age of fixed assets A comparison of accumulated depreciation to depreciation expense that estimates the number of years, on average, that the company has used its fixed assets.

$$\text{Average Age} = \frac{\text{Accumulated Depreciation}}{\text{Depreciation Expense}}$$

The ratio divides the accumulated depreciation balance by the amount of annual depreciation expense to approximate the number of years that the assets have already been depreciated. A higher number means that the assets are older. Like the average useful life ratio, the average age ratio works best when the company uses the straight-line method.

Calculating McDonald's 2008 ratios requires the cost of the fixed assets and their accumulated depreciation balances at the end of 2008. These are found on the balance sheet. It also requires depreciation expense for 2008. This is found in the company's Property and Equipment note to its financial statements. Each account balance is shown in Exhibit 8-7.

$$\text{Average Life} = \frac{31,152.4}{1,161.6} = 26.8$$

$$\text{Average Age} = \frac{10,897.9}{1,161.6} = 9.4$$

The ratios show that McDonald's fixed assets, on average, have about a 27-year expected life and are currently about 9 years old. Now, we have to be careful here not to read too much into these numbers. In its first note to its financial statements, McDonald's reports that it assumes lives of up to 40 years for buildings, up to 15 years for restaurant equipment, and up to 10 years for other equipment. Like many companies, McDonald's has various fixed assets with various useful lives. While this makes the average life and age ratios very general estimates, the calculations do allow us to draw the general conclusion that the company's fixed assets are relatively new. On average, the company has used its fixed assets for about one-third of their useful lives. Thus, we would not expect McDonald's to have abnormally high expenditures for repairing or replacing fixed assets in the near future.

LO6 Fixed Assets and Cash Flows

Another important aspect of fixed assets is their effect on a company's cash flows. Fixed assets affect cash flows the most when they are purchased. Because companies often purchase significant amounts of fixed

A negative number for **capital expenditures** indicates that a company is investing in operating assets.

assets each year, the cash paid for them is reported as a separate line item in the investing activities section of the statement of cash flows. The line item is often labeled as Capital Expenditures or something similar. McDonald's is a little more specific, reporting the following on the first line of its investing activities section:

McDonald's 2008 Capital Expenditures from the Statement of Cash Flows

in millions	2008	2007	2006
Property and equipment expenditures	$(2,135.7)	$(1,946.6)	$(1,741.9)

The negative number signifies a cash outflow. In 2008, McDonald's spent over $2.1 billion in cash to purchase fixed assets. In the two previous years, the company spent about $1.9 billion and $1.7 billion. For the three years combined, this totals over $5.8 billion in cash paid for fixed assets.

A natural question arising from this data is where the company got the $5.8 billion it needed for these investments in fixed assets. Did it borrow the money or did it have it on hand? We can get an idea of where the money came from by looking one line above the capital expenditures. There we find the cash provided by operating activities, which is summarized as follows:

McDonald's 2008 Operating Cash Flows from the Statement of Cash Flows

in millions	2008	2007	2006
Cash provided by operations	$5,917.2	$4,876.3	$4,341.5

In each year, McDonald's generated more cash from operating activities than it spent for fixed assets. For example, in 2008 the company generated $5.9 billion in cash from operations while it paid out $2.1 billion for fixed assets. This means that the company was able to finance its growth with money generated from profitable operations. When a company's capital expenditures exceed its cash from operating activities, the company

L ook at Home Depot's statement of cash flows in Appendix C. How much cash has the company spent to acquire fixed assets over the past three years in total? Compare Home Depot's capital expenditures in the most recent year to its cash from operations.

According to the investing activities section of its statement of cash flows, Home Depot spent a total of $8,947 capital expenditures over the past three years ($1,847 + $3,558 + $3,542 = $8,947).

Home Depot's capital expenditures in the most recent year were $1,847 million while its cash generated from operations was $5,528. Thus, it appears that Home Depot generated enough cash to pay for its growth in fixed assets without having to borrow the cash or dip into its reserves.

must get the needed cash from some other place. Either it must use its cash reserves or borrow the money from a creditor. Being able to generate enough cash to pay for new fixed assets is a good sign for McDonald's.

LO7 Intangible Assets

I n addition to fixed assets, companies often possess other long-term assets known as intangible assets. An **intangible asset** is a resource that is used in operations for more than one year but has no physical substance. A patent is a good example. A **patent** is the right, granted by the United States Patent Office, for the holder of the patent to manufacture, sell, or use a particular product or process exclusively for a limited period of time. Although the right of exclusive use has no physical properties, it can be a very valuable resource to the holder. Consider the pharmaceutical industry. When a company develops a new drug that is approved by the Food and Drug Administration, which will be more valuable—the equipment that manufactures the drug or the patent that provides for exclusive manufacturing and selling of the drug? Pharmaceutical companies will likely tell you that the patent is most valuable to them.

You are probably familiar with other intangible assets. For example, a **trademark** or **trade name** is the right, granted by the United States Patent Office, for a company to use exclusively a name, symbol, or phrase to identify the company. Often, you can tell if something is registered as a trademark if it has a small ™ or ® beside the name or symbol. Wendy's/Arby's Frosty™ is an example. No other company, without permission from Wendy's/Arby's, can lawfully use the name Frosty™ in association with an ice cream drink. The Nike swoosh™ is another example, as is the script Coca-Cola™.

Another recognizable intangible is a copyright. A **copyright** is the right, granted by the United States Copyright Office, to reproduce or sell an artistic or published work. The publisher of this book owns the copyright to the material in the book and can reproduce and sell it as it pleases. The material cannot be reproduced by someone else lawfully without the permission of the publisher.

A third intangible with which you may be familiar is a franchise. A **franchise** is the right, granted by the franchisor, to operate a business under the trade name of the franchisor. Examples of franchises are all around you. For example, whenever you visit a McDonald's, you may be entering into a restaurant that is owned by an individual (the franchisee) who has purchased from

Intangible asset A resource that is used in operations for more than one year but that has no physical substance.

Patent The right to manufacture, sell, or use a particular product or process exclusively for a limited period of time.

Trademark (trade name) The right to use exclusively a name, symbol, or phrase to identify a company.

Copyright The right to reproduce or sell an artistic or published work.

Franchise The right to operate a business under the trade name of the franchisor.

The Nike swoosh is a well known example of a trademark.

McDonald's Corporation (the franchisor) the right to operate the restaurant.

Recording Intangible Assets

Like all other assets, intangible assets are recorded at their acquisition costs. However, what is included as an acquisition cost can vary given the type of intangible asset and how it is acquired.

Externally Acquired The easiest case is when an intangible asset is acquired through an external transaction. For example, suppose that a company purchases a product patent from another company for $100,000. Because the patent is purchased in an arm's length transaction with another company, the cost of the patent is the purchase price. In general, if an intangible asset is acquired through an external transaction, its cost is the purchase price.

A common example of an intangible that is created through an external transaction is goodwill. Goodwill is created when one company buys another company and pays more than the value of the net assets of the purchased company. **Goodwill** is equal to the excess of the purchase price over the value of the purchased net assets. For example, suppose that Buyer Company purchases Seller Company for $8 million when the value of Seller Company's net assets is $6 million. In this transaction, Buyer Company pays $8 million and records $6 million of new assets and $2 million of goodwill. A condensed form of the entry Buyer Company would make to record this transaction would be as follows:

Net Assets of Seller Company	6,000,000	
Goodwill	2,000,000	
Cash		8,000,000
(To record the purchase of Seller)		

Assets	=	Liabilities	+	Equity
+6,000,000				
+2,000,000				
−8,000,000				

The above entry records the decrease in cash resulting from the purchase and the increase in net assets acquired through the purchase. The difference of $2 million is debited to Goodwill, which increases that asset account. The result of the entry is an increase and decrease to assets.

To understand what goodwill represents, think about why a company would pay a premium for another company. The purchasing company might want to acquire the other company's customers, its reputation, its employees, its market share, or its research. Whatever the reason, the purchasing company is paying for something intangible that the other company possesses. This intangible value is what goodwill represents. Note here that goodwill can be recorded by a company *only* when it purchases another company. Goodwill created internally by a company cannot be recorded as an asset because its cost cannot be reliably determined. Only through an independent purchase can the value of goodwill be objectively measured.

Goodwill can be a large asset on the balance sheets of companies that have acquired other companies. Wendy's/Arby's is a good example. On its 2008 balance sheet, the company reports over $853 million in goodwill. Most of this goodwill was created when Wendy's International was purchased by Triarc, the parent company of Arby's. With total assets of approximately $4.6 billion, goodwill represents about 18% of assets. McDonald's also has a large balance in goodwill. It reports over $2.2 billion in goodwill on total assets of over $28 billion. Goodwill makes up about 8% of McDonald's assets.

Internally Generated In the previous two examples, intangible assets were purchased externally and therefore recorded at their purchase prices. When an intangible asset is developed internally, the accounting is slightly different. The initial cost of an internally generated intangible asset is limited to the legal and administrative fees to establish the asset.

To illustrate, suppose that a company's researchers spend $150,000 creating a patentable product. To register the patent, the company spends $10,000. In this case, the cost of the patent is only $10,000. The $150,000 of research and development must be expensed in the period it is incurred, not added to the cost of the asset. While many disagree with this accounting treatment, it is another application of conservatism. It is very difficult to know whether particular research and development costs will result in productive assets and how long those assets might last. Given this uncertainty, excluding research and development costs from the cost of an internally developed intangible asset reduces the likelihood that the intangible asset is overstated.

Goodwill An intangible asset equal to the excess that one company pays to acquire the net assets of another company.

Once an intangible asset is acquired and recorded, it is often challenged by other companies. For example, patent holders often must defend their rights against companies manufacturing similar products. When a company incurs costs to successfully defend the legality of its assets, such costs should be added to the cost of the asset. You can see this treatment in company disclosures. For example, eSpeed, Inc., a provider of business-to-business electronic solutions, discloses in its notes that "[i]ntangible assets consist of purchased patents, costs incurred in connection with the filing and registration of patents and *the costs to defend and enforce our rights under patents.*"

Amortizing Intangible Assets

Like fixed assets that are depreciated, intangible assets with limited useful lives are amortized. **Amortization** is the process of spreading out the cost of an intangible asset over its useful life. Two examples of intangible assets with limited lives are patents and copyrights. Patents are granted for up to 20 years, and copyrights are granted for the life of the creator plus 70 years. Companies usually use the straight-line method for amortization.

To illustrate, suppose that a company possesses a $60,000 patent that has the maximum legal life of 20 years. The company believes that the patent will be useful for only 12 years and will then be worthless. Amortization expense at the end of each year would be $5,000 ($60,000 ÷ 12) and would be recorded as follows:

End of year	Amortization Expense	5,000	
	Patent		5,000

Assets	=	Liabilities	+	Equity
−5,000				−5,000

The result of this entry is an increase to expenses and a decrease to assets. Notice that the entry records amortization expense based on the 12-year useful life, not the 20-year legal life. Amortization should be based on the shorter of the legal life or useful life. Notice also that the entry directly reduces the patent account. Unlike fixed assets, the amortization of intangible assets does not require the use of an accumulated amortization contra-account.

Amortization applies only to intangible assets with limited lives. Assets with indefinite lives such as trademarks and goodwill are instead examined periodically to check for impairment. This is similar to the impairment of fixed assets. In general, if the market value of the intangible asset permanently falls below its cost, then the asset is impaired. In such a case, the company records a loss on impairment and reduces the asset to its market value. As you can imagine, determining whether an intangible asset is impaired is a very subjective process and requires a great deal of judgment. In such cases, it is important for accountants to follow guiding principles such as conservatism, relevance, and reliability.

Amortization The process of spreading out the cost of an intangible asset over its useful life.

STUDY TOOLS
CHAPTER 8

CHAPTER REVIEW CARD
- ❏ Learning Objective and Key Concept Reviews
- ❏ Key Definitions and Formulas

ONLINE (Located at 4ltrpress.cengage.com/acct)
- ❏ Flash Cards and Crossword Puzzles
- ❏ Conceptual and Computational Interactive Quizzes
- ❏ E-Lectures
- ❏ Static, Algorithmic, and Additional Homework Activities (as directed by your instructor)

1. Acquisition Cost   LO1

Prince's Pipe Co. purchases equipment with a list price of $22,000. Regarding the purchase, Prince:
- Received a 2% discount off the list price
- Paid shipping costs of $800
- Paid $1,750 to install the equipment, $1,200 of which was for a unique stand for the equipment
- Paid $2,800 to insure the equipment, $300 for delivery transit, and $2,500 for a two-year policy to cover operations
- Paid $600 to have the manufacturer train employees on safety features

Required
Determine the acquisition cost of the equipment.

2. Acquisition Cost   LO1

Orange & Blue Inc. incurred the following expenditures when purchasing land: $47,000 purchase price; $4,500 in taxes; $2,000 of sales commissions; and $13,000 for clearing and grading, of which $8,000 was for removing an old building.

Required
Determine the acquisition cost of the equipment.

3. Depreciation Methods   LO2

Xing, Inc., purchases a delivery truck on January 1 for $25,000. The truck has an estimated useful life of five years and an estimated salvage value of $2,500.

Required
For both the straight-line and double-declining-balance methods of depreciation, prepare a schedule of depreciation expense, accumulated depreciation, and net book value over the life of the asset. Advise Xing, Inc., of the advantages/disadvantages of the two depreciation methods.

4. Depreciation Methods   LO2

Phigam Steel purchases a machine on January 1 for $30,000. The machine has an estimated useful life of seven years, during which time it is expected to produce 114,800 units. Salvage value is estimated at $1,300. The machine produces 15,500 and 16,200 units in its first and second years of operation, respectively.

Required
Calculate depreciation expense for the machine's first two years using the straight-line, double-declining-balance, and units-of-activity methods of depreciation.

5. Change in Estimates   LO2, 3

On January 1, 2010, Roosters Co. purchases equipment for $30,000 and estimates a useful life of eight years and a salvage value of $2,000. On January 1,
2012, Roosters revises the equipment's useful life from eight years to five years. Roosters uses the straight-line method of depreciation.

Required
a. Calculate depreciation expense for 2011 and 2012.
b. Recalculate 2012 depreciation expense assuming that Roosters leaves the useful life at eight years but reduces the salvage value to $0.

6. Capital/Revenue Expenditures   LO3

A company incurs the following expenditures related to currently owned fixed assets:
- Annual pressure washing of building, $5,000
- New engine in delivery truck, $4,500
- Repair of water damage caused by leaking roof, $3,500
- New tires on tractor, $2,000
- Addition of 1,000 square feet of office space, $22,000
- Modifications to machinery to improve efficiency, $7,200

Required
Identify each expenditure as a capital or revenue expenditure.

7. Disposal   LO4

Ellis Industries sells a building that has an original cost of $200,000 and an accumulated depreciation balance of $100,000.

Required
Prepare the journal entry to record the sale assuming the sales price was (a) $100,000, (b) $95,000, and (c) $108,000.

8. Disposal   LO2, 4

On January 1, 2010, A&G Company pays $40,000 for equipment with a 10-year estimated life and a $5,000 estimated salvage value. On January 1, 2014, A&G sells the equipment for $18,500.

Required
Calculate the gain or loss on the sale assuming A&G uses the straight-line method of depreciation. Where should the gain or loss on the sale be presented on the income statement?

9. Evaluate Fixed Assets   LO5

In its 2004 annual report, Nike reported the following information (in millions): beginning total assets $6,821.1; ending total assets $7,891.6; beginning property, plant, and equipment $2,988.8 (at cost); ending property, plant, and equipment $3,132.3 (at cost); beginning accumulated depreciation $1,293.3; revenues $12,253.1; and depreciation expense of $252.1.

Required
a. Calculate the fixed asset turnover ratio of Nike Corporation.

b. Calculate the average useful life of Nike's fixed assets at the end of 2004.

c. Calculate the average age of Nike's fixed assets at the end of 2004.

10. Evaluate Fixed Assets LO5

The following data was taken from the annual financial statements of Grizzle Company:

	Revenues	Fixed Asset NBV
2004	4,889	150
2005	5,897	201
2006	6,583	245
2007	8,563	395
2008	10,589	524
2009	13,584	687
2010	14,555	793

Required

Calculate the fixed asset turnover ratio for the years presented. What does the trend in the ratio tell you about the company's performance?

11. Intangible Assets LO7

Phoebe Inc. incurred the following expenditures:
- Research and development costs of $60,000 were incurred to develop a new patentable product.
- Phoebe paid $1,000 in application fees for the patent.
- Phoebe paid $12,000 in legal fees to register the awarded patent.
- Phoebe incurred $5,000 in legal fees to successfully defend the patent against a competitor.

Required

Determine the total cost of the patent.

PROBLEMS

12. Depreciation Methods LO2, 4

Development Industries purchased a depreciable asset for $50,000 on January 1, 2010. The asset has a five-year useful life and a $10,000 estimated salvage value. The company will use the straight-line method of depreciation for book purposes. However, Development will use the double-declining-balance method for tax purposes. Assume a tax rate of 30%.

Required

a. Prepare depreciation schedules using the straight-line and double-declining-balance methods of depreciation for the useful life of the asset.

b. Calculate the 2010 tax savings from the use of the accelerated depreciation method for tax purposes.

c. Under the straight-line method of depreciation, what is the gain or loss if the equipment is sold (1) at the end of 2012 for $30,000 or (2) at the end of 2013 for $16,000?

d. How is the gain or loss on the disposal of the equipment presented in the financial statements?

13. Various Transactions LO1, 2, 3, 4

On January 1, 2010, Ravioli, Inc., purchased a building for a cash price of $192,000 and accrued property taxes of $14,950. The building is estimated to have a useful life of 10 years and no salvage value. On the same day, Ravioli paid $25,450 in cash plus sales tax of $2,290 for a new delivery truck that is estimated to have a useful life of five years and a salvage value of $2,200. Another $1,100 was paid to paint the truck company colors with the company logo. Over the next several years, the following events related to these fixed assets occurred.

1/1/2011	Uncovered new information which caused the estimated life of the truck to be reduced to three total years instead of five years.
6/30/2011	Repaired air conditioning system which broke down for one week, $500.
1/1/2012	Renovated bottom floor of the building for $15,000, adding three years useful life to the building.
1/1/2013	Sold building for $163,000.
9/1/2013	Sold truck for $5,350.

Required

Prepare all entries for 2010 through 2013. Ravioli records annual depreciation expense on 12/31.

14. Evaluate Fixed Assets LO5

The following information was available from the 2008 financial statements of Papa John's Pizza:

	2008	2007
Net property and equipment	$ 189,992	$ 198,957
Total assets	386,468	401,817
Depreciation expense	31,800	30,600
Cost of property and equipment	388,080	408,074
Accumulated depreciation	198,088	209,117
Total revenues	1,132,087	1,063,595

Required

Calculate and interpret (1) horizontal and vertical analyses of fixed assets and depreciation expense, (2) fixed asset turnover ratio, and (3) average life and average age of fixed assets.

CASE

15. Research and Analysis LO1, 5, 6

Access the 2008 annual report for Columbia Sportswear Company by clicking on the *Investor Relations*, *Financial Information*, and *Annual Reports* links at www.columbia.com.

Required

1. Examine the company's balance sheet and conduct horizontal and vertical analyses of net property, plant, and equipment.
2. Calculate the company's 2008 fixed asset turnover ratio. Also, calculate the company's average age and useful life ratios at the end of 2008. Cost and accumulated depreciation data can be found in Note 4 to the financial statements. Depreciation and amortization expense can be found in Note 15.
3. Examine the company's statement of cash flows. How much cash did the company spend on property, plant, and equipment over the three years presented?
4. Based on your answers above, write a paragraph explaining your opinion of Columbia's fixed asset position. Use your answers as supporting facts.

Liabilities

Introduction

The generation and payment of liabilities is common to every business. Some are generated daily and paid quickly. Others are paid over time and often require the payment of interest. Still others must be estimated, and some never come to fruition. This chapter examines the accounting for such liabilities. It focuses first on how some common current liabilities are generated and reported. It then examines long-term liabilities with a specific focus on the issuance of, interest on, and payment of bonds. It also discusses the obligations associated with leases and considers the treatment of potential obligations that may or may not become liabilities. As in previous chapters, the final section of the chapter focuses on the analysis of a company's position regarding its obligations. The appendix covers bond pricing and the effective interest method for bond amortization.

LO1 Current Liabilities

A current liability is an obligation of a business that is expected to be satisfied or paid within one year. Current liabilities can arise from regular business operations such as the purchase of inventory, the compensation of employees, the repayment of debt, and the incurrence of taxes. Most current liabilities, such as accounts payable and notes payable, will be satisfied through the payment of cash. Others, such as deferred revenues in which a customer prepays for a service to be performed later, will be satisfied through the performance of the service. The following sections present the accounting for some of the more common types of current liabilities.

Current liability An obligation of a business that is expected to be satisfied or paid within one year.

Learning Objectives

After studying the material in this chapter, you should be able to:

LO1 Describe the recording and reporting of various current liabilities.

LO2 Describe the reporting of long-term liabilities and the cash flows associated with those liabilities.

LO3 Understand the nature of bonds and record a bond's issuance, interest payments, and maturity.

LO4 Account for a bond that is redeemed prior to maturity.

LO5 Understand additional liabilities such as leases and contingent liabilities.

LO6 Evaluate liabilities through the calculation and interpretation of horizontal, vertical, and ratio analyses.

LO7 Appendix: Determine a bond's issuance price.

LO8 Appendix: Record bond interest payments under the effective interest method.

Taxes Payable

When conducting business, corporations generate a variety of tax obligations to federal, state, and local taxing

A deposit in a bank is an asset to the customer, but it is a liability to the bank.

© LESTER LEFKOWITZ/STONE/GETTY IMAGES

authorities. One example is the income tax. Like individuals, corporations are subject to federal taxation of their income. And like individuals, they often wait until later to pay the bill, which creates a current liability. For example, suppose a company has $25,000 of annual income tax expense and plans to pay it in the next period. The company would make the following journal entry at year end to record the expense in the proper period:

Year-end	Income Tax Expense	25,000	
	Income Tax Payable		25,000
	(To record the income tax expense)		

Assets	=	Liabilities	+	Equity
		+25,000		−25,000

Current liabilities arise from regular business operations such as the purchase of inventory, the compensation of employees, the repayment of debt, and the incurrence of taxes.

The entry increases both Income Tax Expense and Income Tax Payable. The result of the entry is a reduction to equity and an increase to liabilities.

Another example is sales taxes. Each time a company makes a retail sale, it collects sales tax according to state and/or local regulations. Because the company remits the taxes to the appropriate authority at some later date, the company must record a liability when the sale is made. To illustrate, suppose that a company sells a $1,000 item and collects an 8% sales tax. The following entry records the sale and the resulting liability:

Cash	1,080	
Sales		1,000
Sales Tax Payable		80
(To record sale of merchandise)		

Assets	=	Liabilities	+	Equity
+1,080		+80		+1,000

The entry increases Cash for the $1,080 received from the customer, increases Sales for the $1,000 earned from the sale, and increases Sales Tax Payable for the $80 of tax collected and now owed to the taxing authorities. Notice that the company does not incur any expense related to the sales tax. The sales tax liability is created only because the company has collected sales tax on behalf of the taxing authority.

A third type of tax that generates a current liability is payroll taxes. When paying employee wages, employers must withhold income taxes and Social Security (FICA) taxes owed by the employee. The employer then remits those taxes to the taxing authorities. To illustrate, suppose that an employee earns a monthly salary of $10,000. Based on the employee's filing status, the company must withhold 15% of the salary for federal income taxes, 12% for state income taxes, and 7.65% for

Note payable A liability generated by the issuance of a promissory note to borrow money.

Social Security taxes. On payday, the company would prepare the following entry:

Salaries Expense	10,000	
Federal Income Taxes Payable		1,500
State Income Taxes Payable		1,200
FICA Taxes Payable		765
Cash		6,535
(To record payment of salary)		

Assets	=	Liabilities	+	Equity
−6,535		+1,500		−10,000
		+1,200		
		+ 765		

The entry increases Salaries Expense for the $10,000 salary earned by the employee for the month. However, the employee is paid only $6,535. The difference is the amount that the employee owes in taxes. On behalf of the employee, the employer withholds those taxes and records the resulting liabilities. As a result of this entry, assets decrease, liabilities increase, and equity decreases for the amount of the total salaries expense.

In addition to withholding taxes on behalf of employees, employers must also pay Social Security taxes of 7.65% on employee wages. These additional taxes are an added expense for the employer. Along with the preceding entry, the employer would make the following entry to record the additional tax expense and the current liability:

Payroll Tax Expense	765	
FICA Taxes Payable		765
(To record employer share of FICA taxes)		

Assets	=	Liabilities	+	Equity
		+765		−765

Notes Payable

Chapter 6 introduced the concept of a promissory note, which is a written promise to pay a specific sum of money at some date in the future. That chapter focused on the party that accepted the note in exchange for cash. That is, the accounting for notes receivable was demonstrated. This chapter focuses on the party that accepts cash in exchange for the note. That is, the accounting for notes payable is demonstrated.

When a company issues a promissory note to borrow money, the company generates a **note payable**. Depending on the terms of the promissory note, a note payable can be classified as either a current liability or a long-term liability. If the note is payable within a year, it is a current liability. Otherwise, it is a long-term liability. The accounting for a note payable consists of recording the note, recording any interest that must be paid to the creditor, and recording the payment of the note.

To illustrate, suppose that on March 1 Brown Company borrows $30,000 by signing an 8%, 6-month note with Miller Street Bank. The note calls for interest to be paid when the note is repaid on August 31. On March 1, Brown would make the following entry to record the note:

Mar. 1	Cash	30,000	
	Note Payable		30,000
	(To record the note)		

| Assets | = | Liabilities | + | Equity |
| +30,000 | | +30,000 | | |

In this entry, Brown increases both Cash and Note Payable for $30,000. As a result, both assets and liabilities increase. Since this note matures within a year, the note payable would be reported as a current liability.

On August 31, Brown must pay Miller Street Bank the original $30,000 borrowed plus the interest on the note. Interest over the six months is calculated as follows:

Interest = Principal × Annual Rate of Interest × Time Outstanding
= $30,000 × 0.08 × 6/12 months
= $1,200

Therefore, Brown would pay $31,200 to the bank and make the following entry on August 31:

Aug. 31	Note Payable	30,000	
	Interest Expense	1,200	
	Cash		31,200
	(To record payment of note and interest)		

| Assets | = | Liabilities | + | Equity |
| −31,200 | | −30,000 | | −1,200 |

In this entry, Brown increases Interest Expense to reflect the cost of borrowing the $30,000 over the six months. Brown also decreases the Note Payable account because the note is being paid. Finally, Brown decreases Cash for the payment of principal and interest. Because of the entry, Brown's assets, liabilities, and equity decrease.

Current Portion of Long-Term Debt

Companies that borrow money on a long-term basis often pay principal on a short-term basis. The **current**

portion of long-term debt represents the portion of a long-term liability that will be paid within one year. To illustrate, suppose that a company borrows $500,000 from a bank through a 10-year promissory note. Because the note is payable in 10 years, the company classifies it as a long-term liability. In year 10, the note is reclassified as a current liability because it will be satisfied in a year.

Suppose instead that the bank requires the company to repay the principal in installments of $50,000 per year plus interest. In that case, when the note is signed, the company has a long-term liability of $450,000 and a current liability of $50,000. Since the company must pay $50,000 each year until the note is repaid, the company will report $50,000 as Current Portion of Long-Term Debt each year.

As you consider these two examples, keep in mind that regardless of how the liability is classified on the balance sheet, the company is borrowing and repaying $500,000. The classification of the note payable as current or long-term does not affect the borrowing or repayment of the note. It only affects how the payable is reported on the balance sheet. However, this balance sheet reporting is important because it tells users of the financial statements what obligations will require payment in the short term.

Reporting Current Liabilities

Current liabilities are reported in a separate section on a classified balance sheet. The following is the current liabilities section of the 2008 balance sheet of Advance Auto Parts:

Advance Auto Parts' 2008 Current Liabilities	
(*in thousands*)	
Bank overdrafts	$ 20,588
Current portion of long-term debt	1,003
Financed vendor accounts payable	136,386
Accounts payable	791,330
Accrued expenses	372,510
Other current liabilities	43,177
Total	$1,364,994

Current portion of long-term debt The portion of a long-term liability that will be paid within one year.

Advance Auto Parts reports over $1.3 billion in current liabilities. This total is made up mostly of accounts payable and accrued expenses. Accounts payable normally represents what a company owes vendors for inventory that it stocks in its stores. It is not surprising to see a large balance in accounts payable for a retailer like Advance Auto Parts. Accrued expense is another name for a liability that is created when recording an unpaid expense. Advance Auto Parts' balance sheet doesn't report what activities created the accrued expenses. However, Note 10 to the company's financial statements shows that the liabilities arise from various operating activities related to payroll, product returns, insurance, and taxes.

Advance Auto Parts' 2008 Accrued Expense Note	
(in thousands)	
Payroll and related benefits	$ 75,471
Warranty reserves	28,662
Capital expenditures	26,299
Self-insurance reserves	90,554
Taxes payable	69,714
Other	81,810
Total accrued expenses	$372,510

To provide some comparison, the 2008 current liabilities section of O'Reilly Automotive's balance sheet is as follows:

O'Reilly Automotive's 2008 Current Liabilities	
(in thousands)	
Accounts payable	$ 736,986
Self-insurance reserve	65,170
Accrued payroll	60,616
Accrued benefits and withholdings	38,583
Other current liabilities	144,015
Current portion of long-term debt	8,131
Total	$1,053,501

Long-term liability Any obligation of a business that is expected to be satisfied or paid in more than one year.

> The most common and largest long-term liabilities often arise from borrowing money.

Similar to Advance Auto Parts' current liabilities, O'Reilly's is made up of various operating obligations, with the largest being accounts payable.

LO2 Long-Term Liabilities

A **long-term liability** is any obligation of a business that is expected to be satisfied or paid in more than one year. Like current liabilities, the type and size of long-term liabilities can vary across companies. However, the most common and largest long-term liabilities often arise from borrowing money. This is the case for Advance Auto Parts. The following shows the company's condensed liabilities from its 2008 balance sheet.

Advance Auto Parts' 2008 Condensed Liabilities	
(in thousands)	
Total current liabilities	$1,364,994
Long-term debt	455,161
Other long-term liabilities	68,744
Total liabilities	$1,888,899

Advance Auto Parts reports two long-term liabilities. The first and largest is long-term debt. The balance sheet reports a total obligation of over $455 million, but it does not reveal how or why this long-term debt was generated or when it must be repaid. Such information is disclosed in the notes to the company's financial statements.

Advance Auto Parts' 2008 Condensed Long-term Debt Note	
(in thousands)	
Revolving credit facility due October 2011	$251,500
Term loan due October 2011	200,000
Other	4,664
	$456,164
Less: Current portion of long-term debt	(1,003)
Total long-term debt	$455,161

A borrower "sells" or "issues" a bond and records a liability. A creditor "buys" a bond and records an investment.

While the balance sheet reports the balance in long-term liabilities, the statement of cash flows reports the cash flows associated with those liabilities in the financing activities section. The following are excerpts from Advance Auto Parts' financing activities section of its 2008 statement of cash flows. These contain the significant cash flows resulting from the generation and repayment of the company's long-term liabilities.

The note discloses that the company's total long-term debt is comprised primarily of two types of debt. The first is a revolving credit facility, which is a type of loan that does not require fixed principal payments during the term of the loan. (Your personal credit card is an example of revolving credit.) According to its note, Advance Auto Parts can borrow up to $750,000 on the credit facility. At the end of 2008, however, it has borrowed only $251,500. The second type of debt is a $200,000 term loan. This is simply an interest-bearing loan with principal due at maturity. Advance Auto Parts discloses that the entire proceeds from the term loan were used to repurchase shares of its common stock. Both the revolving credit facility and the term loan are due in October 2011.

Excerpts from Advance Auto Parts' 2008 Statement of Cash Flows			
(*in thousands*)	2008	2007	2006
Early extinguishment of debt	—	—	($433,775)
Borrowings under credit facilities	$438,600	$495,400	$678,075
Payments on credit facilities	($488,100)	($471,200)	($205,800)

This information reveals that Advance Auto Parts experienced significant debt-related cash inflows and cash outflows over the three-year period. However, while there was significant annual activity, the net effect was relatively small. In 2006, the company borrowed $678 million from its credit facility, but it also paid over $433 million to extinguish previous debt and over $205 million to repay its credit facility. As a result, it experienced a small net cash inflow from these 2006 activities. The same is true in 2007. Advance Auto Parts borrowed $24 million more than it repaid during the

HOME DEPOT ANALYSIS

Look at Home Depot's balance sheet and statement of cash flows in Appendix C. Using both statements, explain what happened to short-term debt during 2008.

Home Depot paid off its entire short-term debt in 2008. The balance sheet shows the balance going from $1,747 in 2007 to $0 in 2008. The statement of cash flows shows a $1,732 cash outflow for short-term debt during 2008. Although the numbers are not exactly the same, they demonstrate that the activity associated with the payments of short-term debt are shown on the financial statements.

Exhibit 9-1 Example Bond Certificate

© Terri Miller/E-Visual Communications, Inc.

year. In 2008, it paid more than it borrowed, resulting in a $49 million cash outflow during the year.

LO3 **Bonds**

A tool that companies such as Advance Auto Parts often use to borrow money on a long-term basis is a bond. A **bond** is a financial instrument in which a borrower promises to pay future interest and principal to a creditor in exchange for the creditor's cash today. The borrower "sells" or "issues" the bond and records a liability. The creditor "buys" the bond and records an investment.

The terms and features of a bond are determined by the borrowing entity and can vary widely. However, all bonds have a face value, a stated interest rate, and a maturity date.

Bond A financial instrument in which a borrower promises to pay future interest and principal to a creditor in exchange for the creditor's cash today.

Face value The amount that is repaid at maturity of a bond.

Stated interest rate The contractual rate at which interest is paid to the creditor.

Maturity date The date on which the face value must be repaid to the creditor.

Market (or effective) rate of interest The rate of return that investors in the bond markets demand for bonds of similar risk.

The **face value** is the amount that the borrowing company wants to borrow. It is also the amount that must be repaid to the creditor upon maturity of the bond. Another name for face value is principal value. The **stated interest rate** is the contractual rate at which interest is paid to the creditor. Other names for stated rate include face rate, nominal rate, contractual rate, or coupon rate. Along with this stated rate, a bond will specify the timing of interest payments. These will usually be annually or semiannually. The **maturity date** is the date on which the face value must be repaid to the creditor. These three terms, which do not change over the life of the bond, are disclosed on the certificate that is given to the creditor or the creditor's trustee when the bond is purchased. An example certificate is shown in Exhibit 9-1.

Although these terms establish both the amount to be paid at maturity (the face value) and the amount of interest to be paid each period (the stated interest rate), they do not establish the issuance price of the bonds. A bond's issuance price is a function of these terms as well as a fourth item, the market rate of interest.

The **market (or effective) rate of interest** is the rate of return that investors in the bond markets demand on bonds of similar risk. The market rate is based on many complicated factors, including current and expected economic conditions. However, its relation to a bond's issuance price is relatively straightforward.

When a bond pays interest at a rate that is equal to what creditors demand in the market, the creditors will buy the bond at its face value. Creditors are getting the return that they demand, so no adjustment to price is needed. As a result, the borrower receives face value. We say that such bonds are issued at par value.

When a bond pays interest at a rate that is lower than what creditors demand, the creditors will purchase the bond only if the price is discounted. By discounting the price, the borrower is effectively increasing the rate of interest that the creditor earns. In fact, the bond will sell only when the price is reduced enough so that the effective interest rate that the creditor earns equals the market rate of interest. Bonds that are issued for less than face value are issued at a *discount*.

When a bond pays interest at a rate that is higher than what creditors demand, the borrower will sell the bond only if the price is raised. By raising the price, the borrower effectively lowers the rate of interest that the creditor earns. In fact, the bond will sell only when the price is raised enough so that the effective interest rate that the creditor earns equals the market rate of interest. Bonds that are issued for more than face value are issued at a *premium*.

be paid semiannually on July 1 and January 1. Because the market rate of interest is also 6%, the bonds sell at face value.

Recording the Issuance In this example, York would record the bond issuance with a simple and straightforward entry to increase Cash and Bonds Payable:

Jan. 1 2010	Cash	100,000	
	Bonds Payable		100,000
	(To record bonds issued at face value)		

Assets	=	Liabilities	+	Equity
+100,000		+100,000		

Note that this entry is practically the same as the entry recording the note payable earlier in the chapter. This should make sense since a bond is really just a more formalized note payable.

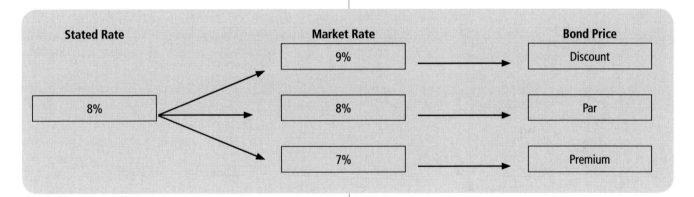

Actual issuance prices are calculated using present value computations. The chapter appendix illustrates these calculations. Here, you should simply understand that bonds sell for whatever price is necessary to make the effective rate of interest equal to the market rate of interest. Sometimes they sell for face value, sometimes at a discount, and sometimes for a premium. The following sections demonstrate how to account for a bond's issuance, the periodic interest payments, and the maturity of bonds under each scenario.

Bonds Issued at Face Value

To illustrate a bond issued at face value, suppose that on January 1, 2010, York Products sells bonds with a face value of $100,000. The bonds carry a 6% interest rate and a January 1, 2025, maturity date. Interest is to

Recording Interest Payments Once the bond is issued, York must pay interest on July 1 and January 1 of each year. For any bond, the amount of interest paid each period is a product of the face value, the stated interest rate, and the length of the payment period. In this example, interest is paid every six months, or semiannually, so the amount paid is $3,000, calculated as follows:

$$\text{Interest Paid} = \text{Face Value} \times \text{Stated Interest Rate} \times \text{Time Outstanding}$$
$$= \$100,000 \times 0.06 \times 6/12 \text{ months}$$
$$= \$3,000$$

Therefore, on July 1, York would record its interest payment with the following entry.

July 1	Interest Expense	3,000	
2010	Cash		3,000
	(To record payment of interest)		

Assets	=	Liabilities	+	Equity
−3,000				−3,000

York increases Interest Expense to reflect the cost of borrowing over the six months and decreases Cash to reflect the payment made to the bondholders. The overall effect of the transaction is a decrease to York's assets and equity.

The next $3,000 interest payment is scheduled for January 1, 2011. However, assuming that York has a December 31 year-end, two entries are required. The first is a December 31 adjusting journal entry that accrues the interest expense and records the related payable so that the expense is properly matched to the period in which the money was used. The second entry records York's payment on January 1, 2011. These two entries are shown as follows:

Dec. 31	Interest Expense	3,000	
2010	Interest Payable		3,000
	(To record accrual of interest)		

Assets	=	Liabilities	+	Equity
		+3,000		−3,000

Jan. 1	Interest Payable	3,000	
2011	Cash		3,000
	(To record payment of interest)		

Assets	=	Liabilities	+	Equity
−3,000		−3,000		

Note that the interest expense is matched to 2010 and that the overall effect of the two entries is to decrease assets and equity by the amount of the interest paid. This is the same overall effect as the July 1 interest entry.

Interest is paid and recorded in the same manner every July 1 and December 31/January 1 for 15 years through the January 1, 2025, maturity date. Over time, York will make 30 payments of $3,000 for a total of $90,000 of interest paid. Thus, the total cost of borrowing the $100,000 over the 15 years is $90,000.

Recording the Maturity On the January 1, 2025, maturity date, York would record the repayment of the bonds in addition to the last interest payment.

Jan. 1	Bonds Payable	100,000	
2025	Cash		100,000
	(To record repayment of the bonds)		

Assets	=	Liabilities	+	Equity
−100,000		−100,000		

Bonds Issued at a Discount

To illustrate a bond issued at a discount, suppose that on January 1, 2010, Agnew Company issues bonds with a face value of $200,000, a stated interest rate of 7%, and a maturity date of December 31, 2014. Interest is payable semiannually on June 30 and December 31. At the time of issuance, the market rate of interest is higher than the stated rate of 7%, and the bonds sell at a price of $196,000, or a $4,000 discount. At such a price, the bonds are said to have sold at 98, meaning that they were issued at 98% of face value ($200,000 × 98% = $196,000).

Recording the Issuance Agnew would record the issuance as follows:

Jan. 1	Cash	196,000	
	Discount on Bonds Payable	4,000	
	Bonds Payable		200,000
	(To record bonds issued at a discount)		

Assets	=	Liabilities	+	Equity
+196,000		+200,000		
		−4,000		

In this entry, Agnew increases Cash for the $196,000 received from the investors. Agnew also increases Bonds Payable to reflect the new obligation that it has. Notice that Bonds Payable is recorded at the bond's face value of $200,000. The Bonds Payable account is *always* recorded at the amount that will ultimately be repaid, which is face value. The difference of $4,000 is recorded in an account called Discount on Bonds Payable, which is a contra-liability account. Its balance is subtracted from the Bonds Payable account to yield the book value or carrying value of the bonds. As a result, both assets and liabilities increase by only $196,000.

After issuance, the bonds would be reported on the balance sheet as follows.

	Jan. 1, 2010
Bonds payable	$200,000
Less: Discount on bonds payable	4,000
Carrying value	$196,000

Notice that the carrying value of $196,000 at the time of issuance is equal to the cash received at issuance. This will always be the case at issuance, regardless of the price of the bond.

Recording Interest Payments Agnew's bonds call for semiannual interest payments over the life of the bonds. Each payment is calculated as follows:

$$\text{Interest Paid} = \text{Face Value} \times \text{Stated Interest Rate} \\ \times \text{Time Outstanding}$$
$$= \$200,000 \times 0.07 \times 6/12 \text{ months}$$
$$= \$7,000$$

Note that this $7,000 interest payment is calculated the same way as the bond issued at face value. Whether a bond is issued at face value, at a discount, or at a premium, interest paid on a bond is always: face value × stated interest rate × time outstanding.

However, unlike the face value scenario, interest expense will be greater than interest paid. Recall that Agnew received only $196,000 at issuance but must repay $200,000 at maturity. That $4,000 discount is therefore an additional cost to Agnew that must be amortized over the life of the bond. To amortize the discount is to gradually reduce the discount balance and add the amount amortized to interest expense. Therefore, at each interest payment date, interest expense will be greater than interest paid.

There are two methods to amortize the discount on bonds payable—the straight-line method and the effective interest method. Because the straight-line method is easier to compute and is often close to the results from the effective interest method, the straight-line method is demonstrated here. However, the effective interest method is also demonstrated in the chapter appendix.

Under the **straight-line method of amortization**, an equal amount of the discount is amortized each time interest is paid. The amount amortized is calculated as follows:

$$\text{Discount Amortized} = \frac{\text{Discount at Issuance}}{\text{Number of Interest Payments}}$$

With a $4,000 discount and 10 semiannual interest payments, Agnew must amortize $400 ($4,000 ÷ 10) each payment. As a result, Agnew's interest expense for each period is $7,400 ($7,000 interest paid + $400 discount amortized). With this information, Agnew can make the following entry to record the first semiannual interest payment on June 30.

June 30	Interest Expense	7,400	
	Discount on Bonds Payable		400
	Cash		7,000
	(To record the payment of interest)		

Assets	=	Liabilities	+	Equity
−7,000		+400		−7,400

The entry affects three accounts. First, Cash is decreased for the amount paid to the creditor. Second, the Discount on Bonds Payable account is decreased (or "amortized") by $400, resulting in a remaining balance of $3,600. Third, Interest Expense is increased by $7,400 to record the expense associated with the interest paid and the discount amortized. The effect of this entry is to decrease equity by $7,400 (the amount of expense), to decrease assets by $7,000 (the cash paid), and to increase liabilities by $400 (the discount amortized).

It may be counterintuitive to you that liabilities would *increase* as a result of the preceding interest entry. However, remember that the contra-liability Discount on Bonds Payable, which was first created for $4,000, is now only $3,600. Therefore, the carrying value of the bonds has increased by $400 because of the interest payment entry. This is illustrated as follows:

	Issuance	June 30, 2010
Bonds payable	$200,000	$200,000
Less: Discount on bonds payable	4,000	3,600
Carrying value	$196,000	$196,400

The carrying value will continue to increase by $400 each interest payment date as the discount is amortized. After ten total payments, the discount will be fully amortized (that is, it will have a zero balance), and the carrying value of the bonds will equal the face value of $200,000.

This movement of the carrying value from issuance price to face value is best illustrated in the schedule found in Exhibit 9-2. It is called an **amortization schedule**

Straight-line method of amortization
Method that amortizes an equal amount of the discount or premium each time interest is paid.

Amortization schedule A schedule that illustrates the amortization of a bond discount or premium over the life of a bond.

Exhibit 9-2 Amortization Schedule—Bonds Issued at a Discount

Interest Payment	Interest Paid	Discount Amortized	Interest Expense	Unamortized Discount	Carrying Value
				$4,000	$196,000
1	$ 7,000	$ 400	$ 7,400	3,600	196,400
2	7,000	400	7,400	3,200	196,800
3	7,000	400	7,400	2,800	197,200
4	7,000	400	7,400	2,400	197,600
5	7,000	400	7,400	2,000	198,000
6	7,000	400	7,400	1,600	198,400
7	7,000	400	7,400	1,200	198,800
8	7,000	400	7,400	800	199,200
9	7,000	400	7,400	400	199,600
10	7,000	400	7,400	0	200,000
	$70,000	$4,000	$74,000		

because it provides the details of the discount amortization and the resulting expense amounts and carrying values.

As you review the amortization schedule, note that it provides the dollar amounts for each semiannual interest entry. The first three columns provide the amounts of cash to be paid, discount to be amortized, and interest expense to be recognized each six months. Because the straight-line method of amortization is used, the amounts are the same each period. Thus, Agnew would make the same interest entry every six months until the bonds mature.

Note also that the schedule confirms that the total cost of borrowing is a combination of the interest paid and the original discount. Total interest expense over the life of the bonds is $74,000, which is the sum of interest paid ($70,000) and the original discount ($4,000). When bonds are issued at a discount, total interest expense will *always* exceed interest paid by the amount of the discount. An alternate calculation of the total cost of borrowing is as follows:

Interest payments ($200,000 × 7% × 6/12)	$ 7,000
× Number of payments	× 10
= Total interest paid	$70,000
+ Discount	4,000
Total cost of borrowing	$74,000

Recording the Maturity Agnew must repay $200,000 on December 31, 2014, to satisfy its obligation. The entry to repay the bonds requires a decrease to both Cash and the Bonds Payable account.

Dec. 31 2014	Bonds Payable	200,000	
	Cash		200,000
	(To record repayment of the bonds)		

Assets	=	Liabilities	+	Equity
−200,000		−200,000		

Bonds Issued at a Premium

To illustrate the accounting for a bond issued at a premium, suppose that on January 1, 2010, McCarthy Company issues bonds with a face value of $50,000, a stated interest rate of 8%, and a maturity date of December 31, 2012. Interest is payable semiannually on June 30 and December 31. At the time of issuance, the market rate of interest is lower than the stated rate of 8%, and the bonds sell at a price of $50,600, or a $600 premium. At such a price, the bonds are said to have sold at 101.2, meaning that they were issued at 101.2% of face value ($50,000 × 101.2% = $50,600).

Recording the Issuance McCarthy would record the issuance as follows:

Jan. 1	Cash	50,600	
	Premium on Bonds Payable		600
	Bonds Payable		50,000
	(To record bonds issued at a premium)		

Assets	=	Liabilities	+	Equity
+50,600		+50,000		
		+600		

In this entry, McCarthy increases Cash for the $50,600 received from creditors. McCarthy also increases Bonds Payable for the face value of $50,000. The $600 received in excess of the face value is recorded in an account called Premium on Bonds Payable. The balance in Premium on Bonds Payable is added to the Bonds Payable account to yield the bond's carrying value. The calculation of McCarthy's carrying value after issuance is shown as follows:

	Jan. 1, 2010
Bonds payable	$50,000
Plus: Premium on bonds payable	600
Carrying value	$50,600

As a result of this entry, McCarthy's assets and liabilities increase by $50,600.

Recording Interest Payments McCarthy's bonds call for semiannual interest payments over the life of the bonds. Each payment is calculated as follows:

Interest Paid = Face Value × Stated Interest Rate × Time Outstanding

$$= \$50,000 \times 0.08 \times 6/12 \text{ months}$$

$$= \$2,000$$

Like the discount example, McCarthy's interest payment will differ from its interest expense. McCarthy received $50,600 at issuance but must repay only $50,000 at maturity. The $600 premium is a reduction in McCarthy's cost. Like the discount example, the premium should be amortized over the life of the bond. As a result, at each interest payment date, interest expense will be less than interest paid.

The following is the amortization calculation using the straight-line method.

$$\text{Premium Amortized} = \frac{\text{Premium at Issuance}}{\text{Number of Interest Payments}}$$

With a $600 premium and 6 semiannual interest payments, McCarthy must amortize $100 ($600/6) each payment. Therefore, interest expense for each period is $1,900 ($2,000 interest paid − $100 premium amortized). This leads to the following entry to record the first semiannual interest payment on June 30.

June 30	Interest Expense	1,900	
	Premium on Bonds Payable	100	
	Cash		2,000
	(To record the payment of interest)		

Assets	=	Liabilities	+	Equity
−2,000		−100		−1,900

The entry affects three accounts. First, Cash is decreased for the $2,000 payment. Second, the Premium on Bonds Payable account is amortized or decreased by $100, leaving a remaining balance of $500. Third, Interest Expense is increased by $1,900 to record the expense associated with the interest paid and the premium amortized. The effect of this entry is to decrease equity by $1,900 (the amount of expense), to decrease assets by $2,000 (the cash paid), and to decrease liabilities by $100 (the premium amortized).

After the entry, the carrying value of the bonds would be reported as follows:

	Issuance	June 30, 2010
Bonds payable	$50,000	$50,000
Plus: Premium on bonds payable	600	500
Carrying value	$50,600	$50,500

The bonds' carrying value is $100 smaller after the first interest payment. The carrying value will continue to decrease by $100 each interest payment date as the premium is amortized. After six total payments, the premium will be fully amortized and the carrying value of the bonds will equal the face value of $50,000. The amortization schedule in Exhibit 9-3 illustrates the change in the carrying value of the bonds over time.

Like the amortization schedule for bonds issued at a discount, the first three columns in the schedule provide the amounts of cash to be paid, premium to be amortized, and interest expense to be recognized each six months. Because of the straight-line method of amortization, the amounts are the same each period. Thus, McCarthy would make the same interest entry every six months until the bonds mature.

The schedule also illustrates that the total cost of borrowing is comprised of interest paid and the original premium. Total interest expense over the life of the bonds is $11,400, which is the amount of interest

Exhibit 9-3 Amortization Schedule—Bonds Issued at a Premium

Interest Payment	Interest Paid	Premium Amortized	Interest Expense	Unamortized Premium	Carrying Value
				$600	$50,600
1	$ 2,000	$100	$ 1,900	500	50,500
2	2,000	100	1,900	400	50,400
3	2,000	100	1,900	300	50,300
4	2,000	100	1,900	200	50,200
5	2,000	100	1,900	100	50,100
6	2,000	100	1,900	0	50,000
	$12,000	$600	$11,400		

paid ($12,000) less the original premium ($600). When bonds are issued at a premium, total interest paid will *always* exceed interest expense by the amount of the premium. An alternate calculation of the total cost of borrowing is as follows.

Interest payments ($50,000 × 8% × 6/12)	$ 2,000
× Number of payments	× 6
= Total interest paid	12,000
− Premium	600
Total cost of borrowing	$11,400

Recording the Maturity   McCarthy must repay $50,000 on December 31, 2012, to satisfy its obligation. The entry to repay the bonds requires a decrease to both Cash and Bonds Payable:

Dec. 31 2012	Bonds Payable	50,000
	Cash	50,000
	(To record repayment of the bonds)	

Assets	=	Liabilities	+	Equity
−50,000		−$50,000		

LO4 Redeeming a Bond Before Maturity

Sometimes a bond is redeemed or retired before maturity. This can occur when the bond has a feature that allows the borrowing company to "call" or retire the bonds at a certain price. The call price is usually stated as a percentage of face value. For example, a call price of 105 means that the bonds can be retired by paying the creditor 105% of the face value of the bonds.

Bonds are retired early for various reasons. A company may simply want to reduce future interest expense or take advantage of falling interest rates by replacing existing bonds with less costly bonds. Whatever the reason, the accounting for the early retirement of a bond consists of the following three steps:

1. Update the carrying value of the bond.

2. Calculate gain or loss on the retirement.

3. Record the retirement.

The first step is to update the carrying value of the bond. Often this means that the bond must be amortized for a partial period. For example, if a bond is retired three months after the last interest payment date, the bond would be amortized for those three months to update the carrying value. Interest payable for the three months would also be recorded and would be paid in addition to the call price.

The second step is to calculate any gain or loss on retirement by comparing the carrying value to the call price. When the carrying value exceeds the call price, the company is paying less than the value of the liability. In that case, the company records a gain on the redemption. In contrast, when the call price exceeds the carrying value, the company is paying more than the value of the liability. In that case, the

A company may retire bonds early to reduce future interest expense or take advantage of falling interest rates by replacing existing bonds with less costly bonds.

company records a loss on the redemption. This is summarized as follows:

> Gain on Redemption =
>   Carrying value > Call price
>
> Loss on Redemption =
>   Call price > Carrying value

To illustrate, suppose that Doyle Township issues a $20,000 eight-year bond on January 1, 2010, to fund the conversion of a warehouse to a youth activity center. The bond has a stated interest rate of 5% and is callable at 103 any time after 2014. The bond pays interest semiannually on June 30 and December 31. The bond sells for $19,200, or an $800 discount. A condensed amortization schedule is presented in Exhibit 9-4.

schedule, the December 31, 2016, carrying value of the bond is $19,900 (after the interest payment). Therefore, the gain or loss on redemption is calculated as follows:

Call price	$20,600
Less: Carrying value on Dec. 31, 2016	19,900
Loss on redemption	$ 700

Doyle would record the redemption with the following journal entry:

Dec. 31 2016	Bonds Payable	20,000	
	Loss on Redemption	700	
	Discount on Bonds Payable		100
	Cash		20,600
	(To record redemption of the bond)		

Assets	=	Liabilities	+	Equity
−20,600		−$20,000 + 100		−700

This entry first decreases the Bonds Payable account by its face value of $20,000. Because Doyle no longer has the bond, it also decreases the remaining $100 balance in the Discount on Bonds Payable. The entry then reduces Cash for the amount paid to retire the bond and records

Exhibit 9-4 Condensed Amortization Schedule—Bond Issued at a Discount

Interest Payment	Interest Paid	Discount Amortized	Interest Expense	Unamortized Discount	Carrying Value
				$800	$19,200
6/30/10	$1,000	$50	$1,050	750	19,250
12/31/10	1,000	50	1,050	700	19,300
⋮	⋮	⋮	⋮	⋮	⋮
6/30/15	1,000	50	1,050	250	19,750
12/31/15	1,000	50	1,050	200	19,800
6/30/16	1,000	50	1,050	150	19,850
12/31/16	1,000	50	1,050	100	19,900
6/30/17	1,000	50	1,050	50	19,950
12/31/17	1,000	50	1,050	0	20,000

Now suppose that Doyle decides to retire the bond a year early on December 31, 2016. The bond's call price of 103 means that Doyle can retire the bond by paying the bondholder 103% of face value, or $20,600 ($20,000 × 103%). According to the amortization

a $700 Loss on Redemption to reflect the loss on retiring the bond. This loss account is reported on the income statement, usually as an other or nonoperating expense. The overall effect of the entry is to decrease assets, liabilities, and equity.

A financial crisis can often be an advantage to a company, and these current economic conditions are no exception.

The value of much corporate debt has been depressed lately—so much so that some companies have saved millions of dollars in both interest and debt-repayment costs. According to a *Wall Street Journal* article ("Firms Move to Scoop Up Own Debt," by Serena Ng; August 24, 2009), companies including Beazer Homes USA Inc., Hexion

Specialty Chemicals Inc., Harrah's Entertainment Inc., and Tenet Healthcare Corp. have bought portions of their debt at significant discounts to the debt's face value. The following table demonstrates the discounts paid to satisfy debt obligations. As a result of these buybacks, many companies recognized material gains on their income statements.

Bond Buybacks

Some companies are buying their own debt in the open market at discounted prices.

	Bonds purchased (in millions)		
	Face value	Amount paid	Cents on the dollar
Hexion Sepcialty Chemicals	$288	$63	22
Hovnanian Enterprises	578	223	39
Harrah's Entertainment	788	378	48
Beazer Homes USA	116	58	50
Tenet Healthcare	68	60	88

Source: Standard & Poor's Leveraged Commentary & Data, Company fillings

LO5 Additional Liabilities

The next two sections examine two additional types of liabilities that are common to many organizations: lease liabilities and contingent liabilities.

Leases

When companies acquire fixed assets, they have a few ways to pay for them. One option is to pay with cash on hand. Another option is to issue notes or bonds to raise the necessary capital. A third option, which is the focus of this section of the text, is to use lease financing.

A **lease** is a contractual agreement in which the lessee obtains the right to use an asset by making periodic payments to the lessor. One of the major advantages of lease financing is its flexibility. Terms of usage, time limits, and payments are a few of the many aspects of lease contracts that can vary. As a result, one lease can look very different from another. However, from an accounting perspective, there are only two main types of leases—operating leases and capital leases.

An **operating lease** is a contract in which the lessee obtains the right to use an asset for a limited period of time but does not acquire ownership of the asset. Ownership remains with the lessor. As a result, the lessee does not record any asset or liability associated with the lease but simply records rent expense as lease payments are made. A common example of an operating lease is the leasing of an automobile from a dealership.

Operating leases can be very popular with companies because they are a form of off-balance-sheet financing. **Off-balance-sheet financing** occurs when a

---

Lease A contractual agreement in which the lessee obtains the right to use an asset by making periodic payments to the lessor.

Operating lease A contract in which the lessee obtains the right to use an asset for a limited period of time but does not acquire ownership of the asset.

Off-balance-sheet financing Occurs when a company's future obligations regarding an asset are not reported as a liability on the balance sheet.

One of the major advantages of lease financing is its flexibility. Terms of usage, time limits, and payments are a few of the many aspects of lease contracts that can vary.

company's future obligations regarding an asset are not reported as a liability on the balance sheet. A common example is a noncancelable operating lease. Although such lease obligations are not reported on the balance sheet, accounting rules require that the future lease payments be disclosed in the notes to the financial statements. The following is a portion of Advance Auto Parts' Note 13 that covers Lease Commitments:

Excerpt from Advance Auto Parts' 2008 Lease Commitments Note

At January 3, 2009, future minimum lease payments due under noncancelable operating leases with lease terms ranging from 1 year to 20 years through the year 2028 for all open stores are as follows:

(in thousands)	Total
2009	$ 282,967
2010	247,640
2011	226,361
2012	202,022
2013	177,500
Thereafter	1,012,744
	$2,149,234

The note discloses that Advance Auto Parts is committed to over $2 billion in future operating lease payments, with over $282 million coming due in the current year. This $2 billion in future lease payments is an example of off-balance-sheet financing. Advance Auto Parts is obligated to pay $2 billion in the future to use certain assets, but the obligation does not appear on the balance sheet. If it did, total liabilities for Advance Auto Parts would increase 114%, from $1,888,899 to $4,038,133. As you can see, off-balance-sheet financing can be significant.

In contrast to operating leases, a **capital lease** is a contract in which the lessee obtains enough rights to use and control an asset such that the lessee is in substance the owner of the asset. Because of this effective ownership, accounting rules require that the leased asset and the lease obligation be recorded by the lessee and reported on the balance sheet. This is why such contracts are called *capital* leases—because the asset is capitalized on the balance sheet. The actual entries associated with a capital lease and the criteria for determining whether a contract is a capital lease will be left to more advanced accounting courses.

Contingent Liabilities

A **contingent liability** is an obligation that arises from an existing condition whose outcome is uncertain and whose resolution depends on a future event. A good example of a contingent liability is a product warranty. The "existing condition" is the company's promise

Capital lease A contract in which the lessee obtains enough rights to use and control an asset such that the lessee is in substance the owner of the asset.

Contingent liability An obligation that arises from an existing condition whose outcome is uncertain and whose resolution depends on a future event.

HOME DEPOT ANALYSIS

Look at Home Depot's debt and leases notes in Appendix C. How much does the company owe under capital leases? What is the amount of future minimum lease payments under operating leases? Which of the two amounts is reported on the balance sheet?

In its debt note, Home Depot reports a $417 million obligation related to capital leases. In its leases note, it discloses that it has over $8.7 billion in future payments under operating leases. Even though Home Depot will pay out much more in operating leases, only the obligations related to capital leases are reported on the balance sheet as a liability.

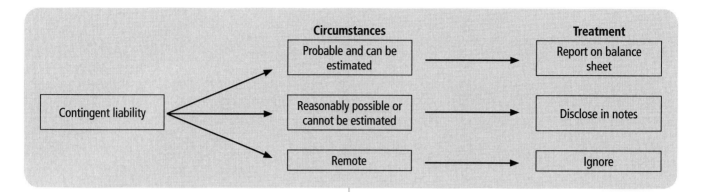

Circumstances		Treatment
Probable and can be estimated	→	Report on balance sheet
Reasonably possible or cannot be estimated	→	Disclose in notes
Remote	→	Ignore

that it will replace the product or refund the price. The uncertain outcome is whether the product will be defective, and the resolution depends on both the product malfunctioning and the customer returning it. Another example is legal action against a company, which is an uncertain condition whose resolution depends on future events (e.g., a jury verdict).

Accounting rules state that a contingent liability should be recorded and reported on the balance sheet if it is *probable* that the liability will be incurred and it can be reasonably estimated. A warranty meets these two conditions. Most merchandisers or manufacturers will have defective products that customers return, and most can reasonably estimate their future warranty claims by reviewing historical claims. As a result, most companies include warranty obligations among their liabilities.

For companies like Advance Auto Parts, warranty liabilities are not large enough to be reported as a separate item on the balance sheet. Rather, they are usually combined with other liabilities. To illustrate, consider again Advance Auto Parts' 2008 accrued expenses note to its financial statements.

Advance Auto Parts' 2008 Accrued Expenses Note

(*in thousands*)	
Payroll and related benefits	$ 75,471
Warranty reserves	28,662
Capital expenditures	26,299
Self-insurance reserves	90,554
Taxes payable	69,714
Other	81,810
Total accrued expenses	$372,510

Effective December 30, 2007, the Company began including in its warranty reserve the warranty obligation on certain other products sold in addition to batteries.

Advance Auto Parts shows that the 2008 balance in accrued expenses as reported on the balance sheet

includes over $28 million of warranty obligations. The note also discloses that 2008 was the first year that the company included nonbattery warranties in its liability.

While probable contingent liabilities are recorded as liabilities, those that have only a *remote* probability of occurring can be ignored. Companies are not generally required to record or disclose any information regarding remote contingent liabilities. If they were, companies would likely have to list so many potential liabilities that the notes to the financial statements would be many pages longer!

Those contingent liabilities that lie in between probable and remote—that is, those that are *reasonably possible*—are disclosed in the notes to the financial statements. This same treatment is required of liabilities that are probable but cannot be reasonably estimated. Note that disclosing something in the notes brings it to the attention of investors, but it does not result in a change to a company's liabilities.

The following is an excerpt from Advance Auto Parts' contingencies note to its 2008 financial statements. It describes a contingency whose occurrence is at least reasonably possible but whose amount cannot be reasonably estimated:

Excerpt from Advance Auto Parts' 2008 Contingencies Note

The Company is involved in various types of legal proceedings arising from claims of employment discrimination or other types of employment matters as a result of claims by current and former employees. The damages claimed against the Company in some of these proceedings are substantial. Because of the uncertainty of the outcome of such legal matters and because the Company's liability, if any, could vary widely, including the size of any damages awarded if plaintiffs are successful in litigation or any negotiated settlement, the Company cannot reasonably estimate the possible loss or range of loss which may arise.

LO6 Evaluating a Company's Management of Liabilities

As a company operates its business, it will generate liabilities. In fact, the generation of liabilities is usually the easy part of a business. It is the repayment of those liabilities that can create significant problems.

The following sections examine the liabilities of Advance Auto Parts to see how well it can meet its obligations. The examination will require information from the company's balance sheet. The required information is found in Exhibit 9-5, excerpted from Advance Auto Parts' 2008 Annual Report.

Exhibit 9-5 Account Balances from Advance Auto Parts' 2008 Annual Report

Source	Accounts	2008	2007
Balance Sheet	Current assets	$1,807,626	$1,682,825
	Total assets	2,964,065	2,805,566
	Current liabilities	1,364,994	1,225,928
	Total liabilities	1,888,899	1,781,771

Horizontal and Vertical Analyses

An easy and useful place to start an examination of liabilities is with horizontal and vertical analyses. Recall from Chapter 2 that horizontal analysis calculates the dollar change in an account balance, defined as the current year balance less the prior year balance, and divides that change by the prior year balance to yield the percentage change. Vertical analysis divides each account balance by a base account, yielding a percentage. The base account is total assets for balance sheet accounts and net sales or total revenues for income statement accounts. These calculations are summarized as follows:

Horizontal Analysis

$$\text{Dollar change in account balance} = \text{Current year balance} - \text{Prior year balance}$$

$$\text{Percentage change in account balance} = \frac{\text{Dollar change}}{\text{Prior year balance}}$$

Vertical Analysis

$$\text{Percentage} = \frac{\text{Account Balance}}{\text{Total Assets}} \text{ (Balance Sheet)} \quad \text{or} \quad \frac{\text{Account Balance}}{\text{Net Sales or Revenue}} \text{ (Income Statement)}$$

Given Advance Auto Parts' financial information in Exhibit 9-5, horizontal and vertical analyses of liabilities result in the following.

Horizontal Analysis

	Change	Percentage Change
Total Liabilities	$\frac{1,888,899 - 1,781,771}{1,781,771} = \frac{107,128}{1,781,771}$	$\frac{107,128}{1,781,771} = 6.0\%$

Vertical Analysis

	2008	2007
Total Liabilities	$\frac{1,888,899}{2,964,065} = 63.7\%$	$\frac{1,781,771}{2,805,566} = 63.5\%$

The calculations show a fairly stable position with regard to liabilities. Horizontal analysis shows a 6.0% increase in liabilities. However, vertical analysis shows that total liabilities as a percentage of total assets was virtually unchanged over the two years. In both years, almost two-thirds of every dollar of assets was generated through debt. So, although liabilities are increasing, they are doing so at the same rate as assets.

For comparison, the horizontal and vertical analyses of liabilities for Advance Auto Parts, O'Reilly Automotive, and Pep Boys are shown as follows.

		Horizontal Analysis	Vertical Analysis
Liabilities	Advance Auto Parts	6.0%	63.7%
	O'Reilly	178.1%	45.6%
	Pep Boys	1.4%	72.7%

You can see that Advance Auto Parts' liabilities grew more than Pep Boys' but nothing like O'Reilly's. (O'Reilly acquired another company during 2008, so its numbers changed dramatically in 2008.) Also, you can see that Advance Auto Parts is in the middle of the two competitors when it comes to liabilities as a percentage of assets (vertical analysis).

In addition to an analysis of total liabilities, it is usually a good idea to conduct horizontal and vertical analyses on some of the larger individual liabilities to identify any potential areas of concern. For Advance Auto Parts, the two largest liabilities are accounts payable and long-term debt. (These balances are not reported in this text.) In 2008, accounts payable increased 14.9% while long-term debt decreased 9.9%. These changes appear to be reasonable given an overall increase of 6.0%.

Current Ratio

Liquidity refers to a company's ability to pay off its obligations in the near future. Many parties are interested in a company's liquidity. For example, a loan officer would be interested in whether a company could pay monthly interest. A vendor would want to know if it could expect prompt payment. Employees are concerned with their employer's ability to satisfy payroll. One way to measure a company's liquidity is to calculate the current ratio.

The **current ratio** compares a company's current assets to its current liabilities as follows:

$$\text{Current Ratio} = \frac{\text{Current Assets}}{\text{Current Liabilities}}$$

By comparing what a company expects to turn into cash within a year to what it expects to pay within the year, this ratio suggests how well a company can pay its short-term liabilities. A higher current ratio indicates a greater ability to satisfy current obligations.

Advance Auto Parts' 2008 current ratio is calculated as follows:

$$\frac{\$1,807,626}{\$1,364,994} = 1.32$$

© ISTOCKPHOTO.COM/MLADEN MLADENOV

Liquidity A company's ability to pay off its obligations in the near future.

Current ratio Compares a company's current assets to its current liabilities and measures its ability to pay current obligations.

Solvency A company's ability to continue in business in the long term by satisfying its long-term obligations.

Debt to assets ratio Compares a company's total liabilities to its total assets and measures its ability to satisfy its long-term obligations.

> ## When interpreting the current ratio, it is a good idea to gauge whether a company can turn its current assets into cash.

The 1.32 ratio shows that at the end of 2008, Advance Auto Parts had $1.32 in current assets for every dollar of current liabilities. That is, Advance Auto Parts had more than enough current assets to satisfy its obligations coming due in the following year. The company's 2007 ratio was almost exactly the same ($1,682,825/$1,225,928 = 1.37). By way of comparison, O'Reilly's 2008 current ratio was 1.78 and Pep Boys' was 1.33.

When interpreting the current ratio, it is a good idea to gauge whether a company can turn its current assets into cash. For example, a company that cannot sell its inventory cannot generate cash to pay its obligations. This could be a risk for Advance Auto Parts. Over $1.6 billion of its $1.8 billion of current assets is inventory. One way to gauge the impact of inventory is to calculate the inventory turnover ratio.

Recall from Chapter 7 that the inventory turnover ratio is calculated as follows: Cost of Goods Sold/Average Inventory. Advance Auto Parts' inventory turnover ratio is 1.7, meaning that the company sells through its inventory 1.7 times during the year. This is similar to industry standards, so it appears that Advance Auto Parts should not have a problem turning its inventory into cash and paying off its obligations.

Debt to Assets Ratio

Solvency refers to a company's ability to continue in business in the long term by satisfying its long-term obligations. While predicting whether a company will survive in the long term is very difficult, we can get an idea of a company's prospects by calculating the debt to assets ratio. The **debt to assets ratio** compares a company's total liabilities to its total assets. It is calculated as follows:

$$\text{Debt to Assets Ratio} = \frac{\text{Total Liabilities}}{\text{Total Assets}}$$

This ratio takes all of the obligations a company reports and divides by all of the assets the company reports, yielding the percentage of assets that are provided by debt. Thus, the ratio is a good indicator of a company's capital structure. **Capital structure** refers to the mix of debt and equity that a company uses to generate its assets. Since debt must be repaid, a company that uses more debt has a riskier capital structure and therefore a greater risk of being unable to meet its obligations.

Advance Auto Parts' 2008 debt to assets ratio is calculated as follows:

$$\frac{\$1,888,899}{\$2,964,065} = 0.637$$

The 0.637 ratio shows that at the end of 2008, 63.7% of Advance Auto Parts' assets were generated through debt. In comparison, O'Reilly's ratio was 0.456 in 2008 and Pep Boys' was 0.727. Whether a ratio of 0.637, 0.456, or 0.727 is good or bad for a company depends on many factors. Some companies willingly expose themselves to liabilities and the risk that comes with them in order to provide a greater chance of significant profits. Others purposely reduce their risk by limiting the use of debt. Neither strategy is right or wrong. They are just different. This issue will be discussed in more detail in Chapter 12. At this point, you should simply recognize that Advance Auto Parts

> A bond's issuance price will always be the present value of future cash flows discounted back at the current market rate of interest.

appears to have more risk of insolvency than O'Reilly and less risk than Pep Boys.

As you consider the debt to assets ratios, you may recognize the numbers from earlier in the chapter. They are the same as those generated in the vertical analysis of total liabilities. In fact, the debt to assets ratio is equivalent to a vertical analysis of total liabilities. Both the debt to assets ratio and vertical analysis divide total liabilities by total assets and are interpreted the same. So, when you conduct a vertical analysis, you already have the debt to assets ratio.

Capital structure The mix of debt and equity that a company uses to generate its assets.

HOME DEPOT ANALYSIS

Using Home Depot's information in Appendix C, calculate and interpret (1) horizontal and vertical analyses of liabilities, (2) the current ratio, and (3) the debt to assets ratio.

(1) *Horizontal Analysis*

$$(\$23,387 - \$26,610)/\$26,610 = -12.2\%$$

Vertical Analysis

$$\$23,387/\$41,164 = 56.8\%$$

The −12.2% horizontal analysis reflects a decreasing amount of obligations. The 56.8% vertical analysis of total liabilities shows that a little over half of the company's assets are generated through liabilities, with the rest generated through equity.

(2) *Current Ratio*

$$\$13,362/\$11,153 = 1.20$$

The 1.20 Current Ratio indicates that Home Depot has $1.20 in current assets for every $1 of current liabilities. It appears that the company can pay off its current liabilities with its current assets. Since most of Home Depot's current assets are tied up in inventory, it will be important for the company to continue to sell its inventory.

(3) *Debt to Assets Ratio*

$$\$23,387/\$41,164 = 56.8\%$$

The 56.8% Debt to Assets Ratio indicates that Home Depot has 57 cents in liabilities for every $1 of assets. This is a reasonable capital structure, comprised of almost half debt and half equity.

LO7 Appendix—Determining a Bond's Issuance Price

Calculating the issuance price of a bond requires the conversion of a bond's future cash flows into today's dollars. A conventional interest-paying bond has two types of future cash flows: the one-time principal payment made at maturity and the periodic interest payments made each year. The bond's issuance price will always be the present value of those future cash flows discounted back at the current market rate of interest.

To illustrate, suppose that the market rate of interest is 8% when Bowman Corporation issues a $100,000 4-year bond that pays interest annually at a rate of 10%. The future cash flows of this bond are represented graphically as follows:

(r = 8%) is 3.3121. Therefore, the present value of the $10,000 payments is $33,121 ($10,000 × 3.3121).

Adding these two present values together yields $106,621. So, the bond sells for a premium. This calculation, along with similar calculations for 10% and 12% market rates are shown in Exhibit 9-6.

Exhibit 9-6 Calculations of Bond Issuance Prices

	Premium Case 8% market rate	Par Value Case 10% market rate	Discount Case 12% market rate
Present value of a single payment of $100,000	$ 73,500	$ 68,300	$63,550
Present value of an annuity of $10,000	33,121	31,700	30,373
Issuance price	$106,621	$100,000	$93,923

Note that the prices calculated confirm that bonds are issued for (1) a premium when the stated interest rate exceeds the market rate, (2) face value when the

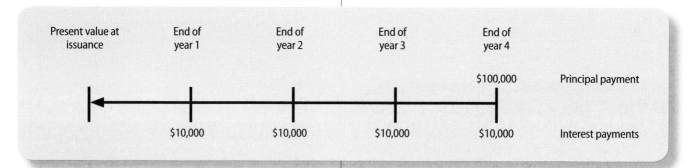

Present value at issuance	End of year 1	End of year 2	End of year 3	End of year 4	
				$100,000	Principal payment
	$10,000	$10,000	$10,000	$10,000	Interest payments

The $100,000 principal payment is a single payment made at the end of year four. Therefore, it is discounted back four periods at an 8% rate using the appropriate factor found in Exhibit A-4, Present Value of $1. The factor for four periods (n = 4) and a rate of 8% (r = 8%) is 0.7350. Therefore, the present value of the $100,000 payment is $73,500 ($100,000 × 0.7350).

The $10,000 interest payments are made at the end of each of the next four years. Therefore, they constitute an annuity that is discounted back four periods at an 8% rate using the appropriate factor found in Exhibit A-9: Present Value of an Ordinary Annuity. The factor for four periods (n = 4) and a rate of 8%

two rates are equal, and (3) a discount when the market interest rate exceeds the stated rate.

LO8 Appendix—Effective Interest Method of Amortization

When a bond is issued at a discount or premium, the discount or premium must be amortized over the life of the bond. The following sections demonstrate the effective interest method of amortization.

The **effective interest method of amortization** amortizes the bond discount or premium so that interest expense each period is a constant percentage of the bond's carrying value. Under this method, interest expense is calculated by multiplying the bond's carrying value by the market rate of interest at issuance by the time outstanding.

Effective interest method of amortization Method that amortizes the bond discount or premium so that interest expense each period is a constant percentage of the bond's carrying value.

When a bond is issued at a discount or premium, the discount or premium must be amortized over the life of the bond.

> Interest Expense = Carrying Value × Market Rate of Interest at Issuance × Time Outstanding

Once interest expense is known, the amount of discount or premium amortized is the difference between interest expense and interest paid.

> Discount Amount Amortized
> = Interest Expense − Interest Paid
>
> Premium Amount Amortized
> = Interest Paid − Interest Expense

To illustrate, refer to the Bowman example, starting first with the discount case.

Discount Example

In the discount case for the Bowman bonds, the market rate of interest was 12% and the $100,000 bond was issued for $93,923, resulting in a discount of $6,077. The issuance would be recorded with the following entry:

Jan. 1	Cash	93,923	
	Discount on Bonds Payable	6,077	
	Bonds Payable		100,000
	(To record bonds issued at a discount)		

Assets	=	Liabilities	+	Equity
+93,923		+100,000		
		−6,077		

At the end of the first year, interest expense, interest paid, and the amount of the discount amortized would be calculated as follows. Note that "time outstanding" is omitted from the calculations because interest is paid annually.

Interest Expense	Carrying value × Market rate	$93,923 × 12%	$11,271
Interest Paid	Face value × Stated rate	$100,000 × 10%	$10,000
Discount Amortized	Interest expense − Interest paid	$11,271 − $10,000	$1,271

With these values, Bowman would record the following entry on the first interest payment date:

Payment 1	Interest Expense	11,271	
	Discount on Bonds Payable		1,271
	Cash		10,000
	(To record the payment of interest)		

Assets	=	Liabilities	+	Equity
−10,000		+1,271		−11,271

Because the Discount on Bonds Payable account is reduced by this entry, the carrying value of the bonds will increase. As a result, the amount of interest expense for the second interest payment will increase as well. In fact, interest expense will continue to increase each period as the bond's carrying value increases toward the face value of $100,000. To illustrate this fact, a full amortization schedule for this bond is shown in Exhibit 9-7 (with the numbers rounded for presentation purposes):

Exhibit 9-7 Amortization Schedule of Bond Discount Using Effective Interest Method

Interest Payment	Interest Paid	Discount Amortized	Interest Expense	Unamortized Discount	Carrying Value
				$6,077	$ 93,923
1	$10,000	$1,271	$11,271	4,806	95,194
2	10,000	1,423	11,423	3,383	96,617
3	10,000	1,594	11,594	1,789	98,211
4	10,000	1,789	11,789	0	100,000
	$40,000	$6,077	$46,077		

Note that, like the straight-line method of amortization, the effective method amortizes the bond discount to zero, resulting in an ending carrying value equal to the face value. But, unlike the straight-line method, interest expense and the amount amortized under the effective interest method are different each period. Again, this is because the effective interest method makes sure that interest expense is a constant percentage (12%) of the current carrying value.

Premium Example

In the premium case, the market rate of interest was 8% and the $100,000 bond was issued for $106,621, resulting in a premium of $6,621. The issuance would be recorded with the following entry:

		Jan. 1	Cash	106,621	

```
Jan. 1   Cash                                106,621
            Premium on Bonds Payable                    6,621
            Bonds Payable                             100,000
            (To record bonds issued at a premium)

         Assets    =    Liabilities    +    Equity
         +106,621       +100,000
                        +6,621
```

At the end of the first year, interest expense, interest paid, and the amount of the discount amortized would be calculated as follows:

Exhibit 9-8 Amortization Schedule of Bond Premium Using Effective Interest Method

Interest Payment	Interest Paid	Discount Amortized	Interest Expense	Unamortized Discount	Carrying Value
				$6,621	$106,621
1	$10,000	$1,470	$ 8,530	5,151	105,151
2	10,000	1,588	8,412	3,563	103,563
3	10,000	1,715	8,285	1,848	101,848
4	10,000	1,848	8,152	0	100,000
	$40,000	$6,621	$33,379		

Interest Paid	Face value × Stated rate	$100,000 × 10%	$10,000
Interest Expense	Carrying value × Market rate	$106,621 × 8%	$8,530
Premium Amortized	Interest paid − Interest expense	$10,000 − $8,530	$1,470

With these values, Bowman would record the following entry on the first interest payment date:

```
Payment 1   Interest Expense               8,530
               Premium on Bonds Payable        1,470
               Cash                                   10,000
               (To record the first bond payment)

            Assets    =    Liabilities    +    Equity
            −10,000        −1,470              −8,530
```

Because the carrying value of the bonds decreases as a result of this entry, the amount of interest expense for the second interest payment will also decrease. Interest

expense will continue to decrease each period as the bond's carrying value decreases toward the face value of $100,000. To illustrate, a full amortization schedule for this bond is shown in Exhibit 9-8 (with the numbers rounded for presentation purposes).

Note that like the straight-line method of amortization, the effective method amortizes the bond premium to zero, resulting in an ending carrying value equal to the face value. But, unlike the straight-line method, interest expense and the amount amortized are different each period under the effective method. Again, this is because the effective interest method makes sure that interest expense is a constant percentage (8%) of the current carrying value.

STUDY TOOLS
CHAPTER 9

CHAPTER REVIEW CARD
- ❑ Learning Objective and Key Concept Reviews
- ❑ Key Definitions and Formulas

ONLINE (Located at 4ltrpress.cengage.com/acct)
- ❑ Flash Cards and Crossword Puzzles
- ❑ Conceptual and Computational Interactive Quizzes
- ❑ E-Lectures
- ❑ Static, Algorithmic, and Additional Homework Activities (as directed by your instructor)

EXERCISES

1. Current Liabilities   LO1

Jones Hardware Store has total receipts for the day of $12,550. This total includes 7% sales tax on all sales.

Required

Calculate sales tax payable and prepare the journal entry to record the sales.

2. Current Liabilities   LO1

On March 1, Azalea Golf borrows $30,000 on a 6-month, 6% note from Augusta Bank. Assume interest is paid at the maturity of the note.

Required

Prepare (a) the journal entry to record the receipt of cash from the note, (b) the journal entry to record the accrual of interest if Azalea prepares financial statements on June 30, and (c) the journal entry to record the repayment of the note at maturity.

3. Current Liabilities   LO1

The employees of Pinehurst Company earned wages of $80,000 during the month of June. The following were withholdings related to these salaries: $5,000 for Social Security (FICA), $3,000 for state income tax, and $7,700 for federal income tax.

Required

Prepare (a) the journal entry to record the payment of these salaries assuming they are paid on June 30 and (b) the journal entry to record Pinehurst Company's additional payroll tax expense for June.

4. Recording Bonds and Interest   LO2, 3

Johnson Galleries issued $500,000 of 10-year bonds on January 1, 2010. The bonds pay 8% interest semi-annually on July 1 and January 1. The market rate of interest on the date of issuance was 8%.

Required

a. Prepare all journal entries necessary in 2010.
b. How would the issue price change if the market rate was lower than 8%? Higher than 8%?
c. What will be recorded in 2010 in the financing section of the statement of cash flows?

5. Recording Bonds at a Premium and a Discount   LO3

On January 1, 2010, Hampton Inc. issues $3 million, 5-year, 10% bonds with interest payable on July 1 and January 1. Hampton prepares financials on December 31 and amortizes any discount or premium using the straight-line method.

Required

Prepare all journal entries necessary in 2010 assuming the bonds were issued at (a) 96 and (b) 103.

6. Bond Amortization   LO3

On January 1, 2010, Thompson Company issues $4 million, 5-year, 8% bonds with interest payable on June 30 and December 31. Thompson amortizes any discount or premium using the straight-line method.

Required

Prepare a bond amortization schedule assuming the bonds were issued at (a) 101 and (b) 97.

7. Bond Redemption   LO4

After making a semiannual interest payment, the carrying value of Woods Company's bonds were as follows:

Bonds payable	$1,500,000
Less: Discount on bonds payable	80,000
Carrying value	$1,420,000

Required

a. Calculate the gain or loss on redemption assuming Woods redeems the bonds at 101.
b. Prepare the journal entry to record the redemption.
c. Can any company redeem the bonds they issue at any time? Explain.
d. Why might a company want to redeem its bonds before maturity?

8. Leases   LO5

Glennon Incorporated needs a new piece of equipment for its factory. Instead of purchasing the asset, the company chooses to enter into a 5-year operating lease with annual payments of $50,000. Assume each lease payment is made on December 31.

Required

a. Prepare the journal entry to record the first annual lease payment.
b. What are the financial reporting advantages of an operating lease over a capital lease?
c. Why might Glennon have chosen to lease the equipment instead of buying it?

9. Contingent Liabilities   LO5

Tanner Toys had sales of $2,500,000 during 2010. In 2009, 5% of sales were returned for a refund, but Tanner believes that recent product changes will reduce warranty expense to about 3% of 2010 sales.

Required

a. What amount is Tanner expecting to refund customers for purchases made in 2010?
b. Should this amount be reported as a liability on the financial statements? Why or why not?
c. Is Tanner using a reasonable means to estimate warranty expense?

10. Evaluate Liabilities   LO6

The following financial data were reported by Verizon Wireless for two recent years ($ in millions):

Verizon Wireless Balance Sheet (partial)		
	Current	Prior
Current assets	$2,290	$ 669
Current liabilities	2,257	2,172
Total liabilities	9,801	9,854
Total assets	5,131	6,200

Required

Conduct horizontal and vertical analyses of Verizon's accounts and calculate the current and debt to assets ratios for each year. How would the most recent ratios change if Verizon decided to pay off $1 billion of current liabilities with cash?

11. Appendix—Bond Interest and Amortization   LO7, 8

On January 1, 2010, Tallakson Company issues a $50,000, 5-year, 8% bond with interest payable annually on December 31. The market interest rate at issuance is 10%. Tallakson uses the effective interest method of amortization.

Required

a. Determine the issuance price of the bond by using the appropriate table(s) in Appendix A.
b. Prepare the entry for the first interest payment on December 31, 2010.
c. Prepare an amortization schedule for the bond.

PROBLEMS

12. Recording and Reporting Current Liabilities   LO1

The following is a list of liability accounts on the ledger of Chop House Incorporated on January 1:

Sales Tax Payable	$ 7,500
Accounts Payable	9,500
Unearned Service Revenue	16,500

The following transactions occurred during the month of January:

Jan. 1 Borrowed $25,000 from Atlanta Bank on a 6-month, 6% note.
9 Provided service for customers who had paid $6,000 in advance.
15 Paid state treasurer for sales taxes collected in December, $7,500.
18 Bought inventory on credit for $12,000.
23 Sold goods on credit for $3,000, plus 7% sales tax.

The employees of the Chop House earned gross salaries of $45,000 during January. Withholdings were $2,500 for Social Security, $4,000 for federal income

tax, and $1,900 for state income tax. Salaries earned in January will be paid during February.

Required:

a. Prepare journal entries for the January transactions.
b. Prepare adjusting entries at January 31 for the salaries expense, payroll tax expense, and notes payable.
c. Create the current liability section of the balance sheet at January 31.

13. Bond Presentation, Interest, and Redemption   LO2, 3, 4

The following is an excerpt taken from the December 31, 2009, balance sheet of the Wimbledon Company:

Current liabilities	
Bond interest payable	$ 64,000
Long-term liabilities	
Bonds payable	1,600,000
Less: Discount on bonds payable	(30,000)
Carrying value	1,570,000

The bonds have a stated interest rate of 8% and mature on January 1, 2015. Interest is paid semiannually on July 1 and January 1. The bonds are callable at 105 on any semiannual interest date.

Required:

a. Prepare the journal entry to record the payment of bond interest on January 1, 2010.
b. Prepare the journal entry to amortize the bond discount and pay the interest on July 1, 2010.
c. Prepare the journal entry to record the redemption of the bonds on July 1, 2010, after the interest has been paid.
d. Prepare the adjusting journal entry for December 31, 2010, assuming that the bonds were not redeemed.

14. Analyzing Liabilities   LO6

Explorer Corporation's board of directors is having its annual meeting to analyze the performance of the firm. One area the board is focusing on is total liabilities. The following are selected items of the December 31, 2010, balance sheet.

	2010	2009
Total assets	$935,870	$902,225
Total liabilities	575,430	562,855
Total equity	360,440	339,370

Required:

Conduct horizontal and vertical analyses of total liabilities and interpret the results. Explain whether or not Explorer should be pleased with its financial position based on these calculations.

15. Research and Analysis   LO1, 2, 5, 6

Access the 2008 annual report for Amazon by clicking on the *Investor Relations* and *Annual Reports and Proxies* links at www.amazon.com.

Required:

1. Examine the company's balance sheet and conduct horizontal and vertical analyses of all liability account balances, including total liabilities.
2. Examine the financing activities section of the company's statement of cash flows. Over the past three years, did the company borrow or repay debt more?
3. Calculate the company's current ratio and debt to assets ratios for 2008 and 2007.

4. Examine the company's long-term debt note. What type of debt was eliminated during 2008? According to the last paragraph of the note, how much cash did Amazon pay to retire the debt? How was the remainder retired?
5. Based on your answers above, write a paragraph explaining your opinion of Amazon's liability position. Use your answers as supporting facts.

- All exercises and problems from the text are available online in static and algorithmic versions.
- Additional multiple choice, exercises, problems, and cases are available online in CengageNOW or as an enrichment module that can be customized into this text.

Stockholders' Equity

Introduction

This chapter examines the accounting for stockholders' equity. It begins with a discussion of the corporate form of business. It then examines how companies account for common stock and any cash or stock dividends distributed on that stock. After discussing preferred stock, preferred stock dividends, and treasury stock, the chapter concludes with a discussion on how to analyze a company's equity position.

LO1 The Corporate Form of Business

Chapter 2 introduced the three major forms of business—the sole proprietorship, the partnership, and the corporation. The following sections describe some of the characteristics of the corporate form of business that distinguish it from sole proprietorships and partnerships. These corporate characteristics are as follows:

- Separate legal entity
- Ability to raise capital
- Limited liability of owners
- Transferability of ownership
- Double taxation
- Regulation

Learning Objectives

After studying the material in this chapter, you should be able to:

LO1 Describe the characteristics of the corporate form of business.

LO2 Describe the characteristics of common stock and how it is recorded and reported.

LO3 Understand cash dividends, stock dividends, and stock splits.

LO4 Describe the characteristics of preferred stock and how it receives preference in dividends.

LO5 Describe the characteristics of treasury stock and how it is recorded and reported.

LO6 Evaluate equity through the calculation and interpretation of horizontal, vertical, and ratio analyses.

Separate Legal Entity

A corporation is a separate legal entity. It is formed under state law by submitting articles of incorporation to a state government and requesting the establishment of a corporate entity. The articles describe the business of the corporation and request authority to sell ownership interests (that is, stock) in the corporation. Once the articles are approved, the state grants a corporate charter that effectively creates a new legal entity. In most cases, this new legal entity can buy, own, and sell assets in its name and can also borrow money. It can sue and be sued. In other words, it has most of the rights and responsibilities of an individual in society.

Google became a publicly traded corporation in 2004 when it sold stock to the public for the first time. It raised $1.6 billion in that initial public offering (IPO).

© ALEX SEGRE/ALAMY

Ability to Raise Capital

Many sole proprietorships and partnerships have limited access to the capital needed to successfully operate or expand their businesses. In contrast, corporations can access capital through the sale of stock to investors, who then become stockholders. Most corporations begin by selling stock privately to a few owners. And while many corporations stay privately owned, others "go public" by offering stock to the public through an initial public offering (IPO). Such public offerings can generate substantial amounts of capital. For example, Google, Inc., raised over $1.6 billion in its 2004 IPO. If needed, a corporation can continue to raise capital in the future by selling additional stock. Google followed its IPO with a second stock offering in 2005, raising another $4.2 billion in capital. The ability to access capital through the sale of stock is certainly an advantage of the corporate form of business.

Stockholders normally have no personal liability for the corporation's obligations beyond their investment in the corporation's stock.

Limited Liability of Owners

Under a sole proprietorship and a general partnership, owners are personally liable for the actions and obligations of their businesses. However, stockholders normally have no personal liability for the corporation's obligations beyond their investment in the corporation's stock. If a corporation defaults and cannot meet its obligations, creditors cannot seek the assets of the stockholders as compensation for the corporate default. They can only pursue the assets of the corporation. As a result of this limited liability, stockholders stand to lose only the amount of their investments. This limited liability of owners is a significant advantage of the corporate form of business.

Transferability of Ownership

Another advantage of the corporate form of business is the ease with which ownership can be transferred. When a sole proprietor wants to transfer his or her ownership to another individual, the business itself must be sold. When a partner wants to transfer an ownership interest to another investor, usually all other partners must agree. Once the transfer occurs, a new partnership is formed. In both of these cases, the transfer of ownership can be burdensome.

In contrast, when stockholders of a publicly traded corporation want to transfer ownership to another investor, they need only to sell the stock to other investors. Such sales usually occur through an open stock exchange such as the New York Stock Exchange (NYSE) or the National Association of Securities Dealers Automated Quotes (NASDAQ). They can be accomplished by calling a broker or logging onto a website such as E*TRADE and executing a sell order. Hundreds of millions of shares of stock are bought and sold every day.

Double Taxation

While the corporate form has several advantages over sole proprietorships and partnerships, it does have some disadvantages. One is the double taxation of income.

A corporation's income is taxed at the federal and state levels. Dividends paid to stockholders are also taxed on the stockholders' personal tax returns. As a result, a corporation's income that is paid in dividends is taxed twice—once at the corporate level and a second time at the personal stockholder level. In contrast, the income of sole proprietorships and partnerships is reported only on personal tax returns and is therefore taxed only once—at the personal level.

To illustrate double taxation, suppose that a corporation earns $1.0 billion in pre-tax earnings and is subject to a 40% corporate tax rate. The corporation would pay $400 million in corporate taxes. Suppose further that the corporation distributed all $600 million of its remaining profits to its stockholders, who all had personal tax rates of 25%. The stockholders would pay $150 million in personal taxes. As a result, the corporation's pre-tax income of $1 billion is taxed twice for a total of $550 million in taxes.

HOME DEPOT ANALYSIS

Look at Home Depot's Balance Sheet in Appendix C. What tells you that Home Depot is a corporation?

You can tell in two ways. First, the balance sheet shows balances in common stock, which means that the company has stockholders and is therefore a corporation. Second, the company name refers to Home Depot, Inc. The "Inc." stands for Incorporated. Home Depot does not report where it is incorporated on its balance sheet, but it is incorporated in the state of Delaware.

> Common stock is sold in shares. That is, each unit of stock is called a "share" of stock.

Regulation

Another disadvantage of the corporation is the extent of regulation. Consider some of the reporting requirements of a publicly traded corporation such as Walgreens. Walgreens must file numerous reports with the Securities and Exchange Commission. These include audited annual financial statements on Form 10-K, unaudited quarterly financial statements on Form 10-Q, and any notifications of significant events, such as the hiring of a new chief executive officer or the announcement of a dividend or the closing of a factory on Form 8-K. There are many other reporting and legal requirements arising from state laws, stock exchange regulations, the Internal Revenue Service, and Congress. Adherence to and compliance with laws and regulations consume significant amounts of the time, labor, and resources of corporations.

LO2 Common Stock

One of the distinguishing characteristics of the corporation is its ability to sell capital stock to investors to raise funds. The amount raised by issuing capital stock is called **contributed capital** because the funds are contributed by investors in exchange for an ownership claim on company assets. The most common type of capital stock is appropriately named **common stock**. Investors who purchase common stock are called stockholders and are the owners of the corporation.

Authorized, Issued, and Outstanding Shares

Common stock is sold in shares. That is, each unit of stock is called a "share" of stock. There are three ways in which a company describes its shares of stock:

- Authorized shares
- Issued shares
- Outstanding shares

Authorized shares refers to the number of shares of stock that a company can legally issue. This capacity is set in the corporate charter filed with the state. Usually, corporations request authority to sell more shares than initially needed so that they do not have to amend the corporate charter to issue additional shares.

Issued shares refers to the number of shares a company has distributed to owners to date. Notice that the description "sold shares" is not used. Common stock is not always distributed via a sale. For example, some stock is issued to employees as part of their compensation. Thus, the description "issued shares" is used.

Outstanding shares refers to the number of shares that have been issued and are still held by someone other than the issuing company. When you hear news about a company's stock price rising or falling, the news is referring to a company's outstanding shares. The difference between a company's issued and outstanding shares is usually the number of shares the company has repurchased from investors, which is called treasury stock. Treasury stock is discussed later in this chapter.

Companies usually disclose the number of authorized, issued, and outstanding shares on their balance sheets or in the notes to their financial statements. You will see this in the section covering the reporting of common stock.

Stockholder Rights

When a corporation issues common stock, it usually grants to stockholders the following four rights:

- the right to vote
- the right to participate proportionally in dividends
- the right to participate proportionally in residual assets
- the right of preemption

Contributed capital The amount of capital raised by issuing stock to investors in exchange for an ownership claim on company assets.

Common stock The most common type of capital stock.

Authorized shares The number of shares of stock that a company can legally issue.

Issued shares The number of shares a company has distributed to owners to date.

Outstanding shares The number of shares that have been issued and are still held by someone other than the issuing company.

The *right to vote* ensures that a stockholder can participate in company governance by voting on issues and actions that require owner consent or approval. An example of such an action is the election of a corporation's board of directors.

The *right to participate proportionally in dividends* ensures that stockholders receive an appropriate amount of any dividends declared by the company. For example, if a stockholder owns 25% of a corporation's common stock, he or she has the right to receive 25% of any dividend the company distributes.

The *right to participate proportionally in residual assets* ensures that stockholders receive an appropriate amount of assets upon liquidation of the company. For example, if a stockholder owns 10% of a corporation's common stock when the company ceases operations and liquidates, he or she has the right to receive 10% of all residual assets.

The *right of preemption* ensures that stockholders can maintain their ownership percentage when new stock is issued. For example, if a company decides to issue additional shares of common stock, a stockholder who owns 15% of all shares of common stock has the right to purchase 15% of the new issuance. Because of the recordkeeping burden of this right and the ease with which an investor can purchase stock in the marketplace, this right may be withheld from stockholders.

Par Value

A corporation normally assigns to its common stock a value known as a par value. **Par value** is an arbitrary value that determines an entity's legal capital. Legal capital is the amount of capital that a state requires a corporation to maintain in order to protect creditor claims. Most companies set par value very low. For example, Walgreens has a $0.078125 par value for its common stock, while CVS has a $0.01 par value. Although most states still require corporations to set par values for their stock, the value has lost much of its legal significance over time. However, as the following section demonstrates, par value still affects both the recording and reporting of common stock.

> **Par value** An arbitrary value that determines an entity's legal capital.

Recording Common Stock

Because a stock's par value is usually set very low, most common stock is issued for more than par value. When this occurs, a company uses two equity accounts to record the stock issuance—one account for the par value and a second account for the excess paid over par value.

To illustrate, suppose that a company issues 100 shares of $1 par value stock for $5 per share on April 5. The company would record this issuance as follows:

April 5	Cash	500	
	Common Stock		100
	Additional Paid-In Capital		400
	(To record sale of $1 par stock)		

Assets	=	Liabilities	+	Equity
+500				+100
				+400

This entry increases Cash for the amount received and divides the increase in equity into two accounts. The Common Stock account is increased for $100, which is the par value of the stock ($1 par × 100 shares issued). The $400 excess paid over par value is recorded in Additional Paid-In Capital. Since both Common Stock and Additional Paid-In Capital are equity accounts, this entry increases the company's assets and equity.

While most companies set a par value for their stock, some do not because their state of incorporation does not require it. Stock without a par value is called no-par stock. For no-par stock, the entire issuance is recorded directly into the common stock account. To illustrate, consider the previous example, except that the stock has no par value. The company would record the issuance as follows:

April 5	Cash	500	
	Common Stock		500
	(To record sale of no-par stock)		

Assets	=	Liabilities	+	Equity
+500				+500

Everything in the entry is the same as previously, except that Common Stock is increased for the entire issuance price rather than just the par value.

L ook at Home Depot's balance sheet in Appendix C. How many shares of common stock does Home Depot have authorized, issued, and outstanding at the end of 2008? What is the stock's par value? Has the company properly recorded the par value of common stock? Calculate the total capital contributed to the company through the issuance of stock.

Home Depot has 10 billion shares authorized, but only 1,707 million issued and 1,696 million outstanding at the end of 2008. The par value of the common stock is $0.05 per share. The common stock account has a balance of $85 million, which is equivalent to 1,707 issued shares times $0.05 par value per share (1,707 × $0.05 = $85). Adding the $85 million to the $6,048 balance in Paid-In Capital yields the total capital received from the issuance of common stock ($85 + $6,048 = $6,133). Home Depot has received over $6 billion from the issuance of common stock.

Walgreens has slightly over 989 million shares of common stock outstanding at the end of 2008.

Reporting Common Stock

A company's balances in both common stock and additional paid-in capital are reported in the stockholders' equity section of the balance sheet. Shown below is the stockholders' equity section of Walgreens' balance sheet as of August 31, 2008.

Walgreens reports an $80 million balance in common stock and a $575 million balance in paid-in capital at the end of 2008. Adding these two amounts together yields $655 million, which is the amount of contributed capital Walgreens has generated to date from the issuance of common stock. This number is much smaller than the balance in retained earnings, which indicates that Walgreens has generated much more equity from profitable operations than from contributed capital.

The textual description also provides information about Walgreens' shares. It discloses that Walgreens stock has a par value of $0.078125 and that the company has the authority to issue 3.2 billion shares. At the end of 2008, Walgreens had issued slightly over 1 billion shares. Note that multiplying the number of

Walgreens' 2008 Stockholders' Equity

(In millions, except shares and per share amounts)	2008	2007
Shareholders' Equity		
Preferred stock, $.0625 par value; authorized 32 million shares; none issued	$ —	$ —
Common stock, $.078125 par value; authorized 3.2 billion shares; issued 1,025,400,000 shares in 2008 and 2007	80	80
Paid-in capital	575	559
Employee stock loan receivable	(36)	(52)
Retained earnings	13,792	12,027
Accumulated other comprehensive income (loss)	9	(4)
Treasury stock at cost, 36,223,782 shares in 2008 and 34,258,643 shares in 2007	(1,551)	(1,506)
Total Shareholders' Equity	$ 12,869	$11,104

shares issued by the par value yields the balance in the common stock account (1,025,400,000 × $0.078125 = $80,109,375, which is rounded to $80 million on the balance sheet). So, Walgreens has recorded its stock issuances as described in the previous example.

One additional reported item that relates to common stock is treasury stock. Treasury stock is common stock that has been repurchased by the company. Treasury stock will be covered later in the chapter, but notice here that Walgreens discloses over 36 million shares in treasury stock. This means that Walgreens has slightly over 989 million shares of common stock outstanding at the end of 2008. The actual calculation of outstanding shares follows:

	2008
Common shares issued shares	1,025,400,000
Less: Shares in treasury stock	36,223,782
Common shares outstanding	989,176,218

LO3 Dividends

The goal of any corporation is to generate profits. Once generated, a company must decide whether or not to distribute those profits to its owners through dividends. A **dividend** is a distribution of profits to owners. The decision to distribute any dividend rests with the company's board of directors, which is the group of individuals elected by stockholders to govern the company and represent the interests of all owners. The board will consider many factors in its decisions, including the financial condition of the company, the cash available for dividends, and the company's past

Dividend A distribution of profits to a corporation's owners.

Cash dividend A distribution of cash to stockholders.

Date of declaration The date on which a corporation's board of directors declares a dividend.

Payment date The date on which a dividend will be distributed.

Date of record The date that determines who receives the dividend; the stock's owner on the date of record receives the dividend.

The goal of any corporation is to generate profits. Once generated, a company must decide whether or not to distribute those profits to its owners through dividends.

history of dividends. When dividends are distributed, they are stated as a per share amount and are paid only on outstanding shares of stock.

When and how a company distributes dividends is called a company's dividend policy. A company's policy can often be found on its website. Walgreens is an example. It reports that it "typically pays dividends in March, June, September, and December" and that checks are "customarily mailed on approximately the 12th of each of these months." In other words, like many companies, Walgreens pays a dividend each quarter.

Dividends are normally paid in cash, but they can also be paid in other forms such as stock. The following sections discuss the practice of distributing dividends, starting with the most common type—the cash dividend.

Cash Dividends

As the name suggests, a **cash dividend** is a distribution of cash to stockholders. When a corporate board decides that a cash dividend is warranted, it will declare publicly that a dividend will be distributed. The date on which the board declares the dividend is called the **date of declaration**. On this date, the board legally obligates the company to pay the dividend, so a liability is created. The board's declaration will also include the payment date and the date of record. The **payment date** is the date on which the dividend will be distributed. The **date of record** determines who receives the dividend. The stock's owner on the date of record receives the dividend.

Exhibit 10-1 contains a press release from Walgreens announcing the declaration of a quarterly dividend of $0.1125 per share. Each of the three dates can be identified: declaration (Jan. 9), record (Feb. 18), and payment (March 12).

Recording Cash Dividends The recording of cash dividends usually requires two entries. The first entry records the declaration of the dividend and the resulting liability. The second entry records the actual distribution on the payment date.

To illustrate, suppose that a company with 1,000,000 outstanding shares of stock declares a $0.05 per share dividend on November 3. The dividend is payable on November 30 to stockholders of record on November 21.

On the date of declaration, the company obligates itself to pay a $50,000 dividend (1,000,000 × $0.05). This obligation would be recorded as follows:

Nov. 3	Retained Earnings	50,000	
	Dividends Payable		50,000
	(To record declaration of dividend)		

Assets	=	Liabilities	+	Equity
		+50,000		−50,000

The entry decreases Retained Earnings because dividends reduce retained earnings. The entry also increases Dividends Payable, which is a current liability. The result of the entry is a reduction in equity and an increase in liabilities.

The distribution of cash on the payment date would be recorded as follows:

Nov. 30	Dividends Payable	50,000	
	Cash		50,000
	(To record payment of dividend)		

Assets	=	Liabilities	+	Equity
−50,000		−50,000		

This entry is simply a payment of an obligation. Both Dividends Payable and Cash are decreased for the amount of the payment. As a result, both assets and liabilities decrease.

Note that no entry is made on the date of record because no accounting transaction occurs on that date.

The date of record only determines who will receive the dividend. Therefore, it is a date with administrative importance only.

Reporting Cash Dividends Companies usually report their dividends on two financial statements. Dividends *declared* during the year are reported on the statement of stockholders' equity. Recall that dividends reduce retained earnings, so they are reported in the retained earnings column of the statement of stockholders' equity. The following is the retained earnings column of Walgreens' 2008 statement of stockholders' equity.

Retained Earnings Column of Walgreens' 2008 Statement of Stockholders' Equity	
Shareholders' Equity (in millions)	**Retained Earnings**
Balance, August 31, 2005	$ 8,836
Net earnings	1,751
Cash dividends declared ($.2725 per share)	(275)
Balance, August 31, 2006	$10,312
Net earnings	2,041
Cash dividends declared ($.3275 per share)	(326)
Balance, August 31, 2007	$12,027
Net earnings	2,157
Cash dividends declared ($.3975 per share)	(394)
FIN No. 48 adoption impact	2
Balance, August 31, 2008	$13,792

The statement provides both the per share and total dollar value of dividends declared during each year. Notice that dividends per share are increasing each year, from $0.2725 to $0.3275 to $0.3975. This results in greater total dividends each year, from $275 million to $326 million to $394 million. Dividends are presented as negative numbers because they are subtracted from retained earnings.

Dividends *paid* during the year are reported on the statement of cash flows. Because a cash dividend is a distribution of assets to an owner, dividends are considered to be a financing activity. Therefore, they are reported in the financing activities of the statement of cash flows. The following is the financing activities section of Walgreens' 2008 statement of cash flows.

Because dividends are cash outflows, they are shown as negative numbers on the statement of cash flows. Note that the amount of dividends paid is not the

Financing Activities Section of Walgreens' 2008 Statement of Cash Flows

	2008	2007	2006
Cash Flows from Financing Activities			
Net (payment) proceeds from short-term borrowings	(802)	850	—
Net proceeds from issuance of long-term debt	1,286	—	—
Payments of long-term debt	(28)	(141)	—
Stock purchases	(294)	(1,064)	(669)
Proceeds related to employee stock plans	210	266	319
Cash dividends paid	(376)	(310)	(263)
Bank overdrafts	—	(214)	214
Other	(29)	(13)	(14)
Net cash used for financing activities	$ (33)	$ (626)	$(413)

same as the amount of dividends declared. For example, the $376 million of dividends paid in the most recent year is less than the $394 million of dividends declared and reported on the statement of stockholders' equity. In fact, dividends paid are less than dividends declared in each year of the three years presented. This occurs because Walgreens' last quarterly dividend of each fiscal year is paid in the next fiscal year, and dividends have increased each year.

Stock Dividends

While cash dividends are by far the most common type of dividend, some companies distribute stock dividends. A **stock dividend** is a distribution of a company's common stock to existing stockholders. Stock dividends are declared by a company's board of directors and are usually stated in percentage terms. For example, a

> **Stock dividend** A distribution of a company's common stock to existing stockholders.

10% stock dividend means that the company will issue additional shares equal to 10% of the current outstanding shares. So, an investor owning 10,000 shares will receive 1,000 additional shares (10,000 × 10%).

At first glance, a stock dividend appears to be a great value to stockholders because they receive more shares. However, some argue that a stock dividend has very little value to stockholders because they are not receiving any assets—they are receiving only stock. Furthermore, because all stockholders receive the same percentage increase in shares, a stock dividend does not change a stockholder's ownership percentage. Finally, a stock dividend usually results in a reduction to the market price of individual shares such that the total market value of a stockholder's holdings remains unchanged. For example, a company distributing a 100% stock dividend will double the shares of stock outstanding, but this will usually result in the stock's market value being cut in half. As a result, each stockholder will have a higher number of shares but no additional monetary value.

So why do companies distribute stock dividends? There are a couple of potential reasons. First, a stock dividend can substitute for a cash dividend when a company does not have enough cash on hand. This

HOME DEPOT ANALYSIS

Look at Home Depot's Statement of Stockholders' Equity and Statement of Cash Flows in Appendix C. What was the total and per share amount of dividends declared in the most recent year? What was the total amount of dividends paid during the year?

Home Depot declared $1,521 million, or $0.90 per share, in dividends in the most recent year. It also paid $1,521 million.

motivation can be especially strong when a company is trying to maintain a long and uninterrupted streak of declaring dividends. Second, a company may want to reduce the market price of its stock to keep its stock price in an "affordable" range for the average investor. Distributing more shares in the marketplace brings down the price of each individual share.

Like cash dividends, a stock dividend is paid out of retained earnings. However, unlike a cash dividend, a stock dividend is not a distribution of assets. It is a distribution of common stock. As a result, a stock dividend simply transfers an amount from retained earnings to contributed capital (that is, common stock and additional paid-in capital). The amount transferred depends on whether the dividend is considered small or large.

A *small stock dividend* is a distribution of 25% or less of the existing outstanding shares. Small stock dividends are recorded at the market value of the stock on the date of declaration. A *large stock dividend* is a distribution of more than 25% of the existing outstanding shares. Large stock dividends are recorded at the par value of the stock.

Recording Small Stock Dividends
To illustrate a small dividend, suppose that Bethany Technologies declares a 15% stock dividend on June 1 to be distributed on June 28 to stockholders of record on June 14. On June 1, Bethany has 100,000 shares of $1 par common stock outstanding, and the stock is trading at $10 per share. Because the dividend is small, it is recorded at the market value of the stock on the date of declaration. Thus, the amount of the dividend would be calculated as follows:

Outstanding shares	100,000
× Stock dividend	× 15%
Shares to be issued	15,000
× Market value per share	× $10
Value of stock dividend	$150,000

On the date of declaration, Bethany would make the following entry:

June 1	Retained Earnings	150,000	
	Common Stock to Be Distributed		15,000
	Additional Paid-In Capital		135,000
	(To record declaration of small stock dividend)		

Assets = Liabilities + Equity
−150,000
+15,000
+135,000

This entry decreases Retained Earnings for the amount of the dividend and increases two contributed capital accounts. The first is Common Stock to Be Distributed. This account is exactly like Common Stock, except that the words "to Be Distributed" are added to indicate that the stock has yet to be issued. The account is recorded at the par value of the stock. The second is Additional Paid-In Capital, which is increased for the value of the dividend that exceeds par value—in this case, $135,000. The effect of the entry is a change in specific equity accounts, but no change in total equity. That again is the nature of a stock dividend. It is a transfer of equity between accounts, not a distribution of assets.

On the payment date, Bethany would make the following entry:

June 28	Common Stock to Be Distributed	15,000	
	Common Stock		15,000
	(To record payment of dividend)		

Assets = Liabilities + Equity
−15,000
+15,000

This entry simply decreases Common Stock to Be Distributed and increases Common Stock to reflect that the stock has been issued. Like the first entry, there is no effect on total equity as a result of this second entry.

Recording Large Stock Dividends
To illustrate a large dividend, suppose that Bethany Technologies declares a 50% dividend instead of 15%. Because the dividend is large, it is recorded at the par value of the stock. Thus, the amount of the dividend would be calculated as follows:

Outstanding shares	100,000
× Stock dividend	× 50%
Shares to be issued	50,000
× Par value per share	× $1
Value of stock dividend	$50,000

On the date of declaration, Bethany would make the following entry:

ook at Home Depot's Statement of Stockholders Equity in Appendix C. Did the company issue any stock during the years presented? Was the issuance a stock dividend?

Home Depot issues stock in each of the years presented. The stock was issued under employee stock purchase and option plans, not under a stock dividend.

June 1	Retained Earnings	50,000	
	Common Stock to Be Distributed		50,000
	(To record declaration of large		
	stock dividend)		

Assets	=	Liabilities	+	Equity
				−50,000
				+50,000

This entry decreases Retained Earnings and increases Common Stock to Be Distributed for the amount of the dividend. Because the dividend is recorded at par value, the entry does not affect Additional Paid-In

Capital. As in the case of the small dividend, total equity is not affected by this entry.

On the payment date, Bethany would make the following entry to reflect that the stock has been distributed:

June 28	Common Stock to Be Distributed	50,000	
	Common Stock		50,000
	(To record payment of dividend)		

Assets	=	Liabilities	+	Equity
				−50,000
				+50,000

Stock Splits

When a company wants to decrease the market price of its stock to make it more affordable, it can use a stock split instead of a stock dividend. A **stock split** is

Stock split An increase in a company's shares of stock according to some specified ratio.

hile companies often split their stock to make the price more affordable to the average investor, one company takes the exact opposite approach. Berkshire Hathaway, the company made famous by its founder, Warren Buffett, has never split its stock. As a result, the value of each share of stock is quite high. During the month of August 2009, the value of one share of stock was approximately $100,000!

According to the company's website, the company does not split its stock so that it can attract high-quality investors who "think of themselves as business owners and invest in companies with the intention of staying a long time." The company continues that it wants owners who "keep their eyes focused on business results, not market prices." The company concludes that "(s)plitting the stock would . . . downgrade the quality of our shareholder population and encourage a market price less consistently related to intrinsic business value."

© AP IMAGES/NATI HARNIK

Source: FocusInvestor.com, http://www.focusinvestor.com/brkfaq.htm#Q8.

> Usually, preferred stockholders relinquish the right to vote in exchange for preference to dividends and preference to assets upon liquidation of the company.

an increase in a company's shares of stock according to some specified ratio. For example, a company that declares a 2-for-1 split recalls all shares from existing stockholders and issues two shares in return, effectively doubling the shares outstanding. As result of this increased supply of shares, the market price of the stock usually falls proportionally. In a 2-for-1 split, the stock price would be cut in half.

Stock splits are very similar to stock dividends in that they both result in additional shares outstanding. In fact, a 2-for-1 stock split is the same as a 100% stock dividend. However, there are important differences. First, a stock split is not an accounting transaction, so no entry is recorded. Second, stock splits apply to all authorized shares, not just those shares outstanding. Whether a share is outstanding, is in treasury stock, or is authorized but unissued, it is split according to the ratio. Third, a stock split results in a proportional change in the par value of the stock. For example, a company declaring a 2-for-1 stock split on its $0.50 par value stock would reduce its par value in half to $0.25. The reduction in the per share par value then allows total par value to remain unchanged.

To illustrate, suppose that Constance Enterprises declares a 3-for-1 stock split when it has 50,000 shares of its $1.50 par common stock outstanding and 200,000 authorized. Before the stock splits, the share price is $60. After the split, Constance would have 150,000 shares outstanding, 600,000 shares authorized, and a par value of $0.50. The stock would trade at $20 per share.

LO4 Preferred Stock

While all corporations issue common stock, many also authorize the sale of preferred stock. **Preferred stock** is a form of capital stock that receives one or more priorities over common stock. Usually,

preferred stockholders relinquish the right to vote in exchange for preference to dividends and preference to assets upon liquidation of the company. Preference to dividends means that preferred stockholders receive their dividends before common stockholders receive any dividends.

Recording Preferred Stock

Because it is a form of contributed capital, preferred stock is recorded in the same manner as common stock. To illustrate, suppose that a company issues 500 shares of $5 par value preferred stock for $15 per share on August 23. The company would record this issuance as follows:

Aug. 23	Cash	7,500	
	Preferred Stock		2,500
	Additional Paid-In Capital		5,000
	(To record sale of preferred stock)		

Assets	=	Liabilities	+	Equity
+7,500				+2,500
				+5,000

This entry increases Cash for $7,500, which is the amount paid by the investor. Preferred Stock is increased for $2,500, which is the par value of the stock ($5 par × 500 shares issued). Additional Paid-In Capital is then increased for the excess paid over par value, which is $5,000 ($7,500 − $2,500). As a result of this entry, both assets and equity increase.

Reporting Preferred Stock

A company's balances in both preferred stock and additional paid-in capital are reported in the stockholders' equity section of the balance sheet. The following shows Walgreen's preferred stock balances from its 2008 balance sheet.

Walgreens' 2008 Preferred Stock		
	2008	2007
Preferred stock, $.0625 par value; authorized 32 million shares; none issued	$ —	$ —

> **Preferred stock** A form of capital stock that receives one or more priorities over common stock.

Walgreens reports a zero balance in preferred stock for both years. Although the company is authorized to issue 32 million shares of $0.0625 par value preferred stock, it has not yet issued any.

Cash Dividends on Preferred Stock

When a company has both preferred and common stock outstanding, cash dividends must be allocated between the two. Because preferred stockholders have dividend preference, they are paid first, followed by common stockholders. The amount that is allocated to preferred stockholders depends on the dividend rate and whether the stock is cumulative or noncumulative.

The dividend rate refers to the annual dividend amount that preferred stockholders normally receive. The rate is usually set as a dollar amount per share or as a percentage of par value. For example, preferred stock may carry a dividend of $2 per share or a dividend of 6% of par value.

All preferred stock is either cumulative or noncumulative. **Cumulative preferred stock** carries the right to receive current-year dividends and all unpaid dividends from prior years before dividends are paid to common stockholders. This means that if a company fails to pay a dividend one year, the missed dividend will be paid the next time dividends are declared. The accumulated value of unpaid prior-year dividends is called **dividends in arrears**. Note that dividends in arrears is not a liability because dividends are declared at the discretion of the board of directors and become a legal obligation only when declared. Nonetheless, because dividends in arrears are informative, they are disclosed in the notes to the financial statements.

Noncumulative preferred stock carries the right to receive current-year dividends only. If a company does not declare a dividend in a particular year, noncumulative preferred stockholders lose the right to that annual dividend forever. As a result, a company

with noncumulative preferred stock will not have dividends in arrears.

To illustrate the allocation of dividends to preferred and common stockholders, suppose that Stover Inc. has the following two types of stock:

Common stock, $2 par, 100,000 shares outstanding

5% Preferred stock, $10 par, 20,000 shares outstanding

Suppose further that Stover does not pay dividends in 2009 or 2010 but declares $64,000 of dividends in 2011. The allocation of the 2011 dividend depends on whether the preferred stock is cumulative or noncumulative.

Cumulative Preferred Stock If Stover's stock is cumulative, the preferred stockholders receive not only the current-year annual dividend but also the two years of dividends in arrears. The annual dividend on preferred stock is $0.50 per share ($10 par × 5%) and $10,000 in total ($0.50 per share × 20,000 shares). Therefore, $30,000 is allocated to preferred stockholders, with the remainder going to common stockholders. These calculations are illustrated as follows:

Preferred stock is cumulative	Preferred	Common
Dividends in arrears—Year 2009	$10,000	
Dividends in arrears—Year 2010	10,000	
Current-year preferred dividend	10,000	
Distribute remainder to common ($64,000 − $30,000)		$34,000
Total allocated in 2011	$30,000	$34,000

Once the allocation of dividends is calculated, Stover would record the declaration and payment of the dividend as follows:

Date of Declaration	Retained Earnings	64,000	
	Common Stock Dividend Payable		34,000
	Preferred Stock Dividend Payable		30,000
	(To record declaration of dividend)		

Assets	=	Liabilities	+	Equity
		+34,000		−64,000
		+30,000		

Cumulative preferred stock Stock that carries the right to receive current-year dividends and all unpaid dividends from prior years before dividends are paid to common stockholders.

Dividends in arrears The accumulated value of unpaid prior-year dividends.

Noncumulative preferred stock Stock that carries the right to receive current-year dividends only.

Payment	Common Stock Dividend Payable	34,000	
Date	Preferred Stock Dividend Payable	30,000	
	Cash		64,000
	(To record payment of dividend)		

Assets	=	Liabilities	+	Equity
−64,000		−34,000		
		−30,000		

As is the case with any cash dividend, the net overall result of the declaration and payment of the dividend is a decrease in Stover's equity and its assets.

Noncumulative Preferred Stock If Stover's stock is noncumulative, the preferred stockholders receive only the current-year annual dividend. The missed dividends in 2009 and 2010 are irrelevant to the calculation for the current year. Therefore, only $10,000 is allocated to preferred stockholders, with the remainder going to common stockholders. These calculations are illustrated as follows.

Preferred stock is cumulative	Preferred	Common
Current-year preferred dividend	$10,000	
Distribute remainder to common ($64,000 − $10,000)		$54,000
Total allocated in 2011	$10,000	$54,000

LO5 **Treasury Stock**

Like any investor, a corporation can purchase shares of its own common stock in the marketplace. The common stock that a company reacquires from stockholders is **treasury stock**. Because shares of treasury stock are no longer held by an external investor,

© ISTOCKPHOTO.COM/JAMES C. PRUITT

One of the most common reasons that a company repurchases its common stock is to acquire shares that can be issued to employees under stock compensation plans.

they are no longer outstanding. However, they are still considered to be issued.

The practice of purchasing treasury stock is commonplace in publicly traded companies today. One of the most common reasons is to acquire shares that can be issued to employees under the company's stock compensation plans. Walgreens is an excellent example. The following shows the common stock column of Walgreens' statement of stockholders' equity. This column reports the number of shares of common stock outstanding.

Common Stock Column of Walgreens' 2008 Statement of Stockholders' Equity	
	Common Stock Shares
Balance, August 31, 2005	1,013,512,047
Treasury stock purchases	(15,033,000)
Employees stock purchases and option plans	9,383,072
Balance, August 31, 2006	1,007,862,119
Treasury stock purchases	(23,842,749)
Employees stock purchases and option plans	7,121,987
Balance, August 31, 2007	991,141,357
Treasury stock purchases	(8,000,000)
Employees stock purchases and option plans	6,034,861
Balance, August 31, 2008	989,176,218

In each year presented, Walgreens reports significant purchases of treasury shares, which reduce the shares outstanding, and significant distributions to employees, which increase shares outstanding. Because Walgreens has purchased more shares than it has distributed during these three years, its total number of outstanding shares has decreased from over 1 billion at the end of 2005 to less than 1 billion at the end of 2008.

Recording Treasury Stock

Companies record the purchase of treasury stock using either the cost method or the par value method. Because most companies use the cost method, it will be

> **Treasury stock** Common stock that a company reacquires from its stockholders.

demonstrated. Under the **cost method**, treasury stock is recorded at its cost of acquisition.

To illustrate, suppose that Bahakel Inc. purchases 1,000 shares of its own common stock on May 3 when the stock is trading for $32 per share. Bahakel would record the purchase as follows:

May 3	Treasury Stock	32,000	
	Cash		32,000
	(To record purchase of treasury stock)		

Assets	=	Liabilities	+	Equity
−32,000				−32,000

The entry increases Treasury Stock and decreases Cash for the $32,000 paid to acquire the stock. Notice that Treasury Stock is increased with a debit. Treasury Stock is a contra-equity account because it represents a reduction of capital. Its balance is therefore subtracted from Bahakel's total equity. As a result of this entry, both assets and equity decrease.

Treasury stock is sometimes reissued at a later date. To illustrate how such a reissuance would be recorded, suppose that Bahakel reissued 100 shares of its treasury stock for $40 per share on July 22. Bahakel would record this transaction as follows:

July 22	Cash	4,000	
	Treasury Stock		3,200
	Additional Paid-In Capital		800
	(To record issuance of treasury stock)		

Assets	=	Liabilities	+	Equity
+4,000				+3,200
				+ 800

Cost method A method of recording the purchase of treasury stock at its cost of acquisition.

This entry increases Cash for the $4,000 received from investors. It then decreases Treasury Stock for the cost of the shares that are reissued. The stock was originally repurchased for $32 per share, so Treasury Stock is decreased by $3,200 (100 shares × $32 cost per share). The difference between the cash received and the cost of the treasury stock represents additional contributed capital beyond the cost of the stock. Therefore, Additional Paid-In Capital is increased for the $800 difference. Note that although it appears that Bahakel has generated a gain on the sale of treasury stock, accounting rules prohibit the recording of a gain or loss on treasury stock transactions. As a result of this entry, both assets and equity increase.

Reporting Treasury Stock

A company's balance in treasury stock is reported in the stockholders' equity section of the balance sheet. The following shows Walgreen's treasury stock balances from its 2008 balance sheet.

Walgreens' 2008 Treasury Stock		
	2008	**2007**
Treasury stock at cost, 36,223, 782 shares in 2008 and 34,258,643 shares in 2007	(1,551)	(1,506)

Walgreens reports a little over $1.5 billion in treasury stock in both years. Because treasury stock is a contra-equity account, its balance is reported as a negative number. The textual description contains the words "at cost," which indicates that Walgreens uses the cost method to account for its treasury stock. It also discloses that at the end of 2008, Walgreens owned more than 36 million shares of treasury stock. This means that Walgreens has paid about $42.82 on average per share of treasury stock ($1,551,000,000 balance ÷ 36,223,782 shares).

HOME DEPOT ANALYSIS

ook at Home Depot's Balance Sheet in Appendix C. How many shares of treasury stock does Home Depot have at the end of 2008? Does Home Depot use the cost or par value method? What is the average cost of each share of treasury stock?

Home Depot shows 11 million shares of treasury stock at the end of 2008. Home Depot reports its treasury shares "at cost." Thus, Home Depot uses the cost method and spent $372 million to acquire the 11 million shares. The average cost per share of treasury stock is therefore $33.82 ($372 ÷ 11).

Because a company's equity represents the owners' claim on corporate assets, stockholders are particularly interested in a company's ability to manage its equity.

LO₆ Evaluating a Company's Management of Equity

Because a company's equity represents the owners' claim on corporate assets, stockholders are particularly interested in a company's ability to manage its equity. Some of the issues that are important to most stockholders are as follows:

1. How does the company generate equity for stockholders?

2. How does the company reward its stockholders through dividends?

3. How does the company's equity affect its cash flows?

The following sections examine these three issues for Walgreens. The examination will require information from the company's balance sheet, income statement, statement of stockholders' equity, and statement of cash flows. The required information is found in Exhibit 10-2, excerpted from Walgreens' 2008 Annual Report. All amounts are in millions except the per share data.

Exhibit 10-2 Account Balances from Walgreens' 2008 Annual Report

Source	Accounts	2008	2007
Balance Sheet	Total assets	$ 22,410	$ 19,314
	Total equity	12,869	11,104
Income Statement	Net income	$ 2,157	$ 2,041
	Earnings per share	2.18	2.03
Statement of Stockholders' Equity	Cash dividends declared	$ 394	$ 326
	Dividends per share	0.3975	0.3275
	Common shares outstanding	989	991

Horizontal and Vertical Analyses

A good place to start the analysis of accounts receivable is horizontal and vertical analyses. Recall from Chapter 2 that horizontal analysis calculates the dollar change in an account balance, defined as the current-year balance less the prior-year balance, and divides that change by the prior-year balance to yield the percentage change. Vertical analysis divides each account balance by a base account, yielding a percentage. The base account is total assets for balance sheet accounts and net sales or total revenues for income statement accounts. These calculations are summarized as follows:

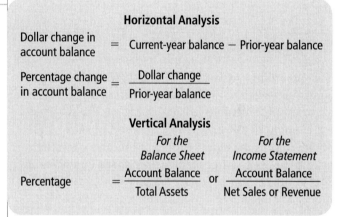

Horizontal Analysis

$$\text{Dollar change in account balance} = \text{Current-year balance} - \text{Prior-year balance}$$

$$\text{Percentage change in account balance} = \frac{\text{Dollar change}}{\text{Prior-year balance}}$$

Vertical Analysis

$$\text{Percentage} = \frac{\text{Account Balance}}{\text{Total Assets}} \text{ (For the Balance Sheet)} \text{ or } \frac{\text{Account Balance}}{\text{Net Sales or Revenue}} \text{ (For the Income Statement)}$$

Given Walgreens' financial data in Exhibit 10-2, horizontal and vertical analyses result in the following.

Horizontal Analysis

	Change	Percentage Change
Stockholders' equity	$\dfrac{\begin{array}{r}12,869 \\ -11,104\end{array}}{1,765}$	$\dfrac{1,765}{11,104} = 15.9\%$

Vertical Analysis

	2008	2007
Stockholders' equity	$\dfrac{12,869}{22,410} = 57.4\%$	$\dfrac{11,104}{19,314} = 57.5\%$

The horizontal analysis reveals that total equity increased by $1,765 million during 2008, which is an increase of 15.9% from the prior year. The vertical analysis shows that total equity as a percentage of total assets was stable at a little over 57% in each year. So, while total equity increased, it stayed the same when compared to assets. Although not reported in this chapter, a closer look at specific equity accounts reveals that the majority of

Walgreens' increase in equity was due to an increase in retained earnings. This shows that Walgreens increased its equity through profitable operations.

For comparison purposes, the 2008 horizontal and vertical analyses of CVS are listed below. Walgreens experienced greater growth in equity during the year, but both companies maintain close to the same percentage of equity to total assets.

Total Equity	Horizontal Analysis	Vertical Analysis
Walgreens	15.9%	57.4%
CVS	10.4%	56.7%

Earnings per Share

The preceding analysis shows that Walgreens' total equity grew due to profitable operations. This is what all stockholders want—greater claims on assets resulting from profitable operations. Another measure of the ability to generate equity through profitable operations is earnings per share. **Earnings per share** compares a company's net income to the number of shares of common stock outstanding. It is calculated as follows:

$$\text{Earnings per Share} = \frac{\text{Net Income}}{\text{Average Number of Common Shares Outstanding}}$$

where average common shares outstanding is:

$$\frac{\text{Beginning shares outstanding} + \text{Ending shares outstanding}}{2}$$

Earnings per share is a useful ratio because it "standardizes" earnings by a company's size. The ratio can therefore be used to compare the profitability of companies of vastly different sizes.

Earnings per share A comparison of a company's net income to the number of shares of common stock outstanding that measures the ability to generate equity through profitable operations.

Return on equity A comparison of a company's net income to total stockholders' equity that measures the ability to use existing equity to generate additional equity.

Walgreens' earnings per share is calculated as follows using the information in Exhibit 10-2.

$$\frac{2{,}157}{(989 + 991) \div 2} = 2.18$$

The 2.18 ratio reveals that Walgreens earned $2.18 in profit for every share of common stock outstanding during the year. This is an improvement over the last two years, when the company earned only $2.03 and $1.73 of earnings per share. However, it is slightly less than the $2.23 earnings per share of its competitor, CVS.

Accounting standards require that companies disclose their annual earnings per share in their financial statements. Like most companies, Walgreens reports its ratio at the bottom of its income statement.

Return on Equity

Another measure of a company's ability to generate equity is return on equity. **Return on equity** compares a company's net income to its total stockholders' equity and provides an indication of how well a company uses its existing equity to generate additional equity. Stockholders naturally want this ratio to be as high as possible. It is calculated as follows:

$$\text{Return on Equity} = \frac{\text{Net Income}}{\text{Average Stockholders' Equity}}$$

where average stockholders' equity is:

$$\frac{\text{Beginning equity} + \text{Ending equity}}{2}$$

Walgreens' return on equity is calculated as follows from the information in Exhibit 10-2:

$$\frac{2{,}157}{(12{,}869 + 11{,}104) \div 2} = 18.0\%$$

The 18.0% ratio indicates that for every dollar of equity held during 2008, Walgreens generated almost 18 cents of additional equity through profitable operations. This compares favorably to CVS's return on equity of 9.7% over the same period. Walgreens was successful in effectively using its existing equity to generate more equity for stockholders.

Dividend Payout Ratio

In addition to examining how well a company generates additional equity, stockholders often examine how a company pays out that equity through dividends. One ratio to do this is the dividend payout ratio.

The **dividend payout ratio** compares a company's dividends to its earnings. The ratio demonstrates the percentage of earnings a company has decided to distribute to owners through cash dividends. The ratio can be calculated in one of two ways, depending on how a company reports its dividend information. If a company reports only the dollar amount of annual dividends, the ratio is calculated by dividing total dividends by net income. If a company reports a dividend per share number, the ratio is calculated by dividing dividends per share by earnings per share. Either way, the result will be the same (except for small differences due to the rounding of per share values). Both calculations are as follows.

$$\text{Dividend Payout Ratio} = \frac{\text{Dividends}}{\text{Net Income}} \quad \text{or} \quad \frac{\text{Dividends per Share}}{\text{Earnings per Share}}$$

Walgreens reports both total and per share earnings on its income statement and total and per share dividends on its statement of stockholders' equity. These amounts are included in Exhibit 10-2 and are used to calculate Walgreens' dividend payout ratio as follows:

Calculation based on totals:

$$\frac{394}{2,157} = 18.3\%$$

Calculation based on per share amounts:

$$\frac{0.3975}{2.18} = 18.2\%$$

A ratio of 18.3% indicates that for every dollar of earnings during 2008, Walgreens declared about 18 cents in cash dividends. This is greater than CVS' ratio of 11.6%. However, an 18.3% ratio is not necessarily better than an 11.6% ratio. The ratios simply reflect each company's dividend policy. For 2008, Walgreens paid out more of

its earnings than did CVS. Thus, stockholders who want to receive more of the profits in dividends would prefer Walgreens. However, stockholders who want the company to plow more earnings back into operations instead of paying more dividends would prefer CVS.

Dividend Yield

In addition to knowing what percentage of earnings is paid in dividends, stockholders want to know how much their investment in a company's stock returns to them. Stockholders generate a return on their investment in two ways—an increase in the stock price and a receipt of dividends. The return from receiving dividends can be calculated with the dividend yield ratio. The **dividend yield ratio** divides dividends per share by the market price per share of stock as follows:

$$\text{Dividend Yield} = \frac{\text{Dividends per share}}{\text{Market Price per share}}$$

According to Exhibit 10-2, Walgreens reports dividends per share of $0.3975 on its 2008 statement of stockholders' equity. Market price information can be found on most any financial website. We will use the stock price of $45.07, which is the closing price on the last day of the preceding fiscal year (August 31, 2007). As a result, the dividend yield reveals the return to a stockholder who bought the stock at the beginning of the fiscal year ending August 31, 2008.

$$\frac{0.3975}{45.07} = 0.9\%$$

The 0.9% ratio indicates that an investment in Walgreens stock on August 31, 2007, would yield a return from dividends equal to about one cent for each dollar invested. This compares to a dividend yield for CVS of 0.6%. Thus, the yield for Walgreens is higher.

> **Dividend payout ratio** A comparison of a company's dividends to its earnings that measures the percentage of current earnings distributed to owners.
>
> **Dividend yield ratio** A comparison of dividends per share to the market price per share of stock that measures the percentage return from dividends.

HOME DEPOT ANALYSIS

Using Home Depot's information in Appendix C, calculate and interpret (1) horizontal and vertical analyses of total equity, (2) earnings per share, (3) return on equity, (4) dividend payout ratio, and (5) dividend yield, assuming a market price of $45.

(1) Horizontal Analysis

$$($17,777 - $17,714)/$17,714 = 0.4\%$$

Vertical Analysis

$$$17,777/$41,164 = 43.2\%$$

The 0.4% horizontal analysis reflects virtually no change in Home Depot's total equity. The 43.1% vertical analysis shows that a little less than half of the company's assets are generated through equity.

(2) Earnings per Share

$$$2,260/(1,696 + 1,690)/2 = $1.34$$

The $1.34 earnings per share indicates that Home Depot earned over one dollar in income for each share of stock outstanding. This ratio is lower than each of the previous two years, which reveals that the company has been less profitable this year, given its size.

(3) Return on Equity

$$$2,260/($17,777 + $17,714)/2 = 12.7\%$$

The 12.7% return on equity ratio indicates that Home Depot earned almost 13 cents in income for every $1 of equity. Such a return gives the company many options. One option is to pay dividends to the owners, while another is to retain the profits and grow the company. Home Depot pays dividends, so it is doing both—rewarding its stockholders through dividends and growing the company.

(4) Dividend Payout Ratio

$$$1,521/$2,260 = 67.3\% \quad \text{or} \quad $0.90/$1.34 = 67.3\%$$

The 67.3% dividend payout ratio indicates that Home Depot paid to owners approximately 67 cents for every dollar it earned during the year. In the two preceding years, the company's ratio was 38.9% and 24.2%. The predominant reason for the increase is that Home Depot's income decreased during that time, thereby increasing the payout ratio.

(5) Dividend Yield

$$$0.90/$45 = 2.0\%$$

The 2.0% dividend yield indicates that Home Depot's dividend yield was two percent of the stock's value.

Stockholders' Equity and Cash Flows

When examining a company's equity, it is always important to analyze how equity has been used to generate or use cash. Equity can significantly affect a company's cash through the issuance of stock, the purchase of treasury stock, and the payment of cash dividends. Each of these activities is reported in the financing activities section of the statement of cash flows. The following is the financing activities of Walgreens' 2008 statement of cash flows.

Walgreens' activity affected cash flows in all three years presented. Over the three years, Walgreens has paid $2,567 million in cash to repurchase its stock ($294 + $1,604 + $669). It has also paid out $949 million in cash dividends ($376 + $310 + $263). This totals over $3 billion that has been paid out to stockholders over three years. This is a significant amount of cash.

Financing Activities Section of Walgreens' 2008 Statement of Cash Flows

	2008	2007	2006
Cash Flows from Financing Activities			
Net (payment) proceeds from short-term borrowings	(802)	850	—
Net proceeds from issuance of long-term debt	1,286	—	—
Payments of long-term debt	(28)	(141)	—
Stock purchases	(294)	(1,064)	(669)
Proceeds related to employee stock plans	210	266	319
Cash dividends paid	(376)	(310)	(263)
Bank overdrafts	—	(214)	214
Other	(29)	(13)	(14)
Net cash used for financing activities	$ (33)	$ (626)	$(413)

In addition to examining the statement of cash flows, it can be beneficial to examine the notes to the financial statements to find additional information with cash flow consequences. In Walgreens' stockholders' equity note, it discloses the following information:

The note discloses details of Walgreens' stock repurchase program. The note states that the 2004 repurchase program has been fully executed but that the company has some capacity remaining in its 2007 repurchase program. Therefore, Walgreens may very well continue its payments of cash to stockholders in the next few years.

Excerpts from Walgreens' 2008 Stockholders' Equity Note

On January 10, 2007, the Board of Directors approved a new stock repurchase program ("2007 repurchase program"), pursuant to which up to $1,000 million of the company's common stock may be purchased prior to the expiration date of the program on January 10, 2011. This program was announced in the company's report on Form 8-K, which was filed on January 11, 2007. During fiscal 2008, the company purchased no shares related to the 2007 repurchase program, compared to $345 million of shares purchased in 2007.

On July 14, 2004, the Board of Directors announced a stock repurchase program ("2004 repurchase program") of up to $1,000 million, which has been completely executed. The company purchased $343 million of shares related to the 2004 repurchase program in fiscal 2007. An additional $294 million of shares were purchased to support the long-term needs of the employee stock plans, which compares to $375 million in fiscal 2007.

HOME DEPOT ANALYSIS

Look at Home Depot's Statement of Cash Flows in Appendix C. How much cash has the company paid in dividends and for the repurchase of stock over the past three years?

According to the financing activities section of its statement of cash flows, Home Depot has paid $17,569 million over the past three years to repurchase stock and $4,625 million in dividends, for a total cash outflow of $22,194 million.

STUDY TOOLS
CHAPTER 10

CHAPTER REVIEW CARD
- ❑ Learning Objective and Key Concept Reviews
- ❑ Key Definitions and Formulas

ONLINE (Located at 4ltrpress.cengage.com/acct)
- ❑ Flash Cards and Crossword Puzzles
- ❑ Conceptual and Computational Interactive Quizzes
- ❑ E-Lectures
- ❑ Static, Algorithmic, and Additional Homework Activities (as directed by your instructor)

EXERCISES

1. Corporate Form of Business   LO1

How does each of the following characteristics relate to the corporate form of business?
a. Separate legal entity
b. Liability of owners
c. Ability to raise capital
d. Transferability of ownership
e. Taxation
f. Regulation

2. Recording Common Stock   LO2

Cox Corporation issued 40,000 shares of $5 par common stock for $10 per share on March 1 and 75,000 shares for $6 per share on July 1.

Required
Prepare the journal entries to record the stock issuances.

3. Recording Stock Transactions   LO2, 4, 5

Irons Incorporated entered into the following stock transactions.

Apr. 5	Issued 30,000 shares of $3 par value common stock for $180,000.
May 31	Purchased 1,000 shares of treasury stock for $50,000.
Oct. 1	Issued 3,000 shares of $40 par value preferred stock for $65 per share.

Required
Prepare the journal entries to record the transactions. Use the cost method to account for the purchase of treasury stock.

4. Stock Terminology   LO2, 5

The stockholders' equity section of Lester Company's balance sheet follows:

Stockholders' equity	
Common stock, 500,000 shares authorized,	
450,000 shares issued	$ 450,000
Additional paid-in capital	4,050,000
Retained earnings	1,425,000
Treasury stock, at cost, 16,000 shares	(480,000)
Total stockholders' equity	$5,445,000

Required
a. How many shares of common stock are authorized, issued, and outstanding?
b. What is the par value of the common stock?
c. How much in total capital has Lester received from the issuance of stock?
d. What is the average cost of a share of treasury stock?

5. Cash Dividends   LO3

On December 15, Taylor Corporation declared a cash dividend of $0.77 per share to be paid on January 15 to stockholders of record on December 31. Taylor has 154 million shares of common stock outstanding.

Required
Identify the date of declaration, the date of record, and the payment date, and prepare all necessary journal entries on those dates.

6. Cash Dividends   LO3, 4

Cope Company declares a $90,000 dividend. Cope's common stock has a $5 par value and 80,000 shares outstanding. Cope's preferred stock is 5%, $12 par, and there are 20,000 shares outstanding. Cope has not paid dividends in the past three years. Cope's preferred stock is cumulative.

Required
a. Determine how the $90,000 in dividends should be allocated to preferred and common stockholders.
b. Prepare the journal entry that would be recorded on the date of declaration.
c. Determine how the $90,000 in dividends should be allocated to preferred and common stockholders, assuming that the preferred stock is noncumulative.

7. Stock Dividends   LO3

Hudson High Rises declared a 10% stock dividend on July 1 to be distributed on August 1 to stockholders of record on July 15. On July 1, Hudson has 1,000,000 authorized shares and 250,000 outstanding shares. Hudson's $2 par stock is trading at $15 per share on July 1.

Required
a. Prepare all necessary journal entries to record the stock dividend.
b. Prepare all necessary journal entries to record the stock dividend, assuming the percentage was 30% instead of 10%.

8. Treasury Stock   LO5

On January 15, Capital Corporation purchased 2,000 shares of its own common stock when the stock was trading at $45. On June 15, Capital Corporation reissued 500 of these same shares for $50 per share.

Required
Prepare the journal entries to record the purchase and reissuance of the treasury stock. Use the cost method.

9. Stock Dividends versus Stock Splits   LO3

Morgan Incorporated is looking to increase its number of shares outstanding of common stock to bring down its stock price. The board of directors is trying to decide if a 2-for-1 stock split or a 100% stock dividend is more appropriate. Morgan's stockholders' equity follows:

Common stock, $2 par, 100,000 shares	
issued and outstanding	$ 200,000
Additional paid-in capital	660,000
Retained earnings	775,000
Total stockholders' equity	$1,635,000

Required
a. Assess the pros and cons of the stock split versus the stock dividend.
b. Create a new stockholders' equity section if Morgan chooses (1) a stock dividend or (2) a stock split.

10. Evaluate Equity LO6

The following is selected financial information for Lee Incorporated:

(in millions)	2010	2009
Average common stockholders' equity	$3,430.5	$2,921.6
Dividends declared on common stock	125.5	104.3
Net income	775.9	691.4

Required
a. Calculate the return on equity for Lee Incorporated for 2010 and 2009.
b. Calculate the dividend payout ratio for 2010 and 2009.
c. Compare the financial performance for the two years and comment on which year was more successful, based on these measures, and possible reasons why.

11. Evaluate Equity LO6

Laura's Boutique is trying to calculate different financial measures to analyze its performance. The net income for the year was $80 million. There are 150 million shares issued and 125 million shares outstanding.

Required
a. Calculate earnings per share for the year.
b. Interpret the results of this calculation. What could the company possibly do to improve this financial measure?

12. Evaluate Equity LO6

The following is from the financial statements of Boutwell Boomerangs from the last two years:

	2010	2009
Total assets	$1,685	$1,730
Total liabilities	900	875
Total stockholders' equity	785	855

Required
Conduct a horizontal and vertical analysis for both years.

13. Evaluate Equity LO6

Kristi's Kites provided the following information from its financial statements:

Net income	$164,500
Average number of common shares outstanding	235,000
Average stockholders' equity	$576,000

Required
Calculate the earnings per share and return on equity for Kristi's Kites. How are the two profitability ratios different?

14. Evaluate Equity LO6

Kay Company's stock on the last day of the year was $39. Kay reported dividends per share of $0.49 and total dividends of $637,000 on its statement of stockholders' equity. Net income for the year was $4,000,000. The average number of common shares outstanding is 1,300,000.

Required
a. Calculate the dividend payout ratio and the dividend yield for Kay Company.
b. Where do you find dividends paid in the statement of cash flows?

PROBLEMS

15. Recording and Reporting Equity LO2, 3, 5, 6

Camp Corporation had the following balances in its stockholders' equity at January 1:

Common stock, $2 par value, 450,000 shares	
issued	$ 900,000
Additional paid-in capital	1,200,000
Retained earnings	2,225,000
Treasury stock, at cost, 8,000 shares	48,000

During the year, Camp Corporation had the following transactions related to stockholders' equity:

Mar. 1	Issued 200,000 shares of common stock for cash at $8 per share.
July 1	Declared a 10% stock dividend, payable August 1. The stock was trading at $7 per share on July 1.
Aug. 15	Declared a $0.50 per share cash dividend to stockholders of record on September 1, payable September 15.
Oct. 1	Bought back 6,000 shares of common stock for $45,000.
Dec. 31	Calculated net income for the year to be $520,000.

Required
a. Prepare the journal entries to record the transactions.
b. Prepare Camp's December 31 stockholders' equity section.
c. Calculate earnings per share for the year.

16. Evaluating Equity LO6

The following are financial measures from the financial statements of Brown Buildings for the past two years:

	2010	2009
Total assets	$4,255,350	$3,895,700
Total liabilities	2,050,150	1,980,300
Total stockholders' equity	2,205,200	1,915,400

Required

a. Conduct a horizontal analysis of Brown Buildings. Comment on your findings and possible reasons for these findings.
b. Conduct a vertical analysis for both years for Brown Buildings. Compare and briefly interpret the results of the two years.

17. Evaluating Equity LO6

Olson Outlet Malls is trying to determine if its equity is comparable to other malls in the area.

	2010	2009
Total assets	$1,374,000	$1,506,000
Total liabilities	$588,000	$732,000
Total stockholders' equity	$786,000	$774,000
Net income	$198,500	
Average number of common shares outstanding	266,000	
Average stockholders' equity	$780,000	
Market price of stock	$21	
Total dividends	$59,000	
Dividends per share	$0.223	

Required

a. Conduct horizontal and vertical analyses for Olson.
b. Calculate the earnings per share and return on equity.
c. Calculate the dividend payout ratio and the dividend yield.

CASE

18. Research and Analysis LO2, 3, 5, 6

Access the 2008 annual report for Tootsie Roll Industries by clicking on the *Company Information* and *Financial Information* links at www.tootsie.com.

Required

1. Examine the company's balance sheet and conduct horizontal and vertical analyses of the company's total shareholders' equity.
2. Calculate the company's 2008 return on equity ratio. Using the dividend and price data found on page 28 of the annual report, calculate the company's 2008 dividend yield from cash dividends assuming that an investor purchased the stock at the low price during the first quarter of 2008.
3. Examine the company's statement of retained earnings and determine the value of stock dividends declared during 2008.
4. Examine the financing activities section of the company's statement of cash flows. How would you characterize the company's activity over the past three years?
5. Based on your answers above, write a paragraph explaining your opinion of Tootsie Roll's 2008 equity position. Use your answers as supporting facts.

REMEMBER

- All exercises and problems from the text are available online in static and algorithmic versions.
- Additional multiple choice, exercises, problems, and cases are available online in CengageNOW or as an enrichment module that can be customized into this text.

MAKING IT REAL!

ACCT will prepare you for the real world by showing you how accounting information is used to make business decisions.

Throughout the text, take a look at the Making It Real features that highlight everyday businesses.

GO ONLINE!
Visit 4ltrpress.cengage.com/acct to:

- Study an **online continuing case about a realistic coffee shop**.
- View 14 videos from the **Experience Accounting Video** series!

The brief Experience Accounting Videos demonstrate how today's companies fuel better business performance. Several of the companies featured include:

BP: Process Costing
Washburn Guitars: Job-Order Costing
Hard Rock Café: Capital Investments
Cold Stone Creamery: Activity-Based Costing
High Sierra: Budgets & Profit Planning
Boyne Resorts: Cost-Volume-Profit Analysis
Navistar: Relevant Costs
Zingerman's Deli: Cost Behavior

COLD STONE CREAMERY   HIGH SIERRA   Washburn GUITARS

ACCT

Statement of
Cash Flows

Introduction

As discussed in Chapter 1, the statement of cash flows provides information on how a company generates and distributes cash over a period of time. This chapter examines the purpose and format of the statement of cash flows and also demonstrates how the statement is prepared. The chapter concludes with an analysis of how to use the statement to generate useful information about a company and its cash.

LO1 The Statement of Cash Flows

One of the most important resources of any company is cash. If a company cannot generate sufficient cash, its ability to continue operations is significantly limited. As a result, management, investors, and creditors want to know how a company is managing its cash. How did the company use its cash? How did it generate cash? What are the prospects of the company paying a cash dividend? Will the company be able to satisfy its upcoming interest and loan obligations? Does the company have enough cash to expand its manufacturing facilities? Answers to these and other questions can be found through an examination of the statement of cash flows.

The **statement of cash flows** is a financial statement that summarizes a company's inflows and outflows of cash over a period of time. Its purpose is to inform users on how and why a company's cash changed during the period. So that it is as informative as possible, the statement groups and reports cash flows in three major categories: operating, investing, and financing. Cash flows from each of the three categories are then combined to determine the company's net change in cash and cash equivalents. This net change will be equal to the difference between the beginning and ending cash and cash equivalents balances from the balance sheet. Note that from this point forward, the term *cash* will be used to represent cash and cash equivalents.

Statement of cash flows A financial statement that summarizes a company's inflows and outflows of cash over a period of time with a purpose to inform users on how and why a company's cash changed during the period.

Learning Objectives

After studying the material in this chapter, you should be able to:

LO1 Describe the purpose and format of the statement of cash flows.

LO2 Describe the process of preparing the statement of cash flows.

LO3 Prepare the operating activities section of the statement of cash flows using the direct method.

LO4 Prepare the operating activities section of the statement of cash flows using the indirect method.

LO5 Prepare the investing activities section of the statement of cash flows.

LO6 Prepare the financing activities section of the statement of cash flows.

LO7 Evaluate the statement of cash flows through the calculation and interpretation of ratio analyses.

One of the keys to success for a company like Under Armour is to convert its merchandise into cash.

© TERRI MILLER/E-VISUAL COMMUNICATIONS, INC.

The basic structure of the statement is as follows:

Cash Flows Provided (Used) by Operating Activities
+/− Cash Flows Provided (Used) by Investing Activities
+/− Cash Flows Provided (Used) by Financing Activities
Net Increase (Decrease) in Cash
+ Cash, Beginning of Year
Cash, End of Year

The following sections discuss the three groupings of cash flows. For illustration purposes, Exhibit 11-1 contains Under Armour, Inc.'s statement of cash flows for the year ending December 31, 2008. All dollar amounts are in thousands.

Exhibit 11-1 Under Armour, Inc.'s 2008 Statement of Cash Flows

**Under Armour, Inc. and Subsidiaries
Consolidated Statements of Cash Flows
(In thousands)**

	Year Ended December 31,		
	2008	**2007**	**2006**
Cash flows from operating activities			
Net income	$ 38,229	$ 52,558	$ 38,979
Adjustments to reconcile net income to net cash provided by (used in) operating activities			
Depreciation and amortization	21,347	14,622	9,824
Unrealized foreign currency exchange rate (gains) losses	5,459	(2,567)	161
Loss on disposal of property and equipment	15	—	115
Stock-based compensation	8,466	4,182	1,982
Deferred income taxes	(2,818)	(4,909)	(6,721)
Changes in reserves for doubtful accounts, returns, discounts and inventories	8,711	4,551	3,832
Changes in operating assets and liabilities:			
Accounts receivable	2,634	(24,222)	(20,828)
Inventories	(19,497)	(83,966)	(26,504)
Prepaid expenses and other assets	(7,187)	(2,067)	(3,997)
Accounts payable	16,957	11,873	8,203
Accrued expenses and other liabilities	(5,316)	11,825	10,681
Income taxes payable and receivable	2,516	3,492	(5,026)
Net cash provided by (used in) operating activities	$ 69,516	$(14,628)	$ 10,701
Cash flows from investing activities			
Purchase of property and equipment	$ (38,594)	$(33,959)	$(15,115)
Purchase of intangible assets	(600)	(125)	—
Purchase of trust-owned life insurance policies	(2,893)	—	—
Proceeds from sales of property and equipment	21	—	—
Purchases of short-term investments	—	(62,860)	(89,650)
Proceeds from sales of short-term investments	—	62,860	89,650
Net cash used in investing activities	$ (42,066)	$(34,084)	$(15,115)
Cash flows from financing activities			
Proceeds from revolving credit facility	$ 40,000	$ 14,000	—
Payments on revolving credit facility	(15,000)	(14,000)	—
Proceeds from long-term debt	13,214	11,841	$ 2,119
Payments on long-term debt	(6,490)	(2,973)	(2,413)
Payments on capital lease obligations	(464)	(794)	(1,840)
Excess tax benefits from stock-based compensation arrangements	2,131	6,892	11,260
Proceeds from exercise of stock options and other stock issuances	1,990	3,182	3,544
Payments of debt financing costs	—	—	(260)
Payments received on notes from stockholders	—	—	169
Net cash provided by financing activities	$ 35,381	$ 18,148	$ 12,579
Effect of exchange rate changes on cash and cash equivalents	(1,377)	497	(487)
Net increase (decrease) in cash and cash equivalents	$ 61,454	$(30,067)	$ 7,678
Cash and cash equivalents			
Beginning of year	40,588	70,655	62,977
End of year	$102,042	$ 40,588	$ 70,655

One of the most important resources of any company is cash. If a company cannot generate sufficient cash, its ability to continue operations is significantly limited.

Cash Flows from Operating Activities

Cash flows provided (used) by operating activities are those cash inflows and outflows arising from the company's operations. These inflows and outflows are sometimes called operating cash flows and would include the following:

- Cash inflows from sales or services

- Cash outflows for operating items such as inventory purchases, salaries, insurance, and supplies

Basically, any cash flow associated with a company's revenues or expenses should be considered an operating cash flow. Because of this, the net cash flow from operating activities can be thought of as net income on a cash basis.

Operating cash flows are reported first on the statement of cash flows. Like most companies, Under Armour reports operating cash flows using the indirect method. The indirect method calculates operating cash flows by adjusting net income from an accrual basis to a cash basis. This calculation will be demonstrated in a later section. For now, you should simply note that many of the adjustments in Exhibit 11-1 involve accounts associated with operations—depreciation expense, accounts receivable, inventory, accounts payable, and income taxes. Under Armour generated over $69 million of cash from operations in 2008.

Cash Flows from Investing Activities

Cash flows provided (used) by investing activities are those cash inflows and outflows arising from the acquisition and disposal of non-current assets. They are often called investing cash flows and would include the following:

- Cash inflows from the sale of property, facilities, equipment, or investments

- Cash outflows for the purchase of property, facilities, equipment, or investments

Investing cash flows are reported after operating activities. Exhibit 11-1 reveals that Under Armour experienced net cash outflows of over $42 million in 2008. The main contributor to that total was over $38 million for the purchase of property and equipment. In fact, in each of the years presented, the bulk of Under Armour's net investing cash outflows resulted from these purchases. This makes sense for a company that is growing.

Cash Flows from Financing Activities

Cash flows provided (used) by financing activities are those cash inflows and outflows associated with the generation and return of capital. These are often called financing cash flows and would include the following:

- Cash inflows from borrowings or stock issuances

- Cash outflows to satisfy debt obligations or to repurchase treasury stock

- Cash outflows for dividends to stockholders

Basically, any cash flows associated with debt or equity (other than interest payments) are considered to be financing cash flows.

Financing cash flows are reported after investing cash flows. Exhibit 11-1 reveals that Under Armour generated over $35 million in cash in 2008 from financing activities. The majority of that net inflow came from a revolving credit facility and some long term debt. According to the statement, Under Armour borrowed $40 million and repaid $15 million of the credit facility during the year. It also borrowed over $13 million and repaid over $6 million of debt during the year. As a result, the company added to its cash balance by adding to its liabilities.

> **Cash flows provided (used) by operating activities** Cash inflows and outflows arising from the company's operations; sometimes called operating cash flows.
>
> **Cash flows provided (used) by investing activities** Cash inflows and outflows arising from the acquisition and disposal of non-current assets; often called investing cash flows.
>
> **Cash flows provided (used) by financing activities** Cash inflows and outflows associated with the generation and return of capital; often called financing cash flows.

Net Increase (Decrease) in Cash

After a company reports its operating, investing, and financing cash flows, it sums the three and reconciles the company's beginning and ending cash balances. The following is a condensed version of Under Armour's statement of cash flows, showing only the major subtotals:

Under Armour's 2008 Condensed Statement of Cash Flows

	2008	2007	2006
Net cash provided by (used in) operating activities	$ 69,516	$(14,628)	$ 10,701
Net cash used in investing activities	(42,066)	(34,084)	(15,115)
Net cash provided by financing activities	35,381	18,148	12,579
Effect of exchange rate changes on cash and cash equivalents	(1,377)	497	(487)
Net increase (decrease) in cash and cash equivalents	61,454	(30,067)	7,678
Cash, beginning of year	40,588	70,655	62,977
Cash, end of year	$102,042	$ 40,588	$70,655

Under Armour's net increase in cash during 2008 was over $61 million. This increase consisted of the sum of operating, investing, and financing cash flows as well as an additional adjustment for exchange rate changes. While exchange rate adjustments are not covered in this chapter, they are often necessary for companies such as Under Armour that conduct business in various currencies. Adding the 2008 increase of over $61 million to the beginning balance of cash of over $40 million yields the 2008 year-end balance in cash of $102 million. Both the $40 million and $102 million can be found in the first row of Under Armour's 2008 balance sheet.

Additional Disclosures

All publicly traded companies prepare the statement of cash flows using a format similar to what has been described. In some cases, companies must also make one or both of the following two disclosures.

- Significant non-cash investing or financing activities

- Cash paid for interest and taxes

The first disclosure relates to significant investing or financing transactions in which no cash is exchanged. Examples would include the purchase of property through the issuance of mortgage debt, the conversion of long-term debt into common stock, or the payment of dividends by the issuance of stock. Even though such transactions do not involve cash, they are important for properly understanding a company's cash flows. Therefore, they must be disclosed either on the face of the statement or in the notes to the financial statements. Although they are not shown in Exhibit 11-1, Under Armour makes the following disclosures on its statement of cash flows.

Under Armour's 2008 Disclosures of Non-Cash Financing and Investing Activities

	2008	2007	2006
Fair market value of shares withheld in consideration of employee tax obligations relative to stock-based compensation	$ —	$ —	$ 734
Purchase of property and equipment through certain obligations	2,486	1,110	2,700
Issuance of warrants in partial consideration for intangible asset	—	—	8,500
Settlement of outstanding accounts receivable with property and equipment	—	—	350
Reversal of unearned compensation and additional paid in capital due to adoption of SFAS 123R	—	—	715

The only significant non-cash activity reported in 2008 is the purchase of property and equipment through certain obligations. While the schedule does not provide further explanation on the nature of the obligations, it does reveal that the company acquired over $2 million in fixed assets by creating future obligations rather than paying cash.

The second disclosure relates to interest and taxes. When a company uses the indirect method to report operating cash flows, the amount of interest and taxes paid are not shown on the statement. However, accounting standards require that companies disclose the amount of interest and taxes paid. Companies like Under Armour often disclose this information at the bottom of their statements of cash flows. Although they are not shown in Exhibit 11-1, the final two rows of Under Armour's statement are as follows.

Under Armour's 2008 Disclosure of Interest and Taxes Paid			
	2008	2007	2006
Cash paid for income taxes	$29,561	$30,502	$20,522
Cash paid for interest	1,444	525	531

LO2 Preparing the Statement of Cash Flows

Chapter 4 discussed the preparation of the income statement, the statement of retained earnings, and the balance sheet. Each of these statements is prepared with numbers from an adjusted trial balance. That is, they are prepared by rearranging numbers already provided by the accounting system.

MAKING IT REAL

Companies cannot function without adequate cash. Therefore, the statement of cash flows is of special interest to stakeholders such as investors and creditors who must determine if the company has the ability to continue operations. The statement of cash flows informs financial statement users on how cash was used and generated during a period.

Hertz Global Holdings Inc. was recently included in a list of 20 corporations with the highest probability of declaring bankruptcy within the next twelve months. As a result of this publication, Hertz is suing the publisher, Audit Integrity, a Los Angeles-based research and risk-modeling firm, for defamation resulting from "the publication of false and harmful information."

Hertz counters its inclusion on this list with several financial indicators. They cite successful stock and debt offerings, refinancing ahead of schedule, and most notably, improved cash flow. Using improved cash flow as an argument for financial health establishes the importance of the information contained in the statement of cash flows. Without the information provided by the statement of cash flows, Hertz would have a much harder time proving that it is a going concern and would have a much weaker position in its defamation lawsuit.

Josh Beckerman, "Somebody Told Me You Had A Term Loan," Wall Street Journal Blogs, accessed at http://blogs.wsj.com/privateequity/2009/10/01/somebody-told-me-you-had-a-term-loan/?blog_id=107&post_id=5524

HOME DEPOT ANALYSIS

Look at Home Depot's Statement of Cash Flows in Appendix C. In the most recent year, what were the company's net cash flows from operating, investing, and financing activities? Also, what amount of cash was paid for capital expenditures and dividends in the most recent year? Finally, how much did the company pay in income taxes in the most recent year?

In the most recent year, Home Depot generated net cash flows of $5,528 from operating activities and used net cash flows of $1,729 from investing activities and $3,680 from financing activities. During the most recent year, the company paid $1,847 for capital expenditures, $1,521 for dividends, and $1,265 for income taxes.

The preparation of the statement of cash flows is different. First, information is collected from a variety of sources. Second, preparing the statement requires an examination of the changes in all non-cash accounts. To understand why, consider the fundamental accounting equation:

$$Assets = Liabilities + Equity$$

Cash can be isolated by breaking it out from other assets to yield the following:

$$Cash + Non\text{-}Cash\ Assets = Liabilities + Equity$$

Moving non-cash assets from the left side of the equation to the right side then results in the following:

$$Cash = Liabilities + Equity - Non\text{-}Cash\ Assets$$

Using Δ to denote a change, this equation can also be rewritten to show that the change in cash for a given period is equal to the changes in all other non-cash accounts (liabilities, equity, and non-cash assets):

$$\Delta\ Cash = \Delta\ Liabilities + \Delta\ Equity - \Delta\ Non\text{-}cash\ Assets$$

As a result, to explain a company's change in cash, you must explain the changes in the company's non-cash accounts. And to do that, you need the following three items:

- A comparative balance sheet

- An income statement

- Additional information on changes in account balances

A comparative balance sheet provides the beginning and ending balances of all non-cash accounts, from which changes for the period are calculated. An income statement provides a company's revenue and

To explain a company's change in cash, you must explain the changes in the company's non-cash accounts.

expense balances for the period. These balances are used to prepare the operating activities section of the statement of cash flows. Additional information on changes in account balances is needed to determine if a balance changed because of non-cash activity. For example, the issuance of stock to satisfy a debt obligation changes both equity and liability balances, but cash is not affected. Knowledge of such significant non-cash transactions keeps one from erroneously concluding that the company received cash for the issuance of stock and paid cash for the retirement of the debt.

Direct and Indirect Methods for Operating Cash Flows

When preparing the statement of cash flows, all companies report cash flows from operating, investing and financing activities. The manner in which cash flows from investing and financing activities are reported is the same for all companies. However, companies can report their cash flows from operating activities using one of two methods:

- Direct Method

- Indirect Method

Under the **direct method**, a company calculates and reports its cash inflows from operations followed by its cash outflows for operations. Typically, cash outflows are broken out into a few categories including cash payments for inventory, operating expenses, interest, and taxes. The difference between inflows and outflows is the company's net cash flow from operating activities. The method is called "direct" because both inflows and outflows are shown directly on the statement.

Under the **indirect method**, a company reports its cash flows from operating activities by adjusting its net income from an accrual basis to a cash basis. The method is called "indirect" because it does not directly report cash inflows and cash outflows from operations. Rather, it reports the adjustments necessary to convert net income to the net cash flow from operating activities. Adjustments typically arise from non-cash

Direct method Method of reporting cash flows from operating activities in which cash inflows and outflows from operations are reported separately on the statement of cash flows.

Indirect method Method of reporting cash flows from operating activities in which net income is adjusted from an accrual basis to a cash basis.

revenues and expenses and/or changes in current assets and current liabilities.

Both the indirect and direct methods will yield the same net cash flows from operating activities. The only difference between the methods is the manner in which cash flows are reported. Because accounting standards require that companies using the direct method must also disclose their cash flows under

the indirect method, the vast majority of companies choose the indirect method.

Example Data

To demonstrate how to prepare a statement of cash flows, the information for Hardin Supply Company in Exhibit 11-2 will be used. Note that Hardin provides both an income statement and a comparative balance sheet and that all numbers are in thousands. For simplicity, references to thousands will be omitted in the discussions. Additional information will be provided as needed.

Exhibit 11-2 Hardin Supply Company Financial Statements

Hardin Supply Company
Income Statement
For the Year Ended December 31, 2009
(in thousands)

Sales		$432
Cost of goods sold		281
Gross profit		$151
Operating expenses:		
Depreciation expense	$25	
Insurance expense	14	
Salaries expense	63	
Utilities expense	28	130
Operating income		$ 21
Gain on sale of equipment		1
Income before taxes		$ 22
Income tax expense		8
Net income		$ 14

Hardin Supply Company
Comparative Balance Sheet
December 31, 2009

	2009	2008
Cash and cash equivalents	$ 18	$ 45
Accounts receivable	45	41
Inventory	101	92
Prepaid insurance	11	15
Total current assets	$175	$193
Investments	22	0
Property and equipment, at cost	232	166
Less: Accumulated depreciation	(57)	(37)
Total assets	$372	$322
Accounts payable	$ 37	$ 29
Salaries payable	21	21
Utilities payable	27	22
Taxes payable	0	7
Total current liabilities	$ 85	$ 79
Long-term debt	45	0
Total liabilities	$130	$ 79
Common stock	$165	$165
Treasury stock	(10)	0
Retained earnings	87	78
Total equity	$242	$243
Total liabilities and equity	$372	$322

LO3 Reporting Cash Flows from Operating Activities— Direct Method

This section demonstrates the calculation of cash flows from operating activities under the direct method.

When reporting operating cash flows under the direct method, companies calculate and report cash receipts from operating activities and cash payments for operating activities. Cash receipts are calculated by converting revenues from the income statement to cash collections. Cash payments are calculated by converting expenses from the income statement to cash payments.

The following sections demonstrate this conversion process. The first section considers cash receipts from customers. The next sections consider cash payments in three main groups: cash paid for inventory, for operating expenses, and for income taxes. For each calculation, two approaches are demonstrated—one focusing on the changes in account balances and another using a debit/credit approach.

Cash Received from Customers

Hardin's income statement shows that the company generated $432 in sales during the year. To determine cash receipts from those sales, the balance sheet account related to sales—accounts receivable—must be examined.

Hardin's balance sheet shows that accounts receivable increased $4 during the year. The accounts receivable account increases when sales are made but no cash is collected. Therefore, a $4 increase means that $4 of Hardin's $432 of sales were not collected during the year. Therefore, cash collections were $428.

Sales for the period	$432
Less: Increase in accounts receivable	4
Cash collected from sales	$428

Note that had Hardin's accounts receivable decreased during the year, the decrease would have been added to sales.

The conversion of sales to cash collections can be summarized as follows:

Balance from Income Statement	Adjustment	Balance for Statement of Cash Flows
Sales	− Increase in accounts receivable or + Decrease in accounts receivable	= Cash collected from sales

A second approach for calculating cash receipts from sales is to prepare the journal entry that Hardin would hypothetically make if it recorded its annual sales and the change in receivables in only one entry.

Given sales of $432, Hardin would credit Sales for $432. Hardin would also debit Accounts Receivable for $4 to reflect the increase in the account. To balance the entry, Hardin would debit Cash for $428. Thus, cash collections from sales are $428.

Hypothetical Entry	Accounts Receivable	4	
	Cash	428	
	Sales		432

Cash Paid for Inventory

Hardin's income statement shows that the company had $281 of cost of goods sold during the year. To convert this expense to cash paid for inventory, Hardin must first calculate total purchases for the period and then calculate the cash paid for those purchases.

To calculate purchases, Hardin must examine the inventory account. Inventory increased by $9 during the year. An increase in inventory means that Hardin bought more inventory than it sold. Therefore, Hardin must have purchased $290 of inventory during the year.

Inventory sold during the period	$281
Plus: Increase in inventory	9
Inventory purchased during the period	$290

Note that had Hardin's inventory decreased during the year, the decrease would have been subtracted from inventory to calculate purchases.

To calculate cash paid for these purchases, Hardin must examine accounts payable. Accounts payable increased $8 during the year. The accounts payable account increases when purchases are made but no cash is paid. Therefore, Hardin must have paid for only $282 of its $290 in purchases.

Inventory purchased during the period	$290
Less: Increase in accounts payable	8
Cash paid to suppliers for the period	$282

Note that had Hardin's accounts payable decreased during the year, the decrease would have been added to purchases to calculate cash paid.

The conversion of cost of goods sold to cash paid for inventory can be summarized as shown on the next page.

Cash paid for inventory can also be determined by preparing the entry that Hardin would hypothetically make to record the activity in the cost of goods sold, inventory, and accounts payable accounts.

Given cost of goods sold of $281, Hardin would debit Cost of Goods Sold for $281. Hardin would also debit Inventory $9 for its increase during the year and credit Accounts Payable $8 for its increase during the year. To balance the entry, Hardin would credit Cash for $282. Thus, cash paid for inventory is $282.

Balance from Income Statement	Adjustment		Adjustment		Balance for Statement of Cash Flows
Cost of goods sold	+ Increase in inventory or − Decrease in inventory	= Purchases	− Increase in accounts payable or + Decrease in accounts payable		= Cash paid for inventory

Hypothetical Entry	Cost of Goods Sold	281	
	Inventory	9	
	Accounts Payable		8
	Cash		282

Cash Paid for Operating Expenses

Hardin's income statement shows several operating expenses. The following sections demonstrate how operating expenses are converted to cash paid. The first section illustrates an expense related to a current asset. The second section illustrates two expenses relating to current liabilities.

Insurance Expense Hardin's income statement shows $14 of insurance expense during the year. To determine the cash paid for insurance, the related balance sheet account—prepaid insurance—must be examined.

Prepaid insurance decreased $4, meaning that Hardin used $4 of insurance it had purchased in a previous period. As a result, cash paid for insurance in the current period was only $10.

Insurance expense for the period	$14
Less: Decrease in prepaid insurance	4
Cash paid for insurance	$10

Note that had Hardin's prepaid insurance increased during the year, the increase would have been added to insurance expense.

The conversion of insurance expense to cash paid for insurance is summarized at the bottom of this page.

Using the entry approach to calculate cash payments for insurance, Hardin would debit Insurance Expense for $14 and credit Prepaid Insurance for $4. Cash would then be credited to balance the entry, showing cash payments for insurance to be $10.

Hypothetical Entry	Insurance Expense	14	
	Prepaid Insurance		4
	Cash		10

Salaries Expense and Utilities Expense Hardin's income statement shows $63 of salaries expense and $28 of utilities expense during the year. To determine the cash paid for these operating expenses, the related balance sheet accounts—salaries payable and utilities payable—must be examined.

Salaries payable did not change during the year, so Hardin must have paid exactly $63 to employees.

Salaries expense for the period	$63
Change in salaries payable	0
Cash paid to employees	$63

Balance from Income Statement	Adjustment	Balance for Statement of Cash Flows
Insurance expense	+ Increase in prepaid insurance or − Decrease in prepaid insurance	= Cash paid for insurance

Utilities payable increased $5 during the year, meaning that Hardin incurred utilities during the year for which it did not pay. Therefore, Hardin paid only $23 for utilities during the year.

Utilities expense for the period	$28
Less: Increase in utilities payable	5
Cash paid for utilities	$23

Note that had Hardin's utilities payable decreased during the year, the decrease would have been added to utilities expense.

The conversion of these operating expenses to cash paid for salaries and utilities can be summarized as follows:

Balance from Income Statement	Adjustment	Balance for Statement of Cash Flows
Salaries expense	− Increase in salaries payable or + Decrease in salaries payable	= Cash paid for salaries
Utilities expense	− Increase in utilities payable or + Decrease in utilities payable	= Cash paid for utilities

Using the entry approach to calculate the cash payments for salaries, Hardin would debit Salaries Expense for $63. Nothing is recorded for Salaries Payable because the account balance was unchanged. Cash is then credited to balance the entry, showing cash payments to be $63.

Hypothetical Entry	Salaries Expense	63	
	Cash		63

For utilities, Hardin would debit Utilities Expense for $28 and credit Utilities Payable for $5. Cash would be credited to balance the entry, showing cash payments to be $23.

Hypothetical Entry	Utilities Expense	28	
	Utilities Payable		5
	Cash		23

Cash Paid for Taxes

Hardin's income statement shows $8 of income tax expense during the year. To determine the cash paid for taxes, the related balance sheet account—taxes payable—must be examined.

Taxes payable decreased $7 during the year, meaning that Hardin paid not only current-year taxes of $8, but also $7 of prior-year taxes. Thus, taxes paid in this period were $15.

Income tax expense for the period	$ 8
Plus: Decrease in taxes payable	7
Cash paid for taxes	$15

Note that had Hardin's taxes payable increased during the year, the increase would have been subtracted from income tax expense.

The conversion of income tax expense to cash paid for taxes is summarized at the bottom of this page.

To calculate cash payments using the entry method, Hardin would debit Income Tax Expense for $8 and debit Taxes Payable for $7. Cash would be credited to balance the entry, showing cash payments to be $15.

Hypothetical Entry	Income Tax Expense	8	
	Taxes Payable	7	
	Cash		15

Other Revenues and Expenses

Hardin's income statement contains two additional items: depreciation expense and gain on sale of equipment. For

Balance from Income Statement	Adjustment	Balance for Statement of Cash Flows
Income tax expense	− Increase in taxes payable or + Decrease in taxes payable	= Cash paid for taxes

the following reasons, these items are ignored under the direct method.

Recall from Chapter 8 that depreciation expense is a non-cash charge, meaning that cash is not affected when depreciation is recorded. As a result, depreciation expense is not included when preparing the operating activities section under the direct method. This is always the case.

Recall also from Chapter 8 that a gain on the sale of equipment occurs when cash received from the sale exceeds the equipment's book value. Because the sale of equipment is an investing activity, all cash received from the sale will be reported as a cash inflow from investing activities. As a result, the gain on the sale is not included when preparing the operating activities section under the direct method. The same would be true for a loss on the sale of equipment.

Net Operating Cash Flows

Based on the previous calculations, Hardin's operating activities section of its statement of cash flows is shown in Exhibit 11-3. A summary of adjustments used to generate the numbers is found in Exhibit 11-4.

Exhibit 11-3 Hardin's Operating Cash Flows Using the Direct Method

Cash flows from operating activities		2009
Cash receipts from customers		$428
Less cash payments:		
To suppliers	$282	
To employees	63	
For insurance	10	
For utilities	23	
For taxes	15	393
Net cash provided by operating activities		$ 35

The indirect method calculates and reports net cash flows from operating activities by adjusting net income from an accrual basis to a cash basis.

LO4 Reporting Cash Flows from Operating Activities— Indirect Method

This section demonstrates the calculation of cash flows from operating activities under the indirect method.

When reporting operating cash flows under the indirect method, companies calculate and report net cash flows from operating activities by adjusting net income from an accrual basis to a cash basis. This requires many adjustments, but they can be grouped into three main types:

- Non-cash effects on net income
- Gains and losses from investing and/or financing activities
- Changes in current assets and liabilities

The following sections demonstrate these adjustments using the Hardin Supply Company information in Exhibit 11-2.

Exhibit 11-4 Summary of Adjustments Used in the Direct Method

Balance from Income Statement	Adjustment		Balance for Statement of Cash Flows
Sales	− Increase in accounts receivable	OR + Decrease in accounts receivable	= Cash collected from sales
Cost of goods sold	+ Increase in inventory	OR − Decrease in inventory	= Cash paid for inventory
	and		
	− Increase in accounts payable	OR + Decrease in accounts payable	
Operating expenses	+ Increase in current asset	OR − Decrease in current asset	= Cash paid for operations
	or		
	− Increase in current liability	OR + Decrease in current liability	
Income tax expense	− Increase in taxes payable	OR + Decrease in taxes payable	= Cash paid for taxes

Adjustments for Non-Cash Items

Accrual-based net income often includes expenses that have no related cash consequences. The most common example is depreciation expense, which is an allocation of the historical cost of a fixed asset. While depreciation reduces accrual-based net income, it does not result in any cash payment. Therefore, to adjust net income to a cash basis, the effect of depreciation must be removed from net income. This is accomplished by adding depreciation expense back to net income. Other examples of non-cash expenses are amortization expense, bad debt expense, and impairment losses.

The general adjustment for all non-cash expenses is therefore as follows:

> **Adjustment rule for non-cash expenses**
> Add back to net income all non-cash expenses

Hardin Supply Company's income statement in Exhibit 11-2 shows only one non-cash expense: depreciation expense of $25. Therefore, the $25 would be added back to net income.

Adjustments for Gains and Losses from Investing and Financing Activities

Sometimes, a company's net income will include a gain or loss arising from an investing or financing activity. For example, a company might generate a gain from the sale of equipment or a loss from the sale of an intangible asset. Another company might generate a gain from the early retirement of debt or a loss from a bond redemption.

When such activity occurs, the entire cash inflow associated with the transaction will be reported as either an investing or financing cash flow. As a result, the effect of the gain or loss must be removed from net income so that operating cash flows are not affected by the transaction. Gains must be subtracted from income, and losses must be added back to income.

> **Adjustment rules for gains and losses from investing and financing activities**
> Subtract from net income any gains arising from investing or financing activities
> Add back to net income any losses arising from investing or financing activities

Hardin's income statement shows only one gain or loss from an investing or financing activity: a $1 gain on the sale of equipment. Because the cash received from the sale will be reported as an investing cash flow, the effect of the gain must be removed from income. Therefore, income is reduced by $1.

Adjustments for Current Assets and Current Liabilities

The third type of adjustment involves the changes in a company's current assets and current liabilities. Current assets and current liabilities change during a period because a company's revenues do not equal cash received and its expenses do not equal cash paid.

For example, a change in accounts receivable means that a company's cash collections do not equal its sales revenue. If accounts receivable increases, sales revenue is greater than cash collections. If accounts receivable decreases, cash collections are greater than sales revenue. Likewise, a change in salaries payable means that a company's cash payments do not equal its salaries expense. If salaries payable increases, salaries expense is greater than cash payments. If salaries payable decreases, cash payments are greater than salaries expense.

Because the indirect method adjusts accrual-based income to cash-based income, these differences must be removed from accrual-based net income. That is, the revenues and expenses of net income must be adjusted so that they reflect cash receipts and cash payments. This is accomplished with the following adjustments:

> **Adjustment rules for current assets and current liabilities**
> Add a decrease in current assets to net income
> Subtract an increase in current assets from net income
> Add an increase in current liabilities to net income
> Subtract a decrease in current liabilities from net income

Hardin's balance sheet shows changes in several current assets and current liabilities. The following sections describe the adjustment that each change requires.

Change in Accounts Receivable Hardin's balance sheet shows a $4 increase in accounts receivable. Accounts receivable increases when sales are made without receiving cash. Therefore, $4 of Hardin's reported sales revenue was not collected in cash and must be removed from revenues. Removing $4 from revenue is accomplished by subtracting $4 from net income.

Change in Inventory Hardin's balance sheet shows that inventory increased by $9 during the year.

Inventory increases when a company purchases more inventory that it sells. Therefore, Hardin must have purchased $9 more in inventory than it sold during the year. So that net income reflects all payments for purchases, the $9 must be added to cost of goods sold. This results in a reduction to net income of $9.

Change in Prepaid Insurance Hardin's balance sheet shows a decrease in prepaid insurance of $4. Prepaid insurance decreases when a company uses insurance that it has already purchased. Thus, a decrease of $4 means that Hardin used $4 of insurance that it purchased in a previous period. As a result, insurance expense is $4 greater than the cash paid for insurance and should be reduced to reflect the cash paid for insurance. Reducing expenses by $4 is accomplished by adding $4 to net income.

Change in Accounts Payable Hardin's balance sheet shows that accounts payable increased by $8 during the year. Accounts payable increases when inventory is purchased without paying cash, so an $8 increase means that Hardin did not pay for $8 of its purchases calculated previously. Therefore, the $8 must be removed from expenses. This is accomplished by adding $8 to net income.

Change in Utilities Payable Hardin's balance sheet shows an increase of $5 in utilities payable. Utilities payable increases when a company incurs utilities expense but does not pay cash. Thus, the $5 increase means that Hardin's expenses are $5 greater than the cash paid. As a result, the $5 of expenses must be removed from net income. This is accomplished by adding $5 to net income.

Change in Taxes Payable Hardin's balance sheet shows that taxes payable decreased $7 during the period to end at a zero balance. Taxes payable decreases when a company pays not only for current-period taxes but also prior-period taxes. The $7 decrease therefore means that Hardin paid $7 more than it expensed. As a result, the $7 should be added to expenses. This is accomplished by subtracting $7 from net income.

Net Operating Cash Flows

The six adjustments from changes in current assets and current liabilities, along with the two adjustments for non-cash items, are shown in Exhibit 11-5. The adjustments result in $35 in net cash provided by operating

activities. If you are learning both the direct and indirect methods, you should note that the $35 is the same as calculated under the direct method.

Exhibit 11-5 Hardin's Operating Cash Flows Using the Indirect Method

Cash flows from operating activities		2009
Net income		$14
Adjustments to reconcile net income to		
net cash provided by operating activities		
Depreciation expense	$25	
Gain on sale of equipment	(1)	
Increase in accounts receivable	(4)	
Increase in inventory	(9)	
Decrease in prepaid insurance	4	
Increase in accounts payable	8	
Increase in utilities payable	5	
Decrease in taxes payable	(7)	21
Net cash provided by operating activities		$35

LO5 Computing Cash Flows from Investing Activities

This section demonstrates the calculation of cash flows from investing activities. Recall that investing activities include the purchase and sale of non-current assets such as fixed assets, intangible assets, and long-term investments.

To calculate cash flows from investing activities, all changes in non-current assets must be examined. In general, an increase in a non-current asset suggests a purchase and therefore a cash outflow. A decrease suggests a sale and therefore a cash inflow. However, to be sure, any available information on the changes must be examined to determine whether the change resulted from a non-cash transaction or whether the change was the net effect of both increases and decreases to the account.

To illustrate, consider again Hardin's balance sheet in Exhibit 11-2. It shows three non-current asset accounts: "Investments, Fixed Assets, and Accumulated Depreciation." In the following sections, each account balance is examined to determine Hardin's cash flows from investing activities.

Investing activities include the purchase and sale of non-current assets such as fixed assets, intangible assets, and long-term investments.

Investments

According to Hardin's balance sheet, investments increased $22. Without any information to the contrary, it is assumed that Hardin bought investments for $22 cash. Thus, a cash outflow of $22 from the purchase of investments is reported in investing activities.

Equipment

Hardin's balance sheet shows a $66 increase in equipment during the year. Thus, Hardin must have purchased equipment during the year. Hardin's income statement shows a $1 gain on the sale of equipment. Thus, Hardin must have sold equipment during the year. As a result, there are both cash inflows and outflows related to equipment. Each will be considered separately.

Cash Inflows Hardin discloses that the $1 gain on the sale of equipment arose from selling equipment with a cost of $10 and accumulated depreciation of $5 for $6. Thus, a $6 inflow from the sale of equipment should be included in investing activities. Note here that the gain from the sale is ignored. Only the cash flow from the sale is of interest at this point. The gain is accounted for in operating activities.

Cash Outflows Hardin's equipment account increased $66 during the year. Absent any additional information, it would be assumed that Hardin purchased $66 in equipment for cash. However, Hardin's additional information discloses that equipment with a cost of $10 was sold during the year. Therefore, Hardin must have purchased $76 in equipment during the year. The calculation of purchases is shown as follows.

Beginning balance	$166		
Plus: Purchases	??	⟶	?? = $76
Less: Sales	10		
Ending balance	$232		

Accumulated Depreciation

Recall from Chapter 8 that accumulated depreciation is the account that collects depreciation expense. Therefore it changes when either depreciation expense is recorded or fixed assets are sold. Depreciation expense does not affect cash, and any sale of equipment is already considered when examining the equipment account. Therefore, the change in the accumulated depreciation account can be ignored.

Summary of Investing Cash Flows

The three cash flows from investing activities are shown in Exhibit 11-6. The three items resulted in a net cash outflow from investing activities of $(92). Hardin was using its cash to invest in additional non-current assets.

Exhibit 11-6 Hardin's Investing Cash Flows

Cash flows from investing activities	2009
Purchase of equipment	$(76)
Sale of equipment	6
Purchase of investments	(22)
Net cash used in investing activities	$(92)

LO6 Computing Cash Flows from Financing Activities

This section demonstrates the calculation of cash flows from financing activities. Recall that financing activities include generating and repaying capital to investors and creditors. Common financing activities include the issuance of stock or debt and the repurchase of stock, the payment of dividends, and the repayment of debt. Note that although payments of dividends to stockholders are considered a financing activity, payments of interest to creditors are not. Because interest is an expense that is reported on the income statement, payments for interest are reported as operating activities rather than financing activities.

To calculate cash flows from financing activities, the balances for long-term liabilities, equity accounts, and dividends must be examined. In general, an increase in a liability or an equity account such as common stock suggests a cash inflow from either borrowing or selling stock. A decrease in a liability or an increase in treasury stock or dividends suggests a cash outflow from payments to creditors or investors. However, to be sure, any available information on the changes must be examined to determine whether the change resulted from a non-cash transaction or whether the change was the net effect of both increases and decreases to the account.

To illustrate, consider again Hardin's balance sheet in Exhibit 11-2. It shows one long-term liability and three equity accounts. Hardin provides no additional information regarding the accounts. In the following sections, each account balance is examined to determine Hardin's cash flows from financing activities.

Long-Term Debt

According to Hardin's balance sheet, long-term debt increased $45 during the year. Absent any information to the contrary, it is assumed that Hardin borrowed $45 in cash. Thus, a cash inflow of $45 from the issuance of debt is reported in financing activities.

Common Stock

Hardin's balance sheet shows no change in the common stock account. Thus, absent any additional information, it is assumed there was no effect on cash from the common stock account.

Treasury Stock

Hardin's balance sheet shows a $10 increase in treasury stock. Recall from Chapter 10 that the treasury stock account records the cost of a company's own stock that has been repurchased. Absent any additional information telling us otherwise, it is assumed that Hardin purchased the stock for $10 cash. Thus, a cash outflow of $10 from the purchase of treasury stock is reported in financing activities.

Retained Earnings

The fourth and final account is retained earnings. Recall from earlier chapters that the retained earnings

> Common financing activities include the issuance of stock or debt and the repurchase of stock, the payment of dividends, and the repayment of debt.

balance is affected by two things—net income and dividends declared. Net income increases the balance while dividends decrease the balance. Hardin's balance sheet shows that retained earnings increased $9 during the year, from $78 to $87. Hardin's income statement shows that net income was $14. Therefore dividends declared can be calculated as follows:

Retained earnings, beginning balance	$78
Plus: Net income	14
Less: Dividends declared	?? → ?? = $5
Retained earnings, ending balance	$87

Now that dividends declared are known, the amount paid can be calculated. If dividends were not paid, the balance sheet would show a balance in dividends payable in current liabilities. Neither year shows a balance, so all $5 of the dividends must have been paid. Thus, a cash outflow of $5 from the payment of dividends is reported in financing activities.

Net Financing Cash Flows

The three cash flows from financing activities are shown in Exhibit 11-7. The three items resulted in a net cash inflow from financing activities of $30. Hardin generated $30 more from financing activities than it paid.

Exhibit 11-7 Hardin's Financing Cash Flows

Cash flows from financing activities	2009
Issuance of long-term debt	$45
Payment of dividends	(5)
Purchase of treasury stock	(10)
Net cash provided by financing activities	$30

> The statement of cash flows reports how a company generated and used its cash during the year.

Complete Statement of Cash Flows— Indirect Method

Hardin's final statement of cash flows, using the indirect method, is shown in Exhibit 11-8. The net decrease in cash of $27 corresponds to the change in the cash account from Hardin's balance sheet.

Exhibit 11-8 Hardin Supply Company Statement of Cash Flows

**Hardin Supply Company
Statement of Cash Flows
For the Year Ended December 31, 2009**

Cash flows from operating activities		
Net income		$ 14
Adjustments to reconcile net income to net cash provided by operating activities		
Depreciation expense	$ 25	
Gain on sale of equipment	(1)	
Increase in accounts receivable	(4)	
Increase in inventory	(9)	
Decrease in prepaid insurance	4	
Increase in accounts payable	8	
Increase in utilities payable	5	
Decrease in taxes payable	(7)	21
Net cash provided by operating activities		$ 35
Cash flows from investing activities		
Purchases of equipment	$(76)	
Sale of equipment	6	
Purchases of investments	(22)	
Net cash used in investing activities		(92)
Cash flows from financing activities		
Issuance of long-term debt	$ 45	
Payment of dividends	(5)	
Purchase of treasury stock	(10)	
Net cash provided by financing activities		30
Net decrease in cash		$(27)
Cash, beginning of the year		45
Cash, end of the year		$ 18

Free cash flow The excess cash a company generates beyond what it needs to invest in productive capacity and pay dividends to stockholders.

LO7 Analyzing a Company's Statement of Cash Flows

The statement of cash flows reports how a company generated and used its cash during the year. As a result, the statement can be used to answer many question about a company's cash. Two of the broader questions that can be addressed are as follows:

1. Is the company able to generate enough cash to grow?

2. Is the company able to generate enough cash to satisfy its obligations?

The following sections examine these questions for Under Armour. The examination will require the information from the company's statement of cash flows and notes to the financial statements. The required information is found in Exhibit 11-9, which is excerpted from Under Armour's 2008 Annual Report.

Exhibit 11-9 Account Balances from Under Armour's 2008 Annual Report

Source	Accounts	2008	2007
Statement of Cash Flows	Cash flows from operating activities	$44,157	$42,929
	Capital expenditures	38,594	33,959
	Dividends	0	0
Notes to Financial Statements	Average debt maturing in next five years	$ 4,027	

Free Cash Flow

When assessing a company's cash flows, a commonly used calculation is free cash flow. **Free cash flow** is the cash a company generates in excess of its investments in productive capacity and payments to stockholders in the form of dividends. Free cash flow is a measure of a company's ability to generate cash for expansion, for other forms of improved operations, for the repayment of debt, or for increased returns to stockholders. While free cash flow can be defined in many ways, the most straightforward definition is as follows:

HOME DEPOT ANALYSIS

ook at Home Depot's Statement of Cash Flows and the last paragraph in Note 6 in Appendix C. Calculate and interpret (1) free cash flow and (2) cash flow adequacy ratio.

(1) Free cash flow:

$$\$5{,}528 - \$1{,}847 - \$1{,}521 = \$2{,}160$$

Home Depot generated $2,160 million in free cash flow in the most recent year. This cash could be used for further expansion, to pay down debt balances, or for other purposes determined by company management.

(2) Cash flow adequacy ratio:

$$\$2{,}160/\$1{,}068 = 2.0$$

The 2.0 cash flow adequacy ratio indicates that Home Depot can pay twice as much as the average debt coming due in the next five years. Thus, the company currently has adequate cash flow to service its maturing debt. [Note: The $1,068 balance is determined by taking the average debt maturing in the next five years: ($1,800 + $1,000 + $1,000 + $240 + $1,300)/5.]

Cash flows from operating activities
Less: Capital expenditures
Less: Dividends
Free cash flow

The calculation starts with cash flows from operating activities, which is a measure of a company's ability to generate cash from its current operations. It then subtracts capital expenditures, which refers to the cash that a company spends on fixed assets during the year, and dividends, which are payments to stockholders during the year. The cash that remains is "free" to be used as the company chooses.

Under Armour's 2008 free cash flow is calculated as follows from the information in Exhibit 11-5:

	2008	2007
Cash flows from operating activities	$69,516	$(14,628)
– Capital expenditures	38,594	33,959
– Dividends	0	0
Free cash flow	$30,922	$(48,587)

In 2008, Under Armour generated positive free cash flow. That is, it generated more cash from operations than it paid for property and equipment and dividends. As a result, the company generated cash that was free to be used for other purposes. However, Under Armour generated negative free cash flow in 2007. It experienced a negative cash flow from operations, meaning

© TERRI MILLER/E-VISUAL COMMUNICATIONS, INC.

that it spent more cash than it generated for operations. A review of the company's statement of cash flows in Exhibit 11-1 shows that the negative cash flow from operations was caused primarily by the purchase of inventory.

Cash Flow Adequacy Ratio

A second ratio that is commonly used to assess a company's cash is the cash flow adequacy ratio. The **cash flow adequacy ratio** compares free cash flow to the

> **Cash flow adequacy ratio** Compares free cash flow to the average amount of debt maturing in the next five years and measures the ability to pay maturing debt.

average amount of debt maturing in the next five years. It is calculated as follows:

$$\text{Cash flow adequacy ratio} = \frac{\text{Free cash flow}}{\text{Average amount of debt maturing in five years}}$$

Because this ratio compares free cash flow to maturing debt, it represents a company's ability to generate enough cash to pay its debt. In general, companies would like this ratio to be higher rather than lower. All other things equal, a higher ratio indicates a greater ability to generate sufficient cash from operations to pay upcoming debt.

Under Armour's 2008 cash flow adequacy ratio is calculated as follows.

$$\frac{30{,}922}{4{,}027} = 7.7$$

The 7.7 ratio indicates that Under Armour generated over $7.70 in free cash flow for every $1 of debt maturing in each of the next five years. Thus, it appears that Under Armour is generating sufficient cash to service its upcoming debt payments.

STUDY TOOLS
CHAPTER 11

CHAPTER REVIEW CARD

❏ Learning Objective and Key Concept Reviews

❏ Key Definitions and Formulas

ONLINE (Located at 4ltrpress.cengage.com/acct)

❏ Flash Cards and Crossword Puzzles

❏ Conceptual and Computational Interactive Quizzes

❏ E-Lectures

❏ Static, Algorithmic, and Additional Homework Activities (as directed by your instructor)

1. Classify Cash Flows LO1

A company enters into the following transactions:
a. Issued $25,000 par value common stock in exchange for cash.
b. Issued a long-term note in exchange for a machine worth $45,000.
c. Received $21,000 in cash from accounts receivable.
d. Paid $7,500 on accounts payable.
e. Issued $50,000 par value common stock upon conversion of convertible bonds with a face value of $50,000.
f. Declared and paid a cash dividend of $78,000.
g. Sold an investment costing $10,000 for $10,000 in cash

Required
Classify each of the preceding transactions as a cash inflow or a cash outflow from operating activities, investing activities, or financing activities, or as a non-cash transaction.

2. Classify Cash Flows LO1

A company enters into the following transactions:
a. Interest is paid on a note payable.
b. Salaries are paid to the company's employees.
c. Bonds are issued in exchange for cash.
d. Income taxes are paid by the company.
e. New heavy machinery is purchased with cash.
f. Convertible bonds are issued in exchange for land.
g. Cash dividends are paid to stockholders.
h. The common stock of another company is purchased as an investment.
i. The company purchases its own common stock on the market and retires it.
j. Common stock is given to the bank in return for cancellation of a note.
k. An amount due from a customer is collected.
l. Intangible assets are purchased from another company for cash.

Required
Indicate whether each transaction would appear under operating activities, investing activities, or financing activities. Also note if a transaction is a significant non-cash transaction that would require additional disclosure.

3. Classify Cash Flows LO1

A company entered into the following transactions:
a. Purchased new machinery for $24,000 cash.
b. Paid an account payable of $2,500 relating to inventory with cash.
c. Recorded cash sales of $52,000 for the period.
d. Purchased a new warehouse for $275,000. The seller of the building accepts 10,000 shares of common stock as payment.
e. Issued bonds at face value of $25,000.
f. Purchased 200 shares of the company's own stock on the open market for $7,000.
g. Purchased a new light truck for $18,000 by signing a 180-day note payable.
h. Collected cash of $3,000 from a customer in satisfaction of accounts payable.
i. Sold 250 shares of Microsoft stock for its book value of $25,000.
j. Paid $2,000 for renewal of the volcano insurance policy.
k. Paid dividends of $5,000 in cash.

Required
Classify each transaction as a cash inflow or outflow from operating activities, investing activities, or financing activities, or as an item reported in a supplemental schedule of the statement of cash flows.

4. Calculate Cash Collections LO3

McDoogle Company's balance sheet showed an accounts receivable balance of $75,000 at the beginning of the year and $97,000 at the end of the year. McDoogle reported sales of $1,150,000 on its income statement.

Required
Using the direct method, determine the amount that McDoogle will report as cash collections in the operating activities section of the statement of cash flows.

5. Calculate Cash Paid for Purchases LO3

JANH Company's balance sheet included an inventory balance of $105,000 at 12/31/09 and $142,000 at 12/31/10. Accounts payable balances were $78,000 and $47,000 at 12/31/09 and 12/31/10, respectively. JANH's accounts payable only relate to inventory purchases. Cost of goods sold as reported on the 2010 income statement was $885,000.

Required
Using the direct method, determine the amount that JANH will report as cash paid for inventory in the operating activities section of the statement of cash flows.

6. Calculate Cash Paid for Operating Expenses LO3

The following information is available for a company's rent and income taxes.

Prepaid rent, beginning of year	$25,000
Prepaid rent, end of year	31,000
Rent expense	40,000
Cash paid for rent during the year	??
Income taxes payable, beginning of year	25,000
Income taxes payable, end of year	31,000
Income tax expense	40,000
Cash payments for income taxes	??

Required
Calculate the missing information.

7. Classify Adjustments Under the Indirect Method LO4

A company that uses the indirect method to report operating activities experiences the following events.
a. Decrease in accounts payable.
b. Increase in accounts receivable.
c. Purchase of a new conveyer belt system.
d. Purchase of and retirement of common stock.
e. Gain on the sale of old conveyer belt system.
f. Depreciation expense.
g. Increase in inventory.
h. Increase in bonds payable.
i. Bad debt expense.

Required
Indicate whether each item should be added to net income, deducted from net income, or not reported in the operating activities section of the statement of cash flows.

8. Prepare Operating Cash Flows Under the Indirect Method LO4

The following information was reported by Shady Imports Company:

	2010	2009
Accounts receivable	$55,000	$47,000
Inventory	35,000	45,000
Prepaid insurance	12,000	10,000
Accounts payable	22,000	15,000
Income taxes payable	10,000	14,000
Interest payable	12,000	9,000
Net income	45,000	
Depreciation expense	25,000	

Required
Prepare the operating activities section of the statement of cash flows using the indirect method and explain why cash flows from operating activities is more or less than net income.

9. Classifying Transactions Under the Indirect Method LO4, 5, 6

The following is a list of transactions and changes in account balances that occurred during the year.
a. Income taxes payable decreased.
b. Paid cash in satisfaction of a matured bond payable.
c. Paid a cash dividend.
d. Accounts payable increased.
e. Accounts receivable doubled before returning to the beginning of the year balance.
f. Sold equipment for cash at a gain.
g. Purchased a new warehouse by issuing bonds.
h. Purchased inventory for cash.
i. Purchased own stock in open market and retired it to the treasury.

Required
Assuming the indirect method for operating activities, indicate whether each transaction would be included in operating activities, investing activities, financing activities, non-cash disclosures, or not reported. Note that some transactions may impact multiple sections.

10. Calculate Cash Flows from Investing Activities LO5

The following information is taken from the balance sheet of Cheese Wheel Company:

	2010	2009
Equipment	$85,000	$120,000
Accumulated depreciation (equipment)	50,000	55,000

Depreciation expense of $15,000 was reported on the income statement for 2010. Equipment with an original cost of $35,000 was sold for its book value.

Required
Compute the amount of cash received from the sale of the equipment.

11. Calculate Cash Flows from Investing Activities LO5

The following transactions occurred during the year.
a. A new warehouse was purchased for cash in the amount of $110,000.
b. The company's own stock was purchased on the open market and placed in treasury stock.
c. An old warehouse costing $80,000 was sold for $45,000, resulting in a gain of $5,000.
d. The company purchased stock in Boston Beer Inc. for $7,500 cash.
e. Stock of Tazer Inc. was sold for $12,500, resulting in a gain of $7,500.

Required
Use this information to compute cash flows from investing activities.

12. Calculate Cash Flows from Financing Activities LO6

The following transactions occurred during the year.
a. Common stock was issued in exchange for a new heavy truck.
b. A cash dividend of $20,000 was paid.
c. A 90-day note payable was issued for $5,000 cash.
d. $25,000 was paid to acquire the company's own stock for retirement.
e. Depreciation expense for the year was $30,000.
f. Bonds with a face value of $25,000 were issued at par.

Required
Use this information to compute cash flows from financing activities.

13. Analyzing Cash Flows LO7

Lowball Ltd. and Cheapskate Inc. are both no-frills, discount distribution companies. The following financial information regarding each company is available:

	Lowball	Cheapskate
Cash flows from operating activities	$225,000	$225,000
Net income	125,000	125,000
Capital expenditures	50,000	65,000
Dividends declared and paid	30,000	10,000
Average amount of debt maturing in 5 years	20,000	30,000

Required
a. Indicate which company generated more free cash flow.
b. Indicate which company has the better cash flow adequacy ratio.

PROBLEMS

14. Prepare Operating Cash Flows Under the Direct Method LO3

The following information is provided for HMG Company.

Balances at 12/31	2010	2009
Accounts Receivable	$ 2,500	$ 1,500
Inventory	26,000	32,000
Maintenance Supplies	2,000	1,000
Accounts Payable	4,000	3,000
Taxes Payable	2,000	3,500
Interest Payable	1,500	2,500
2010 Income Statement		
Revenue		$80,000
Cost of goods sold		55,000
Gross profit		$25,000
General and admininstrative expense		6,000
Depreciation expense		2,000
Total operating expenses		$ 8,000
Income before interest and taxes		$17,000
Interest expense		4,000
Income before taxes		$13,000
Income tax expense		4,000
Net income		$ 9,000

Required
Prepare the operating activities section of the statement of cash flows using the direct method.

15. Prepare a Statement of Cash Flows Using the Indirect Method LO4, 5, 6

The comparative balance sheet for Two Kicks Company is as follows:

Comparative Balance Sheet at 12/31/10

	2010	2009
Cash and cash equivalents	$ 65,000	$ 45,000
Accounts receivable	50,000	55,000
Inventory	125,000	175,000
Property, plant, and equipment	930,000	745,000
Accumulated depreciation	(270,000)	(200,000)
Total assets	$900,000	$820,000
Accounts payable	$110,000	$105,000
Bonds payable (long-term)	180,000	200,000
Total liabilities	$290,000	$305,000
Common stock	$350,000	$280,000
Retained earnings	260,000	235,000
Total stockholders' equity	610,000	515,000
Total liabilities and stockholders' equity	$900,000	$820,000

The following additional information is available:
a. Net income for 2010 was $50,000.
b. Cash dividends of $25,000 were paid during the year.
c. A portion of outstanding bonds matured and were redeemed for cash by the bondholders. No new bonds were issued during the year.
d. Common stock was issued for cash.
e. Property and equipment were purchased for cash. No long term assets were sold during the year.
f. The change in accumulated depreciation is a result of depreciation expense.

Required
Prepare a statement of cash flows for the year using the indirect method for the operating activities section.

16. Prepare a Statement of Cash Flows LO3, 4, 5

Available financial information for Blue Bomber Company is as follows:

Comparative Balance Sheet at 12/31/10

	2010	2009
Cash and cash equivalents	$ 75,000	$ 45,000
Accounts receivable	45,000	55,000
Inventory	200,000	175,000
Prepaid insurance	30,000	35,000
Total current assets	$ 350,000	$ 310,000
Property, plant, and equipment	$ 800,000	$ 720,000
Accumulated depreciation	(240,000)	(170,000)
Total property, plant, and equipment	$ 560,000	$ 550,000
Total assets	$ 910,000	$ 860,000
Accounts payable	$ 110,000	$ 115,000
Accrued salaries	10,000	35,000
Total current liabilities	$ 120,000	$ 150,000
Bonds payable	$ 180,000	$ 230,000
Total liabilities	$ 300,000	$ 380,000
Common stock	$ 350,000	$ 250,000
Retained earnings	260,000	230,000
Total stockholders' equity	$ 610,000	$ 480,000
Total liabilities and stockholders' equity	$910,000	$860,000

Income Statement For the Year Ended 12/31/10	
Revenue	$450,000
Cost of goods sold	(225,000)
Gross profit	$225,000
Depreciation expense	(70,000)
Other operating expenses	(30,000)
Income before interest and taxes	$125,000
Interest expense	(20,000)
Income before taxes	$105,000
Income tax expense	(30,000)
Net Income	$ 75,000

The following additional information is available:
a. Cash dividends of $45,000 were declared and paid during the year.
b. Equipment was purchased for cash.
c. A portion of bonds payable matured and was paid with cash.
d. Common stock was issued for cash.

Required
Prepare a statement of cash flows for Blue Bomber for 2010 using the direct method for the operating activities section. In a separate schedule, show the operating activities section using the indirect method.

CASE

17. Research and Analysis   LO1, 7

Access the 2008 annual report for Callaway Golf Company by clicking on the *Investor Relations* and *Annual Reports* links at www.callawaygolf.com.

Required
1. Examine the company's statement of cash flows and identify the major cash inflows and outflows in investing and financing activities.
2. Calculate the company's free cash flow in each of the past three years.
3. Based on your answers above, write a paragraph explaining what Callaway has been doing with its cash over the past three years.

REMEMBER

- All exercises and problems from the text are available online in static and algorithmic versions.
- Additional multiple choice, exercises, problems, and cases are available online in CengageNOW or as an enrichment module that can be customized into this text.

Financial Statement
Analysis

Introduction

The first eleven chapters of this book examined the various aspects of financial accounting, which is the process of identifying, measuring, and communicating economic information to permit informed decisions. This chapter demonstrates how to analyze the products of this process—the income statement, the balance sheet, the statement of stockholders' equity, and the statement of cash flows—to make informed decisions about a company. That is, the chapter focuses on financial statement analysis. It will use the financial statements of Best Buy as an example.

Learning Objectives

After studying the material in this chapter, you should be able to:

LO1 Understand the nature of financial statement analysis.

LO2 Calculate and interpret horizontal and vertical analyses.

LO3 Assess profitability through the calculation and interpretation of ratios.

LO4 Assess liquidity through the calculation and interpretation of ratios.

LO5 Assess solvency through the calculation and interpretation of ratios.

LO6 Calculate and interpret a DuPont analysis.

LO1 Financial Statement Analysis

Financial statement analysis is the process of applying analytical tools to a company's financial statements to understand the company's financial health. The goal of such an analysis is to provide some context for understanding the accounting numbers on the financial statements. Ultimately, financial analysis should help an investor, creditor, or any other interested party better understand a company's financial position and therefore make better decisions about the company. Enabling good decisions is one goal of financial accounting, and it should be the product of financial statement analysis.

Financial analysis requires the following:

- Financial information
- Standards of comparison
- Analysis tools

Financial statement analysis The process of applying analytical tools to a company's financial statements to understand the company's financial health.

Financial Information

All publicly traded companies must prepare audited financial statements each year and file them with the Securities and Exchange Commission. These statements include the income statement, the balance sheet, the statement of stockholders'

Financial statement analysis can help investors understand how effectively and efficiently a company like Best Buy is profiting from its customers.

© CHRIS RANK/BLOOMBERG VIA GETTY IMAGES

equity, and the statement of cash flows. Financial statements contain multiple years of data for comparative purposes and are the starting point for any analysis.

In addition to financial statements, companies provide other information that should be consulted to augment a financial analysis. For example, a company's notes to its financial statements will provide further explanation of items on the financial statements and additional disclosures not included on the statements. A company's Management's Discussion and Analysis (MD&A) will contain management's commentary on many aspects of company operations and future plans. Even company press releases, earnings conference calls, and notifications of stockholder meetings can contain helpful information. Finally, it is always a good idea to consult independent, third-party analysis.

In this chapter, the financial information provided by Best Buy Co., Inc. will be used to illustrate the process of financial analysis. Our focus will be predominantly on information from

> Enabling good decisions is one goal of financial accounting, and it should be the product of financial statement analysis.

the income statement and the balance sheet. As a result, only those two statements are shown in the text. However, when information beyond those statements is required, it will be provided in the text.

Standards of Comparison

When conducting a financial analysis, there should be some benchmarks for comparison. The most common benchmark is the prior year(s) of the same company. This is often called an intracompany comparison because it is a comparison within a company. Horizontal analysis is an excellent example of an intracompany analysis.

Another common benchmark is competitors. Comparisons among competitors are often called intercompany comparisons because they are between companies. Vertical analysis is an excellent tool for intercompany analysis because it removes the effect of company size.

A final benchmark is industry standards. Often, industry benchmarks can be obtained from financial websites.

The analysis in this text will use both intracompany and intercompany comparisons. For intercompany comparisons, the text will use Best Buy's smaller competitor, hhgregg.

Analysis Tools

There are many analysis tools used to conduct a financial analysis. Three of the more common are the following: horizontal analysis, vertical analysis, and ratio analysis. Horizontal analysis is a comparison of a company's financial results across time. Vertical analysis is a comparison of financial balances to a base account from the same company. Ratio analysis is a comparison of different balances from the financial statements to provide the context to understand the financial results. Typically, multiple individual ratios are grouped together to assess

Horizontal analysis An analysis technique that calculates the change in an account balance from one period to the next and expresses that change in both dollar and percentage terms.

a company's profitability, its ability to satisfy its debts, and its ability to survive in the long term.

The remainder of this text demonstrates and discusses horizontal, vertical, and ratio analyses of Best Buy's 2008 financial statements.

LO2 Horizontal and Vertical Analyses

Horizontal Analysis

Horizontal analysis was first introduced in Chapter 2. Recall that horizontal analysis is a technique that compares account balances over time. Formally, **horizontal analysis** is an analysis technique that calculates the change in an account balance from one period to the next and expresses that change in both dollar and percentage terms. The actual calculations are as follows.

$$\text{Dollar change in account balance} = \text{Current year balance} - \text{Prior year balance}$$

$$\text{Percentage change in account balance} = \frac{\text{Dollar change}}{\text{Prior year balance}}$$

Horizontal analysis is a simple but powerful analysis tool. It reveals significant changes in account balances and therefore identifies items for further investigation. For example, an unusually large increase in operating expenses focuses attention on why those expenses increased so much. That is the nature of horizontal analysis—it often provides the right questions to ask.

Horizontal analysis is calculated for both the balance sheet and the income statement. Changes in critical account balances—such as inventory for a retailer or liabilities for a company in financial trouble—are usually examined first. Also examined are any significant changes in other account balances. Insignificant changes are often ignored because they would not affect decision making. For example, an account that grows from $1 million to $3 million experiences a 200% increase, but such an increase is immaterial to a $50 billion company.

Balance Sheet Analysis Exhibit 12-1 contains a horizontal analysis of a condensed version of Best Buy's 2008 balance sheet.

The analysis shows positive changes in all asset accounts except for cash and cash equivalents. Overall,

Horizontal analysis is a simple but powerful analysis tool. It often provides the right question to ask.

Best Buy added $3 billion in total assets, which represents a 24.1% growth rate. The company experienced the largest dollar and percentage changes in receivables and goodwill. Receivables represent uncollected sales, so an increase can be a troubling sign and should be investigated further. Goodwill is an intangible asset that is created when a company purchases another company at a premium. Best Buy's notes indicate that it experienced significant international acquisitions during the year, which caused goodwill to increase.

The analysis also shows positive changes in all liability accounts. Overall, total liabilities increased by almost the same dollar amount as total assets. However, because total liabilities were smaller than total assets,

the percentage change in liabilities was greater at 35.2%. In effect, Best Buy grew its assets by growing its liabilities. Whether the company can pay off these liabilities is a question to consider further when conducting ratio analysis.

An examination of equity shows a large increase in the company's largest equity account, retained earnings. Such an increase is the result of profitable operations and is a sign of strong financial performance. There is also a significant increase in the company's additional paid-in capital account. According to the company's statement of shareholders' equity, this increase was a result of issuing stock to employees.

Overall, the horizontal analysis shows a growing company that financed its growth predominantly through increases in liabilities, but also through profitable operations. Of potential concern is the large growth in receivables.

Income Statement Analysis Exhibit 12-2 contains a horizontal analysis of a condensed version of Best Buy's 2008 income statement.

Exhibit 12-1 Horizontal Analysis of Best Buy's 2008 Condensed Balance Sheet

$ in millions, except per share amounts	February 28, 2009	March 1, 2008	$ Change	% Change
Assets				
Current Assets				
Cash and cash equivalents	$ 498	$ 1,438	$ (940)	−65.4%
Receivables	1,868	549	1,319	240.3%
Merchandise inventories	4,753	4,708	45	1.0%
Other current assets	1,073	647	426	65.8%
Total current assets	8,192	7,342	850	11.6%
Property and Equipment, net	4,174	3,306	868	26.3%
Goodwill	2,203	1,088	1,115	102.5%
Other Assets	1,257	1,022	235	23.0%
Total Assets	$15,826	$12,758	$3,068	24.1%
Liabilities and Shareholders' Equity				
Current Liabilities				
Accounts payable	$ 4,997	$ 4,297	$ 700	16.3%
Short-term debt	783	156	627	401.9%
Other current liabilities	2,655	2,316	339	14.6%
Total current liabilities	8,435	6,769	1,666	24.6%
Long-Term Liabilities	2,748	1,505	1,243	82.6%
Total liabilities	$11,183	$ 8,274	$2,909	35.2%
Shareholders' Equity				
Common stock, $.10 par value: Authorized—1 billion shares; Issued and outstanding—413,684,000 and 410,578,000 shares, respectively	41	41	0	0.0%
Additional paid-in capital	205	8	197	2,462.5%
Retained earnings	4,714	3,933	781	19.9%
Accumulated other comprehensive income (loss)	(317)	502	(819)	−163.2%
Total shareholders' equity	4,643	4,484	159	3.6%
Total Liabilities and Shareholders' Equity	$15,826	$12,758	$3,068	24.1%

Exhibit 12-2 Horizontal Analysis of Best Buy's 2008 Condensed Income Statement

$ in millions, except per share amounts

For the Fiscal Years Ended	February 28, 2009	March 1, 2008	$ Change	% Change
Revenue	$45,015	$40,023	$4,992	12.5%
Cost of goods sold	34,017	30,477	3,540	11.6%
Gross profit	10,998	9,546	1,452	15.2%
Selling, general and administrative expenses	8,984	7,385	1,599	21.7%
Restructuring charges and impairments	144	—	144	—
Operating income	1,870	2,161	(291)	−13.5%
Other income (expense)				
Investment income and other	35	129	(94)	−72.9%
Investment impairment	(111)	—	(111)	—
Interest expense	(94)	(62)	(32)	51.6%
Earnings from continuing operations before income tax expense	1,700	2,228	(528)	−23.7%
Income tax expense	674	815	(141)	−17.3%
Other expenses	23	6	17	283.3%
Net earnings	$ 1,003	$ 1,407	$ (404)	−28.7%

The analysis shows that revenue increased 12.5% while cost of goods sold increased only 11.6%. This is good news. Any time a company can increase sales faster than the cost of those sales, it can increase profitability for its owners. The effect of these two growth rates is a 15.2% increase in gross profit.

However, the news is not all good. Operating expenses increased 21.7% during the year. Furthermore, the company experienced restructuring charges and impairments in 2008 that it did not have in 2007. As a result, operating income was 13.5% lower than the prior year, and net earnings was 28.7% lower.

Overall, Best Buy's growth in operating costs and a few one-time charges prevented it from maintaining the gains generated in gross profit. Nonetheless, the company was profitable in 2008, and it appears poised for continued profits in the future.

MAKING IT REAL

A retailer can grow sales by adding new stores and/or increasing sales in existing stores. A horizontal analysis does not distinguish between those two sources of sales growth. It only shows total sales growth. Because investors want to know how much of the growth is attributable to each source, companies disclose "same-store" or "comparable-store" sales in their Management's Discussion and Analysis (MD&A). Same-store sales represent the growth in sales for stores that were open all year in both years presented. In its MD&A, Best Buy reports that the increase in sales revenue "was driven primarily by the acquisition of Best Buy Europe... and the net addition of 214 new stores. These gains were partially offset by a 1.3% comparable store sales decline..." So, of Best Buy's 12.47% growth in sales, all came from new stores and the acquisition of Best Buy Europe. Stores that were open for 2008 and 2007 experienced a decline in sales.

Vertical Analysis

Vertical analysis was also introduced in Chapter 2. Recall that vertical analysis is a technique that compares account balances within one year. Formally, **vertical analysis** is an analysis technique that states each account balance on a financial statement as a percentage of a base amount on the statement. The base account is total assets for the balance sheet and either sales or revenues for the income statement. The actual calculation is as follows.

	For the Balance Sheet		For the Income Statement
Percentage =	$\dfrac{\text{Account balance}}{\text{Total Assets}}$	or	$\dfrac{\text{Account balance}}{\text{Net Sales or Revenue}}$

Like horizontal analysis, vertical analysis is a simple but powerful tool. The dividing of each account balance by either assets or revenues accomplishes two purposes. First, it shows the relative importance of each account to the company. Second, it standardizes the account balances by firm size so that companies of different sizes can be compared.

To illustrate, suppose a company with $10 million in total assets has $1 million in cash while another company with $100 billion in assets has $10 billion in cash. The $100 billion company has more cash, but it is also a much bigger company. A vertical analysis would show that each company has 10% of its assets in cash ($1/$10 = $10/$100 = 10%). By dividing by total assets, the analysis makes possible a meaningful comparison of two companies of vastly different sizes. Because vertical analysis removes the effect of size, an analysis prepared on a financial statement is appropriately called a common-size financial statement.

Balance Sheet Analysis   Exhibit 12-3 contains a vertical analysis of Best Buy's condensed 2008 balance sheet.

Exhibit 12-3 Vertical Analysis of Best Buy's 2008 Condensed Balance Sheet

$ in millions, except per share amounts	February 28, 2009		March 1, 2008	
Assets				
Current Assets				
Cash and cash equivalents	$ 498	3.2%	$ 1,438	11.8%
Receivables	1,868	11.8%	549	4.3%
Merchandise inventories	4,753	30.0%	4,708	36.9%
Other current assets	1,073	6.8%	647	5.1%
Total current assets	8,192	51.8%	7,342	57.6%
Property and Equipment, net	4,174	26.4%	3,306	25.9%
Goodwill	2,203	13.9%	1,088	8.5%
Other Assets	1,257	7.9%	1,022	8.0%
Total Assets	$15,826	100.0%	$12,758	100.0%
Liabilities and Shareholders' Equity				
Current Liabilities				
Accounts payable	$ 4,997	31.6%	$ 4,297	33.7%
Short-term debt	783	5.0%	156	1.2%
Other current liabilities	2,655	16.8%	2,316	18.2%
Total current liabilities	8,435	53.3%	6,769	53.1%
Long-Term Liabilities	2,748	5.0%	1,505	11.8%
Total liabilities	$11,183	70.7%	$ 8,274	64.9%
Shareholders' Equity				
Common stock, $.10 par value: Authorized 1 billion shares; Issued and outstanding—413,684,000 and 410,578,000 shares, respectively	$ 41	0.3%	$ 41	0.3%
Additional paid-in capital	205	1.3%	8	0.1%
Retained earnings	4,714	29.8%	3,933	30.8%
Accumulated other comprehensive income (loss)	(317)	−2.0%	502	3.9%
Total shareholders' equity	4,643	29.3%	4,484	35.2%
Total Liabilities and Shareholders' Equity	$15,826	100.0%	$12,758	100.0%

Vertical analysis An analysis technique that states each account balance on a financial statement as a percentage of a base amount on the statement.

The analysis shows large percentages of assets in both inventory and property and equipment. Such percentages are not surprising given that Best Buy is a retailer. Of some concern is the increased percentage associated with receivables (4.3% in 2007 versus 11.8% in 2008) and the decreased percentage associated with cash (11.3% in 2007 versus 3.2% in 2008). The ability of Best Buy to collect cash from its receivables should be monitored.

The analysis of liabilities and equity shows that about half (53.3%) of the company's assets are generated by current liabilities, with the majority of those liabilities in accounts payable. In total, 70.7% of Best Buy's assets are generated by liabilities. This is a slight increase from 2007, when 64.9% of assets were generated by liabilities. In both years, about 30% of assets were generated through profitable operations that were retained in the business.

Overall, the vertical analysis shows a healthy balance sheet, with the possible exception of the growing receivables.

Income Statement Analysis   Exhibit 12-4 contains a vertical analysis of Best Buy's condensed 2008 income statement.

Everyone associated with a company—stockholders, creditors, employees, suppliers—wants the company to generate profits.

increases in operating expenses. Operating expenses were 20.0% of revenue in 2008 and 18.5% in 2007. It cost Best Buy more to operate its business in 2008. Overall, Best Buy was profitable during 2008, but it was less profitable than in 2007 (3.5% in 2007 versus 2.2% in 2008).

Now that horizontal and vertical analyses have been conducted on both the income statement and the balance sheet, attention can be shifted to ratio analyses, starting with an analysis of Best Buy's profitability.

LO3 **Profitability Analysis**

One of the most important aspects of any financial analysis is profitability. Everyone associated with a company—stockholders, creditors,

Exhibit 12-4 Vertical Analysis of Best Buy's 2008 Condensed Income Statement

$ in millions, except per share amounts For the Fiscal Years Ended	February 28, 2009		March 1, 2008	
Revenue	$45,015	100.0%	$40,023	100.0%
Cost of goods sold	34,017	75.6%	30,477	76.2%
Gross profit	10,998	24.4%	9,546	23.9%
Selling, general and administrative expenses	8,984	20.0%	7,385	18.5%
Restructuring charges and impairment	144	0.3%	—	0.0%
Operating income	1,870	4.2%	2,161	5.4%
Other income (expense)				
Investment income and other	35	0.1%	129	0.3%
Investment impairment	(111)	−0.3%		0.0%
Interest expense	(94)	−0.2%	(62)	−0.2%
Earnings from continuing operations before income tax expense	1,700	3.8%	2,228	5.6%
Income tax expense	674	1.5%	815	2.0%
Other expenses	23	0.1%	6	0.0%
Net earnings	$ 1,003	2.2%	$ 1,407	3.5%

The analysis shows that cost of goods sold is approximately 75.6% of sales revenue, leaving a 2008 gross profit of 24.4%, or about a quarter for each dollar of sales. This is a slight improvement over 2007, when the company generated gross profit of 23.9%. However, the improvement in gross profit is offset by

employees, suppliers—wants the company to generate profits. To determine a company's profitability, one can look at net income, but that tells only a portion of the story. It does not reveal how efficiently and effectively those profits were generated. To find out, one must compare net income to other company values such as sales, assets, equity, outstanding shares, and market prices.

The following ratios are commonly used to analyze profitability. Note that each ratio compares net income to some other financial aspect of the company. Because each ratio reveals something different about a company's income, they are best used in tandem so that a broad understanding of a company's profitability can be obtained.

Profitability Ratio	Relationship
Profit Margin	Income to Sales
Return on Equity	Income to Stockholders' Equity
Return on Assets	Income to Total Assets
Earnings per Share	Income to Shares Outstanding
Price to Earnings	Income to Stock Price

In the following sections, the text will explain each ratio and show the calculation for Best Buy's most recent year. Unless otherwise noted, data for each calculation is obtained from Exhibits 12-1 or 12-2. Immediately after the calculation, Best Buy's ratios for the current and prior two years and hhgregg's current and prior year ratios will be provided for comparison purposes. After all ratios are presented, a summary of what was learned from the ratios about Best Buy's profitability will be provided.

Profit Margin

The **profit margin ratio** compares net income to net sales and measures the ability of a company to generate profits from sales. A higher ratio indicates a greater ability to generate profits from sales.

$$\text{Profit Margin} = \frac{\text{Net Income}}{\text{Net Sales}}$$

$$\frac{\$1,003}{\$45,015} = 2.2\%$$

	2008	2007	2006
Best Buy	2.2%	3.5%	3.8%
hhgregg	2.6%	1.7%	

Best Buy's 2008 profit margin is 2.2%, meaning that the company generated a little over two cents of profit for every dollar of sales in 2008. While profitable in 2008, Best Buy was not as profitable as in prior years. It was also not as profitable as hhgregg in 2008.

Return on Equity

The **return on equity ratio** compares net income to the average balance in stockholders' equity during the year. The ratio represents how effectively a company uses the equity provided by stockholders during the year to generate additional equity for its owners. Stockholders naturally want this ratio to be as high as possible.

$$\text{Return on Equity} = \frac{\text{Net Income}}{\text{Average Stockholders' Equity}}$$

where average equity is as follows:

$$\frac{\text{Beginning equity} + \text{Ending equity}}{2}$$

$$\frac{\$1,003}{(\$4,643 + \$4,484)/2} = 22.0\%$$

	2008	2007	2006
Best Buy	22.0%	26.3%	24.0%
hhgregg	35.3%	43.7%	

The 2008 ratio of 22% shows that Best Buy generated close to one quarter in profits for every dollar of resources provided by stockholders. This is similar to, but slightly lower than, the ratios in the prior two years. Such an annual return will result in a doubling of equity in approximately four years. Notice also that hhgregg's return on equity greatly exceeds Best Buy's.

Return on Assets

The **return on assets ratio** compares net income to average total assets during the year. It represents a company's ability to generate profits from its entire resource base, not just those resources provided by owners. Like the return on equity, investors would like the ratio as high as possible.

Profit margin ratio Compares net income to net sales and measures the ability to generate profits from sales.

Return on equity ratio Compares net income to average stockholders' equity and measures the ability to generate profits from equity.

Return on assets ratio Compares net income to average total assets and measures the ability to generate profits from assets.

The price to earnings ratio provides an indication of current investor perceptions of the company.

$$\text{Return on Assets} = \frac{\text{Net Income}}{\text{Average Total Assets}}$$

where average assets is as follows:

$$\frac{\text{Beginning total assets} + \text{Ending total assets}}{2}$$

$$\frac{\$1,003}{(\$15,826 + \$12,758)/2} = 7.0\%$$

	2008	2007	2006
Best Buy	7.0%	11.2%	11.1%
hhgregg	12.8%	10.4%	

The 2008 ratio of 7.0% shows that Best Buy generated about seven cents in profits for every dollar of assets it possessed during the year. This was lower than both 2007 and 2006 and lower than hhgregg's ratio. Best Buy was not as effective in the current year at using its existing resources to generate profits.

Earnings per Share

Earnings per share compares a company's net income to the average number of shares of common stock outstanding during the year. The ratio represents the return on each share of stock owned by an investor. Although companies normally disclose earnings per share on their income statements, the calculation will be demonstrated nonetheless.

Earnings per share Compares net income to common stock outstanding and represents profits generated per share of stock.

Price to earnings ratio Compares net income to a company's stock price and provides an indication of investor perceptions of the company.

$$\text{Earnings per Share} = \frac{\text{Net Income}}{\text{Average Number of Common Shares Outstanding}}$$

where average outstanding shares is as follows:

$$\frac{\text{Beginning outstanding shares} + \text{Ending outstanding shares}}{2}$$

The beginning and ending outstanding shares are collected from the textual information on the balance sheet and are rounded to millions as follows: 413,684,000 = 413.7 million and 410,578,000 = 410.6 million.

$$\frac{\$1,003}{(413.7 + 410.6)/2} = \$2.43$$

	2008	2007	2006
Best Buy	$2.43	$3.20	$2.86
hhgregg	$1.12	$0.70	

The $2.43 value shows that Best Buy earned $2.43 in profits for every share of common stock outstanding during the year. While this is lower than the prior two years, it is more than double hhgregg's earnings per share of $1.12.

Price to Earnings Ratio

The **price to earnings ratio** compares net income to the current market price of the company's common stock. Because a company's stock price represents the value of the company per share of stock, the ratio uses earnings per share rather than net income. It is also the first ratio in which income is in the denominator rather than the numerator. That is why the ratio is called price to earnings rather than earnings to price.

$$\text{Price to Earnings Ratio} = \frac{\text{Current Stock Price per Share}}{\text{Earnings per Share}}$$

Because the price to earnings ratio uses stock prices, it provides an indication of current investor perceptions of the company. For example, a price to earnings ratio of 10 means that investors are willing to pay ten times current earnings per share to buy one share of stock. A ratio of 15 means that investors will pay fifteen times current earnings. A higher price to earnings ratio generally indicates that investors are more optimistic about the future prospects of a company. A lower ratio generally indicates that investors are less optimistic about the company's future.

The following calculation of Best Buy's 2008 price to earnings ratio uses the $28.82 stock price at the close of business on February 28, 2009, the end of the company's fiscal year.

$$\frac{\$28.82}{\$2.43} = 11.9$$

	2008	2007	2006
Best Buy	11.9	13.4	16.2
hhgregg	12.5	16.3	

Best Buy's ratio of 11.9 shows that a share of Best Buy's stock was selling for almost 12 times earnings per share at the close of its most recent fiscal year. This is a decrease from the prior two years. Thus, while investors are still willing to pay a premium for current earnings, they are willing to pay less of a premium than before. This indicates a slight decrease in perceptions about the future prospects of the company.

A company must maintain the ability to pay its liabilities as they come due.

Summary of Profitability

Based on the five ratios examined, it is clear that Best Buy is profitable. However, its profitability has declined over time and is the lowest in the current year. This is a trend to watch closely, especially in an industry that depends on consumer spending.

LO4 Liquidity Analysis

A major concern in any financial analysis is an assessment of a company's liquidity. **Liquidity** refers to the ability of a company to satisfy its short-term obligations. A company must maintain the ability to pay its liabilities as they come due. Failing to do so can result in additional expenses and, ultimately, bankruptcy. As a result, everyone associated with a company—stockholders, creditors, employees, suppliers—wants to see adequate liquidity.

The following ratios are commonly used to assess a company's liquidity. While each ratio reveals information

> **Liquidity** The ability of a company to satisfy its short-term obligations.

HOME DEPOT ANALYSIS

Using Home Depot's information in Appendix C, calculate Home Depot's profitability ratios and make a general assessment about the company's profitability. Home Depot's stock price on February 2, 2009, was $21.57.

Profit Margin: Net Income/Sales
= $2,260 ÷ $71,288 = 3.17%

Return on Equity: Net Income/Average Stockholders' Equity = $2,260 ÷ [($17,777 + $17,714) ÷ 2] = 12.74%

Return on Assets: Net Income/Average Total Assets = $2,260 ÷ [($41,164 + $44,324) ÷ 2] = 5.29%

Earnings per Share: Net Income/Average Outstanding Shares = $2,260 ÷ [(1,707 + 1,698) ÷ 2] = $1.33

Price to Earnings Ratio: Stock Price/Earnings per Share = $21.57 ÷ $1.34 = 16.1

Home Depot shows many positive signs of profitability. It earns over three cents for every dollar of sales, almost thirteen cents for every dollar provided by stockholders, and $1.33 for every outstanding share of common stock. With a 16.1 price to earnings ratio, stockholders appear optimistic about Home Depot's future prospects.

on its own, using the ratios in tandem provides a much richer understanding of liquidity. Note that each ratio focuses on some aspect of either current liabilities or current assets.

Liquidity Ratios	Relationship
Current Ratio	Current Assets to Current Liabilities
Quick Ratio	Cash-like Assets to Current Liabilities
Receivables Turnover Ratio	Sales to Accounts Receivable
Inventory Turnover Ratio	Cost of Goods Sold to Inventory

As in the previous section on profitability, the following sections will explain and calculate each ratio for Best Buy using data from Exhibits 12-1 and 12-2. A comparison of Best Buy's and hhgregg's ratios will follow each calculation. After all ratios are presented, a summary of what was learned about Best Buy's liquidity will be provided.

Current Ratio

The **current ratio** is one of the most frequently used ratios in financial analysis. It compares current assets to current liabilities. It therefore compares assets that should be turned into cash within one year to liabilities that should be paid within one year. A higher ratio indicates more assets available to satisfy current obligations and therefore greater liquidity.

$$Current\ Ratio = \frac{Current\ Assets}{Current\ Liabilities}$$

$$\frac{\$8,192}{\$8,435} = 0.97$$

	2008	2007	2006
Best Buy	0.97	1.08	1.44
hhgregg	1.68	1.21	

Best Buy's ratio of 0.97 shows that it had 97 cents in current assets for every dollar of current liabilities. This

Current ratio Compares current assets to current liabilities and measures the ability to pay current obligations.

Quick ratio Compares cash and near-cash assets to current liabilities and measures the ability to pay current liabilities immediately.

Receivables turnover ratio Compares credit sales to average accounts receivable and measures the ability to make and collect sales.

is lower than both prior years, meaning that Best Buy is becoming less liquid over time. In contrast, hhgregg is becoming more liquid over time.

While the trend in Best Buy's liquidity should be monitored, a ratio near one is not a cause for alarm. In fact, many investors would be critical of maintaining a current ratio that is too high. They would rather the company keep only an adequate amount of assets in current assets and invest the rest in more productive and higher-yielding assets such as property, equipment, or investments.

Quick Ratio

While the current ratio is an excellent measure of liquidity, it does have some limitations. In particular, current assets often include inventory that must be sold before cash can be generated to pay off current liabilities. Because of this, several additional ratios are used to provide more detail regarding a company's liquidity. One is the quick ratio.

The **quick ratio** compares a company's cash and near-cash assets, called *quick assets,* to its current liabilities. Quick assets include cash, short-term investments, and accounts receivable. Sometimes called the *acid-test ratio,* the quick ratio measures the degree to which a company could pay off its current liabilities immediately. Like the current ratio, a higher quick ratio indicates greater liquidity.

$$Quick\ Ratio = \frac{Cash + Short\text{-}term\ Investments + Accounts\ Receivable}{Current\ Liabilities}$$

$$\frac{\$498 + \$11 + \$1,868}{\$8,435} = 0.28$$

	2008	2007	2006
Best Buy	0.28	0.30	0.69
hhgregg	0.32	0.18	

Best Buy's ratio of 0.28 shows that at the end of its fiscal year, the company had 28 cents in cash and near-cash assets for every dollar of current liabilities. This indicates that Best Buy could pay 28% of its current liabilities if they came due immediately. Although current liabilities will not likely come due immediately, the ratio is low compared to the ratio from 2006. This is an issue to continue to monitor.

Receivables Turnover Ratio

The **receivables turnover ratio** compares a company's credit sales during a period to its average accounts receivable balance during that period. It measures a company's ability to make and collect sales. A higher turnover ratio means that the company is better able to generate and collect sales. Therefore, a higher ratio generally leads to better liquidity. Because credit sales are not usually reported by companies, the ratio uses net sales as a substitute.

$$\text{Receivables Turnover Ratio} = \frac{\text{Net Sales}}{\text{Average Accounts Receivables}}$$

where average accounts receivable is as follows:

$$\frac{\text{Beginning accounts receivable} + \text{Ending accounts receivable}}{2}$$

$$\frac{\$45,015}{(\$1,868 + \$549)/2} = 37.2$$

	2008	2007	2006
Best Buy	37.2	73.0	72.1
hhgregg	76.0	56.8	

Best Buy's ratio of 37.2 is much lower than its previous two ratios and hhgregg's current-year ratio. This is cause for some concern. Why has Best Buy's ability to collect its receivables decreased so much in one year? One clue is the substantial increase in receivables—from $549 million in 2007 to $1,868 million. The horizontal analysis in Exhibit 12-1 shows this to be a 240.3% increase. The vertical analysis in Exhibit 12-2 shows that receivables as a percentage of assets jumped from 4.3% to 11.8%. Such a change in receivables should be investigated further to determine whether there is a significant problem with collections.

Inventory Turnover Ratio

The **inventory turnover ratio** compares a company's cost of goods sold during a period to its average inventory balance during that period. It reveals how many times a company is able to sell its inventory balance in a period. In general, companies want this ratio to be higher because it indicates that the company sold more inventory while maintaining less inventory on hand. This means that the company generated more sales revenue while reducing the costs of stocking inventory on the shelves.

$$\text{Inventory Turnover Ratio} = \frac{\text{Cost of Goods Sold}}{\text{Average Inventory}}$$

where average inventory is as follows:

$$\frac{\text{Beginning inventory} + \text{Ending inventory}}{2}$$

$$\frac{\$34,017}{(\$4,753 + \$4,708)/2} = 7.19$$

	2008	2007	2006
Best Buy	7.19	6.98	7.38
hhgregg	6.99	7.03	

A 7.19 ratio shows that during 2008 Best Buy sold more than seven dollars of inventory for every dollar of inventory it had on its shelves. Notice that this is similar to prior years and is similar to hhgregg. It appears that Best Buy's ability to sell inventory is stable.

Inventory turnover ratio Compares cost of goods sold to average inventory and measures the ability to sell inventory.

HOME DEPOT ANALYSIS

Using Home Depot's information in Appendix C, calculate Home Depot's liquidity ratios and make a general assessment about the company's liquidity.

Current Ratio: Current Assets/Current Liabilities
= $13,362 ÷ $11,153 = 1.20

Quick Ratio: (Cash + Short-term Investments + Accounts Receivable)/Current Liabilities
= ($519 + $6 + $972) ÷ $11,153 = 0.13

Receivables Turnover: Net Sales/Average Accounts Receivable
= $71,288 ÷ [($972 + $1,259) ÷ 2] = 63.9

Inventory Turnover: Cost of Goods Sold/Average Inventory = $47,298 ÷ [($10,673 + $11,731) ÷ 2] = 4.22

While Home Depot carries more in current assets than current liabilities, the quick ratio shows that the company does not maintain very high levels of quick assets given current liabilities. However, the inventory turnover ratio indicates that the company is successful in selling its inventory. Therefore, Home Depot appears to have adequate liquidity.

If a company cannot satisfy its obligations and becomes insolvent, it can fall into bankruptcy, which can result in significant losses to investors and creditors.

Summary of Liquidity Analysis

Based on the four ratios examined, it appears that Best Buy has sufficient liquidity. The majority of its current assets are tied up in inventory, but it appears that the company is selling through its inventory adequately. Of potential concern is the increase in accounts receivable. While not yet a threat to liquidity, it is a trend to watch closely.

LO5 Solvency Analysis

A third component of any financial analysis is an examination of solvency. **Solvency** refers to a company's ability to satisfy its long-term obligations. If a company cannot satisfy its obligations and becomes *insolvent*, it can fall into bankruptcy, which can result in significant losses to investors and creditors. Therefore, both investors and creditors are interested in assessing solvency.

A company's solvency is related to its use of financial leverage. **Financial leverage** refers to the degree to which a company obtains capital through debt rather than equity in an attempt to increase returns to stockholders. Leverage is beneficial to stockholders when the return on borrowed funds exceeds the cost of borrowing those funds. In that case, leverage is positive. It is harmful, or negative, when the cost of borrowing the funds exceeds the return on those borrowed funds. As a company uses more financial leverage, it creates an opportunity for greater returns to stockholders, but it also creates greater solvency risk.

Although it is impossible to know whether a company will or will not be able to pay future obligations and remain solvent, the following three ratios can provide some indication of a company's general solvency.

> **Financial leverage** The degree to which a company obtains capital through debt rather than equity in an attempt to increase returns to stockholders.
>
> **Debt to assets ratio** Compares total liabilities to total assets and measures the percentage of assets provided by creditors.

Solvency Ratios	Relationship
Debt to Assets	Total Liabilities to Total Assets
Debt to Equity	Total Liabilities to Total Equity
Times Interest Earned	Net Income to Interest Expense

As in the previous sections, the following sections will explain and calculate each ratio for Best Buy using data from Exhibits 12-1 and 12-2. A comparison of Best Buy's and hhgregg's ratios will follow each calculation. After all ratios are presented, a summary of what was learned about Best Buy's solvency will be provided.

Debt to Assets Ratio

The **debt to assets ratio** compares a company's total liabilities to its total assets and yields the percentage of assets provided by creditors. As such, the ratio provides a measure of a company's capital structure. Capital structure refers to the manner in which a company has financed its assets—either through debt or equity—and is also an indication of how much financial leverage a company is using. Since debt and any related interest must be repaid, companies with a higher percentage of assets provided by creditors have a riskier capital structure. In other words, they are using more financial leverage, and they therefore have a greater risk of insolvency.

$$\text{Debt to Assets Ratio} = \frac{\text{Total Liabilities}}{\text{Total Assets}}$$

$$\frac{\$11,183}{\$15,826} = 0.71$$

	2008	2007	2006
Best Buy	0.71	0.65	0.54
hhgregg	0.64	0.75	

Best Buy's ratio of 0.71 shows that a little over 70 cents of every dollar of assets are generated through liabilities. This ratio is higher than in both prior years, indicating an increasingly risky capital structure and greater use of financial leverage. The ratio is similar to hhgregg's 0.64 ratio, but notice that hhgregg is moving in the exact opposite direction. Its ratio is decreasing, showing that it is taking on a less risky capital structure over time.

Debt to Equity Ratio

The **debt to equity ratio** compares a company's total liabilities to its total equity. Like the debt to assets ratio, this ratio provides a measure of a company's capital structure and financial leverage by directly comparing the two aspects of capital structure—liabilities and equity. Higher debt to equity ratios indicate a riskier capital structure and therefore greater risk of insolvency. Companies with higher debt to equity ratios are also said to be highly leveraged.

$$\text{Debt to Equity Ratio} = \frac{\text{Total Liabilities}}{\text{Total Equity}}$$

$$\frac{\$11,183}{\$4,643} = 2.41$$

	2008	2007	2006
Best Buy	2.41	1.85	1.19
hhgregg	1.80	3.04	

Best Buy's ratio of 2.41 shows that it had almost two and a half dollars of liabilities for every dollar of equity at the end of the most recent year. This is higher than in the previous two years, indicating that its capital structure is becoming more dependent on liabilities and therefore more risky. In contrast, hhgregg's ratio is decreasing, indicating a lower reliance on liabilities and therefore lower risk. As you can see, the interpretation of the debt to equity ratio is the same as the debt to assets ratio.

Times Interest Earned

In addition to examining a company's capital structure, it is wise to assess whether a company can pay the interest on its debt. To answer this question, many use the times interest earned ratio.

The **times interest earned ratio** compares a company's net income to its interest expense. It shows how well a company can pay interest out of current-year earnings. As such, it helps creditors and investors determine whether a company can service its current debt by making its required interest payments.

$$\text{Times Interest Earned Ratio} = \frac{\text{Net Income} + \text{Interest Expense} + \text{Income Tax Expense}}{\text{Interest Expense}}$$

> **Debt to equity ratio** Compares total liabilities to total equity and measures a company's capital structure and financial leverage.
>
> **Times interest earned ratio** Compares net income to interest expense and measures the ability to pay interest out of current earnings.

HOME DEPOT ANALYSIS

Using Home Depot's information in Appendix C, calculate Home Depot's solvency ratios and make a general assessment about the company's solvency.

Debt to Assets Ratio: Total Liabilities/Total Assets = $23,387 ÷ $41,164 = 0.57

Debt to Equity Ratio: Total Liabilities/Total Equity = $23,387 ÷ $17,777 = 1.32

Times Interest Earned: Net Income + Interest Expense + Income Tax Expense/Interest Expense = ($2,260 + $624 + $1,278) ÷ $624 = 6.67

According to these ratios, Home Depot finances its assets with more liabilities than equity. However, the times interest earned ratio shows that the company can comfortably pay interest expense with current year earnings. Thus, Home Depot's solvency appears secure.

Note that the ratio adjusts net income by adding back interest expense and income tax expense. These are added back to "gross up" income to the amount of earnings that were available to make interest payments. Once this adjustment is made, the ratio yields the number of times that current interest payments could be made out of current earnings. A higher ratio indicates a greater ability to make payments, and therefore less risk of insolvency.

$$\frac{\$1,003 + \$94 + \$674}{\$94} = 18.8$$

	2009	2008	2007
Best Buy	18.8	36.8	69.7
hhgregg	9.8	6.3	

Best Buy's ratio of 18.8 indicates that the company earned many times more than its interest expense. Specifically, for every dollar of interest expense, the company earned almost nineteen dollars in profits. Even though the ratio is lower in the current year than prior years, it is higher than hhgregg's ratio and represents a comfortable coverage of interest.

Summary of Solvency

Based on the three ratios examined, it appears that Best Buy's capital structure is trending toward more debt. Thus, its solvency risk has increased, and it is a trend to watch. However, it appears that Best Buy can currently handle the increased risk.

LO6 DuPont Analysis

All investors want to maximize the returns on their investments in a company. An investor's return is measured by the return on equity. To better understanding how the return was generated, investors often conduct a DuPont analysis.

A **DuPont analysis** provides insight into how a company's return on equity was generated by decomposing the return into three components: operating efficiency, asset effectiveness, and capital structure. The actual calculations of the analysis are as follows.

DuPont analysis Decomposes a company's return on equity into measures of operating efficiency, asset effectiveness, and capital structure.

DuPont Analysis

Operating Efficiency		Asset Effectiveness		Capital Structure		Return on Equity
$\dfrac{\text{Net Income}}{\text{Sales}}$	$\times$	$\dfrac{\text{Sales}}{\text{Assets}}$	$\times$	$\dfrac{\text{Assets}}{\text{Equity}}$	$=$	$\dfrac{\text{Net Income}}{\text{Equity}}$

The first component is a company's operating efficiency. It is calculated as net income divided by sales, which is also known as the profit margin ratio. This component reveals a company's ability to turn sales into profits. The higher the ratio, the more efficient a company is in turning sales into profits.

The second component is a company's effectiveness at using its assets. It is calculated as sales divided by assets. This ratio is commonly known as the asset turnover ratio. It measures the ability of a company to generate sales from its asset base. The higher the ratio, the more effective a company is in generating sales given its assets.

The third component is a company's capital structure. For this analysis, it is calculated as assets divided by equity. This ratio is similar to the debt to assets and debt to equity ratios in that it measures how a company has generated its assets. The higher the ratio, the more a company is financing its assets with debt rather than equity. So, a higher ratio means more financial leverage and a riskier capital structure. Sometimes, this ratio is called the leverage multiplier.

Best Buy's most recent DuPont analysis is shown as follows. Also shown are the results of the same analysis for the prior year. Note that the return on equity numbers are slightly different than those calculated previously in the text because a DuPont analysis does not use average equity in the calculation of return on equity.

**Best Buy
DuPont Analysis
2008**

Net Income Sales		Sales Assets		Assets Equity		Net Income Equity
$\dfrac{\$1,003}{\$45,015}$	$\times$	$\dfrac{\$45,015}{\$15,826}$	$\times$	$\dfrac{\$15,826}{\$4,643}$	$=$	$\dfrac{\$1,003}{\$4,643}$
0.022	$\times$	2.84	$\times$	3.41	$=$	0.216

2007

0.035	$\times$	3.14	$\times$	2.85	$=$	0.314

The analysis shows clearly why Best Buy's return to its owners decreased from 2007 to 2008. Despite having a larger leverage multiplier in 2008 (3.41 versus 2.85), Best Buy generated less sales from its asset base (2.84 versus 3.14) and less profits from those sales (0.022 versus 0.035). Quite simply, profits from sales were down in 2008, resulting in a lower return on equity.

One of the main benefits of a DuPont analysis is the ability to ask what-if questions. For example, what if Best Buy was able to squeeze out another $.02 of profit on each dollar of sales? How would that affect the return to owners? The analysis shows that the 2008 return would increase to 0.407 (0.042 × 2.84 × 3.41).

Alternatively, what if Best Buy took a riskier leverage position by increasing its assets to equity ratio from 3.41

to 4.0? Is that in the best interests of owners? Assuming nothing else changes, the answer is yes. The return on equity would rise to 0.250 (0.022 × 2.84 × 4.00).

Finally, what if the market for electronics took a significant downturn and Best Buy was only able to generate sales of 1.5 times assets on hand? Would that significantly affect the return to investors? The analysis shows that it would. The return would fall almost in half to 0.113 (0.022 × 1.50 × 3.41).

Like all ratio analyses, the DuPont analysis is a helpful tool for providing feedback on past performance and expectations for future performance. As such, it is relevant information that can affect the decision making of managers, investors, and creditors.

HOME DEPOT ANALYSIS

Using Home Depot's information in Appendix C, conduct a DuPont analysis. What would happen to Home Depot's return on equity if it could generate one additional cent of profit from sales?

If Home Depot could increase its profit margin by one penny, it would increase the return to its owners from 12.7% to 16.9% (0.042 × 1.73 × 2.32). A small change in profits can create large changes in stockholder returns.

Net Income / Sales	×	Sales / Assets	×	Assets / Equity	=	Net Income / Equity
$2,260 / $71,288	×	$71,288 / $41,164	×	$41,164 / $17,777	=	$2,260 / $17,777
0.032	×	1.73	×	2.32	=	0.127

STUDY TOOLS
CHAPTER 12

CHAPTER REVIEW CARD
- ❏ Learning Objective and Key Concept Reviews
- ❏ Key Definitions and Formulas

ONLINE (Located at 4ltrpress.cengage.com/acct)
- ❏ Flash Cards and Crossword Puzzles
- ❏ Conceptual and Computational Interactive Quizzes
- ❏ E-Lectures
- ❏ Static, Algorithmic, and Additional Homework Activities (as directed by your instructor)

1. Horizontal Analysis   LO2

The following asset information is available for BSI Inc.

	2009	2008
Cash	$ 35,000	$ 60,000
Accounts receivable	60,000	55,000
Inventory	125,000	175,000
Total current assets	$220,000	$290,000
Property and equipment	175,000	150,000
Total assets	$395,000	$440,000

Required
Calculate a horizontal analysis of BSI's assets.

2. Horizontal Analysis   LO2

The income statements of Crisp Corp. for the past two years are as follows:

Income Statements
For the Years Ending December 31

	2009	2008
Revenues	$300,000	$250,000
Cost of goods sold	125,000	100,000
Gross profit	$175,000	$150,000
Operating expenses	75,000	50,000
Income before interest and taxes	$100,000	$100,000
Interest expense	35,000	15,000
Income before taxes	$ 65,000	$ 85,000
Income tax expense	25,000	30,000
Net income	$ 40,000	$ 55,000

Required
Calculate and interpret a horizontal analysis of Crisp's income statements.

3. Vertical Analysis   LO2

The following asset information is available for LOC Inc.

	2009	2008
Cash	$ 15,000	$ 10,000
Accounts receivable	30,000	25,000
Inventory	75,000	75,000
Total current assets	120,000	110,000
Property and equipment	205,000	210,000
Total assets	$325,000	$320,000

Required
Calculate a vertical analysis of assets for both years.

4. Vertical Analysis   LO2

The income statements of High Noon Corp. for the past two years are as follows:

Income Statements
For the Years Ending December 31

	2009	2008
Revenues	$725,000	$700,000
Cost of goods sold	345,000	385,000
Gross profit	$380,000	$315,000
Operating expenses	175,000	180,000
Income before interest and taxes	$205,000	$135,000
Interest expense	45,000	40,000
Income before taxes	$160,000	$ 95,000
Income tax expense	55,000	30,000
Net income	$105,000	$ 65,000

Required
Calculate and interpret a vertical analysis of High Noon's income statements.

5. Identify Ratios   LO3, 4, 5

Identify each of the following ratios as a profitability, liquidity, or solvency ratio.

_____ Return on equity
_____ Debt to assets ratio
_____ Times interest earned
_____ Quick ratio
_____ Inventory turnover ratio
_____ Price to earnings ratio
_____ Profit margin
_____ Current ratio
_____ Debt to equity ratio

6. Interpret Ratios   LO3, 4, 5

The following information is available for Warmouth Enterprises.

	2009	2008
Profit margin	8.7%	8.3%
Return on assets	10.2%	10.4%
Price to earnings ratio	13.5	12.0
Quick ratio	0.8	0.9
Inventory turnover ratio	5.5	7.2
Receivable turnover ratio	11.3	15.5
Times interest earned	7.2	6.4

Required
For each ratio, indicate whether the change in the ratio is favorable or unfavorable and why.

7. Define Ratios   LO3, 4, 5

Identify the appropriate ratio for each of the following descriptions.
a. Shows the return to each share of stock owned by an investor
b. Measures the difference between quick assets and current liabilities
c. Measures the ability of a company to generate profits from sales
d. Provides a measure of a company's capital structure

e. Shows a company's ability to generate profits from its entire resource base
f. Gives information as to how a company manages its inventory
g. Measures a company's capital structure using liabilities and equity
h. Shows how effectively a company uses its current equity to generate additional equity
i. Gives a less strict measure of a company's ability to meet its short-term obligations
j. Shows how well a company can pay interest on debt out of current-year earnings
k. Measures a company's ability to make and collect sales
l. Provides an indication of current investor perceptions of the company

8. Profitability Ratios   LO3

The following financial information about Cloudburst Co. is available:

Sales	$600,000
Net income	130,000
Average total assets	900,000
Average stockholders' equity	440,000

The following additional information is available:
- 500,000 shares of common stock were outstanding during the year.
- The stock was recently trading for $5.00 per share.

Required:
Compute the following ratios: profit margin, return on equity, return on assets, earnings per share, and price to earnings.

9. Profitability Ratios   LO3

The following financial information about NGC Company is available:

Net income	$ 150,000
Common shares outstanding, January 1	400,000
Common shares outstanding, December 31	500,000
Market price at December 31	$ 10.00
Sales	$ 945,000
Total assets, January 1	$ 800,000
Total assets, December 31	$1,000,000
Stockholders' equity, January 1	$ 450,000
Stockholders' equity, December 31	$ 475,000

Required
Compute and interpret the following ratios: profit margin, return on equity, return on assets, earnings per share, and price to earnings.

10. Liquidity Ratios   LO4

The following information was taken from the financial statements of Connor Cookers and Olson Ovens:

(in millions)	2009	2008
Total current assets		
Connor Cookers	$ 46,448	$249,664
Olson Ovens	155,117	153,188
Cash		
Connor Cookers	24,311	48,936
Olson Ovens	28,894	28,406
Accounts receivable		
Connor Cookers	8,216	186,766
Olson Ovens	114,645	114,511
Inventory		
Connor Cookers	13,921	13,962
Olson Ovens	11,578	10,271
Current liabilities		
Connor Cookers	69,036	74,457
Olson Ovens	80,220	85,037
Revenues (sales)		
Connor Cookers	207,349	194,655
Olson Ovens	160,123	176,896
Cost of goods sold		
Connor Cookers	80,153	79,411
Olson Ovens	76,740	71,561

Required
For each company, compute the following 2009 ratios: receivable turnover ratio, inventory turnover ratio, current ratio, and quick ratio. Based in your calculations, discuss the liquidity of each company.

11. Solvency Ratios   LO5

The following information was taken from the financial statements of TKO Company:

	2009	2008
Total assets	$200,000	$125,000
Total liabilities	75,000	75,000
Total equity	125,000	50,000
Net income before interest and taxes	35,000	30,000
Interest expense	7,000	7,500

Required
Compute the debt to assets ratio, the debt to equity ratio, and times interest earned for both years.

12. Solvency Ratios   LO5

The following financial information regarding Foshee Flapjacks is available:

	2009
Total assets	$530,000
Total liabilities	140,000
Total stockholders' equity	390,000

2009 Income Statement

Revenue	$ 250,000
Cost of goods sold	125,000
Gross profit	$ 125,000
Operating expenses	40,000
Income before interest and taxes	85,000
Interest expense	10,000
Income before taxes	$ 75,000
Income tax expense	25,000
Net income	$ 50,000

Required

Compute the following ratios: debt to assets, debt to equity, and times interest earned. Discuss the solvency of Foshee Flapjacks. Does the company rely more on equity or debt to finance its operations?

13. DuPont Analysis LO6

The following financial information about Carbon Company is available:

	2009
Total average assets	$200,000
Total average equity	125,000
Sales	35,000
Net income	7,000

Required

Prepare a DuPont analysis for Carbon Company.

14. DuPont Analysis LO6

The following financial information about Cole's Colas, Inc., is available:

	2009
Total average assets	$350,000
Total average equity	190,000
Sales	55,000
Net income	9,000

Required

Prepare a DuPont analysis for Cole's Colas and interpret each component of the analysis.

PROBLEMS

15. Analyzing Financial Statements LO2, 3, 4, 5

The following financial information is available for Last Chance Repossessions Company as of December 31, 2009.

Comparative Balance Sheet

	2009	2008
Cash	$ 15,000	$ 10,000
Accounts receivable	30,000	25,000
Inventory	75,000	75,000
Prepaid insurance	10,000	15,000
Total current assets	$130,000	$125,000
Property and equipment	$500,000	$400,000
Accumulated depreciation	100,000	85,000
Total property and equipment	$400,000	$315,000
Total assets	$530,000	$440,000
Accounts payable	$ 40,000	$ 50,000
Other current liabilities	25,000	40,000
Total current liabilities	$ 65,000	$ 90,000
Bonds payable	$ 75,000	$150,000
Total liabilities	$140,000	$240,000
Common stock	$290,000	$150,000
Retained earnings	100,000	50,000
Total stockholders' equity	$390,000	$200,000
Total liabilities and stockholders' equity	$530 000	$440,000

2009 Income Statement

Revenue	$400,000
Cost of goods sold	210,000
Gross profit	$190,000
Operating expenses	55,000
Income before interest and taxes	$135,000
Interest expense	15,000
Income before taxes	$120,000
Income tax expense	50,000
Net income	$ 70,000

Required

Calculate all profitability, liquidity, and solvency ratios (except earnings per share, price to earnings, and debt to equity) and comment on Last Chance's overall profitability, liquidity, and solvency.

16. Analyzing Financial Statements LO2, 3, 4, 5

Amanda's Anchors has applied for a loan from a local bank. The bank is basing its decision on the following information.

Ratio	Industry Average
Current ratio	1.5
Quick ratio	0.80
Receivable turnover ratio	18
Inventory turnover ratio	20
Debt to assets ratio	0.56
Times interest earned	6.52
Profit margin	10.25%
Return on assets	11.50%
Return on equity	20.30%

Amanda's Anchors
Income Statement
For the Year Ended December 31, 2009

Revenues	$600,000
Cost of goods sold	350,000
Gross profit	$250,000
Operating expenses	100,000
Income before interest and taxes	$150,000
Interest expense	25,000
Income before taxes	$125,000
Income tax expense	65,000
Net income	$ 60,000

Amanda's Anchors
Balance Sheet

	December 31, 2009	December 31, 2008
Cash	$ 75,000	$ 60,000
Accounts receivable	30,000	20,000
Inventory	30,000	20,000
Prepaid insurance	5,000	5,000
Total current assets	$140,000	$105,000
Property and equipment	$600,000	$550,000
Accumulated depreciation	140,000	110,000
Total property and equipment	$460,000	$440,000
Total assets	$600,000	$545,000
Accounts payable	$ 60,000	$ 60,000
Other current liabilities	40,000	45,000
Total current liabilities	$100,000	$105,000
Bonds payable	$150,000	$150,000
Total liabilities	$250,000	$255,000
Common stock	$250,000	$250,000
Retained earnings	100,000	40,000
Total stockholders' equity	$350,000	$290,000
Total liabilities and stockholders' equity	$600,000	$545,000

Required

For Amanda's Anchors, calculate the ratios for which the bank has an industry average. After comparing Amanda's ratios to the industry averages, should the bank approve the loan? Why or why not?

CASE

17. Research and Analysis   LO1, 3, 4, 5, 6

Access the 2008 annual report for Dick's Sporting Goods by clicking on the *About Dick's Sporting Goods*, *Investor Relations*, and *Annual Reports* links at www.dickssportinggoods.com.

Required

1. Examine the company's income statement and balance sheet and calculate all profitability, liquidity, and solvency ratios for 2008. To calculate the price to earnings ratio, use the high stock price for the fiscal quarter ended January 31, 2009 (found on page 76).
2. Based on your answers above, write a paragraph explaining your opinion of the financial health of Dick's Sporting Goods.
3. Calculate a DuPont analysis and explain what would happen to the company's return on equity if it was able to improve return on sales by one penny.

REMEMBER

- All exercises and problems from the text are available online in static and algorithmic versions.
- Additional multiple choice, exercises, problems, and cases are available online in CengageNOW or as an enrichment module that can be customized into this text.

Appendix A
Investments

common stock meet this criteria. The accounting for investments that are greater than 20% is left to more advanced textbooks.

To illustrate the accounting for investments, the following four events associated with investments will be considered.

- Purchasing the investment
- Recording periodic investment income
- Reporting the investment on the balance sheet
- Selling the investment

Recording the Purchase of Investments

Like other assets, investments are recorded at the cost of acquisition. To illustrate, suppose that on January 1, 2009, Abernathy Inc. purchases the following investments: a $100,000 20-year bond issued by the city of Decatur, 6,000 shares of Eagle Company common stock for $60,000, and 500 shares of C & L Inc. common stock for $10,000. Abernathy would record the purchases as follows.

Jan. 1 2009	Investment in Decatur Bonds	100,000	
	Investment in Eagle Company	60,000	
	Investment in C & L Inc.	10,000	
	Cash		170,000
	(To record purchase of investments)		

Assets	=	Liabilities	+	Equity
+100,000				
+60,000				
+10,000				
−170,000				

The entry increases each investment account for the cost of each security and reduces Abernathy's Cash account for the total cost of the purchase. Because Abernathy has simply exchanged cash for other assets, total assets remain unchanged.

Learning Objectives

After studying the material in this chapter, you should be able to:

LO1 Identify and understand the accounting for different types and classifications of investments.

Investments

Companies commonly invest in other entities by purchasing debt securities or equity securities issued by those entities.

A *debt security* is a financial instrument issued by an entity (such as a corporation, a municipality, or a university) to borrow cash from another entity. A common example of a debt security is a bond. When a company invests in a debt security, it is in effect loaning cash to the borrowing entity. In return, the investing company usually receives periodic interest payments from the borrowing entity. In most cases, the investing company can sell the debt security at any time or hold it until it matures.

An *equity security* is a financial instrument issued by an entity to raise capital in exchange for an ownership interest in the entity. A common example of an equity security is common stock issued by a corporation. When a company invests in an equity security, it is entitled to any dividends paid by the issuing entity. Most equity securities can be sold at almost any time.

This appendix focuses on how to account for investments in debt securities and investments in equity securities in which the investor does not have a significant influence over the target company. Usually, investments of less than 20% of the target company's

Recording Investment Income

Investment income from debt or equity securities is recorded when earned. Because debt securities pay interest and equity securities distribute dividends, periodic investment income will be recorded as either interest revenue or dividend revenue. Both interest revenue and dividend revenue are reported on the income statement, usually as part of other revenues and expenses.

To illustrate, suppose that Abernathy receives $5,000 of interest on the Decatur bonds on June 30 and $3,000 of cash dividends from Eagle Company on September 15. Abernathy would record the receipts as follows.

June 30	Cash	5,000	
	Interest Revenue		5,000
	(To record receipt of interest)		

Assets	=	Liabilities	+	Equity
+5,000				+5,000

Sept. 15	Cash	3,000	
	Dividend Revenue		3,000
	(To record receipt of dividends)		

Assets	=	Liabilities	+	Equity
+3,000				+3,000

In both entries, Abernathy increases Cash to reflect the cash that is flowing into the company from its investments. The first entry increases Interest Revenue while the second increases Dividend Revenue. In both entries, assets and equity increase. Similar entries would be made each time interest or dividends are received.

Reporting Investments on the Balance Sheet

Like other assets, investments are reported on the balance sheet. However, the manner in which they are reported depends on how they are classified. Accounting rules require that investments in debt securities and equity securities without significant influence be classified into one of the following three categories. Each category is based on what management intends to do with the investments.

- Held-to-Maturity Securities
- Trading Securities
- Available-for-Sale Securities

Held-to-maturity securities are those securities that an investor has the positive intent and ability to hold

until they mature. Since equity securities such as common stock do not mature, only debt securities can be classified as held-to-maturity securities. Investments in held-to-maturity securities are reported on the balance sheet at their historical costs. They are reported as non-current assets.

Trading securities are those securities that an investor intends to sell in the near term. Either debt or equity securities can be classified as trading securities. However, common stock is the most common type of trading security. Trading securities are reported on the balance sheet at their market values. This is an exception to the cost principle, but it is allowed because market values of most equity securities are objectively measured and easily known. Trading securities are included in current assets.

Available-for-sale securities are those securities that a company does not intend to hold to maturity but also does not intend to sell in the near term. In other words, an available-for-sale security is any security that is neither a held-to-maturity security nor a trading security. Either debt or equity securities can be classified as available-for-sale securities. Like trading securities, available-for-sale securities are reported on the balance sheet at their market values. Available-for-sale securities are usually reported as non-current assets.

Because trading and available-for-sale securities are reported at their market values, adjustments may be necessary at the balance sheet date. For example, if the market value of a trading security is greater than its cost, the investment account must be increased. If the market value of an available-for-sale security is less than its cost, the investment account must be decreased.

To illustrate, suppose that Abernathy is preparing its balance sheet on December 31, 2009. It has decided to hold the Decatur bonds for the full 20 years, to sell the Eagle investment within 90 days, and to hold the C & L investment indefinitely. The following table contains each investment, its classification, its cost and market values as of December 31, and any resulting unrealized gain or loss.

Investment	Classification	Original Cost	Dec. 31 Market Value	Unrealized gain or (loss)
Decatur	Held-to-maturity	$100,000	$99,000	$ (1,000)
Eagle	Trading	60,000	64,300	4,300
C & L	Available-for-sale	10,000	9,800	(200)

The unrealized gain or loss is the difference between an investment's cost and its market value. When the market value exceeds the cost, Abernathy has an unrealized gain. When the cost exceeds the market value, Abernathy has an unrealized loss. The term *unrealized* is used because Abernathy still owns the investments. A gain or loss is *realized* only when an investment is sold and cash is received.

Because the Decatur bonds are classified as held-to-maturity, they are reported at their cost of $100,000. The market value and the unrealized loss are ignored, and no adjustment is needed.

Because the Eagle investment is classified as trading, it must be reported at its market value of $64,300. Therefore, Abernathy must adjust the investment account with the following entry.

Dec. 31 2009	Investment in Eagle Company	4,300	
	Unrealized Gain on Trading Securities		4,300
	(To adjust investment to market value)		

Assets	=	Liabilities	+	Equity
+4,300				+4,300

In this entry, Abernathy first increases the investment account by $4,300 so that the balance in the account rises from $60,000 to $64,300. Abernathy then increases Unrealized Gain on Trading Securities to reflect the increase in the value of Abernathy's investment. Unrealized gains or losses on trading securities are treated like any other revenue or expense—they are included in the calculation of net income. In this case, the gain would be reported in other revenues on the income statement, which results in an increase to equity.

Because the C & L investment is classified as available-for-sale, it too must be reported at its market value. However, the adjustment is a little different than the Eagle example.

Dec. 31	Unrealized Gain/Loss on Available-for-Sale Securities	200	
	Investment in C & L Inc.		200
	(To adjust investment to market value)		

Assets	=	Liabilities	+	Equity
−200				−200

In this entry, Abernathy decreases the investment account by $200 so that the balance in the account decreases from $10,000 to $9,800, the market value. Abernathy then debits Unrealized Gain/Loss on Available-for-Sale Securities to reflect the decrease in the

value of Abernathy's investment. Unlike the unrealized gain account used for the trading security, this unrealized gain/loss account for available-for-sale securities is not included in the calculation of net income. Rather, it is reported on the balance sheet as an increase or decrease to equity. Specifically, it is reported as a component of Accumulated Other Comprehensive Income, a line item within the stockholders' equity section of the balance sheet. Note that the account can have either a debit or credit balance. A debit balance represents unrealized losses to date while a credit balance represents unrealized gains to date.

After both adjustments are made, the investment balances on the December 31 balance sheet would appear as follows.

Investments on December 31 Balance Sheet	
Current assets	
Trading securities	$ 64,300
Noncurrent assets	
Held-to-maturity securities	100,000
Available-for-sale securities	9,800

Recording the Sale or Maturity

The recording of the maturity or sale of an investment also depends on how the investment is classified. The following sections demonstrate how each classification is handled.

Held-to-Maturity Securities When a held-to-maturity security matures, a company must record the cash that is received at maturity and eliminate the investment account. When a held-to-maturity security is sold, a company must record the cash from the sale, eliminate the investment account, and record any difference as a gain or loss from the sale.

To illustrate a maturity, suppose that Abernathy holds the Decatur bonds until they mature. Abernathy will record the receipt of $100,000 as follows.

At maturity	Cash	100,000	
	Investment in Decatur Bonds		100,000
	(To record maturity of bonds)		

Assets	=	Liabilities	+	Equity
+100,000				
−100,000				

In this entry, Abernathy is simply increasing Cash and decreasing the investment account. Because Abernathy is exchanging one asset for another, total assets remain unchanged.

To illustrate a sale, suppose that Abernathy sells the Decatur bonds for $101,000 immediately after an interest payment. Abernathy will record the sale as follows.

Cash	101,000	
Gain on Sale of Investment		1,000
Investment in Decatur Bonds		100,000
(To record sale of bonds)		

Assets	=	Liabilities	+	Equity
+101,000				+1,000
−100,000				

In this entry, Abernathy increases Cash for the amount received, eliminates the investment account, and increases Gain on Sale of Investment for the difference of $1,000.

Trading Securities   When a trading security is sold, any cash received is recorded, the investment account is eliminated, and any gain or loss on the sale is recorded.

To illustrate, suppose that on February 15, 2010, Abernathy sells its investment in Eagle Company when the market value of the investment is $65,200. Abernathy would make the following entry to record the sale.

Feb. 15	Cash	65,200	
2010	Investment in Eagle Company		64,300
	Gain on Sale of Investment		900
	(To record sale of investment at a gain)		

	Assets	=	Liabilities	+	Equity
	+65,200				+900
	−64,300				

In this entry, Abernathy first increases Cash for the amount received from the sale. It then decreases Investment in Eagle Company by $64,300 since that was its balance on December 31. The difference between the cash received and the current account balance is the amount of gain realized on the sale. Therefore, Gain on Sale of Investment is increased by $900. As a result of this sale, both assets and equity increased $900.

Note in this example that Abernathy's total gain on the value of the investment was $5,200 (sales price − cost = $65,200 − $60,000 = $5,200). A portion of that gain ($4,300) was included in net income in the prior period when the investment was adjusted to its market value. The remainder of the gain ($900) was included in net income when the investment was sold. So, the $5,200 total gain was spread across two accounting periods.

Available-for-Sale Securities   When an available-for-sale security is sold, any cash received is recorded, the investment and any existing unrealized gain or loss are eliminated, and any realized gain or loss on the sale is recorded.

To illustrate, suppose that Abernathy sells its investment in C & L Inc. for $9,700 on March 8, 2010. At the time of the sale, Abernathy would make the following entry.

Mar. 8	Cash	9,700	
2010	Loss on Sale of Investment	300	
	Unrealized Gain/Loss on Available-for-Sale Securities		200
	Investment in C & L Inc.		9,800
	(To record sale of investment at a gain)		

	Assets	=	Liabilities	+	Equity
	+9,700				−300
	−9,800				+200

In this entry, Abernathy increases Cash for the amount of cash received. Because the Investment in C & L Inc. account was adjusted to $9,800 on December 31, Abernathy decreases the account by $9,800 to eliminate it. Furthermore, the Unrealized Gain/Loss balance of $200 that was created on December 31 is also eliminated since Abernathy no longer has that unrealized loss. Finally, Abernathy records a realized loss on the investment of $300. This is the difference between the amount received from the sale and the original cost of the investment. This $300 loss is included in the calculation of net income along with other expenses and revenues.

HOME DEPOT ANALYSIS

Look at the Short-Term Investments paragraph in Home Depot's first note in Appendix C. How does Home Depot classify and report its investments?

Home Depot states that short-term investments are classified as available-for-sale securities. Therefore, they are reported at fair (or market) values.

1. Investment Classifications LO₁

Below is a list of the various investments of Baldy Corporation:
1. Shares of GM stock to be held indefinitely
2. State bonds that will be held until they mature
3. Corporate bonds that the company might or might not sell
4. 15-year Nike bonds that the company plans to sell quickly
5. Target common stock which the company is actively trying to sell

Required

Identify each of the investments as held-to-maturity, available-for-sale, or trading securities.

2. Debt Security Investment LO₁

On January 1, 2009, the Hackman Company purchases $300,000 of 8% bonds for face value. Hackman plans to hold the bonds until they mature on January 1, 2016. Interest is paid semiannually on June 30 and December 31. Hackman's year-end is December 31.

Required

a. How should Hackman classify its investment? Explain your answer.
b. Prepare all appropriate journal entries for 2009. Be sure to include any necessary adjusting entry at year-end.

3. Equity Security Investment LO₁

On December 1, 2009, Wallace, Inc., purchases 500 shares of King Corporation common stock at $30 per share. Wallace plans to sell it at a profit as soon as it rises in value. On December 22, King declares a dividend of $1 per share to be paid on January 5, 2010. At December 31, 2009, King's stock was trading at $35 per share. Wallace sells the stock at $34 per share on January 15, 2010.

Required

a. How should Wallace classify its investment? Explain your answer.
b. Prepare all necessary journal entries from the purchase of the stock to its sale.
c. What is the effect of these transactions on the 2009 and 2010 income statements?

4. Equity Security Investment LO₁

On January 31, 2009, the Coburn Company purchases 10,000 shares of Hughes Corporation common stock at $10 per share. Coburn plans to hold the stock for an extended period of time rather than place it in its active trading portfolio. At December 31, 2009,

Hughes common stock is trading at $8 per share. On March 31, 2010, Coburn sells the stock for $90,000.

Required

a. How should Coburn classify its investment? Explain your answer.
b. Prepare all necessary journal entries from the purchase of the stock through to its sale.
c. What is the effect of these transactions on the 2009 and 2010 income statements?

5. Effect on Net Income LO₁

The following is a list of possible events:
1. Trading securities appreciate in value over the course of the year.
2. Held-to-maturity securities are redeemed at maturity.
3. Available-for-sale securities are sold for less than their market value.
4. Available-for-sale securities appreciate in value during the current period.
5. Interest payments are received in the current year.
6. Trading securities are sold at a value greater than market value.

Required

Identify whether each item increases, decreases, or has no effect on net income for the current period.

6. Investment Entries LO₁

Huang, Inc., enters into the following transactions during 2009:

Jan. 1   Purchased $100,000, 6%, 10-year corporate bonds at face value. The bonds pay interest annually on December 31. Huang plans to hold the bonds to maturity.

Mar. 31   Purchased 500 shares of Bubbles, Inc., common stock at $30 per share. Huang plans to hold the shares indefinitely.

Nov. 15   Purchased 300 shares of Libor, Inc., common stock at $45 per share. Huang plans to sell these shares in January.

Dec. 8   Received a dividend of $1 per share on the Libor, Inc., stock.

Dec. 31   Received interest payment on the corporate bonds purchased on January 1.

Dec. 31   Noted the following market values: Bubbles stock—$40 per share; Libor stock—$44 per share; corporate bonds—$98,000.

Required

a. Prepare all appropriate journal entries associated with Huang's investments during 2009, including any necessary adjustments at year-end.
b. Determine the net effect on 2009 net income of all investment activity.

Appendix B
Time Value of Money

Introduction

When decisions are affected by cash flows that are paid or received in different time periods, it is necessary to adjust those cash flows for the time value of money (TVM). Because of our ability to earn interest on money invested, we would prefer to receive $1 today rather than a year from now. Likewise, we would prefer to pay $1 a year from now rather than today. A common technique used to adjust cash flows received or paid in different time periods is to discount those cash flows by finding their present value. The **present value (PV)** of cash flows is the amount of future cash flows discounted to their equivalent worth today. To fully understand the calculations involved in finding the present value of future cash flows, it is necessary to step back and examine the nature of interest and the calculation of interest received and paid. Interest is simply a payment made to use someone else's money. When you invest money in a bank account, the bank pays you interest for the use of your money for a period of time. If you invest $100 and the bank pays you $106 at the end of the year, it is clear that you earned $6 of interest on your money (and 6 percent interest for the year).

Future Value

Mathematically, the relationship between your initial investment (present value), the amount in the bank at the end of the year (future value), and the interest rate (r) is as follows:

$$FV_{(Year\ 1)} = PV(1 + r)$$

In our example, $FV_{(Year\ 1)} = 100(1 + 0.06) = \$106$. If you leave your money in the bank for a second year, what happens? Will you earn an additional $6 of interest? It depends on whether the bank pays you simple interest or compound interest. **Simple interest** is interest on the invested amount only, whereas **compound interest** is interest on the invested amount plus interest on previous interest earned but not withdrawn. Simple interest is sometimes computed on short-term investments and debts (that is, those that are shorter than six months to a year). Compound interest is typically computed for financial arrangements longer than one year. We will assume that interest is compounded in all examples in this book. Extending the future-value formula to find the amount we have in the bank in two years gives us the following formula:

$$FV_{(Year\ 2)} = PV(1 + r)(1 + r)$$

or

$$FV_{(Year\ 2)} = PV(1 + r)^2$$

In our example, $FV_{(Year\ 2)} = 100(1 + 0.06)^2$, or $112.36. We earned $6.36 of interest in Year 2—$6 on our original $100 investment and $0.36 on the $6 of interest earned but not withdrawn in Year 1 ($6 × 0.06).

In this example, we have assumed that compounding is on an annual basis. Compounding can also be calculated semiannually, quarterly, monthly, daily, or even continually. Go back to our original $100 investment in the bank. If the bank pays 6 percent interest compounded semiannually instead of annually, we would have $106.09 after one year. Note that the interest rate is typically expressed as a percentage rate per year. We are

> **Present value (PV)** The amount of future cash flows discounted to their equivalent worth today.
>
> **Simple interest** Interest on the invested amount only.
>
> **Compound interest** Interest on the invested amount plus interest on previous interest earned but not withdrawn.

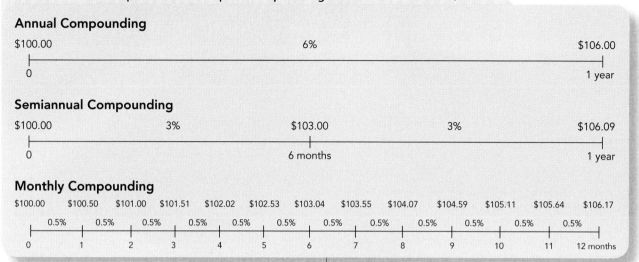

Exhibit B-1 The Impact of More Frequent Compounding on the Future Value of $100

Annual Compounding

$100.00	6%	$106.00
0		1 year

Semiannual Compounding

$100.00	3%	$103.00	3%	$106.09
0		6 months		1 year

Monthly Compounding

$100.00 $100.50 $101.00 $101.51 $102.02 $102.53 $103.04 $103.55 $104.07 $104.59 $105.11 $105.64 $106.17

0.5% 0.5% 0.5% 0.5% 0.5% 0.5% 0.5% 0.5% 0.5% 0.5% 0.5% 0.5%

0   1   2   3   4   5   6   7   8   9   10   11   12 months

really earning 3 percent for each semiannual period, not 6 percent. It is usually easier to visualize the concept of interest rate compounding graphically, with the help of time lines. Exhibit B-1 graphically demonstrates the impact of annual, semiannual, and monthly compounding of the 6 percent annual rate on our original $100 investment.

Mathematically, our formula for future value can once again be modified slightly to account for interest rates compounded at different intervals. $FV_{(n \text{ periods in the future})} = PV(1 + r)^n$, where n is the number of compounding periods per year multiplied by the number of years, and r is the annual interest rate divided by the number of compounding periods per year. Before the advent of

handheld calculators and computers, tables were developed to simplify the calculation of FV by providing values for $(1 + r)^n$ for several combinations of n and r. These tables are still commonly used, and an example is provided in Exhibit B-2. The factors in Exhibit B-2 are commonly referred to as cumulative factors (CF) and are simply calculations of $(1 + r)^n$ for various values of n and r.

Using this new terminology, the future value formula is simply

$$FV_{(n \text{ periods in the future})} = PV(CF_{n,r})$$

Exhibit B-2 Future Value of $1

n/r	0.5%	1%	2%	3%	4%	5%	6%	7%	8%	10%	12%
1	1.0050	1.0100	1.0200	1.0300	1.0400	1.0500	1.0600	1.0700	1.0800	1.1000	1.1200
2	1.0100	1.0201	1.0404	1.0609	1.0816	1.1025	1.1236	1.1449	1.1664	1.2100	1.2544
3	1.0151	1.0303	1.0612	1.0927	1.1249	1.1576	1.1910	1.2250	1.2597	1.3310	1.4049
4	1.0202	1.0406	1.0824	1.1255	1.1699	1.2155	1.2625	1.3108	1.3605	1.4641	1.5735
5	1.0253	1.0510	1.1041	1.1593	1.2167	1.2763	1.3382	1.4026	1.4693	1.6105	1.7623
6	1.0304	1.0615	1.1262	1.1941	1.2653	1.3401	1.4185	1.5007	1.5869	1.7716	1.9738
7	1.0355	1.0721	1.1487	1.2299	1.3159	1.4071	1.5036	1.6058	1.7138	1.9487	2.2107
8	1.0407	1.0829	1.1717	1.2668	1.3686	1.4775	1.5938	1.7182	1.8509	2.1436	2.4760
9	1.0459	1.0937	1.1951	1.3048	1.4233	1.5513	1.6895	1.8385	1.9990	2.3579	2.7731
10	1.0511	1.1046	1.2190	1.3439	1.4802	1.6289	1.7908	1.9672	2.1589	2.5937	3.1058
11	1.0564	1.1157	1.2434	1.3842	1.5395	1.7103	1.8983	2.1049	2.3316	2.8531	3.4785
12	1.0617	1.1268	1.2682	1.4258	1.6010	1.7959	2.0122	2.2522	2.5182	3.1384	3.8960
24	1.1272	1.2697	1.6084	2.0328	2.5633	3.2251	4.0489	5.0724	6.3412	9.8497	15.1786
36	1.1967	1.4308	2.0399	2.8983	4.1039	5.7918	8.1473	11.4239	15.9682	30.9127	59.1356
48	1.2705	1.6122	2.5871	4.1323	6.5705	10.4013	16.3939	25.7289	40.2106	97.0172	230.3908

With 6 percent annual compounding, our $100 investment grows to

$$\$100(CF_{1,6\%}) =$$
$$\$100(1.060) = \$106.00$$

With 6 percent semiannual compounding,

$$\$100(CF_{2,3\%}) =$$
$$\$100(1.0609) = \$106.09$$

With 6 percent monthly compounding,

$$\$100(CF_{12,.5\%}) =$$
$$\$100(1.0617) = \$106.17$$

Most financial calculators will compute future value after the user inputs data for present value, the annual interest rate, the number of compounding periods per year, and the number of years. For example, using a business calculator to compute the future value of $100.00 with 6 percent annual compounding requires the following steps:

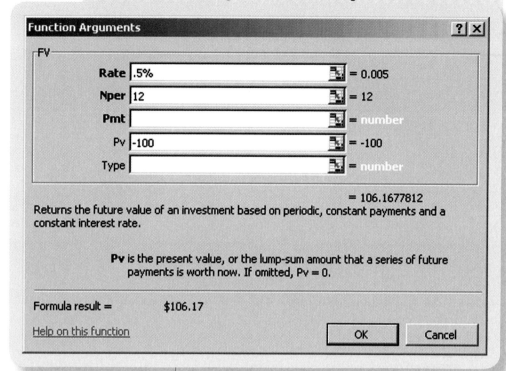

Keys	Display	Description
1 [P/YR]	1.00	Sets compounding periods per year to 1 because interest is compounded annually
100 [±] [PV]	−100.00	Stores the present value as a negative number
6.0 [I/YR]	6.0	Stores the annual interest rate
1 [N]	1	Sets the number of years or compounding periods to 1
[FV]	106.00	Calculates the future value

Calculating the future value of $100 with 6 percent monthly compounding simply requires changing both the compounding periods per year (*P/YR*) and number of compounding periods (*N*) to 12.

Keys	Display	Description
12 [P/YR]	12	Sets compounding periods per year to 12
12 [N]	12	Sets the number of compounding periods to 12
[FV]	106.17	Calculates the future value

Likewise, many spreadsheet programs have built-in functions (formulas) that calculate future value. The Excel function called FV simply requires input of an interest rate (Rate), number of compounding periods (Nper), and present value (Pv) in the following format: =FV(Rate, Nper, Pmt, Pv, Type).[1] Entries for Pmt and Type are not applicable to simple future-value problems. To calculate the future value of $100 in one year at 6 percent interest compounded monthly, enter =FV(.5%,12,−100). Excel returns a value of $106.17 (see Exhibit B-3).

Present Value

A present value formula can be derived directly from the future value formula. If

$$FV_{(n \text{ periods in the future})} = PV(1 + r)^n$$

then

$$PV = \frac{FV}{(1 + r)^n} \quad \text{or} \quad PV = FV\left(\frac{1}{(1 + r)^n}\right)$$

Just as a cumulative factor table was developed to calculate $(1 + r)^n$, present value tables calculate $1 \div (1 + r)^n$

[1] Built-in functions can be accessed in Microsoft Excel by clicking on the Paste function icon, clicking on *financial*, and then scrolling down to the desired function.

Exhibit B-4 Present Value of $1

n/r	0.5%	1%	2%	3%	4%	5%	6%	7%	8%	10%	12%
1	0.9950	0.9901	0.9804	0.9709	0.9615	0.9524	0.9434	0.9346	0.9259	0.9091	0.8929
2	0.9901	0.9803	0.9612	0.9426	0.9246	0.9070	0.8900	0.8734	0.8573	0.8264	0.7972
3	0.9851	0.9706	0.9423	0.9151	0.8890	0.8638	0.8396	0.8163	0.7938	0.7513	0.7118
4	0.9802	0.9610	0.9238	0.8885	0.8548	0.8227	0.7921	0.7629	0.7350	0.6830	0.6355
5	0.9754	0.9515	0.9057	0.8626	0.8219	0.7835	0.7473	0.7130	0.6806	0.6209	0.5674
6	0.9705	0.9420	0.8880	0.8375	0.7903	0.7462	0.7050	0.6663	0.6302	0.5645	0.5066
7	0.9657	0.9327	0.8706	0.8131	0.7599	0.7107	0.6651	0.6227	0.5835	0.5132	0.4523
8	0.9609	0.9235	0.8535	0.7894	0.7307	0.6768	0.6274	0.5820	0.5403	0.4665	0.4039
9	0.9561	0.9143	0.8368	0.7664	0.7026	0.6446	0.5919	0.5439	0.5002	0.4241	0.3606
10	0.9513	0.9053	0.8203	0.7441	0.6756	0.6139	0.5584	0.5083	0.4632	0.3855	0.3220
11	0.9466	0.8963	0.8043	0.7224	0.6496	0.5847	0.5268	0.4751	0.4289	0.3505	0.2875
12	0.9419	0.8874	0.7885	0.7014	0.6246	0.5568	0.4970	0.4440	0.3971	0.3186	0.2567
24	0.8872	0.7876	0.6217	0.4919	0.3901	0.3101	0.2470	0.1971	0.1577	0.1015	0.0659
36	0.8356	0.6989	0.4902	0.3450	0.2437	0.1727	0.1227	0.0875	0.0626	0.0323	0.0169
48	0.7871	0.6203	0.3865	0.2420	0.1522	0.0961	0.0610	0.0389	0.0249	0.0103	0.0043

for various combinations of n and r. These factors are called discount factors, or DFs. An example of a DF table is provided in Exhibit B-4. Our PV formula can now be rewritten as follows:

$$PV = FV(DF_{n,r})$$

Now we are ready to calculate the present value of a future cash flow. For example, how much must be invested today at 8 percent compounded annually to have $1,000 in two years? Mathematically,

$$PV = \$1,000\left(\frac{1}{(1 \times 0.08)^2}\right) = \$857.34$$

or using the DF table,

$$PV = \$1,000(DF_{2,.08}) = \$1,000(0.8573) = \$857.30 \text{ (rounded)}$$

Once again, the frequency of compounding affects our calculation. Just as more frequent compounding *increases* future values, increasing the frequency of compounding decreases present values. This is demonstrated in Exhibit B-5 for annual, semiannual, and quarterly compounding.

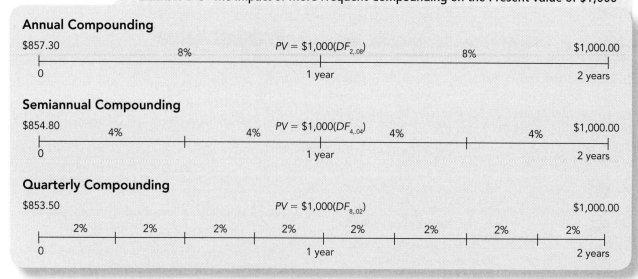

Exhibit B-5 The Impact of More Frequent Compounding on the Present Value of $1,000

Annual Compounding

$857.30   8% $PV = \$1,000(DF_{2,.08})$ 8% $1,000.00

0   1 year   2 years

Semiannual Compounding

$854.80   4%   4% $PV = \$1,000(DF_{4,.04})$ 4%   4% $1,000.00

0   1 year   2 years

Quarterly Compounding

$853.50 $PV = \$1,000(DF_{8,.02})$ $1,000.00

2%   2%   2%   2%   2%   2%   2%   2%

0   1 year   2 years

Using a business calculator to compute present value is similar to computing future value. For example, the present value of $1,000 received or paid in two years at 8 percent compounded quarterly requires the following steps:

Keys	Display	Description
4 [P/YR]	4.00	Sets the compounding periods per year to 4
1,000 [FV]	1000.00	Stores the future value as a positive number
8.0 [I/YR]	8.0	Stores the annual interest rate
8 [N]	8.0	Sets the number of compounding periods to 8
[PV]	−853.49	Calculates the present value

In Microsoft Excel, the built-in function is called PV and requires input of the applicable interest rate (Rate), number of compounding periods (Nper), and future value (Fv) in the following format: =PV(Rate, Nper, Pmt, Fv, Type). In the previous example, entering =PV(2%,8,−1000) returns a value of $853.49. Note once again that Pmt and Type are left blank in simple present value problems, as they were in future value calculations (see Exhibit B-6).

When *FV* and *PV* are known, either formula can be used to calculate one of the other variables in the equations (*n* or *r*). For example, if you know that your $100

bank deposit is worth $200 in six years, what rate of interest compounded annually did you earn? Using the mathematical present value formula,

$$PV = FV\left(\frac{1}{(1 + r)^n}\right) \quad \text{or} \quad \$100 = \$200\left(\frac{1}{(1 + r)^6}\right)$$

Simplifying by dividing each side by $100, $1 = 2 \div (1 + r)^6$, and multiplying each side by $(1 + r)^6$, the equation is simplified to $(1 + r)^6 = 2$. The value of *r* can be calculated by using a financial calculator or mathematically by using logarithmic functions.[2] When using a business calculator, the following steps are typical:

Keys	Display	Description
1 [P/YR]	1.00	Sets compounding periods per year to 1
200 [FV]	200	Stores the future value
100 [±] [PV]	−100	Stores the present value as a negative number
2 [N]	2.0	Sets the number of compounding periods to 2
[I/YR]	0.122462	Calculates the annual interest rate

The tables can also be used to solve for *n* and *r*. Using our table formula, $PV = FV(DF_{n,r})$, if $PV = 100$ and $FV = 200$, *DF* must be equal to 0.5. If we know that *n* is equal to 6, we can simply move across the table until we find a factor close to 0.5. The factor at 12 percent is 0.5066. If we examine the factors at both 10 percent (0.5645) and 14 percent (0.456), we can infer that the actual interest rate will be slightly higher than 12 percent. Our logarithmic calculation is 12.2462 percent. In Microsoft Excel, the RATE function requires input of Nper, Pv, and Fv in the following format:

[2]In logarithmic form, $(1 + r)^6 = 2$ can be rewritten as $\log(1 + r)^6 = \log 2$, or $6 \log(1 + r) = \log 2$. Therefore, $\log(1 + r) = \log 2 \div 6$, which simplifies to $\log(1 + r) = 0.1155245$. Switching back to the equivalent exponential form, $e0.1155245 = (1 + r)$, $(1 + r) = 1.122462$, and $r = 0.122462$ (12.2462%).

Exhibit B-6 Finding the Present Value Using the PV Function in Excel

Function Arguments [?][X]

PV

Rate	2%	= 0.02
Nper	8	= 8
Pmt		= number
Fv	-1000	= -1000
Type		= number

= 853.4903712

Returns the present value of an investment: the total amount that a series of future payments is worth now.

Fv is the future value, or a cash balance you want to attain after the last payment is made.

Formula result = $853.49

Help on this function   [OK]   [Cancel]

Exhibit B-7 Finding the Interest Rate Using the RATE Function in Excel

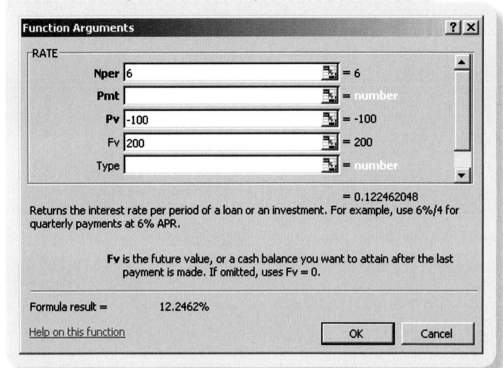

=RATE(Nper, Pmt, Pv, Fv, Type, Guess). Because Excel uses an iterative trial-and-error method to calculate the interest rate, Guess provides a starting point. It is generally not necessary but may be required in complicated problems. Entering =RATE(6,−100,200) returns an interest rate of 12.2462 percent (see Exhibit B-7).

The calculation of n is done in a similar fashion. If we know that our investment earns 12 percent but do not know how long it will take for our $100 to grow to $200, mathematically, we have the following:

$$PV = FV\left(\frac{1}{(1 + r)^n}\right)$$

or

$$\$100 = \$200\left(\frac{1}{(1 + 0.12)^n}\right)$$

Solving the equation by using logarithms or a financial calculator gives us an n of 6.116 years.[3] Using the

DF formula, DF must again be equal to 0.5. If r is known to be 12 percent, we simply move down the 12 percent column until we find a DF close to 0.5. Not surprisingly, we find a factor of 0.5066 for an n of 6. Examining the factors for an n of 5(0.5674) and 7(0.4523), we can infer that the actual time will be something slightly greater than 6 years. The NPER function in Microsoft Excel requires input of Rate, Pmt, Pv, Fv, and Type in the following format: =NPER(12%,−100, 200), and returns a value of 6.116 years. Note that Pv is entered as a negative amount and that Pmt and Type are not necessary, as this is essentially a present value problem (see Exhibit B-8).

Exhibit B-8 Finding the Number of Periods Using the NPER Function in Excel

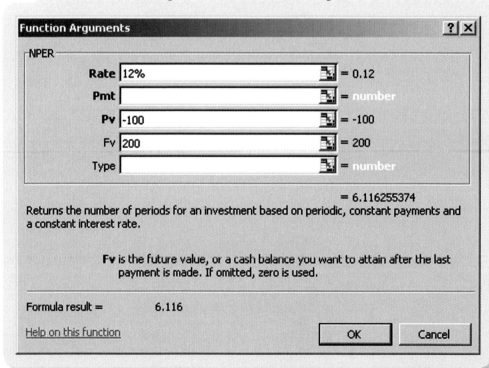

[3]Using a business calculator, simply input 1 P/YR, 200 FV, 100 PV, and 12 I/YR and solve for n. In logarithmic form, $(1 + 0.12)^n = 2$ can be rewritten as $\log(1 + 0.12)^n = \log 2$, or $n \log 1.12 = \log 2$. Therefore, $n = (\log 2) \div (\log 1.12) = 6.116$.

Annuities

An **annuity** is a series of cash flows of equal amount paid or received at regular intervals.[4] Common examples include mortgage and loan payments. The present value of an ordinary annuity (PVA) is the amount invested or borrowed today that will provide for a series of withdrawals or payments of equal amount for a set number of periods. Conceptually, the present value of an annuity is simply the sum of the present values of each withdrawal or payment. For example, the present value

The mathematical formula for PVA can be derived from the formula for PV and is equal to:

$$PVA_{n,r} = R\left(\frac{1 - \frac{1}{(1 + r)^n}}{r}\right)$$

where R refers to the periodic payment or withdrawal (commonly called a rent). Calculated values for various combinations of n and r are provided in Exhibit B-9.

Exhibit B-9 Present Value of an Ordinary Annuity

n/r	0.50%	1%	2%	3%	4%	5%	6%	7%	8%	10%	12%
1	0.9950	0.9901	0.9804	0.9709	0.9615	0.9524	0.9434	0.9346	0.9259	0.9091	0.8929
2	1.9851	1.9704	1.9416	1.9135	1.8861	1.8594	1.8334	1.8080	1.7833	1.7355	1.6901
3	2.9702	2.9410	2.8839	2.8286	2.7751	2.7232	2.6730	2.6243	2.5771	2.4869	2.4018
4	3.9505	3.9020	3.8077	3.7171	3.6299	3.5460	3.4651	3.3872	3.3121	3.1699	3.0373
5	4.9259	4.8534	4.7135	4.5797	4.4518	4.3295	4.2124	4.1002	3.9927	3.7908	3.6048
6	5.8964	5.7955	5.6014	5.4172	5.2421	5.0757	4.9173	4.7665	4.6229	4.3553	4.1114
7	6.8621	6.7282	6.4720	6.2303	6.0021	5.7864	5.5824	5.3893	5.2064	4.8684	4.5638
8	7.8230	7.6517	7.3255	7.0197	6.7327	6.4632	6.2098	5.9713	5.7466	5.3349	4.9676
9	8.7791	8.5660	8.1622	7.7861	7.4353	7.1078	6.8017	6.5152	6.2469	5.7590	5.3282
10	9.7304	9.4713	8.9826	8.5302	8.1109	7.7217	7.3601	7.0236	6.7101	6.1446	5.6502
11	10.6770	10.3676	9.7868	9.2526	8.7605	8.3064	7.8869	7.4987	7.1390	6.4951	5.9377
12	11.6189	11.2551	10.5753	9.9540	9.3851	8.8633	8.3838	7.9427	7.5361	6.8137	6.1944
24	22.5629	21.2434	18.9139	16.9355	15.2470	13.7986	12.5504	11.4693	10.5288	8.9847	7.7843
36	32.8710	30.1075	25.4888	21.8323	18.9083	16.5469	14.6210	13.0352	11.7172	9.6765	8.1924
48	42.5803	37.9740	30.6731	25.2667	21.1951	18.0772	15.6500	13.7305	12.1891	9.8969	8.2972

of an annuity of $100 paid at the end of each of the next four years at an interest rate of 10 percent looks like this:

```
PVA   $100      $100      $100      $100
    10%  ───  10%  ───  10%  ───  10%  ───
├─────────┼─────────┼─────────┼─────────┤
0       1 year   2 years   3 years   4 years
```

Although cumbersome, the present value of an annuity can be calculated by finding the present value of each $100 payment, using the present value table on page B-4 (see Exhibit B-4).

$PVA = \$100(DF_{1,.10}) + \$100(DF_{2,.10}) + \$100(DF_{3,.10}) +$
$\quad \$100(DF_{4,.10})$

$\quad = \$100(0.9091) + \$100(0.8264) + \$100(0.7513) +$
$\quad \$100(0.6830)$

$\quad = \$316.98$

The PVA formula can therefore be rewritten as follows:

$$PVA = R(DFA_{n,r})$$

As previously discussed, common examples of annuities are mortgages and loans. For example, say you are thinking about buying a new car. Your bank offers to loan you money at a special 6 percent rate compounded monthly for a 24-month term. If the maximum monthly payment you can afford is $399, how large a car loan can you get? In other words, what is the present value of a $399 annuity paid at the end of each of the next 24 months, assuming an interest rate of 6 percent compounded monthly?

---

[4]An ordinary annuity is paid or received at the end of each period, whereas an annuity due is paid or received at the beginning of each period. In examples throughout this book, we will assume the annuity is ordinary.

Annuity A series of cash flows of equal amount paid or received at regular intervals.

Using a time line, the problem looks like this:

PVA $399 $399 $399 $399 $399 $399 $399 $399 $399 $399 $399 $399 $399 $399 $399 $399 $399 $399 $399 $399 $399 $399 $399 $399

0.5% 0.5% 0.5% 0.5% 0.5% 0.5% 0.5% 0.5% 0.5% 0.5% 0.5% 0.5% 0.5% 0.5% 0.5% 0.5% 0.5% 0.5% 0.5% 0.5% 0.5% 0.5% 0.5% 0.5%

0   24 months

Mathematically,

$$PVA_{24,.005} = 399\left(\frac{1 - \dfrac{1}{(1 + 0.5)^{24}}}{0.005}\right)$$

Using the DFA table,

$$PVA_{24,.005} = \$399(DFA_{24,.005}) = \$399(22.5629) = \$9{,}002.60$$
(rounded)

The following steps are common when using a business calculator:

Keys	Display	Description
12 P/YR	12.00	Set periods per year
2×12 N	24.00	Stores number of periods in loan
0 PV	0	Stores the amount left to pay after 2 years
6 I/YR	6	Stores interest rate
399 ± PMT	−399.00	Stores desired payment as a negative number
PV	9,002.58	Calculates the loan you can afford with a $399 per month payment

In Microsoft Excel, the PV function is used to calculate the present value of an annuity, with additional entries for the payment amount (Pmt) and type of annuity (Type). The payment is entered as a negative number, and the annuity type is 0 for ordinary and 1 for an annuity due. The format is therefore PV(Rate, Nper, Pmt, Fv, Type). Entering =PV(.5%,24,−399,0,0) returns a value of $9,002.58 (see Exhibit B-10).

The PVA formula can also be used to calculate R, r, and n if the other variables are known. This is most easily accomplished using the DFA table or using a financial calculator. If the car you want to buy costs $20,000 and you can afford a $3,000 down payment (your loan balance is $17,000), how much will your 36 monthly payments be, assuming that the bank charges you 6 percent interest compounded monthly?

Using the DFA table,

$$PVA_{36,.005} = R(DFA_{36,.005})$$
$$\$17{,}000 = R(32.871)$$
$$R = \$517.17$$

The following steps are common when using a business calculator:

Keys	Display	Description
12 P/YR	12.00	Set periods per year
3×12 N	36.00	Stores number of periods in loan
0 PV	0	Stores the amount left to pay after 3 years
6 I/YR	6	Stores interest rate
17,000 PV	17,000	Stores amount borrowed
PMT	−517.17	Calculates the monthly payment

In Microsoft Excel, the calculation is simply =PMT (.005,36,−17000,0,0) (see Exhibit B-11).

In a similar fashion, assume that a used-car dealer offers you a "special deal" in which you can borrow $12,000 with low monthly payments of $350 per month for 48 months. What rate of interest are you being charged in this case? Using the DFA table,

$$PVA_{48,.??} = \$350(DFA_{48,.??})$$
$$\$12{,}000 = 350(DFA_{48,.??})$$
$$DFA_{48,.??} = 34.2857$$

Looking at the row for an n of 48, we see that a DFA of 34.2857 is about halfway between an r of 1 percent and r of 2 percent (closer to 1 percent), which means that you are being charged an annual rate of almost 18 percent (1.5% × 12)—not such a good deal after all! Using a business calculator, observe the following:

Keys	Display	Description
12 P/YR	12.00	Set periods per year
4×12 N	48.00	Stores number of periods in loan
0 PV	0	Stores the amount left to pay after 4 years
12,000 PV	12,000	Stores amount borrowed
350 ± PMT	−350	Stores the monthly payment
I/YR	17.60	Calculates the annual interest rate

Exhibit B-10 Finding the Present Value of an Annuity
Using the PV Function in Excel

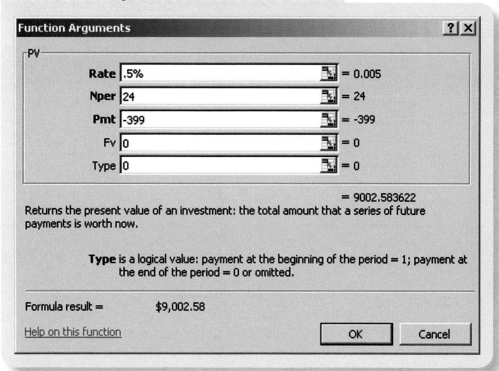

Exhibit B-11 Finding the Payment Using the PMT
Function in Excel

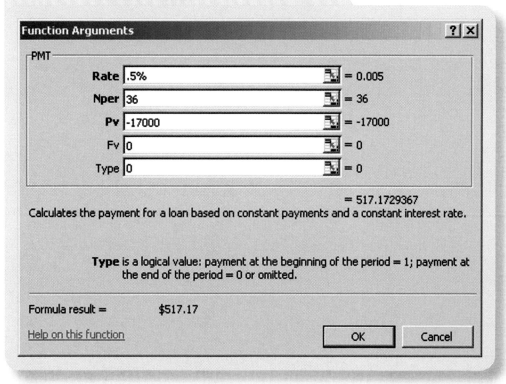

In Excel, =RATE(48, −350,12,000,0) generates a monthly rate of 1.4667 percent and an annual rate of 17.60 percent. The use of the RATE function requires that the payments are the same each period. Excel's IRR function is more flexible, allowing different payments. However, each payment has to be entered separately. For example, if the car is purchased for $17,000 with annual payments of $4,000, $5,000, $6,000, and $7,000 at the end of each of the next four years, the interest rate charged on the car loan can be calculated by using the IRR function (see Exhibit B-12).

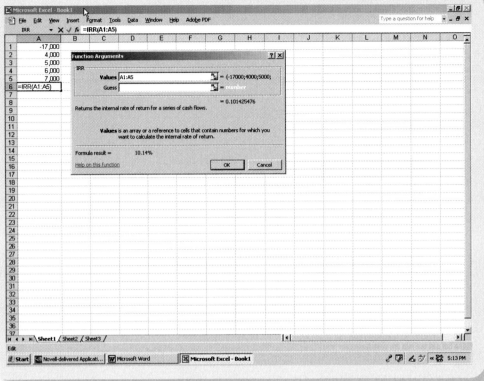

2008 Annual Report

Item 8. Financial Statements and Supplementary Data.

Management's Responsibility for Financial Statements

The financial statements presented in this Annual Report have been prepared with integrity and objectivity and are the responsibility of the management of The Home Depot, Inc. These financial statements have been prepared in conformity with U.S. generally accepted accounting principles and properly reflect certain estimates and judgments based upon the best available information.

The financial statements of the Company have been audited by KPMG LLP, an independent registered public accounting firm. Their accompanying report is based upon an audit conducted in accordance with the standards of the Public Company Accounting Oversight Board (United States).

The Audit Committee of the Board of Directors, consisting solely of outside directors, meets five times a year with the independent registered public accounting firm, the internal auditors and representatives of management to discuss auditing and financial reporting matters. In addition, a telephonic meeting is held prior to each quarterly earnings release. The Audit Committee retains the independent registered public accounting firm and regularly reviews the internal accounting controls, the activities of the independent registered public accounting firm and internal auditors and the financial condition of the Company. Both the Company's independent registered public accounting firm and the internal auditors have free access to the Audit Committee.

Management's Report on Internal Control over Financial Reporting

Our management is responsible for establishing and maintaining adequate internal control over financial reporting, as such term is defined in Rules 13a-15(f) promulgated under the Securities Exchange Act of 1934, as amended. Under the supervision and with the participation of our management, including our chief executive officer and chief financial officer, we conducted an evaluation of the effectiveness of our internal control over financial reporting as of February 1, 2009 based on the framework in *Internal Control – Integrated Framework* issued by the Committee of Sponsoring Organizations of the Treadway Commission (COSO). Based on our evaluation, our management concluded that our internal control over financial reporting was effective as of February 1, 2009 in providing reasonable assurance regarding the reliability of financial reporting and the preparation of financial statements for external purposes in accordance with generally accepted accounting principles. The effectiveness of our internal control over financial reporting as of February 1, 2009 has been audited by KPMG LLP, an independent registered public accounting firm, as stated in their report which is included on page 26 in this Form 10-K.

/s/ FRANCIS S. BLAKE

Francis S. Blake
Chairman &
Chief Executive Officer

/s/ CAROL B. TOMÉ

Carol B. Tomé
Chief Financial Officer &
Executive Vice President – Corporate Services

Report of Independent Registered Public Accounting Firm

The Board of Directors and Stockholders
The Home Depot, Inc.:

We have audited The Home Depot Inc.'s internal control over financial reporting as of February 1, 2009, based on criteria established in *Internal Control – Integrated Framework* issued by the Committee of Sponsoring Organizations of the Treadway Commission (COSO). The Home Depot Inc.'s management is responsible for maintaining effective internal control over financial reporting and for its assessment of the effectiveness of internal control over financial reporting, included in the accompanying Management's Report on Internal Control Over Financial Reporting. Our responsibility is to express an opinion on the Company's internal control over financial reporting based on our audit.

We conducted our audit in accordance with the standards of the Public Company Accounting Oversight Board (United States). Those standards require that we plan and perform the audit to obtain reasonable assurance about whether effective internal control over financial reporting was maintained in all material respects. Our audit included obtaining an understanding of internal control over financial reporting, assessing the risk that a material weakness exists, and testing and evaluating the design and operating effectiveness of internal control based on the assessed risk. Our audit also included performing such other procedures as we considered necessary in the circumstances. We believe that our audit provides a reasonable basis for our opinion.

A company's internal control over financial reporting is a process designed to provide reasonable assurance regarding the reliability of financial reporting and the preparation of financial statements for external purposes in accordance with generally accepted accounting principles. A company's internal control over financial reporting includes those policies and procedures that (1) pertain to the maintenance of records that, in reasonable detail, accurately and fairly reflect the transactions and dispositions of the assets of the company; (2) provide reasonable assurance that transactions are recorded as necessary to permit preparation of financial statements in accordance with generally accepted accounting principles, and that receipts and expenditures of the company are being made only in accordance with authorizations of management and directors of the company; and (3) provide reasonable assurance regarding prevention or timely detection of unauthorized acquisition, use, or disposition of the company's assets that could have a material effect on the financial statements.

Because of its inherent limitations, internal control over financial reporting may not prevent or detect misstatements. Also, projections of any evaluation of effectiveness to future periods are subject to the risk that controls may become inadequate because of changes in conditions, or that the degree of compliance with the policies or procedures may deteriorate.

In our opinion, The Home Depot, Inc. maintained, in all material respects, effective internal control over financial reporting as of February 1, 2009, based on criteria established in *Internal Control – Integrated Framework* issued by the Committee of Sponsoring Organizations of the Treadway Commission.

We also have audited, in accordance with the standards of the Public Company Accounting Oversight Board (United States), the Consolidated Balance Sheets of The Home Depot, Inc. and subsidiaries as of February 1, 2009 and February 3, 2008, and the related Consolidated Statements of Earnings, Stockholders' Equity and Comprehensive Income, and Cash Flows for each of the fiscal years in the three-year period ended February 1, 2009, and our report dated March 26, 2009 expressed an unqualified opinion on those consolidated financial statements.

/s/ KPMG LLP

Atlanta, Georgia
March 26, 2009

Report of Independent Registered Public Accounting Firm

The Board of Directors and Stockholders
The Home Depot, Inc.:

We have audited the accompanying Consolidated Balance Sheets of The Home Depot, Inc. and subsidiaries as of February 1, 2009 and February 3, 2008, and the related Consolidated Statements of Earnings, Stockholders' Equity and Comprehensive Income, and Cash Flows for each of the fiscal years in the three-year period ended February 1, 2009. These Consolidated Financial Statements are the responsibility of the Company's management. Our responsibility is to express an opinion on these Consolidated Financial Statements based on our audits.

We conducted our audits in accordance with the standards of the Public Company Accounting Oversight Board (United States). Those standards require that we plan and perform the audit to obtain reasonable assurance about whether the financial statements are free of material misstatement. An audit includes examining, on a test basis, evidence supporting the amounts and disclosures in the financial statements. An audit also includes assessing the accounting principles used and significant estimates made by management, as well as evaluating the overall financial statement presentation. We believe that our audits provide a reasonable basis for our opinion.

In our opinion, the Consolidated Financial Statements referred to above present fairly, in all material respects, the financial position of The Home Depot, Inc. and subsidiaries as of February 1, 2009 and February 3, 2008, and the results of their operations and their cash flows for each of the fiscal years in the three-year period ended February 1, 2009, in conformity with U.S. generally accepted accounting principles.

As discussed in Note 7 to the consolidated financial statements, effective January 29, 2007, the beginning of the fiscal year ended February 3, 2008, the Company adopted Financial Accounting Standards Board Interpretation No. 48, *Accounting for Uncertainty in Income Taxes*.

We also have audited, in accordance with the standards of the Public Company Accounting Oversight Board (United States), The Home Depot, Inc.'s internal control over financial reporting as of February 1, 2009, based on criteria established in *Internal Control – Integrated Framework* issued by the Committee of Sponsoring Organizations of the Treadway Commission (COSO), and our report dated March 26, 2009 expressed an unqualified opinion on the effectiveness of the Company's internal control over financial reporting.

/s/ KPMG LLP

Atlanta, Georgia
March 26, 2009

THE HOME DEPOT, INC. AND SUBSIDIARIES

CONSOLIDATED STATEMENTS OF EARNINGS

amounts in millions, except per share data	Fiscal Year Ended[1]		
	February 1, 2009	February 3, 2008	January 28, 2007
NET SALES	$71,288	$77,349	$79,022
Cost of Sales	47,298	51,352	52,476
GROSS PROFIT	**23,990**	25,997	26,546
Operating Expenses:			
Selling, General and Administrative	17,846	17,053	16,106
Depreciation and Amortization	1,785	1,702	1,574
Total Operating Expenses	19,631	18,755	17,680
OPERATING INCOME	**4,359**	7,242	8,866
Interest and Other (Income) Expense:			
Interest and Investment Income	(18)	(74)	(27)
Interest Expense	624	696	391
Other	163	—	—
Interest and Other, net	769	622	364
EARNINGS FROM CONTINUING OPERATIONS BEFORE PROVISION FOR INCOME TAXES	**3,590**	6,620	8,502
Provision for Income Taxes	1,278	2,410	3,236
EARNINGS FROM CONTINUING OPERATIONS	**2,312**	4,210	5,266
EARNINGS (LOSS) FROM DISCONTINUED OPERATIONS, NET OF TAX	**(52)**	185	495
NET EARNINGS	**$ 2,260**	$ 4,395	$ 5,761
Weighted Average Common Shares	1,682	1,849	2,054
BASIC EARNINGS PER SHARE FROM CONTINUING OPERATIONS	**$ 1.37**	$ 2.28	$ 2.56
BASIC EARNINGS (LOSS) PER SHARE FROM DISCONTINUED OPERATIONS	**$ (0.03)**	$ 0.10	$ 0.24
BASIC EARNINGS PER SHARE	**$ 1.34**	$ 2.38	$ 2.80
Diluted Weighted Average Common Shares	1,686	1,856	2,062
DILUTED EARNINGS PER SHARE FROM CONTINUING OPERATIONS	**$ 1.37**	$ 2.27	$ 2.55
DILUTED EARNINGS (LOSS) PER SHARE FROM DISCONTINUED OPERATIONS	**$ (0.03)**	$ 0.10	$ 0.24
DILUTED EARNINGS PER SHARE	**$ 1.34**	$ 2.37	$ 2.79

(1)   Fiscal years ended February 1, 2009 and January 28, 2007 include 52 weeks. Fiscal year ended February 3, 2008 includes 53 weeks.

See accompanying Notes to Consolidated Financial Statements.

THE HOME DEPOT, INC. AND SUBSIDIARIES

CONSOLIDATED BALANCE SHEETS

amounts in millions, except share and per share data	February 1, 2009	February 3, 2008
ASSETS		
Current Assets:		
Cash and Cash Equivalents	$ 519	$ 445
Short-Term Investments	6	12
Receivables, net	972	1,259
Merchandise Inventories	10,673	11,731
Other Current Assets	1,192	1,227
Total Current Assets	13,362	14,674
Property and Equipment, at cost:		
Land	8,301	8,398
Buildings	16,961	16,642
Furniture, Fixtures and Equipment	8,741	8,050
Leasehold Improvements	1,359	1,390
Construction in Progress	625	1,435
Capital Leases	490	497
	36,477	36,412
Less Accumulated Depreciation and Amortization	10,243	8,936
Net Property and Equipment	26,234	27,476
Notes Receivable	36	342
Goodwill	1,134	1,209
Other Assets	398	623
Total Assets	**$41,164**	**$44,324**
LIABILITIES AND STOCKHOLDERS' EQUITY		
Current Liabilities:		
Short-Term Debt	$ —	$ 1,747
Accounts Payable	4,822	5,732
Accrued Salaries and Related Expenses	1,129	1,094
Sales Taxes Payable	337	445
Deferred Revenue	1,165	1,474
Income Taxes Payable	289	60
Current Installments of Long-Term Debt	1,767	300
Other Accrued Expenses	1,644	1,854
Total Current Liabilities	11,153	12,706
Long-Term Debt, excluding current installments	9,667	11,383
Other Long-Term Liabilities	2,198	1,833
Deferred Income Taxes	369	688
Total Liabilities	23,387	26,610
STOCKHOLDERS' EQUITY		
Common Stock, par value $0.05; authorized: 10 billion shares; issued 1.707 billion shares at February 1, 2009 and 1.698 billion shares at February 3, 2008; outstanding 1.696 billion shares at February 1, 2009 and 1.690 billion shares at February 3, 2008	85	85
Paid-In Capital	6,048	5,800
Retained Earnings	12,093	11,388
Accumulated Other Comprehensive Income (Loss)	(77)	755
Treasury Stock, at cost, 11 million shares at February 1, 2009 and 8 million shares at February 3, 2008	(372)	(314)
Total Stockholders' Equity	17,777	17,714
Total Liabilities and Stockholders' Equity	**$41,164**	**$44,324**

See accompanying Notes to Consolidated Financial Statements.

THE HOME DEPOT, INC. AND SUBSIDIARIES

CONSOLIDATED STATEMENTS OF STOCKHOLDERS' EQUITY AND COMPREHENSIVE INCOME

amounts in millions, except per share data	Common Stock Shares	Common Stock Amount	Paid-In Capital	Retained Earnings	Accumulated Other Comprehensive Income (Loss)	Treasury Stock Shares	Treasury Stock Amount	Stockholders' Equity	Total Comprehensive Income
BALANCE, JANUARY 29, 2006	**2,401**	**$120**	**$ 7,149**	**$ 28,943**	**$ 409**	**(277)**	**$ (9,712)**	**$ 26,909**	
Cumulative Effect of Adjustment Resulting from the Adoption of SAB 108, net of tax	—	—	201	(257)	—	—	—	(56)	
ADJUSTED BALANCE, JANUARY 29, 2006	**2,401**	**$120**	**$ 7,350**	**$ 28,686**	**$ 409**	**(277)**	**$ (9,712)**	**$ 26,853**	
Net Earnings	—	—	—	5,761	—	—	—	5,761	$5,761
Shares Issued Under Employee Stock Plans	20	1	351	—	—	—	—	352	
Tax Effect of Sale of Option Shares by Employees	—	—	18	—	—	—	—	18	
Translation Adjustments	—	—	—	—	(77)	—	—	(77)	(77)
Cash Flow Hedges	—	—	—	—	(22)	—	—	(22)	(22)
Stock Options, Awards and Amortization of Restricted Stock	—	—	296	—	—	—	—	296	
Repurchase of Common Stock	—	—	—	—	—	(174)	(6,671)	(6,671)	
Cash Dividends ($0.675 per share)	—	—	—	(1,395)	—	—	—	(1,395)	
Other	—	—	(85)	—	—	—	—	(85)	
Comprehensive Income									$5,662
BALANCE, JANUARY 28, 2007	**2,421**	**$121**	**$ 7,930**	**$ 33,052**	**$ 310**	**(451)**	**$(16,383)**	**$ 25,030**	
Cumulative Effect of the Adoption of FIN 48	—	—	—	(111)	—	—	—	(111)	
Net Earnings	—	—	—	4,395	—	—	—	4,395	$4,395
Shares Issued Under Employee Stock Plans	12	1	239	—	—	—	—	240	
Tax Effect of Sale of Option Shares by Employees	—	—	4	—	—	—	—	4	
Translation Adjustments	—	—	—	—	455	—	—	455	455
Cash Flow Hedges	—	—	—	—	(10)	—	—	(10)	(10)
Stock Options, Awards and Amortization of Restricted Stock	—	—	206	—	—	—	—	206	
Repurchase of Common Stock	—	—	—	—	—	(292)	(10,815)	(10,815)	
Retirement of Treasury Stock	(735)	(37)	(2,608)	(24,239)	—	735	26,884	—	
Cash Dividends ($0.90 per share)	—	—	—	(1,709)	—	—	—	(1,709)	
Other	—	—	29	—	—	—	—	29	
Comprehensive Income									$4,840
BALANCE, FEBRUARY 3, 2008	**1,698**	**$ 85**	**$ 5,800**	**$ 11,388**	**$ 755**	**(8)**	**$ (314)**	**$ 17,714**	
Net Earnings	—	—	—	2,260	—	—	—	2,260	$2,260
Shares Issued Under Employee Stock Plans	9	—	68	—	—	—	—	68	
Tax Effect of Sale of Option Shares by Employees	—	—	7	—	—	—	—	7	
Translation Adjustments	—	—	—	—	(831)	—	—	(831)	(831)
Cash Flow Hedges	—	—	—	—	(1)	—	—	(1)	(1)
Stock Options, Awards and Amortization of Restricted Stock	—	—	176	—	—	—	—	176	
Repurchase of Common Stock	—	—	—	—	—	(3)	(70)	(70)	
Cash Dividends ($0.90 per share)	—	—	—	(1,521)	—	—	—	(1,521)	
Other	—	—	(3)	(34)	—	—	12	(25)	
Comprehensive Income									$1,428
BALANCE, FEBRUARY 1, 2009	**1,707**	**$ 85**	**$ 6,048**	**$ 12,093**	**$ (77)**	**(11)**	**$ (372)**	**$ 17,777**	

See accompanying Notes to Consolidated Financial Statements.

THE HOME DEPOT, INC. AND SUBSIDIARIES

CONSOLIDATED STATEMENTS OF CASH FLOWS

amounts in millions	Fiscal Year Ended[1]		
	February 1, 2009	February 3, 2008	January 28, 2007
CASH FLOWS FROM OPERATING ACTIVITIES:			
Net Earnings	$ 2,260	$ 4,395	$ 5,761
Reconciliation of Net Earnings to Net Cash Provided by Operating Activities:			
Depreciation and Amortization	1,902	1,906	1,886
Impairment Related to Rationalization Charges	580	—	—
Impairment of Investment	163	—	—
Stock-Based Compensation Expense	176	207	297
Changes in Assets and Liabilities, net of the effects of acquisitions and disposition:			
Decrease in Receivables, net	121	116	96
Decrease (Increase) in Merchandise Inventories	743	(491)	(563)
(Increase) Decrease in Other Current Assets	(7)	109	(225)
(Decrease) Increase in Accounts Payable and Accrued Liabilities	(646)	(465)	531
Decrease in Deferred Revenue	(292)	(159)	(123)
Increase (Decrease) in Income Taxes Payable	262	—	(172)
(Decrease) Increase in Deferred Income Taxes	(282)	(348)	46
Increase (Decrease) in Other Long-Term Liabilities	306	186	(51)
Other	242	271	178
Net Cash Provided by Operating Activities	5,528	5,727	7,661
CASH FLOWS FROM INVESTING ACTIVITIES:			
Capital Expenditures, net of $37, $19 and $49 of non-cash capital expenditures in fiscal 2008, 2007 and 2006, respectively	(1,847)	(3,558)	(3,542)
Proceeds from Sale of Business, net	—	8,337	—
Payments for Businesses Acquired, net	—	(13)	(4,268)
Proceeds from Sales of Property and Equipment	147	318	138
Purchases of Investments	(168)	(11,225)	(5,409)
Proceeds from Sales and Maturities of Investments	139	10,899	5,434
Net Cash (Used in) Provided by Investing Activities	(1,729)	4,758	(7,647)
CASH FLOWS FROM FINANCING ACTIVITIES:			
(Repayments of) Proceeds from Short-Term Borrowings, net	(1,732)	1,734	(900)
Proceeds from Long-Term Borrowings, net of discount	—	—	8,935
Repayments of Long-Term Debt	(313)	(20)	(509)
Repurchases of Common Stock	(70)	(10,815)	(6,684)
Proceeds from Sale of Common Stock	84	276	381
Cash Dividends Paid to Stockholders	(1,521)	(1,709)	(1,395)
Other Financing Activities	(128)	(105)	(31)
Net Cash Used in Financing Activities	(3,680)	(10,639)	(203)
Increase (Decrease) in Cash and Cash Equivalents	119	(154)	(189)
Effect of Exchange Rate Changes on Cash and Cash Equivalents	(45)	(1)	(4)
Cash and Cash Equivalents at Beginning of Year	445	600	793
Cash and Cash Equivalents at End of Year	$ 519	$ 445	$ 600
SUPPLEMENTAL DISCLOSURE OF CASH PAYMENTS MADE FOR:			
Interest, net of interest capitalized	$ 622	$ 672	$ 270
Income Taxes	$ 1,265	$ 2,524	$ 3,963

(1) Fiscal years ended February 1, 2009 and January 28, 2007 include 52 weeks. Fiscal year ended February 3, 2008 includes 53 weeks.

See accompanying Notes to Consolidated Financial Statements.

NOTES TO CONSOLIDATED FINANCIAL STATEMENTS

1.   SUMMARY OF SIGNIFICANT ACCOUNTING POLICIES

Business, Consolidation and Presentation

The Home Depot, Inc. and its subsidiaries (the "Company") operate The Home Depot stores, which are full-service, warehouse-style stores averaging approximately 105,000 square feet in size. The stores stock approximately 30,000 to 40,000 different kinds of building materials, home improvement supplies and lawn and garden products that are sold to do-it-yourself customers, do-it-for-me customers, home improvement contractors, tradespeople and building maintenance professionals. At the end of fiscal 2008, the Company was operating 2,274 stores, which included 1,971 The Home Depot stores, 34 EXPO stores, five Yardbirds stores and two THD Design Center stores in the United States, including the Commonwealth of Puerto Rico and the territories of the U.S. Virgin Islands and Guam ("U.S."), 176 The Home Depot stores in Canada, 74 The Home Depot stores in Mexico and 12 The Home Depot stores in China. On January 26, 2009, the Company announced plans to close the EXPO, THD Design Center and Yardbirds stores as part of the Company's focus on its core business. The Consolidated Financial Statements include the accounts of the Company and its wholly-owned subsidiaries. All significant intercompany transactions have been eliminated in consolidation.

Fiscal Year

The Company's fiscal year is a 52- or 53-week period ending on the Sunday nearest to January 31. Fiscal year ended February 1, 2009 ("fiscal 2008") includes 52 weeks, fiscal year ended February 3, 2008 ("fiscal 2007") includes 53 weeks and fiscal year ended January 28, 2007 ("fiscal 2006") includes 52 weeks.

Use of Estimates

Management of the Company has made a number of estimates and assumptions relating to the reporting of assets and liabilities, the disclosure of contingent assets and liabilities, and reported amounts of revenues and expenses in preparing these financial statements in conformity with accounting principles generally accepted in the U.S. Actual results could differ from these estimates.

Fair Value of Financial Instruments

The carrying amounts of Cash and Cash Equivalents, Receivables, Short-Term Debt and Accounts Payable approximate fair value due to the short-term maturities of these financial instruments. The fair value of the Company's investments is discussed under the caption "Short-Term Investments" in this Note 1. The fair value of the Company's Long-Term Debt is discussed in Note 6.

Cash Equivalents

The Company considers all highly liquid investments purchased with original maturities of three months or less to be cash equivalents. The Company's Cash Equivalents are carried at fair market value and consist primarily of high-grade commercial paper, money market funds and U.S. government agency securities.

Short-Term Investments

Short-Term Investments are recorded at fair value based on current market rates and are classified as available-for-sale.

Accounts Receivable

The Company has an agreement with a third-party service provider who directly extends credit to customers, manages the Company's private label credit card program and owns the related receivables. We evaluated the third-party entities holding the receivables under the program and concluded that they should not be consolidated by the Company in accordance with the provisions of Financial Accounting Standards Board ("FASB") Interpretation No. 46(R), "Consolidation of Variable Interest Entities." The agreement with the third-party service provider expires in 2018, with the Company having the option, but no obligation, to purchase the receivables at the end of the agreement. The deferred interest charges incurred by the Company for its deferred financing programs offered to its customers are included in Cost of Sales. The interchange fees charged to the Company for the customers' use of the cards and the profit sharing with the third-party administrator are included in Selling, General and Administrative expenses ("SG&A"). The sum of the three is referred to by the Company as "the cost of credit" of the private label credit card program.

In addition, certain subsidiaries of the Company extend credit directly to customers in the ordinary course of business. The receivables due from customers were $37 million and $57 million as of February 1, 2009 and February 3, 2008, respectively. The Company's valuation reserve related to accounts receivable was not material to the Consolidated Financial Statements of the Company as of the end of fiscal 2008 or 2007.

Merchandise Inventories

The majority of the Company's Merchandise Inventories are stated at the lower of cost (first-in, first-out) or market, as determined by the retail inventory method. As the inventory retail value is adjusted regularly to reflect market conditions, the inventory valued using the retail method approximates the lower of cost or market. Certain subsidiaries, including retail operations in Canada, Mexico and China, and distribution centers record Merchandise Inventories at the lower of cost or market, as determined by a cost method. These Merchandise Inventories represent approximately 18% of the total Merchandise Inventories balance. The Company evaluates the inventory valued using a cost method at the end of each quarter to ensure that it is carried at the lower of cost or market. The valuation allowance for Merchandise Inventories valued under a cost method was not material to the Consolidated Financial Statements of the Company as of the end of fiscal 2008 or 2007.

Independent physical inventory counts or cycle counts are taken on a regular basis in each store and distribution center to ensure that amounts reflected in the accompanying Consolidated Financial Statements for Merchandise Inventories are properly stated. During the period between physical inventory counts in stores, the Company accrues for estimated losses related to shrink on a store-by-store basis based on historical shrink results and current trends in the business. Shrink (or in the case of excess inventory, "swell") is the difference between the recorded amount of inventory and the physical inventory. Shrink may occur due to theft, loss, inaccurate records for the receipt of inventory or deterioration of goods, among other things.

Income Taxes

The Company provides for federal, state and foreign income taxes currently payable, as well as for those deferred due to timing differences between reporting income and expenses for financial statement purposes versus tax purposes. Federal, state and foreign tax benefits are recorded as a reduction of income taxes. Deferred tax assets and liabilities are recognized for the future tax consequences attributable to temporary differences between the financial statement carrying amounts of existing assets and liabilities and their respective tax bases. Deferred tax assets and liabilities are measured using enacted income tax rates expected to apply to taxable income in the years in which those temporary differences are expected to be recovered or settled. The effect of a change in income tax rates is recognized as income or expense in the period that includes the enactment date.

The Company and its eligible subsidiaries file a consolidated U.S. federal income tax return. Non-U.S. subsidiaries and certain U.S. subsidiaries, which are consolidated for financial reporting purposes, are not eligible to be included in the Company's consolidated U.S. federal income tax return. Separate provisions for income taxes have been determined for these entities. The Company intends to reinvest substantially all of the unremitted earnings of its non-U.S. subsidiaries and postpone their remittance indefinitely. Accordingly, no provision for U.S. income taxes for these non-U.S. subsidiaries was recorded in the accompanying Consolidated Statements of Earnings.

Depreciation and Amortization

The Company's Buildings, Furniture, Fixtures and Equipment are recorded at cost and depreciated using the straight-line method over the estimated useful lives of the assets. Leasehold Improvements are amortized using the straight-line method over the original term of the lease or the useful life of the improvement, whichever is shorter. The Company's Property and Equipment is depreciated using the following estimated useful lives:

	Life
Buildings	5-45 years
Furniture, Fixtures and Equipment	3-20 years
Leasehold Improvements	5-45 years

Capitalized Software Costs

The Company capitalizes certain costs related to the acquisition and development of software and amortizes these costs using the straight-line method over the estimated useful life of the software, which is three to six years. These costs are included in Furniture, Fixtures and Equipment in the accompanying Consolidated Balance Sheets. Certain development costs not meeting the criteria for capitalization are expensed as incurred.

Revenues

The Company recognizes revenue, net of estimated returns and sales tax, at the time the customer takes possession of merchandise or receives services. The liability for sales returns is estimated based on historical return levels. When the Company receives payment from customers before the customer has taken possession of the merchandise or the service has been performed, the amount received is recorded as Deferred Revenue in the accompanying Consolidated Balance Sheets until the sale or service is complete. The Company also records Deferred Revenue for the sale of gift cards and recognizes this revenue upon the redemption of gift cards in Net Sales. Gift card breakage income is recognized based upon historical redemption patterns and represents the balance of gift cards for which the Company believes the likelihood of redemption by the customer is remote. During fiscal 2008, 2007 and 2006, the Company recognized $37 million, $36 million and $33 million, respectively, of gift card breakage income. This income is recorded as other income and is included in the accompanying Consolidated Statements of Earnings as a reduction in SG&A.

Services Revenue

Net Sales include services revenue generated through a variety of installation, home maintenance and professional service programs. In these programs, the customer selects and purchases material for a project and the Company provides or arranges professional installation. These programs are offered through the Company's stores. Under certain programs, when the Company provides or arranges the installation of a project and the subcontractor provides material as part of the installation, both the material and labor are included in services revenue. The Company recognizes this revenue when the service for the customer is complete.

All payments received prior to the completion of services are recorded in Deferred Revenue in the accompanying Consolidated Balance Sheets. Services revenue was $3.1 billion, $3.5 billion and $3.8 billion for fiscal 2008, 2007 and 2006, respectively.

Self-Insurance

The Company is self-insured for certain losses related to general liability, product liability, automobile, workers' compensation and medical claims. The expected ultimate cost for claims incurred as of the balance sheet date is not discounted and is recognized as a liability. The expected ultimate cost of claims is estimated based upon analysis of historical data and actuarial estimates.

Prepaid Advertising

Television and radio advertising production costs, along with media placement costs, are expensed when the advertisement first appears. Included in Other Current Assets in the accompanying Consolidated Balance Sheets are $18 million and $31 million, respectively, at the end of fiscal 2008 and 2007 relating to prepayments of production costs for print and broadcast advertising as well as sponsorship promotions.

Vendor Allowances

Vendor allowances primarily consist of volume rebates that are earned as a result of attaining certain purchase levels and advertising co-op allowances for the promotion of vendors' products that are typically based on guaranteed minimum amounts with additional amounts being earned for attaining certain purchase levels. These vendor allowances are accrued as earned, with those allowances received as a result of attaining certain purchase levels accrued over the incentive period based on estimates of purchases.

Volume rebates and certain advertising co-op allowances earned are initially recorded as a reduction in Merchandise Inventories and a subsequent reduction in Cost of Sales when the related product is sold. Certain advertising co-op allowances that are reimbursements of specific, incremental and identifiable costs incurred to promote vendors' products are recorded as an offset against advertising expense. In fiscal 2008, 2007 and 2006, gross advertising expense was $1.0 billion, $1.2 billion and $1.2 billion, respectively, which was recorded in SG&A. Specific, incremental and identifiable advertising co-op allowances were $107 million, $120 million and $83 million for fiscal 2008, 2007 and 2006, respectively, and were recorded as an offset to advertising expense in SG&A.

Cost of Sales

Cost of Sales includes the actual cost of merchandise sold and services performed, the cost of transportation of merchandise from vendors to the Company's stores, locations or customers, the operating cost of the Company's sourcing and distribution network and the cost of deferred interest programs offered through the Company's private label credit card program.

The cost of handling and shipping merchandise from the Company's stores, locations or distribution centers to the customer is classified as SG&A. The cost of shipping and handling, including internal costs and payments to third parties, classified as SG&A was $501 million, $571 million and $545 million in fiscal 2008, 2007 and 2006, respectively.

Goodwill and Other Intangible Assets

Goodwill represents the excess of purchase price over the fair value of net assets acquired. The Company does not amortize goodwill, but does assess the recoverability of goodwill in the third quarter of each fiscal year by determining whether the fair value of each reporting unit supports its carrying value. The fair values of the Company's identified reporting units were estimated using the present value of expected future discounted cash flows.

The Company amortizes the cost of other intangible assets over their estimated useful lives, which range from 1 to 20 years, unless such lives are deemed indefinite. Intangible assets with indefinite lives are tested in the third quarter of each fiscal year for impairment. The Company recorded no impairment charges for goodwill or other intangible assets for fiscal 2008, 2007 or 2006.

Impairment of Long-Lived Assets

The Company evaluates the carrying value of long-lived assets when management makes the decision to relocate or close a store or other location, or when circumstances indicate the carrying amount of an asset may not be recoverable. A store's assets are evaluated for impairment by comparing its undiscounted cash flows with its carrying value. If the carrying value is greater than the undiscounted cash flows, a provision is made to write down the related assets to fair value if the carrying value is greater than the fair value. Impairment losses are recorded as a component of SG&A in the accompanying Consolidated Statements of Earnings. When a location closes, the Company also recognizes in SG&A the net present value of future lease obligations, less estimated sublease income.

In fiscal 2008, the Company recorded $580 million of asset impairments and $252 million of lease obligation costs as part of its Rationalization Charges. See Note 2 for more details on the Rationalization Charges. The Company also recorded impairments on the other closings and relocations in the ordinary course of business, which were not material to the Consolidated Financial Statements in fiscal 2008, 2007 and 2006.

Stock-Based Compensation

Effective January 30, 2006, the Company adopted the fair value recognition provisions of Statement of Financial Accounting Standards ("SFAS") No. 123(R), "Share-Based Payment" ("SFAS 123(R)"), using the modified prospective transition method. Under the modified prospective transition method, the Company began expensing unvested options granted prior to fiscal 2003 in addition to continuing to recognize stock-based compensation expense for all share-based payments awarded since the adoption of SFAS 123 "Accounting for Stock-Based Compensation" in fiscal 2003. During fiscal 2006, the Company recognized additional stock compensation expense of approximately $40 million as a result of the adoption of SFAS 123(R). Results of prior periods have not been restated.

The per share weighted average fair value of stock options granted during fiscal 2008, 2007 and 2006 was $6.46, $9.45 and $11.88, respectively. The fair value of these options was determined at the date of grant using the Black- Scholes option-pricing model with the following assumptions:

	Fiscal Year Ended		
	February 1, 2009	February 3, 2008	January 28, 2007
Risk-free interest rate	2.9%	4.4%	4.7%
Assumed volatility	33.8%	25.5%	28.5%
Assumed dividend yield	3.5%	2.4%	1.5%
Assumed lives of option	6 years	6 years	5 years

Derivatives

The Company uses derivative financial instruments from time to time in the management of its interest rate exposure on long-term debt and its exposure on foreign currency fluctuations. The Company accounts for its derivative financial instruments in accordance with SFAS No. 133, "Accounting for Derivative Instruments and Hedging Activities."

Comprehensive Income

Comprehensive Income includes Net Earnings adjusted for certain revenues, expenses, gains and losses that are excluded from Net Earnings under accounting principles generally accepted in the U.S. Adjustments to Net Earnings and Accumulated Other Comprehensive Income consist primarily of foreign currency translation adjustments.

Foreign Currency Translation

Assets and Liabilities denominated in a foreign currency are translated into U.S. dollars at the current rate of exchange on the last day of the reporting period. Revenues and Expenses are generally translated using average exchange rates for the period and equity transactions are translated using the actual rate on the day of the transaction.

Segment Information

The Company operates within a single reportable segment primarily within North America. Net Sales for the Company outside of the U.S. were $7.4 billion for fiscal 2008 and 2007 and were $6.3 billion for fiscal 2006. Long-lived assets outside of the U.S. totaled $2.8 billion and $3.1 billion as of February 1, 2009 and February 3, 2008, respectively.

2.   RATIONALIZATION CHARGES

In fiscal 2008, the Company reduced its square footage growth plans to improve free cash flow, provide stronger returns for the Company and invest in its existing stores to continue improving the customer experience. As a result of this store rationalization plan, the Company determined that it would no longer pursue the opening of approximately 50 U.S. stores that had been in its new store pipeline. The Company expects to dispose of or sublet these pipeline locations over varying periods. The Company also closed 15 underperforming U.S. stores in the second quarter of fiscal 2008, and the Company expects to dispose of or sublet those locations over varying periods.

Also in fiscal 2008, the Company announced that it would exit its EXPO, THD Design Center, Yardbirds and HD Bath businesses in order to focus on its core The Home Depot stores. The Company expects to close 34 EXPO Design Center stores, five Yardbirds stores, two THD Design Center stores and seven HD Bath locations in the first quarter of fiscal 2009, and expects to dispose or sublet those locations over varying periods. These steps will impact approximately 5,000 associates in those locations, their support functions and their distribution centers.

The Company also restructured its support functions to better align the Company's cost structure with the current economic environment. These actions impacted approximately 2,000 associates.

The Company recognized $951 million in total pretax charges for fiscal 2008 related to these actions. The significant components of the total expected charges and charges incurred to date are as follows (in millions):

	Total Expected Charges	Fiscal 2008 Charges	Estimated Remaining Charges
Asset impairments	$ 580	$580	$ —
Lease obligation costs, net	336	252	84
Severance	82	78	4
Other	103	41	62
Total	$1,101	$951	$150

Inventory markdown costs in Other are included in Cost of Sales in the accompanying Consolidated Statements of Earnings and costs related to asset impairments, lease obligations, severance and other are included in SG&A expenses. Asset impairment charges, including contractual costs to complete certain assets, were determined based on fair market value using market data for each individual property. Lease obligations represent the present value of contractually obligated rental payments offset by estimated sublet income, and therefore are not generally incremental uses of cash.

Activity related to Rationalization Charges for fiscal 2008 was as follows (in millions):

	Fiscal 2008 Charges	Cash Uses	Non-cash Uses	Accrued Balance, February 1, 2009
Asset impairments	$580	$—	$542	$ 38
Lease obligation costs, net	252	39	—	213
Severance	78	6	—	72
Other	41	18	3	20
Total	$951	$63	$545	$343

3. CHANGE IN ACCOUNTING PRINCIPLE

During fiscal 2008, the Company implemented a new enterprise resource planning ("ERP") system, including a new inventory system, for its retail operations in Canada. Along with this implementation, the Company changed its method of accounting for Merchandise Inventories for its retail operations in Canada from the lower of cost (first-in, first-out) or market, as determined by the retail inventory method, to the lower of cost or market using a weighted-average cost method. As of the end of fiscal 2008, the implementation of the new inventory system and related conversion to the weighted-average cost method for Canadian retail operations was complete.

The new ERP system allows the Company to utilize the weighted-average cost method, which the Company believes will result in greater precision in the costing of inventories and a better matching of cost of sales with revenue generated. The effect of the change on the Merchandise Inventories and Retained Earnings balances was not material. Prior to the inventory system conversion, the Company could not determine the impact of the change to the weighted-average cost method and therefore, could not retroactively apply the change to periods prior to fiscal 2008.

4. DISPOSITION AND ACQUISITIONS

On August 30, 2007, the Company closed the sale of HD Supply. The Company received $8.3 billion of net proceeds for the sale of HD Supply and recognized a $4 million loss, net of tax, in fiscal 2007. In fiscal 2008, the Company finalized working capital adjustments related to the sale and recorded a loss of $52 million, net of tax.

In connection with the sale, the Company purchased a 12.5% equity interest in the newly formed HD Supply for $325 million. In fiscal 2008, the Company determined its 12.5% equity interest in HD Supply was impaired and recorded a $163 million charge to write-down the investment, which is included in Interest and Other, net, in the accompanying Consolidated Statements of Earnings.

Also in connection with the sale, the Company guaranteed a $1.0 billion senior secured loan ("guaranteed loan") of HD Supply. The fair value of the guarantee, which was determined to be approximately $16 million, is recorded as a liability of the Company and included in Other Long-Term Liabilities. The guaranteed loan has a term of five years and the Company is responsible for up to $1.0 billion and any unpaid interest in the event of non-payment by HD Supply. The guaranteed loan is collateralized by certain assets of HD Supply.

In accordance with Statement of Financial Accounting Standards No. 144, "Accounting for the Impairment or Disposal of Long-Lived Assets" ("SFAS 144"), the Company reclassified the results of HD Supply as discontinued operations in its Consolidated Statements of Earnings for all periods presented.

The following table presents Net Sales and Earnings of HD Supply through August 30, 2007 and the losses on disposition which have been classified as discontinued operations in the Consolidated Statements of Earnings for fiscal 2008, 2007 and 2006 (amounts in millions):

	Fiscal Year Ended		
	February 1, 2009	February 3, 2008	January 28, 2007
Net Sales	$ —	$7,391	$11,815
Earnings Before Provision for Income Taxes	$ —	$ 291	$ 806
Provision for Income Taxes	—	(102)	(311)
Loss on Discontinued Operations, net	(52)	(4)	—
Earnings (Loss) from Discontinued Operations, net of tax	$(52)	$ 185	$ 495

The Company made no acquisitions during fiscal 2008. The aggregate purchase price for acquisitions in fiscal 2007 and 2006 was $25 million and $4.5 billion, respectively, including $3.5 billion for Hughes Supply in fiscal 2006. The Company recorded Goodwill related to the HD Supply businesses of $20 million and $2.8 billion for fiscal 2007 and 2006, respectively, and recorded no Goodwill related to its retail businesses for fiscal 2007 and $229 million for fiscal 2006.

5.   STAFF ACCOUNTING BULLETIN NO. 108

In fiscal 2006, the Company adopted Staff Accounting Bulletin No. 108, "Considering the Effects of Prior Year Misstatements when Quantifying Misstatements in Current Year Financial Statements" ("SAB 108"). SAB 108 addresses the process of quantifying prior year financial statement misstatements and their impact on current year financial statements. The provisions of SAB 108 allowed companies to report the cumulative effect of correcting immaterial prior year misstatements, based on the Company's historical method for evaluating misstatements, by adjusting the opening balance of retained earnings in the financial statements of the year of adoption rather than amending previously filed reports. In accordance with SAB 108, the Company adjusted beginning Retained Earnings for fiscal 2006 in the accompanying Consolidated Financial Statements for the items described below. The Company does not consider these adjustments to have a material impact on the Company's consolidated financial statements in any of the prior years affected.

Historical Stock Option Practices

During fiscal 2006, the Company requested that its Board of Directors review its historical stock option granting practices. A subcommittee of the Audit Committee undertook the review with the assistance of independent outside counsel, and it has completed its review. The principal findings of the 2006 review were as follows:

- All options granted in the period from 2002 through the present had an exercise price based on the market price of the Company's stock on the date the grant was approved by the Board of Directors or an officer acting pursuant to delegated authority. During this period, the stock administration department corrected administrative errors retroactively and without separate approvals. The administrative errors included inadvertent omissions of grantees from lists that were approved previously and miscalculations of the number of options granted to particular employees on approved lists.

- All options granted from December 1, 2000 through the end of 2001 had an exercise price based on the market price of the Company's stock on the date of a meeting of the Board of Directors or some other date selected without the benefit of hindsight. The February 2001 annual grant was not finally allocated to recipients until several weeks after the grant was approved. During this period, the stock administration department also corrected administrative errors retroactively and without separate approvals as in the period 2002 to the present.

- For annual option grants and certain quarterly option grants from 1981 through November 2000, the stated grant date was routinely earlier than the actual date on which the grants were approved by a committee of the Board of Directors. In almost every instance, the stock price on the apparent approval date was higher than the price on the stated grant date. The backdating occurred for grants at all levels of the Company. Management personnel, who have since left the Company, generally followed a practice of reviewing closing prices for a prior period and selecting a date with a low stock price to increase the value of the options to employees on lists of grantees subsequently approved by a committee of the Board of Directors.

- The annual option grants in 1994 through 2000, as well as many quarterly grants during this period, were not finally allocated among the recipients until several weeks after the stated grant date. Because of the absence of records prior to 1994, it is unclear whether allocations also postdated the selected grant dates from 1981 through 1993. Moreover, for many of these annual and quarterly grants from 1981 through December 2000, there is insufficient documentation to determine with certainty when the grants were actually authorized by a committee of the Board of Directors. Finally, the Company's stock administration department also retroactively added employees to lists of approved grantees, or changed the number of options granted to specific employees, without authorization of the Board of Directors or a board committee, to correct administrative errors.

- Numerous option grants to rank-and-file employees were made pursuant to delegations of authority that may not have been effective under Delaware law.

- In numerous instances, and primarily prior to 2003, beneficiaries of grants who were required to report them to the SEC failed to do so in a timely manner or at all.

- The subcommittee concluded that there was no intentional wrongdoing by any current member of the Company's management team or its Board of Directors.

The Company believes that because of these errors, it had unrecorded expense over the affected period (1981 through 2005) of $227 million in the aggregate, including related tax items. In accordance with the provisions of SAB 108, the Company decreased beginning Retained Earnings for fiscal 2006 by $227 million within the accompanying Consolidated Financial Statements.

As previously disclosed, the staff of the SEC began in June 2006 an informal inquiry into the Company's stock option practices, and the Office of the U.S. Attorney for the Southern District of New York also requested information on the subject. On December 10, 2008, the SEC stated in a letter to the Company that it did not intend to take any action as a result of the inquiry. The SEC matter is therefore now closed, and the Company has not received any communication from the Office of the U.S. Attorney since 2006.

The Company does not believe that the effect of the stock option adjustment was material, either quantitatively or qualitatively, in any of the years covered by the review of these items. In reaching that determination, the following quantitative measures were considered (dollars in millions):

Fiscal Year	Net After-Tax Effect of Adjustment	Reported Net Earnings	Percent of Reported Net Earnings
2005	$ 11	$ 5,838	0.19%
2004	18	5,001	0.36
2003	18	4,304	0.42
2002	21	3,664	0.57
1981-2001	159	14,531	1.09
Total	$227	$33,338	0.68%

Vendor Credits

The Company records credits against vendor invoices for various issues related to the receipt of goods. The Company previously identified that it was not recording an allowance for subsequent reversals of these credits based on historical experience. Beginning Retained Earnings for fiscal 2006 was decreased by $30 million in the accompanying Consolidated Financial Statements to reflect the appropriate adjustments to Merchandise Inventories and Accounts Payable, net of tax.

Impact of Adjustments

The impact of each of the items noted above, net of tax, on fiscal 2006 beginning balances are presented below (amounts in millions):

	Cumulative Effect as of January 30, 2006		
	Stock Option Practices	Vendor Credits	Total
Merchandise Inventories	$ —	$ 9	$ 9
Accounts Payable	—	(59)	(59)
Deferred Income Taxes	11	20	31
Other Accrued Expenses	(37)	—	(37)
Paid-In Capital	(201)	—	(201)
Retained Earnings	227	30	257
Total	$ —	$ —	$ —

6. DEBT

The Company has commercial paper programs that allow for borrowings up to $3.25 billion. All of the Company's short-term borrowings in fiscal 2008 and 2007 were under these commercial paper programs. In connection with the commercial paper programs, the Company has a back-up credit facility with a consortium of banks for borrowings up to $3.25 billion. The credit facility, which expires in December 2010, contains various restrictive covenants, all of which we are in compliance. None of the covenants are expected to impact the Company's liquidity or capital resources.

Short-Term Debt under the commercial paper programs was as follows (dollars in millions):

	February 1, 2009	February 3, 2008
Balance outstanding at fiscal year-end	$ —	$1,747
Maximum amount outstanding at any month-end	$1,771	$1,747
Average daily short-term borrowings	$ 403	$ 526
Weighted average interest rate	3.4%	5.0%

The Company's Long-Term Debt at the end of fiscal 2008 and 2007 consisted of the following (amounts in millions):

	February 1, 2009	February 3, 2008
3.75% Senior Notes; due September 15, 2009; interest payable semi-annually on March 15 and September 15	$ 999	$ 998
Floating Rate Senior Notes; due December 16, 2009; interest payable on March 16, June 16, September 16 and December 16	750	750
4.625% Senior Notes; due August 15, 2010; interest payable semi-annually on February 15 and August 15	998	998
5.20% Senior Notes; due March 1, 2011; interest payable semi-annually on March 1 and September 1	1,000	1,000
5.25% Senior Notes; due December 16, 2013; interest payable semi-annually on June 16 and December 16	1,245	1,244
5.40% Senior Notes; due March 1, 2016; interest payable semi-annually on March 1 and September 1	3,047	3,017
5.875% Senior Notes; due December 16, 2036; interest payable semi-annually on June 16 and December 16	2,959	2,959
Capital Lease Obligations; payable in varying installments through January 31, 2055	417	415
Other	19	302
Total debt	11,434	11,683
Less current installments	1,767	300
Long-Term Debt, excluding current installments	$ 9,667	$11,383

During fiscal 2008 and 2007, the Company entered into interest rate swaps, accounted for as fair value hedges, with notional amounts of $3.0 billion, that swapped fixed rate interest on the Company's $3.0 billion 5.40% Senior Notes for variable rate interest equal to LIBOR plus 60 to 149 basis points. In fiscal 2008, the Company received $56 million to settle these swaps, which will be amortized to reduce net Interest Expense over the remaining term of the debt.

At February 1, 2009, the Company had outstanding an interest rate swap, accounted for as a cash flow hedge, with a notional amount of $750 million that swaps variable rate interest on the Company's $750 million floating rate Senior Notes for fixed rate interest at 4.36% that expires on December 16, 2009. At February 1, 2009, the approximate fair value of this agreement was a liability of $21 million, which is the estimated amount the Company would have paid to settle the interest rate swap agreement.

The Senior Notes may be redeemed by the Company at any time, in whole or in part, at a redemption price plus accrued interest up to the redemption date. The redemption price is equal to the greater of (1) 100% of the principal amount of the Senior Notes to be redeemed, or (2) the sum of the present values of the remaining scheduled payments of principal and interest to maturity.

Additionally, if a Change in Control Triggering Event occurs, as defined by the terms of the Floating Rate Senior Notes and 5.25% Senior Notes issuance (together the "December 2006 Issuance"), holders of the December 2006 Issuance have the right to require the Company to redeem those notes at 101% of the aggregate principal amount of the notes plus accrued interest up to the redemption date.

The Company is generally not limited under the indentures governing the Senior Notes in its ability to incur additional indebtedness or required to maintain financial ratios or specified levels of net worth or liquidity. However, the indenture governing the Senior Notes contains various restrictive covenants, none of which is expected to impact the Company's liquidity or capital resources.

Interest Expense in the accompanying Consolidated Statements of Earnings is net of interest capitalized of $20 million, $46 million and $47 million in fiscal 2008, 2007 and 2006, respectively. Maturities of Long-Term Debt are $1.8 billion for fiscal 2009, $1.0 billion for fiscal 2010, $1.0 billion for fiscal 2011, $24 million for fiscal 2012, $1.3 billion for fiscal 2013 and $6.3 billion thereafter. As of February 1, 2009, the market value of the Senior Notes was approximately $10.0 billion.

7. INCOME TAXES

The components of Earnings from Continuing Operations before Provision for Income Taxes for fiscal 2008, 2007 and 2006 were as follows (amounts in millions):

| | Fiscal Year Ended | | |
	February 1, 2009	February 3, 2008	January 28, 2007
United States	$3,136	$5,905	$7,915
Foreign	454	715	587
Total	$3,590	$6,620	$8,502

The Provision for Income Taxes consisted of the following (amounts in millions):

| | Fiscal Year Ended | | |
	February 1, 2009	February 3, 2008	January 28, 2007
Current:			
Federal	$1,283	$2,055	$2,557
State	198	285	361
Foreign	85	310	326
	1,566	2,650	3,244
Deferred:			
Federal	(209)	(242)	(2)
State	(56)	17	(1)
Foreign	(23)	(15)	(5)
	(288)	(240)	(8)
Total	$1,278	$2,410	$3,236

The Company's combined federal, state and foreign effective tax rates for fiscal 2008, 2007 and 2006, net of offsets generated by federal, state and foreign tax benefits, were approximately 35.6%, 36.4% and 38.1%, respectively.

The reconciliation of the Provision for Income Taxes at the federal statutory rate of 35% to the actual tax expense for the applicable fiscal years was as follows (amounts in millions):

	Fiscal Year Ended		
	February 1, 2009	February 3, 2008	January 28, 2007
Income taxes at federal statutory rate	$1,257	$2,317	$2,976
State income taxes, net of federal income tax benefit	92	196	234
Other, net	(71)	(103)	26
Total	$1,278	$2,410	$3,236

The tax effects of temporary differences that give rise to significant portions of the deferred tax assets and deferred tax liabilities as of February 1, 2009 and February 3, 2008, were as follows (amounts in millions):

	February 1, 2009	February 3, 2008
Current:		
Deferred Tax Assets:		
Property and equipment	$ 85	$ —
Accrued self-insurance liabilities	143	155
Other accrued liabilities	490	601
Current Deferred Tax Assets	718	756
Deferred Tax Liabilities:		
Accelerated inventory deduction	(114)	(118)
Other	(118)	(113)
Current Deferred Tax Liabilities	(232)	(231)
Current Deferred Tax Assets, net	486	525
Noncurrent:		
Deferred Tax Assets:		
Accrued self-insurance liabilities	317	285
State income taxes	118	105
Capital loss carryover	65	56
Net operating losses	71	52
Other	222	54
Valuation allowance	(12)	(7)
Noncurrent Deferred Tax Assets	781	545
Deferred Tax Liabilities:		
Property and equipment	(1,068)	(1,133)
Goodwill and other intangibles	(78)	(69)
Other	—	(31)
Noncurrent Deferred Tax Liabilities	(1,146)	(1,233)
Noncurrent Deferred Tax Liabilities, net	(365)	(688)
Net Deferred Tax Assets (Liabilities)	$ 121	$ (163)

Current deferred tax assets and current deferred tax liabilities are netted by tax jurisdiction and noncurrent deferred tax assets and noncurrent deferred tax liabilities are netted by tax jurisdiction, and are included in the accompanying Consolidated Balance Sheets as follows (amounts in millions):

	February 1, 2009	February 3, 2008
Other Current Assets	$ 491	$ 535
Other Assets	4	—
Other Accrued Expenses	(5)	(10)
Deferred Income Taxes	(369)	(688)
Net Deferred Tax Assets (Liabilities)	$ 121	$(163)

The Company believes that the realization of the deferred tax assets is more likely than not, based upon the expectation that it will generate the necessary taxable income in future periods and, except for certain net operating losses discussed below, no valuation reserves have been provided.

At February 1, 2009, the Company had state and foreign net operating loss carryforwards available to reduce future taxable income, expiring at various dates from 2010 to 2028. Management has concluded that it is more likely than not that the tax benefits related to the net operating losses will be realized. However, certain foreign net operating losses are in jurisdictions where the expiration period is too short to be assured of utilization. Therefore, a $12 million valuation allowance has been provided to reduce the deferred tax asset related to net operating losses to an amount that is more likely than not to be realized. Total valuation allowances at February 1, 2009 and February 3, 2008 were $12 million and $7 million, respectively.

As a result of its sale of HD Supply, the Company incurred a tax loss, resulting in a net capital loss carryover of approximately $187 million. The tax loss on sale resulted primarily from the Company's tax basis in excess of its book investment in HD Supply. The net capital loss carryover will expire if not used by 2012. However, the Company has concluded that it is more likely than not that the tax benefits related to the capital loss carryover will be realized based on its ability to generate adequate capital gain income during the carryover period. Therefore, no valuation allowance has been provided.

The Company has not provided for U.S. deferred income taxes on approximately $1.3 billion of undistributed earnings of international subsidiaries because of its intention to indefinitely reinvest these earnings outside the U.S. The determination of the amount of the unrecognized deferred U.S. income tax liability related to the undistributed earnings is not practicable; however, unrecognized foreign income tax credits would be available to reduce a portion of this liability.

On January 29, 2007, the Company adopted FASB Interpretation No. 48, "Accounting for Uncertainty in Income Taxes — an Interpretation of FASB Statement No. 109" ("FIN 48"). Among other things, FIN 48 requires application of a "more likely than not" threshold to the recognition and derecognition of tax positions. It further requires that a change in judgment related to prior years' tax positions be recognized in the quarter of such change. The adoption of FIN 48 reduced the Company's Retained Earnings by $111 million. As a result of the implementation, the gross amount of unrecognized tax benefits at January 29, 2007 for continuing operations totaled $667 million. A reconciliation of the beginning and ending amount of gross unrecognized tax benefits for continuing operations is as follows (amounts in millions):

	February 1, 2009	February 3, 2008
Unrecognized tax benefits balance at beginning of fiscal year	$ 608	$ 667
Additions based on tax positions related to the current year	67	66
Additions for tax positions of prior years	231	25
Reductions for tax positions of prior years	(142)	(115)
Reductions due to settlements	(65)	(31)
Reductions due to lapse of statute of limitations	(4)	(4)
Unrecognized tax benefits balance at end of fiscal year	$ 695	$ 608

The gross amount of unrecognized tax benefits as of February 1, 2009 includes $401 million of net unrecognized tax benefits that, if recognized, would affect the annual effective income tax rate.

During fiscal 2008, the Company decreased its interest accrual associated with uncertain tax positions by approximately $19 million and paid interest of approximately $12 million. During fiscal 2007, the Company increased its interest accrual associated with uncertain tax positions by approximately $32 million and paid interest of approximately $8 million. Total accrued interest as of February 1, 2009 and February 3, 2008 is $109 million and $140 million, respectively. There were no penalty accruals during fiscal 2008 or 2007. Interest and penalties are included in net interest expense and operating expenses, respectively. Our classification of interest and penalties did not change as a result of the adoption of FIN 48.

The Company's income tax returns are routinely examined by domestic and foreign tax authorities. These audits generally include queries regarding the cost recovery of certain assets, which may result in timing differences. During 2007, the IRS completed its examination of the Company's fiscal 2003 and 2004 income tax returns, with the exception of certain issues that are currently under appeal. During 2008, the IRS began its examination of the Company's U.S. federal income tax returns for fiscal years 2005 and 2006. The Canadian governments, including various provinces, are currently auditing income tax returns for the years 2004 through 2005. Also, during 2008, the company entered into an Advance Pricing Agreement which settled a transfer pricing issue for the years 2004 through 2008 related to intangible assets provided from the U.S. There are also ongoing U.S. state and local audits covering tax years 2001 to 2006. At this time, the Company does not expect the results from any income tax audit to have a material impact on the Company's financial statements.

The Company believes that certain adjustments under appeal for the completed IRS examination, as well as certain state audits, will be agreed upon within the next twelve months. The Company has classified approximately $18 million of the reserve for unrecognized tax benefits as a short-term liability in the accompanying Consolidated Balance Sheets. Final settlement of these audit issues may result in payments that are more or less than these amounts, but the Company does not anticipate the resolution of these matters will result in a material change to its consolidated financial position or results of operations.

8. EMPLOYEE STOCK PLANS

The Home Depot, Inc. 2005 Omnibus Stock Incentive Plan ("2005 Plan") and The Home Depot, Inc. 1997 Omnibus Stock Incentive Plan ("1997 Plan" and collectively with the 2005 Plan, the "Plans") provide that incentive and non-qualified stock options, stock appreciation rights, restricted shares, performance shares, performance units and deferred shares may be issued to selected associates, officers and directors of the Company. Under the 2005 Plan, the maximum number of shares of the Company's common stock authorized for issuance is 255 million shares, with any award other than a stock option reducing the number of shares available for issuance by 2.11 shares. As of February 1, 2009, there were 205 million shares available for future grants under the 2005 Plan. No additional equity awards may be issued from the 1997 Plan after the adoption of the 2005 Plan on May 26, 2005.

Under the terms of the Plans, incentive stock options and non-qualified stock options are to be priced at or above the fair market value of the Company's stock on the date of the grant. Typically, incentive stock options and non-qualified stock options vest at the rate of 25% per year commencing on the first or second anniversary date of the grant and expire on the tenth anniversary date of the grant. Certain of the non-qualified stock options also include performance options which vest on the later of the first anniversary date of the grant and the date the closing price of the Company's common stock has been 25% greater than the exercise price of the options for 30 consecutive trading days. The Company recognized $47 million, $61 million and $148 million of stock-based compensation expense in fiscal 2008, 2007 and 2006, respectively, related to stock options.

Restrictions on the restricted stock issued under the Plans generally lapse according to one of the following schedules: (1) the restrictions of the restricted stock lapse over various periods up to five years, (2) the restrictions on 25% of the restricted stock lapse upon the third and sixth anniversaries of the date of issuance with the remaining 50% of the restricted stock lapsing upon the associate's attainment of age 62, or (3) the restrictions on 25% of the restricted stock lapse upon the third and sixth anniversaries of the date of issuance with the remaining 50% of the restricted stock lapsing upon the earlier of the associate's attainment of age 60 or the tenth anniversary date. The restricted stock also includes the Company's performance shares, the payout of which is dependent on the Company's total shareholders return percentile ranking compared to the performance of individual companies included in the S&P 500 index at the end of the three-year performance cycle. Additionally, certain awards may become non-forfeitable upon the attainment of age 60, provided the associate has had five years of continuous service. The fair value of the restricted stock is expensed over the period during which the restrictions lapse. The Company recorded stock-based compensation expense related to restricted stock of $109 million, $122 million and $95 million in fiscal 2008, 2007 and 2006, respectively.

In fiscal 2008, 2007 and 2006, there were 641 thousand, 593 thousand and 417 thousand deferred shares, respectively, granted under the Plans. Each deferred share entitles the person to one share of common stock to be received up to five years after the vesting date of the deferred shares, subject to certain deferral rights of the associate. The Company recorded stock-based compensation expense related to deferred shares of $9 million, $10 million and $37 million in fiscal 2008, 2007 and 2006, respectively.

As of February 1, 2009, there were 2.5 million non-qualified stock options outstanding under non-qualified stock option plans that are not part of the Plans.

The Company maintains two Employee Stock Purchase Plans ("ESPPs") (U.S. and non-U.S. plans). The plan for U.S. associates is a tax-qualified plan under Section 423 of the Internal Revenue Code. The non-U.S. plan is not a Section 423 plan. As of February 1, 2009, there were 15 million shares available under the plan for U.S associates and 21 million shares available under the non-U.S. plan. The purchase price of shares under the ESPPs is equal to 85% of the stock's fair market value on the last day of the purchase period. During fiscal 2008, there were 3 million shares purchased under the ESPPs at an average price of $19.74. Under the outstanding ESPPs as of February 1, 2009, employees have contributed $6 million to purchase shares at 85% of the stock's fair market value on the last day (June 30, 2009) of the purchase period. The Company recognized $11 million, $14 million and $17 million of stock-based compensation in fiscal 2008, 2007 and 2006, respectively, related to the ESPPs.

In total, the Company recorded stock-based compensation expense, including the expense of stock options, ESPPs, restricted stock and deferred stock units, of $176 million, $207 million and $297 million, in fiscal 2008, 2007 and 2006, respectively.

The following table summarizes stock options outstanding at February 1, 2009, February 3, 2008 and January 28, 2007, and changes during the fiscal years ended on these dates (shares in thousands):

	Number of Shares	Weighted Average Exercise Price
Outstanding at January 29, 2006	84,032	$37.24
Granted	257	39.53
Exercised	(10,045)	28.69
Canceled	(8,103)	40.12
Outstanding at January 28, 2007	66,141	$38.20
Granted	2,926	37.80
Exercised	(6,859)	28.50
Canceled	(9,843)	40.68
Outstanding at February 3, 2008	52,365	$38.98
Granted	5,226	26.09
Exercised	(777)	22.55
Canceled	(4,800)	39.14
Outstanding at February 1, 2009	52,014	$37.91

The total intrinsic value of stock options exercised was $4 million, $63 million and $120 million in fiscal 2008, 2007 and 2006, respectively. As of February 1, 2009, there were approximately 52 million stock options outstanding with a weighted average remaining life of 4 years and an intrinsic value of $1.4 million. As of February 1, 2009, there were approximately 42 million options exercisable with a weighted average exercise price of $39.33, a weighted average remaining life of 4 years, and no intrinsic value. As of February 1, 2009, there were approximately 51 million shares vested or expected to ultimately vest. As of February 1, 2009, there was $47 million of unamortized stock-based compensation expense related to stock options which is expected to be recognized over a weighted average period of 3 years.

The following table summarizes restricted stock outstanding at February 1, 2009 (shares in thousands):

	Number of Shares	Weighted Average Grant Date Fair Value
Outstanding at January 29, 2006	5,308	$35.76
Granted	7,575	41.37
Restrictions lapsed	(1,202)	38.03
Canceled	(1,551)	39.00
Outstanding at January 28, 2007	10,130	$39.20
Granted	7,091	39.10
Restrictions lapsed	(2,662)	39.01
Canceled	(2,844)	39.37
Outstanding at February 3, 2008	11,715	$39.14
Granted	7,938	27.14
Restrictions lapsed	(1,251)	34.37
Canceled	(2,115)	34.86
Outstanding at February 1, 2009	16,287	$34.22

As of February 1, 2009, there was $320 million of unamortized stock-based compensation expense related to restricted stock which is expected to be recognized over a weighted average period of 3 years. The total fair value of restricted stock shares vesting during fiscal 2008, 2007 and 2006 were $33 million, $103 million and $48 million, respectively.

9. LEASES

The Company leases certain retail locations, office space, warehouse and distribution space, equipment and vehicles. While most of the leases are operating leases, certain locations and equipment are leased under capital leases. As leases expire, it can be expected that, in the normal course of business, certain leases will be renewed or replaced.

Certain lease agreements include escalating rents over the lease terms. The Company expenses rent on a straight-line basis over the lease term which commences on the date the Company has the right to control the property. The cumulative expense recognized on a straight-line basis in excess of the cumulative payments is included in Other Accrued Expenses and Other Long-Term Liabilities in the accompanying Consolidated Balance Sheets.

The Company had a lease agreement under which the Company leased certain assets totaling $282 million. This lease was originally created under a structured financing arrangement and involved two special purpose entities. The Company financed a portion of its new stores opened in fiscal years 1997 through 2003 under this lease agreement. Under this agreement, the lessor purchased the properties, paid for the construction costs and subsequently leased the facilities to the Company. The Company recorded the rental payments under the terms of the operating lease agreements as SG&A in the accompanying Consolidated Statements of Earnings.

The $282 million lease agreement expired in fiscal 2008, and the Company exercised its option to purchase the assets under this lease for $282 million. As a result of this purchase, the Company paid off $282 million of Long-Term Debt included in the structured financing arrangement and reclassified $282 million from Long-Term Notes Receivable to Property and Equipment in the accompanying Consolidated Balance Sheets.

Total rent expense, net of minor sublease income for fiscal 2008, 2007 and 2006 was $846 million, $824 million and $768 million, respectively. Certain store leases also provide for contingent rent payments based on percentages of sales in excess of specified minimums. Contingent rent expense for fiscal 2008, 2007 and 2006 was approximately $5 million, $6 million and $9 million, respectively. Real estate taxes, insurance, maintenance and operating expenses applicable to the leased property are obligations of the Company under the lease agreements.

The approximate future minimum lease payments under capital and all other leases at February 1, 2009 were as follows (in millions):

Fiscal Year	Capital Leases	Operating Leases
2009	$ 88	$ 804
2010	89	724
2011	89	642
2012	89	572
2013	89	522
Thereafter through 2097	922	5,474
	1,366	$8,738
Less imputed interest	949	
Net present value of capital lease obligations	417	
Less current installments	16	
Long-term capital lease obligations, excluding current installments	$ 401	

Short-term and long-term obligations for capital leases are included in the accompanying Consolidated Balance Sheets in Current Installments of Long-Term Debt and Long-Term Debt, respectively. The assets under capital leases recorded in Property and Equipment, net of amortization, totaled $309 million and $327 million at February 1, 2009 and February 3, 2008, respectively.

10.   EMPLOYEE BENEFIT PLANS

The Company maintains active defined contribution retirement plans for its employees (the "Benefit Plans"). All associates satisfying certain service requirements are eligible to participate in the Benefit Plans. The Company makes cash contributions each payroll period up to specified percentages of associates' contributions as approved by the Board of Directors.

The Company also maintains a restoration plan to provide certain associates deferred compensation that they would have received under the Benefit Plans as a matching contribution if not for the maximum compensation limits under the Internal Revenue Code. The Company funds the restoration plan through contributions made to a grantor trust, which are then used to purchase shares of the Company's common stock in the open market.

The Company's contributions to the Benefit Plans and the restoration plan were $158 million, $152 million and $135 million for fiscal 2008, 2007 and 2006, respectively. At February 1, 2009, the Benefit Plans and the restoration plan held a total of 20 million shares of the Company's common stock in trust for plan participants.

11.   BASIC AND DILUTED WEIGHTED AVERAGE COMMON SHARES

The reconciliation of basic to diluted weighted average common shares for fiscal 2008, 2007 and 2006 is as follows (amounts in millions):

	Fiscal Year Ended		
	February 1, 2009	February 3, 2008	January 28, 2007
Weighted average common shares	1,682	1,849	2,054
Effect of potentially dilutive securities:			
Stock Plans	4	7	8
Diluted weighted average common shares	1,686	1,856	2,062

Stock plans include shares granted under the Company's employee stock plans as described in Note 8 to the Consolidated Financial Statements. Options to purchase 52.2 million, 43.4 million and 45.4 million shares of common stock at February 1, 2009, February 3, 2008 and January 28, 2007, respectively, were excluded from the computation of Diluted Earnings per Share because their effect would have been anti-dilutive.

12. COMMITMENTS AND CONTINGENCIES

At February 1, 2009, the Company was contingently liable for approximately $695 million under outstanding letters of credit and open accounts issued for certain business transactions, including insurance programs, trade contracts and construction contracts. The Company's letters of credit are primarily performance-based and are not based on changes in variable components, a liability or an equity security of the other party.

The Company is a defendant in numerous cases containing class-action allegations in which the plaintiffs are current and former hourly associates who allege that the Company failed to provide work breaks. The complaints generally seek unspecified monetary damages, injunctive relief or both. Class or collective-action certification has yet to be addressed in most of these cases. The Company has reached a tentative settlement with the plaintiffs in certain of these cases, subject to court approval. The reserve recorded by the Company for these cases is not material to the consolidated financial statements. The Company cannot reasonably estimate the possible loss which may arise from the remainder of these lawsuits. These matters, if decided adversely to or settled by the Company, individually or in the aggregate, may result in a liability material to the Company's consolidated financial condition or results of operations. The Company is vigorously defending itself against these actions.

13. QUARTERLY FINANCIAL DATA (UNAUDITED)

The following is a summary of the quarterly consolidated results of operations from continuing operations for the fiscal years ended February 1, 2009 and February 3, 2008 (dollars in millions, except per share data):

	Net Sales	Gross Profit	Earnings (Loss) from Continuing Operations	Basic Earnings per Share from Continuing Operations	Diluted Earnings per Share from Continuing Operations
Fiscal Year Ended February 1, 2009:					
First Quarter	$17,907	$ 6,072	$ 356	$0.21	$0.21
Second Quarter	20,990	6,964	1,202	0.72	0.71
Third Quarter	17,784	5,994	756	0.45	0.45
Fourth Quarter	14,607	4,960	(2)	0.00	0.00
Fiscal Year	$71,288	$23,990	$2,312	$1.37	$1.37
Fiscal Year Ended February 3, 2008:					
First Quarter	$18,545	$ 6,263	$ 947	$0.48	$0.48
Second Quarter	22,184	7,341	1,521	0.78	0.77
Third Quarter	18,961	6,339	1,071	0.59	0.59
Fourth Quarter	17,659	6,054	671	0.40	0.40
Fiscal Year	$77,349	$25,997	$4,210	$2.28	$2.27

Note: The quarterly data may not sum to fiscal year totals.

ACCT

Index

F

G

H

I

Learning Objectives		Key Concepts
LO1	Describe the four assumptions made when communicating accounting information.	When communicating accounting information, accountants assume that the activities of a company can be separated from those of the owners, that economic information can be effectively communicated in dollars over short periods of time, and that the business will continue into the foreseeable future.
LO2	Describe the purpose and structure of an income statement and the terms and principles used to create it.	An income statement reports a company's revenues and expenses over a period of time. A revenue is an inflow of resources from providing services, while an expense is an outflow of resources from providing services. Revenues are recorded when they are earned (revenue recognition principle), and expenses are recorded when they are incurred (matching principle). When revenues exceed expenses, a company generates net income.
LO3	Describe the purpose and structure of a balance sheet and the terms and principles used to create it.	A balance sheet reports a company's assets, liabilities, and equity accounts at a point in time. An asset is a resource of a business. A liability is an obligation of a business. Equity is the difference between assets and liabilities. Assets are recorded at their costs (cost principle). Assets are always equal to liabilities plus equity.
LO4	Describe the purpose and structure of a statement of retained earnings and how it links the income statement and the balance sheet.	A statement of retained earnings reports the change in a company's retained earnings balance over a period of time. The statement links the income statement and the balance sheet. Net income reported on the income statement is used to calculate the retained earnings balance reported on the balance sheet.
LO5	Describe the purpose and structure of a statement of cash flows and the terms and principles used to create it.	A statement of cash flows reports a company's sources and uses of cash over a period of time. Cash inflows and outflows are categorized into operating, investing, or financing activities.
LO6	Describe the qualitative characteristics that make accounting information useful.	Accounting information is useful only if it possesses several qualitative characteristics. It should be understandable, relevant, reliable, easily comparable, and consistent across time.
LO7	Describe the conceptual framework of accounting.	The conceptual framework is the collection of concepts that guide the practice of accounting. It includes the principles followed, the assumptions made, and the terms and statements used to communicate accounting information. It also includes the qualitative characteristics that make the information useful.

Key Definitions

Accounting The process of identifying, measuring, and communicating economic information to permit informed judgments and decisions. (p. 2)

Asset An economic resource that is objectively measurable, results from a prior transaction, and will provide future economic benefit. (p. 7)

Balance sheet A financial statement that reports a company's assets, liabilities, and equity at a specific point in time. (p. 8)

Comparability The ability to use accounting information to compare or contrast the financial activities of different companies. (p. 12)

Conceptual framework of accounting The collection of concepts that guide the manner in which accounting is practiced. (p. 14)

Conservatism The manner in which accountants deal with uncertainty regarding economic situations. (p. 13)

Consistency The ability to use accounting information to compare or contrast the financial activities of the same entity over time. (p. 12)

Contributed capital The resources that investors contribute to a business in exchange for ownership interest. (p. 7)

Cost principle The principle that assets should be recorded and reported at the cost paid to acquire them. (p. 7)

Dividends Profits that are distributed to owners. (p. 8)

Economic entity assumption Accountants assume that the financial activities of a business can be separated from the financial activities of the business's owner(s). (p. 3)

Equity The difference between a company's assets and liabilities, representing the share of assets that is claimed by the company's owners. (p. 7)

Expense A decrease in resources resulting from the sale of goods or provision of services. (p. 5)

Going concern assumption Accountants assume that a company will continue to operate into the foreseeable future. (p. 4)

Income statement A financial statement that reports a company's revenues and expenses over a specific period of time. (p. 6)

Liability An obligation of a business that results from a past transaction and will require the sacrifice of economic resources at some future date. (p. 7)

Key Definitions (continued)

Matching principle The principle that expenses should be recorded in the period resources are used to generate revenues. (p. 5)

Materiality The threshold at which a financial item begins to affect decision making. (p. 13)

Monetary unit assumption Accountants assume that the dollar is the most effective means to communicate economic activity. (p. 4)

Relevance The capacity of accounting information to make a difference in decisions. (p. 12)

Reliability The extent to which accounting information can be depended upon to represent what it purports to represent, both in description and in number. (p. 12)

Retained earnings Profits that are retained in the business. (p. 8)

Revenue An increase in resources resulting from the sale of goods or the provision of services. (p. 5)

Revenue recognition principle The principle that a revenue should be recorded when a resource has been earned. (p. 5)

Statement of cash flows A financial statement that reports a company's sources and uses of cash over a specific period of time. (p. 10)

Statement of retained earnings A financial statement that reports the change in a company's retained earnings over a specific period of time. (p. 9)

Time period assumption Accountants assume that economic information can be meaningfully captured and communicated over short periods of time. (p. 4)

Understandability The ability of accounting information to "be comprehensible to those who have a reasonable understanding of business…and are willing to study the information with reasonable diligence." (p. 11)

Demonstration Problem

On August 1, Sarah begins a tutoring service that she will operate for four months. With $40 borrowed from a friend and $100 of her own money, she purchases a $120 accounting textbook and $8 of school supplies. Sarah promises to pay her friend $1 at the end of each month and to pay back the full $40 at the end of December.

Sarah charges $20 per tutoring session. During August, she conducted ten sessions and bought $10 of additional school supplies. At the end of the month, Sarah has not collected on four of the ten sessions, and she has $5 of school supplies left over. Prepare Sarah's income statement and statement of retained earnings for the month ending August 31 and her balance sheet on August 31.

Key Formulas

Income Statement	Revenues − Expenses = Net Income or Net Loss
Balance Sheet	Assets = Liabilities + Equity
Statement of Retained Earnings	Retained Earnings, Beginning Balance +/− Net Income/Loss − Dividends = Retained Earnings, Ending Balance
Statement of Cash Flows	Cash Flows Provided (Used) by Operating Activities +/− Cash Flows Provided (Used) by Investing Activities +/− Cash Flows Provided (Used) by Financing Activities = Net Increase (Decrease) in Cash

Demonstration Problem Solution

Sarah's Tutoring Service
Income Statement
For the Month Ending August 31

Revenues:		$200
Expenses:		
Depreciation (textbook)	$ 30	
Supplies	13	
Interest	1	
Total expenses		44
Net income		$156

Sarah's Tutoring Service
Statement of Retained Earnings
For the Month Ending August 31

Retained earnings, August 1	$ 0
Add: Net income	156
Less: Dividends	0
Retained earnings, August 31	$156

Sarah's Tutoring Service
Balance Sheet
August 31

Cash	$121	
Accounts receivable	80	
Textbook	90	
Supplies	5	
Total assets		$296
Note payable	$ 40	
Total liabilities		$ 40
Contributed capital	$100	
Retained earnings	156	
Total equity		256
Total liabilities and equity		$296

Visit **4ltrpress.cengage.com/acct** for additional study tools!

reviewcard

Learning Objectives	Key Concepts	Key Definitions
LO1 Describe the three major forms of business.	The three major forms of business are sole proprietorship, partnership, and corporation. A sole proprietorship is owned by one person. A partnership is owned by multiple partners. A corporation is established in a state and is owned by investors who purchase the corporation's stock. Corporations whose stock is available to the public at large are called public corporations.	**American Institute of Certified Public Accountants** The professional organization of certified public accountants whose board establishes rules that are often more technical and more specific to certain industries. (p. 23) **Classified balance sheet** A type of balance sheet that groups together accounts of similar nature and reports them in a few major classifications. (p. 24) **Common-size financial statement** A statement in which all accounts have been standardized by the overall size of the company. (p. 31) **Contributed capital** The amount of equity a company generates through the sale of stock to investors. (p. 26)
LO2 Define generally accepted accounting principles and their origins.	Generally accepted accounting principles are the accounting standards, rules, principles, and procedures that comprise authoritative practice for financial accounting. They have been developed over time by several regulatory bodies, including the Securities and Exchange Commission, the Financial Accounting Standards Board, and the American Institute of Certified Public Accountants.	**Corporation** A separate legal entity that is established by filing articles of incorporation in a state. (p. 22) **Cost of sales** The cost of the inventory sold during a period. (p. 27) **Current asset** Any asset that is reasonably expected to be converted to cash or consumed within one year of the balance sheet date. (p. 24) **Current liability** An obligation that is reasonably expected to be satisfied within one year. (p. 26)
LO3 Describe the main classifications of assets, liabilities, and equity in a classified balance sheet.	A classified balance sheet summarizes an entity's financial position at a point in time by grouping similar asset, liability, and equity accounts together and reporting them in several major classifications. Assets are classified into current assets, long term investments, fixed assets, intangible assets, and other assets. Liabilities are classified into current liabilities and long term liabilities. Equity is classified into contributed capital and retained earnings.	**Financial Accounting Standards Board** The standard setting body whose mission is "to establish and improve standards of financial accounting and reporting for the guidance and education of the public, including issuers, auditors, and users of financial information." (p. 23) **Fixed assets** The tangible resources that are used in a company's operations for more than one year and are not intended for resale. (p. 24)
LO4 Describe the main subtotals of income on a multi-step income statement.	A multi-step income statement calculates income in multiple steps by grouping certain revenues and expenses together and calculating several subtotals of income. These subtotals include gross profit, operating profit, income before taxes, and net income.	**Generally accepted accounting principles** The accounting standards, rules, principles, and procedures that comprise authoritative practice for financial accounting. (p. 22)

Learning Objectives	Key Concepts	Key Definitions (continued)
LO5 Analyze the balance sheet and the income statement using horizontal and vertical analyses.	Horizontal analysis calculates the change in an account balance from one period to the next and expresses that change in both absolute and percentage terms. Because a horizontal analysis shows the growth or decline in each account, it is useful for identifying trends. Vertical analysis states each account balance as a percentage of some base account—sales on the income statement and total assets on the balance sheet. Because a vertical analysis standardizes each account by a measure of company size, it is useful in comparing different companies. The product of a vertical analysis is called a common-size statement.	**Gross profit** The profit that a company generates when considering only the sales price and the cost of the product sold. (p. 27)
		Horizontal analysis A method of analyzing a company's account balances over time by calculating absolute and percentage changes in each account. (p. 29)
		Income before taxes The profit that a company generates when considering all revenues and expenses except for income taxes. (p. 28)
		Independent auditor's report A report, prepared by a certified public accountant for the public shareholder, stating an opinion on whether the financial statements present fairly, in conformity with GAAP, the company's financial condition and results of operations and cash flows. (p. 37)
LO6 Describe the purpose of a statement of stockholders' equity.	The statement of stockholders' equity shows the changes in all equity accounts, including retained earnings and contributed capital, over a period of time.	**Intangible asset** A resource that is used in operation for more than one year, is not intended for resale, and has no physical substance. (p. 25)
		International Accounting Standards Board A board, similar to the FASB, whose mission is to develop a single set of high quality standards requiring transparent and comparable information. (p. 23)
LO7 Describe the types of information usually disclosed along with financial statements.	In addition to its financial statements, a company will include the following in its annual report distributed to stockholders: notes to the financial statements, the auditor's report, and management's discussion and analysis.	**International Financial Reporting Standards** Standards issued by the International Accounting Standards Board. (p. 23)
		Long-term investments The investments in the common stock or debt of another entity that will not be sold within a year. (p. 24)
		Long-term liability An obligation that is not expected to be satisfied within one year. (p. 26)
		Management's Discussion and Analysis A discussion and analysis of the financial activities of the company by the company's management. (p. 38)
		Multi-step income statement Calculates income by grouping certain revenues and expenses together and calculating several subtotals of income. (p. 27)
		Net income The final income measure after the provision for income taxes is subtracted from income before taxes. (p. 29)
		Notes to the financial statements The additional textual and numerical information immediately following the financial statements. (p. 36)

Key Formulas

Operating expenses Recurring expenses that a company incurs during normal operations. (p. 28)

Operating profit The profit that a company generates when considering both the cost of the inventory and the normal expenses incurred to operate the business. (p. 28)

Other assets Resources that do not fit well into one of the other asset classifications or are small enough that they do not warrant separate reporting. (p. 25)

Other revenue and expenses Revenues and expenses generated outside of normal operations. (p. 28)

Partnership A business that is formed when two or more proprietors join together to own a business. (p. 21)

Provision for income taxes The amount of income tax expense for a given period. (p. 29)

Public corporation A separate legal entity in which ownership is available to the public at large. (p. 22)

Retained earnings The amount of equity a company generates by being profitable and retaining those profits in the business. (p. 26)

Sales revenue The resources that a company generates during a period from selling its inventory. (p. 27)

Securities and Exchange Commission The federal agency charged to protect investors and maintain the integrity of securities markets. (p. 22)

Single-step income statement Calculates total revenues and total expenses and then determines net income in one step by subtracting total expenses from total revenues. (p. 26)

Sole proprietorship A business owned by one person. (p. 20)

Statement of stockholders' equity A financial statement that shows how and why each equity account in the company's balance sheet changed from one year to the next. (p. 34)

Vertical analysis A method of comparing a company's account balances within one year by dividing each account balance by a base amount to yield a percentage. (p. 31)

Classified balance sheet	Assets
	  Current assets
	  Long-term investments
	  Fixed assets
	  Intangible assets
	  Other assets
	    <u>Total assets</u>
	
	Liabilities and Equity
	  Current liabilities
	  <u>Long-term liabilities</u>
	    Total liabilities
	  Contributed capital
	  <u>Retained earnings</u>
	    Total equity
	    <u>Total liabilities and equity</u>

Multi-step income statement	Net sales or revenues <u>− Cost of goods sold</u> Gross profit <u>− Operating expenses</u> Operating profit +/− Other revenues and expenses Income before taxes <u>− Income tax expense</u> <u>Net income</u>

Horizontal Analysis

$$\text{Dollar change in account balance} = \text{Current year balance} - \text{Prior year balance}$$

$$\text{Percentage change in account balance} = \frac{\text{Dollar change}}{\text{Prior year balance}}$$

Vertical Analysis

	For the Balance Sheet	For the Income Statement
Percentage	$\dfrac{\text{Account balance}}{\text{Total Assets}}$	$\dfrac{\text{Account balance}}{\text{Net Sales or Revenue}}$

Demonstration Problem

The following items were taken from the financial statements of Columbia Sportswear Company. Use the items to prepare a multi-step income statement for the year ending December 31 and a classified balance sheet at December 31. For each statement, prepare a vertical analysis. All dollar amounts are in thousands of dollars.

Accounts payable	$ 62,432
Accounts receivable	206,024
Accrued liabilities	43,789
Cash and cash equivalents	264,585
Common stock	205,465
Cost of sales	511,101
Current portion of long-term debt	4,596
Deferred tax asset, current	17,442
Deferred tax liability, long-term	7,716
Goodwill	12,157
Income tax expense	70,548
Income taxes payable	8,069
Intangibles and other assets	24,475
Interest expense	1,627
Interest revenue	2,107
Inventories	126,808
Long-term debt	16,335
Net sales	951,786
Prepaid expenses and other current assets	6,028
Property, plant, and equipment	126,247
Retained earnings	435,364
Selling, general and administrative expenses	250,496

Demonstration Problem Solution

Columbia Sportswear Company
Income Statement
For the Year Ending December 31

Net sales	$951,786	100.0%
Cost of sales	511,101	53.7%
Gross profit	$440,685	46.3%
Selling, general, and administrative expenses	250,496	26.3%
Operating profit	$190,189	20.0%
Other revenues and expenses:		
Interest revenue	2,107	0.2%
Interest expense	(1,627)	0.2%
Income before income tax	$190,669	20.0%
Income tax expense	70,548	7.4%
Net income	$120,121	12.6%

Columbia Sportswear Company
Balance Sheet
December 31

Assets

Current assets:		
Cash and cash equivalents	$264,585	33.8%
Accounts receivable, net	206,024	26.3%
Inventories, net	126,808	16.2%
Deferred tax asset	17,442	2.2%
Prepaid expenses and other current assets	6,028	0.8%
Total current assets	$620,887	79.2%
Property, plant, and equipment, net	126,247	16.1%
Intangibles and other assets	24,475	3.1%
Goodwill	12,157	1.6%
Total assets	$783,766	100.0%

Liabilities and Shareholders' Equity

Current liabilities:		
Accounts payable	$ 62,432	8.0%
Accrued liabilities	43,789	5.6%
Income taxes payable	8,069	1.0%
Current portion of long-term debt	4,596	0.6%
Total current liabilities	$118,886	15.2%
Long-term debt	16,335	2.1%
Deferred tax liability	7,716	1.0%
Total liabilities	$142,937	18.2%
Shareholders' equity:		
Common stock	$205,465	26.2%
Retained earnings	435,364	55.6%
Total shareholders' equity	$640,829	81.8%
Total liabilities and shareholders' equity	$783,766	100.0%

reviewcard

CHAPTER 3
Recording Accounting Transactions

Learning Objectives		Key Concepts
LO1	Describe the purpose of an accounting information system.	The purpose of an accounting information system is to identify economic events to be recorded, to measure and record those events, and to process the resulting information so that financial statements can be prepared.
LO2	Analyze the effect of accounting transactions on the accounting equation.	All accounting transactions must affect at least two accounts so that the fundamental accounting equation remains in balance. This is known as the dual nature of accounting.
LO3	Understand how T-accounts and debits and credits are used in a double-entry accounting system.	The double entry accounting system uses debits and credits to record accounting transactions. For every transaction, total debit entries must equal total credit entries. Asset, expense, and dividend accounts have debit balances, so they are increased with debit entries and decreased with credit entries. Liability, equity, and revenue accounts have credit balances, so they are increased with credit entries and decreased with debit entries.
LO4	Describe the purpose of the journal, ledger, and trial balance.	Accounting transactions are recorded in the general journal, which captures information chronologically. Information in the general journal is posted to the general ledger, which summarizes information by account. Balances from the general ledger are listed on a trial balance, which contains all account balances and proves that debit balances equal credit balances.
LO5	Record and post accounting transactions and prepare a trial balance and financial statements.	After determining which accounts are affected by an accounting transaction, the transaction is recorded and posted. Once all transactions are posted, a trial balance is prepared, from which financial statements are prepared.

Key Definitions

Account An accounting record that accumulates the activity of a specific item and yields the item's balance. (p. 45)

Accounting information system The system that identifies, records, summarizes, and communicates the various transactions of a company. (p. 44)

Accounting transaction Any economic event that affects a company's assets, liabilities or equity at the time of the event. (p. 44)

Chart of accounts The list of accounts that a company uses to capture its business activities. (p. 45)

Credit The right side of an account. (p. 51)

Debit The left side of an account. (p. 51)

Dual nature of accounting Every accounting transaction affects at least two accounts. (p. 46)

Journal A chronological record of transactions. (p. 54)

Ledger A collection of accounts and their balances. (p. 55)

Trial balance A listing of accounts and their balances at a specific point in time. (p. 55)

Key Exhibit

Debit and Credit Rules	Type of Account	Normal Balance	Increase with a	Decrease with a
	Asset	Debit	Debit	Credit
	Liability	Credit	Credit	Debit
	Equity	Credit	Credit	Debit
	Revenue	Credit	Credit	Debit
	Expense	Debit	Debit	Credit
	Dividend	Debit	Debit	Credit

Demonstration Problem

The following transactions occurred during the first month of operations for Auburn Windows, Inc. Prepare all necessary journal entries, post the information to the ledger, and prepare a trial balance at March 31.

Mar. 1 Issued 15,000 shares of common stock for $20,000 cash.

1 Purchase a used truck for $7,200 cash.

3 Purchased cleaning supplies for $5,000 cash.

5 Paid $2,400 cash on a one-year insurance policy effective March 1.

12 Billed customers $4,800 for cleaning services.

Mar. 20 Paid $2,300 cash for employee salaries.

21 Collected $4,000 cash from customers billed on March 12.

25 Billed customers $5,200 for cleaning services.

31 For the month, paid for and used $600 of fuel.

31 Declared and paid $200 cash dividend.

Demonstration Problem Solution

Mar. 1	Cash	20,000	
	Common Stock		20,000
	(Initial investment by owner)		
Mar. 1	Equipment	7,200	
	Cash		7,200
	(Purchase of equipment)		
Mar. 3	Supplies	5,000	
	Cash		5,000
	(Purchase of supplies)		
Mar. 5	Prepaid Insurance	2,400	
	Cash		2,400
	(Purchase of insurance policy)		
Mar. 12	Accounts Receivable	4,800	
	Service Revenue		4,800
	(Provide services on account)		
Mar. 20	Salaries Expense	2,300	
	Cash		2,300
	(Pay employees)		
Mar. 21	Cash	4,000	
	Accounts Receivable		4,000
	(Collect receivables from customers)		
Mar. 25	Accounts Receivable	5,200	
	Service Revenue		5,200
	(Provide services on account)		
Mar. 31	Fuel Expense	600	
	Cash		600
	(Pay for fuel consumed)		
Mar. 31	Dividends	200	
	Cash		200
	(Pay for dividends)		

Cash

20,000	7,200
4,000	5,000
	2,400
	2,300
	600
	200
6,300	

Accounts Receivable

4,800	4,000
5,200	
6,000	

Equipment

7,200
7,200

Prepaid Insurance

2,400
2,400

Supplies

5,000
5,000

Common Stock

20,000
20,000

Service Revenue

4,800
5,200
10,000

Salaries Expense

2,300
2,300

Fuel Expense

600
600

Dividends

200
200

Trial Balance
March 31

Cash	$ 6,300	
Accounts Receivable	6,000	
Prepaid Insurance	2,400	
Supplies	5,000	
Equipment	7,200	
Common Stock		$20,000
Service Revenue		10,000
Fuel Expense	600	
Salaries Expense	2,300	
Dividends	200	
Totals	$30,000	$30,000

Visit **4ltrpress.cengage.com/acct** for additional study tools!

reviewcard

Learning Objectives

LO1 Describe how income is measured and reported under the accrual and cash bases of accounting.

LO2 Identify the four major circumstances in which adjusting journal entries are necessary.

LO3 Record and post adjusting journal entries, and prepare an adjusted trial balance and financial statements.

LO4 Describe the purpose of the closing process and prepare closing entries.

LO5 Describe the steps of the accounting cycle.

Key Concepts

The cash basis records revenues when cash is received and expenses when cash is paid. The accrual basis records revenues when they are earned and expenses when they are incurred. Although both bases result in the same income over the long term, the accrual basis best reflects income over short periods of time, so it is required by GAAP.

Adjusting journal entries are necessary to record revenues that have been earned and expenses that have been incurred. The four scenarios in which adjusting entries arise are (1) a deferred revenue—revenue is earned after cash is received, (2) an accrued revenue—revenue is earned before cash is received, (3) a deferred expense—an expense is incurred after cash is paid, and (4) an accrued expense—an expense is incurred before cash is paid.

At the end of an accounting period, adjusting journal entries are prepared to properly record revenues and expenses. Once these entries are posted to the ledger, an adjusted trial balance is prepared, from which financial statements are created.

The purpose of the closing process is to (1) update the Retained Earnings account to reflect all revenues, expenses, and dividends from the period and (2) prepare all revenue, expense, and dividend accounts for the next period by setting their balances to zero. The closing process is accomplished through "closing entries" recorded in the journal after financial statements are prepared.

The steps in accounting cycle are as follows: (1) journalize and post transactions, (2) prepare a trial balance, (3) journalize and post adjusting entries, (4) prepare an adjusted trial balance, (5) prepare financial statements, (6) journalize and post closing entries, (7) prepare a post-closing trial balance.

Key Definitions

Accounting cycle The sequence of steps in which an accounting information system captures, processes and reports a company's accounting transactions during a period. (p. 82)

Accrual basis of accounting Records revenues when they are earned and records expenses when they are incurred. (p. 66)

Adjusting journal entries Entries made in the general journal to record revenues that have been earned but not recorded and expenses that have been incurred but not recorded. (p. 69)

Cash basis of accounting Records revenues when cash is received and records expenses when cash is paid. (p. 66)

Closing entries Entries made in the journal and posted to the ledger that eliminate the balances in all temporary accounts and transfer those balances to the Retained Earnings account. (p. 81)

Closing process The process of transferring all revenue, expense, and dividend account balances to the Retained Earnings account. (p. 80)

Temporary accounts Accounts that accumulate balances only for the current period. (p. 80)

Demonstration Problem

Given the following March 31 Unadjusted Trial Balance and the additional information at the end of the month, prepare all necessary adjusting journal entries and prepare an Adjusted Trial Balance as of March 31.

Unadjusted Trial Balance
March 31

	Debit	Credit
Cash	$ 6,300	
Accounts Receivable	6,000	
Equipment	7,200	
Prepaid Insurance	2,400	
Supplies	5,000	
Common Stock		$20,000
Service Revenue		10,000
Fuel Expense	600	
Salaries Expense	2,300	
Dividends	200	
Totals	$30,000	$30,000

Additional Information:

1. Depreciation on truck is $150 monthly.

2. One-twelfth of the insurance expired during the month.

3. An inventory count shows $1,000 of cleaning supplies on hand at March 31.

4. Earned but unpaid employee salaries were $250 on March 31.

Demonstration Problem Solution

Adjusting Journal Entries on March 31

1	Depreciation Expense	150	
	Accumulated Depreciation		150

(To record depreciation on the truck: $150 is given)

2	Insurance Expense	200	
	Prepaid Insurance		200

(To record expired insurance: $2,400 × 1/12)

3	Supplies Expense	4,000	
	Supplies		4,000

(To record supplies used: $5,000 − $1,000)

4	Salaries Expense	250	
	Salaries Payable		250

(To record salaries earned but not paid: $250 is given)

Adjusted Trial Balance
March 31

	Debit	Credit
Cash	$ 6,300	
Accounts Receivable	6,000	
Equipment	7,200	
Prepaid Insurance	2,200	
Supplies	1,000	
Accumulated Depreciation		$ 150
Salaries Payable		250
Common Stock		20,000
Service Revenue		10,000
Depreciation Expense	150	
Fuel Expense	600	
Insurance Expense	200	
Salaries Expense	2,550	
Supplies Expense	4,000	
Dividends	200	
Totals	$30,400	$30,400

Learning Objectives	Key Concepts	Key Definitions
LO1 Describe the role of internal control in a business.	Internal control is management's system of policies and procedures that helps it operate efficiently and effectively, report financial information reliably, and comply with laws and regulations. The Sarbanes-Oxley Act of 2002 requires publicly traded companies to assess annually the effectiveness of their internal control. An auditor must also assess management's own assessment.	**Bank reconciliation** The process of reconciling the differences between the cash balance on a bank statement and the cash balance in a company's records. (p. 94) **Cash** A medium of exchange. (p. 98) **Cash equivalent** Any investment that is readily convertible into cash and has an original maturity of three months or less. (p. 98)
LO2 Describe the five components of internal control.	The report *Internal Control—Integrated Framework* provides guidance on good internal control practices. Internal control consists of five components—the control environment, risk assessment, control activities, information and communication, and monitoring. For internal control to be effective, each component must operate effectively.	**Control activities** The policies and procedures established to address the risks that threaten the achievement of organizational objectives. (p. 92) **Control environment** The atmosphere in which the members of an organization conduct their activities and carry out their responsibilities. (p. 91) **Credit memorandum** An addition to the cash balance on the bank statement for items such as the collection of interest. (p. 95)
LO3 Understand two methods of internal control over cash—bank reconciliations and petty cash funds.	Two methods of internal control over cash are bank reconciliations and petty cash funds. A bank reconciliation is the process of reconciling the cash balance shown on the bank statement with the cash balance shown in a company' records. Common items of reconciliation include deposits in transit, outstanding checks, credit memoranda, and debit memoranda. The purpose of a bank reconciliation is to confirm the accuracy of cash records and to determine the actual balance in cash. A petty cash fund is an amount of cash kept on hand for minor expenditures. Once established, a petty cash fund keeps receipts as expenditures are made. It is periodically replenished by bringing the total cash in the fund back to the original amount.	**Debit memorandum** A subtraction from the cash balance on the bank statement for items such as service charges. (p. 95) **Deposit in transit** A deposit that has been made by the company but has not cleared the bank as of the statement date. (p. 94) **Free cash flow** The excess cash a company generates beyond what it needs to invest in productive capacity and pay dividends to stockholders. (p. 102) **Information and communication** Required for the open flow of relevant information throughout an organization. (p. 93) **Internal control** The system of policies and procedures used in a company to promote efficient and effective operations, reliable financial reporting, and compliance with laws and regulations. (p. 88)
LO4 Describe the reporting of cash.	Cash is a medium of exchange that can take many forms. A cash equivalent is any investment that (1) is readily convertible into a specific amount of cash and (2) will mature in three months or less from the date it was acquired. Examples of cash equivalents can include Treasury Bills, certificates of deposit, etc. These cash equivalents are reported along with cash in current assets on the balance sheet.	**Internal control report** Annual report in which management states its responsibility for internal control and provides an assessment of its internal control. (p. 89) **Monitoring** The assessment of the quality of an organization's internal control. (p. 93) **Outstanding check** A check that has been distributed by the company but has not cleared the bank as of the statement date. (p. 94)

Learning Objectives

LO5 Evaluate cash through the calculation and interpretation of horizontal, vertical, and ratio analyses.

Key Concepts

Free cash flow shows the amount of cash that a company generates after it has paid for investments in property and equipment and for dividends to shareholders. More free cash flow gives a company more flexibility to expand or to provide greater returns to shareholders.

Key Definitions (continued)

Petty cash fund An amount of cash kept on hand to pay for minor expenditures. (p. 97)

Restricted cash Cash a company has restricted for a specific purpose. (p. 98)

Risk assessment The identification and analysis of the risks that threaten the achievement of organizational objectives. (p. 92)

Demonstration Problem

Bank Reconciliation

At the end of January, Estess shows a cash balance of $67,650. The January 31 bank statement shows a balance of $64,170. Estess discovers the following.

1. Deposits of $4,250 and $2,300 made on January 30 and January 31, respectively, do not appear on the January bank statement.
2. Checks written in late January for $620 (No. 1983), $950 (No.1986), and $1,200 (No. 1989) do not appear on the January bank statement.
3. The bank showed a $200 customer check deposited by Estess and returned to the bank for nonsufficient funds (NSF), charged a $50 service fee, and collected a $500 receivable from one of Estess' customers.
4. A check that Estess wrote cleared the bank at $300 but was erroneously recorded in Estess' books at $350.

Prepare a bank reconciliation for Estess.

Key Formulas

Horizontal Analysis	Dollar change in account balance = Current year balance − Prior year balance
	$\text{Percentage change} = \dfrac{\text{Dollar change}}{\text{Prior year balance}}$
Vertical Analysis	$\text{Percentage} = \dfrac{\text{Cash}}{\text{Total Assets}}$
Free Cash Flow	Cash Flows from Operating Activities Less: Capital Expenditures Less: Dividends Free Cash Flow

Demonstration Problem Solution

Estess Enterprises
Bank Reconciliation
January 31

Balance per bank statement		$64,170
Add deposits in transit:		
January 30	$4,250	
January 31	2,300	6,550
Deduct outstanding checks:		
No. 1983	$ 620	
No. 1986	950	
No. 1989	1,200	2,770
Actual cash balance		$67,950
Balance per company records		$67,650
Add:		
Collection of receivable	$ 500	
Error by Estess	50	550
Deduct:		
Service fee	$ 50	
NSF check	200	250
Actual cash balance		$67,950

Learning Objectives		Key Concepts	Key Definitions
LO1	Describe the recording and reporting of receivables.	Receivables are current assets reported at net realizable value, which is equal to the expected cash receipts from total receivables. Net realizable value is calculated as total receivables less the allowance for bad debts.	**Account receivable** An amount owed by a customer who has purchased the company's product or service. (p. 106)
LO2	Understand the methods used to account for uncollectible receivables.	There are two methods to account for uncollectible receivables: the direct write-off method and the allowance method. Under the direct write-off method, bad debt expense is recorded when a receivable is deemed to be uncollectible and is removed from the company's records. Because the method does not follow the matching principle, it is not allowable under generally accepted accounting principles unless the amount of bad debts is immaterial. Under the allowance method, bad debt expense is estimated and recorded at the end of each accounting period and an allowance is set up for future write-offs. When a receivable is deemed uncollectible, both the specific receivable and the allowance account are decreased for the value of the receivable.	**Aging schedule** A listing of accounts receivable by their ages. (p. 114) **Allowance for bad debts** The dollar amount of receivables that a company believes will ultimately be uncollectible. (p. 111) **Allowance method** Method in which companies use two entries to account for bad debt expense—one to estimate the expense and a second to write off receivables. (p. 110) **Allowance ratio** A comparison of the allowance account to receivables that measures the percentage of receivables that are expected to be uncollectible in the future. (p. 116) **Bad debt expense** The expense resulting from the inability to collect accounts receivable. (p. 109) **Days-in-receivables ratio** A conversion of the receivables turnover ratio that expresses a company's ability to generate and collect receivables in days. (p. 116)
LO3	Understand the methods for estimating bad debt expense.	Bad debt expense can be estimated with the percentage of sales approach or the percentage of receivables approach. Under percentage of sales, bad debt expense is a set percentage of sales for the period. This approach has the advantage of matching expenses to revenues well. Under percentage of receivables, bad debt expense is a function of receivables at the end of the period. This approach has the advantage of creating a very meaningful net realizable value. An aging schedule is a more refined version of the percentage of receivables approach.	**Direct write-off method** Method in which bad debt expense is recorded when a company determines that a receivable is uncollectible and removes it from its records. (p. 110) **Net realizable value** The amount of cash that a company expects to collect from its total accounts receivable. (p. 108) **Note receivable** An asset created when a company accepts a promissory note. (p. 118)
LO4	Evaluate accounts receivable through the calculation and interpretation of horizontal, vertical, and ratio analyses.	The receivables turnover ratio shows how effective a company is at generating and collecting its accounts receivable during a period. The days-in-receivables ratio converts the turnover ratio into a number of days. The allowance ratio shows the percentage of receivables that a company expects will not be collected.	**Percentage-of-receivables approach** Method that estimates bad debt expense as a percentage of receivables. (p. 113) **Percentage-of-sales approach** Method that estimates bad debt expense as a percentage of sales. (p. 112) **Promissory note** A written promise to pay a specific sum of money on demand or at some specific date in the future. (p. 117)
LO5	Understand the accounting for notes receivable.	A note receivable is created when a company accepts a promissory note. Accounting for a note requires the recording of the note, the accrual of any interest earned, and the recording of collection.	**Receivables turnover ratio** A comparison of credit sales to receivables that measures a company's ability to generate and collect receivables. (p. 116)

Key Formulas

Percentage-of-Sales Approach	Bad debt expense = Sales × Percentage
Percentage-of-Receivables Approach	Bad debt expense = [Receivables × Percentage] + or − Allowance for Bad Debts balance
Receivables Turnover Ratio	$\dfrac{\text{Credit Sales}}{\text{Average Receivables}}$
Average receivables	$\dfrac{\text{Beginning Receivables} + \text{Ending Receivables}}{2}$
Days-in-Receivables Ratio	$\dfrac{365}{\text{Receivables Turnover Ratio}}$
Allowance Ratio	$\dfrac{\text{Allowance for Bad Debts}}{\text{Gross Accounts Receivable}}$
Horizontal Analysis	Dollar change in account balance = Current year balance − Prior year balance $\dfrac{\text{Percentage change}}{\text{in account balance}} = \dfrac{\text{Dollar change}}{\text{Prior year balance}}$
Vertical Analysis	For the Balance Sheet: $\text{Percentage} = \dfrac{\text{Account Balance}}{\text{Total Assets}}$ For the Income Statement: $\dfrac{\text{Account Balance}}{\text{Net Sales or Revenue}}$
Interest on Notes Payable	Principal × Annual Rate of Interest × Time Outstanding

Demonstration Problem

Bad debt estimation and write-off

Lambert Golf Supplies provides the following partial balance sheet and income statement information for 2010. Assume that Lambert uses the *allowance method* for recording bad debts.

Gross accounts receivable at 12/31	$11,760
Allowance for bad debts at 12/31	138 credit
Net sales for 2010	75,200
Receivables written off during 2010	800

Required:

1. Prepare the journal entry that Lambert made during 2010 to write off the $800 in receivables.

2. Prepare the journal entry to record bad debt expense for 2010 if Lambert estimates that 1% of net sales will be uncollectible. Calculate the resulting net realizable value of receivables.

3. Prepare the journal entry to record bad debt expense for 2010 if Lambert estimates that 5% of receivables will be uncollectible. Calculate the resulting net realizable value of receivables.

4. Assume that instead of the allowance method, Lambert uses the direct write-off method. What would Lambert recognize as bad debt expense for 2010?

Demonstration Problem Solution

1.
Accounts Receivable	800	
Allowance for Bad Debts		800

2.
Bad Debt Expense ($75,200 × 1%)	752	
Allowance for Bad Debts		752

Net Realizable Value:

Gross accounts receivable	$11,760
Less: Allowance ($138 + $752)	890
Net realizable value	$10,870

3.
Bad Debt Expense [($11,760 × 5%) − $138]	450	
Allowance for Bad Debts		450

Net Realizable Value:

Gross accounts receivable	$11,760
Less: Allowance	450
Net realizable value	$11,310

4. The $800 that was written off during the year.

Visit **4ltrpress.cengage.com/acct** for additional study tools!

review card CHAPTER 7
Inventory

Learning Objectives	Key Concepts	Key Definitions
LO1 Describe inventory and how it is recorded, expensed, and reported.	Inventory is a current asset that is recorded at its cost of acquisition, which can include purchase discounts, returns and allowance, and transportation-in. Inventory becomes an expense when it is sold.	**Days-in-inventory ratio** Converts the inventory turnover ratio into a measure of days by dividing the turnover ratio into 365 days. (p. 139)

First-in, first-out method Calculates the cost of goods sold based on the assumption that the first unit of inventory available for sale is the first unit sold. (p. 129) |
| **LO2** Calculate the cost of goods sold using different inventory costing methods. | Companies can use one of four costing methods to determine cost of goods sold: specific identification, first-in, first-out (FIFO), last-in, first-out (LIFO), and moving average. Specific identification determines cost of goods sold from the costs of actual units sold. FIFO assumes that the first units available for sale are included in cost of goods sold. LIFO assumes that the last units available for sale are included in cost of goods sold. Moving average assumes that the cost of inventory sold is the average cost of all inventory available for sale. | **Gross profit method** A method of estimating inventory using a company's gross profit percentage to estimate the cost of goods sold and then ending inventory. (p. 136)

Inventory A tangible resource that is held for resale in the normal course of operations. (p. 124)

Inventory turnover ratio Compares the cost of goods sold during a period to the average inventory balance during that period and measures the ability to sell inventory. (p. 139)

Last-in, first-out method Calculates the cost of goods sold based on the assumption that the last unit of inventory available for sale is the first unit sold. (p. 130) |
| **LO3** Understand the income and tax effects of inventory cost flow assumptions. | When inventory costs are rising, the LIFO costing method will result in the highest cost of goods sold while the FIFO costing method will result in the smallest cost of goods sold. The LIFO method is often used because of the tax deferral resulting from the higher cost of goods sold. The amount of taxes a company has deferred can be approximated through examination of the LIFO reserve. | **LIFO reserve** The difference between the LIFO inventory reported on the balance sheet and what inventory would be if reported on a FIFO basis. (p. 134)

Lower-of-cost-or-market rule Requires inventory to be reported on the balance sheet at its market value if the market value is lower than the inventory's cost. (p. 137)

Moving average method Calculates the cost of goods sold based on the average unit cost of all inventory available for sale. (p. 131) |
| **LO4** Analyze the effects of inventory errors. | An error in calculating ending inventory will result in a misstatement of cost of goods sold and thus, net income. In addition, since ending inventory becomes beginning inventory the following year, the error will also misstate cost of goods sold and net income the following year in the opposite direction. | **Net purchases** Gross purchases plus transportation-in less purchase returns and allowances and purchase discounts. (p. 141)

Periodic inventory system Updates the inventory account only at the end of an accounting period. (p. 126)

Perpetual inventory system Updates the inventory account each time inventory is bought or sold. (p. 126) |
| **LO5** Demonstrate how inventory is estimated. | Using the gross profit method, ending inventory can be estimated by first estimating cost of goods sold and subtracting it from cost of goods available for sale. Cost of goods sold is estimated by subtracting the usual gross profit on sales from actual sales. | **Purchases** An account used to accumulate the cost of all purchases. (p. 140)

Purchase Discounts An account that accumulates the cost reductions generated from vendor discounts granted for prompt payments. (p. 141) |

Learning Objectives		Key Concepts	Key Definitions
LO6	Apply the lower-of-cost-or-market rule to inventory.	If the market value of inventory falls below its cost, the lower-of-cost-or-market rule requires a company to write down its inventory to the market value. This rule can be applied to individual inventory items or to groups of items.	**Purchase Returns and Allowances** An account that accumulates the cost of all inventory returned to vendors as well as the cost reductions from vendor allowances. (p. 140)
LO7	Evaluate inventory through the calculation of horizontal, vertical, and ratio analyses.	The inventory turnover ratio indicates how fast a company sells its inventory. The days in inventory ratio shows how many days on average it takes a company to sell its inventory.	**Specific identification method** Determines the cost of goods sold based on the actual cost of each inventory item sold. (p. 129)
LO8	Appendix: Record purchases and calculate the cost of goods sold under a periodic system.	Companies can use one of four costing methods to determine cost of goods sold: specific identification, first-in, first-out (FIFO), last-in, first-out (LIFO), and weighted average. Specific identification determines cost of goods sold from the costs of actual units sold. FIFO assumes that the first units available for sale are included in cost of goods sold. LIFO assumes that the last units available for sale are included in cost of goods sold. Weighted average assumes that the cost of inventory sold is the average cost of all inventory available for sale.	**Tax deferral** A temporary delay in the payment of income taxes. (p. 133) **Transportation-in** An account that accumulates the transportation costs of obtaining the inventory. (p. 140)

Key Formulas

Moving or Weighted Average Unit Cost

$$\frac{\text{Cost of Goods Available for Sale}}{\text{Units Available for Sale}}$$

Horizontal Analysis

Dollar change in account balance = Current-year balance − Prior-year balance

$$\frac{\text{Percentage change}}{\text{in account balance}} = \frac{\text{Dollar change}}{\text{Prior-year balance}}$$

Vertical Analysis

	For the Balance Sheet	For the Income Statement
Percentage =	$\dfrac{\text{Account Balance}}{\text{Total Assets}}$	$\dfrac{\text{Account Balance}}{\text{Net Sales or Revenue}}$

Inventory Turnover Ratio

$$\frac{\text{Cost of Goods Sold}}{\text{Average Inventory}}$$

Average Inventory

$$\frac{\text{Beginning Inventory} + \text{Ending Inventory}}{2}$$

Days-in-Inventory Ratio

$$\frac{365}{\text{Inventory Turnover Ratio}}$$

Cost of Goods Sold Model

Beginning Inventory
+ Purchases
―――――――――――――
Cost of Goods Available for Sale
− Ending Inventory
―――――――――――――
Cost of Goods Sold

Visit **4ltrpress.cengage.com/acct** for additional study tools!

Learning Objectives	Key Concepts	Key Definitions
LO1 Describe fixed assets and how they are recorded, expensed, and reported.	Fixed assets are recorded at cost, expensed over their useful lives by depreciation, and reported on the balance sheet at net book value, which is the asset's cost less its accumulated depreciation.	**Accumulated depreciation** The cumulative amount of depreciation expense recognized to date on a fixed asset. (p. 150) **Amortization** The process of spreading out the cost of an intangible asset over its useful life. (p. 170) **Average age of fixed assets** A comparison of accumulated depreciation to depreciation expense that estimates the number of years, on average, that the company has used its fixed assets. (p. 166)
LO2 Calculate and compare depreciation expense using straight-line, double-declining-balance, and units-of-activity methods.	All depreciation methods depreciate an asset's net cost over its useful life, but they differ in the amount of depreciation expense recognized each year. Straight-line yields the same expense each year. Double-declining-balance accelerates the expense to early years. Units-of-activity bases the expense on asset usage.	**Average useful life of fixed assets** A comparison of the cost of fixed assets to depreciation expense that estimates the number of years, on average, that a company expects to use its fixed assets. (p. 166) **Capital expenditure** An expenditure that increases the expected useful life or productivity of a fixed asset. (p. 159)
LO3 Understand the effects of adjustments that may be made during a fixed asset's useful life.	When an estimate on an existing fixed asset is changed, depreciation expense from that point forward is based on the new estimate. Expenditures that significantly increase a fixed asset's useful life or productive capacity are added to the asset's cost. When a fixed asset's market value falls permanently below its net book value, the asset is impaired and must be written down to market value.	**Copyright** The right to reproduce or sell an artistic or published work. (p. 168) **Cost** The historical cost of a fixed asset being depreciated. (p. 153) **Depreciable cost** The difference between an asset's cost and its salvage value. (p. 153) **Depreciation** The process of systematically and rationally allocating the cost of a fixed asset over its useful life. (p. 150)
LO4 Record the disposal of fixed assets.	When disposing of fixed assets, companies record a gain on disposal when the asset is sold for more than its net book value. A loss is recorded when it is sold for less than net book value.	**Depreciation expense** The portion of a fixed asset's cost that is recognized as an expense in the current period. (p. 150) **Depreciation method** The method used to calculate depreciation expense, such as the straight-line method, the double-declining-balance method, and the units-of-activity method. (p. 153)
LO5 Evaluate fixed assets through the calculation and interpretation of horizontal, vertical, and ratio analyses.	The fixed asset turnover ratio shows how effective a company is at using its fixed assets to produce revenues. The average age and average useful life ratios provide an indication of the remaining life of a company's fixed assets.	**Double-declining-balance method** A depreciation method that accelerates depreciation expense into the early years of an asset's life. (p. 154) **Fixed asset** A tangible resource that is expected to be used in operations for more than one year and is not intended for resale. (p. 148)
LO6 Describe the cash flow effect of acquiring fixed assets.	Cash paid for fixed assets is reported as a separate line item in the investing activities section of the statement of cash flows. A negative number indicates that a company is buying fixed assets.	**Fixed asset turnover ratio** A comparison of total revenues to the average net book value of fixed assets that measures the productivity of fixed assets. (p. 165)
LO7 Describe intangible assets and how they are recorded, expensed, and reported.	Intangible assets are recorded at their cost and amortized over their useful lives. An internally developed intangible asset is recorded only for those costs necessary to register it.	

Franchise The right to operate a business under the trade name of the franchisor. (p. 168)

Goodwill An intangible asset equal to the excess that one company pays to acquire the net assets of another company. (p. 169)

Intangible asset A resource that is used in operations for more than one year but that has no physical substance. (p. 168)

Net book value The unexpired cost of a fixed asset, calculated by subtracting depreciation expense to date from the cost of the fixed asset. (p. 152)

Patent The right to manufacture, sell, or use a particular product or process exclusively for a limited period of time. (p. 168)

Revenue expenditure An expenditure that maintains the expected useful life or the productivity of a fixed asset. (p. 159)

Salvage value An estimate of the value of a fixed asset at the end of its useful life. (p. 153)

Straight-line method A depreciation method that results in the same amount of depreciation expense each year of the asset's useful life. (p. 153)

Trademark (trade name) The right to use exclusively a name, symbol, or phrase to identify a company. (p. 168)

Units-of-activity method A depreciation method in which depreciation expense is a function of the actual usage of the asset. (p. 156)

Useful life The length of time a fixed asset is expected to be used in operations. (p. 153)

Key Formulas

Straight-Line Method

$$\text{Depreciation Expense} = \frac{\text{Cost} - \text{Salvage Value}}{\text{Useful Life}}$$

Double-Declining-Balance Method

$$\text{Depreciation Expense} = \text{Depreciation Rate} \times \text{Net Book Value}$$
$$= (\text{Straight-Line Rate} \times 2)$$
$$\times (\text{Cost} - \text{Accumulated Depreciation})$$

Units-of-Activity Method

$$\text{Depreciation Expense per Unit} = \frac{\text{Cost} - \text{Salvage Value}}{\text{Useful Life in Units}}$$

$$\text{Depreciation Expense} = \text{Depreciation Expense per Unit} \times \text{Actual Units of Activity}$$

Net Book Value   Cost − Accumulated Depreciation

Disposals

Gain on Disposal:
   Proceeds from Sale > Net Book Value

Loss on Disposal:
   Proceeds from Sale < Net Book Value

Fixed Asset Turnover Ratio

$$\frac{\text{Total Revenues}}{\text{Average Net Book Value of Fixed Assets}}$$

where average net book value is:

$$\frac{\text{Beginning Net Book Value} + \text{Ending Net Book Value}}{2}$$

Average Useful Life Ratio

$$\text{Average Useful Life} = \frac{\text{Cost of Fixed Assets}}{\text{Depreciation Expense}}$$

Average Age Ratio

$$\text{Average Age} = \frac{\text{Accumulated Depreciation}}{\text{Depreciation Expense}}$$

Demonstration Problem

Rooney Inc. purchases a new machine for $37,750. The machine has a useful life of 10 years and a salvage value of $2,750. Rooney estimates that the machine will be used for 17,500 hours.

a. Calculate the machine's annual depreciation expense using the straight-line method.

b. Calculate depreciation expense for the first three years of the asset's life using the double-declining-balance method.

c. Assuming that the machine is used for 3,000 hours one year, calculate depreciation expense for that year using the units-of-activity method.

d. Suppose that after five years of straight-line depreciation, Rooney increases the machine's useful life an additional two years. Calculate depreciation expense for year six.

e. Suppose instead that after six years of straight-line depreciation, Rooney sells the machine for $16,300. Calculate the gain or loss on the sale.

Demonstration Problem Solution

a.   ($37,750 − $2,750) / 10 = $3,500 depreciation expense per year

b.   Double-declining rate = (100% ÷ 10) × 2 = 20%
Year 1: 20% × $37,750 = $7,550 depreciation expense
Year 2: 20% × ($37,750 − $7,550) = $6,040 depreciation expense
Year 3: 20% × ($37,750 − $7,550 − $6,040) = $4,832 depreciation expense

c.   ($37,750 − $2,750) / $17,500 = $2 depreciation expense per hour
3,000 hours × 2 = $6,000 depreciation expense

d.

Cost of the asset	$37,750
Less: Accumulated depreciation for five years ($3,500 × 5)	17,500
Net book value at time of revision	$20,250
Less: Salvage value	2,750
Remaining depreciable cost	$17,500
Divided by remaining useful life (5 years + 2 more years)	÷ 7
Depreciation expense for year 6	$ 2,500

e.

Cost of the asset	$37,750
Less: Accumulated depreciation for six years ($3,500 × 6)	21,000
Net book value at time of revision	$16,750
Sales price	16,000
Loss on sale	$ 750

reviewcard

Learning Objectives	Key Concepts	Key Definitions
LO1 Describe the recording and reporting of various current liabilities.	A current liability is an obligation that is reasonably expected to be satisfied or paid within one year. Current liabilities are reported on the balance sheet and include obligations relating to the purchase of inventory, the compensation of employees, the repayment of debt, and the incurrence of taxes.	**Amortization schedule** A schedule that illustrates the amortization of a bond discount or premium over the life of a bond. (p. 183)
LO2 Describe the reporting of long-term liabilities and the cash flows associated with those liabilities.	Long-term liabilities are reported on the balance sheet. The cash received from the issuance of long-term liabilities is reported in the financing activities section of the statement of cash flows.	**Bond** A financial instrument in which a borrower promises to pay future interest and principal to a creditor in exchange for the creditor's cash today. (p. 180)
LO3 Understand the nature of bonds and record a bond's issuance, interest payments, and maturity.	A bond payable is a long-term liability created when a company issues bonds. All bonds have a face value, a stated interest rate, and a maturity date. Interest is paid based on the stated rate and face value. Bonds are often issued at a discount or premium because the stated rate of interest differs from the market rate of interest at the time of issuance. The discount or premium is amortized over the life of the bond.	**Capital lease** A contract in which the lessee obtains enough rights to use and control an asset such that the lessee is in substance the owner of the asset. (p. 189) **Capital structure** The mix of debt and equity that a company uses to generate its assets. (p. 193) **Contingent liability** An obligation that arises from an existing condition whose outcome is uncertain and whose resolution depends on a future event. (p. 189) **Current liability** An obligation of a business that is expected to be satisfied or paid within one year. (p. 174)
LO4 Account for a bond that is redeemed prior to maturity.	When a bond is paid prior to the maturity date, a gain is realized when the amount paid is greater than the bond's carrying value. A loss is realized when the amount paid is less than the bond's carrying value.	**Current portion of long-term debt** The portion of a long-term liability that will be paid within one year. (p. 177) **Current ratio** Compares a company's current assets to its current liabilities and measures its ability to pay current obligations. (p. 192)
LO5 Understand additional liabilities such as leases and contingent liabilities.	A lease is an agreement in which the lessee obtains the right to use an asset by making periodic payments to the lessor. Operating leases are like rental contracts, and no liability is recorded by the lessee. Capital leases are like purchases, and the lease liability is recorded by the lessee. A contingent liability is an obligation arising from an existing condition whose outcome is uncertain and whose resolution depends on a future event. Whether a contingent liability is recorded, disclosed, or ignored depends on the likelihood that the liability will occur and the ability to estimate it.	**Debt to assets ratio** Compares a company's total liabilities to its total assets and measures its ability to satisfy its long-term obligations. (p. 192) **Effective interest method of amortization** Method that amortizes the bond discount or premium so that interest expense each period is a constant percentage of the bond's carrying value. (p. 194) **Face value** The amount that is repaid at maturity of a bond. (p. 180) **Lease** A contractual agreement in which the lessee obtains the right to use an asset by making periodic payments to the lessor. (p. 188)
LO6 Evaluate liabilities through the calculation and interpretation of horizontal, vertical, and ratio analyses.	The current ratio shows a company's liquidity, or its ability to pay its short term obligations. The debt to assets ratio shows a company's capital structure and therefore its risk of long-term solvency.	**Liquidity** A company's ability to pay off its obligations in the near future. (p. 192) **Long-term liability** Any obligation of a business that is expected to be satisfied or paid in more than one year. (p. 178)

Learning Objectives

		Key Concepts
LO7	Appendix: Determine a bond's issuance price.	A bond's issuance price is determined by converting the bond's future cash flows to present day values. The principal value is discounted back at the present value of a single sum. The interest payments are discounted back at the present value of an annuity.
LO8	Appendix: Record bond interest payments under the effective interest method.	The effective interest method amortizes any bond discount or premium so that interest expense is equal to the carrying value of the bond times the market rate of interest.

Key Formulas

Interest Payment on Notes Payable

Principal × Annual Interest Rate × Time Outstanding

Interest Payment on Bonds Payable

Face Value × Stated Interest Rate × Time Outstanding

Bond Discount or Premium Amortized Each Payment (Straight-Line Method)

$$\frac{\text{Discount or Premium at Issuance}}{\text{Number of Interest Payments}}$$

Bond Interest Expense (Straight-Line Method)

If Discount: Interest Payment + Discount Amortized
If Premium: Interest Payment − Premium Amortized

Bond Carrying Value

If Discount: Face Value − Unamortized Discount
If Premium: Face Value + Unamortized Premium

Bond Interest Expense (Effective Interest Method)

Carrying Value × Market Interest Rate × Time Outstanding

Bond Discount or Premium Amortized Each Payment (Effective Interest Method)

If Discount: Interest Expense − Interest Paid
If Premium: Interest Paid − Interest Expense

Horizontal Analysis

$$\text{Percentage change in account balance} = \frac{\text{Current year balance} - \text{Prior year balance}}{\text{Prior year balance}}$$

Vertical Analysis

$$\text{Percentage} = \underset{\text{For the Balance Sheet}}{\frac{\text{Account Balance}}{\text{Total Assets}}} \quad \text{or} \quad \underset{\text{For the Income Statement}}{\frac{\text{Account Balance}}{\text{Net Sales or Revenue}}}$$

Current Ratio

$$\frac{\text{Current Assets}}{\text{Current Liabilities}}$$

Debt to Assets Ratio

$$\frac{\text{Total Liabilities}}{\text{Total Assets}}$$

Key Definitions (continued)

Market (or effective) rate of interest The rate of return that investors in the bond markets demand for bonds of similar risk. (p. 180)

Maturity date The date on which the face value must be repaid to the creditor. (p. 180)

Note payable A liability generated by the issuance of a promissory note to borrow money. (p. 176)

Off-balance-sheet financing Occurs when a company's future obligations regarding an asset are not reported as a liability on the balance sheet. (p. 188)

Operating lease A contract in which the lessee obtains the right to use an asset for a limited period of time but does not acquire ownership of the asset. (p. 188)

Solvency A company's ability to continue in business in the long term by satisfying its long-term obligations. (p. 192)

Stated interest rate The contractual rate at which interest is paid to the creditor. (p. 180)

Straight-line method of amortization Method that amortizes an equal amount of the discount or premium each time interest is paid. (p. 183)

Visit **4ltrpress.cengage.com/acct** for additional study tools!

Learning Objectives		Key Concepts	Key Definitions
LO1	Describe the characteristics of the corporate form of business.	The corporation is a separate legal entity formed under state law. Advantages include the limited liability of the owners, the ability to raise capital by the sale of stock to investors, and the ease of transferring ownership by selling one's stock. Disadvantages include double taxation and increased regulation.	**Authorized shares** The number of shares of stock that a company can legally issue. (p. 203) **Cash dividend** A distribution of cash to stockholders. (p. 206) **Common stock** The most common type of capital stock. (p. 203) **Contributed capital** The amount of capital raised by issuing stock to investors in exchange for an ownership claim on company assets. (p. 203)
LO2	Describe the characteristics of common stock and how it is recorded and reported.	Common stock is the basic form of capital stock that is issued for ownership in a corporation. Shares held by entities other than the corporation are called outstanding shares. Most common stock has a par value, which is an arbitrary value that determines an entity's legal capital. When recording common stock, the common stock account is increased for the par value of the stock, while the additional paid-in capital account is increased by the excess paid over par value. The balances associated with common stock are reported in the stockholders' equity section of the balance sheet.	**Cost method** A method of recording the purchase of treasury stock at its cost of acquisition. (p. 214) **Cumulative preferred stock** Stock that carries the right to receive current-year dividends and all unpaid dividends from prior years before dividends are paid to common stockholders. (p. 212) **Date of declaration** The date on which a corporation's board of directors declares a dividend. (p. 206) **Date of record** The date that determines who receives a dividend; the stock's owner on the date of record receives the dividend. (p. 206) **Dividend** A distribution of profits to a corporation's owners. (p. 206)
LO3	Understand cash dividends, stock dividends, and stock splits.	A cash dividend is a distribution of earnings to the owners in the form of cash. A stock dividend is a distribution of a company's own common stock to existing shareholders. Small stock dividends are recorded at market value, while large stock dividends are recorded at par value. A stock split is the decrease or increase in the number of shares authorized, issued, and outstanding through some specified ratio, such as 2-for-1.	**Dividend payout ratio** A comparison of a company's dividends to its earnings that measures the percentage of current earnings distributed to owners. (p. 217) **Dividend yield ratio** A comparison of dividends per share to the market price per share of stock that measures the percentage return from dividends. (p. 217) **Dividends in arrears** The accumulated value of unpaid prior-year dividends. (p. 212) **Earnings per share** A comparison of a company's net income to the number of shares of common stock outstanding that measures the ability to generate equity through profitable operations. (p. 216)
LO4	Describe the characteristics of preferred stock and how it receives preference in dividends.	Preferred stock is a form of capital stock that receives priorities over common stock. Most preferred stock relinquishes the right to vote in exchange for preference to dividends and residual assets. Preferred stock is recorded in a similar manner as common stock and is reported in the stockholders' equity section of the balance sheet.	**Issued shares** The number of shares a company has distributed to owners to date. (p. 203) **Noncumulative preferred stock** Stock that carries the right to receive current-year dividends only. (p. 212)

Learning Objectives	**Key Concepts**	**Key Definitions** (continued)
LO5 — Describe the characteristics of treasury stock and how it is recorded and reported.	Treasury stock is common stock that has been repurchased by the company. Treasury stock is recorded at cost. Because the treasury stock account represents the amount of capital returned to shareholders, it is reported in the stockholders' equity section of the balance sheet as a negative number.	**Outstanding shares** The number of shares that have been issued and are still held by someone other than the issuing company. (p. 203)
		Par value An arbitrary value that determines an entity's legal capital. (p. 204)
		Payment date The date on which a dividend will be distributed. (p. 206)
LO6 — Evaluate equity through the calculation and interpretation of horizontal, vertical, and ratio analyses.	Earnings per share shows a company's profitability per share of stock outstanding and is easily comparable across different companies. Return on equity shows the ability of a company to effectively use capital provided by stockholders to generate income. The dividend payout ratio shows what percentage of earnings is distributed to owners. The dividend yield shows the percentage return dividends provide on an investment in the company's stock.	**Preferred stock** A form of capital stock that receives one or more priorities over common stock. (p. 211)
		Return on equity A comparison of a company's net income to total stockholders' equity that measures the ability to use existing equity to generate additional equity. (p. 216)
		Stock dividend A distribution of a company's common stock to existing stockholders. (p. 208)
		Stock split An increase in a company's shares of stock according to some specified ratio. (p. 210)
		Treasury stock Common stock that a company reacquires from its stockholders. (p. 213)

Key Formulas

Earnings per Share	$$\dfrac{\text{Net Income}}{\text{Average Number of Common Shares Outstanding}}$$
Average Common Shares Outstanding	$$\dfrac{\text{Beginning shares outstanding} + \text{Ending shares outstanding}}{2}$$
Return on Equity	$$\dfrac{\text{Net Income}}{\text{Average Stockholders' Equity}}$$
Average Equity	$$\dfrac{\text{Beginning equity} + \text{Ending equity}}{2}$$
Dividend Payout Ratio	$$\dfrac{\text{Dividends}}{\text{Net Income}} \quad \text{or} \quad \dfrac{\text{Dividends per Share}}{\text{Earnings per Share}}$$
Dividend Yield	$$\dfrac{\text{Dividends per share}}{\text{Market Price per share}}$$
Horizontal Analysis	$$\dfrac{\text{Percentage change}}{\text{in account balance}} = \dfrac{\text{Dollar change}}{\text{Prior-year balance}}$$
Vertical Analysis	For the Balance Sheet / For the Income Statement $$\text{Percentage} = \dfrac{\text{Account Balance}}{\text{Total Assets}} \quad \text{or} \quad \dfrac{\text{Account Balance}}{\text{Net Sales or Revenue}}$$
Stock Dividend	If Small: Outstanding Shares × Percentage × Market Value If Large: Outstanding Shares × Percentage × Par Value

Learning Objectives		Key Concepts	Key Definitions
LO1	Describe the purpose and format of the statement of cash flows.	The statement of cash flows summarizes a company's inflows and outflows of cash over a period of time. It reports cash flows in three major categories: operating, investing, and financing activities. The net cash flows from these three activities is equal to the change in cash from the balance sheet.	**Cash flow adequacy ratio** Compares free cash flow to the average amount of debt maturing in the next five years and measures the ability to pay maturing debt. (p. 241)
LO2	Describe the process of preparing the statement of cash flows.	The process of preparing the statement of cash flows involves the collection of information from a company's comparative balance sheet and income statement and the explanation of the changes in the account balances.	**Cash flows provided (used) by financing activities** Cash inflows and outflows associated with the generation and return of capital; often called financing cash flows. (p. 227)
LO3	Prepare the operating activities section of the statement of cash flows using the direct method.	The direct method of reporting net cash flows from operating activities calculates cash inflows from customers and subtracts cash outflows from operations, interest, and taxes.	**Cash flows provided (used) by investing activities** Cash inflows and outflows arising from the acquisition and disposal of non-current assets; often called investing cash flows. (p. 227)
LO4	Prepare the operating activities section of the statement of cash flows using the indirect method.	The indirect method of reporting net cash flows from operating activities adjusts net income from an accrual basis to a cash basis. Required adjustments include non-cash expenses, gains and losses from investing and financing activities, and changes in current assets and current liabilities.	**Cash flows provided (used) by operating activities** Cash inflows and outflows arising from the company's operations; sometimes called operating cash flows. (p. 227) **Direct method** Method of reporting cash flows from operating activities in which cash inflows and outflows from operations are reported separately on the statement of cash flows. (p. 230)
LO5	Prepare the investing activities section of the statement of cash flows.	Net cash flows from investing activities are calculated by examining all changes in non-current assets. Those changes involving an exchange of cash are included as investing cash flows.	**Free cash flow** The excess cash a company generates beyond what it needs to invest in productive capacity and pay dividends to stockholders. (p. 240) **Indirect method** Method of reporting cash flows from operating activities in which net income is adjusted from an accrual basis to a cash basis. (p. 230)
LO6	Prepare the financing activities section of the statement of cash flows.	Net cash flows from financing activities are calculated by examining all changes in long-term liabilities, equity accounts, and dividends. Those changes involving an exchange of cash are included as financing cash flows.	**Statement of cash flows** A financial statement that summarizes a company's inflows and outflows of cash over a period of time with a purpose to inform users on how and why a company's cash changed during the period. (p. 224)
LO7	Evaluate the statement of cash flows through the calculation and interpretation of ratio analyses.	Free cash flow is a measure of a company's ability to generate cash for expansion, improvements, repayment of debt, and/or increased returns to stockholders. The cash flow adequacy ratio measures a company's ability to generate enough cash to pay the average amount of debt maturing in each of the next five years.	

Cash flow adequacy ratio	$\dfrac{\text{Free cash flow}}{\text{Average amount of debt maturing in five years}}$

Cash received from customers:

Service revenue + decrease in accounts receivable

= $40,000 + $1,000 = $41,000

Cash paid to employees:

Salaries expense − increase in salaries payable

= $13,000 − $4,000 = $9,000

Cash paid for income taxes:

Income tax expense +/− change in income tax payable

= $2,000 + $0 = $2,000

Cash paid for equipment:

Change in equipment balance is attributable to equipment bought for cash = $27,000

Cash paid for dividends:

Beginning retained earnings + net income − dividends = ending retained earnings

$25,000 + $5,000 − ?? = $26,000   ?? = $4,000

Demonstration Problem

A company provides the following comparative balance sheets and income statement. Prepare the company's statement of cash flows for the year using the direct method for operating cash flows. In a supplemental schedule, show operating cash flows under the indirect method. Assume that the change in equipment was caused by a purchase of equipment for cash.

Income Statement
For the Year Ended December 31, 2009

Service revenue	$ 40,000
Depreciation expense	(20,000)
Salaries expense	(13,000)
Income before taxes	$ 7,000
Income tax expense	(2,000)
Net income	$ 5,000

Balance Sheet
December 31, 2009

	2009	2008
Cash and cash equivalents	$ 1,000	$ 2,000
Accounts receivable	7,000	8,000
Equipment	100,000	73,000
Accumulated depreciation	(55,000)	(35,000)
Total assets	$ 53,000	$ 48,000
Salaries payable	$ 5,000	$ 1,000
Common stock	22,000	22,000
Retained earnings	26,000	25,000
Total liabilities and stockholders' equity	$ 53,000	$ 48,000

Statement of Cash Flows
For the Year Ended December 31, 2009

Cash flows from operating activities		
Cash receipts from customers		$ 41,000
Less cash payments:		
to employees	$ (9,000)	
for taxes	(2,000)	(11,000)
Net cash provided by operating activities		$ 30,000
Cash flows from investing activities		
Cash paid for equipment	$ (27,000)	
Net cash used in investing activities		(27,000)
Cash flows from financing activities		
Cash paid for dividends	$ (4,000)	
Net cash used in financing activities		(4,000)
Net decrease in cash and cash equivalents		$ (1,000)
Cash, beginning of year		2,000
Cash, end of year		$ 1,000

Supplemental schedule:

Operating cash flows using the indirect method

Net income		$ 5,000
Adjustments to reconcile net income to cash provided by operating activities:		
Depreciation expense	$ 20,000	
Decrease in accounts receivable	1,000	
Increase to salaries payable	4,000	25,000
Net cash provided by operating activities		$ 30,000

Learning Objectives		Key Concepts	Key Definitions
LO1	Understand the nature of financial statement analysis.	Financial analysis is the process of applying analytical tools to a company's financial statements to understand the company's financial health. The goal of financial analysis is to provide the context necessary to understand a company's financial information and to make good decisions. Financial analysis requires financial information, standards of comparison, and analysis tools such as horizontal analysis, vertical analysis, and ratio analysis.	**Current ratio** Compares current assets to current liabilities and measures the ability to pay current obligations. (p. 258) **Debt to assets ratio** Compares total liabilities to total assets and measures the percentage of assets provided by creditors. (p. 260) **Debt to equity ratio** Compares total liabilities to total equity and measures a company's capital structure and financial leverage. (p. 261)
LO2	Calculate and interpret horizontal and vertical analyses.	Horizontal analysis is used to compare both the dollar change and the percent change of an account balance from one period to the next. Vertical analysis is used to compare account balances within one year by expressing them as a percentage of a base amount on the financial statement.	**DuPont analysis** Decomposes a company's return on equity into measures of operating efficiency, asset effectiveness, and capital structure. (p. 262) **Earnings per share** Compares net income to common stock outstanding and represents profits generated per share of stock. (p. 256)
LO3	Assess profitability through the calculation and interpretation of ratios.	Profitability refers to the ability of a company to generate profits effectively and efficiently. The following five ratios are commonly used to assess a company's profitability: profit margin, return on equity, return on assets, earnings per share, and price to earnings. Each of these ratios compares net income to some other financial aspect of the company in question.	**Financial leverage** The degree to which a company obtains capital through debt rather than equity in an attempt to increase returns to stockholders. (p. 260) **Financial statement analysis** The process of applying analytical tools to a company's financial statements to understand the company's financial health. (p. 248)
LO4	Assess liquidity through the calculation and interpretation of ratios.	Liquidity refers to the ability of a company to satisfy its short-term obligations. The following four ratios are commonly used to assess a company's liquidity: current ratio, quick ratio, receivable turnover ratio, and inventory turnover ratio. Each of these ratios focuses on some aspect of either current assets or current liabilities.	**Horizontal analysis** An analysis technique that calculates the change in an account balance from one period to the next and expresses that change in both dollar and percentage terms. (p. 250) **Inventory turnover ratio** Compares cost of goods sold to average inventory and measures the ability to sell inventory. (p. 259) **Liquidity** The ability of a company to satisfy its short-term obligations. (p. 257)
LO5	Assess solvency through the calculation and interpretation of ratios.	Solvency refers to the ability of a company to satisfy its long-term obligations and therefore to continue in business over the long term. The following three ratios are commonly used to assess a company's solvency: debt to assets ratio, debt to equity ratio, times interest earned.	**Price to earnings ratio** Compares net income to a company's stock price and provides an indication of investor perceptions of the company. (p. 256) **Profit margin ratio** Compares net income to net sales and measures the ability to generate profits from sales. (p. 255)
LO6	Calculate and interpret a DuPont analysis.	A DuPont analysis decomposes a company's return on equity into three parts: operational efficiency, asset effectiveness, and leverage. The analysis reveals how a company generated its return to stockholders and allows a stockholder to determine how the return would be affected by changes in operations, asset use, or capital structure.	**Quick ratio** Compares cash and near-cash assets to current liabilities and measures a company's ability to pay current liabilities immediately. (p. 258) **Receivables turnover ratio** Compares credit sales to average accounts receivable and measures the ability to make and collect sales. (p. 258)

Key Definitions (continued)

Return on assets ratio Compares net income to average total assets and measures the ability to generate profits from assets. (p. 255)

Return on equity ratio Compares net income to average stockholders' equity and measures the ability to generate profits from equity. (p. 255)

Times interest earned ratio Compares net income to interest expense and measures the ability to pay interest out of current earnings. (p. 261)

Vertical analysis An analysis technique that states each account balance on a financial statement as a percentage of a base amount on the statement. (p. 253)

Demonstration Problem

The following information was taken from past financial statements of The Gillette Company.

	Current Year	Prior Year
Current assets	$ 3,650	$ 3,797
Quick assets	1,952	2,314
Total assets	9,955	9,863
Current liabilities	3,658	3,488
Total liabilities	7,731	7,603
Total stockholders' equity	2,224	2,260
Net sales	9,252	
Cost of sales	3,708	
Income before interest and taxes	2,028	
Interest expense	54	
Net income	1,385	
Other information:		
Common stock shares outstanding	1,007	1,044
Stock price at year end	$ 23.55	

Calculate all profitability, liquidity, and solvency ratios for the current year.

Demonstration Problem Solution

Profitability ratios:

Profit margin	$1,385 ÷ $9,252	15.0%
Return on equity	$1,385 ÷ [($2,224 + $2,260) ÷ 2]	61.8%
Return on assets	$1,385 ÷ [($9,955 + $9,863) ÷ 2]	14.0%
Earnings per share	$1,385 ÷ [(1,007 + 1,044) ÷ 2]	$1.35
Price to earnings	$23.55 ÷ $1.35*	17.4

* EPS is taken from the above calculation

Liquidity ratios:

Current ratio	$3,650 ÷ $3,658	1.00
Quick ratio	$1,952 ÷ $3,658	0.53
Receivables turnover ratio	$9,252 ÷ [($920 + $1,202) ÷ 2]	8.72
Inventory turnover ratio	$3,708 ÷ [($1,094 + $928) ÷ 2]	3.67

Solvency ratios:

Debt to assets	$7,731 ÷ $9,955	0.78
Debt to equity	$7,731 ÷ $2,224	3.48
Time interest earned	$2,028 ÷ $54	37.56

Key Formulas

Profitability Ratios

$$\text{Profit Margin} = \frac{\text{Net Income}}{\text{Net Sales}}$$

$$\text{Return on Equity} = \frac{\text{Net Income}}{\text{Average Stockholders' Equity}}$$

$$\text{Return on Assets} = \frac{\text{Net Income}}{\text{Average Total Assets}}$$

$$\text{Earnings per Share} = \frac{\text{Net Income}}{\text{Average Number of Common Shares Outstanding}}$$

$$\text{Price to Earnings Ratio} = \frac{\text{Current Stock Price per Share}}{\text{Earnings per Share}}$$

Liquidity Ratios

$$\text{Current Ratio} = \frac{\text{Current Assets}}{\text{Current Liabilities}}$$

$$\text{Quick Ratio} = \frac{\text{Cash} + \text{Short-term Investments} + \text{Accounts Receivable}}{\text{Current Liabilities}}$$

$$\text{Receivables Turnover Ratio} = \frac{\text{Net Sales}}{\text{Average Accounts Receivables}}$$

$$\text{Inventory Turnover Ratio} = \frac{\text{Cost of Goods Sold}}{\text{Average Inventory}}$$

Solvency Ratios

$$\text{Debt to Assets Ratio} = \frac{\text{Total Liabilities}}{\text{Total Assets}}$$

$$\text{Debt to Equity Ratio} = \frac{\text{Total Liabilities}}{\text{Total Equity}}$$

$$\text{Times Interest Earned Ratio} = \frac{\text{Net Income} + \text{Interest Expense} + \text{Income Tax Expense}}{\text{Interest Expense}}$$

DuPont Analysis

Operating Efficiency		Asset Effectiveness		Capital Structure		Return on Equity
$\dfrac{\text{Net Income}}{\text{Sales}}$	×	$\dfrac{\text{Sales}}{\text{Assets}}$	×	$\dfrac{\text{Assets}}{\text{Equity}}$	=	$\dfrac{\text{Net Income}}{\text{Equity}}$

comprehensive review

A. **Economic entity:** Financial activities of a business can be separated from the financial activities of the business's owner(s).

B. **Time period assumption:** Economic information can be meaningfully captured and communicated over short periods of time, such as one month or one quarter.

C. **Going concern assumption:** A company will continue to operate into the foreseeable future.

D. **Monetary unit assumption:** The dollar is the most effective means to communicate economic activity.

E. **Revenue recognition principle:** Revenue should be recorded when a resource has been earned. A resource is earned when either the sale of the good or the provision of the service is substantially complete and collection is reasonably assured.

   Example: Lawn Service, Inc., mowed 10 lawns at $20 each in June. Total revenue that would be recognized is $200.

F. **Matching principle:** Expenses should be recorded in the period resources are used to generate revenues.

G. **Cost principle:** Assets should be recorded and reported at the cost paid to acquire them.

H. **Cash basis of accounting:** Records revenue when cash is received and records expenses when cash is paid.

I. **Accrual basis of accounting:** Records revenue when they are earned and records expenses when they are incurred. This is the application of revenue recognition and matching principle.

FINANCIAL STATEMENTS

A. **Income Statement**
   1. The financial statement that shows a company's assets, liabilities, and equity at a specific point in time.
   2. A financial statement that shows a company's revenues and expenses over a specific period of time.
   3. Its purpose is to demonstrate the financial success or failure of the company over a specific period of time.
   4. **Basic Structure of the Statement:**
      Revenues > Expenses = Net Income or
      Revenues < Expenses = Net Loss.
      Example: Net Sales = $2,000M, Cost of Sales = $1,000M, Interest = $500M, and Depreciation = $200M. Net Income would equal $300M or ($2,000 − $1,000 − $500 − $200).

Exhibit 1-1 Income Statement for Lawn Service, Inc.

Lawn Service, Inc.
Income Statement
For the Month Ending June 30

Revenues		$400
Expenses:		
Fuel	$185	
Interest	1	
Depreciation	70	
Total expenses		256
Net income		$144

B. **Statement of Retained Earnings**
   1. The financial statement that shows a company's assets, liabilities, and equity at a specific point of time.
   2. Shows the change in a company's retained earnings over a specific period of time.
   3. Reports how equity is growing as a result of profitable operations and is distributed in the form of dividends.
   4. The statement of retained earnings links the income statement and the balance sheet.
   5. **Basic Structure of Statement:**
      Retained Earnings, Beginning Balance
      +/− Net Income/Loss
      − Dividends
      = Retained Earnings, Ending Balance
      Example: In 2009, Lawn Service, Inc. reported $50 million of net income and paid $20 million of dividends to shareholders during the year. The previous retained earnings were $800 million. How much is 2009 Retained Earnings?

Retained Earnings, Beginning Balance	$800
+/− Net Income/Loss	$50
− Dividends	($20)
= Retained Earnings, Ending Balance	$830

Exhibit 1-3 Statement of Retained Earnings for Lawn Service, Inc.

Lawn Service, Inc.
Statement of Retained Earnings
For the Month Ending June 30

Retained earnings, June 1	$ 0
+ Net income	144
− Dividends	0
Retained earnings, June 30	$144

C. **Balance Sheet:**
   1. Its purpose is to show, at a given point in time, a company's resources and its claims against those resources.
   2. Referred to as a snapshot in time.
   3. **Asset:** An economic resource that is objectively measurable, that results from a prior transaction, and that will provide future economic benefit. Examples are Cash, Inventory, and Supplies.
   4. **Liability:** An obligation of a business that results from a past transaction and will require the sacrifice of economic resources at some future date. Examples are Accounts Payable, Notes Payable, and Taxes Payable.
   5. **Equity:** The difference between a company's assets and liabilities and represents the share of assets that are claimed by the company's owners. Examples are Contributed Capital (resources that investors contribute to a business in exchange for ownership interest) and Retained Earnings (equity generated and retained from profitable operations).
   6. **Basic Structure of Statement:**
      Assets = Liabilities + Equity

D. **Relationship Among Financial Statements:** When preparing financial statements, the income statement must be prepared first, followed by statement of retained earnings and then the balance sheet.

Exhibit 2-1 Bed Bath & Beyond Classified Balance Sheet

BED BATH & BEYOND INC. AND SUBSIDIARIES
Consolidated Balance Sheets
(in thousands, except per share data)

	February 28, 2009	March 1, 2008
Assets		
Current assets:		
Cash and cash equivalents	$ 668,209	$ 224,084
Short-term investment securities	2,000	—
Merchandise inventories	1,642,339	1,616,981
Other current assets	250,251	238,646
Total current assets	2,562,799	2,079,711
Long-term investment securities	221,134	326,004
Property and equipment, net	1,148,435	1,121,906
Other assets	336,475	316,472
Total assets	$4,268,843	$3,844,093
Liabilities and Shareholders' Equity		
Current liabilities:		
Accounts payable	$ 514,734	$ 570,605
Accrued expenses and other current liabilities	247,508	258,989
Merchandise credit and gift card liabilities	165,621	171,252
Current income taxes payable	25,105	13,266
Total current liabilities	952,968	1,014,112
Deferred rent and other liabilities	227,209	192,778
Income taxes payable	88,212	75,375
Total liabilities	1,268,389	1,282,265
Shareholders' equity:		
Preferred stock—$0.01 par value; authorized - 1,000 shares; no shares issued or outstanding	—	—
Common stock—$0.01 par value; authorized - 900,000 shares; issued 314,678 and 312,229 shares, respectively;	3,147	3,122
Additional paid-in capital	878,568	813,568
Retained earnings	4,154,921	3,729,766
Treasury stock, at cost	(2,031,642)	(1,983,590)
Accumulated other comprehensive loss	(4,540)	(1,038)
Total shareholders' equity	3,000,454	2,561,828
Total liabilities and shareholders' equity	$ 4,268,843	$ 3,844,093

Exhibit 1-4 Relationship Among Financial Statements

Income Statement

Revenues	$400
– Expenses	256
Net income	$144

Statement of Retained Earnings

Retained earnings, June 1	$ 0
+ Net income	144
– Dividends	0
Retained earnings, June 30	$144

Balance Sheet

Total assets	$444
Liabilities	200
Contributed capital	100
Retained earnings	144
Total liabilities and equity	$444

E. Statement of Cash Flows

1. A financial statement that reports a company's sources and uses of cash over a specific period of time.
2. Its main purpose is to inform users about how and why a company's cash changed during the period.
3. Reports a company's cash inflows and outflows from its operating, investing, and financing activities.
   a. **Financing activities:** Generating and repaying cash from creditors and investors.
      Example: Owner contributed $100 to Lawn Service, Inc. The $100 is considered a cash inflow from financing activities.
   b. **Investing activities:** The buying and selling of revenue-generating assets.
      Example: A lawn mower is purchased for $300. The $300 is considered a cash outflow from investing activities.
   c. **Operating activities:** The operation of a business such as the purchase of supplies, payment of employees, and the sale of products.
      Example: An employee spent $100 gas to operate lawn mower. The $100 is considered a cash outflow from operating activities.
   d. **Basic Structure of the Statement:**
      Cash Inflows Provided (Used) by Operating Activities
      +/– Cash Flows Provided (Used) by Investing Activities
      +/– Cash Flows Provided (Used) by Financing Activities
      = Net Increase (Decrease) in Cash
   e. **Direct Method:** A company calculates and reports its cash inflows from operations followed by its cash outflows for operations.

Exhibit 11-3 Hardin's Operating Cash Flows Using the Direct Method

Cash flows from operating activities		2009
Cash receipts from customers		$428
Less cash payments:		
To suppliers	$282	
To employees	63	
For insurance	10	
For utilities	23	
For taxes	15	393
Net cash provided by operating activities		$ 35

f. Indirect Method: A company reports cash flows from operating activities by adjusting its net income from an accrual basis to the cash basis.

Exhibit 11-5 Hardin's Operating Cash Flows Using the Indirect Method

Cash flows from operating activities		2009
Net income		$14
Adjustments to reconcile net income to		
net cash provided by operating activities		
Depreciation expense	$25	
Gain on sale of equipment	(1)	
Increase in accounts receivable	(4)	
Increase in inventory	(9)	
Decrease in prepaid insurance	4	
Increase in accounts payable	8	
Increase in utilities payable	5	
Decrease in taxes payable	(7)	21
Net cash provided by operating activities		$35

QUALITATIVE CHARACTERISTICS OF ACCOUNTING INFORMATION

A. **Understandability:** Accounting information should be comprehensible by those willing to spend a reasonable amount of time studying it.

B. **Relevance:** Accounting information should have the capacity to affect decisions.

C. **Reliability:** Accounting information should be dependable to represent what it purports to represent.

D. **Comparability:** Accounting information should be comparable across different companies.

E. **Consistency:** Accounting information should be comparable across different times periods within a company.

F. **Materiality:** The threshold over which an item could begin to affect decisions.

G. **Conservatism:** When uncertainty exists, accounting information should present the least optimistic alternative.

FIXED ASSETS

A. **Recording Fixed Asset:** Includes all costs incurred to get the asset delivered, installed, and ready to use. Examples of expenditures are purchase price and delivery costs.

Journal Entry:

Delivery Truck	XXX	
Cash		XXX
(To record the purchase of the truck)		

B. **Depreciation:** The process of allocating the cost of a fixed asset over its useful life.

Journal Entry:

Depreciation Expense	XXX	
Accumulated Depreciation		XXX
(To record depreciation expense)		

C. **Net book value:** The unexpired cost of a fixed asset, calculated by subtracting accumulated depreciation from the cost of the fixed asset.

SHOW CONDENSED DATA on bottom, right hand side of page 152 (2008 note)

Property and equipment, at cost	$1,977,253
Accumulated depreciation and amortization	(206,881)
Net property and equipment	$1,770,372

D. **Calculating Depreciation Expense**

1. **Straight-line method:**

$$\text{Depreciation Expense} = \frac{\text{Cost} - \text{Salvage Value}}{\text{Useful Life}}$$

2. **Double-Declining-Balance:**

Depreciation Expense =
(Straight-Line Rate $\times$ 2) $\times$ (Cost $-$ Accumulated Depreciation)

3. **Units-of-activity method:**

Depreciation Expense = Depreciation Expense per unit $\times$ Units of Activity

$$\text{Depreciation Expense per unit} = \frac{\text{Cost} - \text{Salvage Value}}{\text{Useful Life in Units}}$$

BONDS

A. **Bond:** A financial instrument in which a borrower promises to pay future interest and principal to a creditor in exchange for the creditor's cash today.

B. **Bond Issuance**

1. **Par Value:** When a bond pays interest at a rate that is equal to what creditors demand in the market, the creditors will buy at its face value (Stated Interest Rate = Market Interest Rate).

Journal Entry:

Cash	XXX	
Bonds Payable		XXX

2. **Discount:** Bonds that are issued for less than face value are issued at a *discount* (Stated Rate < Market Rate).

Journal Entry:

Cash	XXX	
Discount on Bonds Payable	XXX	
Bonds Payable		XXX

3. **Premium:** Bonds issued for more than face value are issued at a *premium* (Stated Rate > Market Rate)

Journal Entry:

Cash	XXX	
Premium on Bonds Payable		XXX
Bonds Payable		XXX

comprehensivereview

STOCKHOLDERS' EQUITY

A. Common Stock: The most common type of capital stock.

Journal Entry:

Cash	XXX	
Common Stock		XXX
(To record sale of stock at par value)		

Suppose a company issues 100 shares of $1 par value stock for $5 per share on April 5.

Cash	500	
Common Stock		100
Additional Paid-In Capital		400

B. Treasury Stock: Common stock that a company reacquires from it stockholders.

Journal Entry:

Treasury Stock	XXX	
Cash		XXX
(To record purchase of treasury stock)		

C. Dividend: A distribution of profits to owners.

Journal Entries:

Retained Earnings	XXX	
Dividends Payable		XXX
(To record declaration of dividend)		
Dividends Payable	XXX	
Cash		XXX
(To record payment of dividend)		

BUSINESS FORMS

A. Sole proprietorship: A business owned by one person and is the most common type of business in the United States.

B. Partnership: A business that is formed when two or more proprietors join together to own a business.

C. Corporation: A separate legal entity that is established by filing articles of incorporation in a state.

SINGLE-STEP VERSUS MULTI-STEP INCOME STATEMENT

A. Single-step income statement: Calculates total revenues and total expenses and then determines net income in one step by subtracting total expenses from total revenues (or Revenues — Expenses = Net Income or Net Loss).

B. Multi-step income statement: Calculates income by grouping certain revenues and expenses together and calculating several subtotals of income: gross profit, operating profit, income before taxes, and net income.

HORIZONTAL AND VERTICAL ANALYSES

A. Horizontal Analysis: Method of analyzing a company's account balances over time.

Formulas:

Dollar Change in Account Balance: Current Year Balance — Prior Year Balance

Percentage Change in Account Balance: $\dfrac{\text{Dollar Change}}{\text{Prior Year Balance}}$

Example

	2009	2008	%
Merchandise Inventories	$1,642,339	$1,616,981	1.6%*

*$1,642,339 — $1,616,981 = $25,358; $25,238/$1,616,981 = 1.6%

B. Vertical Analysis: Method of comparing a company's account balances within one year.

Formulas:

$$\text{Percentage} = \dfrac{\text{Balance Sheet}}{\text{Account Balance}} \text{ or } \dfrac{\text{Income Statement}}{\text{Account Balance}}$$
$$\dfrac{\text{Account Balance}}{\text{Total Assets}} \quad \dfrac{\text{Account Balance}}{\text{Net Sales or Revenue}}$$

Example

	2009	%
Merchandise inventories	$1,642,339	38.5%*
Total Assets	$4,268,843	100.0%

*$1,642,339 / $4,268,843 = 38.5%

Exhibit 2-2 Bed Bath & Beyond Multi-step Income Statement

Consolidated Statements of Earnings
Bed Bath & Beyond Inc. and Subsidiaries

	FISCAL YEAR ENDED		
	February 28, 2009	March 1, 2008	March 3, 2007
(in thousands)			
Net sales	$7,208,340	$7,048,942	$6,617,429
Cost of sales	4,335,104	4,123,711	3,782,027
Gross profit	2,873,236	2,925,231	2,835,402
Selling, general and administrative expenses	2,199,340	2,087,209	1,946,001
Operating profit	673,896	838,022	889,401
Interest income	9,412	27,210	43,478
Earnings before provision for income taxes	683,308	865,232	932,879
Provision for income taxes	258,185	302,424	338,635
Net earnings	$ 425,123	$ 562,808	$ 594,244

TRANSACTION ANALYSIS AND RECORDING TRANSACTIONS

A. An **accounting transaction** is any economic event that affects a company's assets, liabilities, and equity at the time of the event. Every accounting transaction must affect at least two accounts (also known as dual nature of accounting).

KEY INFORMATION

1. Circle Films issues 3,000 shares of common stock to investors for $15,000 cash.
2. Circle Films purchases a video camera for $9,000.
3. Circle Films receives a $1,500 payment immediately after filming a customer's wedding.
4. Circle Films receives a $2,000 deposit from a customer to film her parents' fiftieth wedding anniversary.
5. Circle Films paid $250 cash to run an ad in the local paper.

TRANSACTION SUMMARY:

ASSETS	=	LIABILITIES	+	EQUITY
#1 + $15,000 cash				+ $15,000 common stock
#2 − $9,000 cash + $9,000 equipment				
#3 + $1,500 cash				+ $1,500 retained earnings
#4 + $2,000 cash		+ $2,000 unearned revenue		
#5 − $250 cash				− $250 retained earnings

B. A **journal** is a chronological record of transactions. Entries recorded in the journal are called journal entries.

GENERAL JOURNAL (Using key information above)

Transaction	Account Names and Explanation	Debit	Credit
#1	Cash	15,000	
	Common Stock		15,000
#2	Equipment	9,000	
	Cash		9,000
#3	Cash	1,500	
	Service Revenue		1,500
#4	Cash	2,000	
	Unearned Revenue		2,000
#5	Advertising Expense	250	
	Cash		250

C. A **trial balance** is a listing of accounts and their balances at a specific point in time.

Circle Films
Trial Balance
XXX

	Debit	Credit
Cash	9,250	
Equipment	9,000	
Unearned Revenue		2,000
Common Stock		15,000
Service Revenue		1,500
Advertising Expense	250	0
Total	18,500	18,500

THE T-ACCOUNT

A. All accounts can be characterized or represented in the following form known as a T account due to its resemblance to a capital T.

B. The left side of an account is the debit side. The right side of an account is the credit side.

Examples of T-Account Mechanics

Asset		Liability		Equity	
1,000	5,000	2,000	6,000	7,000	2,000
4,000	3,000	1,000	4,000		3,000
8,000		3,000			3,000
5,000			4,000		1,000

C. To increase an account balance, record on the same side as the normal balance. To decrease an account balance, record on the opposite side as the normal balance.

Exhibit 3-3 Summary of Debit and Credit Rules

Type of Account	Normal Balance	Increase with a	Decrease with a
Asset	Debit	Debit	Credit
Liability	Credit	Credit	Debit
Equity	Credit	Credit	Debit
Revenue	Credit	Credit	Debit
Expense	Debit	Debit	Credit
Dividend	Debit	Debit	Credit

UNCOLLECTIBLE RECEIVABLES

A. **Bad Debt Expense:** The expense resulting from the inability to collect accounts receivable.

B. **Direct write-off method:** Bad debt expense is recorded when a company determines that a receivable is uncollectible and removes it from its records. GAAP prohibits the use of direct method because it violates the matching principle.

Recording Bad Debt Expense & Write Off Receivable: On April 2, 2011, Thompson Inc. determines that Brandon LLC will be unable to pay its receivable amounting to $4,000.

April 2011	Bad Debt Expense	4,000	
	Accounts Receivable—Brandon LLC		4,000

C. **Allowance method:** Method in which companies use two entries to account for bad debt expense—one to estimate the expense and a second to write off receivables.

1. **Recording Bad Debt:** Based on past experience, Duncan Sports estimates that $8,000 of 2009 sales will not be collected.

End of 2009	Bad Debt Expense	8,000	
	Allowance for Bad Debts		8,000
	(To record bad debt expense)		

2. **Recording a Write-Off:** Suppose that Duncan Sports determines in 2010 that a $2,500 receivable from William Johnson is uncollectible and decides to write it off the books.

2010	Allowance for Bad Debts	2,500	
	Accounts Receivable—William Johnson		2,500
	(To record write-off)		

3. Recording the Recovery of a Write-Off: Suppose William Johnson pays his bill in full later during 2010.

2010	Accounts Receivable—William Johnson	2,500	
	Allowance For Bad Debts		2,500
	(To reverse the original write-off)		
	Cash	2,500	
	Accounts Receivable—William Johnson		2,500
	(To collect the receivable)		

RATIOS

A. Allowance Ratio: Allowance for Bad Debts/Gross Accounts Receivable.

B. Fixed Asset Turnover Ratio = Total Revenues/Average Net Book Value of Fixed Assets

C. Cash Flow Adequacy Ratio: Free cash flow/Average amount of debt maturing in five years

D. Free Cash Flow: Cash flows from operating activities − Capital expenditures − Dividends

Profitability

E. Profit Margin: Net Income/Net Sales

F. Return on Equity: Net Income/Average Stockholders' Equity

G. Return on Assets: Net Income/Average Total Assets

H. Earnings per Share: Net Income/Average Number of Common Shares Outstanding.

I. Price to Earnings Ratio: Current Market Price per Share/Earnings per Share

Liquidity

J. Current Ratio: Current Assets/Current Liabilities

K. Quick Ratio: (Cash + Short-term Investments + Accounts Receivable)/Current Liabilities

L. Receivables Turnover Ratio: Net Sales/Average Accounts Receivables

M. Days-in-Receivables Ratio: 365/Receivables Turnover Ratio

N. Inventory Turnover Ratio: Cost of Goods Sold/Average Inventory

O. Days-in-Inventory Ratio: 365/Inventory Turnover Ratio

Solvency

P. Debt to Assets = Total Liabilities/Total Assets

Q. Debt to Equity = Total Liabilities/Total Equity

R. Times Interest Earned = (Net Income + Interest Expense + Income Tax Expense)/Interest Expense

DuPont Analysis

S. Return on Equity = Operating Efficiency × Asset Effectiveness × Capital Structure

RECORDING INVENTORY

A. Perpetual inventory system: Updates the inventory account each time inventory is bought or sold.

Entries:

Suppose that Devon Gifts purchases $20,000 of inventory on account on Oct. 10.

Oct. 10	Inventory	20,000	
	Accounts Payable		20,000
	(To record purchase of inventory)		

Suppose that Devon pays a third-party carrier $300 to transport the inventory to its warehouse on Oct. 10.

Oct. 10	Inventory	300	
	Cash		300
	(To record transportation-in)		

Suppose that on Oct. 12 Devon is granted a $1,000 reduction in the cost of the merchandise due to blemishes on the inventory.

Oct. 12	Accounts Payable	1,000	
	Inventory		1,000
	(To record purchase allowance granted by vendor).		

Suppose Devon pays its remaining $19,000 bill to the vendor on Oct. 15, which qualifies Devon for a 1% discount.

Oct. 15	Accounts Payable	19,000	
	Inventory		190*
	Cash		18,810
	(To record payment)		

*$19,000 × .01

On Nov. 2, Devon sells inventory costing $400 for $600 cash.

Nov. 2	Cash	600	
	Sales		600
	Cost of Goods Sold	400	
	Inventory		400
	(Record the sale of inventory)		

B. Periodic inventory system: Updates the inventory account only at the end of an accounting period.

INVENTORY COSTING METHODS

A. Specific identification: Determines cost of goods sold based on the actual cost of each inventory item.

B. First-in, first-out (FIFO) method: Calculates cost of goods sold based on the assumption that the first unit of inventory available for sale is the first unit sold.

C. Last-in, first-out (LIFO) method: Calculates cost of goods sold based on the assumption that the last unit of inventory available for sale is the first unit sold.

D. Moving average method: Calculates cost of goods sold based on the average unit cost of all inventory available for sale.

$$\text{Average Unit Cost} = \frac{\text{Cost of Goods Available for Sale}}{\text{Units Available for Sale}}$$

In a period of rising inventory prices	Ending Inventory	Cost of Goods Sold
FIFO yields:	Highest	Lowest
Moving average yields:	Middle	Middle
LIFO yields:	Lowest	Highest